Transactions
of the
Royal
Historical
Society

SIXTH SERIES

XII

CAMBRIDGE
UNIVERSITY PRESS

Published by the Press Syndicate of the University of Cambridge
The Edinburgh Building, Cambridge CB2 2RU, United Kingdom
40 West 20th Street, New York, NY 10011–4211, USA
477 Williamstown Road, Port Melbourne, VIC 3207, Australia
Ruiz de Alarcón 13, 28014 Madrid, Spain

A catalogue record for this book is available from the British Library

First published 2002

ISBN 0 521 81561 4 hardback

SUBSCRIPTIONS. The serial publications of the Royal Historical Society, *Royal Historical Society Transactions* (ISSN 0080–4401) and Camden Fifth Series (ISSN 0960–1163) volumes may be purchased together on annual subscription. The 2002 subscription price (which includes postage but not VAT) is £63 (US$102 in the USA, Canada and Mexico) and includes Camden Fifth Series, volumes 19, 20 and 21 (published in July, October and December) and Transactions Sixth Series, volume 12 (published in December). Japanese prices are available from Kinokuniya Company Ltd, PO Box 55, Chitose, Tokyo 156, Japan. EU subscribers (outside the UK) who are not registered for VAT should add VAT at their country's rate. VAT registered subscribers should provide their VAT registration number.

Subscription orders, which must be accompanied by payment, may be sent to a bookseller, subscription agent or direct to the publisher: Cambridge University Press, The Edinburgh Building, Shaftesbury Road, Cambridge CB2 2RU, UK; or in the USA, Canada and Mexico: Cambridge University Press, Journals Fulfillment Department, 110 Midland Avenue, Port Chester, NY 10573–4930, USA. Prices include delivery by air.

SINGLE VOLUMES AND BACK VOLUMES. A list of Royal Historical Society volumes available from Cambridge University Press may be obtained from the Humanities Marketing Department at the address above.

Printed and bound in the United Kingdom by Butler & Tanner Ltd, Frome and London

CONTENTS

PAGE

Presidential Address: England and the Continent in the Ninth
    Century: I, Ends and Beginnings   1
    Janet L. Nelson

Some Pardoners' Tales: The Earliest English Indulgences   23
    Nicholas Vincent

Travellers and the Oriental City, c. 1840–1920   59
    Mark Mazower

Individualising the Atlantic Slave Trade: The Biography of
    Mahommah Gardo Baquaqua of Djougou (1854)   113
    Robin Law

The Myths of the South Sea Bubble   141
    Julian Hoppit

The Place of Tudor England in the Messianic Vision of
    Philip II of Spain   167
    (*The Prothero Lecture*)
    Geoffrey Parker

The Charity of Early Modern Londoners   223
    Ian W. Archer

Matrix of Modernity?   245
    (*The Colin Matthew Memorial Lecture*)
    Roy Porter

ENGLISH POLITENESS: CONDUCT, SOCIAL RANK AND MORAL VIRTUE, C. 1400–
C. 1900: A CONFERENCE HELD AT THE HUNTINGTON LIBRARY, SAN MARINO,
CALIFORNIA, USA, 14–15 SEPTEMBER 2001, AND THE INSTITUTE OF HIS-
TORICAL RESEARCH, UNIVERSITY OF LONDON, 24 NOVEMBER 2001

Introduction   263
    John Tosh

From *Civilitas* to Civility: Codes of Manners in Medieval and
    Early Modern England   267
    John Gillingham

Rank, Manners and Display: The Gentlemanly House,
    1500–1750   291
    Nicholas Cooper

The Uses of Eighteenth-Century Politeness   311
    Paul Langford

Polite 'Persons': Character, Biography and the Gentleman   333
    Philip Carter

Topographies of Politeness   355
    R. H. Sweet

Polite Consumption: Shopping in Eighteenth-Century England   375
    Helen Berry

Creating a Veil of Silence? Politeness and Marital Violence in
    the English Household   395
    Elizabeth Foyster

Courses in Politeness: The Upbringing and Experiences of Five
    Teenage Diarists, 1671–1860   417
    Anthony Fletcher

The Brash Colonial: Class and Comportment in Nineteenth-
    Century Australia   431
    Penny Russell

Gentlemanly Politeness and Manly Simplicity in Victorian
    England   455
    John Tosh

Report of Council for 2001–2002   473

Transactions of the RHS 12 (2002), pp. 1–21 © 2002 Royal Historical Society
DOI: 10.1017/S0080440102000014   Printed in the United Kingdom

TRANSACTIONS OF THE
ROYAL HISTORICAL SOCIETY

PRESIDENTIAL ADDRESS

By Janet L. Nelson

ENGLAND AND THE CONTINENT IN THE NINTH CENTURY: I, ENDS AND BEGINNINGS

READ 24 NOVEMBER 2001

ABSTRACT. This essay begins by celebrating the achievement of Wilhelm Levison, whose *England and the Continent in the Eighth Century* has both inspired and provoked new generations of explorers. The essay goes on to argue that the historiography of the earlier Middle Ages has been haunted by quests for the end of the Roman Empire. Recent attempts at periodisation, Marxist and other, have extended Rome's decline to span the ninth century, with the Carolingian heyday both truncated and belittled, while Anglo-Saxon England has been split down the middle by representations of the Vikings' impact as a re-run of the fifth-century barbarian onslaught. Since 1989, abundant and diverse historiographical takes, cross-cultural, interdisciplinary and comparative, have made it possible to see the ninth century as a formative and defining period in European history, not least because of multiple contacts between England and the Continent. The last part of the essay examines the pontificate of Leo III (795–816), to show England and the Continent meeting, figuratively speaking, in Rome. A wider world of connections is brought into view and the scene set for further explorations.

'IN MY beginning is my end'[1] is one of those deep sayings that sets the mind working overtime – and over time. First, in my present situation, it makes me reflect that the beginning of one president's stint is necessarily an end to another's. Peter Marshall's lectures have adorned and enriched the last four years' programmes of this Society, and of course its *Transactions* too. Great wisdom, scholarship worn lightly, intercontinental breadth, compelling explanatory power: these made Peter's lectures as memorable as his whole presidency has proved memorable in expanding the Society's size and scope, and, more

---

[1] T. S. Eliot, 'East Coker', *The Four Quartets* (1944), 15. The tag was a well-used later medieval and early modern *memento mori*.

important still, its vision of what it can and should be doing for History. Peter's successor self-evidently has an impossible act to follow.[2] All that can be said is that this one will be different, thanks to the Society's excellent practice of choosing as successive presidents specialists in different times and places. So, we now skip back a millennium, from India and America to western Europe, from an age of western European global cultural dominance to a world in which Latin Christendom, small, disparate, poor, was peripheral to the great Eurasian landmass, where the shots were called in Baghdad and Ch'ang-an.[3] The Royal Historical Society takes all that and more in its stride, just as, following the injunction of the psalmist's text in Hebrew that adorns the Gustav Tuck theatre in University College, London, it 'considers the years of each generation'.[4] Enough, in this context, about a beginning being an end.

Let me instead pursue the thought in another context. My title, as early medievalists here will have recognised, perhaps with a frisson of alarm at what may look like sheer cheek on my part, echoes Wilhelm Levison's *England and the Continent in the Eighth Century*. Levison escaped from Germany in 1939, just in time, and received a welcome in Durham, then as since, a bastion of medieval learning. In 1943, Oxford invited Levison to deliver the Ford Lectures, which became the book published posthumously in 1947. In his preface, he wrote: 'I have tried to some extent to connect up Continental and English research. May these pages ... contribute to join again broken links, when the works of peace have resumed their place lost in the turmoil of war.'[5] And Levison recalled 'with grateful mind' his old pre-war colleagues at the Monumenta Germaniae Historica (MGH), 'many of whom did not bow the knee to Baal, but remained faithful till the hour of parting could no longer be avoided'. My beginning is a salute to his memory. His death was indeed the ending of a magnificent chapter in the history of early medieval scholarship. Of course, the Monumenta has long since revived again, and flourished, but that was a never-to-be-repeated pioneering age when Levison and Bruno Krusch between them published the seven magnificent volumes of the MGH Scriptores rerum Merovingicarum, and Levison completed the first part of the revision

---

[2] This is the apt moment to acknowledge, too, James Holt and Rees Davies, two medievalists among recent past presidents of the Society, both exemplary, both inimitable.

[3] See *The Times Atlas of World History*, ed. G. Barraclough, 4th rev. edn G. Parker (1993), 108–9: 'The Eurasian world in 814'.

[4] The Society owes thanks to UCL for making this beautiful theatre available for our lectures in London. I owe the translation of the Hebrew to the kindness of my UCL colleague David d'Avray.

[5] W. Levison, *England and the Continent in the Eighth Century* (Oxford, 1947), vi. There is a thought-provoking entry on Levison (by F. Lifshitz) in *Encyclopedia of Historians and Historical Writing*, ed. K. Boyd (1999), I, 717–18.

of Wattenbach's nineteenth-century monumental *Deutschlands Geschichtsquellen im Mittelalter*. No wonder an MGH colleague recalled Levison as 'the tireless one' *(der Unermüdlich)*.[6] No wonder early medievalists remember Levison with grateful mind. No wonder that more than one of us has wished that Levison had lived to write the sequel to his masterwork. As it is, *England and the Continent in the Eighth Century* contains no more than a few tantalising forays into the ninth.

There is a further sense, too, in which a subject came to an end not just in Levison's work, but around 800. The well-documented eighth-century connections woven by four generations of Anglo-Saxon missionaries on the Continent were becoming attenuated, or transformed, as the Frankish Church assumed responsibility for its own mission. A great age of missionary saints' Lives ended too. To read the Continuator of Bede is to realise, painfully, that Bede's act was impossible to continue.[7] In Francia, the Continuator of Fredegar who stopped work in 768 had no successor.[8] Thread-bare annals replaced history on both sides of the Channel.[9] The death of Alcuin in 804 did not just put a stop to his letter-writing, so depriving us of the richest source we have for Anglo-Continental relations in the late eighth century, but the Northumbrian annals nourished by information from Francia stopped approximately then too.[10] It becomes curiously less easy to write a story of Anglo-Continental connections in the ninth century than for the eighth century – or even the seventh.

As for seizing the ninth century as a substantive subject in itself, there is another kind of obstacle: periodisation, History's handy organiser, but also its bane. Marc Bloch, in 1942, noted the carving-up of the past by centuries as a 'rather recent fashion', 'all the more insidious because it has no rational basis'.[11] What Georges Duby called the magic of the double zero still casts its spell – witness the syllabus I have taught for thirty-two years at King's College London. Frustration may account

---

[6] Walther Holtzmann, 'Vorwort' to Levison's revised vol. 1 of W. Wattenbach, *Deutschlands Geschichtsquellen im Mittelalter* (Weimar, 1952), vii.

[7] *Venerabilis Bedae Opera Historica*, ed. C. Plummer (Oxford, 1896), 361–3, trans. J. McClure and R. Collins, *Bede: The Ecclesiastical History of the English People* (Oxford, 1994), 296–8, and comment, xxi–ii.

[8] R. Collins, 'Deception and Misrepresentation in Early Eighth-Century Frankish Historiography: Two Case Studies', in *Karl Martell in seiner Zeit*, ed. J. Jarnut, U. Nonn and M. Richter, Beihefte der *Francia* (Sigmaringen, 1994), 227–47; *idem*, *Fredegar*, Authors of the Middle Ages, 13 (Aldershot, 1996).

[9] M. McCormick, *Les 'Annales' du haut moyen âge*, Typologie des sources du haut moyen âge occidental xiv (Turnhout, 1975).

[10] D. Rollason, *Sources for York History to AD 1100*, The Archaeology of York 1 (York, 1998); *idem*, 'Symeon's Contribution to Historical Writing in Northern England', and J. Story, 'Symeon as Annalist', in *Symeon of Durham: Historian of Durham and the North*, ed. D. Rollason (Stamford, 1998), 1–13, 202–13.

[11] M. Bloch, *The Historian's Craft*, trans. P. Puttnam (Manchester, 1954), 149.

for the proliferation of 'long centuries' (the long eighteenth century set the trend) that sprawl imperialistically across double-zero frontiers. The ninth century recently had its first four decades nabbed by foragers from the long eighth: maybe no bad thing.[12] But what the ninth century has suffered excessively from is periodisation's dead hand. It has been the victim of two great efforts at revisionism. Marx rethought Antiquity as a slave-based mode and the Middle Ages as feudalism. Unclarity about where, when and how you got from one to the other (not to mention, in feudalism's case, confusion with non-Marxist meanings) has evoked a great deal of debate. That most magical of multiple zeros, the year one thousand, has seemed to many historians, especially in France, the most natural of frontiers. Under the great neo-Marxian sign of *mutation féodale*, that frontier could remain upstanding when other walls crumbled, leaving the ninth century firmly on the antique side.[13] Marc Bloch began *Feudal Society* with the ninth century in order to emphasise, not a beginning, but an end.[14] In his view, the ninth century completed the unfinished business of the fifth, as a second age of invasions by Saracens, Vikings and Magyars finished off the remnants of the Roman empire. This was scene-setting. For Bloch's book, centred on the eleventh to thirteenth centuries, was about a new world. Overwhelmed by prescience of the destruction to follow, Charlemagne, as imagined by Michael Wallace-Hadrill, could only lament, *Dieus ... si penuse est ma vie* – though he had to do so in the words of a twelfth-century text (the Song of Roland), not a ninth-century one.[15] Wallace-Hadrill followed the logic of Bloch's periodisation. The ninth and tenth centuries inevitably featured in *The Barbarian West* (and in so much other text-book writing on the earlier Middle Ages) as a dying fall. See also Georges Duby's answer in 1980 to his own question, what, really, was the Carolingian empire? – 'a village chiefdom extended to the limits of the universe; from the edge of impenetrable forests that sheltered outlaws, where every autumn men took their herds of pigs and bands of huntsmen ventured, through clearings where starving peasants struggled to produce what they were forced to take to the residences of their lords, those specialists in fighting whom their warlord-

---

[12] *The Long Eighth Century*, ed. I. L. Hanson and C. Wickham (Leiden, 2000).
[13] C. Wickham, 'The Other Transition: From the Ancient World to Feudalism', *Past and Present*, 103 (1984), 3–36; *idem*, 'Mutations et révolutions aux environs de l'an mil', *Médiévales*, 21 (1991), 27–38; T. N. Bisson, 'The Feudal Revolution', *Past and Present*, 144 (1995), 6–42; cf. D. Barthélemy and S. White, 'Debate: The Feudal Revolution', *Past and Present*, 152 (1996), 196–223; T. Reuter, C. Wickham and the rejoinder of Bisson, 'Debate: The Feudal Revolution', *Past and Present*, 155 (1997), 176–225; and D. Barthélemy, *La mutation de l'an mil a-t-elle eu lieu?* (Paris, 1997), 13–28.
[14] M. Bloch, *La société féodale* (2 vols., Paris, 1939–41), English trans. J. Anderson (1961).
[15] J. M. Wallace-Hadrill, *The Barbarian West*, 3rd rev. edn (1967), 114.

king led every spring on plundering raids'.[16] Where, really, was the link between this primitive capital accumulation and the new age of feudal growth after the year 1000? In such a context, Carolingian renewal of the Roman empire could only seem at best a fantasy, at worst a fake. In the historiographies of Germany, of Italy, of Spain, all for quite different reasons that Marx would have termed superstructural, but which also have a lot to do with modern national preoccupations, the big medieval break-points have *post*dated the ninth century: Germany's first Reich, Italy's urban civilisation, Spain's *reconquista*.

In a second area, too, revisionism became fossilised in a way that offered nothing for the ninth century. For the francophone Belgian Henri Pirenne, medieval European towns were the creation of *homo oeconomicus* in the tenth and eleventh centuries. The breed was new. An absence of continuity, of any organic or structural link, between the key economic institutions of Antiquity and the Middle Ages, was the key argument of *Mohammed and Charlemagne*. The rise of Islam, and the Arab conquests of the seventh and eighth centuries ended the Roman empire for good by destroying a trading and cultural community centred on the Mediterranean.[17] In economic terms, this end was followed by no new beginning, but a caesura: a period of no markets, but instead of rural autarky, associated with what we would call under-development, in Francia, the heartland of Charlemagne's empire. Here belong Duby's outlaws, pigs and huntsmen, impenetrable forests, starving peasants and miserable clearings. Because Pirenne left his book unfinished when he died in 1935, and its latter part remained only a sketch, between his earlier work and this final one no bridge was ever built. Into that void fell the ninth century. At the same time, of course, Pirenne acknowledged cultural and ideological innovation in the eighth-century Franks' *entente cordiale* with the Church. *Mohammed and Charlemagne* ends here, with new monarchy. Pirenne could not have written the rest of the ninth century in these terms, any more than could his younger contemporaries Louis Halphen and François-Louis Ganshof, who took up Pirenne's story. New monarchy was shortlived because (I quote Halphen) 'neither Charlemagne nor his counsellors were capable of forming a clear idea of the objective to be aimed at'. Charlemagne

---

[16] G. Duby, *Des sociétés médiévales*, Leçon inaugurale au Collège de France, prononcée le 4 décembre 1970 (Paris, 1971), p. 23.

[17] H. Pirenne, *Mahomet et Charlemagne* (1937), trans. B. Meall (1939). Recent radical rethinking is exemplified in P. Delogu, 'Reading Pirenne Again', in *The Sixth Century*, ed. R. Hodges and W. Bowden (Leiden, 1998), 15–40; P. Hordern and N. Purcell, *The Corrupting Sea: A Study of Mediterranean History* (Oxford, 2000), 153–72; and, especially relevant to the ninth century, M. McCormick, *Origins of the European Economy: Communications and Commerce AD 300–900* (Cambridge, 2002), all with fine bibliographies.

'had no idea of system', but simply responded to events.[18] The result – and the word recurs depressingly in the writings of the late 1940s – was decomposition. Charlemagne's old, decaying body (he died at the age of sixty-five in 814) represented the premature aging of his state.[19] And to the Old World historians of the late 1940s, it mirrored the state of the post-war Continent. Looking back from 1990 and from the New World, Norman Cantor castigated the 'post-Nazi era anti-intellectualism of [the Austrian] Heinrich Fichtenau (Hitler was a phony, so Charlemagne had be a phony, too), and the sour British vulgarity of Wallace-Hadrill (they were all barbarians, and intelligence never prevails in history anyway)'.[20] Things could only get better.

The post-war historiographical upswing began and throve where you would have expected: in the areas of high culture, the Church and Christianisation in regions and localities rather than at the level of kingdom or empire. The ninth century was the focus of new attention from theologians, historians of thought including political thought, of script, of art and ritual and the Christian life. While the bulk of the work was Continental,[21] there were important contributions from this side of the Channel where two men in particular were productive and inspirational: Michael Wallace-Hadrill (let me as quickly as possible rescue his name from the charge of sour vulgarity, ethnically labelled or otherwise) and Walter Ullmann, who, like Levison, came to Britain in 1939 and stayed. If you seek their monument, look about you! Most of the earlier medieval historians currently working in this country are their intellectual children and grandchildren.[22] Their influence internationally was and still is large.

[18] L. Halphen, *Charlemagne et l'empire carolingien* (Paris, 1947; repr. with postface by P. Riché 1995), 423, and cf. 424, 412.

[19] F.-L. Ganshof, 'L'échec de Charlemagne' ('Charlemagne's failure'), and 'The last period of Charlemagne's reign: a study in decomposition', both in his collected papers trans. J. Sondheimer, *The Carolingians and the Frankish Monarchy* (1971), chs. 12 and 13; and see also H. Fichtenau, *The Carolingian Empire* (Oxford, 1957; originally published in German in 1949), 177–87.

[20] N. F. Cantor, *Inventing the Middle Ages: The Lives, Works and Ideas of the Great Medievalists of the Twentieth Century* (Cambridge, 1991), 139.

[21] The works of B. Bischoff in his collected *Mittelalterliche Studien*, I and II (Stuttgart, 1966–7); J. Fleckenstein, *Die Hofkapelle der deutschen Könige* (2 vols., Stuttgart, 1957–66); J. Semmler, 'Studien zum *Supplex Libellus* und zur anianischen Reform in Fulda', *Zeitschrift für Kirchengechichte*, 119 (1958), 268–98. These three in *Karl der Grosse: Idee und Wirklichkeit*, ed. W. Braunfels (5 vols., Düsseldorf, 1965), vols. I and II; and P. Riché in his collected papers, *Instruction et vie religieuse dans le haut moyen âge* (Aldershot, 1981), are exemplary, in both senses.

[22] This emerges from the historiographical review by R. Collins, 'The Carolingians and the Ottonians in an Anglophone World', *Journal of Medieval History*, 22 (1996), 97–114. There is an entry for Ullmann (by F. Lifshitz), but not, alas, for Wallace-Hadrill, in *Encyclopedia of Historians*, ed. Boyd, II, 1212–13. The third great inspiring presence for my

And yet in 1989, quite soon after their deaths, Richard Sullivan, a North American grand old man of earlier medieval history surveying the international historiography of the preceding three decades or so, detected 'a malaise in Carolingian studies'. He was polite enough to write of a problem rather than an error, but he was absolutely clear that a crisis had arisen out the Carolingianists' very achievement: in producing a great deal of research intended to support their prior conviction that the Carolingian age was one of beginnings, and innovation, Carolingianists had actually proved the opposite. Their findings, far from sustaining the 'unique, organic character' of the Carolingian period, had splintered it beyond repair by demonstrating 'cultural plurality'. The Carolingianists' cognitively dissonant experience had produced, Sullivan thought, 'a kind of aimlessness', an 'absence of cohesion', 'uncertainty' – in short, 'something amiss'.[23] Sullivan, perceptibly, grew impatient with the Carolingianists' prior conviction: it became a previous conviction. Sullivan's tone, in 1989, was appropriately judgemental. Few Carolingianists then aged forty or over remained with knuckles unrapped. Yet Sullivan's justice was more remedial than punitive. What he prescribed for these recidivists was an *annaliste* boot camp, distance runs while carrying thirty-five kilos' weight of *grandes thèses* through indefinitely prolonged late Antiquity, immersions in icy post-Roman *longues durées*, ending with a short, sharp douche of *révolution féodale*. They – we – would emerge convinced of 'a long historical continuum reaching forward from late antiquity, a continuum in which the Carolingian age constituted a not so distinctive segment'. The failed model of Carolingian change would be replaced by a new ' "excavation" of structural foundations', from the bottom up — hence diminishing the role of elites and of ' "high" civilisation', and privileging 'the "little" people whose lives constitute the essence of society's basic structures [characterised by] immobility over the *longue durée*'. 'Enduring economic, social and mental structures ... little affected by the allegedly decisive events clustered around 750' (he referred to the fall of Byzantine Ravenna to the Lombards, and the accession in Francia of the first Carolingian king) persisted down to c. 1000, increasingly moribund. Sullivan finally, and to me rather surprisingly, endorsed the *annaliste/marxisant* variant of the dead hand. So much for the innovative ninth century – if

generation of British earlier medievalists was Karl Leyser. See the entry (by T. Reuter), in *Encyclopedia of Historians*, ed. Boyd, I, 721–2.

[23] R. Sullivan, 'The Carolingian Age: Reflections on its Place in the History of the Middle Ages', *Speculum*, 64 (1989), 267–306, at 268, and for quotations below, 281, 285–7, 297–8, 303. It is instructive to compare two earlier historiographical staging-posts: the two volumes of *Nascita dell'Europa ed Europa carolingia: un'equazione da verificare*, Settimane di Studi del Centro Italiano sull'alto Medioevo XXVII (Spoleto, 1981), and the review article of D. Bullough, '*Europae pater*: Charlemagne and his Achievement in the Light of Recent Scholarship', *English Historical Review*, 85 (1970), 59–105.

Sullivan was right. But I do not believe Sullivan was right, either in the diagnosis, for cultural plurality can coexist with organic unity, nor in the prescription, for I think we shall not look at the little people *instead of* elites, any more than we should look at men *instead of* women and gender. I am for the inclusive view, and I hope to convince you that it shows the ninth century's formative impact in the history of Europe.

But before pursuing that agenda, I want to apply the Sullivan method to the historiography of ninth-century England, which he excluded. Looking back from 1989, we would have to start, not post-war, but mid-war, in 1943, with F. M. Stenton's Anglo-Saxon chronicling of 'the evolution of an effective monarchy', and 'the advance of the English peoples towards political unity'.[24] Here is a ninth century of shadow, of *dis*unity, corruption, violence within, making the Anglo-Saxon kingdoms easy prey to Viking depredation and destruction from without, but also a ninth century of sunshine, not least in its coverage of the reign of Alfred, who in successfully resisting the Vikings created a state and a corpus of Old English vernacular literature, and set Englishkind (*Angelcynn*) again on the progressive road.[25] Stenton can stand, too, for the inclusion in historical studies of numismatics. Not himself a numismatist, he recognised the importance of coinage as evidence of the Anglo-Saxon economy and of the state. One reason for Alfred's consistent interest in London, and his 'restoration' of the city in 886, was that he knew the value of its mint.[26] After the war, Dorothy Whitelock's publication of *English Historical Documents*, volume 1, a landmark of erudition, gave undergraduates easy access to a treasure-hoard of evidence, including some of the Continental narrative sources with a bearing on Anglo-Saxon history.[27] Even in those decades,

---

[24] F. M. Stenton, *Anglo-Saxon England* (Oxford, 1943). The quotations come from the third edition (1971), 259.

[25] See P. Wormald, 'Bede, the Bretwaldas and the Origins of the *Gens Anglorum*', in *Ideal and Reality in Frankish and Anglo-Saxon Society: Studies Presented to J. M. Wallace-Hadrill*, ed. P. Wormald *et al.* (Oxford, 1983), 99–129, building on but also critiquing Stenton; and S. Foot, 'The Making of *Angelcynn*: English Identity before the Norman Conquest', *TRHS*, 6th series, 6 (1996), 25–50.

[26] Stenton's pioneering interest in this field was recognised in the presentation to him of a Festschrift edited by R. H. M. Dolley, *Anglo-Saxon Coins: Studies Presented to F. M. Stenton* (Oxford, 1961). The most recent work also acknowledges (though it revises) Stenton: see M. Blackburn, 'The London Mint in the Reign of Alfred', in *Kings, Currency and Alliances: History and Coinage of Southern England in the Ninth Century*, ed. M. Blackburn and D. Dumville (Woodbridge, 1998), 105–24.

[27] D. Whitelock, *English Historical Documents c. 500-1042*, 1 (1955; 2nd rev. edn, 1979). For a thoughtful review of the second edition, see K. Leyser, 'The Anglo-Saxons "At Home" ', in *Anglo-Saxon Studies in Archaeology and History*, 11 ed. D. Brown, J. Campbell and S. C. Hawkes (British Archaeological Reports, British Series XCII, Oxford, 1981), 237–42, reprinted in Leyser's collected papers, posthumously published as *Communications and Power in Medieval Europe*, ed. T. Reuter (2 vols., London, 1994), 1, 105–10.

historians of Anglo-Saxon England did, sometimes, look across the Channel, not just, as Levison had done for the eighth century, to show the multiplicity of contacts, or, as Stenton and Whitelock did, to track evidence bearing on England, but, as well, to make substantial comparisons and contrasts, as James Campbell and Patrick Wormald both did for the tenth and eleventh centuries.[28] For the ninth century, though, Michael Wallace-Hadrill's shining example apart,[29] what strikes me is the relative lack of such comparative approaches before c. 1989, a tendency accentuated, paradoxically, by one of the most positive aspects of Anglo-Saxon studies already in those decades: their inter-disciplinarity. Talking to archaeologists of the middle Saxon period did not incline historians of ninth-century Wessex to look across the Channel (though in their defence, it must be said that there were few Continental archaeologists specialising in the ninth century to talk to in those days, which helps explain why both Quentovic and Pont-de-l'Arche were excavated, in the end, by English archaeologists).[30] Talking to Old English specialists did not incline the historian of ninth-century Wessex to look across to the Continent either; and that, I am afraid, remains for me a limitation of Anglo-Saxon historiography in North America where the great majority of specialists come out of the literary and linguistic rather than the historical stable. What has the Sullivan method revealed for England then? No sign of aimlessness, certainly, and plenty of cohesion – perhaps too much.

My response to historiographical developments *since* 1989? Bliss was it in that dawn to be alive, but to be middle aged may allow (by analogy with wine) a more intense savouring of change and difference.

---

[28] J. Campbell, 'England, France, Flanders and Germany: Some Comparisons and Connections', in *Ethelred the Unready: Papers from the Millenary Conference*, ed. D. Hill (British Archaeological Reports, British Series LIX, Oxford, 1978), 255–70, and *idem*, 'The Significance of the Anglo-Norman State in the Administrative History of Western Europe', in *Histoire comparée de l'administration (IVe–XVIIIe siècle)*, ed. W. Paravicini and K. F. Werner, Beihefte der *Francia* IX (Munich, 1980), 117–34, both reprinted in J. Campbell, *Essays in Anglo-Saxon History* (1986), chs. 12 and 11; P. Wormald, 'Æthelwold and his Continental Counterparts', in *Bishop Æthelwold: His Career and Influence*, ed. B. A. E. Yorke (Woodbridge, 1988), 13–42.

[29] J. M. Wallace-Hadrill, 'The Franks and the English in the Ninth Century: Some Common Historical Interests', *History*, 35 (1950), 202–18, reprinted in J. M. Wallace-Hadrill, *Early Medieval History* (1975), 201–16. This was the inspiration behind J. L. Nelson, ' "A King across the Sea": Alfred in Continental Perspective', *TRHS*, 36 (1986), 45–68, reprinted in J. L. Nelson, *Rulers and Ruling Families in Early Medieval Europe* (Aldershot, 1999), ch. 1.

[30] R. Hodges, 'Trade and Market Origins in the Ninth Century: Relations between England and the Continent', in *Charles the Bald: Court and Kingdom*, ed. M. Gibson and J. L. Nelson (2nd edn, Aldershot, 2000), 203–23; B. Dearden, 'Charles the Bald's Fortified Bridge at Pîtres (Seine): Recent Archaeological Investigations', *Anglo-Norman Studies*, 11 (1989), 107–11; *idem*, 'Pont-de-l'Arche or Pîtres? A Location and Archaeomagnetic Dating for Charles the Bald's Fortifications on the Seine', *Antiquity*, 64 (1990), 567–71.

Little over a decade ago, Sullivan looked in vain, he said, for diversity in scholarship on the ninth century. Since then, how he must have enjoyed seeing a hundred flowers bloom in England (and Britain more widely) and on the Continent *and* in North America! Over the past decade or so, Carolingianists and Anglo-Saxonists alike have proved incorrigibly productive and innovative. What is more, there seems to me to have been a lot more to-ing and fro-ing across the Channel intellectually and therefore literally too,[31] and a lot less fog. Historians of Anglo-Saxon England are no longer insular (if they ever were). Some evidently know their ways round Brescia and Rome, Benevento and Monte Gargano just as well as Southampton, London and Canterbury.[32] 'Historians of Anglo-Saxon England' are in some cases intrepid Continentals following Levison and Ullmann into lands across the sea, but for happier because entirely positive reasons and from choice,[33] just as ninth-century Continental history has long been a specialism of choice for some born and bred on this side of the Channel and further afield too. Benefits in all cases have been mutual. 1989 was a vintage year in one other quite specific sense: Rosamond McKitterick's *The Carolingians and the Written Word* challenged us all to look afresh at the multiplicity, and multiple concerns, of ninth-century writers and readers, lay as well as clerical.[34] From that, much has followed (and will follow), not least from this author herself.[35]

[31] There is an instructive comparison to be made with the relatively limited participation of British scholars in post-war scholarship on earlier medieval Continental Europe of the immediate post-war decades, and the increased traffic of the 1980s and *a fortiori* the 1990s. See, for instance, the volumes of the Spoleto Settimane held from 1952 onwards by the Centro Italiano di Studi sull'alto medioevo at Spoleto (published 1954 onwards). Much to be welcomed are inter-institutional collaborations set up over the past decade involving Dutch, Belgian, German and French scholars, young and old, with British and American counterparts. The ongoing effects of the 'Transformation of the Roman World' project are perceptible here: see below, n. 53. There is still a long way to go, however, and British scholars of the younger generation are likely to be more, not less, hampered by a deficit in modern-language skills that has become a national disgrace.

[32] See for instance S. Keynes, 'Anglo-Saxon Entries in the "Liber Vitae" of Brescia', in *Alfred the Wise: Studies in Honour of Janet Bately*, ed. J. Roberts and J. L. Nelson (Woodbridge, 1997), 99–119; J. Story, 'Cathwulf, Kingship and the Royal Abbey of St Denis', *Speculum*, 74 (1999), 1–22; A. Thacker, '*Peculiaris patronus noster*: The Saint as Patron of the State in the early Middle Ages', in *The Medieval State: Essays Presented to James Campbell*, ed. J. R. Maddicott and D. M. Palliser (2000), 1–24.

[33] See for instance A. Scharer, 'The Writing of History at King Alfred's Court', *Early Medieval Europe*, 5 (1996), 177–206; S. Lebecq, 'Les marchands aux longs cours et les formes de leur organization dans l'Europe du nord et du nord-ouest aux VIIe–XIe siècles', *Voyages et voyageurs à Byzance et en Occident du VIe au XIe siècle*, ed. A. Dierkens and J.-M. Sansterre (Geneva, 2000), 321–37.

[34] R. McKitterick, *The Carolingians and the Written Word* (Cambridge, 1989).

[35] R. McKitterick, 'Constructing the Past in the Early Middle Ages: The Case of the Royal Frankish Annals', *TRHS*, 6th series, 7 (1997), 101–30; *idem*, 'Political Ideology in

Since 1989, too, wider geographical boundaries-of-the-mind have been dismantled: 'England and the Continent' no longer means (if it ever did) just England and Francia. Scandinavia is self-evidently integral to Europe's Viking age, and the Vikings' impact continues to be vigorously and fruitfully debated.[36] Nowadays western Europeanists compare notes with Byzantinists on a ninth century that some Mediterranean specialists are insisting saw a revival of contacts between East and West. A new agenda looms, in consequence, of making models to link, or otherwise accommodate, the economies of northern and southern Europe.[37] Hoary historiographical constructs are being targeted, none more effectively than associated fiefs and vassals by Susan Reynolds, who includes the ninth century in her sights.[38] Other boundaries too have been subverted: fine new work in ecclesiastical and intellectual and art history, sometimes all three at once, has been launched directly into the historical mainstream.[39] Biblical exegesis and liturgy have come in from the cold to the cutting edge, and the ninth century begins to look as creative as the late Margaret Gibson foresaw it would.[40] New interdisciplinary currents from anthropology and gender studies have run strongly in social and religious history.[41] The religious

---

Carolingian Historiography', in *The Uses of the Past in the Earlier Middle Ages*, ed. Y. Hen and M. Innes (Cambridge, 2000), 162–74.

[36] Between them, contributors to *The Oxford Illustrated History of the Vikings*, ed. P. Sawyer (Oxford, 1997), and *Cultures in Contact: Scandinavian Settlement in England in the Ninth and Tenth Centuries*, ed. D. Hadley and J. D. Richards (Turnhout, 2000), unsettle orthodoxies, provoke comparisons and offer new entrées.

[37] C. Wickham, 'Ninth-Century Byzantium through Western Eyes', in *Byzantium in the Ninth Century: Dead or Alive?*, ed. L. Brubaker (Aldershot, 1998), 245–56; J. Shepard, 'Courts in East and West', in *The Medieval World*, ed. P. Linehan and J. L. Nelson (2001), 14–36; McCormick, *Origins of the European Economy* (which triumphantly delivers the promise of its subtitle, rather less so, that of its title).

[38] S. Reynolds, *Fiefs and Vassals: The Medieval Evidence Reinterpreted* (Oxford, 1994).

[39] Both L. Brubaker, *Vision and Meaning in Ninth-Century Byzantium* (Cambridge, 1999), and C. Chazelle, *The Crucified God in the Carolingian Era* (Cambridge, 2001), offer rich comparative insights.

[40] M. Gibson, 'The Continuity of Learning, c. 850–1050', *Viator*, 6 (1975), 1–13. See further D. Ganz, *Corbie in the Carolingian Renaissance* (Sigmaringen, 1990); D. A. Bullough, *Carolingian Renewal* (Manchester, 1992); J. Cavadini, *The Last Christology of the West: Adoptionism in Spain and Gaul, 785–820* (Philadelphia, 1993); *The Gentle Voices of Teachers: Aspects of Learning in the Carolingian Age*, ed. R. E. Sullivan (Columbus, OH, 1995); J. J. Contreni, 'Carolingian Biblical Culture', in *Iohannes Scottus Eriugena: The Bible and Hermeneutics*, ed. G. Van Riel *et al.* (Louvain, 1996), 1–23. Two important recent editions with excellent commentary are A. L. Harting-Corrêa, *Walahfrid Strabo's Liber de exordiis et incrementis* (Leiden, 1995), and A. Freeman with P. Meyvaert, *Opus Caroli Regis contra synodum (Libri Carolini)*, Monumenta Germaniae Historica, Concilia aevi Karolini, Supplementum 1 (Hannover, 1998).

[41] See on ninth-century social and political relations R. Le Jan, *Famille et pouvoir dans le monde franc (VIIe–Xe siècle): essai d'anthropologie sociale* (Paris, 1994); *La royauté et les élites dans l'Europe carolingienne*, ed. R. Le Jan (Lille, 1998); M. Innes, 'Charlemagne's Will: Piety,

dimension of guilds (which make their first appearance in the long ninth century) links them with prayer-association and arrangements for the commemoration of the dead in which lay people and ecclesiastics were mutually bound.[42] *Libri Vitae*, 'books of life', recording the names of persons to be liturgically commemorated are among the most impressive of the ninth century's written survivals; and while work on these has been ongoing since long before 1989, recent research has added qualitative as well as quantitative value.[43] Confronting those myriad names (a prosopographer's dream challenge!), many of them in clusters representing groups of local or occupational associates, or kin (including dead children), and reflecting on how they came to be listed and how they were remembered thereafter, you are tempted to charge historians of later periods with misappropriation of the discovery of the individual, and the discovery of childhood. The research project at Durham on the *Liber Vitae* kept by St Cuthbert's community will at last put the spotlight on this unique Anglo-Saxon example of the genre in

---

Politics and the Imperial Succession', *English Historical Review*, 112 (1997), 833–55; *idem*, 'Memory, Orality and Literacy in an Early Medieval Society', *Past and Present*, 158 (1998), 3–36; *idem*, *State and Society in the Early Middle Ages: The Middle Rhine Valley 400–1000* (Cambridge, 2000), which, title notwithstanding, focuses on the ninth century. With a similar focus, see P. E. Dutton, *The Politics of Dreaming in the Carolingian Empire* (Lincoln, NE, 1994); M. de Jong, *In Samuel's Image: Child Oblation in the Early Medieval West* (Leiden, 1996); J. L. Nelson, 'Monks, Secular Men, and Masculinity c. 900', in *Masculinity in Medieval Europe*, ed. D. Hadley (1997), 121–42; G. Bührer-Thierry, ' "Just Anger" or "Vengeful Anger"? The Punishment of Blinding in the Early Medieval West', in *Anger's Past: The Social Uses of an Emotion in the Middle Ages*, ed. B. H. Rosenwein (Cornell, 1998), 75–91; S. Airlie, 'Private Bodies and the Body Politic in the Divorce Case of Lothar II', *Past and Present*, 161 (1999), 1–38; P. E. Kershaw, 'Illness, Power and Prayer in Asser's Life of King Alfred', *Early Medieval Europe*, 10 (2001), 201–24; and the review article of P. Stafford, 'Parents and Children in the Early Middle Ages', *Early Medieval Europe*, 10 (2001), 257–71. See also S. Thiébaux's fine new edition with commentary of Dhuoda's *Liber Manualis* (Cambridge, 1998).

[42] J. L. Nelson, 'Peers in the Early Middle Ages', in *Law, Laity and Solidarities: Essays in Honour of Susan Reynolds*, ed. P. Stafford, J. L. Nelson and J. Martindale (Manchester, 2001), 27–46, where I engage with the work of O. G. Oexle, especially his '*Conjuratio* und Gilde im frühen Mittelalter', in *Gilden und Zünfte: Kaufmännische und gewerbliche Genossenschaften*, ed. B. Schwineköper (Sigmaringen, 1985), 151–214, and 'Gilde und Kommune: Über die Entstehung von "Einung" und "Gemeinde" als Grundformen des Zusammenlebens in Europa', in *Theorien kommunalen Ordnung in Europa*, ed. P. Blickle (Oldenburg, 1996), 75–97.

[43] See the new Monumenta edition of *Der Memorial und Liturgiecodex von San Salvatore/ Santa Giulia in Brescia*, ed. D. Geuenich *et al.* (Munich, 2000), and for some of the individuals therein, Keynes, 'Anglo-Saxon Entries', and C. La Rocca and L. Provero, 'The Dead and their Gifts: The Will of Eberhard, Count of Friuli, and his Wife Gisela', in *Rituals of Power: From Late Antiquity to the Early Middle Ages*, ed. F. Theuws and J. L. Nelson (Leiden, 2000), 225–80. On *Libri Vitae* and the work of K. Schmid and J. Wollasch, see J. Gerschow, '*Societas et Fraternitas*: A Report on a Research-Project Based at the Universities of Freiburg and Münster', *Nomina*, 12 (1988–9), 153–71, and *idem*, *Die Gedenküberlieferung der Angelsachsen: Mit einem Katalog der Libri vitae und Necrologien* (Berlin, 1988).

the ninth century, and, not least, its impressive list of *nomina reginarum et abbatissarum*, 'queens and abbesses': that conjuncture is significant, and for even more reasons than Levison saw in 1943.[44] Several recent museum exhibitions in England and on the Continent have showcased – and for hundreds of thousands of people – the ninth century's material culture. Immense research efforts have gone into all this.[45] Archaeologists, thank goodness, have been ever-ready to inject theoretical stiffening into interdisciplinary debate.[46] Both thence, and via new investigations of written texts, students of the ninth century have become not just hot on towns but hot on the causes of towns.[47] By similar routes, the ninth-century peasantry have acquired more variegated features: some can be seen not just multiplying in what can be seen, now, in the ninth century, as monogamous Christian relationships, but potentially thriving as well.[48] And ninth-century

---

[44] Levison, *England and the Continent*, 28; cf. Stafford, 'Queens, Nunneries and Reforming Churchmen: Gender, Religious Status and Reform in Tenth- and Eleventh-Century England', *Past and Present*, 163 (1999), 3–35, and *idem*, 'Powerful Women in the Early Middle Ages: Queens and Abbesses', in *The Medieval World*, ed. Linehan and Nelson, 398–415.

[45] See *The Transformation of the Roman World AD 400–900*, ed. L. Webster and M. Brown (1997), including the catalogues of five linked exhibitions in 1997 at Cologne, Thessaloniki, Leiden, Stockholm and London (see below, n. 53). There was a further series of five exhibitions on the theme 'Charlemagne: The Making of Europe', in 1999–2001, at Paderborn, Barcelona, Brescia, Split and York. Among the catalogues for these were: *Kunst und Kultur der Karolingerzeit: Karl der Grosse und Papst Leo III. in Paderborn*, ed. C. Stiegemann and M. Wemhoff (2 vols., Mainz, 1999); *Il futuro dei Longobardi: L'Italia e le costruzione dell'Europa di Carlo Magno*, ed. C. Bertelli and G. P. Brogiolo (Brescia, 2000); *Alcuin and Charlemagne: The Golden Age of York*, ed. E. Hartley (York, 2001). For comparative reflections on the Paderborn Exhibition, and an exhibition on 'Alfred the Great: London's Forgotten King' at the Museum of London, also in 1999, see J. L. Nelson, 'Two Exhibitions', *History Workshop Journal*, 50 (2000), 295–9.

[46] See J. Moreland, 'Concepts of the Early Medieval Economy', in Hanson and Wickham, *The Long Eighth Century*, 1–34, and C. Loveluck, 'Aspects of Rural Settlement Hierarchy in the Age of Charlemagne: An Archaeological Perspective', in *Charlemagne*, ed. J. Story (2002, forthcoming). I am very grateful to Chris Loveluck for letting me see a copy of this paper in advance of publication. For further interdisciplinary insights, see O. Bruand, 'Circulation monétaire et pouvoirs politiques locaux sous les Mérovingiens et les Carolingiens (du VIIe au IXe siècles)', in *L'argent au moyen âge*, Actes du XXIIIe Congrès de la Société des historiens médiévistes de Clermont-Ferrand (Paris, 1998), 47–59.

[47] A. Verhulst, *The Rise of Cities in North-West Europe* (Cambridge, 1999); R. Hodges, *Towns and Trade in the Age of Charlemagne* (2000).

[48] See J.-P. Devroey, 'Femmes au miroir des polyptyques: une approche des rapports du couple dans l'exploitation rurale dépendante entre Seine et Rhin au IXe siècle', *Femmes et pouvoirs des femmes à Byzance et en Occident (VIe–XI siècles)*, ed. S. Lebecq *et al.* (Lille, 1999), 227–50; *idem*, 'Men and Women in Early Medieval Serfdom: The Ninth-Century North Frankish Evidence', *Past and Present*, 166 (2000), 3–30; Y. Morimoto, 'Aspects of the Early Medieval Peasant Economy', in *The Medieval World*, ed. Linehan and Nelson, 605–20. See also H.-W. Goetz, 'Serfdom and the Beginnings of a "Seigneurial System" in the Carolingian Period', *Early Medieval Europe*, 2 (1993), 29–52.

nobilities have been more intensively and sympathetically viewed as elites and notables with varied local obligations rather than a monochrome and monotonously exploitative ruling class.[49] For a historian of material culture, graves and wills (and the ninth century has striking examples of both)[50] have exceptional evidentiary value as well as their own pathos. 'Consider the years of each generation ...'

For me, most heartening of all have been the ways that the old historical staples of the ninth century, that is, politics, political structures, political ideas, law and historical writing, have been renovated through new perspectives, cross-cultural, interdisciplinary and comparative. One example can stand for many: Patrick Wormald's re-reading of the Laws of Alfred (c. 890) in such a wide-lens context.[51] And in this context, you cannot have too much of a good thing. In Anglo-Saxon historiography nowadays, comparison of English with Irish, Welsh and Scottish history is proving not an alternative to but complementary to the Continental sort, and often as fruitful, not least in Viking studies. It may seem ungrateful to lament that two very recent and especially useful comparisons, John Maddicott's of two Anglo-Saxon kingdoms, Timothy Reuter's of England with Germany, deal respectively with the seventh–eighth centuries and the long tenth century;[52] but it can only be a matter of time before someone subjects the long ninth century to similar treatment. It would certainly be ungrateful to mourn the ending of the European Science Foundation-funded Transformation of the Roman World project (1993-8), or to regret that the ninth century constituted its chronological tail-end. Maybe the ninth-century brigade were lucky to be there at all, but they clung on tenaciously, and a general note of ninth-century innovativeness resonates in results published so far.[53] In all the above, the academic community of this country,

[49] See S. Airlie, 'The Aristocracy', in *The New Cambridge Medieval History*, vol. II, ed. R. McKitterick (Cambridge, 1995), 431–50, and the contributions by S. Airlie, P. Fouracre, R. Le Jan, J. L. Nelson, J. Roberts and T. Reuter to *Nobles and Nobility in Medieval Europe*, ed. A. Duggan (Woodbridge, 2000), Part I: 'Early Middle Ages', 17–98.

[50] For instances of graves, in J. L. Nelson, *Charles the Bald* (1992), 6; *idem*, 'Carolingian Royal Funerals', in *Rituals of Power*, ed. Theuws and Nelson, 167–8; G. Halsall, 'The Viking Presence in England? The Burial Evidence Reconsidered', in *Cultures in Contact*, ed. Hadley and Richards, 259–76. For wills, Nelson, 'The Wary Widow', in *Property and Power in Early Medieval Europe*, ed. W. Davies and P. Fouracre (Cambridge, 1995), 82–113; La Rocca and Provero, 'The dead and their gifts'.

[51] P. Wormald, *The Making of English Law: King Alfred to the Twelfth Century, I: Legislation and its Limits* (Oxford, 1999), 265–85.

[52] J. R. Maddicott, 'Two Frontier States: Northumbria and Wessex, c. 650–750', in *The Medieval State*, ed. Maddicott and Palliser, 25–46; T. Reuter, 'The Making of England and Germany, 850–1050: Points of Comparison and Difference', in *Medieval Europeans: Studies in Ethnic Identity and National Perspectives in Medieval Europe*, ed. A. P. Smyth (Basingstoke, 1998), 53–70.

[53] I. N. Wood, 'Report: The European Science Foundation's Programme on the

embodied not least in the Fellows of this Society, can say it has done its bit. Two special sources of mellow enjoyment for the likes of me are first, the contributions of so many younger scholars, some already Fellows of the Society, others no doubt future ones; and second, the collaborations with Continental colleagues, for I really do believe that the future of medieval historical scholarship is European or it is nothing.

All periodisation is artifice, but it is not arbitrary. Johannes Fried in 1991 dated the formation of Europe from 840 to 1046, 'the break-up of the Carolingian Empire and the rise of nation-states'.[54] R. I. Moore in 2000 placed the first European revolution squarely in the eleventh and twelfth centuries, when sustained economic growth was founded on urbanisation.[55] For Robert Bartlett, the making of Europe, which he also memorably saw in terms of Europeanisation, began c. 950 and was complete by 1300: among its traits were shared saint-cults, shared economic and governmental tools in the form of coins and charters and shared educational practices embodied in universities.[56] Any model has to take account of the intensity or dominance of these features vis-à-vis other and older ones, and also of their diffusion over time. Travel around Europe and you find the Middle Ages beginning at different dates in Poland, Hungary, Denmark, Ireland, while the Dark Ages, now barely visible in academic history books, used to end at different dates in England and France, Germany and Italy, and still do on television and in museums. With all that in mind, I want to argue for the ninth century (long or short) as a fundamentally formative and defining period; and I do so, less by challenging the periodisations of Fried, Moore and Bartlett, than by borrowing and reassigning their criteria. That is, I would see medieval states (though I would not call them nation-states), urbanisation, saint-cults, coins and charters and educational practices as either new, or acquiring a new significance in ninth-century Carolingian kingdoms and in England, to be diffused from then on, in varied forms, elsewhere in Europe. That is to claim a lot for the ninth century. Over the next three lectures, and courtesy of the work of many colleagues, I hope to substantiate the claim by another look at the defining features, but also at processes not just of diffusion but of *fusion*, through new encounters, new appropriations and new blends (what I intend to do for Fried *et al.* is what, for instance, the Anglo-Saxons did for the Franks, and the Scandinavians for the

---

Transformation of the Roman World and the Emergence of Early Medieval Europe', *Early Medieval Europe*, 6 (1997), 217–27.

[54] J. Fried, *Die Formierung Europas 840–1046* (Munich, 1991), 2.

[55] R. I. Moore, *The First European Revolution, c. 970–1215* (2000), esp. 30–9.

[56] R. Bartlett, *The Making of Europe: Conquest, Colonization and Cultural Change 950–1350* (1993), esp. 269–92.

Anglo-Saxons *and* the Franks) and in new contexts (here violence will loom larger than in Levison's view of the eighth century, but so too will prayer-associations and marriages, for mine will be stories of peace as well as war).

In the last bit of *this* paper, I will concentrate on a place, and an institution, where England and the Continent met (figuratively speaking) in the ninth century: Rome, and the papacy, in the pontificate of Leo III (795-816).[57] A Member of the Society has thoughtfully reminded me that today is the 1900th anniversary of the death of St Clement, St Peter's first successor, and that is pleasingly apt for my Roman theme. I focus first on a date with its own magic, the very first day of the ninth century, which was reckoned by those who knew about time-reckoning then to be 25 December 801. Chroniclers started the year on Christmas Day. Maybe not every little English girl or boy knows what happened that day, but I am told that little French and German ones did and do: Charlemagne (or *Karl der Grosse*) was crowned emperor by Pope Leo III in Rome. Some of the time-reckoners had calculated the end of time on 24 December 800.[58] For several years they had been expressing what we moderns can see, with our longer hindsight, as 90s *Angst*. Was Charlemagne defying the experts, or did he reckon on winning each way? This coronation was carefully planned, at least a year and more in advance. Charlemagne's wagon-train, lumbering Romewards in October–November 800, carried gifts for St Peter that were both lavish and extremely heavy, up to 400lb of precious metal in the form of church plate, fixtures and fittings: a headache for the royal Frankish transport corps; but surely suggesting forward planning for a big event.[59]

Who gained most from it? Leo III? Charlemagne? Charlemagne's family? Apart from the main actors, there were many more interested parties, including Anglo-Saxons dependent on Frankish and papal support. There was something for everyone to hope for. One little bundle of evidence that has been relatively little weighed in the balance here consists of three letters that Leo sent Charlemagne in 808 and 809.[60] They are the more precious because relatively little ninth-century

---

[57] See R. Schieffer, 'Charlemagne and Rome', in *Early Medieval Rome and the Christian West: Essays in Honour of Donald Bullough*, ed. J. M. H. Smith (Leiden, 2000), 279–96. For Leo's lavish extensions to the Lateran palace and their iconography, see P. E. Dutton, *Carolingian Civilization* (Peterborough, Ontario, 1993), 50–4.

[58] W. Brandes, '*Tempora periculosa sunt*: Eschatologisches im Vorfeld der Kaiserkrönung Karls der Grossen', in *Das Frankfurter Konzil von 794*, ed. R. Berndt (Mainz, 1997), 49–80; cf. R. Landes, 'The Fear of an Apocalyptic Year 1000', *Speculum*, 70 (2000), 97–145.

[59] *Vita Leonis III* cc. 24, 25, ed. L. Duchesne, C. Vogel (rev. edn, 3 vols., Rome, 1955–7), II, 7–8, trans. R. Davis, *The Lives of the Eighth-Century Popes* (Liverpool, 1992), 191–2.

[60] Monumenta Germaniae Historica, Epistolae v, ed. K. Hampe (Berlin, 1898), Epistolae Leonis III Papae 2, 3 and 4, pp. 89–94 (this one-sided correspondence consists of just ten letters of Leo to Charles).

papal correspondence survives (in fact some 979 probably genuine ninth-century papal letters do survive but they are the tip of a now-lost iceberg).[61] Leo's letters cast retrospective light on what Leo and Charlemagne thought the coronation meant. That they are preserved uniquely in a manuscript which also contains the only two key dossiers that show how Charlemagne's estates were managed suggests an official collection of sorts, and, as we will see, concern with economic resources is a common thread.[62] In the first letter, Leo complains to Charlemagne:

We do not know if it was at your request that your envoys (*missi*) who came to do justice brought with them many men and based them in various cities. Everything that your duke, set in position by you, was accustomed to do in the way of levying [fines] through his jurisdiction in various cases, and which he paid over to us annually in the customary way, these men of your envoys have now been levying. They have also collected heavy taxes from that people, so that the dukes cannot pay over the contributions they owe *us*.[63]

The grounds for complaint are clear, even if the accusation that Charlemagne ordered the envoys' action is decently veiled. The rest of the letter is about Anglo-Saxon matters, and, again, about envoys: Charlemagne's *missi* had seen to the evacuation to Francia of King Eardwulf of Northumbria, who had been driven out of his kingdom (in 806? or slightly later?) by opponents including the archbishop of York and the king of neighbouring Mercia (the Royal Frankish Annals report the exiled king's meeting with Charlemagne at Nijmegen on or about 16 April 808);[64] Leo tells Charlemagne of his joy at Eardwulf's safety: 'he has always been your faithful man', and thanks to his safe escape, 'your [Charlemagne's] imperial defence

[61] This rough calculation was made on the basis of data in P. Jaffé, *Regesta Pontificum Romanorum*, S. Loewenfeld *et al.*, eds. (2nd edn, 2 vols, Berlin, 1885–8), I.

[62] MS Wolfenbüttel, Herzog August Bibliothek, Helmst. 254, also contains the Capitulare *De villis*, and the *Brevium Exempla*: see H. Mordek, *Bibliotheca capitularium regum Francorum manuscripta: Überlieferung und Traditionzusammenhang der fränkischon Herrscherlasse*, Monumenta Germaniae Historica Hilfsmittel xv (Munich, 1995), 946–9. See further K. Verhein, 'Studien zu den Quellen zum Reichsgut der Karolingerzeit', *Deutsches Archiv*, 10 (1953–4), 313–94, at 363–5, and *Deutsches Archiv*, 11 (1954–5), 333–92; and on *De villis*, see J. Martindale, 'The Kingdom of Aquitaine and the Dissolution of the Carolingian Fisc', *Francia*, 11 (1984), 131–91, repr. J. Martindale, *Status, Authority and Regional Power: Aquitaine and France, 9th to 12th Centuries* (Aldershot, 1997), ch. II, 160–2.

[63] Leo III, Ep. 2, p. 89. Some justice was done to the interest of this letter by J. M. Wallace-Hadrill, 'Charlemagne and England', originally in *Karl der Grosse: Idee und Wirklichkeit*, I, 683–98, repr. in Wallace-Hadrill's collected papers, *Early Medieval History* (Oxford, 1975), 155–80.

[64] *Annales regni Francorum* 808, ed. F. Kurze, Monumenta Germaniae Historica, Scriptores rerum Germanicarum in Usum Scholarum (Hannover, 1895), 126.

resounds everywhere in multiple ways'; Leo says that Charlemagne's envoys and his, acting in concert, should see to the Northumbrian king's restoration, which was clearly what Charlemagne wanted. Leo takes the opportunity to observe, with special regret, and perceiving, no doubt, the huge contrast with Charlemagne's firm control of *his* churchmen, that both Anglo-Saxon archbishops, Canterbury as well as York, are in conflict with their respective kings. Leo knows that precisely these circumstances caused archbishops and kings to invoke papal intervention. Charlemagne has asked Leo to require the archbishop of York either to come to Rome to answer for his conduct, or to answer to Charlemagne. Leo replies that he has sent the orders as requested but suggests that *his* envoy would have greater impact if he were to be accompanied by an envoy from Charlemagne. In a situation where *dolositas* (suspicion, guile, treachery – an appropriately slippery word) is rampant, it is vital that Charlemagne and Leo sing from the same hymn sheet: 'ipsi homines [i.e. the archbishop and co.] dolosi sunt, ut ne, missos super missos suscipientes, in dolositate eveniant'.[65] Leo adds a PS: do not make Bishop Jesse of Amiens your envoy again for I regard him as *non idoneus* ('not suitable') both for that job, and for being a confidential adviser. (Given that the bishop of Amiens was one of Charlemagne's very closest advisers, this was frank stuff!) And finally, quiz your (other) envoys especially closely about what they heard when the archbishop of Ravenna invited them to dinner on Palm Sunday (9 April). Leo's letter reveals the multi-tasking of envoys, their capacity, with or without their principal's say-so, to take initiatives which included military and fiscal ones, the close involvement of emperor and pope in Northumbrian politics (Leo offers here the clearest evidence for the implications of Charlemagne's imperial role), the mind-boggling complexity of Italian politics, the intimate interconnectedness of papal and imperial policy and last but not least, this pope's political *nous*. You can think of parallels for a jumped-up and insecure churchman quickly learning the old rules, and experimenting with new ones (Gregory VII, Thomas Becket, Thomas Cranmer), but Leo emerges here as exceptionally resourceful, and that has its own implications for what had happened on 25 December 801.

Leo's second letter, dated 31 December and also of 808 (by modern reckoning), reveals yet more about envoys, this time including one of Leo's own, a man named Aldulf, *de Brittania, natione Saxo*.[66] Aldulf had

---

[65] Leo III, Ep. 2, 90: 'These men are anxious that they may come under suspicion for receiving one lot of *missi*, then another.'

[66] *Annales regni Francorum* 808, 126–7; Leo, Ep. 3, p. 91, names him as 'Hadulf'.

been sent to meet the archbishop of York's envoy in England and accompany him to Rome. On the outward journey, Aldulf had been honourably received by Charlemagne, escorted to the port and given permission to embark. On the inward journey, with the archbishop's envoy in tow, Aldulf had not waited for Charlemagne's envoy to meet him and escort him to the emperor, but had gone hell for leather, like a fugitive (*quasi fugiens*), to Rome. Meanwhile Charlemagne had been waiting for him for several days in vain.[67] Now it was never a good idea to make Charlemagne feel he had been stood up. In fact, Leo knew, the emperor was in a state of 'fury'. Leo apologised for his envoy's 'crude offence against the manners of this world' (*stolida occursio* against *solertia huius saeculi*), and promised that it would not happen again. Charlemagne had of course suspected much more than a breach of diplomatic courtesy: he thought Ardulf was in league with the archbishop's envoy to get to Rome before the Northumbrian king, Charles's protégé. Leo said he was sending Charles the contents of Ardulf's diplomatic bag to prove there was no treachery here; please return them once read, he added, for my files (*pro pignore*). At the same time Leo affirmed his own special responsibility for the English, the Holy Roman Church's people of acquisition. Leo dreaded 'that people's giving the impression that the struggles of my predecessor Pope Gregory are fruitless in my times, and that that be laid to my account at the judgement'. Given the amount of evidence for Leo's involvement in Anglo-Saxon affairs and his sense of papal tradition, I think we can read his anxiety as sincere. Leo thought Charlemagne would share that sense of responsibility: emperor and pope stood shoulder to shoulder.

The third letter, of 809, can be quickly dealt with. Most of it consists of replies to three queries from Charlemagne about three biblical passages, but first, Leo acknowledges receipt of news from Charlemagne brought by Leo's envoy Bishop Sabinus: Leo's earlier envoy Aldulf, after participating in the restoration of the Northumbrian king, and en route for home, had been captured by 'pirates', that is, Vikings. They had taken him to Britain, where he had been ransomed by one of the king of Mercia's men. Bishop Sabinus has brought the news but returned alone 'from regions across the sea', that is, England.[68] Leo expresses to Charlemagne his continuing anxiety about Aldulf's fate. Thanks to the Royal Frankish Annals for this year, though, we know that Aldulf made it back to Rome (the last we hear of him).[69] Embarrassing for Leo that the accident-prone envoy had evidently troubled the emperor again: for it sounds as if Charlemagne saw to

---

[67] Leo III, Ep. 3, 91–2.
[68] Leo III, Ep. 4, 93–4.
[69] *Annales regni Francorum* 808, 128.

Aldulf's transfer from Mercian hands, perhaps very soon after receiving Leo's letter.

These letters (along with other evidence) show an astonishing frequency of transalpine exchanges, implying continuous to-ing and fro-ing of envoys between Aachen and Rome. They also reveal multiple exchanges with Anglo-Saxon England, and a wider world of connections in which Vikings were starting to figure. Like other churchmen, especially bishops, Leo was not aloof from the world, but well versed in its *solertia*. Frequently in touch with Anglo-Saxons, and far though he was, mostly, from Charlemagne, Leo knew that his envoys to England had to travel by way of Charlemagne's court, and have Charlemagne's leave to depart, just as aristocrats needed the ruler's leave to quit assemblies and head for home. Equally, Anglo-Saxons knew that the route to Rome from Quentovic or Rouen must now take them via Aachen. The ninth century opens, then, with the new emperor in his new capital exerting his own centripetal pull across Europe and far beyond. At the same time, the Anglo-Saxons felt more strongly than ever the pull of Rome. Twice in Leo's pontificate, an Anglo-Saxon archbishop went to Rome, the first visits there of Anglo-Saxon bishops in person since the early eighth century. Archbishops engaged in conflicts with kings, and in equally urgent conflicts to control churches founded by lay royals or aristocrats and inherited by their noble kin, needed all the signs of distinction they could get. Papal privileges, exotically inscribed on papyrus, were such signs. But all the papal privileges in the world could not secure ecclesiastical property in the far-flung regions of Christendom against local familial interest. Levison's tart comment on this subject was: 'facts were stronger than theories'.[70] The papacy had its own material worries too. Leo needed the fines and renders that dukes customarily collected and handed over. Writing to the Mercian king Coenwulf, Leo recalled that King Offa, recently deceased, had promised from himself and his successors in perpetuity an annual payment of 365 mancuses, that is 1,095 silver pennies, to St Peter the keybearer of heaven, '*Quod et fecit* – and he did it too!': a sharp reminder to Coenwulf who had just sent only a third that much (120 mancuses).[71] Leo III was a big spender. He invested heavily in the assiduous promotion of papal authority in Rome itself, through lavish gifts to Rome's many churches, and through staging huge, impressive processions. If Leo commanded such resources, his income from Mercian

[70] Levison, *England and the Continent*, 32.
[71] Coenwulf's letter to Leo, and Leo's reply, are edited in A. Haddan and W. Stubbs, *Councils and Ecclesiastical Documents relating to Great Britain and Ireland* (3 vols., 1869–71), III, 521–3, 523–5, trans. D. Whitelock, *English Historical Documents*, I (rev. edn, 1979), 858–62. See N. P. Brooks, *The Early History of the Church of Canterbury* (Leicester, 1984), 123–7, and ch. 7, illuminating the wider context.

kings, and from pilgrim traffic generally, was part of the explanation. But no such material explanation could work without something else: the cult of St Peter himself, to whose tomb, called the *confessio*, beneath the church of St Peter's, awestruck pilgrims were taken. Charlemagne himself had been taken down there at Easter 774 at a critical moment in his early career. Charlemagne's best hope *then* had been for Peter's help. And in the light of that earlier experience, Charlemagne on 25 December 801, but also on 24 December 800 – that is, when, if experts were to be believed, the imminence of the end-time was still a possibility – must have felt confident in and for himself. In Charlemagne's mind, and in the minds of his Frankish contemporaries, there was no incompatibility, no paradox, in holding on, despite papal protests, to what the papacy considered St Peter's lands, or sending envoys to appropriate for his own Italian regime what Leo considered St Peter's dues, and yet, at the same time investing heavily in St Peter's patronage. Likewise, the same Anglo-Saxon king, Offa of Mercia, who allegedly plotted to remove one pope and replace him with another[72] was the same king who instituted the annual payment of what came to be called Peter's Pence. These kings and their counsellors were not incapable of grasping ideas, including the big idea that individual popes and their earthly lordship were to be distinguished from the papal office and its first tenant St Peter, the chosen of Christ. Anglo-Saxon pennies found in Rome are the material residue of faith in powers wielded beyond the grave by the keybearer of heaven. Theories – or beliefs – were stronger than facts.

In the end, though, theories coexisted with facts, more or less comfortably. Leo connived at the restoration of a western empire because 'imperial defence' would thereby be provided, not just for the likes of Eardwulf, but for the papacy itself, if on Charlemagne's terms. Thanks to Leo's realism, the ninth century was on course to be a great age for the papacy. Those 979 papal letters, the vast majority addressed to recipients north of the Alps, were supplied in response to local requests, and they show the strength of new demand for papal authority. Whether imperial power waxed or waned, there was a widening desire that St Peter's patronage 'resound everywhere in multiple ways'. That resonance was as much a part of Europe's making as Charlemagne's ninth-century empire. But those stories and sequels are for other lectures. In my end is my beginning.

---

[72] Codex Carolinus 92, ed. W. Gundlach, Monumenta Germaniae Historica, Epistolae III (Berlin, 1892), 629–30. See Brooks, *The Early History*, 111–27.

Transactions of the RHS 12 (2002), pp. 23–58 © 2002 Royal Historical Society
DOI: 10.1017/S0080440102000026   Printed in the United Kingdom

SOME PARDONERS' TALES:
THE EARLIEST ENGLISH INDULGENCES*

By Nicholas Vincent

READ 26 JANUARY 2001

ABSTRACT. Indulgences have long been studied as a contributory factor to the Protestant Reformation. The present essay focuses attention upon their origins in the eleventh century, and the changes that affected both the theology and the practice of indulgences in the period before 1215. The indulgences issued by English bishops tell us much of the role played in the English Church both by Parisian theology and by post-Gregorian theories of papal monarchy. They shed light upon the 'birth' of purgatory, and upon twelfth-century penitential practice. The present essay also explores the relationship, previously ignored, between the indulgences advertised by pardoners, and the relics of the saints which pardoners were accused of mishandling.

THANKS to Geoffrey Chaucer, the medieval pardoner is a figure familiar to most students of English history. With his pig's bones masquerading as relics of the saints, his indulgences 'come from Rome all hot', his feigned meekness, his tavern humour and his insatiable appetite for silver, Chaucer's pardoner has his counterpart in many other medieval romances, from Adam de la Halle, via Boccacio to John Heywood.[1] Nor is he merely a figure of fiction. At least one of his all-too real confrères, John Tetzel, was to play a significant role in provoking the Protestant Reformation.[2] For a real English pardoner, we could hardly do better than cite the case of John Greve, whose story is told, in Greve's own words, in letters surviving amongst the archives of the corporation of Bridport in Dorset.[3] In the late 1440s,

---

*For assistance in the writing of this essay, I am indebted to Martin Brett, Michael Clanchy, Reinhold Kaiser, Marie and Roger Lovatt, Miri Rubin, Robert Swanson and Patrick Zutshi. Robert Swanson, in particular, made available several as yet unpublished papers with a wealth of references to late medieval indulgences.

[1] Amongst the many studies of the medieval pardoner, the best is that by A. L. Kellogg and L. A. Haselmayer, 'Chaucer's Satire of the Pardoner', *Publications of the Modern Language Association of America*, 46, part 1 (1951), 251–77. See also G. R. Owst, *Preaching in Medieval England* (Cambridge, 1926), 99–110; P. Boussel, *Des reliques et de leur bon usage* (Paris, 1971), 57–66.

[2] N. Paulus, *Johann Tetzel der Ablassprediger* (Mainz, 1899), remains the classic study here.

[3] Dorchester, Dorset Record Office, DC/TB/N4–11, partly printed in *The Sixth Report of the Royal Commission on Historical Manuscripts* (1877), appendix, 495–6.

the men of Bridport set about the rebuilding of their harbour. To raise the necessary money, they approached at least fourteen of the bishops of England and Wales, from whom they obtained letters of indulgence. John Greve was one of the collectors sent out to advertise these letters. A professional who had previously collected on behalf of a leper hospital, Greve found his new quest less than congenial. Writing from 'The Antelope', clearly a tavern at Dartford, in May 1447, Greve had a sorry tale to relate to his employers back in Dorset: no wonder perhaps that his letter is headed 'Jesus Mercy, Mary Help!'[4] Having set out from Bridport, Greve had met with a shady character known as John Banbery, alias John Gyst, who offered to serve as his assistant, collecting whatever money he could on Greve's behalf. At Basingstoke, Greve and Gyst alias Banbery, met and drank with two other colleagues, known as Sterre and Baly, before embarking on their own circuit of Kent and Essex. Money was raised, although not as much as had been hoped. At the prompting of his assistant, Greve was persuaded to farm collection to Banbery at a greatly reduced rate, to supply him with a new set of copies of their indulgences, a crucifix set with a stone of beryl and a suit of new clothes. At Dartford, however, on St George's day, whilst Greve was away preaching in towns roundabouts, Banbery absconded, owing four shillings for his clothes and his crucifix and a further five shillings and twopence for the past six weeks' collection. With him he also took the sealed copies of the episcopal indulgences, perhaps intending to continue to beg alms and to pocket on his own behalf whatever might be given for the work of Bridport harbour.

Pardoners such as Greve and Banbery, Sterre and Baly, lodging in taverns, much concerned with their sartorial appearance and their badges of rank – their jewelled crucifixes and their sealed indulgences – were a familiar feature of the late medieval landscape. The indulgences which they hawked from parish to parish were equally ubiquitous, advertised by all and sundry from the popes to the humblest of individuals. Wherever there was need, there was an indulgence to fit the case: to solicit alms on behalf of the sick and homeless, for widows or for prisoners of the Turks, for leper hospitals and for bridge- and harbour-builders, to encourage attendance at the mass or at particular sermons, to accompany the reading of the psalter or the veneration of religious images, to solicit alms for the poor or prayers for souls in purgatory.[5] Displayed on tomb stones and monumental brasses, in

---

[4] Dorchester, Dorset Record Office, DC/TB/N10, printed in full in *HMC 6th Report*, appendix, 496.

[5] Amongst a great wealth of articles on late medieval English indulgences, see in particular R. N. Swanson, 'Letters of Confraternity and Indulgence in Late Medieval England', *Archives*, 25 (2000), 40–57, which cites much of the best of the most recent secondary literature. For specific studies, either thematic or regional, see, for example,

elaborately decorated flysheets sealed and sold by popes and bishops, read out from more humdrum schedules passed from church to church, recorded in private missals and in letters of pardon which the faithful might elect to carry with them to the grave, indulgences were as common in the fourteenth and fifteenth centuries as the charitable appeals, harrowing or disingenuous as the case may be, that arrive today through the letterboxes of every modern English home.[6] With that love of calculating the incalculable, so typical of fifteenth-century piety – How many angels were there in the celestial hierarchy? How many individual drops of blood had been shed during the scourging and crucifixion of Christ? – a writer in the diocese of Ely attempted around the year 1500 to estimate the full extent of the indulgences that were available from popes and bishops. For the churches and pilgrimages throughout the whole of Christendom, he arrived at the quite astonishing figure of one million, sixty-four thousand and thirty-seven years of indulgence, besides eleven complete remissions of all sin, thirteen partial remissions of a third of penance and any number of lesser awards – more temporal indulgence, in other words, than was estimated to remain between the time of writing and the end of the world.[7] Figures such as this were exceptional. But in most great churches or shrines, pilgrims would have been able to consult publicly posted announcements of the number of days' indulgence that they could

C. Wordsworth, 'On Some Pardons or Indulgences Preserved in Yorkshire, 1412–1527', *Yorkshire Archaeological Journal*, 16 (1902), 369–423; C. Wordsworth, 'Wiltshire Pardons or Indulgences', *Wiltshire Archaeological and Natural History Magazine*, 38 (1913–14), 15–33; N. Orme, 'Indulgences in the Diocese of Exeter 1100–1536', *Report and Transactions of the Devonshire Association*, 120 (1988), 15–32; N. Orme, 'Indulgences in Medieval Cornwall', *Journal of the Royal Institution of Cornwall*, n. s., 2, part 1 (1992), 149–70; R. M. Haines, *Ecclesia Anglicana: Studies in the English Church of the Later Middle Ages* (Toronto, 1989), chs. 11–12; F. Lewis, 'Rewarding Devotion: Indulgences and the Promotion of Images', in *The Church and the Arts: Studies in Church History 28*, ed. D. Wood (Oxford, 1992), 179–94.

[6] For the display of indulgences on tombs and brasses, see G. Marshall, 'The Church of Edvin Ralph and Some Notes on Pardon Monuments', *Transactions of the Woolhope Naturalists Field Club* (1924–6), 40–55. For the elaborately decorated indulgences distributed in England, especially from the papal court at Avignon, see C. N. Cheney, 'Illuminated Collective Indulgences from Avignon', in *Palaeographica diplomatica et archivistica: studi in onore di Giulio Battelli*, Storia e Letteratura Raccolta di Studi e Testi 139–40 (Rome, 1979), II, 353–73; P. N. R. Zutshi, 'Collective Indulences from Rome and Avignon in English Collections', in *Medieval Ecclesiastical Studies in Honour of Dorothy M. Owen*, ed. M. J. Franklin and C. Harper-Bill (Woodbridge, 1995), 281–97. For 'schedula', see R. Graham, 'An Appeal for the Church and Buildings of Kingsmead Priory, circa 1218', *Antiquaries Journal*, 11 (1931), 51–4; R. N. Swanson, 'Fund-Raising for a Medieval Monastery: Indulgences and Great Bricett Priory', *Proceedings of the Suffolk Institute of Archaeology and History*, 40 (2001), 1–7.

[7] *Vetus Liber Archidiaconi Eliensis*, ed. C. L. Feltoe and E. H. Minns, Cambridge Antiquarian Society (1917), 3, with a doomed attempt to unravel the calculation at pp. 209–11. For other such bizarre calculations, including the bloodsheddings of Christ, see J. C. Hirsh, *The Boundaries of Faith: The Development and Transmission of Medieval Spirituality* (Leiden and New York, 1996), 98–9.

expect in return for their offerings of prayer or silver.[8]
For this great inflation of indulgence, the papacy was ultimately to
be held responsible. Whether through greed, as with the fund-raising
for St Peter's Rome that brought Martin Luther to the church door at
Wittenburg, or through the entirely laudable desire to distribute mercy,
the period after 1280 or so witnessed a vast outpouring of indulgences,
and with it a corresponding polemic that attacked such awards as
positively damaging to Christian faith.[9] In official circles, much of the
blame for the system's excesses was assigned not to the papacy or the
bishops, but to ignorant or mendacious pardoners, the travelling-
salesmen of indulgences. Foreigners, or illiterate laymen and women,
preaching with the aid of preposterous false relics − feathers of the
Archangel Gabriel and bread which had been chewed by Christ's own
teeth − pardoners are as frequently criticised in diocesan and conciliar
legislation as they are satirised in fiction.[10] What the pardoner sold or
misrepresented, however, was the indulgence, and the indulgence was
the award made by bishops and popes, ensuring that even today the
standard histories of indulgences, by H. C. Lea and Nicolaus Paulus,
approach their subject either from distinctly hostile and Protestant or
apologetic and Catholic perspectives, with the Reformation never very
far from mind.[11] In what follows, I hope to adopt a rather different

[8] For the public display of the total number of days indulgence available at Glastonbury, for example, see J. Krochalis, '"Magna Tabula": The Glastonbury Tablets', *Arthurian Literature*, 15 (1997), 93–183, esp. 180–3; 16 (1998), 41–82.

[9] In general, and stressing the merciful and for the most part innocent motives of the papacy, see R. W. Southern, *Western Society and the Church in the Middle Ages* (1970), 136–43. For fund-raising for St Peter's, beyond the studies by Paulus, see M. Venard, 'Les ventes d'indulgences au temps de Luther', in *Entre idéal et réalité: actes du colloque international 'Finances et religion du moyen-âge à l'époque contemporaine'*, ed. M. Aubrun et al. (Le Poiré-sur-Vie, 1994), 275–85. For two of the more notoriously generous of papal indulgences, issued by Celestine V at Collemaggio, and for the Portiuncula at Assisi, this last award attributed to Pope Honorius III, see P. Sabatier, *Fratris Francisci Bartholi de Assisio, Tractatus de indulgentia S. Mariae de Portiuncula* (Paris, 1900), esp. clxxxi–clxxxiv, 15–17.

[10] For the excesses attributed to pardoners, see Kellogg and Haselmayer, 'Chaucer's Satire of the Pardoner', 255–9. For angels' feathers, see the satirical accounts cited by Boussel, *Des reliques*, 57–60, noting, amongst others, Boccaccio, 'Decameron', 6th day, tale 10. For bread from the Last Supper, see the eye-witness account of Guibert of Nogent, 'De sanctis et eorum pigneribus', ed. R. B. C. Huygens, Corpus Christianorum Continuatio Mediaevalis 127 (Turnhout, 1993), 98, also in *Patrologiae cursus completus: series Latina*, ed. J.-P. Migne (Paris, 1841–64) [hereafter *PL*], clvi, 621.

[11] H. C. Lea, *A History of Auricular Confession and Indulgences in the Latin Church* (3 vols., 1896), esp. iii; N. Paulus, *Geschichte des Ablasses im Mittelalter* (3 vols., Paderborn, 1923). A rich selection of twelfth-century sources is to be found in L. Hödl, *Die Geschichte der scholastischen Literatur und der Theologie der Schlüsselgewalt, 1. Teil*, Beiträge zur Geschichte der Philosophie und Theologie des Mittelalters 38 (Münster, 1960). Most recently, see C. Neuhausen, *Das Ablasswesen in der Stadt Köln vom 13. bis zum 16. Jahrhundert* (Cologne, 1994), with a useful conspectus of recent writing in German at pp. 12–13.

approach, concentrating as much upon practice as upon theory, and more upon bishops than upon either pardoners or theologians. By focusing attention upon the first century of English indulgences, issued between 1100 and 1215 – a period in their history that has been largely ignored by English historians – I hope to demonstrate why indulgence, as many bishops were to discover, was both too potent and too delicate a practice to be left entirely to schoolsmen or to the devices of the medieval pardoner.

The process by which popes, legates and bishops began to award indulgences, at some time in the eleventh century, preceded by as much as two centuries the full working out of a theological system to justify such awards. As a result, it is not easy to find a definition of indulgence that will suit every case or satisfy the variety of opinions that were expressed upon the subject throughout the twelfth and thirteenth centuries. In essence, however, and here employing the language of thirteenth-century scholastic theory rather than twelfth-century episcopal practice, an indulgence represented the remission, not of sin or wrongdoing (the *culpa*) which only God could judge, nor necessarily of the satisfaction owing for such sin in the afterlife (the *pena*), but, in a phrase that was to become standard, of a certain period of 'enjoined penance': the earthly mortification imposed upon the penitent by his earthly confessor.[12] As such, the award of indulgences has to be approached as merely one aspect of the wider history of penance and confession.

The earliest written indulgence to have survived was identified by Paulus as letters of the archbishop of Arles for the church of St Croix de Montmajour, issued perhaps as early as 1019, promising the remission of up to one third of enjoined penance to those who bestowed alms upon the church.[13] Although the authenticity of the Montmajour indulgence remains subject to doubt,[14] the eleventh century undoubtedly

---

[12] See the definition by Bishop Bouvier, cited by Lea, *Confession and Indulgences*, III, 39: 'The remission of the temporal penalty due to actual sins, already remitted as to their guilt; granted externally to the Sacrament of Penance by those who have the power of distributing the spiritual treasure of the Church.' The classic scholastic formulation, by Thomas Aquinas, 'Summa Theologica', part 3, suppl. q.25 (printed in *Sancti Thomae Aquinatis ... Opera Omnia iussu impensaque Leonis XIII P.M. edita*, XII (Rome, 1906), 48ff), differs from various twelfth-century writers (for example, from Senatus of Worcester, cited below n. 40), in allowing that indulgence might carry away both the earthly satisfaction and the 'pena' that would otherwise be owing in the afterlife. Aquinas is more certain of the salutary effects and the authority by which indulgences are granted than he is of the precise benefits that they confer: an attitude in which he follows most earlier commentators. For general commentary, see the studies by Lea and Paulus cited above.

[13] Paulus, *Ablasses*, I, 135–6, citing L. d'Achery, *Spicilegium sive collectio veterum aliquot scriptorum* (Paris, 1657–77), VI, 427–31.

[14] Lea (*Confession and Indulgences*, III, 137–8) regards the Montmajour indulgence as an imitation of what may be a genuine award made to the church of Correns in 1065. Both

witnessed the development of a system by which popes and bishops offered remission of enjoined penance by substituting a particular indulgenced act of charity or devotion for a set fraction or period of days of the penitential sentence originally imposed upon sinners. It was within this context that Pope Urban II, at the Council of Clermont in 1095, offered indulgence to those prepared to make expedition to the Holy Land.[15] For many centuries before this, it had been allowed that the penances imposed by individual confessors, almost universally expressed as a set number of days or years to be spent fasting on bread and water, might be commuted, on occasion through the payment of a forfeit, either in money or in kind, or elsewhere by the substitution of a shorter but sharper penitential 'shock'.[16] In Anglo-Saxon and Frankish practice, for example, a year's fasting on bread and water might be redeemed for the payment of twenty-six *solidi*, the price of a slave or the recital of 300 masses.[17] Such commutations formed an essential feature of the system of tariffed penance from the time of its origins in the sixth century.[18] Without them, penance itself would have been almost impossible to implement, since the tariffed days of fasting imposed for any particular confession must frequently have exceeded the number of days left in a penitent's lifetime.[19] In imposing penance upon the archbishop of Milan in 1060, for example, Peter Damian

---

awards are remarkable in equating entrance into the churches in question with entry into an earthly prefiguration of purgatory.

[15] For Urban II's crusading indulgence and its pre-history, see J. Richard, 'Urbain II, la prédication de la croisade et la définition de l'indulgence', in *Deus qui mutat tempora: Menschen und Institutionen im Wandel des Mittelalters: Festschrift für Alfons Becker*, ed. E.-D. Hehl et al. (Sigmaringen, 1987), 129–35.

[16] C. Vogel, 'Composition légale et commutations dans le système de la pénitence tarifée', *Revue de droit canonique*, 8 (1958), 289–318, 9 (1959), 1–38, 341–59, reprinted in C. Vogel, *En rémission des péchés: recherches sur les systèmes pénitentiels dans l'église latine*, ed. A. Faivre (1994), ch. 5. For the system of penance as a whole, see the classic studies by H. K. Schmitz, *Die Bussbücher und die Bussdisciplin der Kirche* (2 vols., Mainz, 1883–98); C. Vogel, *La discipline pénitentielle en Gaule des origines à la fin du VIIe siècle* (Paris, 1952); C. Vogel, *Le pécheur et la pénitence au moyen-âge* (Paris, 1969); B. Poschmann, *Penance and the Annointing of the Sick*, trans. T. Courtney (Freiburg and London, 1964), with an excellent introduction in English to the most recent literature by A. Murray, 'Confession before 1215', *TRHS*, 6th ser., 3 (1993), 51–81. For the specific relation between commutation and indulgence, see B. Poschmann, *Der Ablass im Licht der Bussgeschichte* (Bonn, 1948).

[17] Vogel, *En rémission des péchés*, ch. 5, pp. 18, 25–6, 31.

[18] *Ibid.*, ch. 5, pp. 21-3, where Vogel rejects the assumption by earlier writers, for example by J. T. McNeill (*Medieval Handbooks of Penance: A Translation of the Principal 'Libri Poenitentiales'*, ed. J. T. McNeill and H. M. Gamer (New York, 1938; repr. 1990), 48-9), that commutations were a later addition to, and a potentially dangerous dilution of, the system set out in the earlier penitentials.

[19] See the example, cited by Murray, 'Confession before 1215', 60–1, of a man referred to in the Anglo-Saxon Council of Clovesho (747) who had accumulated 300 years of fasting for diverse offences.

clearly intended that his sentence of 100 years of fasting should be commuted in return for a substantial monetary payment.[20] Moreover, in allowing that so many days or years of fasting might be commuted, the Church accepted that the penance of one individual might be discharged by proxy, through the payment of a priest or the endowment of a monastery to discharge the commuted penance.[21] Such practices lie behind most of the great religious foundations of the Middle Ages, and were as common in England as anywhere else in Christendom. Edward the Confessor's refoundation of Westminster Abbey, for example, is said to have been made in commutation of a penitential pilgrimage vowed to Rome.[22]

Both commutation and indulgence represent an exercise of the Church's power to bind and loose, allowing a remission of enjoined penance to those prepared to carry out a particular task newly specified, in lieu of the penance that had originally been imposed. None the less, the grant of indulgences differed from the earlier system of commutation in at least two significant respects. First, it intruded greater papal or episcopal control over the relationship between penitent and confessor, allowing pope or bishop to alter substantially the penance imposed upon sinners, regardless of the terms set by any particular confessor. Secondly, whereas previously the bodily punishment of the sinner was to be discharged either by the sinner in person, or by proxy, in paying for the bodily and spiritual labours of a monk or religious, indulgences allowed far greater control to be exercised by pope or bishop over the precise object of commutation.[23] The grant of indulgences would have been meaningless save as part of a well-established tradition of penance. The indulgence was nothing more than the remission of part of a sentence that had already been imposed, just as in modern legal practice, remission or parole can only be extended to criminals who have already been convicted and sentenced to a set term of imprisonment. Moreover, for indulgences to be issued, like the Montmajour indulgence,

---

[20] Peter Damian writing to the future Pope Gregory VII, in *Sacrorum Conciliorum nova et amplissima collectio*, ed. J. D. Mansi (53 vols., Florence, Venice and Paris, 1759–98) [hereafter Mansi, *Concilia*], XIX, 893; *PL*, CXLV, 97–8.

[21] See, for example, Peter Damian, 'De ordine eremitarum', in *PL*, CXLV, 345.

[22] Ailred of Rievaulx, 'Vita Edwardi', in *PL*, CXCV, 752, whence Leo IX, 'Epistolae', in *PL*, CXLIII 674; P. Jaffé, *Regesta pontificum Romanorum*, ed. S. Loewenfeld, F. Kaltenbrunner and P. Ewald (2 vols., Leipzig, 1885–8) [hereafter Jaffé–Loewenfeld], I, no. 4257.

[23] For the thesis that financial 'amercements' were the chief end of tariffed penance as described in the penitentials, and for the suggestion that the penitentials themselves were intended more for the use of bishops than for local confessors, see F. Kerff, ' "Libri paenitentiales" und kirchliche Strafgerichtsbarkeit bis zum "Decretum Gratiani" Ein Diskussionsverschlag', *Zeitschrift der Savigny-Stiftung für Rechtsgeschichte*, 106, Kanonostische Abteilung 75 (1989), 23–57, with comment, mostly favourable, by Murray, 'Confession before 1215', 56, 61.

in the form of a remission of a specified fraction of penance, or elsewhere by the remission of a set number of days, most often calculated according to a forty-day Lenten standard, it was necessary that penance be susceptible to precise numerical measurement – an interesting indication this, at a time when the average man or woman is assumed to have had only the vaguest idea of their own age measured as a span of years, of the complex mathematical calculations that had to be made if a sinner were to assess their own chances of salvation.[24]

As the system of granting indulgences developed, so we might expect penance to have become measurable in ever more precise, numerical terms: a requirement that reflects the emergence of indulgences out of the system of early medieval penitential tariffs, measured in so many days or years of penitential fast. It is one of the peculiarities of our story that the twelfth century, far from witnessing the evolution of ever more quantified, numerically determined tariffs, saw instead the replacement of the old tariffs by a new style of penance, placing a far greater emphasis upon the sinner's inner contrition and the sincerity with which any penitential act was performed.[25] The ideal form of penance, exceeding even the ambition of Gilbert and Sullivan's *Mikado*, had long been considered to be one in which the punishment was tailored perfectly to fit both the crime and the individual criminal. What changed in the twelfth century was not just the replacement of mechanically tariffed penitential fastings by more personal acts of satisfaction – a tendency already allowed for in the early medieval penitentials – but the intrusion of a far greater emphasis upon contrition rather than penance as the defining feature of repentance. Penance now followed, rather than preceded, absolution. Confession became a far more subtle affair, in which the individual sinner may well have been left bewildered as to the true state of his or her soul. Had confession been properly made? Had there been genuine contrition? With what true feeling had penance been discharged? The very unease and bewilderment that this engendered could be interpreted by the Church in a positive light, since men and women, unsure of the state of their consciences, would be encouraged to engage in more frequent confession. To the individual sinner, however, like so many of the developments transmitted in the twelfth century from the schools to the parish, there was much here that was difficult to understand. What precisely had been achieved by confession? Was the soul now purified, or was the sinner merely compounding damnation by being readmitted to communion whilst still in a state of sin?

---

[24] For the calculation of age, see J. Bedell, 'Memory and Proof of Age in England 1272–1327', *Past and Present*, 162 (1999), 3–27.
[25] For an overview, see P. Anciaux, *La théologie du sacrement de pénitence au XIIe siècle* (Louvain and Gembloux, 1949).

The penitential literature of the twelfth and early thirteeenth centuries disposes of any mere mechanical conception of penance.[26] Even the tag cited by Stephen Langton – 'Bodily ills may be healed by fasting, ills of the mind are driven out by prayer' – would come to appear excessively crude to Langton's pupils.[27] In a tract attributed to one such pupil, Alexander of Stainsby, bishop of Coventry and Lichfield (1224–38), fasts are still enjoined for sins such as gluttony to which they serve as a suitable penance by opposites, but in other cases other penances should be applied: sins of the mouth, such as bearing false witness, should be punished by prayer, sins of the body by bodily mortification, sins of unrighteous violence by acts of righteous bravery, and so forth.[28] None of these penances was very easily susceptible to remission calculated merely as a fraction or a set number of days of the penance enjoined. How for example was a sinner to be remitted a third of a pilgrimage to Jerusalem, or forty days of an enjoined act of charitable benefaction? Furthermore, as Stainsby's tract explains, there were many sins so grave that absolution could not be granted by the parish priest, but only by the bishop or, as in the gravest cases such as violence against priests and bishops, by the pope.[29] Such reservation of penance to papal or episcopal penitentiaries once again reflects the post-Gregorian tendency to annex yet further power to the ultimate authorities within the Church.[30] Henry II and the murderers of Thomas Becket are only the most famous of those who in twelfth-century

[26] For penitentials written by English authors during this period, see Bartholomew of Exeter, 'Penitential', printed with a brief introduction in A. Morey, *Bartholomew of Exeter Bishop and Canonist* (Cambridge, 1937), 163ff; Thomas of Chobham, *Summa Confessorum*, ed. F. Broomfield, Analecta Mediaevalia Namurcensia 25 (Louvain and Paris, 1968); Robert of Flamborough, *Liber Poenitentialis*, ed. J. J. F. Firth (Toronto, 1971).

[27] Langton, 'Questio de satisfactione', printed by Hödl, *Schlüsselgewalt*, 346 lines 87–8: 'Iciunio enim sanantur pestes corporis, oratione eliduntur pestes mentis', quoted in a similar context in the 'Summa' of Robert Courson: V. L. Kennedy, 'Robert Courson on Penance', *Mediaeval Studies*, 7 (1945), 325, with echoes of Jerome, 'Expositio in Marcum', 9 (in *PL*, xxx, 638): 'stultitia ad luxuriam carnis pertinet et ieiunio sanatur et oratione'.

[28] Alexander of Stainsby, 'Tractatus de confessionibus', printed in *Councils and Synods with Other Documents relating to the English Church II: 1205–1313*, ed. F. M. Powicke and C. R. Cheney (2 vols., Oxford, 1964), i, 220–6, quoting the same tag from Jerome as above n. 27, and for commentary, noting Alexander's dependence upon the earlier confessional of William de Montibus, see N. Vincent, 'Master Alexander of Stainsby, Bishop of Coventry and Lichfield, 1224–1238', *Journal of Ecclesiastical History*, 46 (1995), 624–7.

[29] Alexander, 'Tractatus', in *Councils and Synods II*, i, 221–2, 225–6. The papal reservation of matrimonial cases is already implied in a 'questio' 'De satisfactione', attributed to Stephen Langton: Hödl, *Schlüsselgewalt*, 346 lines 52ff.

[30] For papal and episcopal reservation, see J. Longère, 'Les évêques et l'administration du sacrement de pénitence au XIIIe siècle: les cas reservés', in *Papauté, monachisme et théories politiques: études d'histoire médiévale offertes à Marcel Pacaut*, ed. P. Guichard et al. (2 vols., Lyon, 1994), ii, 537–50; Vogel, *En rémission des péchés*, ch. 7, pp. 140–7.

England found themselves subject to papal penance.[31] But were the penances imposed by the pope to be susceptible to mere episcopal indulgence? Could indulgences be applied to 'solemn' penances, which were indefinite in length and which could be ended only by the bishop's licence to the individual penitent?[32]

For all of these reasons, from its beginnings in the eleventh century, the award of indulgences involved a number of potentially self-contradictory elements. Contemporaries were not slow to point these out. Some were already prejudiced against any idea of commutation, let alone of indulgence, demanding that the confessor's sentence be enforced to the letter and not abandoned for some 'silvered penance'.[33] Peter Abelard, with his particular interest in the interior, psychological nature of the intention to sin, is possibly the first theologian to pour scorn upon those bishops, 'shamelessly ablaze with greed', who offered indulgences to great multitudes of sinners at the time of dedicating churches or consecrating altars, remitting a third or a quarter of enjoined penance by virtue of the powers supposedly vested in St Peter and the apostles by Christ. Why be so stingy, Abelard enquires, when if bishops possess the powers to which they lay claim they might just as easily remit a half or indeed the entire penance?[34] Writing towards the end of the twelfth century, Peter the Chanter is almost equally dismissive, citing more than a dozen objections that might be made to such awards. How can the same gift made by the rich man and the poor man alike merit the same indulgence? St Jerome urged the penitent to sleep in sack cloth, not merely to give a penny in alms! How can the archbishop of Reims claim to remit the sins of parishioners who are themselves subjects of the archbishop of Sens? Although it was allowed that one person might take on the penitential burden of another, it could be argued that remission of penance is impossible,

---

[31] For the penance (crusade and religious benefaction, as well as more personal mortifications) imposed upon Henry II by the papal legates, and the more severe sentence of a seventeen-year exile in the Holy Land imposed by the pope on the three murderers of Thomas Becket, see N. Vincent, 'The Murderers of Thomas Becket', in *Bischofsmord im Mittelalter*, ed. N. Frye (Göttingen, forthcoming).

[32] For 'solemn penance', applied in the case of laymen but not priests, involving public expulsion from communion, most usually on Ash Wednesday, to be undertaken once only during a sinner's lifetime, still operative throughout the twelfth and thirteenth centuries, see Vogel, *En rémission des péchés*, ch. 7, pp. 117–21, and especially ch. 8; M. C. Mansfield, *The Humiliation of Sinners: Public Penance in Thirteenth-Century France* (Ithaca, 1995); Aquinas, 'Summa Theologica', part 3, suppl. q. 28 (in Aquinas, *Opera Omnia*, XII, 52–3).

[33] For the claim made of St Hugh of Grenoble (d. 1132) that 'non deargentatem convictis vel confitentibus imposuit penitentiam', see 'Vita Sancti Hugonis', 5.20, in *PL*, CLIII, 776, noticed by Murray, 'Confession before 1215', 74.

[34] *Peter Abelard's Ethics*, ed. D. E. Luscombe (Oxford, 1971), 108–17, esp. 108–11, and for commentary on Peter's theory of the keys, see Hödl, *Schlüsselgewalt*, ch. 3.

since a penance, once decreed, could not be abolished save by the substitution of an equivalent compensation.[35] This last point, which owes much to the contemporary scholastic understanding of change and the impossibility of destruction within substances and forms, led to attempts to explain what happened to penance once it was remitted. One theory was that it passed from the penitent to the pope or bishop awarding indulgence. In this way, in his extraordinary account of the indulgence granted by Pope Eugenius III (1145–53) to the count of Molise, John of Salisbury tells us that the pope, by virtue of the power of the keys, awarded the count complete remission of all his sins, taking their burden upon himself at Judgement Day, and proffering a ring as token of this contract.[36] Not all were satisfied by such an explanation. For example, the Chanter's contemporary, Peter of Poitiers, suggests that in purgatory the merits of one person cannot suffice for the salvation of another, so that the merits of the Church cannot release an individual soul from the satisfaction (the *pena*) due for sin, nor mitigate such satisfaction.[37]

These are just a few of the more significant criticisms levelled at indulgences by twelfth-century writers. Taken together, they reflect the self-contradictions that appeared to weaken the indulgence's force. How could the penitential debt of sinners be satisfied when no equivalent hardship was put in its place? How could a mechanistic, catch-all indulgence satisfy the penance owed by individual sinners? How was it possible that a single act of almsgiving – the offer of alms as insignificant as a penny – could allow the remission of a far more considerable burden of penance? Much of the language of the critics, with its reference to debts and their payments, is distinctly worldly and economic in tone. In employing such language, however, the critics were anxious to distinguish between the spiritual or sacramental function of penance, and what appeared to be the intrusion of a financial consideration linking indulgences to the payment of alms. Nor are such criticisms to be found only in the schools of Paris. In England and amongst English writers, there was clearly just as much unease.

As early as the 1160s, John of Salisbury had launched a tirade against monastic confessors prepared to sell light penances in return for a rich man's silver.[38] With particular regard to indulgences, although there is

---

[35] Peter the Chanter, *Summa de sacramentis et animae consiliis*, part 2, ed. J.-A. Dugauquier, Analecta Mediaevalia Namurcensia 7 (Louvain and Lille, 1957), 190–6.

[36] John of Salisbury, *Historia Pontificalis*, ch. 41, ed. M. Chibnall (London, 1956), 82.

[37] Peter of Poitiers, 'Sentences', 5.20, in *PL*, ccxi, 1270. Elsewhere ('Sentences', 3.16, in *PL*, ccxi, 1076), Peter none the less allows that a priest or bishop might subtract ('subtrahere') part of the 'pena'.

[38] John of Salisbury, *Policraticus*, 7.21, ed. C. C. I. Webb (2 vols., Oxford, 1909), 692–3.

no English conciliar legislation on the subject before 1215, it is easy to detect signs that the practice was regarded with suspicion by at least some English bishops and theologians.[39] Of greatest significance here are the questions sent by Bishop Roger of Worcester (1164–79) to one of his cathedral's monks, Master Senatus. From Senatus's answers, it is apparent that the bishop was concerned by the arbitrary nature of indulgences offered to those who gave alms at the time of church dedications and for such charitable projects as hospitals and the building of bridges, expressing much the same doubts – on the authority that the bishop granting such indulgences possessed over individual penitents, over the equal remissions granted to rich and poor alike, and over the absence of any real knowledge of the penitent's inner contrition – that were to be articulated shortly afterwards by Peter the Chanter. Senatus's reply to these questions is grounded upon the distinction between the offence (culpa), the satisfaction (pena) owing to God which could only be supplied by true confession and contriteness of heart, and that aspect of penance imposed by the earthly confessor. None the less, his judgement ends abruptly with an admission that although such arguments could calm the doubts of the crowd, they might not calm those of the bishop himself.[40] That doubts continued to linger is suggested by a query sent to Pope Alexander III by one of Bishop Roger's contemporaries – probably the archbishop of Canterbury. In reply to a request for guidance as to the effect of a bishop's indulgences upon the subjects of other bishops, the pope replied that indulgences might be extended to all those who lived within the bishop's 'province' but not to those who dwelt in the province of another. Only the confessor (or the superior of the confessor) who originally binds a sinner is entitled to remit that sinner's penance.[41] Preserved in decretal collections, this judgement was later incorporated in the Liber Extra. In the common gloss attached to it, the English canonist Alanus (c. 1206)

---

[39] Before 1215, the chief thrust of English conciliar legislation had lain in an effort to free penance and confession from any taint of simony, rather than in specific concern for indulgences: Councils and Synods with Other Documents relating to the English Church I: Part II, 1066–1204, ed. D. Whitelock, M. Brett and C. N. L. Brooke (Oxford, 1981), 1048 (c. 4), 1062 (c. 4).

[40] P. Delhaye, 'Deux textes de Senatus de Worcester sur la pénitence', Recherches de théologie ancienne et médiévale, 19 (1952), 203–24, editing the passages on indulgences at pp. 206–7, citing an unidentified decree 'in Grangensi concilio', and ending 'si hec discretioni vestre non sederint, vel sedeant ut missilia que iactantur in vulgus ubi qui potest capere capiat' (Matth. 19.12). For commentary, see M. G. Cheney, Roger Bishop of Worcester 1164–1179 (Oxford, 1980), 58–61.

[41] 'Brugensis' 59.1, also in 1 Comp. 5.33.3 ('Quod autem consuluisti'), printed with address to 'Carnot episcopo', by E. Friedberg, Die Canones-Sammlungen zwischen Gratian und Bernhard von Pavia (Leipzig, 1897), 170, and with address to 'archiepiscopo Cantuariensi', in 'Liber Extra' [hereafter X] 5.38.4, printed by E. Friedberg, Corpus Iuris Canonici, II: Decretalium Collectiones (Leipzig, 1881), col. 885.

was to remark 'What these remissions (indulgences) are worth is an old dispute, and is still highly uncertain.'[42] Peter of Blois, the close associate of several English bishops and himself the author of a treatise on penance, takes issue with various claims that had been made for indulgences: for example, that they could be applied to sins which the sinner himself had forgotten (an old theological problem this), or that they could be effective even in the case of offences committed against parents, short of physical violence.[43] Similar questions are addressed, although with a far more positive response, in the work of another English scholar trained at Paris, Thomas of Chobham, writing shortly after 1215. Thomas raises the thorny issue of how a penitent sentenced to pilgrimage or prayers can obtain relaxation from an indulgence expressed in so many days' remission of enjoined penance. Should a penitent in possession of an indulgence of ten days who sets out on a pilgrimage that he knows will take forty days, return after only thirty days on the road?[44] Others, Thomas notes, believe that God alone can know the period of penance owing for any sin.[45]

Thus far we have observed the debate over indulgences as expressed in theory and precept. Such expressions, however, tell us merely what English writers thought about indulgences, and in particular what they thought might be wrong with indulgences in theory. As with so many areas of medieval life – for example in the prolonged debate over the purpose and practical impact of early medieval law codes, or, more recently, in Alexander Murray's questioning of the reality as opposed to what was recorded in penitential literature of the sacrament of confession – we must beware of confusing principles with practice. The time has now come for us to examine what evidence there is for indulgences actually issued in England in the century or so before 1200. This evidence should help us to answer one very obvious question: if

---

[42] In a gloss, noticed by Cheney, *Roger of Worcester*, 61. For the citation of 1 Comp. 5.33.3 (X 5.38.4) in Vincent of Spain's commentary on the Lateran constitution on indulgences, see *Constitutiones concilii quarti Lateranensis una cum comentariis glossatorum*, ed. A. Garcia y Garcia, Monumenta Iuris Canonici Series A: Corpus Glossatorum 2 (Vatican, 1981), 375.

[43] For Peter on indulgences, also querying the validity of awards made by bishops who have since died, and might therefore be in purgatory or hell, see *The Later Letters of Peter of Blois*, ed. E. Revell, Auctores Britannici Medii Aevi 13 (Oxford, 1993), 135–6 (28.2). For further remarks on penance and confession, as applied to the case of King Henry II of England, see Peter, 'Dialogus inter regem Henricum secundum et abbatem Bonevallis', ed. R. B. C. Huygens, *Revue Bénédictine*, 68 (1958), 97–112. Other short, and for the most part jejune, treatises by Peter on penance and confession are to be found in PL, ccvii, 1077–98.

[44] For later, unsuccessful, attempts to resolve this particular problem, see Lea, *Confession and Indulgences*, iii, 85–6.

[45] Chobham, *Summa Confessorum*, 5.9, ed. Broomfield, 208–10.

schoolsmen and theologians were so mistrustful of indulgences, why did bishops, many of them trained in the schools, permit indulgences to flourish and to multiply?

We must begin here with the letters of indulgence issued by successive twelfth-century English bishops. The story that these letters and charters tells is as follows. No genuine episcopal indulgence survives from England for the period before 1066. Where references are made much later to such indulgences, as for example in the claim by the monks of Glastonbury that they possessed indulgences issued by Popes Eleutherius, Celestine I, by Saints Patrick and St Dunstan, these can invariably be dismissed as the result of wishful thinking or outright forgery.[46] Before 1140 or so, indulgences remain very rare. All told, we have barely twenty surviving letters of indulgence purporting to have been issued by English bishops before 1140, the very earliest of them by Archbishop Anselm (between 1101 and 1107) renewing and adding a further three days to a ten-day indulgence awarded by the papal legate John of Tusculum in favour of benefactors of the monks of Bury.[47]

Various general points emerge from these awards. First, there is no evidence that indulgences were known in England prior to 1095 and

[46] Krochalis, ' "Magna Tabula" ', 180–1, a record dating from the early fifteenth century. For other such forged pre-Conquest indulgences, in this instance recited in full, see J. B. Davidson, 'On Some Ancient Documents relating to Crediton Minster', *Report and Transactions of the Devonshire Association*, 10 (1878), 237–54, from a fifteenth-century source; *English Episcopal Acta*, XI: *Exeter 1046–1184*, ed. F. Barlow (Oxford, 1996), no. 2, supposedly before 1072 but with impossible details.

[47] *Feudal Documents of the Abbey of Bury St Edmunds*, ed. D. C. Douglas (1932), 153 no. 171, with commentary by M. Brett, *The English Church under Henry I* (Oxford, 1975), 49, to be dated to the vacancy at Bury between 1101 and 1107. For indulgences, supposedly issued by Archbishop Lanfranc, to Glastonbury and a Canterbury hospital, surviving merely as mentions in later catalogues, see Krochalis, ' "Magna Tabula" ', 180; J. Duncombe and N. Battely, *History and Antiquities of the Three Archiepiscopal Hospitals and Other Charitable Foundations at and near Canterbury* (1785), 254, whence *English Episcopal Acta II:* [hereafter *EEA*] *Canterbury 1162–1190*, ed. C. R. Cheney and B. E. A. Jones (Oxford, 1986), no. 7. In reality, when Lanfranc is found remitting penance, it is on an individual rather than a general basis: *The Letters of Lanfranc Archbishop of Canterbury*, ed. H. Clover and M. Gibson (Oxford, 1979), 110–11 no. 26. For indulgences in the names of Archbishops Ralph (1114–22) and William (1123–36), see *Text of the Book of Llan Dâv*, ed. J. G. Evans (Oxford, 1894), 87; *Liber memorandorum ecclesie de Bernewelle*, ed. J. W. Clark (Cambridge, 1907), 44–5; Norwich, Norfolk Record Office, DCN 40/8 (Cartulary of St Benet) fo. 40r; Cambridge, University Library MS Add. 3020 (Thorney cartulary), fo. 166r, partly noticed by Brett, *English Church*, 67n, 85. I am extremely grateful to Martin Brett for providing these references together with transcripts of the awards. For other early examples, see *English Episcopal Acta VI: Norwich 1070–1214*, ed. C. Harper-Bill (Oxford, 1990), nos. 8, 15–16, 30, 42; *The Charters of Norwich Cathedral Priory I*, ed. B. Dodwell, Pipe Roll Society, n. s., 40 (1974), nos. 107–8, 254; *EEA I: Lincoln 1067–1185*, ed. D. M. Smith (Oxford, 1980), no. 13; *EEA VII: Hereford 1079–1234*, ed. J. Barrow (Oxford, 1993), no. 32; *EEA XIV: Coventry and Lichfield 1072–1159*, ed. M. J. Franklin (Oxford, 1997), no. 10; *The Acta of the Bishops of Chichester 1075–1207*, ed. H. Mayr-Harting, Canterbury and York Society 56 (1964), no. 8.

Urban II's offer of plenary indulgence to those who participated in the First Crusade. The very earliest, by Archbishop Anselm, appears to have been issued in association with a papal legation. The terms of the indulgence are invariably modest, the most generous being of forty days, with only one award of a year, made by the legate Alberic for benefactions made at the dedication of Godstow Abbey, itself reduced to forty days for visitors on the anniversary.[48] Even a forty-day indulgence may appear suspiciously generous, given that many of the awards are for far lesser terms.[49] However, it would be rash to dismiss so great a portion of the evidence as forged, particularly since we are dealing with a period in which there was no fixed standard against which forgery can be judged. Most of the awards are issued for a specified number of days. The only exceptions are indulgences issued by Archbishops Ralph and William of Canterbury, relaxing a quarter or a seventh of penance under various, more complicated conditions.[50] Several indulgences, including a papal award to St Albans, are tacked on to the end of more general confirmations of lands and privileges.[51] Precisely what is being offered is stated differently in different cases. The dispositive verbs 'remit' or 'relax' are most common, although in early examples from Norwich and Chichester, the bishops speak either of 'pardoning' or of a 'pardon' available to the penitents who bring alms.[52] The authority by which the bishop acts is occasionally specified. Bishop Herbert of Norwich, for example, claims to act 'by authority of our office',[53] Richard of London 'paternally'.[54] Bishops Roger of Chester

[48] *EEA I: Lincoln 1067–1185*, no. 33.

[49] For example, the three-day indulgence granted by Anselm to Bury (above n. 47), or that of a single day during each week of fasting granted by Bishop Robert to those giving alms to St Albans: *EEA I: Lincoln 1067–1185*, no. 13.

[50] *Book of Llan Dâv*, 87 ('de onere penitentie sue quod sibi a suis confessoribus impositum est quartam partem ei de misericordia Dei et potestate nostri ministerii confisi relaxamus'); Norwich, Norfolk Record Office, DCN 40/8 fo. 40r ('si in penitentia quinque vel septem vel amplius annorum fuerit et vere confessus extiterit et in penitentia permanserit a Pascha usque ad festum sancti Martini et a natale Domini usque ad capud ieiunii, eodem anno septimana unus ei dies relaxetur. Qui vero in iniuncta penitentia fuerit, triginta dies illi relaxentur per annum, et si penitentiam extra ecclesiam egerint, eisdem diebus intrent ecclesiam'), transcripts courtesy of Martin Brett.

[51] For example, see *EEA I: Lincoln 1067–1185*, no. 33; *Norwich Cathedral Charters I*, no. 107; *Papsturkunden in England*, ed. W. Holtzmann, Abhandlungen der Gesellschaft der Wissenschaften zu Göttingen, Philologisch-Historische Klasse, neue Folge 25, 3. Folge 14–15, 33 (1930–52) [hereafter *PUE*], iii, no. 5.

[52] *Norwich Cathedral Charters I*, nos. 107–8; *Acta of Chichester*, no. 8.

[53] *EEA VI: Norwich 1070–1214*, no. 8, 'auctoritate nostri officii remittimus'.

[54] *EEA XV: London 1076–1187*, ed. F. Neininger (Oxford, 1999), no. 22, 'xx. dies de suis penitentiis paterne remittentes', and for further examples see *Norwich Cathedral Charters I*, no. 254, 'remitto eis ex divino largitione et nostra auctoritate'; *EEA VII: Hereford 1079–1234*, no. 32, 'confisus de misericordia Dei et meritis sanctorum et orationibus fratrum tam ibi quam apud Rading Deo servientibus'; *PUE*, iii, no. 6, 'nos ex parte beati Petri apostolorum principis constituimus'.

and Ralph of Chichester, however, merely claim to relax or remit, with no reference to the authority by which they act.[55] Where a motive for the issue of indulgences is stated or can be discerned, they are issued to increase the devotion and almsgiving of the faithful and above all to ensure public attendance at particular churches and festivals. Indeed, in certain cases, as with the indulgence for visitors to the dedication of Godstow Abbey or another for the translation of an arm relic of St Osyth at London, it is almost certain that indulgences were published in advance of the ceremony itself, precisely to encourage a greater throng of the faithful.[56] Confirmation of this can be obtained from numerous later sources. For example, the life of the Limousin saint Stephen of Obazine records that in 1156, Stephen was offered indulgences by the local bishops well in advance of the dedication of his church, so that as many people as possible might be encouraged to attend: an offer which the saint scrupulously refused.[57]

From this, several implications follow. First, indulgences were intended both to encourage alms and to serve as an early form of rent-a-crowd. As a result of this, from the very beginning, their effectiveness depended upon the indulgence being widely advertised: a fact that allows us to assume the existence of publicists – the forebears of the later pardoners or *questores* – in England at least as early as the first decades of the twelfth century. Secondly, and perhaps most significantly, the issue and the publication of indulgences suggest that the bishops assumed that there were many penitent sinners awaiting the opportunity to respond to the offer contained in the indulgence: a point to which we shall return. Finally, it is worth noting the close association, even as early as the 1120s and 30s, between indulgences and the relics of the saints, for example at London, with the translation of an arm relic of St Osyth, at Leominster by the institution of a feast of relics which the penitent were encouraged to attend and at St Albans by the award of indulgence to visitors on the feast day of the principal saint whose relics were there displayed.[58]

Before the 1140s, indulgences appear in only a minority of the English sees, and seem to have been issued by only a minority of the reigning bishops even within those sees. Our evidence here, of course, is distorted by the loss of most of the ephemeral documentation of the Church.

---

[55] *EEA XIV: Coventry and Lichfield 1072–1159*, no. 10; *Acta of Chichester*, no. 8.

[56] *EEA I: Lincoln 1067–1185*, no. 33; *EEA XV: London 1076–1187*, no. 22.

[57] *Vie de Saint Etienne d'Obazine*, ed. M. Aubrun (Clermont-Ferrand, 1970), 128–31, and for publicity that brought a great multitude of people to St Mary-le-Bow in London a century later, to receive an indulgence offered by Archbishop Boniface of Canterbury, see Matthew Paris, *Chronica Majora*, ed. H. R. Luard (7 vols., 1872–84), v, 351.

[58] *EEA VII: Hereford 1079–1234*, no. 32; *EEA XV: London 1076–1187*, no. 22; *PUE*, III, nos. 5, 6.

Just as more indulgences survive from after the 1140s, so the total number of surviving episcopal charters undergoes a great increase at much this same time. To this extent, the apparent increase in the issue of indulgences after 1140 may be more a function of archival practice than a proof of any real increase in the issue of such documents. It is none the less from the 1140s and 1150s that we have the first evidence of bishops acting in concert, to issue a dozen or more related indulgences for a single beneficiary – the shrine of St Edward the Confessor at Westminster, for example, or the relics of St James at Reading.[59] By contrast to the mere twenty or so indulgences that survive for the whole of England before 1140, Archbishop Theobald of Canterbury is recorded issuing at least twenty-four indulgences between 1139 and 1161.[60] Gilbert Foliot issued at least twenty-three as bishop of Hereford and London between 1148 and 1187.[61] These figures are greatly boosted by the survival of Gilbert's letter collection: a resource lacking for other twelfth-century bishops.[62] Even allowing for evidential distortion, it is apparent not only that more indulgences have survived for the years after 1140, but that this increased rate of survival may suggest a real increase in the rate of issue.

By the end of the twelfth century, there was probably no diocese in England where indulgences could not be found. Moreover, the sheer number of projects that was henceforth supported by indulgences appears to have undergone considerable expansion. Here the indulgences preserved in the letter book of Gilbert Foliot are particularly instructive, not only because they can be assumed to be free from any

---

[59] *Westminster Abbey Charters 1066–c. 1214*, ed. E. Mason, London Record Society 25 (1988), nos. 200, 204, 221, 229; *Reading Abbey Cartularies*, ed. B. R. Kemp, Camden Society, 4th ser., 31–2 (1986–7), I, nos. 183ff.

[60] A. Saltman, *Theobald Archbishop of Canterbury* (London, 1956), nos. 9, 28, 53, 67, 76, 82, 87, 93–4, 114, 188, 213–14, 242–3, 261, 279, 286–8, 293, 308–9, of which no. 288 is reassigned by *EEA II: Canterbury 1162–1190*, no. 45, to Archbishop Thomas. To the charters printed by Saltman should be added a further four awards, some of them previously attributed to Archbishop Thomas, as drawn to my attention by Martin Brett: Cambridge University Library MS Ff.ii.33 (Bury sacrist's cartulary), fo. 134r no. 730; R. Foreville, 'Lettres "extravagantes" de Thomas Becket', *Mélanges d'histoire du moyen âge dédiés à la mémoire de Louis Halphen* (Paris, 1951), 233–4 nos. 11, 12; *Norwich Cathedral Charters I*, 164–5 no. 262.

[61] For the most part merely calendared in *EEA VII: Hereford 1079–1234*, nos. 69, 98, 110; *EEA XV: London 1076–1187*, nos. 83–4, 93, 102–3, 121, 126, 145, 152–3, 168, 176, 178, 184, 189, 207, 210, 218, 225, 228, 248, with full texts printed in *The Letters and Charters of Gilbert Foliot*, ed. A. Morey and C. N. L. Brooke (Cambridge, 1967).

[62] Of the twenty-three indulgences recorded for Bishop Foliot, sixteen would be unknown were it not for the survival of Foliot's letter collection (*EEA XV: London 1076–1187*, nos. 83–4, 102, 121, 126, 145, 153, 168, 176, 178, 184, 210, 218, 225, 228, 248). Note, in addition, that there is no overlap between those indulgences recorded in the letter collection and in sources independent of it, demonstrating that even the tally obtained from the letter collection is likely to be well below the total number of indulgences that Foliot actually awarded.

element of forgery, but because they include a number of awards that, due to their ephemeral nature, would not otherwise survive. Thus we find Gilbert issuing indulgences for those who give support to a converted London Jew; the first examples surviving in England of indulgences issued for the building or repair of bridges and causeways, at London and St Ives, and the earliest English examples of indulgences solicited by foreign alms-seekers: not just the Hospitallers and the Templars, but envoys from the crusader church of Josaphat, reputed the place of the Virgin Mary's earthly burial.[63] Such foreign missions were not themselves new. As early as 1086, the monks of Marchiennes had attempted, with disastrous lack of success, to raise money from England with a tour of the relics of St Eusebius.[64] The subsequent evidence for fund-raising by the canons of Laon Cathedral and the monks of Provins, touring England before 1160 with or without relics, is probably only the tip of a much more considerable iceberg, and suggests both that the authors of such itinerant quests were keen to recruit the support of the English bishops, and that those bestowing alms were encouraged to confess their sins, much as those obtaining indulgence were expected, by definition, to be penitent and confessed.[65] Like indulgences, the itinerant relic quest was a phenomenon that first appears in the eleventh century: both quest and indulgence, let it be noted, were dependent upon there being a ready supply of surplus cash within the economy. It is not until the 1160s, however, that we have any certain proof of an association between foreign *questores* and English episcopal indulgences.[66]

---

[63] For the Jew, and for bridges and causeways, see *Letters and Charters of Gilbert Foliot*, nos. 418–19, 448, whence *EEA XV: London 1076–1187*, nos. 168, 176, 210, 225. For foreign missions, see *Letters and Charters of Gilbert Foliot*, nos. 386, 390, 459, whence *EEA XV: London 1076–1187*, nos. 121, 126, 228.

[64] 'Miracula sanctae Rictrudis', ed. A. Poncelet, *Analecta Bollandiana*, 20 (1901), 455–6. This, together with the other missions to England, is noted in the considerable literature on quests with relics, for which see P. Héliot and M.-L. Chastang, 'Quêtes et voyages de reliques au profit des églises françaises du Moyen Age', *Revue d'histoire ecclésiastique*, 59 (1964), 789–822; 60 (1965), 5–32; N. Herrmann-Mascard, *Les reliques des saints: formation coutumière d'un droit* (Paris, 1975), 296–312; P.-A. Sigal, 'Les voyages de reliques aux XIe et XIIe siècles', *Voyage, quête, pèlerinage dans la littérature et la civilisation médiévales* (Aix-en-Provence and Paris, 1976), 75–104; R. Kaiser, 'Quêtes itinérantes avec des reliques pour financer la construction des églises (XIe–XIIe siècles)', *Le moyen-âge*, 101 (1995), 205–25.

[65] For the Laon 'quest' of 1113, see Herman of Tournai, 'Miracula sanctae Mariae Laudunensis', in *PL*, CLVI, 961–87, with extended English commentary by J. S. P. Tatlock, 'The English Journey of the Laon Canons', *Speculum*, 8 (1933), 454–65, and by Murray, 'Confession before 1215', 66–7 n. 70, 75–9. For the monks of Provins, apparently supported by Archbishop Theobald in their quest of the 1150s, see Peter of Celle, 'Epistolae', 16, 68, in *PL*, CCII, 417–18, 513–14; *The Letters of John of Salisbury, I: The Early Letters (1153–1161)*, ed. W. J. Millor, S. J. and H. E. Butler and C. N. L. Brooke (1955), 54 no. 32.

[66] The claim by Héliot and Chastang, 'Quêtes et voyages de reliques', 797, 814–15, that indulgences were applied to a French relic quest as early as the 1080s, are not

As we have seen, indulgences, like relic quests, assume the existence of itinerant publicists and alms-seekers prepared to advertise the indulgence to the people at large. Foliot's letters supply us with further details of such *questores*, referring, for example, to 'the bearers of the present letters', to *nuncios*, *procuratores* and occasionally to named individuals.[67] At much the same time, we catch our first glimpse of such men, in royal letters, with King Henry II's request for support for collectors from Rochester, Compiègne and Dieppe.[68] Henry II, indeed, is the first English king for whom we have evidence to suggest regular confession and penance during his own lifetime, rather than merely at his deathbed.[69] If we are to believe the words attributed to Henry by Peter of Blois, then the king was troubled in later life by the fear that although he had many times accepted penance with a humble and contrite heart, he had not succeeded in completing any of the penances thus imposed.[70] In 1188, on taking the Cross, we are told that Henry, like his fellow crusaders, was immediately subject to papal indulgence for all penances imposed in confession or owing for forgotten sins.[71] Most remarkably of all, in 1188 as in 1166 when he had first pledged aid to the Holy Land, the king issued letters promising that all who made proper contribution to taxes imposed for the Crusade would be subject to an indulgence, in 1166 remitting a third, and in 1188 half of their enjoined penance.[72] This fiscal application of the crusading indulgence, although sanctioned by the Church, is symptomatic of another important development

substantiated by the source cited: G. Chenesseau, *L'Abbaye de Fleury à St-Benoit-sur-Loire* (Paris, 1931), 128.

[67] *Letters and Charters of Gilbert Foliot*, nos. 352, 363, 386, 390, 418, 424, whence *EEA XV: London 1076–1187*, nos. 83, 102, 121, 126, 168, 178.

[68] *Recueil des actes de Henri II roi d'Angleterre et du de Normandie concernant les provinces françaises et les affaires de France*, ed. L. Delisle and E. Berger (3 vols., Paris, 1916–27), I, no. 151, II, no. 619; *Registrum Roffense*, ed. J. Thorpe (1769), 37. Of these, the Rochester letters are almost certainly spurious or reworked. The licence to Compiègne, although highly peculiar, is probably genuine. For a comparable licence, issued by Louis VII of France to the *questores* of Senlis Cathedral, probably in the 1150s, see A. Luchaire, *Etudes sur les actes de Louis VII* (Paris, 1885), 216–17 no. 363.

[69] See, for example, the confession made by Henry II, before 1165, on the eve of crossing the Channel from Normandy into England: E. P. Sauvage, 'Vitae B. Petri Abrincensis et B. Hamonis monachorum coenobii Saviniacensis', *Analecta Bollandiana*, 2 (1883), 531–2, and for confession and penance undertaken by Henry's mother, the Empress Matilda, see *ibid.*, 546–7.

[70] Peter of Blois, 'Dialogus inter regem Henricum secundum et abbatem Bonevallis' (above n. 43), 112, esp. lines 441–3, 453–4.

[71] William of Newburgh, 'Historia Rerum Anglicarum', 3.23, in *Chronicles of the Reigns of Stephen, Henry II and Richard I*, ed. R. Howlett (4 vols., 1884–9), I, 273.

[72] Newburgh, in *Chronicles*, ed. Howlett, I, 273, applied in 1188 to both confessed and forgotten sins; *The Historical Works of Gervase of Canterbury*, ed. W. Stubbs (2 vols., 1879–80), I, 198–9, applied in 1166 simply to 'tertia pars penitentie'.

that affected indulgences in the twelfth century. Although many indulgences continued to require attendance at particular churches, relics or religious festivals, many others became focused upon almsgiving with no requirement for the almsgiver's attendance at a particular time or place. Bridge-building, for example, which by the end of the twelfth century we can assume to have been heavily indulgenced, and which could be justified in Christian terms by the assistance that bridges supplied to pilgrims, was hardly an enterprise that lent itself to mass attendance at the construction site.[73] At London, as elsewhere in the late twelfth century, we find the establishment of special fraternities, intended to pay for the building of cathedrals and churches.[74] In return for subscription to such projects, members of the fraternity were promised extensive spiritual benefits: indulgence from enjoined penance, participation in special masses and prayers and the prospect that should they die under a sentence that would normally exclude them from burial in holy ground, such restrictions might be relaxed.[75] The association here between money and spiritual benefits is more explicitly stated than in most indulgences. Nor did it go uncriticised. Constitution 57 of the Lateran Council of 1215 was specifically intended to counter the abuse by which fraternity members purchased burial in consecrated ground, whatever the true state of their souls.[76] Even before this, and no doubt wary of the charge of simony that such awards might incur, Gilbert Foliot's statutes for the fraternity at St Paul's had allowed membership and spiritual benefits not merely to those who paid in cash, but to those who were too poor to maintain their financial contributions.[77] Fraternities undoubtedly involved the services of publicists and *questores*. Attempting to establish a fraternity for Lisieux Cathedral in the 1170s, Arnulf of Lisieux recruited the assistance of professional, clerical

---

[73] For indulgenced bridge-building, see Paulus, *Ablasses*, II, 247–62. Beyond the examples from London and St Ives cited above, and the appearance of indulgences for bridges referred to in the decretal letter of Alexander III (above n. 41), by the beginning of the thirteenth century Robert of Flamborough takes it for granted that indulgences were available in large numbers *in ecclesiarum aedificatione vel pontium*: *Liber Poenitentialis*, 5.16, ed. Firth, 276.

[74] In general, see C. R. Cheney, 'Church-Building in the Middle Ages', in C. R. Cheney, *Medieval Texts and Studies* (Oxford, 1973), 359–61.

[75] See, for example, the fraternity established by Gilbert Foliot c. 1175 for rebuilding at St Paul's (*Letters and Charters of Gilbert Foliot*, no. 235, whence *EEA XV: London 1076–1187*, no. 153), or that decreed by Archbishop Baldwin in 1186/7 for the new church of St Thomas at Canterbury: *Chronicles and Memorials of the Reign of Richard I*, II: *Epistolae Cantuarienses*, ed. W. Stubbs (1865), 8–9 no. 8, whence *EEA II: Canterbury 1162–1190*, no. 241.

[76] Lat. IV c. 57, in *Constitutiones concilii quarti Lateranensis*, ed. Garcia y Garcia, 97–8.

[77] *Letters and Charters of Gilbert Foliot*, no. 235 lines 70–4, and see R. Graham, 'An Appeal about 1175 for the Building Fund of St Paul's Cathedral Church', *Journal of the British Archaeological Association*, 3rd ser., 10 (1945–7), 73–6.

collectors, previously involved in fund-raising for the cathedral of Noyon. In a tradition honoured by many later pardoners, the Lisieux *questores* duly absconded, leaving the bishop to answer for their debts.[78]

Building projects were frequently financed from the proceeds of relics and pilgrimage. At least one of Gilbert Foliot's indulgences, for visitors to portions of the shroud of St Cuthbert, reminds us of this continuing association between indulgences and relics.[79] Elsewhere, we find indulgences being employed to encourage attendance at newly instituted feast of relics at Salisbury and Chichester, besides the great series of indulgences preserved for the feast day of St James at Reading and for the shrine of St Edward the Confessor at Westminster.[80] By the end of the century, indulgences were issued as a matter of course, following the canonisation and translation of St Gilbert of Sempringham, and later St William at York and St Edmund at Pontigny.[81]

Throughout our period, and despite the precocious appearance of awards to foreign alms-seekers, the majority of English indulgences were directed towards those bestowing alms upon hospitals, upon the English cathedrals, Benedictine and Augustinian monasteries and at least one collegiate church.[82] Conspicuous by their absence here are the Cistercians and the Premonstratensians, neither of which order is recorded in receipt of a single English indulgence before the 1220s.[83]

---

[78] *The Letters of Arnulf of Lisieux*, ed. F. Barlow, Camden Society, 3rd ser., 61 (1939), 114 no. 63. For an indulgenced fraternity for the cathedral of Bayeux, established by Arnulf's contemporary, Bishop Henry of Bayeux (1165–1205), see *Antiquus cartularius ecclesiae Baiocensis (Livre Noir)*, ed. V. Bourrienne (2 vols., Rouen, 1902–3), I, 58–60 no. 47.

[79] *EEA XV: London 1076–1187*, no. 152.

[80] For indulgences for visitors to the hand of St James, and later to the head of St Philip at Reading, see *Reading Cartularies*, I, nos. 183–201, 210, 217. For episcopal indulgences inspired by the cult of St Edward in the twelfth century, see *Westminster Abbey Charters*, nos. 200, 204, 221, 229. For Chichester, see *EEA II: Canterbury 1162–1190*, no. 103. For Salisbury, see Saltman, *Theobald*, no. 243.

[81] *The Book of St Gilbert*, ed. R. Foreville and G. Keir (Oxford, 1987), 194, 260–2. For the indulgences for the shrine of St William of York, see British Library [BL] MS Cotton Claudius B iii (York Minster cartulary) fos. 53r–4v. For the indulgences for the shrine of St Edmund at Pontigny, now in the Musée de la Ville at Sens series II, see C. H. Lawrence, *St Edmund of Abingdon* (Oxford, 1960), 323–5. Amongst other collections, note the large number of indulgences issued after 1247 for the relic of the Holy Blood granted by King Henry III to Westminster Abbey: N. Vincent, *The Holy Blood: King Henry III and the Westminster Blood Relic* (Cambridge, 2001), 154–64.

[82] For indulgences for the collegiate church of St Martin's London, see *EEA VI: Norwich 1070–1214*, no. 115; *EEA XV: London 1076–1187*, no. 152.

[83] With the exception of an indulgence by Archbishop Hubert Walter to the nuns of Pinley Priory, only later and very loosely attached to the Cistercian order (*EEA III: Canterbury 1193–1205*, ed. C. R. Cheney and E. John (Oxford, 1986), no. 575), the first Cistercian indulgence appears to be that said to have been awarded by Bishop Richard Poer of Salisbury to benefactors of the fabric of Stanley Abbey: *EEA XIX: Salisbury 1217–1228*, ed. B. R. Kemp (Oxford, 2000), no. 384. I know of no indulgence for an English Premonstratensian house earlier than the award by Archbishop Edmund of Canterbury

This may well reflect deliberate abstention from a practice that relaxed the austerity of penance. There had long been a tradition amongst the Cistercians forbidding general begging quests, and in 1195 the general chapter rebuked a Danish abbot for sending out members of his community to beg with relics.[84] Although St Bernard himself had enthusiastically broadcast the papal indulgence for the Second Crusade, he had laid particular stress upon the interior requirements of contrition and confession – yet another reminder that St Bernard and Peter Abelard were but two sides of the same coin – whilst the disastrous aftermath of the Crusade may well have discouraged Bernard's successors from pursuing his example.[85] It is none the less worth remarking that the only Cistercian in our period to have been promoted to an English bishopric, Baldwin of Forde, issued at least two indulgences during his time at Canterbury.[86] One of these, in favour of the proposed college of St Thomas outside Canterbury, is unusually generous in dispensing its recipients from one third of penances of more than seven years, and sixty days of other enjoined penances, to include not only those sins which had been forgotten and which were therefore unconfessed, but offences, short of violence, against parents.[87] Baldwin's indulgence, indeed, is so close to that which was later to earn criticism from Peter of Blois that it is tempting to suggest that it was this Canterbury indulgence, rather than any other, against which Peter reacted.[88] A Cistercian, accustomed to observing the austerity of the monastic cloister, Baldwin may have been all the keener to observe the episcopal custom of indulgences once he ascended the episcopal throne. A similar phenomenon can be observed in the case of St Hugh of Lincoln. There are no English indulgences recorded in our period in favour of the Carthusians, the most austere of all the religious orders to be found in twelfth-century England. None the less, the Carthusian St Hugh appears to have had no qualms in issuing indulgences in his

---

(1234–40) in favour of the building of Bayham Abbey: BL MS Cotton Otho A ii (Bayham cartulary) fos. 49v–50r.

[84] *Statuta capitulorum generalium ordinis Cisterciensis*, ed. J.-M. Canivez, vol. 1, Bibliothèque de la Revue d'Histoire Ecclésiastique, fasc. 9 (Louvain, 1933), 193–4 no. 78, 224 no. 3, noticed by Herrmann-Mascard, *Les reliques*, 307.

[85] G. Constable, 'The Second Crusade as Seen by Contemporaries', *Traditio*, 9 (1953), 247, 251–2; Bernard, 'Epistolae', 363, in *PL*, CLXXXII, 566, incidentally referring to the crusade and its indulgence as the opportunity for 'jubilee', a significant marker in the development of the later theory of the jubilee indulgence, for which see most recently, J. Petersohn, 'Jubiläumsfrömmigkeit vor dem Jubelablass', *Deutsches Archiv für Erforschung des Mittelalters*, 45 (1989), 31–53, esp. p. 34.

[86] *EEA II: Canterbury 1162–1190*, nos. 241, 317.

[87] *Ibid.*, no. 241, printed in full in *Epistolae Cantuarienses*, 8–9 no. 8.

[88] *Later Letters of Peter of Blois*, ed. Revell, 135–6 (28.2). Note that the contemporary fraternity indulgence for Bayeux (above n. 78) also dispenses its recipients from forgotten sins and offences short of violence against parents.

capacity as bishop, including an award of thirteen days indulgence made immediately after his consecration in favour of those attending his enthronement at Lincoln.[89] St Hugh and Baldwin are virtually the only English bishops during our period known to have issued indulgences that exceeded the forty-day maximum otherwise observed.

In light of the decretal of Pope Alexander III, limiting the force of any indulgence to the province of the issuing bishop, we find several late twelfth-century indulgences in which the territorial limitations of the indulgence are clearly spelled out.[90] More rarely, time limits were imposed upon the indulgence's validity.[91] On occasion, the particular types of penance for which indulgence was available are clearly specified, sometimes by distinguishing between penance owing for venal or more serious sins, more often by graduating the award as it might be applied to penances of greater or lesser extent.[92] Although the benefits in such cases must have been almost impossible to calculate, it seems that indulgences could be applied not merely to private penances but to the most solemn sentences imposed publicly for grave and public crimes.

After 1140, we find the first examples of multiple indulgences issued for a single beneficiary, and of joint indulgences, such as that issued at the dedication of the Augustinian Priory of Southwick, totalling up to 100 days issued by three bishops acting in concert.[93] The same period witnesses the first appearance of a system of mutual ratification, by which the bishop of one diocese might agree to recognise whatever awards were made by his episcopal colleagues, thereby extending the

---

[89] *EEA IV: Lincoln 1186–1206*, ed. D. M. Smith (Oxford, 1986), nos. 97–8, p. 204 app. 2 no. 1. The indulgence by Bishop Hugh for the fabric of Lincoln Cathedral is variously calculated in the schedula printed in *Giraldi Cambrensis Opera*, ed. J. S. Brewer (8 vols., 1861–91), VII, 217–19, as eighty days, or as twenty days together with a moiety of venial sins and all forgotten sins.

[90] *Letters and Charters of Gilbert Foliot*, nos. 235, 428, whence *EEA XV: London 1076–1187*, nos. 153, 184.

[91] *EEA III: Canterbury 1193–1205*, no. 428.

[92] For a distinction between venial and other sins, see Gerald of Wales, *Opera*, VII, 218–19; *Antiquus cartularius ecclesiae Baiocensis*, I, 58–60 no. 47 (distinguishing between 'criminales' and 'veniales'). A similar distinction appears in the highly suspect legatine indulgences for Westminster (*PUE*, I, nos. 12, 13), offering forty days for 'criminalium penitentia' and a remission of a third of 'minorum delictorum'. One indulgence issued by Gilbert Foliot as bishop of Hereford (*Letters and Charters of Gilbert Foliot*, no. 340, whence *EEA VII: Hereford 1079–1234*, no. 98) awards forty days indulgence to 'hiis qui in criminali sunt', but only twenty days of ordinary enjoined penance. Several of Gilbert's awards allow twenty or forty days remission for penances of more than seven years, but only ten or twenty days if the penance was of shorter duration: *Letters and Charters of Gilbert Foliot*, nos. 235, 386, 390, 428, 447, whence *EEA XV: London 1076–1187*, nos. 121, 126, 153, 184, 207.

[93] For Southwick, see *EEA VIII: Winchester 1070–1204*, ed. M. J. Franklin (Oxford, 1993), nos. 178–9, and see the joint award of 100 days said to have been made by the four bishops present at the consecration of the new church of Wells in the 1140s: *EEA X: Bath and Wells 1061–1205*, ed. F. M. R. Ramsey (Oxford, 1995), p. 202 app. 1 no. 19.

application of the indulgence beyond the subjects of the bishop who had originally issued it.[94] By this means, implicitly licensed by Pope Alexander III, it was possible for beneficiaries to continue to accumulate indulgences that, when expressed as a total number of days, greatly exceeded the forty-day maximum that was observed in the awards by the vast majority of individual bishops.[95]

Most of the indulgences we have considered so far were intended to apply to penances owed by the living. The idea that indulgences could be purchased by the living to buy the souls of the dead out of purgatory was a much later, fifteenth-century development, and was to prove extremely controversial even then. However, as early as the 1140s, following the death of Peter Abelard, Heloise is said to have sought letters from Peter the Venerable, abbot of Cluny, posthumously absolving Abelard from his sins: letters which are said to have been suspended over Abelard's tomb, and which surely suggest a belief that earthly absolution could still be applied to the sins of those in the afterlife.[96] In England, by much the same time, it is apparent that the living could seek indulgences on their deathbeds, hoping to apply the benefits of such awards to whatever penance might be owing in the afterlife. This is clearly the purpose of an indulgence of Archbishop Theobald, offering 'God's absolution' and fifteen days 'relaxation of the burden of penance' to any inhabitant of Dover who should die during the fishing season.[97] The Cistercian Archbishop Baldwin, in offering indulgence in the 1180s, specifically extended his award to include those who made deathbed gifts, the indulgence in such cases clearly to be applied to the afterlife.[98] Baldwin, indeed, is credited with a sentence, allowing that undischarged

---

[94] For offers to ratify, the earliest made by Archbishop William (c. 1126–8), see Cambridge University Library MS Add. 3020 (Thorney cartulary) fo. 166r; Saltman, *Theobald*, no. 309; *EEA II: Canterbury 1162–1190*, no. 124, and for the bishop of Chichester offering an indulgence for the monks of Reading with the assent of the local diocesan, the bishop of Salisbury, see *Acta of Chichester*, no. 45.

[95] For Alexander's decretal, see above n. 41.

[96] See *The Letters of Peter the Venerable*, ed. G. Constable (Cambridge, MA, 1967), 401–2 nos. 167–8, and for other such absolutions by Abbot Peter, see 324 no. 133. The original sealed letters of absolution supposedly shown at the tomb, are cited in *PL*, CLXXVIII, 91, and re-edited by C. J. Mews and C. S. F. Burnett, 'Les épitaphes d'Abélard et d'Héloïse au Paraclet et au prieuré de St-Marcel à Chalon-sur-Saône', *Studia Monastica*, 27 (1985), 62: 'auctoritate omnipotentis Dei et sanctorum omnium, absolvo eum pro officio ab omnibus peccatis suis'. In general, see M. Clanchy, *Peter Abelard* (Oxford, 1997), 324. For all of these references, I am indebted to Michael Clanchy.

[97] Saltman, *Theobald*, no. 87 (1139 X 1150): 'Si quis vestrum infra terminum piscationis viam universe carnis ingressus fuerit, quantum sua expetit accusatio et ad nos pertinet remissio, absolutionem Dei et nostram habeat et relaxationem quindecim dierum de onere penitentie sue unde penitens et confessus fuerit.'

[98] *Epistolae Cantuarienses*, 8–9 no. 8, and cf. *EEA XVII: Coventry and Lichfield 1183–1208*, ed. M. J. Franklin (Oxford, 1998), no. 76.

penance might be relaxed in the afterlife by indulgences obtained by the sinner before death.[99] Shortly thereafter, Alan of Lille, influenced no doubt by the contemporary debate on the efficacy of prayers for the dead, whose merits were denied by various heterodox or heretical preachers, specifically recommends that sinners who obtain indulgence discharge whatever penance may be enjoined upon them in this life and save their indulgences for use in purgatory.[100] Without some such understanding, it would be hard to explain why so learned a figure as Gerald of Wales, on pilgrimage to Rome around the year 1200, sought out indulgences totalling 100 years: greatly in excess of the number of years that even the self-confident Gerald can have supposed were left to his own lifetime.[101] Robert Courson, whilst denouncing as heretical the idea that indulgences could release the souls of the damned in hell, says nothing against their effect in purgatory.[102] Purgatory, it would seem, was alive and functioning at least as early as the 1150s, with indulgences serving as a significant indication of its pre Le Goffian birth.[103]

Not only do we find more indulgences being issued as the twelfth century advanced, but indulgences of greater complexity, applied to a greater variety of ends. What determined these changes? Some of course may have been generated by the English bishops themselves: both Roger of Worcester and Baldwin of Canterbury were sufficiently concerned by the theology of indulgences to have contributed to scholastic debate. For the rest, two other sources of inspiration are worth considering: Paris and Rome. With respect to Paris, we have

[99] A. Landgraf, 'Cod. Bamberg Patr. 136, Cod. Paris Nat.lat. 3237 und der Magister Alanus', *Philosophisches Jahrbuch*, 54 (1941), 489, citing the gloss in Paris, Bibliothèque Mazarine MS 785 fo. 164v: 'Bal(duinus) Cantuariensis archiepiscopus dicebat huiusmodi relaxationes tantum post mortem locum habere, ut scilicet si penitens morte preventus penitentiam sibi iniunctam non possit consummare, tunc demum locum habeat relaxatio, aliter non.'

[100] Alan of Lille, 'Contra Haereticos', 2.11, in *PL*, CCX, 387–8. Similar recommendations are made by William of Auxerre, Henry of Susa and William of Paris: Lea, *Confession and Indulgences*, III, 45, 123. For the debate over the heretical repudiation of prayers for the dead, see M. Lauwers, ' "Dicunt vivorum beneficia nichil prodesse defunctis": histoire d'un thème polemique (XIe–XIIe siècles)', in *Inventer l'hérésie*, ed. M. Zerner (Nice, 1998), 157–92. The Dominican Saint Bertrand de Garrigue (d. 1230), who initially denied the power of prayers for the dead, found his sleep tormented by visions of those for whom he had thus denied succour: A. Vauchez, 'Heurs et malheurs d'un saint dominicain: les vicissitudes du culte du bienheureux Bertrand de Garrigue (+1230)', *Maisons de Dieu et hommes d'église: florilège en l'honneur de Pierre-Roger Gaussin* (Lyon, 1992), 110.

[101] Gerald, 'De invectionibus', 12, in Gerald, *Opera*, I, 137–8.

[102] Kennedy, 'Robert Courson on Penance', 330.

[103] The classic study by J. Le Goff, *La naissance du purgatoire* (Paris, 1981), translated as *The Birth of Purgatory* (1984), is thus overcautious in asserting (English translation, p. 168) that 'between 1170 and 1200 – possibly as early as 1170–80 and surely by the last decade of the century – Purgatory first emerged'.

seen that the bishops of England issued indulgences in ever greater numbers and of ever greater sophistication, despite the doubts as to the merits of such awards expressed in the Paris schools. By contrast to so much else in twelfth-century English episcopal thought and practice, in which the English bishops merely implemented a pastoral and theological programme devised on the banks of the River Seine, indulgences supply us with a highly unusual spectacle, in which we find the Paris theologians struggling to keep abreast of a practice widely adopted by the bishops of England, France and other Christian realms. When the schoolsmen came to admit the merits of indulgence, as most of the Parisian masters working around 1200 were eventually if somewhat grudgingly to do, it was as a practice dictated by custom and by apostolic authority, rather than as a necessity generated from theological first principles. Even Aquinas founds his justification for indulgences upon the premise that indulgences must be effective because popes and bishops issue such awards.[104] This emphasis in the Parisian account of indulgences upon the authority of the Church, and in particular upon the power of the keys entrusted to Peter, encourages us to trace the cause of the indulgence's development in twelfth-century England not to the banks of the Seine, but to those of the Tiber.

We have seen that indulgences first appear in England in the aftermath of the First Crusade and in association with papal legates. We have suggested, too, that the number of such awards may have increased significantly in the two or three decades after 1140. Here it is at least worth hazarding the suggestion that there was a causal link between the change both in the frequency and the form of indulgences issued after 1140, and the indulgence issued in 1145 by Pope Eugenius III for the Second Crusade.[105] In the awards made by English bishops during the 1150s and 1160s, we find the introduction of phrases that appear to be borrowed directly from Eugenius's crusading bull, *Quantum predecessores*, issued in December 1145, and apparently widely broadcast in England. Rather than promising remission to all who perform the actions recommended in lieu of their enjoined penance, the bull of 1145 is limited to sins for which the penitent has 'made confession with a contrite and humble heart'. Furthermore, in issuing his indulgence, the pope specified that he was acting by the authority awarded to him by

---

[104] Aquinas, 'Summa Theologica', part 3, suppl. q. 25, art. 1, resp. 2 (in *Opera Omnia*, XII, 48): 'Ecclesia generalis non potest errare ... Ecclesia generalis indulgentias approbat et facit, ergo indulgentie aliquid valent. Respondeo dicendum quod ab omnibus conceditur indulgentias aliquid valere, quia impium esset dicere quod ecclesia aliquid vanum faceret.'

[105] For what follows I am indebted to a suggestion first made by Henry Mayr-Harting, *Chichester Acta*, 31-2.

God.[106] These two conditions, limiting indulgence to those who are truly penitent, contrite and confessed, and specifying the authority by which such indulgence is made available, were themselves, of course, influenced by scholastic debate, on the nature of repentance and upon the power of remission. Here, Paris and Rome combined to determine a new formulation of indulgence, rapidly introduced to the language of English episcopal practice. So common do these formulas become that not only can their presence in an episcopal indulgence supposedly issued before 1145 be read as a strong indication of forgery or misdating, but their absence from any award issued after the 1180s or so must raise an equally grave suspicion.[107] By the end of the century, it is rare indeed to find an English indulgence that does not refer explicitly and in standardised terminology both to confession and to authority.

Let us pause for a moment to consider the significance of these references, beginning with confession. Alexander Murray has recently used saints' lives and their attendant miracle stories to advance a bold and compelling thesis. Confession, he suggests, 'though prescribed in the twelfth century, was a usage generally ignored'. The only areas of Europe where Murray allows that lay confession may have been regularly practised in the century before 1215 are northern France in the shadow of the pastoral programme of the Paris schools, and post-Conquest England.[108] Murray's evidence for the spread of confession in England is amply supported by our study of indulgences. Whatever may have been the situation elsewhere, from the 1140s and arguably from even earlier, the very fact that English indulgences call for those that receive them to be penitent, contrite and truly confessed suggests that the bishops who granted them expected the laity at whom they were targeted to be in a fit state to receive indulgence. Furthermore, and despite the criticisms raised by those such as Peter Abelard – who

---

[106] For the text of 'Quantum predecessores' (Jaffé–Loewenfeld no. 8796), see *PL*, CLXXX, 1064; *Monumenta Germaniae Historica Scriptores*, xx (Hanover, 1868), 371–2: 'omnipotentis Dei et beati Petri apostolorum principis auctoritate nobis a Deo concessa talem concedimus ut qui tam sanctum iter devote inceperit et perfecerit sive ibidem mortuus fuerit, de omnibus peccatis suis quibus corde contrito et humiliato confessionem susceperit, absolutionem obtineat et sempiterne retributionis fructum ab omnium remuneratore percipiat'.

[107] For what appear to be genuine references to confession as a condition of indulgence before 1145, see the awards by Archbishop Ralph (before 1122), and Archbishop William (before 1136) (*Book of Llan Dâv*, 87; Norwich, Norfolk Record Office, DCN 40/8 fo. 40r). Of the surviving indulgences issued by Archbishop Theobald, seven refer to neither confession nor to the authority for the award, six are limited to those who are confessed or contrite and twelve refer explicitly to the authority by which the archbishop claimed to act: confession and/or contrition: *Norwich Cathedral Charters I*, no. 262; Saltman, *Theobald*, nos. 9, 76, 87, 114, 266, and arguably no. 242; confessing the merits of God or the saints, or citing authority: Saltman, *Theobald*, nos. 9, 67, 82, 93–4, 213–14, 242, 279, 286–7; Foreville, 'Lettres "extravagantes"', 233–4 no. 11.

[108] Murray, 'Confession before 1215', 51–81, esp. 79–81.

argued that indulgences disrupted the proper relationship between personal confessor and individual penitent – the award of indulgences could be interpreted as a means of lending positive encouragement to the practice of confession. This alone would help to explain its growing appeal to the English bishops. If the laity were to come in large numbers to church dedications, shrines and saints' feast days, and if, to receive the spiritual benefits awarded on these occasions it was necessary that they be properly confessed, then the award of indulgences could be presented not only as a sign that confession was widely practised, but as an incentive to large numbers of men and women to confess and obtain absolution and penance. To this extent, far from appearing a retrograde practice, out of step with the new confessional teachings of the Church, the award of indulgences could serve as yet a further weapon in the Church's struggle to urge practices upon the laity and the parish clergy that were otherwise slow to take root. It is precisely during the period when the issue of indulgences became a regular feature of English church life that we first begin to read of the appointment of diocesan penitentiaries charged, like Master Senatus of Worcester, with hearing confessions.[109]

As for the authority by which popes and bishops claimed the power to offer indulgence, here too there are interesting implications. Not content merely to assume the power to bind and loose invested in Peter and his successors by Christ, those bishops who granted indulgences increasingly chose to style themselves as 'confessing the merits or mercy of such and such a saint', in many cases naming either the patron saints of their diocesan cathedral, or the saints whose relics rested in whatever church was to be made the subject of indulgence.[110] This formula might be read as mere pious platitude, were it not for two things: the association that we have already observed between indulgences and relics, and the scholastic debate upon the nature of the indulgences, their spiritual source and merits. Quite how indulgences could be held to operate in theological terms was a question that occupied writers for much of the twelfth and thirteenth centuries. Popes

---

[109] At Norwich, as at Worcester, it was to one of the cathedral's monks that the bishop deputed the hearing of confessions, and at Norwich too, as early as the 1140s, we hear of an annual 'absolution day' when crowds of penitents were accustomed to gather in the cathedral: *The Life and Miracles of St William of Norwich by Thomas of Monmouth*, ed. A. Jessopp and M. R. James (Cambridge, 1896), 26, 30, 84. For the assumption, implicit in the statutes of the Council of York of 1195, that each diocese would possess a general confessor, see *Councils and Synods I*, II, 1051 (c. 13). For the prior of Huntingdon acting as penitentiary to Bishop Hugh of Lincoln, see *Magna Vita Sancti Hugonis*, ed. D. L. Douie and D. H. Farmer (2 vols., 2nd edn, Oxford, 1985), II, 118–19.

[110] See, amongst a wealth of examples, *EEA VIII: Winchester 1070–1204*, no. 180; *EEA IX: Winchester 1205–1238*, ed. N. Vincent (Oxford, 1994), no. 58; *EEA XVIII: Salisbury 1078–1217*, nos. 54, 106.

and bishops might take it upon themselves to assume liability for the penance owing by their subjects, just as Pope Eugenius is said to have assumed the sins of the count of Molise, in Eugenius's case with a ceremonial gesture reminiscent of the secular contract of fealty.[111] Was the pope or the bishop, however, to be made to suffer in the afterlife for such acts of mercy? The explanation that was to become widely accepted was that indulgences were a gift placed at the Church's disposal through the sufferings and good works of Christ and his saints. Pope or bishop merely dispensed indulgence from the resources of the Church. First fully formulated by the circle around the English Franciscan Alexander of Hales and thence adopted by Thomas Aquinas, this idea of the 'treasury of merits' is generally regarded as an innovation of the 1240s.[112] In fact, it is already anticipated eighty years earlier, in the close association between the offer of indulgence and the bishops' reliance upon the merits and mercy of Christ and particular saints.

By anticipating the later theory, a quite definite association was established between the issue of indulgence and the saints. From this it may have appeared to many as if the penance for sin was transferred, by indulgence, from the individual penitent to the individual saint, physically present in the form of his or her relics. A similar transference is one of the assumptions underlying many of the practices of popular magic, for example in healing cures in which the illness of the invalid is transferred to another object, animate or inanimate as the case may be.[113] Christ himself, in driving out the demons of the Gaderene into a herd of swine, was no stranger to such practices, indeed to Christian minds he was arguably their inventor. Commentators on the Lateran constitutions of 1215 have previously assumed that it was mere coincidence that led the Council to regulate in the same constitution (const. 62) both the display and authentication of relics and the award of indulgences. Beginning with the canonists of the 1220s and thence the compilers of the *Liber Extra*, the two parts of the Lateran constitution were divided one from another and treated as independent decretals, one assigned to the discussion of relics, the other to that of penance.[114] Modern historians have been content to follow this example. Even

[111] Above n. 36.

[112] Lea, *Confession and Indulgences*, III, 19–27, tracing the idea's pre-history.

[113] For the use of relics in 'magical' cures, see V. I. J. Flint, *The Rise of Magic in Early Medieval Europe* (Oxford, 1991), 304–10. For a later example from Normandy of a blend between indulgence schedule and magic charm, listing papal and other indulgences and specifying the curative properties of the relics of St Laurence with respect to certain skin diseases (*sacer ignis*), see M. Sauvage, 'Note sur un billet d'indulgences délivré au XIIIe siècle par l'abbaye de Cordillon (diocèse de Bayeux)', *Bulletin philologique et historique* (1913), 413–15.

[114] X 3.45.2, and X 5.30.14, whence Friedberg, *Decretalium Collectiones* (above n. 41), 650, 888–9, noting that the two sections were already divided by the time of the decretal collection 'Compilatio IV'.

those historians who have written on the medieval profession of
pardoner have portrayed as two distinct phenomena the pardoner's
sale of indulgences and his collection of relics – often decried as false.[115]
In reality, there may have been a highly significant association between
the pardoners' indulgences and the relics that pardoners were accused
of mishandling, sufficient to explain their joint regulation in the
constitution of 1215. Relics were the physical proof of the supernatural
power possessed by the saints, perhaps even the physical instruments
of that power by which indulgences were held to operate. In these
circumstances it is hardly surprising to find relics mingled with indulgences in many pardoners' bags, not merely as gewgaws to draw the
crowd, but perhaps as an essential tool of the pardoner's trade.

In a famous study, Peter Brown has demonstrated how the veneration
of relics challenged the claims of the Church to serve as man's sole
route to salvation. Hence the anxiety shown by the bishops of late
antiquity to translate the shrines and relics of the saints away from
private, family control, to establish them within cathedrals and churches
under the supervision of the priesthood.[116] Even then, the emphasis that
pilgrimage and the cult of the saints placed upon the relationship
between the individual believer and God through the mediation of the
saints continued to pose a challenge to the church authorities. Indulgences can be regarded as offering one response to this challenge,
distinct from but complementary to the reservation to the papacy of
the right to grant or withhold official canonisation.[117] Whereas in the
past, pilgrimage, prayer and almsgiving had been considered sufficient
in themselves to earn favour from the saints, with the development of
the system of indulgences the church authorities could intrude their
own authority within this system, defining through the grant of indulgences the precise spiritual benefits that a pilgrim could hope to obtain
from a visit to any particular saint or shrine. Saints and their relics
could henceforth heal both the physical and the spiritual ills of man. The
bishops of the Plantagenet realm were more famed for administrative
competence than for their ability to work miracles. Their control over
indulgences none the less allowed them to define the precise measure
of spiritual healing that the saints might bestow. For all of these reasons,
as a means of drawing men and women into pious works, almsgiving
and Church attendance, as a spur to confession and penitence, and as

[115] For example, Kellogg and Haselmayer, 'Chaucer's Satire of the Pardoner', 251–77,
and cf. Herrmann-Mascard, Les reliques, 308.

[116] P. Brown, The Cult of the Saints: Its Rise and Function in Latin Christianity (Chicago, 1981),
esp. ch. 2.

[117] For canonisation, see E. W. Kemp, Canonization and Authority in the Western Church
(Oxford, 1948), esp. ch. 5; A. Vauchez, La sainteté en occident aux derniers siècles du moyen-âge
(2nd edn, Paris and Rome, 1988), esp. 25–67.

a means by which the Church authorities could channel the healing powers of the saints into the sponsorship both of episcopal authority and of favoured episcopal projects, it is easy to understand why indulgences should have appealed just as much to the bishops who issued them as to the penitent men and women to whom they were addressed.

If indulgences suited the needs of the English bishops, then they afforded even greater advantages to the popes. From the 1090s onwards, plenary indulgence became the defining feature of what was perhaps the keenest expression of papal authority to have emerged from the entire Gregorian programme: the Crusade. Like the English bishops, the popes were clearly aware of the scholastic criticism of indulgences. Like the bishops, the popes were in no hurry to do away with so useful a device. Where we might most expect to find the Parisian anxiety over indulgences translated into canon law – in the constitutions of the Fourth Lateran Council of 1215, summoned by a Paris-trained pope and attended and informed by any number of Parisian alumni – we in fact find an uncompromising statement of the pope's authority to award remission, with the offer of plenary indulgence from those sins confessed by all the faithful joining or contributing to the forthcoming Crusade.[118] With the Crusade, and the crusading indulgence at the forefront of its proceedings, it is hardly surprising to find the Council brushing aside any scholastic misgivings over the merits of indulgence.

Constitution 62 of the Council, it is true, witnessed the most comprehensive attempt yet to legislate on indulgences. Beginning with a prohibition of the display of relics for financial gain, the constitution proceeds via a common form recommended for episcopal indulgences, *Quoniam ut ait*, to a ban upon indulgences of more than forty days, or more than one year in the case of church dedications, ending with a severe censure of the preaching and loose morals of unlicensed pardoners.[119] But what is perhaps most remarkable here is how little of the Lateran constitution is directly concerned with indulgences. Much the greater part of it is taken up with relics, *questores* and the common form for appeals for alms. The form itself, *Quoniam ut ait*, had been frequently employed in the papal chancery since at least the 1180s, and is to be found in a indulgence, not previously noticed, addressed by Pope Innocent on 27 November 1215, three days before the closure of the Lateran Council, to the province of Canterbury.[120] A similar form, *Cum*

---

[118] Lat. IV c. 71, printed by Garcia y Garcia, *Constitutiones*, 110–18, especially 117–18. For the Parisian influence at the Council, see the classic study by J. W. Baldwin, *Masters, Princes and Merchants: The Social Views of Peter the Chanter and his Circle* (2 vols., Princeton, 1970).

[119] Lat. IV c. 62, printed in Garcia y Garcia, *Constitutiones*, 101–3.

[120] For this indulgence, not previously noticed, in favour of a hospital at Aynho, see

dicat scriptura, appears in an indulgence issued in August 1215 by the English cardinal Robert Courson, then serving as papal legate to France. Courson's indulgence is particularly remarkable for its closing injunction, forbidding the employment of *questores* or pardoners.[121] In his 'Summa', composed at Paris between 1204 and 1208, Courson had devoted considerable attention to indulgences. Rehearsing many of the scholastic objections that we have already encountered, Courson concludes that indulgences do indeed have an effect, albeit an effect that will remain mysterious before death. Courson then passes on to deal at far greater length with the *questores*, the pardoners who make extravagant and even heretical claims for the power of indulgences, and who bring the entire Church into disrepute. Good *questores* must be set apart from the bad. Only appropriate alms are to be solicited. Relics of the saints are not to be exposed by such men merely for profit, or to beg, or to tempt God to work miracles.[122] Drunken, lay and illiterate pardoners had already been criticised in letters of Innocent III and in the statutes of Bishop Odo of Paris, issued before 1208, forbidding preachers from presenting relics save with accompanying testimonials which the parish priest, rather than the pardoner, was to expound to the faithful.[123] In his own legatine statutes, issued at Paris and renewed at Rouen and Bourges after 1212, Courson himself forbade *questuarii* from preaching or carrying relics, save in good causes for which they had obtained letters from their diocesan bishops.[124]

In many ways, the legislation of 1215 had already been anticipated in England, where from at least the 1170s we find examples of episcopal indulgences of such length and such density of scriptural quotation that

---

Oxford, Magdalen College muniments EP/137/1 (Aynho cartulary roll) recto and dorse. For the use of 'Quoniam ut ait' since at least the time of Pope Lucius III in 1184, see Jaffé–Loewenfeld nos. 15331, 15417; P. F. Kehr *et al.*, *Italia Pontificia* (10 vols., Berlin and Turici, 1906–75), II, 193 no. 4; III, 375–6 nos. 1, 4, 5, 7; V, 282 no. 22; VII part 2, 160 no. 1; IX, 171 no. 2, various of these being noticed as Jaffé–Loewenfeld, nos. 15413, 15773, 16132–3; and the letters of Innocent to a Portuguese beneficiary issued in February 1208, noticed by Garcia y Garcia, *Constitutiones*, 103 n. 4.

[121] Melun, Archives départementales de Seine-et-Oise, H supplément (Cartulary of Fontaines-les-Nonnes) fo. IV, printed from an earlier but equally imperfect version, by T. Du Plessis, *Histoire de l'église de Meaux* (2 vols., Paris, 1731), II, 106, ending with the injunction: 'inhibentes ne occasione istarum litterarum pseudo-predicatores, conductitii sive questuarii admittantur'.

[122] Kennedy, 'Robert Courson on Penance', 327–30, esp. 328: 'Dicimus quod predicte absolutiones valent per suffragia ecclesie ad tria scilicet, ad pene diminutionem et ad gratie impetrationem et ad venalium deletionem.'

[123] *PL*, CCXIV, 425–6 no. 450 (with address to the archbishop of Lund), whence (with address to the archbishop of Lyons) X 5.33.11, pd Friedberg, *Decretalium Collectiones*, 852–3, and cf. 'Statutes of Paris' (1196 X 1208), c. 61, printed in *Les statuts synodaux français du XIIIe siècle: tome I, Les statuts de Paris et le synodal de l'Ouest (XIIIe siècle)*, ed. O. Pontal (Paris, 1971), 74–5, where the French translation is misleading.

[124] 'Statutes of Paris' (1212), c. 8, in Mansi, *Concilia*, XXII, 821.

they were clearly intended to be read out as sermons in their own right, depriving the pardoner of any opportunity to improvise some less orthodox sermon of his own.[125] Few English indulgences issued in the twelfth century had exceeded the forty-day limit imposed in 1215, and none had even approached the one year of indulgence permitted by the Council, for the dedication of churches. If we were looking for the author of the Lateran constitution 62, then the Englishman Robert Courson would be our most obvious candidate. For once the practical experience of the English Church, the theology of the Paris schools and the legislative powers of the papacy appear to have been distilled into a single canonical formula. The effect of this formula is clear. Henceforth, the indulgence was established as a customary and properly licensed instrument. Controversy was deflected from the indulgence itself to the unlicensed and increasingly proscribed activities of pardoners, accused of misusing indulgences and relics and of misrepresenting the teachings of the Church.

Confirmation of this is to be found in any number of rulings by the English bishops after 1215, in which it is pardoners, not indulgences, that become the object of episcopal censure, often of extreme severity.[126] Without our straying too far beyond 1215, this development can be clearly traced in the writings of England's most influential Paris-trained bishop of the 1220s: Archbishop Stephen Langton. In his scholastic *questiones* on penance, and founding his teaching upon St Paul's promise to the church of Corinth (2 Corinthians 2.10), 'Whatever you have given, I give also, and what I have given I have done on your behalf', Langton equates St Paul's gift with the award of indulgence, allowing that a bishop and above all the pope may offer forgiveness as a function of his role as successor to the apostles and as merciful provider to the poor and needy.[127] Rather surprisingly for a theologian devoted to the memory of Thomas Becket and nurtured in the Paris schools on that great rallying cry of the Becket conflict, *non iudicabit Dominus bis in idipsum*, Langton continues to allow for what might be considered an element of double judgement in the imposition of penance.[128] Penance is owed to God who alone can determine its proper extent, although

---

[125] See, for example, *Letters and Charters of Gilbert Foliot*, nos. 235, 413, 459, 474; *EEA II: Canterbury 1162–1190*, nos. 103, 224; *EEA IX: Winchester 1205–1238*, no. 58 and note.

[126] For English conciliar legislation directed against pardoners after 1215, see *Councils and Synods II*, I, 128–9 (cc. 17, 19), 352–3 (c. 46), 386 (c. 54), 622–3 (c. 75), 722 (c. 101); II, 1043 (c. 47).

[127] Langton's 'questiones' here, assembled from a series of Parisian manuscripts, are analysed by Hödl, *Schlüsselgewalt*, 342–53.

· [128] For the debate over 'non bis in idipsum', see B. Smalley, *The Becket Conflict and the Schools* (Oxford, 1973), cap. 124 8. For Langton's devotion to the memory of Becket, see A. Duggan, 'The Cult of St Thomas Becket in the Thirteenth Century', in *St Thomas Cantilupe Bishop of Hereford: Essays in his Honour*, ed. M. Jancey (Hereford, 1982), 21–44.

the sentence itself is announced by the earthly and therefore fallible confessor, whose award may not coincide with that imposed in heaven. In such circumstances, it is God's sentence that will be implemented, if necessary in purgatory, although any remission offered by a pope or bishop on earth will be duly honoured by God.[129] The obvious conclusion to be drawn from this, as from the later formulation by Aquinas, is that sinners should seek as many indulgences as possible upon earth, even in excess of penances that they had received in confession. Since God would honour the indulgences, but not necessarily concur with the penances decreed on earth, excess indulgences would serve to offset any penance decreed in the court of heaven which the sinner had not been made aware of before death. No wonder that Gerald of Wales was so keen to claim his one hundred year bounty.

As archbishop of Canterbury, Langton issued at least five indulgences.[130] One of these is modelled directly upon the formulae decreed in the Lateran Council, to which Langton, like Courson before him, adds a specific decree that the indulgence itself was to serve as sermon, with no preacher being allowed to stray from its text.[131] Similar injunctions were made in the indulgences of several of Langton's contemporaries.[132] In 1220, it was to be Langton who solicited what may well be considered the first jubilee indulgence, issued at the translation of the relics of St Thomas Becket at Canterbury, and advertised as a total of 540 days remission of penance bestowed by the

---

[129] Hödl, *Schlüsselgewalt*, 348 lines 68–80.

[130] *Acta Stephani Langton Cantuariensis Archiepiscopi A.D. 1207–1228*, ed. K. Major, Canterbury and York Society 50 (1950), nos. 50, 90, p. 155 no. 8, to which can be added a surviving indulgence for the shrine of St William at York (BL MS Cotton Claudius B iii fo. 53v, also in York Minster Library MS L2(1) fo. 162v), and references to lost indulgences for St Albans, Glastonbury and the shrine of Becket at Canterbury: BL MS Cotton Nero D vii fo. 88r; *Johannis Glastoniensis Chronica sive historia de rebus Glastoniensibus*, ed. T. Hearne (2 vols., Oxford, 1726), II, 383; below n. 133.

[131] *Acta Stephani Langton*, no. 90: 'Nolumus autem quod per has litteras nostras predicator aliquis admittatur, set illa sufficiat predicatio que presentibus litteris continetur.'

[132] *EEA IX: Winchester 1205–1238*, no. 58 (and cf. *Councils and Synods II*, I, 129, c. 19); Cambridge, St John's College muniments MS D9/9; BL MS Cotton Otho A ii fos. 49v–50r; Hereford Cathedral Library muniments no. 2036; *EEA XIII: Worcester 1218–1268*, ed. P. M. Hoskin (Oxford, 1997), no. 111; *Rotuli Hugonis de Welles Episcopi Lincolniensis A.D. MCCIX–MCCXXXV*, ed. W. P. W. Phillimore and F. N. Davis, Canterbury and York Society 1, 3–4 (1907–9), II, 253–4, and for the adoption of the Lateran formula 'Quoniam ut ait', most notably in the indulgences issued by Langton's successor Archbishop Boniface of Canterbury, see for example *EEA VII: Hereford 1079–1234*, no. 344; Cambridge University Library MS D. & C. Peterborough 1 fo. 110r; Hatfield House, Marquess of Salisbury Deeds 110/19; Westminster Abbey MS Domesday fos. 397v–8r. The form was still in use as late as 1299 in an indulgence issued by the Irish Bishop Nicholas of Leighlin for those praying before the tomb of the late Bishop William de la Corner in Salisbury Cathedral: Salisbury Cathedral Library Muniments Press IV Box Indulgences.

pope and by a great host of English and foreign bishops.[133] Taken up by the papacy in 1300, the jubilee indulgence was to have momentous effects over the course of the next two centuries, establishing a hyper-inflation of indulgences that was to contribute in no small part to the Protestant Reformation.[134] Amongst Langton's pupils, we find indulgences issued as a matter of course by Richard Poer at Salisbury, and even more significantly by Alexander of Stainsby as bishop of Lichfield.[135] Stainsby's indulgences are worthy of note, not merely because they were issued in spite of the very sophisticated conception of contrition and penance set out in Stainsby's writings on confession, but because via Stainsby the English tradition of indulgences flows back into the broader stream of European thought. It was Stainsby's one-time protégé, Alexander of Hales, who in the 1240s was to compose the first full theory of the treasury of merit, formulating a theological justification for indulgences that was to become, with the assistance of Thomas Aquinas, the very bedrock of Catholic doctrine thereafter.[136] Indulgences in England did not cease to evolve after 1215. Not only do we have the jubilee indulgence of 1220, but in the 1240s we get our first glimpse of what was afterwards to become a spate of indulgences awarded to those saying prayers for the souls of particular men and women in the afterlife – an important step on the road to the fifteenth-century extension of indulgences to souls in purgatory.[137] None the less, it is the Lateran decrees and their implementation by Langton, Stainsby and Alexander of Hales that supply us with an appropriate point at which to end this survey.

In the past, indulgences and pardoners have too often been treated as a merely picaresque aspect of medieval life, of interest chiefly for the part that they were to play in the sixteenth-century Reformation. I

---

[133] In general, see Duggan, 'The Cult of St Thomas Becket', 37-41; R. Foreville, *Le jubilé de Saint Thomas Becket du XIIIe au XVe siècle (1220-1470)* (Paris, 1958), esp. pp. 165-6; Petersohn, 'Jubiläumsfrömmigkeit', 31-53. For the mention of 540 days, see *The Historical Collections of Walter of Coventry*, ed. W. Stubbs (2 vols., London, 1872-3), II, 246.

[134] Lea, *Confessions and Indulgence*, III, ch. 4.

[135] *EEA XIX: Salisbury 1217-1228*, nos. 258, 272, 309, 348-9, 384, and for Stainsby, see Hereford Cathedral Library Muniments no. 2038; London, Public Record Office E135/6/38; Guilhall Library MS D. & C. St Pauls 25124 no. 4/3; Westminster Abbey MS Domesday fo. 402r; Krochalis, '"Magna Tabula"', 180.

[136] For the connections between Stainsby and Hales, see Vincent, 'Master Alexander of Stainsby', 627.

[137] The earliest English example that I know is the award by Fulk bishop of London, 29 Dec. 1249, for those praying in St Paul's Cathedral for the soul of the late Alexander of Swerford (d. 1246): *Documents Illustrating the History of St Paul's Cathedral*, ed. W. S. Simpson, Camden Society, 2nd ser., 26 (1880), 2-3 no. 3. For an earlier award of seven days indulgence to those saying the Pater Noster three times in the cemeteries of the diocese of Worcester, said to have been awarded in 1242, see *EEA XIII: Worcester 1218-1268*, p. 147 app. 1 no. 22.

hope to have shown here that the first century of English indulgences has far more significant implications and can be put to far more interesting uses than may previously have been supposed. By 1215, the agenda that was to be taken up by Alexander of Hales, Thomas Aquinas and much later by Martin Luther had already been set. Indulgences were accepted as a customary episcopal practice, not because but in spite of the emergence of new theological teachings on contrition, penance and absolution. Developing out of the much older system of tariffed penances and commutations, indulgences were in many ways ill suited to the more subtle penitential psychology of the twelfth and thirteenth centuries. Paris, where this new penitential thinking had greatest influence, resounded with criticisms and anxieties over the very idea of indulgence. Despite this, the indulgence was so useful a tool, both to the papacy and to the bishops, that even the theologians of Paris were forced eventually to admit it as a custom, whose benefits remained mysterious, but whose legitimacy was no longer to be denied. The debate over indulgences, and the indulgences themselves, tell us much: of the application of papal and episcopal authority in the post-Gregorian world, of the practice of confession and of the anxieties of whole masses of repentant sinners, of the interplay between Paris and Rome as influences over the English Church, of the birth of purgatory, of the cult of relics and of the emergence of that pantomime villain, the medieval pardoner. Superficially, a great gulf might appear to divide Chaucer's pardoner or the likes of Greve, Banbery and the Bridport alms-collectors from the solemn deliberations of Innocent III and the Lateran Council of 1215. In reality they are bound together by an instrument, the indulgence, that deserves to be regarded not as some archaic monument to theological folly, but as something far more central to the concerns of the twelfth-century Church.

Transactions of the RHS 12 (2002), pp. 59–111 © 2002 Royal Historical Society
DOI: 10.1017/S0080440102000038   Printed in the United Kingdom

TRAVELLERS AND THE ORIENTAL CITY,
c. 1840–1920
By Mark Mazower

READ 2 MARCH 2001 AT THE UNIVERSITY OF STIRLING

ABSTRACT. This paper explores the way in which nineteenth-century travellers to Salonica conveyed in writing the experience of travel to, and in, this Ottoman city. Their descriptions of the city indicate the power of certain aesthetic tropes in shaping their impressions. The claims of the picturesque were pre-eminent for decades but they coexisted with other rationales for travel – in particular the value of the direct impression conveyed by a landscape impregnated with classical and Biblical associations. Nor were most travellers insensible to the changing political prospects for the Macedonian port. The historical value of such works lies less in their reliability as testimony to the changes in the city itself than in the way they express patterns of authorial cultural taste.

IN THE middle of the nineteenth century, the age of mass travel came to Salonica. There had, of course, been visitors to the city from earliest times. Despite its location off the main trading and communications routes, a steady trickle of pilgrims, missionaries, diplomats and other voyagers made their way through Macedonia. The remarkable French traveller Paul Lucas stayed during his epic journey through the Levant and sent antiquities back to Paris for the king's collection. As the Grand Tour took aristocrats to the shores of the Mediterranean, a few enterprising young gentlemen of the late eighteenth century also made their way to the Ottoman port. James Stuart and Nicholas Revett, commissioned by the Society of Dilettanti to survey and draw the ruins of classical Greece, travelled to Salonica in 1751 and made one of the first depictions we possess of the city. But such trips were few and far between. We possess no more than half a dozen accounts of travels to Salonica published in the entire eighteenth century. In the first half of the nineteenth century the figure rises to about fifteen, and then to more than double that for the half-century after 1850.[1]

This rapid growth was in part a reflection of the new opportunities for, and interest in, travel that opened up to Europeans and, increasingly,

[1] Numbers based on S. H. Weber, *Voyages and Travels in the Near East Made during the XIX Century* (Princeton, NJ, 1952), and *idem*, *Voyages and Travels in Greece, the Near East and Adjacent Regions Made Previous to the Year 1801* (Princeton, NJ, 1953).

Americans, with the coming of steam and rail. Mass literacy too brought new popular markets for the travel book, and industrialisation whetted European appetites for tales of the exotic lands around them. Between 1876 and 1918, the travails of the Ottoman empire brought journalists flocking to Macedonia and new illustrated magazines like the *Illustrated London News*, the immensely popular French travel magazine, *Le tour du monde*, or its cheaper German equivalent, *Globus*, offered an outlet for the kind of educational and entertaining stories which would later form the staple fare of the *National Geographic*. Brigands, monks and pachas filled their pages.

It would be ridiculous to suppose that this body of writing failed utterly in its main purpose which was to enlighten and inform its readers about the realities of life in European Turkey. But much more than the purveying of information was at stake here. Writers were increasingly concerned to convey the experience of travel itself: the subjective dimension became of far greater literary importance than it had ever seemed to eighteenth-century travellers: Paul Lucas, among the most remarkable of these, had not even written his books himself – they had been composed on the basis of his travel notes by French savants who were able to add the classical allusions that more than compensated the readers of his works for the loss of an authentic authorial presence. Such procedures were not unknown in the nineteenth century, but they went against the grain of expectation. The more travel became a matter of routine and timetable, the more the nineteenth-century accounts emphasised the exceptional insights and subjective experiences thereby acquired. Travel increasingly became an opportunity for meditation, reflection and reverie in a world of unprecedently rapid change and transformation. Travel, in particular, to lands dense with classical and Biblical association, was shot through with historical meanings and allusions. It reflected both the doubts and the certainties of the Victorian era.

Travellers to Salonica came to see a remarkable city, but by their presence they changed it too. Their impact reflected the changing balance of power between Christian Europe and the Near East: the travellers were – in their person, in their expectations and demands, in the ideas they popularised – the embodiment of a the political and technological might of Europe itself, and they were not the least of the ways in which that power was projected upon the Ottoman world. As they came in ever-growing numbers to the city by the sea, did the people of Salonica realise how much the city would itself be altered by their depictions, fantasies and beliefs?

Even after travellers began coming to Greece, Egypt and the lands of the Bible, the Ottoman empire's remaining European provinces

remained off the beaten track. Almost no one made their way to
Salonica by land from the north before the end of the nineteenth
century. In 1816 the Reverend Clarke, coming up the coast from
Athens, had noted that 'as we viewed the mountains lying to the north
of Thessalonica, and compared their appearance with the forlorn blank
that characterises all the maps of the country between the Hebrus and
the Axius, we could but regret that they have been so rarely visited by
travellers'. Decades later little had changed when the Austrian consul
von Hahn rode down the Vardar valley from Belgrade in 1858 in the
company of a Serbian army officer, and discovered for the first time
that there were passages through the mountain ranges which previous
geographers had assumed bisected the Balkan peninsula. Von Hahn's
survey, transmitted as a monograph to the Imperial Academy of
Sciences in Vienna, stimulated plans for a rail link between central
Europe and the Aegean. Even as railway fever intensified, there were,
according to the German ethnographer Keipert, still 'vast territories
yet unexplored by European science'. Ottoman officials found this
desire for the unknown hard to understand. The pacha of Salonica
complimented one traveller on his enterprising spirit in venturing where
few Europeans dared go, but recommended next time he try Crete
instead 'for a long stay in winter or spring'. It was, he went on, 'a real
paradise and as interesting in every particular as it was convenient to
travel'.[2]

Even on the more convenient Mediterranean sea or land routes to
the Macedonian port – westwards from Istanbul, or northwards along
the Greek coast – visitors felt they were blazing a trail. 'I am the first
American woman that has ever visited Salonica', one wrote proudly to
her sister in 1839. More than three decades later, travellers were still
unusual. On a steamer from Constantinople, a German passenger fell
into conversation with a French salesman who wanted to know the
purpose of his journey. ' "For amusement?" the latter exclaimed. "To
Salonica? To this boring and most disconsolate of all Eastern one-horse
towns? Can it be?" ' Not everyone thought the benefits outweighed the
dangers of being captured by brigands, murdered by pirates or expiring
to plague, cholera or malaria. 'I think the old motto "Le jeu ne vaut
pas la chandelle", should have due weight with any Englishmen who
are purposing to visit the interior of Turkey', wrote a journalist in 1881.
But there were always those who felt drawn either by the risks, or by

[2] E. D. Clarke, *Travels in Various Countries of Europe, Asia and Africa* (1816), 338; J. G. von
Hahn, 'Reise von Belgrad nach Salonik', *Denkschriften der Kaiserlichen Akademie der Wissenschaften* (Philosophisch-Historische Classe), XI (Vienna, 1861), 1–245; H. Keipert, 'Note
sur des Cartes d'Albanie, de Macedoine et d'Epire', *Bulletin de la societé de géographie*,
15 (Jan.–June 1868), 93; Karl Braun-Wiesbaden, *Eine türkische Reise* (Stuttgart, 1876), II,
96–7.

the sense of being at the centre of events. 'The traveller in pursuit of the picturesque or in flight from the commonplace will find here what he seeks', wrote the journalist-historian, William Miller, in 1898 as the Macedonian Question hotted up. 'Tourists do not come to Macedonia', wrote a young American journalist in 1906, just before the Young Turk revolution broke out, 'but if they did they would find a show that no other part of Europe can produce. Not only is the comic-opera stage outdone in characters, in costumes, and in complexity of plot, but the scene is set in alpine mountains on a vaster scale than Switzerland affords.'[3]

It may have been debatable whether, as von Hahn asserted, culture followed the railway, but there was no doubt that tourism followed steam. The first steam cruise in the Levant took place in 1833; the first steam boat ran down the Danube the following year. By 1840 organised schedules connected the main ports of the Mediterranean on British, French and Austrian lines. The steam revolution ushered in a range of reactions which have, in many ways, remained unchanged from that day to this: on the one hand, the sheer wonder of speed, shortening for example the journey time between the Austrian and Ottoman capitals from three weeks to one, together with the closely connected fear that such acceleration in the pace of travel would destroy its very pleasure and purpose. The regrettable shortening of journey times was not to be checked 'in our hurried century', warned one writer. 'Three days saved in the time for navigation, the railways and roads substituting for sail, these are the attractions against which the immense majority of travellers lack any defence.' When the German scholar Jacob Fallmerayer spent a winter in Salonica in 1841, he boasted that he was 'much more fortunate than other travellers, who are always in a hurry'. On the other hand, it was hard to escape the cultural impact of Europe's technological inventiveness, whether this was viewed in triumph as hastening the global victory of Christian civilisation or with foreboding as destroying cultures and diverse forms of life.[4]

What steam, and later the railway, brought home to all travellers was the frightening pace of change. They were willing to pontificate on this with a readiness that irritated, bemused and occasionally amused members of the society they were so ready to advise. Braun-Wiesbaden, who at least could take the joke against himself, records a conversation he had with the fluent German-speaking pacha of Salonica. Talking of camels, still used in considerable numbers in merchant caravans, the

[3] Anon., 'Letters to my Sister: Letter III: Turkey–Salonica, 1839', *Southern Literary Messenger* (July 1840), 550; Braun-Wiesbaden, *Eine türkische Reise*, II, 129–30; 'Brigandage in Macedonia', *Appleton's Journal*, II: 65 (Nov. 1881), 469–72; W. Miller, *Travels and Politics in the Near East* (1898), xiv; F. Moore, *The Balkan Trail* (1906), 88.
[4] E. Isambert, *Itinéraire descriptif, historique et archéologique de l'Orient* (Paris, 1881), xxii.

visitor opined that after the coming of the railways, 'this animal will disappear like the ichthyosaurus'. 'Perhaps', the pacha replied with a smile. 'Nothing lasts for ever. But the camel is very useful ... especially in Asia.' 'If you stay here a year', his host went on, 'You may become a good Turk. And perhaps by then you'll learn how to deal with camels too.'[5]

Steam made travelling more predictable and easier to plan. Time was standardised. Cockerell, who visited the city in the era of sail, noted absent-mindedly in his diary on 28 September 1810: 'Here I find I have been for some time too late in my dates by a day.' What mattered little then mattered a great deal more in an era of timetables and schedules. Travellers were no longer dependent on the whim or favour of a ship's captain to take them; they could book a passage and turn the voyage into a regular commercial transaction. After the establishment of an independent Greek state in 1830, Greek, Turkish and British ships cooperated in stamping out piracy in the Aegean, and this made the sea passage to Salonica less dangerous than at any time for centuries. As adventurous travellers began to branch out and ventured further south – leaving the Rhineland and Switzerland for the south of France, Italy and the Holy Land, the market responded and the first guidebooks, offering instruction and advice to the lands of Greece and European Turkey, made their appearance.[6]

In the eighteenth century, the guidebook had been unknown. Some travellers to the Levant carried with them a veritable library of useful tomes. 'I am particularly in want of WOOD's *Description of the Ruins of Palmyra and Balbec*, a work very valuable and very scarce, in two volumes in folio', John Tweddell wrote from the Greek archipelago to a friend in 1798. 'There is also a book published lately by ROBINSON, in two volumes octavo – *View of the Ruins of Palmyra in the Desert of Syria* ... Add to this, ANSELM BANDURI's *Imperium Orientale*, DU CANGE's *Constantinopolis Christiana*, BRYANT's *Attack upon Homer's Topography* etc. etc.' The nine-teenth-century traveller was not supposed to escape the duty of extensive reading either. Far from it: Murray's *Handbook* sternly advised the traveller to the Levant to 'refresh his memory by an attentive perusal' of Dr Smith's *Dictionary of Antiquities*, and referred him to Gordon's *History of the Greek Revolution* for the recent background, to Neale's *History of the Holy Eastern Church* for ecclesiastical matters and to Colonel Leake's *Researches in Greece* and Thiersch's *Über die Sprache der Tzakonen* for those hoping to try out their classical Greek on the modern natives. The difference was that this reading was supposed to be done in

[5] Braun-Wiesbaden, *Eine türkische Reise*, 100.
[6] M. Vickers, 'Cockerell at Thessaloniki', *Balkan Studies*, 13:1 (1972), 54.

advance; once en route, the *Handbook* was intended to suffice.[7]

Compendia of earlier voyages like John Pinkerton's multi-volume collection had made older travel narratives available in a relatively cheap but entirely impracticable format; information for armchair or intending travellers might also be obtained from encyclopaedic ancient and modern geographies. *The Modern Traveller*, Josiah Conder's thirty-volume series of country studies – that on *Turkey* appeared in 1827 – was perhaps the first small and useful guide to the towns and regions of the empire for a mass market, but it was not based on firsthand experience. Its sources were all drawn from earlier travel narratives – the section on Salonica was lifted entirely from Henry Holland's description based on a visit there two decades previously – and it remained a geography not a travel guide. A German savant, the Abbé Boué, did traverse European Turkey himself, and published a voluminous work which charted roads and villages in remarkable detail. Boué's extensive studies provided the kind of material travellers required; but the handbook in its modern guise perhaps only emerged with Murray's *Handbook for Travellers in Greece*, which first appeared in 1840. Demand was slow – a new edition appeared only in 1854 – and French and German equivalents took twenty years to appear. But here at last were guides in the modern mode, with tips on how to travel, what to see and where to stay. They responded to travellers' needs, and in the early years relied on expert travellers for their own information, but they also shaped their experiences too. They were designed, in the words of Isambert's 1861 *Itinéraire descriptif, historique et archéologique de l'Orient*, 'to furnish the tourist with all the practical information necessary for a voyage which the new means of transportation facilitate'.[8]

Inspired by 'a scrupulous exactitude in details, a preoccupation with being always useful to the traveller', nothing was to be left to chance. All the practicalities of travel – from the construction of mosquito nets to the procuring of visas, obtaining letters of introduction, equipping oneself with provisions, employing servants and interpreters and bestowing appropriate gifts ('a few pairs of English pistols, knives, pocket-telescopes, toys for children, and ornaments for ladies ... New periodicals, caricatures etc. from London are most prized by English residents in the East') – were laid out. Voyagers were warned of seasonal diseases and the pecularities of local diets. Many travellers returned with advice of their own to pass on. James Baker advised dressing warmly in Macedonia, even in summer, to avoid chills. Emmanuel

---

[7] *Remains of the Late John Tweddell*, ed. R. Twedell (1815), 272–3.
[8] Cf. R. Schiffer, *Oriental Panorama: British Travellers to Nineteenth Century Turkey* (Amsterdam, 1999), 35–8. Also J. Buzard, *The Beaten Track: European Tourism, Literature and the Ways to 'Culture', 1800–1918* (Oxford, 1993).

Miller insisted on a morning coffee, and advocated a diet of cucumbers. The eccentric but highly erudite David Urquhart – among whose claims to fame was the introduction of the Turkish bath to England – advised shaving one's head to 'prevent chills by cooled perspiration', taking as little liquid as possible (for the same reason), and just one meal a day – preferably nothing more than 'pilaf, yaoort [a species of sour milk] and eggs ... the first two form together a light, nutritive and not unpalatable diet'. Everyone carried quinine against the marshy fevers for which Salonica was notorious.[9]

Although Urquhart would have sharply disagreed, the general attitude was that it was important to wear European dress and to avoid being mistaken for a native. 'It is simply ridiculous in an English traveller to assume the Greek or any other Oriental dress', admonished Murray, 'unless he is a *perfect* master of the local language and manners; and even in that improbable case he will still find an *English shooting jacket and wide-awake* the most respectable and respected travelling costume throughout the Levant'. In a society where to be European meant almost automatically to be regarded as a figure of power, this was not altogether unreasonable advice. Caught up in a brawl in the streets of Salonica between local Jews and some Greek sailors, a Greek writer visiting the town in the 1850s escaped harm because 'thanks to our clothes which allowed us to be taken for Franks, the *cawasses* let us enter the [Greek] consulate to ... watch the riot from upstairs'. Nevertheless, it expressed perfectly the attitude of superior detachment with which most travellers from Europe approached the mysteries of the Orient.[10]

Turkish cities, as Ami Boué explained, were particularly confusing to the Western visitor – they lacked public spaces such as squares or boulevards; they were often curiously silent since there was little wheeled traffic; they were dark and deserted at night; and there were no street names or numbers. Maps did not exist. Neither did time – at least as Europeans understood it: there were few or no public clocktowers. On the other hand, there were at least three calendars in use (four indeed if one counted the Jewish), and when one asked the time, one had to specify whether one meant 'alla turca' or 'alla franca'. Travellers were understandably thrown, wrote Lucy Garnett, by being asked: 'At what time is noon today?' In Salonica, of course, there were no less than three Sabbaths observed by the different religions, and the language of the streets was a confusing amalgam of Turkish, Italian and half a

[9] Isambert, *Itinéraire descriptif*, xxxvi; J. Baker, *Turkey* (New York, 1877), 371; E. Miller, *Le mont Athos, Vatopedi, l'île de Thasos* (Paris, 1889), 234; D. Urquhart, *Spirit of the East* (1838), I, 208.

[10] *Handbook for Travellers in Greece* (1854), 7; B. Nicolaidy, *Les turcs et la Turquie contemporaine: itinéraire et compte-rendu de voyages dans les provinces ottomanes* (Paris, 1859), I, 49–50.

dozen other tongues. Having ordered his morning coffee ('una piccola nera alla turca') a German visitor watched a public hanging – the dying man screaming half in Armenian, half in Judeo-Spanish – and read the placard eventually placed on his corpse which detailed his crimes in Turkish, Italian, Armenian and Greek. The mail was intermittent – one traveller at the end of the eighteenth century received a letter sent from England in October the following June – and even with the beginning of a regular steam service, newspapers still took more than a week to reach the city. Manners, it went almost without saying, were very different too: rooms lacked what were regarded elsewhere as basic furnishings such as chairs or tables, food looked odd and table manners were decidedly peculiar: 'Salads appear in great numbers on Turkish tables.' Dishes were a mish-mash of incongruous ingredients. 'If culinary science is foreign to the Turks, the science of dining well is still more unknown', warned one guidebook.[11]

This daunting prospect made it imperative for the traveller to try to feel as secure as possible while there, and to find a place where 'amidst the dirt, decay and disorder of the Orient, one is surrounded by all the cleanliness and comfort of Europe'. Staying in Turkish caravanserais and hans – as Ottoman subjects did – was too awful a prospect for most travellers: they generally only endured these if in the company of Turks – like Warrington Smyth – or when venturing out of Salonica into the hinterland, where nothing else was available. Not that there was a great deal of choice in Salonica itself. Until the 1840s it was customary for most travellers of any standing to present themselves to their consul, who would put them up until they could rent lodgings of their own, usually from a local Christian landlord. Hotels in the European style were unknown before this point. According to Boué, Salonica possessed a café, whose proprietor made available a living room, a bedroom and a gallery on the first floor. Edward Lear, passing through in 1848, records 'a Locanda – a kind of hotel – the last dim shadow of European "accommodation" between Stamboul and Cattaro'. Was this perhaps the Hotel Benedetti, where travellers could enjoy a coffee and cigarette over breakfast in the central courtyard, possibly the same establishment which the Guide Joanne sniffily referred to as 'une mauvaise auberge' run by an Italian? In 1874 James Baker noted 'two hotels, which are moderately comfortable'. It was, however, only nearer the century's end that amenities developed. By 1890 there were several large establishments – the Colombo, the Splendid Palace, the d'Angleterre, the Imperial and the Grand Hotel – in modern buildings fronting the new quay, or in the Frank Quarter, as well as smaller, seedier guesthouses along the road to the station. Old Balkan

[11] A. Boué, *La Turquie d'Europe* (Paris, 1840), II, 326–7.

hands were struck by the change: 'Who talked of Salonica fifty years ago?' asked a French writer in 1888. 'Only the antiquaries. Today her name is on every lip.'[12]

Walking around the town alone was not recommended. Instead, one hired a guide, initially through the consulate, later at the hotel, occasionally off the street. 'This time it was not enough to admire the Oriental sky', writes Auguste Choisy in August 1875, 'I had to get organised, or what came to the same thing, to find someone to do it for me. This organiser of the trip is called a dragoman, and the discovery of the Greek Nikolaki at Salonica was, I believe, arranged by providence.' Nikolaos Hadji-Thomas was, in the words of his satisfied customer, 'the model dragoman: a well-built man of open countenance, loyal, speaking Greek, Turkish, Bulgarian, Italian and able to make himself understood in French'. It was the guide-interpreter, who nego-tiated on the voyager's behalf for horses and provisions, dealt with Ottoman officials and guided him or her through the narrow streets of the lower town to the recognised sights. Until the 1880s – and later still for anyone venturing outside the city gates to promenade or hunt – one might additionally hire a bodyguard – the *cawass*, described by one traveller as 'Life Assurance made flesh' – since, as Braun-Wiesbaden noted during his stay in the city, 'in Europe we pay taxes for the armed force which the State operates on our behalf; here in Turkey it is every man for himself … This system is more expensive [but] it has one advantage, that one gets hand-rolled cigarettes and various other personal services.'[13]

More or less the only activity which the visitor was able to undertake alone was shopping for gifts in the bazaar, one of the largest and most impressive in the Turkish provinces. 'Sightseeing and visiting being accomplished, we had only to look if there was anything in the shops', wrote the Misses Irby and Mackenzie. Then, as now, obtaining souvenirs and presents took up time and energy – avoiding the pestering boot-blacks while browsing among the shoes, belt-knives, 'gaudy pistols', silks, gold-embroidered trousers, rose oil and carpets. However, even this was confusing. Shops were not organised as at home, and there were 'no "Stores" or general shops in which goods of various kinds are collected'. Visitors looking for books about the city were bound to be disappointed, and even postcards and photographs were not easy to obtain. Nor were the goods themselves always what they seemed. One traveller bought some local writing materials, a pair of white half-leather

[12] E. Lear, *Journals of a Landscape Painter in Albania etc.* (1848), 18; anon., 'De Salonique à Belgrade', *Revue des deux mondes*, 85 (1888), 108.

[13] A. Choisy, *L'Asie Mineure et les turcs en 1875: souvenirs de voyage* (Paris, 1876), 13; Braun-Wiesbaden, *Eine türkische Reise*, 135.

slippers and an impressive dagger that looked 'extremely Turkish' – only to discover too late that the blade was stamped with a German mark. The modern traveller's obsession – the search for authenticity – was already obstructed by modern tourism's nightmare creation – consumerism – and local markets were gearing themselves to the visitors far more quickly than the visitors liked to realise. 'We are greeted by importunate tradesmen's boys with cries of "Ver'goot Johnnie, anyting you like, Sair, souvenir Salonik" ', ran one record of the First World War, when the city was crowded with thousands of soldiers, and the locals quickly turned to English in place of the Italian they had been likely to know half a century earlier: 'The Salonician quickly realised the Westerners' weakness for souvenirs, and it was not long before a number of shops were doing excellent business selling cheap modern jewellery and antiques, such as Turkish swords and pistols, Greek daggers, Albanian cartridge-cases and old coins dating from the Byzantine and Roman eras.' Ottoman rule had scarcely ended before its relics were being sold off to the tourists.[14]

In love with the exotic and strange, but fearing them too, these travellers manifested the full ambivalence of their role. As anxious as any modern travel writer to prove they were not mere Cook's tourists, individualists not conformists, they emphasised the daring, courage and hardships involved in a trip to European Turkey. A romantic like Edward Lear was always likely to highlight how far the Balkans were 'remote from the ordinary routine of English travel'. 'Travellers accustomed to the luxurious hotels of civilised Europe can form no idea of what must be endured in the search after the picturesque in the interior of Turkey', wrote Mary Adelaide Walker. Reaching the han in Pella, just outside Salonica, she notes:

> Who has not in these days travelled in Switzerland and Germany, or at least in France, and can remember arriving at the comfortable, well-furnished hotel, where an elegant gentleman meets you on the steps, bows you into the brilliantly-lighted hall, and, conducting you up the carpeted staircase, hands you over to the care of the smart chambermaid, who smoothes the snowy sheets and downy pillow, draws the warm window-curtains, and professes herself ready to attend to your slightest wish?

No such luck in Pella where she described with relish a grumbling innkeeper, clad in 'a ragged caftan, greasy turban and tattered sheepskin cloak', crumbling walls, a broken staircase, rotten flooring and mud

[14] G. Muir Mackenzie and A. P. Irby, *Travels in the Slavonic Provinces of Turkey-in-Europe* (2nd edn, 1877), I, 63; A. Goff and H. Fawcett, *Macedonia: A Plea for the Primitive* (1921), 138–40.

floor spattered with the rain coming in through the roof. 'One must be endowed with a certain dose of energy and courage to travel in the provinces of Turkey in Europe', cautioned the Guide Joanne.[15]

There was also an inverse form of this kind of attitude – the sort of daredevil Regency insouciance cultivated especially by young military men. 'An excursion like ours from Corfu to Salonica is most indescribably delightful', wrote Captain Best in 1842 in his *Excursions in Albania, Comprising a Description of the Wild Boar, Deer and Woodcock Shooting in that Country; and a Journey from Thence to Thessalonica and Constantinople and up the Danube to Pest.*

> I know nothing more exciting (always save and except a good run with a good pack of fox-hounds) and no better or surer cure for ennui, and other ills common to civilised life in the hot seas of the Mediterranean, than a ride of from twelve to sixteen hours a day, at a jog trot, with an enterprising friend or two ... through a wild and partly unknown country, in a magnificent climate, amongst some of the most splendid scenery in the world, rendered doubly interesting by the classical associations connected with it.

David Urquhart agreed – 'no small portion of the pleasures of Eastern travel arises from sheer hardship and privation, which increase so much our real enjoyments'.[16]

We do not know what Salonica's inhabitants thought of the city's landscape since they have left no trace of their views before the twentieth century. One does well to bear in mind Wordsworth's Lake District woman who exclaimed: 'Bless me! Folks are always talking about prospects: when I was young, there was never such a thing named.' But if we can hazard an interpretation of this silence, it probably reflects not only the familiarity which even the most beautiful scenery eventually induces in the minds of those who spend their lives among it, but also, and more importantly, the lack of a literary culture and the absence of a worldview which turned landscape itself and the natural world into an object of aesthetic contemplation. The travellers on the other hand were visitors, and for them the city and its surroundings had all the charm of novelty. In addition, they were also the products of a powerful set of cultural and aesthetic expectations, and where they could, they did their best to live up to these. The landscape and its charms could not fail to attract their attention and

[15] Lear cited by J. Pemble, *The Mediterranean Passion* (Oxford, 1988), 50; anon., 'Letters to my Sister: Letter III, Turkey–Salonica, 1830', 550; M. A. Walker, *Through Macedonia to the Albanian Lakes* (1864), 86.

[16] J. Best, *Excursions in Albania etc.* (1842), 195; Urquhart, *Spirit of the East*, I, 8.

generate a stream of literary effusions. It would not be going too far to say that Western visitors to Salonica saw the city primarily, and sometimes exclusively, as an aesthetic construct rather than as a living society.[17]

Coming by sea, one entered the gulf at whose head the city lay; but before it came into view, there to the right was the mysterious realm of Mount Athos, a mountainous presence falling away to the sea, and on the left, towering above the wooded coastline, the inescapable grandeur of the home of the gods, Olympos itself. Nor did the first glimpse of Salonica ever fail to live up to this remarkable setting. 'The approach to this city from the sea is very imposing', wrote Henry Holland. 'It is seen from a great distance, placed on the acclivity of a steep hill ... surrounded by lofty stone-walls ... and surmounted by a fortress with seven towers. The domes and minarets of numerous mosques rise from the other buildings, environed as usual by cypresses, and giving a general air of splendour to the place.' 'The traveller who approaches it by sea on a summer morning', wrote the more whimsical Reverend Davies, 'might think he was coming to one of those cities of enchantment which he had read of in Eastern romances.'[18] Pretty as a picture, it was generally described in painterly terms:

> At the risk of labouring the expression 'Pearl of the Aegean', as applied to Salonika, one must repeat that whether on account of the cupidity it excited in foreign invaders or on account of its picturesque appearance from the sea, the title is amply justified. So pleasing is its setting and perspective that an artist or anyone with a sense of the beautiful is straightway filled with a desire to maroon himself in the middle of the harbour and endeavour to depict in colour the panorama before him. So perfect is the composition of the picture that it seems to have been controlled and set out from the sea, just as the expert window-dresser directs his scheme from the pavement. The tiers of white, red-roofed houses, interspersed with graceful minarets, stretch in a vast amphitheatre from the upper gallery of the ancient walls down to a proscenium of deep blue sea. With a fringe of boats as the foreground, the mauve-tinted heights in the distance and a middle theme made up of the multi-coloured terraces of the town, the picture seems almost unreal in its perfection.[19]

'It is one of the most picturesque cities from the water that I ever saw',

[17] Wordsworth cited in E. Bohls, *Women Travel Writers and the Language of Aesthetics, 1716–1818* (Cambridge, 1995), 90 and *passim*.

[18] H. Holland, *Travels in the Ionian Islands, Albania, Thessaly, Macedonia etc. during the Years 1812 and 1813* (1815), 310; G. S. Davies, *The Heathen World and St. Paul: St. Paul in Greece* (n.d.), 123.

[19] Goff and Fawcett, *Macedonia*, 128–9.

wrote M. to her sister in 1839. The picturesque was, according to its acolytes, a view which offered a different kind of beauty to the sublime – more romantic, inspiring in the beholder not terror or a sense of human insigificance but rather reverie, fancy and dreams. It required vegetation, gentle inclines, graduated tones and half-glimpsed suggestions of human habitation, if possible accompanied by the desirable sense of decay evoked by ruins or other kinds of remains. Although the ideal of the picturesque had been around for many decades, it was only at this time that it began to be applied to the Orient, popularised in collections of engravings like Julia Pardoe's highly popular *Beauties of the Bosphorus*. W. H. Bartlett, probably the most prolific topographical illustrator of the first half of the century, also jumped on the bandwagon with works such as *Footsteps of our Lord and His Apostles*.[20]

The picturesque style, like any other, demanded work to be fully appreciated. This was not, to be sure, as serious a business as familiarising oneself with the landscape's historical and political associations. Nevertheless, Emile Isambert urged travellers not to disdain prior study of 'some *picturesque and humorous voyages*' as 'a stimulant which will encourage you to head off, and their vividly coloured images will teach you to paint yourselves'. Many travellers sketched or painted and used their accounts as a guide to their own future work or as a substitute for it. Edward Lear was only perhaps the best known of the professional artists who traversed the Balkans in the search for romantic scenery. Indeed, the landscape he produced of the view across the gulf to Olympos from the citadel of Salonica is a fine example of the conventions of the picturesque. Lear, exceptionally, was even able to detect the picturesque amid the squalor of the lower town where, in his words, 'I saw an infinity of picturesque bits, cypresses, and minarets, and latticed houses' despite the cholera epidemic which had silenced the city and eventually drove him out of it.[21]

Until 1869, the city was entirely ringed by walls, making access inconvenient, especially after dark, but lending further beauty to the travellers' first impression. The demolition of the sea wall opened the front up to the ship-bound newcomer. Some liked this – it created, according to the Guide Joanne, for example, 'the most agreeable promenade' in the city, but as modernity fringed the quay with European-style hotels and warehouses, tramlines and street-lights, the search for the picturesque encountered new obstacles. 'The walls which protected the city from the sea have unfortunately been removed in these days of peace', lamented the classicist J. P. Mahaffy, 'more

[20] Anon., 'Letters to my Sister. Letter III: Turkey–Salonica, 1839', 551.
[21] Isambert, *Itinéraire descriptif*, xxxv; Lear, *Journals*, 25. See generally, Buzard, *The Beaten Track*, ch. 1.

convenient no doubt but not half so picturesque.' 'Behind the quay', wrote R. H. Russell in 1896, 'the modern tramway, with busy cars running to and fro, does much to destroy the Eastern atmosphere of the place, forcing you to close your eyes to this feature of the foreground ... before you can believe that you are really in an Oriental port'. Even so, Salonica, for devotees of the picturesque, still conserved those features which had vanished in independent Greece, where in Lear's words, approvingly cited by Murray's *Handbook*, 'war and change' had deprived her of 'the charm of Oriental architecture, the picturesque mosque, the minaret, the fort and the serai'. As Athens and Belgrade erased the traces of their Muslim past, Salonica's 'unmistakably Eastern look' became ever more pronounced, its anomalous character in a European setting ever more seductive. In an odd way, the city was coming to seem more Oriental, the more the world around it changed. Some commentators, trying to alert their readers to the city's changing contemporary significance, reacted angrily to the tyranny of this fashion: 'One ought to flog the fanatics of the picturesque in public were they not anyway reduced to impotence', thundered one journalist. His anger betrayed the continued resilience of a way of experiencing the Levant, which lingered on, as we shall see, well after the First World War. Travellers tried (and largely succeeded) to screen out evidence of modernity and focused on what they had come to see.[22]

From afar, the lovely setting induced reverie, dreams, enchantment, a sense of otherworldliness. The view from the citadel at the top of the town was particularly prone to send writers into a swoon. Having described the 'glorious panorama of old red roofs, graceful minarets, green trees and the blue of the Aegean beyond', Goff and Fawcett paused before the 'towering snow-capped "Home of the Gods" – Mount Olympus' in the distance:

> Such is the picture – so clear that it might almost be a fitting illustration by a fanciful artist to an Eastern fairy tale. For indeed is not the East one huge fairy tale? Are not the white minarets and the mysterious old houses, the storks on the roof, the beggar at the fountain, the very cobble-stones and above all, the deep blue sky and the star-strewn night the very essentials of magic and romance?

The customary illuminations for Ramadan were especially spectacular. To the Oxford geographer Henry Tozer, sailing across the gulf towards Olympos in July 1853, 'the city presented an enchanting sight for each of the tall minarets which rise from among its houses was circled by a ring of glittering lamps ... We watched them gradually lessening, until

---

[22] *Handbook for Travellers in Greece*, 1; J. P. Mahaffy, *Greek Pictures* (1890), 218; Miller, *Travels and Politics*, 365; R. H. Russell, *On the Edge of the Orient* (New York, 1896), 191.

they formed a delicate bright cluster, like a swarm of fire-flies on the horizon.' Even the nasty George Abbott, who could rarely find a good word for anyone or anything, was moved by the prospect from the sea as he looked across the bay one evening and saw the city lit up for the anniversary celebrations for the Sultan Abdul Hamid: the White Tower, he wrote, was like 'a castle in fairyland, such as one loved to dream of in the days of long ago'. The same prospect reminded John Foster Fraser of 'a scene to be occasionally noticed on the drop-curtain of a theatre'.[23]

For some, this first glimpse provided a spell which further investigation could only break: 'It is the oriental city', wrote de Vogüé, 'which one ought to pass from afar in a dream, without approaching it.' This stance was in itself almost an inevitable part of the aesthetic ideal of the picturesque. By definition, it kept humans at an ornamental distance, and guaranteed disappointment, irritation or at the very least, readjustment, once what had been an enchanting prospect hove into closer view. And when the centrepiece of this enchanted image was a city – an anarchic form of human community always likely to provoke fears among the Victorian middle and upper classes – one can understand why, almost without exception, travellers to Salonica found the contrast between their first glimpse and their entry into the reality of a bustling, ployglot commercial centre overpowering. 'Few places can exhibit a greater discrepancy than here between external splendour and internal squalor', Murray's 1884 Handbook flatly stated.[24]

Closer acquaintance immediately brought disenchantment, revulsion and often disgust as a host of unruly gesticulating figures filled the foreground and approached the viewer. Edward Lear, brought by lighter to the slippery wooden-planked quay – before the construction of new docks in the 1890s, it was impossible for large boats to berth by the shore – was flummoxed by the 'crowds of black-turbaned Hebrews at the water's edge' who seized him, his dragoman and his luggage bodily and carried them out of the boat before fighting over who would have the right to carry his belongings to the hotel. Melville, who visited the town briefly a few years later, watched in fascination the 'vast crowd and tumult' when the Austrian steamer arrived from Constantinople: 'Imagine an immense accumulation of the rags of all nations, and all colors rained down on a dense mob, all strugling for huge bales and bundles of rags, gesturing with all gestures and wrangling in all tongues.

---

[23] Goff and Fawcett, Macedonia, 155–7; H. F. Tozer, Researches in the Highlands of Turkey (1869), II, 140–1; G. F. Abbott, The Tale of a Tour in Macedonia (1903), 35; John Foster Fraser, 'Adrianople, Salonika and Monastir', in Turkey and the Balkan States, ed. E. Singleton (New York, 1908), 148; Schtiter, Oriental Panorama, ch. 8, is excellent.

[24] E.-M. de Vogüé, 'La Thessalie', Revue de deux mondes, 31 (1879), 6; Murray cited in B. Gounaris, 'Salonica', Review: Fernand Braudel Center, 16:4 (Fall, 1993), 499–518.

Splashing into the water from the grounded boats.' Should a boat suspected of carrying cholera or plague approach, hundreds of wailing and protesting Jews thronged the quay, trying to prevail upon the Ottoman officials to prohibit its passengers from disembarking. And before the sanctuary of consulate or hostel could be reached, the newcomer had to brave the warehouses, customs sheds, hans, taverns and cafés of the city's business quarter. The newly arrived Mary Adelaide Walker was directed

> through a pond of mud, under a crumbling archway, along some miserably paved, tortuous streets. No Consulate appeared and were beginning to feel rather helpless amidst the clamour of Turkish, Spanish, Greek, Bulgarian, Albanian and various other tongues, when a brisk young man, with an Armenian face, looking delightfully cool, and clean in a complete suit of white, saw our perplexity.

Salvation beckoned and they were rescued.[25]

This was always, though most travellers did not perhaps realise it, a tough working port, a magnet for merchant seamen, naval men and, often indistinguishable from the rest, pirates on leave. Add to this the large numbers of regular troops which passed through on their way to trouble-spots from Albania to the Yemen, the more troublesome irregulars, and it is not surprising that local street life was lacking in the social graces. Yet in fact, crime never features as a problem facing the European traveller, and there is not a single mention of cut-throats, pick-pockets, thieves or the other dangerous lowlifes which haunted English or French metropolitan streets. Street brawls, affrays and riots, when they occurred – which was certainly less often than at home – left Europeans unscathed.

The only form of violence to which they were exposed – stones thrown by small Muslim children in the upper town – was scarcely life-threatening, and generally stopped by the presence of a local adult. Only when a male 'Frank' was stupid enough to try to approach a Muslim woman might he be threatened with worse. 'On our return to the town we met a pretty Turkish girl', wrote a traveller at the end of the eighteenth century, 'about fifteen or sixteen years old. Her eyes, the only part of her which we could see, were the finest I ever beheld. When we approached close to her, one of our company was so imprudent as to make signs to her, which is here the most effectual way to get assassinated.' Even then, much depended upon where and in what spirit such an approach was made. When a Greek doctor and his two friends, having helped a gypsy musician recover from an

[25] Lear, *Journals*, 18–19; H. Melville, *Journals* (Evanston, IL, 1989), 56; Walker, *Through Macedonia*, 31–2.

apoplectic fit in the public gardens outside the city gates – a popular evening recreational jaunt for the moneyed classes – came suddenly upon a group of Muslim women, the incident was more playful than angry:

> The Turkish women, not having had time to replace their yashmaks [veils] which they remove when they are alone, restricted themselves to hiding their faces with whatever was to hand, some behind their large sleeves, others draping the first piece of fabric they saw, some throwing up the folds of their split skirts. They did all that with a refined coquetry which picqued our curiosity and provoked our desire. But as we approached they turned away with the usual cry: 'Here comes harm!'[26]

Once inside the city walls, the marvellous light-filled vista gave way to a grimmer, ill-lit reality – 'suffocating streets, wretched wooden houses, leprous constructions, unmentionable cesspools'. In a setting where even the main street was unimpressive in its dimensions, there were none of the broad avenues, spacious squares or vistas to be enjoyed in the increasingly sanitised and planned urban environments of northern and western Europe. Even the well-disposed Braun-Wiesbaden wrote that 'the interior of the city is disappointing and ... evokes in one an irritated disillusionment'. 'After telling you of the romantic appearance of the city from without', wrote M. to her sister, 'I must not forget to say that the first object I encountered on entering was the *fish* market – a long dark, covered way, redolent with the most disgusting perfumes. Alas! For all romance in a Turkish city.' The bazaar struck one unimpressed tourist as 'quite large but filthy. Streets all narrow, like cow lanes, and smelling like barnyards.' The open drains, which stank in all weathers, the effluent which collected against the walls in the lower town, the mean, crooked streets and poorly paved roads, harsh enough to tax the strongest feet on a day's sight-seeing – this 'sad labyrinth' was more than enough to tax the sympathies of all but the most open-minded visitor. The houses, so attractive from afar, looked ill-built on closer inspection. 'Aspect of streets like those of Five Points', noted Melville, alluding to a notorious slum back home. 'Rotten houses. Smell of rotten wood.' In the centre of the town, the throng of humans and packs of dogs alarmed even experienced travellers like Clarke, who justified his cursory scrutiny of the Arch of Constantine on the grounds that 'it is situate in a very crowded part of the city, which made his stay dangerous, and would have rendered its examination difficult'.[27]

[26] A. Bisani [?], *A Picturesque Tour through Part of Europe, Asia and Africa* (1793), 44; Nicolaidy, *Les turcs et la Turquie contemporaine*, 47.

[27] De Vogüé, 'La Thessalie', 7, Melville, *Journals*, 55; Braun-Wiesbaden, *Eine türkische Reise*, 134; anon., 'Letters to my Sister: Letter III: Turkey–Salonica, 1839', 550; Clarke, *Travels*, 360.

Not everyone was so alarmed, or so harsh in their judgements. Jacob Fallmerayer wrote lovingly of his winter there and felt that 'the mild weather, the quick and sure communications with the West, the lively trade, intermingling of foreigners, the tolerant attitude of the inhabitants of all religions, ease of living and life give a stay in Thessalonica a charm such as few cities in European Turkey possess'. But few visitors shared Fallmerayer's deep interest in the people of the Balkans and their current situation, and few stayed as long as he did unless on business. Only a few older hands – Fanny Blunt, the remarkable wife of the British consul, or Lucy Garnett, a pioneering ethnographer of the Ottoman Balkans – were able to see the life of the city on its own terms and to appreciate its charms, and their explanations enjoyed only a limited circulation compared with the caricatures and clichés offered by Thackeray, Mark Twain and other best-selling Oriental lampooners. Most Europeans remained resolutely uninterested in any reading of the urban culture of the Ottoman empire that did more than confirm their prejudices. The main reason for this was a simple one: they were, in general, far less interested in the present of the place than they were in its past.

The overwhelming reason for travelling to the Near East was to gain insights into the classics and the Bible – the twin mainstays of nineteenth-century European culture – which could only come from looking with one's own eyes upon the places one would otherwise merely have read about in books. Passing amidst dramatic scenery from Thessaly into Macedonia, the Reverend Clarke was put in mind of Alexander the Great. 'Almost the first object on which his sight rested', he wrote, 'was the awful form of *Olympus*, believed to be the throne of Heaven itself ... the grandeur of whose appearance can only be felt by those who come here to view it.' In the words of John Pemble:

> If the British studied the present they did so in order to come closer to the past. Only a few studied the past in order to come closer to the present. Victorian writing on the Mediterranean was dominated by the assumption that the modern South was in some crucial sense not authentic ... always a distortion or remnant of the real South of classical or medieval times.

Greece, according to Murray – as if to illustrate the truth of Pemble's observation –

> has no modern history of such a character as to obscure the vividness of her classical features. A modern history she does indeed possess, various and eventful, but it has been of a destructive not a constructive character. It has left little behind it which can hide the immortal

memorials of the greatness of Hellenic genius ... In all parts of the country, the traveller is, as it were, left alone with antiquity.

It would not be too much to say that the educated European felt far closer in spirit to the ancient inhabitants of the lands through which he passed than he did to those he actually met.[28]

The topography of the Levant had long been referred to in classical terms by travellers there. 'We passed from the gulf Syngiticus to that of Thermaicus, and anchored in the bay of Thermes, Thessalonica or Salonica, in the country of the Myrmidons', wrote Bisani. Many a traveller went to identify classical locations, to verify the accuracy of Greek and Latin historians and to contribute to the refinement of what the eighteenth century knew as 'ancient geography'. Crossing the Vardar on his way to Salonica, Clarke noted that

> it is the AXIUS of *Herodotus*: separating the *Mygdonian* from the *Bottioean* territory ['epi tin Axion potamon hos ourizei chorin tin Mygdonin te kai Bottiaiida', *Herodoti Hist.*lib.vii.cap.123.p.418, ed. *J. Gronov. L.Bat.* 1715' a footnote helpfully confirmed], where Pella stood: and it is now called *Vardar*. The same river is also mentioned, under the name of AXIUS, by the venerable *Scylax*.

(The learned don was not to know that a century later, the river would be officially renamed 'Axios' by a Greek government, under the guidance of a placename committee of scholars – but that is a later part of the story.)[29]

The spectacular view from the upper town across to Olympos inspired a host of historical meditations as one foreigner after another sought to gain access to the mind of the ancients. 'From the mountain on which today the old citadel of Salonica stands, Xerxes saw some two thousand three hundred years ago what today any knowledge-thirsty tourist can see if he doesn't mind the effort of traipsing between debris and boulders, rocks and burned grass, thistles and especially weeds', wrote one, trying to recapture the thoughts of the Persian king, as he planned his invasion of Greece. For the more high-minded Mary Adelaide Walker, 'the sight which inspired Xerxes with the hope of other lands to conquer, may well elevate the mind of the Christian spectator to the world beyond the grave' to that 'wondrous future when even the "mountains shall pass away"'. 'It is sometimes the charm of marvellous or unusual natural beauty which forms the attraction, sometimes the irresistible force of historical or legendary associations', mused the Reverend Davies.

---

[28] Pemble, *The Mediterranean Passion*, 267; *Murray's Handbook*, 1.
[29] Bisani, *Picturesque Tour*, 35; Clarke, *Travels*, 335–7.

At Salonica it is the linking together of both. Neither the full majesty of perfect beauty nor the full strength of historic memories is lacking there. It is the same Olympus as that which ages ago was a landmark of reverence and awe to those who sailed the early seas, seeing in it the home of the gods. It is the same Olympus, empty now of its gods, but still full of its eternal loveliness, on which St. Paul must often have gazed – deep blue in the noonday, purple in the evening – seeing in it the work and beauty of Him who in His strength setteth fast the mountains, and is girded about with power.[30]

Primed by education, expectation and perhaps by special preparatory reading, the traveller there came face to face with history itself – classical, Biblical or in the case of Macedonia, the two together. 'It is history, which for him had till that point been no more than an ideal, an exercise of memory, or for some only a subject for meditation, the history of the first ages of mankind, which suddenly reveals itself in its proper theatre', wrote Isambert.

The East is the cradle of our civilisation ... In the East, everything takes body, assumes its real proportions, ... not only in the sight of the ancient buildings which the hand of time has spared, but also by frequenting those peoples, those races conserved through the centuries which are still the most living monument, the most effective demonstration of what their ancestors bequeathed to us!

The task of civilisation might have been passed to the West, but the East still offered enlightenment.[31]

What was more, it did so not only through the remains of the dead but by the example of the living as well. Those American classicists who between the two world wars travelled among the guslar players of Yugoslavia to learn more about the Homeric epics were far from the first to see the inhabitants of the Balkans as living fossils. Even David Urquhart, a most untypical traveller in the depth of his engagement with the society he travelled through, recommended experiencing the East for 'what I would call the novelty of antiquity'. Lost to 'our times and in our portion of the globe', the 'habits of ancient days still live and breathe' there, he asserted.

There you may dine as people dined at Athens; there may you enjoy the greatest, the lost luxury of antiquity, and bathe as they bathed at Rome; and while there you may look upon, in real flesh and blood, the Homeric visions of three thousand years – may you also

---

[30] Braun-Wiesbaden, *Eine türkische Reise*, 263; Davies, *St. Paul in Greece*, 129; Walker, *Through Macedonia*, 66.

[31] Isambert, *Itinéraire descriptif*, xviii.

behold the living counterpart of our Anglo-Saxon ancestors, as described by Bede, and assist at *gemots* in each parish, as convened by Alfred.[32]

Although it was really the peasantry who preserved the ancient ways best, at least in the nineteenth-century mind, the desire to find the past was so strong that travellers were quite capable of finding it alive and well in the unlikely setting of an Ottoman town as well. 'We set out through the streets of the sleeping town', recalled Demetra Vaka. 'How teeming with history it was. Everything spoke of the past, not the present.' The Jews in particular cast her mind back centuries. 'But it is the same with all the other nationalities one sees in Saloniki: they represent the past not the present ... The history of ages enveloped us.' Sir Austen Layard's famous excavations in Mesopotamia surely lay behind one writer's discovery that 'the Assyrian type was widespread' in Salonica. 'Certain lanes in the bazaar resemble a bas-relief from Nineveh and Babylon', readers were assured, 'where magnificent Assurbanipals sell melons or watermelons.' Another asserted that studying the habits of the city's Greek community would allow one to 'understand the internal life of a Byzantine city'. By 1905, as the lower town became ever more prosperous, noisy and Western in outlook, even the Turkish quarter in the upper town could be enlisted, offering one American correspondent 'truly a Biblical scene though the characters were Mohammedan'.[33]

In such an urban setting, modern life intruded unavoidably. Local peoples and their habits were to be valued for the light they supposedly shed upon the classics; their moving away from this role was not appreciated. It was thus only partly tongue in cheek that Charles Warner wrote, while waiting for the post: 'From whence a mail was expected I do not know. The traveller who sails these seas with a cargo of ancient history resents in these classic localities such attempts to imitate modern fashions. Were the Dardanians or the Moesians to send us letters in a leathern bag?' Like all travellers, those to European Turkey wanted modern amenities and complained if they were not there; but in this case they complained if they were too obtrusive too, for then they threatened that communion between the visitor and his past which was the real purpose of his coming.[34]

Where the devotees of the picturesque met students of the antique was in their passion for ruins and antiquities – objects which combined beauty, a hint of the vanity of things human and scientific usefulness. The Turks, commented Boué in 1840, 'even the most educated, are

[32] Urquhart, *Spirit of the East*, I, 11.

[33] Anon., 'De Salonique à Belgrade', 115; D. Vaka, *The Heart of the Balkans* (New York, 1917), 228; Choisy, *L'Asie Mineure*, 16; Moore, *The Balkan Trail*, 87.

[34] C. D. Warner, *In the Levant* (New York, 1893 edn), I, 479.

unable to comprehend the respect which we attach to a lump, even shapeless, of some beautiful architectural remain'. Of course Salonica, and its surroundings, could not compete with the riches of Greece itself. 'Few monuments to visit, no great ruins', was the judgement of a French guidebook in 1873. Nevertheless, the city's ancient remains had attracted visitors since the early eighteenth century, and continued to do so: the Arch of Constantine, the remarkable caryatids known as Las Incantadas (The Enchanted Ones) and the other standing classical monuments and early churches formed the main attractions of the city according to all the guidebooks. Salonica was, according to even a highly engaged observer of the contemporary scene, 'a city of churches, and ruins, antiquities and mosques. The modern buildings with the exception of a large barracks by the eastern gate, a hospital, the Jesuit college and the Banque Ottomane, are not impressive or solidly built.'[35]

To the antiquarians, the city's modern buildings were in fact often seen merely as locations for ancient remains. The French consul there between 1745 and 1748, Germain, collected a series of classical inscriptions, identified as follows: 'No. 19: Pièce de marbre qui forme le coin de la traverse derrière la taverne de Manoly, au vieux quartier des Francs' − this the only trace in the historical record of Manoli's tavern, which otherwise disappears into oblivion; or: 'No. 20 Pièce de marbre où il y a une inscription: elle sert de base à un pillier de bois qui soutient un auvent, en entrant à la mosquée Isak Pacha, ditte *Allagéa imarêt*, fondation où l'on distribue du pain et du ris pour les pauvres.' Not until another 250 years had passed would these buildings − or what little was left of them − be regarded in their turn as a precious part of the historical record.[36]

Even the city's major remains of antiquity were in ramshackle condition, crumbling, half hidden behind the shacks and shops built around them, a matter for seeming indifference on the part of the Ottoman authorities. Inspecting the Arch of Constantine − as it was then known − a German visitor, his mind no doubt harking back to Berlin, capital of the newly founded Reich of Bismarck and the Hohenzollerns, was struck by the futility of the passion for monumentality and felt

> a shiver at the thought that our beautiful west European towns too might fall into the hands of barbarians, like Salonica today, and that in the future some Australian ... of the 28th century will sit before our mutilated triumphal arch and contemplate matters just as I do here before the arch of Constantine.

[35] Boué, *La Turquie d'Europe*, II, 307; Isambert *Itinéraire descriptif*, 1873 ed., 1873, 498, 714; Braun-Wiesbaden, *Eine türkische Reise*, 240.

[36] *Thessalonikin Filippou Vasilissan* (Thessaloniki, 1985), 730.

Not merely viewing, but saving the ruins for scholarship and civilisation thus impressed itself as an urgent duty for the visiting European. Aware of living in an exciting new era of archaeological discovery, travellers were advised to do their bit, not by carrying away mosaics, coins, sarcophagi fragments and shards but by the serious work of tracing inscriptions and surveying architecture. 'There would be precious discoveries to be made at Salonica for the traveller who seeks to research the numerous inscriptions and the still unpublished monuments scattered among individual houses', the Guide Joanne alerted its readers. Ancient masonry and tombstones were visible in the city walls and even in the walls of private buildings. A large sarcophagus lay in the courtyard of the Hotel Benedetti; dedicatory tablets were found on the property of the dragoman of the British consulate and in the courtyard of the governor's palace. The time had passed for picturesque views, insisted two scholars in 1876; serious measurement and analysis were now what were needed, especially with the upheaval caused by the urban rebuilding projects of the municipality at this time. 'The debris from the demolished walls, monuments of all kinds, which had once been used to reconstruct the gates to the lower part of the city were immediately used in construction of the new quay', reported two scholars anxiously, adding a new concern to the longer-standing worry at the locals' propensity to consign ancient marble fragments to the lime-kiln.[37]

In 1886 Salomon Reinach published his *Conseils aux voyageurs arch-éologues*, in which he advised travellers how to take rubbings of inscriptions, how to take advantage of the new techniques of photography and in particular how to fill in the gaps in maps and charts by recording one's itinerary 'simultaneously in two ways, by means of notes and by drawing'. Many heeded the call. The pages of bulletins, journals and periodicals – of the *Archives des missions scientifiques*, the *Berliner Philologische Wochenschrift* and the *Mitteilungen des Deutschen Archäologischen Instituts* – resounded with the clash of academic debate amidst the rush to publication. 'The appended inscriptions are the outcome of a short visit to Salonica in April of this year', wrote a British classicist in the *Journal of Hellenic Studies* in 1887. 'I copied or impressed as many Greek inscriptions as came my notice in my short stay, the great majority being sepulchral of a commonplace order found in the foundations of houses in the Jewish quarter, and too frequently relegated to the stonemasons' yards to be cut up for modern gravestones.' Hogarth, the Frenchmen Duchesne, Bayet and Perdrizet, the Greek Papageorgiou, the Germans Wolters and Mordtmann were part of the expanding fraternity of scholars who scoured the bazaars, drains, graveyards,

[37] *Thessalonikin Filippou Vasilissan*, 626–7.

alleyways and walls of Salonica in the hunt for inscriptions and the race against time.[38]

The middle decades of the nineteenth century were an exciting time for European archaeology: Schliemann and Layard were household names while in Greece itself the great excavations at Olympia, Delphi and Delos were uncovering major artefacts of the classical era each year. Archaeology inspired poets and satirists, and fresh finds made the pages of the daily press. In Salonica the first generation of committed archaeologists arrived and began to take a more systematic interest in the city's remains. Charles Newton, the British Museum's man in the Levant, came for a cursory inspection in 1853, and noted the *Incantadas* and the Arch of Constantine. 'There are many remains of antiquity in this historical town', reported James Baker, 'and it would offer an admirable field for an archaeological campaign.' Braun-Wiesbaden felt it would 'not be a bad idea for one of the German savants, so preoccupied with Olympia, to make a detour to Salonica. It would only cost him a few days and amply repay the effort. I know no city in Europe which boasts so many antiquities and is so little known for research.'[39]

Archaeology may have been a science, it may have even been international in its research interactions; but there could be little doubt in the nationally rivalrous atmosphere of late nineteenth-century Europe that it was also a profession in the service of the nation. The competition was political as well as professional to appropriate the most illustrious and exciting remains of the past for the new state museums springing up like mushrooms in western Europe. Charles Newton had remarked that 'the most interesting relic of classical antiquity' in Salonica was

> the *Incantadas*. This is the name given to part of a colonnade apparently erected in the time of Hadrian. The colonnade is sup-ported by Corinthian columns half-buried in the ground, above which are square pilasters, each of which has on two faces a figure sculptured in relief. Among these figures are Dionysos, Hermes, Ariadne, Ganymede, Leda, a Bacchante and a Victory.

A century earlier, the colonnade had been drawn by Stuart and Revett in their visit to the city: the picture is the first realistic depiction we possess of the city at all. Newton, who would shortly become Keeper of the Greek and Roman Antiquities at the British Museum, probably had his hands full with excavations at the site of the Mausoleum of Halicarnassus and Didyma. Although he, like previous and subsequent

---

[38] Braun-Wiesbaden, *Eine türkische Reise*, 241–2; S. Reinach, *Conseils aux voyageurs arch-éologues en Grèce et dans l'Orient hellenique* (Paris, 1886), 108–9.
[39] Baker, *Turkey*, 352.

British visitors to the city, was greatly struck by the *Incantadas*, it does not appear that more than a half-hearted effort was ever made to bring them to Britain. They are, however, not to be found in the city today, nor is it even possible to identify the spot where they stood for over a millennium. Defenders of the British Museum's retention of the Elgin Marbles should ponder this little-known chapter in the long squalid saga of the West's plundering of the antiquities of the Levant and learn precisely how the famous caryatids of Salonica – the 'enchanted ones' as some in the town called them, in Judeo-Espagnol, the 'spirits of angels' as they were known in Turkish – flew, or rather were shipped, to their new resting-place in the Louvre.[40]

Travellers had been collecting artefacts in the city at least since the time of Paul Lucas in the early eighteenth century. There was a market in medals and coins, in particular, and local middlemen served as links between supply and demand. Almost all the consuls in the city collected coins, medals and statuary, which could be admired in their homes: after their deaths, they might be repatriated into the gift of one of the national museums, or sold privately. Those on the older Grand Tour could easily accumulate large and rather cumbersome collections of antiquities. When one British gentleman died in Greece in 1799, his effects were found to include:

A box with a white leather covering, containing, amongst other things, the following, namely:
Eighteen ancient vases, lamps of pottery-ware etc. etc.
A box covered with leather, containing (amonst other sundry items,)
A book, entitled, 'The Plains of Troy,'
A little journal, covered with green marbled paper, containing various annotations.
A purse of blue-striped cotton, containing *eighty-seven* medals of brass, great and small, entitled, 'Macedonia'
1 like to the former, containing *one hundred and fifteen* brass medals, great and small, entitled, 'Medals of Greece.'[41]

'Went into the mosque ... Tomb of an old Greek saint shown in the cellar ... mosaic pieces falling. [Brought away several]', runs an entry in Melville's journal. He was not the only one. Carrying away antiquities was a customary part of travelling in classical lands, and some guidebooks even listed the import duties payable back home on such items. Salonica's locals helped, and provided forgeries to meet the strong demand.

[40] C. T. Newton, *Travels and Discoveries in the Levant* (1865), 121.
[41] *Remains of the late John Tweddell*, ed. Twedell, 343–5.

Carrying away large pieces of sculpture, however, was hindered by the fact that there were not very many such items to be found. From time to time the British and French consuls in particular had endeavoured, mostly unsuccessfully, to persuade the Ottoman governor to allow them to remove major pieces. When Adolphus Slade was, like many others, shown round the verde antico carving which was claimed to be the pulpit from which St Paul had preached to the Jews, he found the imam who was guiding him became irritated when Slade proposed to measure it. 'The good priest might have thought that if he allowed me to measure it, I should make a corresponding aperture in the roof, and so convey it away at night', joked Slade. 'It would be seen to much more advantage in London; and I dare say that the sultan would give it to an ambassador, if asked. He certainly does not know of it. A trifling gift afterwards to the pasha, and the Greek bishop of Salonica, would cause it to be embarked without opposition from the people.'[42]

Ten years later, the scenario Slade had joked about came to pass through the unlikely figure of a fifty-one-year-old French savant called Emmanuel Miller, an expert palaeographer with a self-professed 'passion for manuscripts'. Miller had obtained the backing of Napoleon III for a mission to examine the holdings of the libraries of Ottoman Europe, especially among the monasteries of Mount Athos and, no doubt, to collect rare medieval and Byzantine manuscripts to bring back to France. At the time he was Librarian of the French National Assembly; later he would become Professor of Modern Greek in Paris. But that was after the publication of numerous articles, considerable academic politicking and, above all, the fruits of his successful mission to the East.

Teaming up in Constantinople with a photographer-artist compatriot called Guillemet, and deciding to work together, the two men spent two months with the monks on Athos before making a first trip to Salonica. Rested there, Miller continued his search for manuscripts. 'There is a doctor here', he writes, 'very precious for me: he knows everything and no door is closed to him. In a short while he showed me all the antiquities. I also visited the library of the Tchaous monastery ... I found there a large manuscript which I believe will greatly interest the emperor.' The good doctor, a Greek called Prasakakis, was entrusted by Miller with the task of obtaining manuscripts – which required complex local negotiations especially with the Greek archbishop – and 'various other antiquities for the Emperor'. Obtaining originals of medieval manuscripts was not only desirable as a means of impressing Napoleon III back in Paris; it would also save the homesick Miller time

[42] A. Slade, *Record of Travels in Turkey, Greece etc.* (1854), 512.

since 'if I am obliged to copy the manuscript, which is considerable, I'll be obliged to stay in Salonica a long time'.

But the monks would not part easily with their manuscripts: those on Athos had just had some disagreeable experiences with Miller's predecessor, a Paris-based Greek savant called Mynas; those in Salonica, and also in the rock monasteries of Meteora, where Miller took a hair-raising but ultimately fruitless ride, were proving suspicious and reluctant. Bargaining with the pacha was also a trial: Miller had his eyes on a handsome bas-relief. But the pacha refused to take responsibility for allowing this to go, saying he would have to get permission from Istanbul, and dropping heavy hints that he wanted a French decoration – 'an impssible thing' which Miller hesitated to bother the emperor with. Then – good news: 'They *will* lend me the manuscript. *Now*, if I can get some important stones', he wrote to his wife, 'my mission will be worthy of my reputation, which between you and me, is a little burdensome, since they expect great things from me. There are many Greek monasteries in Macedonia, and I have a list: next spring I will make a tour.'

But in fact, Miller's 'rich harvest' – as he termed it – of the following year was to be reaped elsewhere. In the summer of 1864 he visited Thasos, no less beautiful an island than now, but considerably quieter. It was at this time a curious diplomatic anomaly – technically still part of the Ottoman empire and inhabited entirely by Greek Christian villagers, but a personal possession of the ruling Egyptian dynasty, whose founder, Mehmet Ali, had been born in the nearby port of Cavalla. An Egyptian engineer who was mapping the island proved useful to Miller since he 'knows all the stones and monuments which might interest us'. It was on Thasos, amidst its luxuriant vegetation and heavy-drinking villagers, that Miller discovered for the first time the joys of archaeology, the hard but simple life, the discovery of unknown fragments, the pride of the pioneer. The joys, but the sorrows too: some of the locals, he discovered, were angry at his excavations even though 'they burn the most beautiful marbles for building works'. Everywhere he found 'traces of *une belle époque*', but everywhere, too, 'traces of indescribable barbarism'. The workers drank and shirked and only respected 'someone with energy'. And yet 'the life of an archaeologist', he found 'extremely attractive, despite all the suffering ... What emotions one feels when an edge of marble pokes its head out of the soil! Will it be an inscription or a bas-relief? Perhaps a disappointment, merely a simple building block.'

Miller's procedures were not very professional. Despite his fulminations at Turkish inefficiency and sloth, and his description of himself as 'exactitude incarnate', he made no surveys, gave no indication of the location of his finds. Guillemet sometimes took photographs, but soon ran out of glass plates. But Miller's 'archaeological fever' drove him on and soon he had some fifty marbles. 'You see it is a good harvest', he wrote to his wife proudly. 'Sure, many are in poor condition, but where antiquities are concerned, nothing is to be ignored.' The French consul from Philippoupolis who visited him was astonished at the haul. 'You're not taking all this away!' he exclaimed. But then it struck him that 'it is all interesting, and you should not leave anything otherwise the English will grab it'.

Miller could scarcely remove this quantity of stones himself. Orders went out for a boat to be sent from France. Meantime, he visited the ruins at Philippi and turned his thoughts again to Salonica where he decided to work on the local governor, enlisting the consul's help, to obtain permission for the removal of the caryatids. 'As obstacle, I foresee the jealousy of the Greeks and the foreign consuls', he wrote. 'If Fortune wishes that I should take away those statues! Think then: eight statues, of a very fine period, mutilated it is true, but so what?' He was pessimistic, but news of the impending demolition of the city's fortifications made him dizzy with the thought of how much there was to be uncovered. 'I know no longer where I am – past, present, future are all confused in my head.'

Then came exciting news:

Thasos, 10 October 1864
I rush to send you the good, the great news ... The Sultan, through the Grand Vizier, Fuad Pacha, has authorised me to remove and ship to France the eight statues of Salonica which I so wanted.

French diplomacy had done its work: the rest was up to the energetic M. Miller. And as he knew, all his energy would be needed. The population of Salonica was likely to be very angry, and it was not impossible that the Turks would change their mind. He made haste to the town, leaving behind on the beach at Thasos 'two large sarcophagi with very remarkable inscriptions' which were too large for him to get on board. At the French consulate in Salonica, there was a despatch from Paris ordering him to take not merely the statues, but 'the monument as a whole', a decision which left him perplexed since the boat he had been sent was not powerful enough to organise the transportation of five to six tonnes of marble. 'Thus something which could have brought lively satisfaction to Paris', he fretted, 'will be regarded as a job left unfinished.'

The pacha himself was cooperative. He received Miller in a friendly fashion, making him a present of 'an ancient vase' found during the road-building, and assured him he would provide him with everything he wanted – men, soldiers, carts. But the news was spreading round Salonica and there was much upset. 'Already the population is getting agitated and tormented', he wrote on 1 November, just two days after his arrival. 'People are furious that I am going to remove these statues that have deteriorated so badly.' Miller could not understand this: the janissaries had used to fire at them for fun, while the proprietor of the house which had been built around them used to break off pieces to sell to tourists. Having neglected these marvellous pieces, how could the local inhabitants now feel angry if they passed into safer hands? The statues were in an alleyway in the heart of the Jewish quarter: Miller planned to ring off the area with soldiers so that they could work without interruption from the locals.

Once operations began, the problems multiplied. First, the Jewish proprietor of the house where they stood tried to cause trouble. Furious, he declared his opposition and insisted on seeing Miller's firman from the sultan. Miller was just telling him to take up his grievances with the pacha, when the latter arrived on the scene in a carriage, with his mounted escort. 'Everyone dispersed like a flock of pigeons.' That problem was best left to the pacha, who was happy to resolve it, pledging to recompense the owner for any damage. But popular anger did not subside. As the sailors prepared the carts which would take the statues to the waterside, 'the word got around, and the population reacted in an extraordinary fashion – wild rumours, gossip, incredible nonsenses. All the foreign consuls are going to telegraph Constantinople to prevent the removal of the statues.' Offers also came flooding in of antiquities, bas-reliefs, statues, sarcophagi; there was a story that Miller was planning to cart off the Arch of Constantine as well. Not trusting the inhabitants, Miller arranged for a night watch to be set in the street.

As the operations went on day after day, the crowds increased, and it became almost impossible to force a passage through. The removals had become entertainment. Miller was reduced to dreaming of bringing up a fire-hose to quench the spirits of the unruly onlookers. But signs of hostility did not end, either from the Jews or the Turks, who hoped for a counter-order from the sultan. There were assaults on the French sailors, and at one point, on Miller himself. And there were less violent indications of the grief the operation was causing. 'One of [the Turks] played a ridiculous comedy', wrote Miller.

> A *cawass*, a servant, came up to the statue of Victory. He wept and tried to embrace it. Matting almost completely surrounded it; the sailors had left bare only the rear of the statue. Our chap, not seeing anything else, embraced it. Everyone roared with laughter ... He must have been mad or a cretin.

The caryatids stood atop a marble colonnade; getting them down without smashing them was a delicate job and required machinery not easily to be found in Salonica. Eventually a large derrick was found and brought through the narrow alleys to the place, drawn on two carts by four buffaloes. It looked alarmingly rotten, especially since 'the pieces of marble are so immense!' But by 4 November the preparations had been completed and the operation of lifting down the statues could begin. Miller decided to begin with the massive slab which crowned the statues, which was itself split into three sections. A huge crowd watched from the street and hung out of the adjacent houses as the first section was removed and brought to the ground; halfway down, the derrick lost its footing, and the marble fell to the earth, fortunately without smashing. Two statues were removed; again disaster was narrowly averted. But there was a slight accident:

As it touched the ground, the group of two statues received a slight blow and the top section fell, happily, upon the upper part, which is to say that the figure of Victory was unscathed. The marble had evidently long been split, and the pieces were scarcely holding together as we could see from the break.

The upper pediment and the statues themselves were all safely removed. Getting them to the port required a team of eight buffaloes to navigate the poorly paved labyrinth of lanes and alleys, pitted with ruts and filled with slime and rubbish. Through the bazaar the team picked its way between rotting carcasses and their 'foetid odours'. Nauseous, riven with anxiety, suffering from lack of sleep, beset by the throng of onlookers who followed them everywhere, Miller and his team took an hour and a half before emerging at the port where the statues were embarked without difficulty. The blocks which had rested above the statues were heavy, and the Bulgarian carters began to worry about wearing out their buffaloes. A sharp bend nearly halted them; then, face to face with a deep, muddy cesspool which caused the animals to slip and lose their footing, they did. They were forced to leave one block in the bazaar, with a guard, to check that no one stole the rope around it. Eventually it took five teams of buffaloes to get it to the boat, and Miller began to despair of ever shifting the rest.

That left the entablature, the columns and the rest of the monument which Paris had ordered. Miller contemplated sawing through the entablature on which the statues rested, since it was made up of huge blocks. 'Since I have sacrificed so much, I will go through with this ... There is not, I believe, in Paris, another ancient monument of this size.' He had freed one column but found it was so large that it would not fit in the boat. Miller also thought about excavating the site in order to obtain a better idea of what the mysterious edifice had been.

By digging and following the foundations, it would be easy to restore the general plan. But what an effort! What work! Above all when the season is as late as this, with such bad weather! The continual rain we have had for two months now has soaked everything and excavations would be very difficult.

Then came bad news: Paris would not send any more equipment. 'That would have been fine', Miller writes,

at the start when the monument was still in one piece, but now the position is not the same, since all the marbles are in the street and we cannot leave them there. I'd have to break them to free the road but what a deplorable necessity! Then they would be justified in calling us barbarians. Better it would have been to leave the monument and rest content with taking only the statues. To destroy it, take down all the pieces which make it up, then smash them, that is the act of a Vandal.

The rain had been followed by freezing cold, and the buffalo drivers in the nearby villages were even starting to bribe the sailor he sent out to say there were none available. In the meantime, he had the remaining marbles placed along the wall so as not to impede the traffic, and left the four large slabs to one side. Either they could be fetched at a later date, or they could be given to help build the new church of St Nicolas, which was being constructed in the vicinity. By now Miller was exhausted, homesick, fed up. In the middle of December he left for Paris with his marbles, having been forced to leave the larger pieces behind, the columns, and the remains of what had once been the most striking antiquity in the city.[43]

In the city itself fires and urban rebuilding over the next century entirely erased all trace of *Las Incantadas*. Because Miller failed to note the location or to draw a plan of the site, we have no means of knowing exactly where the statues stood or what their function was. Since his day several scholars have attempted to solve the puzzle of the caryatids on the basis of all too little evidence. Miller sent a photograph of the statues to his wife; but that has long since vanished. And the caryatids themselves? They have fared little better. Initially intended to enrich the royal collection of Napoleon III, a latecomer to the museum business, they were only deposited in the Louvre once the idea of a Musée Napoleon III had been abandoned. And because Miller failed to number the pieces he did deliver, the curators had to reconstruct the ensemble themselves. 'When the Miller marbles were sent to France and brought to the Louvre', wrote the *conservateur des Antiques* there in

---

[43] The entire story has been reconstructed from Miller, *Le mont Athos*.

the 1920s, 'they were unfortunately not accompanied by any kind of regular inventory.' Indeed the Louvre's own initial catalogue made matters worse by mixing up pieces from Salonica with others from Thasos, and by failing to note that some pieces Miller had collected in Salonica had not yet been received. After the Second World War, the reconstruction was dismantled, and the pieces were scattered across the Museum where today they may be viewed, some next to the Antioch mosaics, others in the great entrance-hall under the Daru staircase.[44]

The Miller affair left its mark on the local authorities and they tightened up their supervision of the foreign archaeologists. They did not prevent their activities; far from it, there were probably more serious investigations undertaken after 1880 than at any time previously. But, as one scholar reported, 'they have become sufficiently alive to the possible value of archaeological finds no longer to allow the wholesale deporting that has often been practised, more especially by the French'. Major finds were reserved for the Archaeological Museum that Abdul Hamid established in a fine neo-classical building in the Topkapi palace in Constantinople. And a small space was set aside in Salonica itself to store local finds, which formed the nucleus of the city's first archaeological museum. Power and control over the past was slowly passing into the hands of those who ran and lived in the city.

Alongside the rise of archaeology, another shift in approaches to the ancient past was taking place which would have momentous consequences for Salonica. That was the nineteenth-century reappraisal of Byzantine civilisation. However, it took a long time before older, more disparaging attitudes disappeared. To the devotee of neo-classicism, the creed which had held sway in much polite European society since the late eighteenth century, the classical era represented a universal ideal of beauty, and later epochs were a sad degeneration in taste. 'All that is of the pagan period had been byzantined and all that was Byzantine has been mohammedanised', wrote the Misses Irby and Mackenzie dismissively after their two days' sightseeing round the town, 'so that while much may be traced to interest the antiquary, there is scarce beauty enough left to delight the unprofessional traveller.' To this was added the suspicion and scorn of a civilisation whose moral and ecclesiastical principles were held in deep suspicion by the Victorians. Indeed as late as 1893, a Greek scholar noted 'the unfavourable impression which even today is provoked by the name of Byzantium'.[45]

Greek historians contributed to the shift in perceptions, positing a

[44] P. Perdrizet, 'L'Incantada de Salonique', *Monuments et mémoires*, 31 (Paris, 1930), 51–90.
[45] Mackenzie and Irby, *Travels*, 56; D. Bikelas, *La Grèce byzantine et moderne* (Paris, 1893), 4.

continuity of Hellenic culture from classical to modern times, a view which gave the Byzantine world enormous significance as transmitter and protector of classical values, and would guarantee it an important part in the reshaping of late nineteenth-century Greek national consciousness. But Western taste was changing – an increasing appetite for the medieval past, for Genoa, Venice and the Italian city states, which spread slowly to the Levant – and foreign scholars like Bury, Texier and Charles Diehl also played their part. The first architectural surveys of Byzantine remains were published, and the field of Byzantine studies emerged as a separate domain of research. Although the kingdom of Greece did contain some important relics of Byzantine art, it was really in European Turkey that the greatest concentration of art and architecture from this epoch survived. Accounts of the treasures of Mount Athos had been circulating since Robert Curzon's trip in 1837, published to great acclaim in 1849; a few years later, Antonin Proust published a popular account complete with illustrations in an early issue of *Le tour du monde*. For those making the trip to Athos, Salonica was a natural jumping-off point, or a place to recuperate. As for Salonica itself, its churches, wrote the scholarly Tozer in 1869, 'are of the greatest value for the history of art'. This was, for the time, a novel view, and he cited recently published studies of Byzantine architecture in support of it. 'The sole merit of the town', wrote de Vogüé in 1875, 'is to have conserved a series of extremely ancient churches which allow one to follow step by step the evolution of architecture in the first centuries of Christianity ... From this point of view Salonica is a unique museum in the Levant and has no equal except for Rome.' The guidebooks echoed this new view and by 1890, one stressed that there were to be found there 'a group of Byzantine constructions of a richness which equals and even surpasses in certain respects the buildings of Constantinople'.[46]

Most of the mosques, wrote a Benedictine monk in 1908, 'are early churches whose majestic architecture testifies to the power of primitive Christianity in this town'. What particularly struck visitors was that while the most important churches had been turned into mosques, no restrictions were placed by the imams and dervish orders on tourist access. Although the churches were crumbling, mosaic pieces littering the floors, and the columns were sometimes whitewashed or painted, it was the easy-going attitude to Christian visitors, so different from in other Ottoman cities, which seemed most remarkable. 'If the conquerors had showed everywhere the same moderation as at Salonica', wrote one, 'the Orient would be nothing other than a vast museum of inexpressible interest ... Imagine for a moment that one of our Eastern

[46] Tozer, *Researches*, I, 145; de Vogüé, 'La Thessalie', 7.

Catholic churches enclosed the tomb of some dervish, and that one allowed Muslims to make their prayers there.'[47]

For some the Byzantine legacy was about far more than architecture alone. As he reviewed the city's remains, one writer felt

> the mystery of the drowning of a world. Of this rich and magnificent Byzantium which preserved the Roman tradition until the middle of the fifteenth century nothing remains except some mosaics, some arches defaced by a barbarian coating. We ourselves, under the influence of some scholastic prejudice, we write off ten centuries of an admirable civilisation with the term decadence. The term 'Byzantinism' has become the equivalent of tittle-tattle, baseness, cowardice.

What of their efforts to united Christendom, their courage in the face of repeated invasion, the sophistication of their philosophical thought?

> Ignorance alone accepted summary judgements, finding it convenient to tear out some pages of the book of history, even at the cost of making what follows meaningless. Our civilisation above all, so infatuated with itself, likes to pass a sponge over the injustices it has committed, and happily regards as inferiors those it has sacrificed. It does not want to recognise that its indifference has freed endless woes across this beautiful part of the world which was its cradle.[48]

The memory of the Byzantines could thus be deployed to show the weakness of Turkish claims to the city. Greek authors naturally pushed this line. Dimitris Bikelas, a savant based in France, skated over the unpleasant memories of 1204 and argued that the Byzantine empire had been destroyed by its Asiatic enemies not by Europe. With the former the gulf was unbridgeable, not however with the latter. Europeans and Greeks could learn from the memory of Byzantium to band together against those successive waves of invaders – from the Persians to the Arabs and the Turks, who had all been driven by the same religious hatred and the same desire to 'exterminate' the Christian empire.[49]

Others, however, had reservations about the Greeks' rights to claim this legacy. 'There is indeed no part of Greece proper where the splendours of early Byzantine church architecture, and the strange spiritual life of the Greek Church, can be studied as well as Salonica', wrote the classicist J. P. Mahaffy. But the state of the buildings

---

[47] D. Placide de Meester, *Voyage de deux Bénédictins aux monastères du Mont-Athos* (Paris, 1908), 25.

[48] Anon., 'De Salonique à Belgrade', 122–3.

[49] Bikelas, *La Grèce byzantine et moderne*, 27–8.

themselves depressed him; the 'empty and deserted churches show no care for religion, either in the Turks, who now own them, or in the Greeks, who are permitted on certain feasts to assemble in the basilica. All are in shameful neglect and decay.' The old Western suspicions of Eastern Christianity died hard, and Auguste Choisy returned from a visit to the monasteries of Athos convinced that they were 'the elderly testimony of a vanished society ... from which we can evaluate ... the stages of civilisation and the progress of thought'. Even some commentators well disposed to the Greeks felt astonished at how few traces of Greek life remained in the modern city, and wondered how 'Salonica, Greek as it once was, could become a little Israel.'[50]

Salonica's overwhelming significance to the majority of Christian travellers lay not, however, in its ecclesiastical architecture, nor its Byzantine art, but in the fact that it figured in the Bible and had been visited by Paul the Apostle. Following in his steps, Bible in hand, they walked the streets where he had preached. Guides showed them his actual pulpit – 'the chief lion of Salonica', noted Melville. Indeed the demand was so great that the number of such spots multiplied – by the century's end there were six or seven places pointed out to keen pilgrims as hallowed by association with Paul. 'There are also clumps of trees in several parts of the plain', wrote James Baker, 'which are supposed to mark the spots where St. Paul stopped to preach.'[51]

To Salonica's classical associations, wrote Bowen, were added 'the more important Christian interest of St. Paul'. 'The early triumphs of the Gospel', wrote a publication of the Religious Tract Society, 'have at least an equal share with any classical associations in the enthusiasm which leads the traveller to brave the perils of Macedonia and Achaia.' And Macedonia had a particular importance for the devout Victorian, for did it not illustrate the truth of the maxim that 'westward the course of empire takes its way'? Paul had heeded the call of the 'man from Macedonia' – as the Bible said – and come over from Asia, thereby reversing that epic conquest of the East by the West described by Homer with a 'nobler conquest', the conquest of Christianity. 'Out of that expedition, and those words, CHRISTENDOM arose; and because of them England, America and Australia are great today.' It was in Salonica, in other words, that Christianity became European. Comforted by pride in succeeding to such a legacy, the traveller could feel that 'strange, sad, fascination' which experiencing the lands of that Apostolic triumph must inevitably bring, where 'the name of Christ is blasphemed by those who still hold sway over these unhappy lands,

---

[50] Mahaffy, *Greek Pictures*, 219; Choisy, *L'Asie Mineure*, 28; anon., 'De Salonique à Belgrade', 119–20.

[51] Baker, *Turkey*, 349.

and even where professedly honoured, it is amid perversions of a corrupt creed and of ignorant worship'.[52]

Thus dismissive equally of Islam and Orthodox Christianity, confident that Protestantism was the true successor to the pure faith of the early fathers of the Church, the Victorian mind merged the Biblical and the modern landscape. Conybeare and Howson's great Life of the Apostle, like many a family Bible, was illustrated by engravings of the modern Macedonian port. 'The physical features of a spot which was so dear to the man who once worked in its streets, and saw its scenery, are of interest enough to justify me in devoting the remainder of the chapter to a special description of the present aspect of Salonica', wrote the Reverend Davies, who then discussed at length whether the city still looked as it once did to Paul. From afar, was his answer: it was enough that walls, fort, towers conveyed an impression of antiquity, irrelevant that none of these features was less than several centuries too late for the Apostle to have clapped eyes on them. But this landscape was more than mere scenery for many of his readers: it was – more excitingly, more importantly, more urgently – testimony to the Word of God, 'to the truth of the Bible record, and to the wonderful and literal fulfilment of Bible prophecy'.[53]

So important was it to convey the overwhelming visual impact of the place, that illustration became a very important feature of the religious travel literature of the late nineteenth century. Over the century that stretched from Bartlett's *Footsteps of Our Lord* to Morton's *In the Steps of St. Paul*, the illustrated evocation of the Bible lands was a genre for which west European readers possessed an almost insatiable appetite. Steel plate engraving came first – a highly dramatic, even melodramatic medium in the hands of an artist like Bartlett – to be followed in the 1870s by photogravure. Photography was an exciting addition to this spiritual armoury. 'The plain prose of photography', wrote the editor of one of the earliest books of travel photos of the Bible Lands, compared favourably with the 'poetry' of art since it was best able 'to make us perfectly acquainted with the physical characteristics of the Land of Promise and the neighbouring regions', and to convey the 'actual positive truth'. It was not surprising that when Lucy Garnett published an article on Salonica, entitled 'A New Jerusalem' in the *Catholic World* in 1900, the first page was illustrated by a photograph captioned 'St. Paul's Pulpit in Salonica'.[54]

One might have thought that classics and Christianity made an

[52] G. F. Bowen, *Mount Athos, Thessaly and Epirus* (1852), 28; S. G. Green, *Pictures from Bible Lands* (n.d.), v, 171–4.

[53] Davies, *St. Paul in Greece*, 120–5; Green, *Pictures from Bible Lands*, vii.

[54] W. M. Thompson, *The Holy Land, Egypt, Constantinople, Athens etc.* (1862), 4; L. Garnett, 'A New Jerusalem', *Catholic World*, 71:425 (August 1900), 612–17.

unlikely and uncomfortable pair of lenses through which to view the modern city, but in fact most travellers were no more perturbed by the incongruity than the majority of Victorians. The pairing was, after all, basic to west European culture throughout the nineteenth century. Thoughtful Christians were aware that here perhaps they *were* different from the inhabitants of the ancient world. 'The classical Christian student', wrote Green in *Pictures from Bible Lands*, could view the remains of antiquity detached from their spirit; ruins were 'the magnificent records of a vanished lie'; for Paul, on the other hand, they were symbols of 'a dark and evil power'. But in general, they felt so much at home in both worlds that this antagonism meant little to them; only for a new generation of scholars who worshipped classical paganism as an antidote to the pieties of Victorian bourgeois culture would it become again important.[55]

'Let us leave the archaeologist to one side', wrote Nicolaidy in 1859, 'We will occupy ourselves with matters of the present.' A rare attitude this, but certainly not unique. Seeing Salonica in terms of its ancient associations allowed Europeans to employ clear, familiar and distinct categories. Interpreting the modern city was a much more confusing matter. As we have seen, travellers on the whole shied away from this task, but they could scarcely avoid it entirely: they themselves were, after all, symptoms of the rapid change in customs and communications wrought by industrial revolution and its political consequences. As the Guide Joanne reminded its readers: 'The immobile Orient is no longer immobile [and] in the presence of this peaceful invasion of the European spirit, the old world of Islam feels itself renewed.' According to Murray, one of the chief reasons for travelling was to be able to 'form an accurate opinion on that most important question – the present state and future destinies of the Levant'. As the century advanced, the Eastern Question became more and more central to the very peace of Europe. With the great Near Eastern crisis of 1876–7 and the Congress of Berlin the following year, the fate of Ottoman dominion in Europe dominated the headlines. History seemed to be accelerating. 'Look how, in the last three years, humanity – that tireless traveller – has been marching to an unaccustomed tread, holding its book of notes, which it calls history', wrote de Vogüé in 1879.[56]

The second half of the century was dominated by a sense of anticipation, excitement and apprehension about the future. As early as 1845, Fallmerayer felt a 'dark foreboding' among its inhabitants,

[55] Green, *Pictures from Bible Lands*, 173–4.
[56] Nicolaidy, *Les turcs et la Turquie contemporaine*, 26; Isambert, *Itinéraire descriptif*, xx; *Handbook for Travellers in Greece*, 1.

which he attributed to a sense 'that their city stands on weak foundations and has in the current order of things not long to survive'. To Tozer, in 1869, it was evident that 'the present state of things cannot last for ever? So what next?' Miller detected 'a period of expectancy'. Almost everyone, it seemed, felt obliged to play what one traveller sarcastically called 'future music'. A few believed that the Ottoman state would be able to reform itself, and were impressed by the changes that took place in the city in the last quarter of the century; during the Young Turk revolution of 1908, this optimism briefly attracted new supporters. More took a pessimistic line and looked instead to the Great Powers, or to one or another of the subject peoples of the Balkans. But the urge to speculate was common to all.[57]

Salonica became a port of call for those who wished to be able to discern the coming order in Europe, but reading the future in Salonica was especially hard because of the kaleidoscopic complexity of its inhabitants. According to Irby and Mackenzie, whose journey had an avowedly ethnographic goal, 'the Therma of ancient history and Thessalonica of St. Paul's Epistles yields at present the curious instance of a city historically Greek, politically Turkish, geographically Bulgarian and ethnographically Jewish'.[58] Business was carried out in a mix of five or six languages; most shop signs were in two or three; even the bootblacks were more polyglot than the average European visitor. An era shaped increasingly by the precepts of nationalism could not but have difficulty confronting such a prospect. After all, no one was even sure at mid-century how to classify the different groups of the region. German professors argued over Macedonian ethnography and the relative merits of Boué, Kiepert and Sax were vehemently debated. The Ottomans classified their subjects by religion, and ran inefficient censuses. The scholars demanded reliable statistics classified on the basis of speech or 'actual national consciousness', not to mention physical and racial types. None of this was much help to ordinary travellers at a time when most people had scarcely a conception of the difference between 'Greek' (a term often used to mean simply Orthodox Christian) and 'Slav' (a term referring to language, or to pro-Russian affiliation). 'The various non-Mussulman communities', wrote a former consular official in the city, 'had a fairly accurate idea of their own numbers, which they were wont to halve for the purposes of estimating taxes, and to double when it was a question of urging national claims.'[59]

The Victorian sense of duty, however, combined with a basic confidence about the possibility of discovering the truth of the situation

[57] Jakob Philipp Fallmerayer, *Fragmente aus dem Orient* (Stuttgart, 1877), 360; Tozer, *Researches*, I, 393–4.

[58] Mackenzie and Irby, *Travels*, 57.

[59] A. Wratislaw, *A Consul in the East* (1924), 13.

through observation and the accumulation of facts, spurred people on. Gladstone, like many an activist, was basically optimistic: 'Until our own day', he wrote, 'it has never been possible for the people of one country to obtain trustworthy information respecting the contemporary condition of another. The press, the telegraph, the railway, the large and costly development of diplomatic and consular establishments ... have contributed to place within our reach this description of knowledge.' He praised Irby and Mackenzie's book – designed indeed to teach the English reader about the Slavs of European Turkey – for giving the reader not merely 'a theoretical but ... a practical and living knowledge' of the state of the Balkans.[60]

Knowledge, it was probably inevitable in an age of growing racial consciousness, meant first and foremost evaluating the character of the diverse ethnic groups of the city. The most immediately identifiable criterion – at least before the 'Frankish' style began to erase older traditions – was dress. National costumes demarcated the different groups: the baggy roughspun breeches of the 'Bulgarian' villagers, the Albanians in their fustanellas, the black-clad Greeks, above all the distinctive long robes of the Jews. 'One recognises the Jews', noted some visiting Catholic monks, 'by their long kaftans and their dirty and tattered appearance.'[61]

Visitors did not feel twenty-first century inhibitions at generalising about national type and character, physical and mental, and most had strong views about the relative merits of their chosen peoples. 'The population is hotch-potch', wrote Fraser, 'But you have to note the features, the eye, the walk, the general manner, to decide whether this man be a Turk, a Greek, an Armenian, a Bulgarian or a Jew. The shifty eye tells the Armenian, the swagger of demeanour proclaims the Greek, the quiet alertness reveals the Jew.' Physiognomy and physical beauty – especially female – were not the properties of individuals; they revealed the attributes of the race.[62]

Choisy, who liked the Greeks and admired their fortitude and collective spirit, found that they had preserved 'a physiognomy up till now which takes us back before the Turkish invasion, as far as the times of classical antiquity'. Braun-Wiesbaden found 'the Greek women here extremely beautiful ... much more attractive than in the Kingdom of Greece where with the best will I could not discern a national-Hellenic type of female beauty'. Others were less sympathetic and shared the widespread west European sense of disappointment that the modern Greeks had not lived up to the standards set by their

---

[60] Gladstone in *ibid.*, VII–IX.
[61] de Meester, *Voyage*, 20.
[62] Fraser, 'Adrianople, Salonika and Monastir', 149.

predecessors. This disillusionment, the inevitable consequence of a style of philhellenism based largely on familiarity with the classics, had grown since the establishment of independent Greece, the spread of brigandage in border areas and the discovery of the habits of a Church which most Anglicans and Catholics found unattractive. The liberal Bowen, not unsympathetically, felt that 'the Greek character has suffered much from centuries of slavery'. But a similar sensitivity to oppression, in the Macedonian context, could lead equally to anti-Greek conclusions on the part of those sensitive to the plight of the Slav peasantry. Then all the usual stereotypes came into play. 'How strongly differences of race can tell under identical conditions of climate, religion and government, is exemplified in towns where Greeks have been dwelling side by side with Bulgarians for centuries', wrote Irby and Mackenzie. 'The one is commercial, ingenious and eloquent, but fraudulent, dirty, and immoral; the other is agricultural, stubborn, and slow-tongued; but honest, cleanly and chaste.'[63]

Ill-wishers disparaged the Jews in very similar terms. Physical uncleanliness was a sure sign of moral decay. For some, the Jews were living, as they always had, from money-lending and other parasitic activities. The pro-Greek Abbott regarded them, like the Turks, as 'mere residents, birds of passage, though likewise birds of prey' who, 'unless driven away, will remain and continue in the peaceful pursuit of lucre, which is the alpha and omega of their wordly ambition'. Any real knowledge of the city, however, brought different conclusions. Braun-Wiesbaden referred to those 'Jew-devouring' journalists back in Germany who asserted that 'the Jew, or as one now calls them, when one wants to look refined, the "Semites", are unfit for physical work of any kind and averse to it'. Let such writers come to Salonica, he went on, and try to lift the back-breaking loads commonly carried by the teams of Jewish *hamals*: 'I'd like to see the Jew-eater of our paper be the eighth man in one of these *hamal*-consortia to match his strength with these Semites, who can neither read nor write.'[64]

For most observers, the dominating scale of the Jewish presence made it hard to write them off as parasites. 'In terms of the majoriy population and overall character, Salonica is really a city of Israel, and should properly be called Samaria', wrote Fallmerayer. Another writer appealed to the curiosity of 'amateur ethnographers' to explore the 'fate of a Jewish nation left to itself, under the most tolerant of despotisms, forming the majority in a great cosmopolitan city'. There

---

[63] Braun-Wiesbaden, *Eine türkische Reise*, 157; Choisy, *L'Asie Mineure*, 22; Mackenzie and Irby, *Travels*, 69.

[64] Abbott, *Tale of a Tour*, 21–2; Braun-Wiesbaden, *Eine türkische Reise*, 221; Fallmerayer, *Fragmente*, 354.

they seemed different from elsewhere; freed from disdain and insult, they were altered in their behaviour with 'franker, more open demeanours'. Searching for beauty, he found a variety of male types – 'from the Israelite as sharp as steel, pale and thin, eyes set on his work' to 'the sanguine giant, with the large aquiline nose and sensual mouth'. Moving from the 'wisdom of Solomon', however, to the female form was harder and more dangerous: despite their charming costumes, most women he saw were of 'a regular, but banal type – beautiful eyes in a round, pale face'.

> They tell me that the pretty ones stay inside. The Jews are Orientals on this point. At the risk of provoking their jealousy, I crept through the alleyways where their vines and figs provide shelter. By dint of persistence, I discovered a superb daughter of Zion, dark and svelte, bearing herself like a queen, eyes of velvet, holding a broom like a sceptre. I mentally recited the *Nigra sum, sed formosa* ... then I slipped away, because from the neighbouring shacks several Aarons and Isaacs were beginning to watch me with more curiosity than good-will.[65]

Making generalisations about the 'Turks' was perhaps harder. In the first place, the word itself was misleading. The streets were filled with Muslims of all colours, wrote one traveller, from 'the black of Ethiopia' (mostly slaves or their descendants from the Sudan or elsewhere in Africa) to fair-skinned Circassians and Albanians. Like 'Macedonia', the term 'Turk' was one of those words imported by western visitors that confused instead of clarifying. Ottoman officials came from a variety of ethnic backgrounds: indeed in the second half of the century, not a few were likely to be Hungarians, Poles and Germans who had fled the repressive atmosphere of central Europe for a new life in the south. Second, of all the peoples of the city, the Muslims were the hardest to approach and get to know. The wealthier they were, the more likely they were to live above the Via Egnatia in the quiet backlanes of the upper town, where visitors were conspicuous and not especially welcomed. Contacts, especially for men, were limited to official business; some women might be able to engineer an introduction to the *haremlik*, but real conversation and friendship were not available. What is the 'character of the Turk'?, wondered one commentator. It was not easy to say, he felt, not only because of the usual problem of rash generalisation, especially pronounced among travellers, but because almost no foreigner understood Turkish. Since the Turks, especially of the lower classes, spoke fewer languages than the Greeks or the Jews, this posed a particular difficulty. And understanding their 'inner life'

[65] Anon., 'De Salonique à Belgrade', 114–15.

was hard, not only because of the lack of access to the domestic realm but more importantly, because the west European visitor found it hard to understand Islam.[66]

Many travellers took this for granted, and did not much mind. So far as they were concerned, the function of the Islamic presence in the city was – through far-off vistas of mosques and minarets – to provide elements of picturesque interest. Almost no one found Islamic architecture worth a closer look, except where it disguised earlier Christian remains. 'There is very little to see in a mosque', commented Captain Best. The general assumption, in fact, was that the Ottoman conquerors and their descendants were squatting amid the faded glories of earlier architectural achievements. 'The Turks, although they have borrowed much and destroyed more, have built nothing – not even a jail', vituperated Abbott. This was a reference to the most conspicuous symbol of the city – the tower on the south-eastern corner of the sea walls which was known first as the 'Bloody Tower' and then as the 'White Tower', and which is even today used to identify the city – assumed by everyone at this time to have been built by the 'Normans' or the 'Genoese'; in fact, it was just one example of the extensive building programme initiated after 1430 by the Ottoman conquerors.[67]

The character of the city's rulers had to be deduced by their behaviour and their policies towards the city, and here the general opinion was unfavourable. The swamps to the west of the city wafting their 'poisonous exhalations' over its streets, the defective quarantine arrangements, the insanitary alleys, the frequent fires, all testified to an undesirable degree of laissez-faire on the part of the city's administrators. Even the eroded ruins of antiquity seemed to testify to centuries of decay and degeneration. 'The government must be bad which leaves a town so prosperous and busy in such a condition', wrote the sternly improving Arthur Arnold. 'If I were an ardent philhellene I should point to the condition of Salonica as a condemnation of the Moslem rule.' The philhellene George Finlay thought the natural potential of the region enormous: 'Under any government which admitted the possibility of investing capital in the soil with security, it would yield great returns.' The town's prosperity was attributed to the hard work of its labouring population; its squalor to the Ottoman governors.[68]

The burning question was whether the Turk could be 'improved'. Auguste Choisy, an architectural engineer with an interest in 'organ-

---

[66] Braun-Weisbaden, *Eine türkische Reise*, 213–14.

[67] Abbott, *Tale of a Tour*, 13.

[68] R. Arthur Arnold, *From the Levant* (London, 1868), I, 323; J. M. Hussey, *The Journals and Letters of George Finlay* (Athens, 1995), I, 277.

isation', was unconvinced. 'Constantinople, if one would believe the official establishment, will soon be the most European city in Europe', he wrote.

> One dresses in the French style, performs Molière in Turkish ...
> Don't believe a word. The old Turk lives under the guise of the
> reform, only the dress has changed, and that Turk who dresses like
> you, understands your language, does not share your ideas, tastes
> and feelings ... The necessity of knowledge, the spirit of progress,
> these entirely European passions he does not understand.

A brief flurry of municipal activism, and the coming of the railways, made some optimistic. But most felt that reforms were destined to fail, and to destroy what was valuable about the Ottoman ways into the bargain.[69]

Mixing Turkish and European, Eastern and Western, was for most observers, an undesirable idea. Blending cultures or races, after all, was generally felt to foster degeneration: in their different ways, both the Donmeh and the Levantine communities of the city seemed to illustrate the dangers of a confusion of categories and identities. 'Generally speaking, the Greek peasant degenerates in Asia, the Turkish, in Europe;- that is, where they come into contact, both loses his value', wrote Urquhart.

> So the Turk in contact with Europeans and the Europeans among
> the Turks. The two systems, when in juxtaposition, and not under
> the control of a mind that grasps both, are mutually destructive of
> each other ... Ill-will and hatred are the result of intercourse without
> reciprocal sympathy and respect.[70]

In the second half of the nineteenth century, it was evident to most travellers that the tide of history was running against the Turks as Greece, Serbia, Bulgaria and Romania all broke away from their rule. 'The rule of the Ottoman in Macedonia is drawing to a close', stated Miller. The fires in the city struck another traveller as symbolic of the fate of the Turks: 'Thus collapses the Turkish rule and the "European" contemplates the show.' Many visitors had their favourite peoples whom they hoped would win the day. But the more impartial and clear-sighted observers were worried. Writing before the Congress of Berlin, Henry Tozer feared that neither a federation under Turkish rule nor a 'united Christian empire' provided a possible solution to the Balkan dilemma. Greeks and Slavs could not be put together any more than Christians and Turks: Tozer looked forward to 'a Greek and a Slavonic

[69] Choisy, *L'Aise Mineure*, 1–2.
[70] Urquhart, *Spirit of the East*, II, 61.

state, with Salonica as its Aegean port'. When Russian diplomacy nearly created the latter in 1877–8, the other Great Powers acted swiftly to prevent it by whittling down the new Bulgarian state that the Russian defeat of the Ottoman army had called into being. Increasingly, the Macedonian succession was becoming embroiled with the Great Power rivalries and alliance systems that were dominating European diplomacy. 'In Macedonia', warned William Miller, 'there exist the germs of a conflict which may not only herald the dismemberment of the Turkish Empire in Europe but may lead to a fatricidal conflict between the Christian states of the Balkans, or even to that much-dreaded European war, which it has been the object of diplomacy to postpone if it cannot prevent.' Within twenty years, both of these had come to pass.[71]

William Brown to Plumkett, June 1877
My dear Plumkett
Loti is dead. Loti has left this sombre earth where he extravagantly scorched his life. He forgot everything, abandoned everything to follow, with the rapidity that killed him, his *fatum*, his particular destiny.

A sad note which served to introduce:

Salonica.
Loti's Journal. 16 May 1876
... A beautiful May day, bright and sunny, a clear sky ... When the foreign rowboats arrived, the executioners were putting the final touches to their work: six corpses hanging in front of the crowd underwent their horrible final contortion ... Windows, roofs were thick with spectators; on a nearby balcony the Turkish authorities smiled on the familiar spectacle.

Thus, with a characteristic blend of themes – death, Oriental despotism, voyeurism – did one of fin-de-siècle France's most popular novelists begin his first best-seller. There was only one ingredient missing, and this was soon supplied:

One fine spring day, one of the first that we were permitted to circulate in Salonica of Macedonia, a little after the massacres, three days after the hangings, around four in the afternoon, it happened that I stopped before the closed door of an old mosque to watch two storks fighting.
The scene took place in a lane of the old Muslim quarter. Decrepit

[71] Tozer, *Researches*, 1, 393–7; Miller, *Travels and Politics*, 369; Braun-Wiesbaden, *Eine türkiche Reise*, 79.

houses flanked tortuous little paths, half-covered by the projecting *shaknisirs*. Oats pushed between the paving stones, and branches of fresh greenery overhung the roofs. The sky, glimpsed at intervals, was pure and blue. One breathed everywhere the balmy air and sweet smell of May.

The inhabitants of Salonica still displayed a constrained and hostile attitude towards us. The authorities obliged us to carry a sword and full military kit. In the distance, some turbaned men passed the walls, and no woman's head showed itself behind the discreet grilles of the *haremlik*. One would have said it was a dead city.

I felt so perfectly alone that I felt a shock when I perceived near me, behind iron bars, at the height of a man's head, two great green eyes fixed on mine.

The brows were brown, lightly frowning, pushed together so that they nearly joined. The expression in that look was a mixture of energy and naivety. One would have said the glance of a child, it had so much freshness and youth.

The young woman whose eyes they were stood, and displayed to the waist a figure enveloped in a Turkish cape (*feredje*) with long, stiff folds. The cloak was of green silk, embroidered with silver thread. A white veil was carefully wrapped around her head, letting one see nothing but her forehead and her large eyes. Her pupils were green, that sea-green tint of which the poets of the East once sung.

That young woman was Aziyadé.[72]

Pierre Loti was not, despite the Introduction, dead. Loti – the 'lotus' – was the pen-name of a young writer called Julien Viaud, acrobat and adventurer, who was to become, through works such as *Fleurs d'ennui* and *Le roman d'un spahi*, one of the most successful of Europe's fin-de-siècle Orientalists. Although not much to today's taste, his novels of decadent sensibility and exotic seduction were the rage at the end of the nineteenth century. Many others, of course, mined the same vein: indeed, the literature of Oriental fantasy erotica stretched back well before Loti's day. The earlier genre sterotyped the lustful Turkish male able to exert his power over the helpless captives of his harem. But the balance of power had shifted, and literature consciously or unconsciously mirrored the shift. The Turkish man was now reduced to impotence; now it was the West that was penetrating the East. Of this moment Loti was the master storyteller, and it was in Salonica that his literary career took off with a tale of forbidden love, between a Frenchman, himself, and a Muslim woman, member of the harem of a Turkish bey. Loti claimed that the affair described in the novel had really

[72] P. Loti, *Aziyadé* (Paris, 1886), 1–7.

happened. This seems only slightly less likely than the authorial death announcement which began the novel. Nevertheless, Viaud *was* writing from first-hand experience for he had actually been sent to Salonica in 1876 as a naval cadet on a ship sent by the French fleet. The Near Eastern crisis was underway when two consuls were lynched by a mob in the city in controversial circumstances, and the Great Powers reacted by making a demonstration of their power with a little gunship diplomacy. Thus the scene with which the novel opened had some basis in fact. What followed, however, showed how far the city, increasingly romanticised in the minds of its visitors, had taken on a life of its own as a stage-set of subjective imaginative possibilities in the mind of a talented writer.

Taking the form of an epistolary exchange between Loti and two young British naval friends in London, Brown and Plumkett, the story unfolds of Loti's passionate but secretive affair with Aziyadé – despite her being married to a Turkish notable. They are assisted by a third person, a bearded man with 'a very handsome head, a great sweetness in his eyes and resplendent with honesty and intelligence', the Jewish boatman, Samuel. Of course this book is 'about' Salonica, only in the sense in which D'Annunzio's writings are about Venice or Rome. The city, though often well observed, is really the backdrop to Loti's exploration of mood, sensibility, subjectivity and emotion. So much was clear to Loti himself by the way, in whom fin-de-siècle decadence and bored aestheticism were combined with acute self-awareness: in one of the letters in *Aziyadé* supposedly written to him by his sister, she likens him to a 'plaything of illusions ... an illusion in Salonica, an illusion elsewhere'.

Everything in this city is illusion. Loti escapes from the foreigner's trademark – visibility – after being disguised by three elderly Jewish women, who dress him up in Turkish constume, allowing him to wander unremarked through 'an absurd city, the Eastern bazaars, the mosques, the multi-coloured crowds'. Love, embracing Aziyadé on a boat, draped in carpets, floating in the bay at night, is 'drunkenness'. 'You will say that this wants a terrible egoism; I would not disagree', writes Loti. 'But then I came to think that everything that pleases me is worth doing and that one should always spice up life's insipid stew.' When he came to, after the night's delirium, Salonica 'presented a paltry picture. Its minarets had the air of a collection of old candles, set on a dirty, black city where the vices of Sodom flourished'. The city's appearance comes to stand for nothing more than the artist's mood: the world has shrunk to feeling and sensibility. All that matters is to keep *ennui* at bay – 'the disheartening void and the immense *ennui* of life'. Only one thing can transform the landscape of Loti's soul when it comes: 'Something like love was born in these ruins, and the Orient threw its great charm on this reawakening of myself.'

'It was at first nothing more than an inebriation of the imagination and the senses', Loti writes to his friend Brown in London. But then love followed. Gradually, the city's charms impress themselves on the lover.

It was happiness to take a stroll at sunrise. The air was so light, the freshness so delicious, that one had no trouble living. One was, as it were, penetrated by well-being. Some Turks began to circulate, dressed in red gowns, green or orange, in the vaulted lanes of the bazaar, hardly visible in the transparent half-glimmer ... The evening was an enchantment of a different order for the eyes. All was pink or gold. Olympus was tinted as though smouldering or molten, and was reflected in the still sea like a mirror. No smoke in the air. It seemed as though there was no more atmosphere and that the mountains were floating in the void, so clearly delineated were the farthest ridges.

Strange to realise that Loti's novel was published at the same time as Gladstone was praising the possibilities for real knowledge of the peoples of the Balkans. The turn away from positivism at the end of the century, the rise of Bergson and Nietzsche among others, was encouraging a literary trope which veered easily into mysticism and solipsism. 'From our libraries, our laboratories, all our positivism', wrote Barres in *Une enquête aux pays du Levant*, 'j'ai hât d'aller a cet inconnu'. To these writers, the Orient was not the origin of civilisation, but on the contrary, its opposite, the spiritual alternative to Western rationalism, mysterious, unknowable and – in many male minds – feminine. Knowledge was possible, but only of oneself. The only cure for *ennui* was excess. Was not Loti simply carrying to an extreme the romantic style of travel writing – the voyage as internal exploration into the world of feeling, the escape from the conventions of sedentary, bourgeois Europe?

What is striking is the feminisation of the image of Salonica at the fin-de-siècle. Time and again, the city was portrayed as a mysterious woman, coquettish, unknowable, trying her charms on all comers, inconstant, fought over, desired. *La ville convoitée* 'the coveted city' – was the title of the history published by Joseph Nehama on the eve of the Balkan Wars. One journalist, astonished at the rapid commercial expansion of the city saw it as 'an Andromeda who has smashed one of her chains, and half untied, dries her tears and stretches her arms towards her liberator'. Another saw a 'coquette', surrounded by cemeteries, tokens of death. This theme gathered ground during the First World War, as foreign soldiers passed through the city, and death, violence and sex became more inescapable features of daily life than ever before. 'There is something tragic about Salonica', wrote the novelist William McFee, 'She babbles all the tongues of Europe and speaks none of them aright. She has no natural language, no natural air. She is everything and nothing ... She has nothing to give but death, yet the nations fling themselves upon her and quarrel for the honour of her embrace.' Louis Golding, writing just after the 1917 fire, saw it as a kind of divine retribution:

> Modern Salonica was a city of corruption, a city of innuendoes ... The decadence of Eastern and Western Europe gathered here and found a congenial home. The cocottes sitting in the cafes, their green eyes half-opened, their carmine lips set in a patient and significant smile, had lost all the adventurousness of Paris and the rotund complacency of Vienna.[73]

And in his light-hearted skit on Loti – *A Salonique sous l'œil des dieux* – a French officer with the Army of the Orient, stationed in the city, published a love story in which Aziyadé has now become Ayché, who turns to prostitution in response to the opportunities provided by the war. This has brought to the city 'a chosen clientele of officers ... many of whom had read Loti' and who ask a local pimp if he cannot help them meet a Turkish woman. 'For the European man', Frappa continues, 'the Turkish woman is Mystery, Forbidden Love peppered with danger, the anticipation of variation in the unchanging melody of desire'. If we compare this approach to the city with that taken over the previous century, we see a striking change: what was previously regarded by travellers as the least knowable and inaccessible aspect of the city's life has become the centre of the Western erotic imagination; what was formerly regarded as worthy of description has been reduced to the mundane and the banal. The obsession with the city's Oriental nature has not died away; but now, it is found chiefly in the fantasy of a Western conquest of the feminine East. After all, had the West not, by this point, conquered everything else?[74]

18 May.
I am at Salonica barely a week and since then I have been looking for the shadow of Aziyadé. I know I shall never find her, but how not to be obsessed by that simple and marvellous story of love and death?[75]

Pol Roussel, an infantry officer with the Army of the Orient was another of those spellbound by Loti. Having read *Aziyadé* as a young

---

[73] Anon., 'De Salonique à Belgrade', 110; W. McFee, *A Six-Hour Shift* (New York, 1920), 35; L. Golding, 'Colour in Salonica', *English Review*, 27 (1918), 155–7.

[74] J.-J. Frappa, *A Salonique sous l'œil des dieux* (Paris, 1917), 137–8.

[75] P. Roussel, *Salonique au temps de la campagne d'Orient* (Paris, 1925), 167.

man, he was impressed by the affinities between himself and its hero – 'the same way of feeling and of thinking, the same mix of scepticism and naivety, an identical need to love and be loved, a similar disgust of certain conventions, certain obligations, certain habits, the same desire for the infinite'. And like Loti he found 'all the charm of the Orient' working on his senses. 'Behind those hermetically sealed blinds' – he was strolling idly in the Turkish quarter – 'no doubt pretty eyes shone and crimson lips smiled. Ah, mirage of the East! Aziyadé! Loveable fantasies of Loti!' Actually to be traversing the same alleys, amid the same houses – this was for a moment an almost overpowering experience.[76]

Not every visiting soldier or sailor felt as passionately as Roussel the effects of the city, to be sure. Yet at no time in its history did more tourists come to Salonica than in the years between 1915 and 1918, when troops from half a dozen countries poured into the port before moving inland to man the Macedonia front. 'Salonica was now probably the most crowded city in the universe', wrote a British newspaper man. As Roussel's writings showed, their reactions were often like those of other tourists before them. They visited the same sites – at least on days off from the front – and commented in identical fashion on the contrast between that first magical glimpse of the distant skyline, and the frenetic and often bewildering impact of the city at close quarters. They drank in the seafront cafes, and bargained for souvenirs in the bazaar. 'Turkish slippers and fezzes made in Austria, daggers made in Germany, Japanese silks and fans, black amber ornaments advertised as from Erzerum but probably from Germany, ancient coins and vases, ikons and charms – all the junk of the foolish traveller is here', wrote one sceptical onlooker. 'I observe smart British nurses buying souvenirs for friends in Balham and Birmingham, smart subalterns purchasing cigarette-cases and walking-stick handles, daggers and silly old Turkish pistols.'[77]

For these men – and a few women – it was the sheer commercial energy of the place that took them aback. 'The entire city', wrote one officer, 'without elegance, without sexuality, gave itself over to the demon of commerce in a paroxysm.' Hucksters, conmen, hard-bargaining shopkeepers, pimps and loansharks fill the pages of the wartime memoirs of the 'Gardeners of Salonica'. Perhaps nothing captures the mood better than the epic parody of *Hiawatha* – 'Tiadatha' – which an officer in the 6th Wiltshires wrote while there, and which was reprinted ten times in the next fifteen years:[78]

---

[76] Roussel, *Salonique*, 99.

[77] H. Collinson Owen, *Salonika and After* (1919), 20; McFee, *A Six-Hour Shift*, 57.

[78] Captaine Canudo, *Combats d'Orient: Dardanelles-Salonique* (1915–16) (Paris, 1917), 80; O. Rutter, *Tiadatha* (1935), 41.

Tiadatha thought of Kipling,
Wondered if he'd ever been there
Thought 'At least in Rue Egnatia
East and West are met together.'
There were trams and Turkish beggars,
Mosques and minarets and churches,
Turkish baths and dirty cafés,
Picture palaces and kan-kans:
Daimler cars and Leyland lorries
Barging into buffalo wagons,
French and English private soldiers
Jostling seedy Eastern brigands.

In other ways, however, the soldiers made rather unusual tourists. They were not much interested in antiquities, rather more in taverns, cafés, drug dens and the brothels which sprang up all over the western edge of the town. They flocked to night-clubs and cinemas, watched foreign can-can dancers and chanteuses. The lower part of the town was packed as never before, as the city's population temporarily doubled. And among the newcomers were thousands of working-class troops, whose perceptions of their surroundings offered a striking contrast of tone and style with those of the middle classes who had dominated the travel literature of the previous century. One, in the memoirs he typed up as an old man more than six decades later, captures something of this new voice: 'The ship arrived in the Greek port of Salonika just before dawn. From the boat deck, the rising of the morning was a very lovely sight ... so different to the Albert and Victoria docks', recalled Ned Casey, who described himself as 'a misfit soldier', a pale, ill-fed, scrawny working-class Irish boy, nineteen years old, from Canning Town. The contrast he found with 'the cold hard world' of east London hit him from his first steps through the town. He was amused at the local dress: 'they seemd to wear no pants, and had like long whiteskirts tucked between their legs and to me, it looked af they had dropped their bundle before they had time to get seated'. Soon things became even stranger as his boyhood Bible readings came to life:

Another sight that amused me was the sight, of a great big bearded man, his legs scraping along the ground, riding a very small Donkey, while his woman with a bit of rope over her shoulder seem to drag the old along, I had pictures in my prayer book, that looked exactly like the people I saw in this Greek City. I knew that our Lord, who was a carpenter, had a donkey but he let his wife, who was the Virgin Mary ride the Donkey. All my Mates remarked look at that lazy bugger, he ought to be ashamed of himself, treating a tart like that. Christ if that bloke did that along the Barking he would be

pinched, and the Cockney Tarts would cut his love affair off. I was
to see many such sights while stationed in Greece.[79]

The new pace of life – the presence of a huge modern fleet in the bay,
the camps springing up on the city's fringes, the influx of machines,
bureaucracies, languages – seemed to mark the moment at which the
Ottoman spirit of the place vanished. 'Salonica since the war has lost
a little of its *Orientalism*', wrote Roussel. This was modernity, but a
ersatz and tawdry version of the real thing which had tarnished the
old ways and left nothing beautiful in its place: the great fire of 1917
accelerated the process. 'Throughout it was a feverish, make-believe
pleasure', wrote Collinson Owen, 'which never rang true.' It was to
escape this bustling, chaotic atmosphere of the lower town – what
McFee scornfully called 'the casual and irrelevant encounters with the
offscourings of hybrid races' – that Roussel and others made their way
up the hill. The Greeks and the Jews they associated with the Levantine
money-making frenzy that they detested; it was to the old Turkish
quarter that they fled.[80]

'There above the crowds and the noisy throngs were conserved
the traditions of the Orient, the indulgent fatalism and the serene
contemplation, the past in its unchanging setting', lamented Joseph
Vassal in the aftermath of the fire. 'On these desolated ruins, one will
not see again for many a day the groups of old men smoking their
nargileh, playing with their worry beads, the sombre silhouettes of
veiled women.' But even before the fire, the Turkish presence was
being evoked with a new nostalgia. 'What of the Turk, the Turk who
owned Saloniki?' asked Demetra Vaka in 1917, remembering a visit
there many years earlier. 'What did we see of the Turk in Saloniki?
Alas for his past grandeur, we saw him as we saw him all over the
Balkans … He presented the near past, crumbling to pieces before our
eyes. He, to me, was the real pathos of the peninsula.' The citadel
above the city – from where Victorian travellers had dreamed of Xerxes
and St Paul – now saw writers and the journalists finding local colour
in the last traces of Muslim life. For Vaka it was a miserable, ill-clad
Turkish sentry, missing his family in his 'far-distant home', already
perhaps looking forward to his departure; for the *National Geographic* in
1916 it was a singer under the plane trees as he 'poured forth the
melancholy of his heart'. Only now, as the mosques were converted or

[79] 'The Misfit Soldier: A War Story 1914–1918 by … John William Roworth' [Edward
Casey], Imperial War Museum 80/40/1. See also *The Misfit Soldier: Edward Casey's War
Story, 1914–1918*, ed. J. Bourke (Cork, 1999). My thanks to my colleague Joanna Bourke
for showing me this source.

[80] Collinson Owen, *Salonika and After*, 29; Roussel, *Salonique*, 164; McFee, *A Six-Hour
Shift*, 80.

destroyed, and many of the minarets pulled down, did they become noteworthy for the travel writers of the 1920s.[81]

'Much of the old mystery and romance of its narrow streets and quaint silent houses have gone', wrote Goff and Fawcett in 1921. 'The fast decaying fairy-tale book of the East has had a few of its last pages torn from it.' As we have seen, this anxiety about the vanishing picturesque was nothing new. 'Speed destroys impressions', the Guide Joanne had lamented in 1873.

> When the railway is able to transport us in three or four days from London, Paris or Venice to a city like Constantinople without preparation, without any transition, the first impression will be lost, and one will understand the East poorly: truly this will destroy in a few years whatever is left of the 'picturesque'.

What was different was the way the picturesque was now so closely identified with the vanishing traces of Ottoman Islam. Times were changing: new borders curtailed the city's hinterland. The ambitions to turn it into a communications centre between Europe and Asia had been replaced by the realities of its new subordinate status in Greece. 'Instead of being a second capital of the Ottoman Empire', wrote H. C. Woods in 1921, 'It now forms a mere appendage of Athens.' The Eastern Question – the dominant issue for European diplomacy of the past century – was over, and hundreds of thousands of new refugees had come into the city to testify to the cruel terms on which it had been solved. Few travel writers now visited the town, unless it was to appeal to the war memories of the veterans of the Salonica Front. A few such books were published between the two world wars; perhaps the last appeared in 1964. By then, as its veteran author sadly found, 'only one minaret remains and the Turks are all gone'. Blocks of flats were now springing up across the city, indistinguishable from those to be found in 'Lisbon, Stockholm and London'.[82]

The literary centre of gravity had shifted meanwhile from visitors to those for whom the city was home. European literary fashions had spread fast among the Greek and Jewish communities especially at the end of the nineteenth century, and by the interwar years there was a flourishing local literary scene. No longer could one grant the foreign writer any kind of observational privilege. Writing in Greek, the 'generation of the 30s' put the city on the country's cultural map, asserting their specific value against the dominant claims of the capital,

---

[81] J. Vassal, 'Salonique', *Revue de Paris* (Jan.–Feb. 1918), 194–201; Vaka, *The Heart of the Balkans*, 239–40; H. G. Dwight, 'Saloniki', *National Geographic*, 30:3 (1916), 232.

[82] Isambert, *Itinéraire descriptif*, 1873 ed., 495; H. C. Woods, 'Trieste, Salonic and Smyrna', *Fortnightly Review*, 109 (Jan.–June 1921), 818; C. Packer, *Return to Salonika* (1964), 3.

Athens. And in French, Ladino and English, Salonican Jews were also recording their own image of the city. Let us end with a work which captured better than any other the mood of nostalgia for a vanished city that became so powerful in the twentieth century. This was *Farewell to Salonika*, a book published in the United States in 1946 by Leon Sciaky. Born in the Ottoman town in the middle of the reign of Abdul Hamid before emigrating across the Atlantic, he wrote one of the classic immigrant accounts of remembered childhood. Was it coincidence that this most evocative of memoirs begins with the sound of the muezzin calling the faithful to prayer from a neighbourhood minaret at sunset? The call for God's unity had not been heard in the streets of the city from the time of the Greek conquest in 1912. After the First World War, the city's remaining Muslim inhabitants had left. By the time Sciaky wrote his memoir, a second war had intervened, and most of the Jews had gone too.

Transactions of the RHS 12 (2002), pp. 113–40 © 2002 Royal Historical Society
DOI: 10.1017/S008044010200004x   Printed in the United Kingdom

INDIVIDUALISING THE ATLANTIC SLAVE TRADE: THE BIOGRAPHY OF MAHOMMAH GARDO BAQUAQUA OF DJOUGOU (1854)*

By Robin Law

READ 20 MARCH 2001

ABSTRACT. Recent quantitative studies of the Atlantic slave trade tend to marginalise the voices of the enslaved and transported Africans who were its victims, but some sense of their experience is provided by surviving narratives by African-born ex-slaves. This essay draws attention to a neglected example of such narratives, the biography (published in the USA, 1854) of Mahommah Gardo Baquaqua, from Djougou (in modern Bénin), who was enslaved and exported to Brazil in 1845. It explores some of the problems of interpretation raised by this text, especially the relationship between Baquaqua's Muslim upbringing and his conversion to Christianity in the Diaspora.

ALTHOUGH this lecture is delivered under my own name alone, it is the product of a collaborative enterprise of research, with Professor Paul Lovejoy of York University, Canada. During the last two years we have been working on the life of Mahommah Gardo Baquaqua, and in particular on his *Biography*, published in 1854. This work is embodied in a joint publication, comprising an edited reprinting of the 1854 text with other relevant documents, which appeared in the autumn of 2001.[1] This lecture is basically extracted from this larger work. Paul Lovejoy and I have long ago got beyond the point where the paternity of individual ideas, or even of individual turns of phrase, can be sensibly differentiated; so this is in substance a presentation of our joint research, even though the particular form which it takes is my individual responsibility.

Further, this study of Baquaqua is part of a wider project of collaborative research, on 'The Slave Trade of the Nigerian Hinterland', initiated in 1996, which is coordinated by Lovejoy and myself, together

---

*The paper was written while the author held a Lady Davis Visiting Professorship, in conjunction with a Visiting Fellowship in the Harry S. Truman Research Institute for the Advancement of Peace, at the Hebrew University of Jerusalem, Israel, during the academic session 2000/1; thanks to these institutions for their hospitality and support.

[1] Robin Law and Paul E. Lovejoy, *The Biography of Mahommah Gardo Baquaqua: His Passage from Slavery to Freedom in Africa and America* (Princeton, 2001).

with Dr Elisée Soumonni of the National University of Bénin, West Africa. This project is affiliated to the UNESCO Slave Route Project, and is supported by the Social Sciences and Humanities Research Council of Canada, under its Major Collaborative Research Initiatives programme.[2] A central objective of this wider 'Nigerian Hinterland' project is to study the slave trade and its consequences in a truly Atlantic framework, promoting communication and collaboration among historians working in all of the three continents involved, Africa, America and Europe.[3] In our work on Baquaqua, we have drawn upon the networks of international and intercontinental communication which have grown out of the Nigerian Hinterland Project, and have received very generous assistance from scholars based in and/or working on West Africa, Brazil and Haïti, as well as North America and the United Kingdom. Whatever merit may be attributed to the outcome of this research, I therefore hope will be taken as an illustration of both the potential for and the necessity of such a collaborative approach to the study of the Atlantic slave trade.

The lecture is about one individual victim of the Atlantic slave trade, an African who was enslaved and forcibly transported to America in the mid-nineteenth century. Its title, 'Individualising the Atlantic slave trade', warrants some explanatory comment.

In recent years there has been an immense advance in our historical understanding of the Atlantic slave trade. This has been mainly based upon the application of quantitative approaches, most monumentally represented by the Database of slave-trading voyages recently published by Cambridge University Press, including information on over 27,000 transatlantic slaving voyages, thought to represent between two-thirds and three-quarters of the total; some of the implications of which are summarised in the synthetical survey also recently published by Cambridge, by Herbert Klein, one of the co-editors of the Database.[4] For all its evident value, however, this sort of quantitative approach also carries some obvious problems: in particular, that one by-product

---

[2] See the Project's website: http://www.yorku.ca/nhp. The term 'Nigerian Hinterland' is used with reference not only to the Republic of Nigeria, but in a wider sense, to include the Republics of Togo and Bénin to the west, and adjacent parts of Niger and Cameroun to the north and east.

[3] For a programmatic statement, see Robin Law and Paul Lovejoy, 'The Changing Dimensions of African History: Reappropriating the Diaspora', in *Rethinking African History*, ed. Simon McGrath *et al.* (Centre of African Studies, University of Edinburgh, 1997), 181–200.

[4] *The Trans-Atlantic Slave Trade: A Database on CD-Rom*, ed. David Eltis, Stephen D. Behrendt, David Richardson and Herbert S. Klein (Cambridge, 1999); Herbert S. Klein, *The Atlantic Slave Trade* (Cambridge, 1999).

of it is 'effectively to de-centre the voices of the enslaved and transported Africans themselves'.[5]

This is not to say that the experience of the slaves is omitted from the Database, since much of the numerical data in it relates to the slaves (as well as the ships and the crews). It illuminates in particular the conditions under which slaves travelled: for example, questions of spatial crowding on board slave ships, and mortality during the 'Middle Passage' from Africa to America. But the slaves figure in this material mainly as passive victims, rather than as active agents. The editors of the Database themselves stress the issue of 'African agency' as central to the new research made possible by it.[6] The Database does reveal patterns, in terms of variations in supply of slaves both across space and through time, and in the gender and age composition of the exported population, which it seems impossible to account for by European demand, and which must logically reflect conditions in Africa, and perhaps conscious choices by Africans; but the Africans whose decisions might have influenced the level and composition of slave exports were themselves slave merchants, rather than the enslaved persons whom they sold. The agency of the slaves themselves figures in the Database much less; direct evidence of their actions is to be found only in records of shipboard revolts.[7]

It is difficult to contest the fact that, in the Database, enslaved Africans as individuals largely get lost: as the editors themselves acknowledge, the Database does not include a single name of a slave, although it contains those of many thousands of owners and captains of slave ships. This absence of slaves as named individuals does not derive from the nature of databases in general, but from the fact that this particular database is focused on individual voyages, in records of which slaves rarely if ever figure as named individuals. Other databases, relating to slaves in the Americas rather than in the Middle Passage, do deal with slaves as individuals, with identities and names: for example the recently published database of slaves in Louisiana.[8] It is also possible to envisage a database of specifically African-born slaves which would relate to their experience of enslavement in Africa and transportation across the Atlantic, rather than (or as well as) of slavery in the Americas; the construction of such a database is indeed one of the projects of Paul

---

[5] See the author's review of Klein's book, in *Journal of African History*, 41 (2001), 495–7.

[6] Eltis *et al.*, *Database*, 'Introduction'. The argument for African agency is elaborated in the recent study by David Eltis, *The Rise of African Slavery in the Americas* (Cambridge, 2000), ch. 7.

[7] See David Richardson, 'Shipboard Slave Revolts, African Authority and the Atlantic Slave Trade', *William and Mary Quarterly*, 58 (2001), 69–92.

[8] *Louisiana Slave Database, 1719–1820*, ed. Gwendolyn Midlo Hall, in *Databases for the Study of Afro-Louisiana History and Genealogy* (Baton Rouge, LA, 2000).

Lovejoy within the Nigerian Hinterland Project.[9] But even with a dataset of named individuals, a quantitative approach necessarily aggregates and thereby de-individualises them. Quantitative data provide a context in which individual experience can be better understood, but do not convey much sense of that experience.

For a sense of that individual experience, we can turn to a small but significant number of narratives recorded by or from actual victims of slavery and the slave trade. In the USA in the nineteenth century in particular, such narratives by ex-slaves became a significant literary genre. But these accounts are mostly by American-born slaves, which therefore document the experience of slavery (and commonly, emancipation) in the Americas, but not that of enslavement in Africa, transportation through the Middle Passage and cultural adjustment to slave societies in America. For example, what is probably the most distinguished of such slave narratives in a literary sense, and the most significant in its political impact, that of Frederick Douglass (1845), is not only by a man born in America, but is entirely divorced from any sense of his African ancestry.[10]

There are, however, a handful of narratives by African-born former slaves, beginning in the second half of the eighteenth century – the precise number depending upon how narrowly the criteria for inclusion are drawn, since several biographies of ex-slaves are not strictly first-person narratives, told by themselves, but accounts of them given at second hand by European or American writers. The first strictly autobiographical account by an enslaved African appears to be that of James Albert Ukawsaw Gronniosaw, published originally in 1772.[11] The most substantial and best known is certainly that of the prominent Abolitionist activist Olaudah Equiano, published in 1789; Equiano's is the most frequently quoted narrative by an African-born slave (being, for example, the only voice of an enslaved African actually quoted in

[9] Paul Lovejoy, 'Biography as Source Material: Towards a Biographical Archive of Enslaved Africans', in *Source Material for Studying the Slave Trade and the African Diaspora*, ed. Robin Law (Centre of Commonwealth Studies, University of Stirling, 1997), 119–40.

[10] Frederick Douglass, *Narrative of the Life of Frederick Douglass, an American Slave, Written by Himself* (Boston, 1845; and frequently reprinted).

[11] *A Narrative of the Most Remarkable Particulars in the Life of James Albert Ukawsaw Gronniosaw, an African Prince, as Related by Himself* (Bath, 1772; 2nd edn, Bristol, 1774), reprinted in *Black Atlantic Writers of the Eighteenth Century*, ed. Adam Potkay and Sandra Burr (1995), 21–63; and in *Unchained Voices: An Anthology of Black Authors in the English-Speaking World of the Eighteenth Century*, ed. Vincent Carreta (Kentucky, 1996), 32–58. On a looser definition, including third-person accounts substantially based on information supplied by the African subject, the earliest biographical account of an African-born ex-slave would be Thomas Bluett, *Some Memoirs of the Life of Job, Son of Solomon, the High Priest of Boonda in Africa* (1734).

Herbert Klein's book).[12] During the nineteenth century, following the legal banning of the slave trade, there were also a number of narratives by persons who were enslaved and exported from Africa, but who were liberated through the interception of their ships by the anti-slaving squadron of the British navy, and therefore did not complete the Middle Passage and go on to experience slavery in the Americas: among which the best known (although much less often cited than Equiano's) is that of Samuel Ajayi Crowther, written in 1837.[13]

Autobiographical material of this sort of course presents a number of well-known problems of interpretation and evaluation. First, there are questions of authorial status, since many were collaborative works, produced with the assistance of European or Euro-American editors. For example, Gronniosaw's account, although described on the title page of the second (1774) edition as 'written by himself', was in fact, as explained in the Preface, rather 'written down and committed to paper, by the elegant pen of a young Lady of the town of Leominster'. Such cases raise questions, of evidently critical importance but often difficult to resolve, as to the balance of responsibility and control between the African subject and the non-African editor. Whose voice, in fact, are we hearing?[14]

Even where we may feel confident that the ostensible African author did have effective control of the process of production of the text, this does not exhaust the difficulties which such accounts present. Most of them were composed with an explicit polemical intent, as propaganda for the abolition and suppression of the slave trade and/or slavery, which must be supposed to have influenced and perhaps distorted the way in which they presented both their own individual experiences and the character of the societies in Africa from which they originated. And in any case, most of them were written many years after their enslavement and sale into export. Gronniosaw's autobiography, for example, was on his own account recorded no less than forty-five years after his transportation from Africa; Equiano's, thirty-three years later; though Crowther's only sixteen years later. This is bound to raise doubts about how accurately they could have remembered details of their early lives in Africa and their experience of the Middle Passage. And these doubts are compounded by the fact that they had generally undergone profound transformations of outlook in their subsequent lives, commonly

---

[12] *The Life of Olaudah Equiano, or Gustavus Vassa, the African, Written by Himself* (1789; and frequently reprinted).

[13] Originally published as an appendix in *Journals of the Rev. James Frederick Schön and Mr Samuel Crowther Who ... Accompanied the Expedition up the River Niger in 1841* (1842), 289–316.

[14] See William L. Andrews, 'The First Fifty Years of the Slave Narrative, 1760–1810', in *The Art of Slave Narrative: Original Essays in Criticism and Theory* ed. John Sekora and Darwin T. Turner (Macomb IL, 1982), 6–24.

through conversion to Christianity, which must be presumed to have altered the ways in which they remembered and represented their earlier lives. This ambiguity is explicit, for example, in Crowther's account, who wrote of the day of his enslavement as simultaneously 'unhappy' but also 'blessed', the latter because it initiated the process whereby he would be brought to knowledge of the 'true' religion of Christianity.

In some cases, indeed, the detailed content of such memoirs is difficult to accept as reliable. Gronniosaw, for example, claims to have been from Borno, in what is today north-eastern Nigeria, which was a Muslim country; yet he describes its religious practice as pagan.[15] Realisation of the problematical character of Gronniosaw's account is presumably the reason why it is seldom cited by modern scholars. Even Equiano's account, although it offers a generally more plausible as well as a more substantial account of his homeland – Igboland, in modern south-eastern Nigeria – is geographically vague, and includes some material which is difficult to reconcile with what is otherwise known of this area. This is reflected in the difficulty of identifying precisely his community of origin, and consequent disagreement as to where it should be placed.[16] These problems in Equiano's account have led to the suggestion that it might be best understood as a composite construction, rather than a simple autobiography, based in part on information obtained from other slaves of Igbo origin whom Equiano met in the Diaspora, as well as on his own recollections, implying that it might be in part 'imaginative reconstruction or a hotch-potch built up from scraps of information collected from fellow-slaves or ex-slaves'.[17]

Moreover, the possibility of deliberate fraud has also to be considered. When Equiano's autobiography was published in 1789, at least one critic claimed that he had in fact been born in the West Indies, rather than in Africa; and although modern scholars have generally rejected this allegation, the issue has been reopened by the recent discovery that a couple of documents from his early years in England record his place of birth as South Carolina, with the implication that 'his account of Africa [and also, of the Middle Passage] may have been based upon

---

[15] He says its inhabitants worshipped the sun, moon and stars, and did not acknowledge any 'superior power' beyond these; although Gronniosaw himself supposedly inferred the existence of such a supreme deity, this is presented as an idiosyncrasy of his (foreshadowing his later conversion to Christianity).

[16] The claim of Catherine Obianuju Acholonu, *The Igbo Roots of Olaudah Equiano* (Owerri, 1989), to have identified not only Equiano's home village but the particular family in it from which he came, is unconvincing.

[17] A. E. Afigbo, 'Through a Glass Darkly: Eighteenth Century Igbo Society through Equiano's Narrative', in *Ropes of Sand: Studies in Igbo History and Culture* (Ibadan, 1981), 145–86.

oral history and reading, rather than on personal experience'.[18] This would hardly diminish the importance of his text: indeed, the implications of the suggestion that such an account could have been written by somebody born in America for our understanding of the survival of African cultural traditions in the slave societies of the Americas would be staggering; but it would evidently alter the way in which, and the purposes for which, it could be used as a historical source.

The main limitation of such sources, however, is that there are so few of them; and their small number raises the issue of how representative they are of the experience of transported Africans in general. As regards their experience of slavery in the Americas, the few who left personal accounts were certainly not representative. Any slave whose biography was recorded was by definition exceptional, and they were unusual not only in the fact of leaving accounts of themselves, but also in the circumstances which afforded the opportunity for this literary self-representation. These normally included that they had acquired an exceptional competence in a European language, frequently including literacy; and also commonly that they had become free, either through independent accumulation to finance self-redemption (as in Equiano's case), or through attracting favour and patronage from their owners or from other Euro-Americans.

It might be supposed nevertheless that in their earlier experience, of their enslavement in Africa and transportation to America, there is no *a priori* reason why they might not constitute a representative sample. However, it is clear that in certain respects they are not representative of the larger population of enslaved and transported Africans. First, they are overwhelmingly males; most ex-slave narratives are by men, but the paucity of female voices is especially great in the case of those born in Africa.[19] The majority of enslaved Africans were likewise males, probably around two-thirds; but males are disproportionately represented among recorded narratives. Second, such accounts are mostly by persons who were children at the time of their enslavement and transportation: Gronniosaw, for example, was by his own account aged around fifteen when he was taken from Africa; Equiano, only eleven or twelve; and Crowther only thirteen. Children, however, were

---

[18] Vincent Carreta, 'Olaudah Equiano or Gustavus Vassa? New Light on an Eighteenth-Century Question of Identity', *Slavery and Abolition*, 20 (1999), 96–105.

[19] The only extant narratives by African-born females enslaved in the Americas seem to be two very brief accounts recorded in Barbados in 1799, published by Jerome S. Handler, 'Life Histories of Enslaved Africans in Barbados', *Slavery and Abolition*, 19 (1998), 129–40. Phillis Wheatley (lived 1753–84) is a seemingly unique example of a female African-born ex-slave (brought to Boston at the age of eight in 1761) whose own writings were published, but she wrote only poetry (plus a few extant letters), with no significant autobiographical content: see *The Collected Works of Phillis Wheatley*, ed. John C. Shields (Oxford, 1988).

normally a minority among slaves exported, probably under one sixth during the eighteenth century, although rising to perhaps over a third during the nineteenth. This predominance of persons transported as children is probably not accidental, since those brought to America at an early age evidently had more opportunity of acquiring the requisite linguistic and literary skills. Third, the recorded voices are dis-proportionately those of Muslims. On an impressionistic count, maybe almost a half of the African-born slaves and ex-slaves whose biographies were recorded were Muslims; and this too was certainly a very much higher proportion than Muslims represented among the entire enslaved population. The reason for this disproportionate visibility of Muslims is unclear; but it may be that the literacy of Muslims (in Arabic) was likely to attract the attention and patronage of slave-owners and other Europeans, and thus improve their chances both of obtaining freedom and of access to opportunities for literary production.

It seems to be this problem of representativity which has led to the relative neglect of such sources by historians of a quantitative bent. For example, David Eltis, one of the co-editors of the recently published Database, in an earlier work on the illegal slave trade of the nineteenth century, when discussing how the illegality of the trade might have affected conditions in the Middle Passage, noted that one approach to this question might be 'through the eyes of the Africans themselves', in the form of surviving autobiographical accounts by persons who experienced it. But while acknowledging that such accounts represent 'invaluable human records', he observed that they are not only 'few in number', but also questionably representative: 'their authors would have had little hard data on the environment in which they found themselves to enable them to make comparisons'; and after listing the relevant accounts in a footnote, he made no further reference to them.[20] Yet, in the light of the general framework provided by quantitative studies, it ought to be possible to assess how typical the experience of any individual was; and thus to make more effective use of these 'invaluable human records', to flesh out the dehumanised statistics of the databases – thereby 'individualising' our understanding of the slave trade.

Given the scarcity of first-hand narratives by African-born ex-slaves, it might be supposed that any that existed would have been eagerly sought out and minutely studied by interested historians; but curiously, some examples have attracted relatively little attention. This lecture draws attention to one neglected instance of the genre of the ex-slave biography, and explores some of the issues raised by its detailed

[20] David Eltis, *Economic Growth and the Ending of the Transatlantic Slave Trade* (New York, 1987), 125–6.

contents. This was published in Detroit, USA, in 1854, under the title *An Interesting Narrative: Biography of Mahommah G. Baquaqua*. From one perspective, this was merely one of a number of narratives by former slaves published in the USA in the middle decades of the nineteenth century, as noted earlier. On the face of it, moreover, it is not the most substantial or interesting example of the genre. It is a brief work, of only sixty-six pages; and its literary merit is slight. It is written in a simple, indeed naïve style, which reflects not (or not only) the character of the author, but also a deliberate choice, to make it accessible to a wider audience, including specifically children; and its narrative structure is somewhat shapeless and rambling. But as regards its contents, it is of enormous interest.

Baquaqua's *Biography* was unusual among USA ex-slave narratives in two important respects. First, he had been a slave, not in the USA itself, but in Brazil. His arrival in the USA, at New York in 1847, was in fact the occasion of his escape from slavery to freedom; and his subsequent period of residence in the USA was for purposes of education, and restricted to Northern states where slavery was already illegal. As an extended first-hand narrative of the experience of slavery in Brazil, Baquaqua's *Biography* is literally unique.

Second, and for present purposes more critically, unlike most other ex-slaves whose lives were published in the USA during the nineteenth century, Baquaqua had been born in Africa rather than in America; he names his town of origin as 'Zoogoo', which can be identified with Djougou, in the north of the modern Republic of Bénin. His *Biography* therefore covers not only his experience in slavery, and later as a Free Black, in the Americas; but also his enslavement in Africa and transportation through the Middle Passage to America, and indeed his life in Africa prior to his enslavement and export. In fact, the greater part of the *Biography* deals with his life in Africa. The text comprises two parts: first, a general account of the 'manners and customs' of Baquaqua's homeland in Africa, twenty-five pages in length; and second, an account of his individual life, comprising forty pages. Nearly half of the latter deals with his life in Africa, including his enslavement and passage to the coast; the narrative reaches his actual embarkation on the ship which took him to Brazil only at page 42. Nearly two-thirds of the *Biography* therefore deals with his life in Africa, rather than in the Americas. This primary focus on Baquaqua's life in Africa is related to the book's purpose. Although it was in part, like many other ex-slave narratives, an Abolitionist tract, illustrating the evils of slavery and the slave trade by his own experience of them, it was also propaganda for a more personal project, his intended return home to Africa, as a Christian missionary. It concludes with an explicit appeal for funds for this purpose in its final sentence: 'Should a call be given to him to return at once to the land of his birth, he will cheerfully respond, and is sure friends will not be wanting to aid him in his benevolent purpose.'[21]

Baquaqua's biography attracted little interest at the time of its original publication. It does not seem to have circulated widely; and we have traced only a single brief review of it, which was published in the journal *The American Baptist*, an organ of the American Baptist Free Missionary Society, to which Baquaqua was affiliated.[22] It was also long neglected by modern scholars. It was not included in any of the classic anthologies of USA slave narratives, down into the 1990s;[23] and more surprisingly, it was omitted from the anthology of narratives by specifically African-born ex-slaves, published by Philip Curtin in 1967.[24] It seems to have attracted attention only from the 1970s onwards.[25] It was rediscovered first by scholars working on the history of slavery in Brazil, for whom (as noted earlier) Baquaqua's autobiography is a literally unique source; the sections of the *Biography* which deal with his transportation from Africa to Brazil and his life as a slave there were reprinted in anthologies of documents relating to slavery in Brazil (or Latin America more generally) in the 1970s and 80s.[26] The text was also rediscovered by scholars working on African-Americans in the USA: above all, by Allan Austin, who included it in his anthology of biographical material on *African Muslims in Antebellum America*, published in 1984. Although this invaluable sourcebook also seems not to have achieved a wide circulation and has remained relatively little known, Austin discussed Baquaqua's case further in his recent book of the same title.[27]

---

[21] *Biography*, 65. References in the footnotes to Baquaqua's biography are to the original 1854 edition.

[22] 'Biography of Mahommah G. Baquaqua', in *The American Baptist*, 2 Nov. 1854.

[23] E.g. *Slave Testimony: Two Centuries of Letters, Speeches, Interviews and Autobiographies*, ed. John W. Blassingame (Baton Rouge, 1977); *The Classic Slave Narratives*, ed. Henry Louis Gates, Jr (New York, 1987); *I Was Born a Slave: An Anthology of Classic Slave Narratives*, ed. Yuval Taylor (2 vols., Englewood Cliffs, NJ, 1993).

[24] *Africa Remembered: Narratives by West Africans from the Era of the Atlantic Slave Trade*, ed. Philip D. Curtin (Madison, WI, 1967).

[25] As far as has been traced, the first modern notice of it was its inclusion in a bibliography of published material on the slave trade in 1973, which is assumed to be the proximate source of knowledge of it among subsequent scholars: Peter C. Hogg, *The Atlantic Slave Trade and its Suppression: A Classified and Annotated Bibliography of Books, Pamphlets and Periodical Articles* (1973), no. 1500.

[26] *The African in Latin America*, ed. Ann M. Pescatello (New York, 1975), 186–94; *Children of God's Fire: A Documentary History of Black Slavery in Brazil*, ed. Robert Edgar Conrad (Princeton, 1984), 23–9. A Portuguese translation of the entire text was published in Brazil in 1997: Robert Krueger (trans.), *Biografia e narrativa do ex-escravo afro-brasileiro Mahommah G. Baquaqua* (Rio de Janeiro, 1997).

[27] Allan Austin, *African Muslims in Antebellum America: A Sourcebook* (New York, 1984), 655–

The last group of scholars to give attention to the *Biography* have been historians of Africa, including both those interested in the African end of the Atlantic slave trade and those working on the particular region of West Africa from which Baquaqua came – which is ironic, given that the text deals mainly with its subject's life in Africa, rather than in America. This delay is an index of the lack of communication which persisted, until very recently, between historians of Africa, on the one hand, and those studying populations of African origin and descent in the Americas, on the other, which the 'Nigerian Hinterland' project is seeking to address, as noted earlier. Lovejoy and I, therefore, although claiming no credit for the rediscovery of the text (which we ourselves learnt of in the first instance through Austin's work), appear to be the first to look at it from an Africanist perspective.

We first drew upon Baquaqua's text in a paper on the role of the Borgu region (to which Djougou was commercially and politically linked) in the transatlantic slave trade, which was presented at a conference in Parakou, in northern Bénin, in 1999.[28] That might have been the end of our interest, but we also took advantage of this visit to go to Djougou, taking photocopies of the text of Baquaqua's *Biography*, in order to discuss it with authorities on local history and culture. It would be pleasant to be able to record that, like Alex Haley seeking his African 'roots' in the Gambia, we identified Baquaqua's family in Djougou, but we did not.[29] However, we were able to confirm our conclusion (already reached by Austin) that Baquaqua's homeland 'Zoogoo' was to be identified with Djougou, and also that the details of local society and institutions given in his *Biography* were, as far as they could be checked, accurate; and we became convinced that a republication of the text, with extended critical and explanatory commentary, was warranted. Also, we found that the *Biography* was altogether unknown in Djougou, and indeed in the Republic of Bénin more generally; so that we can claim at least to have helped to repatriate his memory to his community of origin.

The remainder of this lecture seeks to do three things: to summarise Baquaqua's career, as documented in the *Biography* and other sources;

89; *African Muslims in Antebellum America: Transatlantic Stories and Spiritual Struggles* (New York and London, 1997), 158–71.

[28] Published as Robin Law and Paul Lovejoy, 'Borgu in the Atlantic Slave Trade', *African Economic History*, 27 (1999), 69–92.

[29] Alex Haley, *Roots* (1977). This is not to suggest that Haley's claim to have identified the particular family, as opposed to the general locality, from which his African ancestor originated is persuasive: for a critique, see Donald R. Wright, 'Uprooting Kunta Kinte: On the Perils of Relying on an Encyclopedic Informant', *History in Africa*, 8 (1981), 205–17.

to consider briefly the question of the authenticity and reliability of the account of his life given in the *Biography*; and to explore some of the issues raised by his representation of the society in Africa from which he came, and his own projected identity as an African.

First, his career, as far as it is known. He was born probably in the late 1820s. At this period, Djougou, his place of birth, was an important centre for interregional trade, and Baquaqua's family belonged to its commercial community: he describes his father as having been a 'traveling merchant',[30] and other members of the family were also involved in long-distance trade. The commercial community in Djougou (and in the wider region of Borgu to which it was connected), which was called Wangara, was non-indigenous, distinguished from the rest of society by its language (Dendi, originating from further north) and its religion, Islam.[31] Baquaqua's account confirms his membership of this Wangara community; most of the items of vocabulary which he cites are identifiable as Dendi, and his family was Muslim. His name reflects this background: the third name, Baquaqua, is presumably a surname or family name and, although not precisely identified, is analogous to names (and titles) current in the area. Of his two personal names, the first, Mahommah, is an African version of the name Muhammad, and advertises his allegiance to Islam; while the second Gardo (by modern spelling, Gado), is his indigenous African name, given in Dendi and other languages of this region to a son born immediately after twins.[32]

As a boy Baquaqua attended Quranic school, but found the discipline of study irksome, twice absconded and evidently did not complete his elementary education. He was also apprenticed for a while to an uncle who was a blacksmith, but did not like this much either – he complains of the hard work of making iron needles. (By way of an aside, it may be said that one of the engaging features of Baquaqua's self-representation in the *Biography* is its candidly unheroic picture of his character, at least in his early life, as idle, self-indulgent and averse to hard work.) Subsequently, probably in his mid-teens, he served as a porter on a long-distance trading journey which took him to the town of Daboya, about 350 km west of Djougou (in modern northern Ghana); there, he was taken captive in a local war, but was redeemed, and returned home to Djougou. He then enlisted as a servant to a local ruler – apparently not the king of Djougou itself, but of a neighbouring

---

[30] *Biography*, 21.

[31] See Denise Brégand, *Commerce caravanier et relations sociales au Bénin: les Wangara du Borgou* (Paris, 1998).

[32] In the *Biography*, 26, Baquaqua notes that he was 'the next born after twins', but without explaining the connection to his name.

subordinate town: probably Soubroukou, 6 km to the south-west.[33] He describes his position in the king's service as that of 'a kind of bodyguard'; but his principal duties seem to have comprised requisitioning provisions for the palace from the local peasantry – as he observes, 'we plundered for a living'.[34]

On a visit to another neighbouring town, 'Zarachoo' (probably Yarakeou, 15 km south-west of Soubroukou), he fell asleep after a drunken party, to find himself kidnapped into slavery. He was taken south through the kingdom of Dahomey to the port of Ouidah, in southern Bénin, and embarked on a ship which took him to Brazil. This probably occurred in 1845 (though this date is not given in the *Biography*, but can be inferred from its combination with information in other sources),[35] when he was probably in his late teens. His transportation into slavery in Brazil at this date was illegal: Portugal, which then still controlled Brazil, had accepted the banning of the slave trade to the north of the Equator by a treaty with Britain in 1815; and after the independence of Brazil in 1822, this treaty had been confirmed by the Brazilian government in 1826. Initially, the slave trade from south of the Equator had remained legal, but in 1831 Brazil had legislated to outlaw any importation of slaves from Africa. However, this legislation was not enforced (until 1850);[36] and – itself a point of some interest – Baquaqua's *Biography* registers no awareness that his importation as a slave was technically illegal under Brazilian law.

The cargo of slaves which included Baquaqua was delivered to the province of Pernambuco, in north-eastern Brazil. He was taken for sale into the capital city Recife, but purchased there by a baker who lived in a nearby town, probably Olinda.[37] He was employed there as a petty trader, hawking bread for his master. But he was later sold on from Pernambuco to Rio de Janeiro, where he was purchased by a ship's captain. This second Brazilian owner is not named in the *Biography*, but is identified in other contemporary sources as Clemente José da Costa,

[33] The town is not named in the *Biography*, but the title of its ruler is given as 'Massa-sa-ba'; although the wording implies that this was a generic title, applied to the rulers of all towns subordinate to Djougou, it was recognised by informants in Djougou (in the form *masasawa*) as the title of the ruler of Soubroukou specifically: fieldwork in Djougou, April 1999.

[34] *Biography*, 31–2.

[35] Baquaqua spent two years in slavery in Brazil (*ibid.*, 59) prior to his departure for the USA, which was in April 1847.

[36] See Leslie M. Bethell, *The Abolition of the Brazilian Slave Trade: Britain, Brazil and the Slave Trade Question, 1807–1869* (Cambridge, 1970).

[37] The town is not named in the *Biography*, 44–6, but is described as situated 'not a great distance from Pernambuco [i.e. Recife]' and on the tidal estuary of a river: Olinda, 10 km north of Recife, at the mouth of the River Berebibe, is the only town close to Recife which fits this description.

master and part-owner of the ship *Lembrança*; in consequence of passing into this man's ownership, Baquaqua acquired the Portuguese name José da Costa, by which he is referred to in USA newspaper reports of 1847. He served as a cabin steward on the *Lembrança*, making two voyages to the south of Brazil. But fatefully for him, in April 1847 the *Lembrança* sailed from Rio de Janeiro with a cargo of coffee for New York, where it arrived on 27 June 1847.[38]

Baquaqua was one of three slaves held on board the ship, together with a man called José da Rocha and a girl, Maria da Costa. According to the *Biography*, he and his fellow-slaves were aware that slavery no longer existed in New York State, and hoped that they might become free on arrival there; he says that the first word he learned in English, on the voyage between Rio and New York, was 'free'.[39] On arrival in New York, Baquaqua made attempts to leave the ship, but was confined in irons on board to prevent escape. His case, however, came to the notice of local Abolitionists, who procured a writ of *habeas corpus* requiring the surrender of the three slaves; the girl Maria then decided that she after all wanted to remain on the ship, but the two men persisted in claiming their freedom. The case was argued out in the New York courts (and reported in local newspapers), during July and August 1847. Interestingly (and surprisingly) the lawyers who appeared for Baquaqua and Rocha did not challenge their status as slaves under Brazilian law, although technically, having been imported from Africa illegally, they were legally free.[40] Instead, they invoked New York State legislation of 1840, which provided that slaves brought into the state by their owners (as opposed to those who ran away) thereby became free. Captain Costa's counsel, however, responded by shifting the argument from their status as slaves to their status as members of the crew, arguing that the extradition of deserting crew members was required by a USA–Brazilian treaty of 1829, and this argument was successful; judgement was given in favour of Captain Costa, and this decision reaffirmed on appeal.

A further appeal was made, but before the third hearing could take

---

[38] The identity of Baquaqua's Brazilian owner and his ship, together with details of their voyage to the New York, are provided by newspaper reports of the ensuing legal proceedings: see esp. the affidavits of Captain Costa and the slaves José da Costa (i.e. Baquaqua) and José da Rocha, printed in the *National Anti-Slavery Standard*, 2 Sept. 1847.

[39] *Biography*, 54.

[40] The Brazilian anti-slave trade law of 1831 provided that anyone introduced from Africa after that date was legally free. The failure to use this argument is odd because the issue of the illegality of their original importation from Africa (in this case, to Cuba) was central to the earlier case (also in New York State) of the slaves involved in the revolt on the ship *Amistad* in 1839, and was the legal basis for their liberation: see Howard Jones, *The Mutiny on the Amistad: The Saga of the Slave Revolt and its Impact on American Abolition, Law and Diplomacy* (revised edn, Oxford, 1988).

place Baquaqua and his fellow-slave were helped to escape from jail, and smuggled out of New York to Boston. They were then offered a choice of passage either to England or to Haïti – they chose Haïti, according to the *Biography*, because the weather there would be better.[41] In Haïti, Baquaqua became attached to the mission of the American Baptist Free Mission Society in the capital Port-au-Prince, entering the service of its local head, the Rev. William Judd, initially as a cook, in early October 1847. Under the influence of living in Judd's household, in March 1848 he was converted to Christianity, and he was baptised into the Baptist Church in July 1848.[42]

The American Baptist Free Mission Society, to which Baquaqua thus became attached, had been formed in 1843, and established its mission in Haïti in 1845. It was in origin an offshoot of the Free Will Baptist movement, from which it had split over the slavery issue. In addition to its Abolitionist commitment, the Free Mission Society engaged in missionary work, among fugitive slaves from the USA resident in Canada, as well as in Haïti. It also had as a central objective the establishment of a mission to Africa, although this was never in the event to be realised. The Free Mission subscribed to the conventional view that missionary enterprise in Africa would have to be entrusted in large part to persons of African descent, mainly on the grounds of the high mortality of white missionaries in Africa. But it was sceptical of the employment for this purpose of African-Americans from the USA, who were held to have been corrupted by the experience of slavery; it was, in particular, highly critical of the settlement of Free Blacks from the USA in West Africa, in what had become (in 1847) the independent Republic of Liberia. It looked to Haïti, with its experience of fifty years of Republican freedom (since the abolition of slavery in the revolution of the 1790s) for Black personnel who could be employed in Africa; and had founded the Haïtian mission largely for this purpose.[43] In this context, the arrival of Baquaqua, an actual African, in the Haïtian mission, seemed a providential gift. From the first, the Rev. Judd sought his conversion, with the explicit hope that he could then be employed as a missionary in Africa; as he observed, 'The circumstances of his escape and final arrival in Port-au-Prince, and his

[41] 'I thought Hayti would be more like the climate of my own country and would agree better with my health and feelings': *Biography*, 56–7.

[42] The account of Baquaqua's period in Haïti in the *Biography*, 57–60, is brief; fuller details can be found in American Baptist Free Mission sources, especially letters of the Rev. Judd and his wife Nancy, printed in the journal *The Christian Contributor and Free Missionary*.

[43] This account of the origins of the Haïti mission is taken from the Annual Report for 1848–9, in Report of the Sixth Annual Meeting of the American Baptist Free Mission Society, 1849 (preserved in the American Baptist Samuel Colgate Historical Library, Rochester, NY).

entrance into my family, are so clearly providential that I can not doubt that but God has some very glorious object to accomplish through him in this connection.'[44] The assumption from the beginning was not that Baquaqua himself would be trained for ordination as a minister, but that he could serve as interpreter and guide to an American missionary. Whether he himself had previously entertained hopes of getting back to Africa is not clear from the records; but on his conversion in July 1848 he embraced the idea with enthusiasm, and repeatedly declared his desire to return to Africa, to spread Christianity in his homeland, beginning with his own family. Baquaqua became, in effect, the Free Mission Society's star convert; an engraving of him (receiving instruction from the Rev. Judd) being used as the frontispiece for a book describing the Society's work published in 1850.[45]

After two years in Haïti, Baquaqua returned to the USA in October 1849, to be enrolled in New York Central College, at McGrawville, NY, a multi-racial institution recently established by the Baptist Free Mission Society, for further education, still with the aim of preparing him for employment as a missionary in Africa. He spent three years in the Primary (i.e. preparatory) Department of the College, but did not proceed to the Academic (university-level) course, for reasons which are not specified in the sources, but perhaps because his progress was considered inadequate for more advanced study. Meanwhile, in 1852, the Free Mission Society had determined that its projected African mission should now be actualised. In this venture, Baquaqua's role was still seen as merely auxiliary, and attention focused on identifying a suitable American minister to undertake the mission; but it proved impossible to find a candidate. At successive Annual Meetings of the Society, in 1853, 1854 and 1855, the Board of the Society reported its failure to recruit a missionary for the African mission. In the meantime, however, efforts were made to raise funds to finance the projected mission, and Baquaqua was enlisted to this end. At the Annual Meeting of the Society in June 1853, he was appointed a member of its Committee on the African Mission, and charged with touring Baptist churches in Pennsylvania and New York State to solicit funds.[46]

By now, however, Baquaqua was losing faith in the Free Mission's ability to deliver on its promise of returning him home. In August 1853 he approached another body, the American Missionary Association

[44] Letter of Rev. W. L. Judd, 28 Oct. 1847, printed in *Christian Contributor*, 22 Dec. 1847.
[45] A. T. Foss and Edward Matthews, *Facts for Baptist Churches* (Utica, NY, 1850).
[46] The account of this period in the USA in the *Biography*, 61–4, is cursory, and in particular omits any reference to Baquaqua's fund-raising activities for the Free Mission Society (this silence probably reflecting his subsequent alienation from the Society, noted later); additional information can be found in the records of the Society, including its journal *The American Baptist*.

(AMA), which already maintained a mission in West Africa, in Sierra Leone (originating with the return of the survivors of the slave revolt on board the ship *Amistad*), in the hope of being taken on; but the AMA seems not to have been impressed with his qualifications (linguistic and moral) for the work, and nothing came of this.[47] He was also becoming disillusioned with USA society, from his experience of racial discrimination: on one occasion, he was threatened with violence when it was believed that he intended to marry a white girl who was a fellow-member of the Baptist Church which he attended in Freetown Corners, near McGrawville.[48] Early in 1854, he emigrated to Canada; and it was from there that he arranged the publication of his *Biography*, across the border in Detroit. Presumably he hoped that the book would raise sufficient support to finance his return to Africa, but in this he was evidently disappointed. At the beginning of 1855 he went on to England, in the hope of getting back to Africa from there. But although he spent at least two years in England, he did not succeed in getting any further; in 1857 he again contacted the Baptist Free Mission Society in the USA, offering his services for their African Mission, but once again this project was shelved, and never came to fruition.[49]

What happened to Baquaqua after 1857 is unfortunately unknown; he would then have been aged only in his early thirties, but we have no idea how much longer he lived, or where he went. It would be agreeable to think that he did in the end succeed in getting back to Africa; but there is no evidence that he did so.

Baquaqua's *Biography* presents many of the same problems as other ex-slave narratives, such as those of Gronniosaw or Equiano. First, the question of authorship is complex. The work as published was avowedly a joint production, involving Baquaqua and an editor, Samuel Moore, a Unitarian minister who had immigrated from Ireland to Michigan, attested otherwise as an Abolitionist publicist. According to the title page, the *Biography* was 'written and revised from his [i.e. Baquaqua's] own words' by Moore; by 'written' is evidently meant 'written down' rather than 'composed', the implication being that Moore put into writing an account given orally by Baquaqua. However, study of the

[47] Eight letters by Baquaqua to the AMA, written from various addresses in New York State between Aug. 1853 and Jan. 1854, are preserved in the AMA Archives, Amistad Research Centre, Tulane University, New Orleans.

[48] This incident is not referred to in the *Biography*, but in one of his letters to the AMA, 26 Oct. 1853.

[49] His departure for England and his subsequent approach to the Free Mission Society are recorded in the Annual Report for 1854–5, in Report of the Twelfth Annual Meeting of the American Baptist Free Mission Society, 1855; and the *New York Free Mission Record*, 13 Feb. 1857.

contents of the book shows that the situation was more complex than this, and that Moore did more than simply record and correct a narrative by Baquaqua. Much of the first part of the book, which gives the general description of Baquaqua's homeland, is in fact written in the third person, though with several illustrative direct quotations from Baquaqua; it is only in the second part, which narrates the history of Baquaqua's own life, that the first-person mode becomes dominant, though here too with frequent third-person interpolations. Parts of the book were evidently composed by Moore, though on the basis of material supplied by Baquaqua; but others represent Baquaqua's voice, albeit as edited by Moore. However, it is clear that, unlike in some other cases of ex-slave biographies, it was Baquaqua who was ultimately in control of the production of the text. This was certainly true in a legal or entrepreneurial, as opposed to a narrowly literary, sense; it is Baquaqua rather than Moore who is identified on the title page as the 'author'; and it was he and not Moore who held legal copyright in the text.

This is not to deny that some parts of the text represent the voice of Moore rather than Baquaqua (as is sometimes detectable, on the basis of substantive content or stylistic difference); or indeed that Moore's editing of Baquaqua's voice may have produced a degree of mis-representation, arising from imperfect communication between the two. There are particular points where the text is either obscure on matters which Baquaqua must have understood clearly, or where it says things about his home society which seem improbable, and these seem best explicable as reflecting misunderstanding by Moore of what he was told by Baquaqua.

Beyond this, the question remains of whether, even to the extent to which we believe that Baquaqua's voice has been accurately transmitted, his account is reliable. Here, a distinction has to be made between the earlier period of his life, including his years as a slave in Brazil as well as his life in Africa, and the period beginning with his arrival in the USA in 1847. For the later period, there is considerable documentation other than the *Biography*, including references in newspaper accounts, as well as the records of the American Baptist Free Mission Society and the AMA; indeed, the documentation in these other sources is fuller than the account in the *Biography*. Although there are discrepancies of detail and differences of emphasis and perspective, broadly this additional material serves to corroborate Baquaqua's own account.

For the period prior to his arrival in the USA, there is no such independent documentation of his individual life, and his account can be evaluated only in the light of more general, contextual information. But here, too, it can be said that what Baquaqua says is generally consistent with what we know (or think we know) of conditions in the town of Djougou from which he originated, in Dahomey through which he was taken to the coast, in the Middle Passage across the Atlantic, and in Brazil where he was held in slavery. By comparison with the problematical case of Equiano, moreover, it can be said that Baquaqua is on the face of it a better source, in that he was recalling his life in Africa after a much shorter interval, less than ten years after his transportation to America. Nor is there, as in the case of Equiano, any reason to doubt that Baquaqua was, as he claimed, a native of Africa, or that his account of his homeland was based on his own recollections. Unlike Equiano's group, the Igbo, who were very numerous in the transatlantic Diaspora, there can have been few (if indeed any) other slaves from Djougou in the Americas from whom Baquaqua could have derived his information.[50]

This is not to deny that there are particular points on which Baquaqua may have sought to misrepresent aspects of his early life. This possibility arose not only from faulty memory or self-aggrand-isement, but also from his interaction with his intended audience. Since his conversion in Haïti in 1848, he had often told parts of his life story to Baptist and Abolitionist audiences; and when he was engaged in fund-raising for the projected mission to Africa during 1853 he is explicitly recorded to have talked about his homeland and his experience of enslavement, liberation and conversion.[51] It was evidently in this context that the idea of a book on his life was conceived; the *Biography* as published can be regarded as a written version of what he had been saying on the Baptist lecture-circuit. Baquaqua had therefore had ample opportunity to learn what his intended audience thought, or wanted to know, about Africa, and to tailor his account accordingly.

There are indeed indications that this led him to change his story over time. One critical point in particular can be identified where this led him into distortion. At the time of his conversion in Haïti in 1848, his Baptist patrons understood him to say that he had been a slave for some considerable time in Africa before he was sold into export;[52] but

---

[50] It is doubtful whether he would have found any fellow-slaves from Djougou in Brazil. In the *Biography*, 40, he records meeting a man at Ouidah whom he knew from Djougou, who had been enslaved and sent to the coast two years earlier, but implies that this man stayed behind in Ouidah when he himself was exported; if he had met any other persons from Djougou subsequently in Brazil, it seems likely that he would have mentioned this. Even slaves from the wider Borgu region were not numerous in Brazil; some slaves from Borgu are documented (under the name 'Bariba') in the province of Bahia, but lists of nationalities of African slaves in Rio de Janeiro do not include the 'Bariba': see Law and Lovejoy, 'Borgu in the Atlantic Slave Trade', 75–6; Mary C. Karasch, *Slave Life in Rio de Janeiro 1808–1850* (Princeton, 1987), 11–21, 371.

[51] See the letter of A. L. P. [= Albert L. Post], Montrose, PA, July 1853, in *The American Baptist*, 28 July 1853.

[52] Letter of Mrs N. A. L. Judd, 24 Mar. 1848, in *Christian Contributor*, 17 May 1848.

the later *Biography* represents him as being taken to the coast directly after his kidnapping, taking only a few weeks in transit. Although this contradiction might be attributed simply to confusion arising from problems of communication (at a time when Baquaqua's English was still poor, and his Baptist friends spoke no Portuguese), it seems more probable that he was indeed held as a slave in Africa prior to export, and that he later chose to suppress this fact. As noted earlier, Baquaqua records that immediately prior to his sale into export, he was employed as a palace bodyguard, for which status he gives the correct indigenous term, *tkiriku* ('cherecoo'). What he does not make clear is that the status of *tkiriku* in Djougou (and in the Borgu region more generally) was that of a slave – although in origin they were not necessarily acquired by purchase or capture; they might include criminals escaping justice by enlisting in palace service.[53] Which of these circumstances applied to Baquaqua himself is a matter for speculation, but he has evidently been less than candid about some aspect of his history. Although he may have sought to conceal his status as a slave in Africa merely in order to present himself in a more favourable light, more serious issues may have been involved. It seems likely that in the USA Baquaqua would have learned that defenders of the slave trade commonly sought to justify it on the grounds that those taken to America were supposedly already enslaved in Africa, so that the trade involved merely an intercontinental transfer of slaves, rather than the enslavement of previously free persons. It may be therefore that he wished to prevent his own individual case being cited in defence of the slave trade.

Baquaqua's account of his life is of interest from many perspectives, including the history of his homeland Djougou; the operation of the African end of the slave trade, in the enslavement of Africans and their delivery to the coast; the experience of the Middle Passage and of slavery in Brazil; and the situation of Free Blacks in the USA. The remainder of this lecture, however, concentrates upon one particular set of issues which his story serves to illuminate, relating to questions of identity in the context of transatlantic transportation: namely, how this particular displaced African conceived his relationship to his African homeland, and more specifically to his originally Muslim background, especially in relation to his subsequent conversion to Christianity.

As noted earlier, the *Biography* is mainly an account of Baquaqua's life in Africa; and this focus is consistent with the fact that he emphasised

---

[53] On *tkiriku*, see Jacques Lombard, *Structures de type 'féodal' en Afrique noire: étude des dynamiques internes et des relations sociales chez les Bariba du Dahomey* (Paris, 1965), 112; Bernd Baldus, 'Responses to Dependence in a Servile Group: The Machube of Northern Benin', in *Slavery in Africa: Historical and Anthropological Perspectives*, ed. Suzanne Miers and Igor Kopytoff (Madison, WI, 1977), 438.

his identity as an African, for example sometimes speaking at public meetings in Haïti and the USA in an African language – which, although nobody in his audience could have understood what he was saying, was evidently dramatically effective. An engraving of himself on the cover of the *Biography* likewise depicts him wearing African robes, again suggesting a self-conscious promotion of an African identity (and in interesting contrast to the engraving of him in the Free Mission publication of 1850, which shows him in European dress). In part, no doubt, this stress on his African origins was calculated, since it was precisely his African background which recommended him to the Free Mission Society for employment as a missionary in Africa. But conversely, his commitment to Christian evangelisation might have been a device to procure his return to Africa. One may ask, what was Baquaqua's priority: to get back to Africa in order to share the gospel of Christianity; or to enlist as a Christian missionary as a means of getting back to Africa?

This question was raised by Allan Austin, whose explicit agenda was to argue that African Muslims who found themselves transported into slavery in America generally remained true to Islam; and that their purported conversions to Christianity, as regularly reported in contemporary accounts, were either misrepresentations or, on the part of the supposed coverts, insincere. In Baquaqua's case, consistently with this general orientation, Austin concluded with the speculation that, if he had succeeded in getting back to Africa, he might have 'reverted to the religion of his youth'. However, the only specific evidence cited in support of this view is the inclusion of a phrase in Arabic in one of Baquaqua's letters to the AMA, which appears to be an incomplete version of the Quranic rubric, *Bismillah al-rahman al-rahim*, 'In the name of God, the compassionate, the merciful'; which Austin interpreted as indicating that 'perhaps he was thinking of going home and returning to his original religion'.[54] This, however, seems an improbable interpretation; in its context, in a letter seeking employment in a mission in Africa, the inclusion of this phrase seems more likely to have been an attempt to illustrate Baquaqua's claimed knowledge of Arabic, and hence his qualifications as an interpreter.

Austin's argument nevertheless serves to pose the interesting and difficult question of how transported African Muslims would have understood the conversion to Christianity which was urged upon them. Islam and Christianity are, after all, variants of a single religious tradition, both derived historically from Judaism. Islam recognises the authority of both the Old and New Testaments (while alleging that

---

[54] Austin, *Transatlantic Stories*, 169, 171, citing Baquaqua's letter to the AMA of 26 Oct. 1853.

these have been falsified in particular details), and thus accepts Jews and Christians as deviant followers of the true revealed religion, 'people of the Book', rather than straightforward Infidels. Islam was founded by Abraham, not Muhammad; and acknowledges both Moses and Jesus as Prophets, precursors to Muhammad. It follows that the content of Christianity was much less distinctive, relative to Islam, than most nineteenth-century Christian missionaries appreciated. As Austin pertinently points out, the Lord's Prayer, a text often recommended for study to converts to Christianity, contains nothing to which a Muslim could not subscribe.[55] The theological differences between Islam and Christianity are in fact narrow, which is not to say that they are unimportant: Muhammad's status as a Prophet is denied by Christians, while that of Jesus as God (together with the consequent doctrine of vicarious salvation through his crucifixion) is rejected by Muslims. Given this similarity of the two religions, it may not be easy to distinguish Baquaqua the Muslim by upbringing in Africa from Baquaqua the Christian by conversion in the Diaspora. As an illustration of the problem, a letter from the Rev. Judd's wife, describing Baquaqua's study of the Bible after his conversion, reports enthusiastically his positive reaction to the story of Abraham and Isaac, evidently without any awareness that this story is also part of the Islamic tradition (alluded to in the Quran), and thus probably already familiar to Baquaqua from his background in Africa.[56]

Parallel ambiguities occur elsewhere in relation to Baquaqua's understanding of Christianity. In this connection, it is important that it was specifically the Baptist version of Christianity to which he was converted. His first acquaintance with Christianity had not, in fact, been with the Baptists in Haïti, but with the Roman Catholic Church in Brazil earlier: as recorded in the *Biography*, while held in slavery in Pernambuco, he was obliged to participate in ceremonies of Christian worship in his owner's household – as was, indeed, normal (and in theory legally obligatory) for slaves in Brazil. Baquaqua himself, however, is dismissive of the superficiality of the Christian instruction he received: 'we were taught to chant some words which we did not know the meaning of'.[57] It may be that this retrospective dismissal of his exposure to Christianity in Brazil reflects his subsequent conversion into the Baptist Church, and his internalisation of the Protestant view that Roman Catholicism was not 'true' Christianity. But maybe something else was involved, which referred back to his earlier Muslim background in Africa. In describing the Christian ceremonies in which he participated in Brazil,

[55] Austin, *Transatlantic Stories*, 136–7.
[56] Letter of Mrs N. A. L. Judd, 13 Nov. 1848, in *Christian Contributor*, 27 Dec. 1848.
[57] *Biography*, 45.

he refers to 'images of clay' before which he and his fellow-slaves were obliged to kneel; and this theme recurs in an account (not recorded in the *Biography*, but in another letter from Mrs Judd) of a conversation which Baquaqua had in Haïti, after his conversion, with a Spanish Roman Catholic, who wore a crucifix, and whom he derided for worshipping a 'wooden god'.[58] Baquaqua's Baptist patrons interpreted his rejection of Roman Catholic 'idolatry' as evidence of the genuineness of his conversion to the Baptist version of Christianity; but it does not seem altogether fanciful to relate it to the fact that rejection of the worship of images in human form is a central tenet of the Islamic religion in which he had been brought up in Africa. The point is not necessarily to deny the sincerity of Baquaqua's conversion to Christianity; but rather to suggest the possibility that this was facilitated by the convergence on critical points between the doctrines of Islam and of Baptism.

This argument can be developed further with regard to a second issue which seems to have been critical in Baquaqua's conversion: that of alcoholic drinks. When he joined the Baptist Free Mission in Haïti in 1847, he clearly had a serious drink problem. This had begun in Africa, and by his own account had indeed been the occasion of his enslavement and transportation. According to the story told in the *Biography*, he was tricked into slavery, being decoyed by supposed friends into a drunken party, from which he woke up to find himself made a slave. As he explicitly reflected, if he had not been drunk, he would not have been enslaved: 'Had it not been that my senses had been taken from me, the chance was that I should have escaped their snares, at least for that time.' His predilection for alcohol surfaces repeatedly in his subsequent narrative, in frequent references to his drinking, which at times served as solace in his misfortune (both in Brazil and in his early days in Haïti), at others got him into trouble with his Brazilian owners and at least once (on his arrival in the USA) emboldened him to resist his slavery. Significantly, his account of his conversion also singles out this issue of drink: 'After my conversion to christianity I gave up drinking and all other kinds of vices'.[59]

The prohibition of alcohol is, of course, a central rule of Islam, as well as of Baptist Christianity; and arguably provides a key to interpreting Baquaqua's attitude towards his Muslim background in Africa, in relation to his conversion to Christianity. A critical passage of the *Biography* for understanding this question occurs in his discussion of warfare in his African homeland, where he observes: 'They drink

---

[58] Letter of Mrs N. A. L. Judd, 21 July 1848, in *Christian Contributor*, 30 Aug. 1848.

[59] *Ibid.*, 35, 58. The *Biography* can indeed be read as a Temperance (as well as an Abolitionist) narrative.

considerably before going to battle, in order to strengthen them and instil them with courage and daring'; but immediately adds a qualificatory aside, 'of course this has no reference to those professing Mahomedanism, as they use no kinds of intoxicating drinks on any occasion'.[60]

To understand and explicate this passage, it requires contextualisation, in relation to the nature of ruling elites in pre-colonial West Africa, and their relationship to Islam. First, ruling elites were commonly warrior aristocracies, whose central purpose in life was the waging of war (and the appropriation of resources as booty, including slaves); in the interior of West Africa, such warrior elites were frequently linked specifically with service as cavalry.[61] Certainly, this was so in the Borgu region, to which Djougou was politically and culturally attached: the ruling elite there, the Wasangari, were essentially a military class, here too serving as cavalry.[62] Second, these warrior elites commonly had a problematic relationship with Islam. In this regard, it is necessary to distinguish between levels of Islamisation in different areas. In some cases, generally in the northern interior, there were societies which were predominantly Muslim, or at least officially Muslim, in the sense that the rulers were Muslims (such as Borno, despite Gronniosaw's misrepresentation to the contrary, noted earlier). In others, generally towards the coast to the south, Islamic influence was non-existent or minimal, and societies remained essentially pagan (such as the Igbo, in this case as correctly described by Equiano). In others, there was significant Islamic influence, with Muslims forming an influential minority, especially prominent in commerce; but the political elite remained non-Muslim. This third, intermediate pattern was generally the situation in what may be called the 'middle interior', including the Borgu region, and Baquaqua's home town of Djougou.

The most substantial study of Islam in this 'middle' region, by Nehemiah Levtzion, is entitled *Muslims and Chiefs in West Africa*; and this title was chosen, not only because relations between Muslims and the ruling establishment were a critical issue in the process of the expansion of Islam, but also because there was a conceptual opposition between the ruling warrior aristocracy and Islam. In Levtzion's formulation, 'the two estates remained distinct ... Members of the chiefly estate came under Islamic influence, but they did not become Muslims ... there is a distinction between being a chief and being a Muslim.'[63] Certainly,

[60] *Ibid.*, 24.

[61] See further Robin Law, *The Horse in West African History: The Role of the Horse in the Societies of Pre-Colonial West Africa* (International African Institute, 1980), ch. 7.

[62] On the Wasangari of Borgu, see esp. Lombard, *Structures de type 'féodal'*.

[63] Nehemiah Levtzion, *Muslims and Chiefs in West Africa: A Study of Islam in the Middle Volta Basin in the Pre-Colonial Period* (Oxford, 1968), 189. The passage quoted refers

this pattern of opposition between the ruling military aristocracy and Islam applies to Borgu, where the identity of the Wasangari elite was based, in part, on their 'rejection of Islam'.[64] This was evidently a matter of ideal types, and not inconsistent with individual chiefs/warriors being, at the level of personal belief, Muslims, but nevertheless was a pervasive concept. In such circumstances, drinking alcohol (especially in public) served as an affirmation of identity as a member of the non-Muslim warrior class. This can be illustrated by the case of Senegambia, in the extreme west of West Africa, where the military ruling elite, known here as *tyeddo*, was overthrown in a 'Muslim Revolution' in the 1860s. A recent study observes of the distinction between the *tyeddo* and their Muslim critics, 'Basic to the difference in life styles was their heavy drinking'; a village chief told a European missionary in 1847, 'We are *tyeddo*; our religion is to drink.'[65] Likewise among the Mossi of Burkina Faso, further east, a non-Muslim will define his religious allegiance by saying, 'I do not pray [i.e. like the Muslims], I drink.'[66]

It may be suggested that it is in this context that Baquaqua's reference to warriors, alcohol and Muslims is best understood. Consider how this opposition between Islam and the warrior ethos played out in his own personal life. First, he was from a Muslim family, and one whose adherence to the religion was evidently more than nominal. Of his father, he records: '[his] manners ... were grave and silent; his religion, Mahommedanism', and he performed the Muslim prayers scrupulously. Moreover, he had an elder brother who was an Islamic scholar: 'His brother was a staunch Mohammedan and well learned in Arabic', and maintained a Quranic school, in which Baquaqua himself was briefly enrolled.[67]

Baquaqua himself, however, was by the standards of his family at best an indifferent Muslim. In childhood, he was placed by his father in an Islamic school, with a career as a scholar in mind: 'he destined him for mosque, intending to bring him up as one of the prophet's faithful followers'. But he left the school to work as an apprentice with his blacksmith uncle, 'not liking school very much'. Later, apparently after this uncle's death, his father once again placed him in school, this time under his own brother; but Baquaqua, as he explains, 'soon ran

---

specifically to the particular case of Gonja (in northern Ghana), but it is explicitly stated that this pattern was, to a greater or lesser degree, replicated elsewhere. In Dagomba (also in northern Ghana), for example, 'there is a clear distinction between being a chief and being a Muslim; that is, being a chief implies not being a real Muslim' (p. 109).

[64] Lombard, *Structures de type 'féodal'*, esp. 224–31, on 'Le Noble et l'Islam'.

[65] Martin A. Klein, 'Social and Economic Factors in the Muslim Revolution in Senegambia', *Journal of African History*, 13 (1972), 419–41.

[66] Personal communication from Christoph Pelzer, Johann Wolfgang Goethe-Universität, Frankfurt-am-Main.

[67] *Biography*, 9–10, 26–7.

away; he did not like the restraint that his brother (the teacher) put upon him ... [he] did not progress very well in learning, having a natural dread of it'. It is clear from his account that he did not complete even the basic elementary education, of learning to read the entire Quran; it appears that he completed only about a third of the text.[68] His subsequent career drew him further away from his Muslim background, especially when he was recruited as a *tkiriku* or bodyguard to a local ruler. Implicitly, this involved abandoning the Muslim and commercial world of his family for the military and non-Muslim milieu of the ruling warrior elite. It was evidently also in this period that he acquired the taste for alcohol which was to be his downfall, since he records being employed in requisitioning palm wine, among other provisions, for the king's use.

How does this experience relate to Baquaqua's subsequent conversion to Christianity? An account of his conversion in another letter by Mrs Judd (much fuller than the brief account in the *Biography*) is explicit in linking his move to Christianity to recollections of his African background. On the night preceding his conversion, he is said to have dreamed of being back in Africa; and his announcement of his conversion on the following day was coupled with an expression of willingness to return home as a Christian missionary. Although the cynical might interpret this to indicate that his profession of Christianity was merely a device to get himself back home, the reported details suggest something more than simple homesickness. Mrs Judd's account of Baquaqua's conversion is conventional enough in stressing his growing consciousness of his own sinfulness, but it is noteworthy that he was understood to be 'referring to his sins in Africa as well as since'. Also, he saw this problem of sin in collective as well as individual terms, as relating to the society in Africa to which he had belonged, rather to himself alone: 'he [said] that he had been thinking about Africa; and how bad the people were there (This he would never admit until lately.) "Now I see the people *very* bad in Africa." '[69]

Baquaqua is thus presented as turning to Christianity out of feelings of guilt at aspects of his earlier life in Africa. The logic of the Baptists' understanding of his state of mind is evidently that he now saw his home society in Africa as degraded and/or backward, and hence in need of Christian redemption. This, however, seems at odds with the

---

[68] The *Biography*, 27, says that pupils had to learn twenty chapters of the Quran; but since it was in fact standard to learn the entire text (over perhaps four years), this is taken to refer only to the extent of Baquaqua's own education. The Quran contains 114 chapters (suras), of unequal length, but for educational purposes it is conventionally divided into sixty sections (*ahzab*): J. S. Trimingham, *Islam in West Africa* (Oxford, 1959), 159, n. 1.

[69] Letter of Mrs N. A. L. Judd, 24 Mar. 1848, in *Christian Contributor*, 17 May 1848.

general thrust of the representation of his African home in the *Biography*, which gives a quite positive account of it. As regards religion in particular, although he frequently refers to Muhammad as a 'false prophet' (unless this wording is due to his editor Moore), his actual description of Muslim worship and practice contains no particular negativity; his dismissive references to African 'superstitions' relate specifically to non-Islamic beliefs.[70] The only really negative observations he makes upon his own society relate to the devastation caused by endemic warfare, including its relationship to the market for captives who could be sold into slavery.[71] As regards his own individual life, likewise, the only explicitly expressed regrets relate to his period as a palace 'bodyguard', or *tkiriku*:

> whilst he was there he became very wicked. But (says he) at that time, I scarce knew what wickedness was; the practises of the soldiers and guards, I am now convinced, was very bad indeed, having full power and authority from the king to commit all kinds of depredations they pleased upon the people without fear of his displeasure or punishment.[72]

Although here he explicitly relates his 'wickedness' only to such looting forays, it is surely also relevant that it was in this context of employment as a palace bodyguard, as noted earlier, that Baquaqua took to drink.

This interpretation is also supported by an account in another of Mrs Judd's letters, of a conversation which Baquaqua had shortly after his arrival in Haïti, even before he joined the Baptist Free Mission (although he was already in contact with it). On seeing a party of soldiers in Port-au-Prince,

> he expressed a strong detestation of war and soldiers, saying, if it was not for war, all these men might be employed in cultivating the land ... He also expressed his opinion concerning the effects of war on the morals of a country. Said he – 'these men have little to do at present. They very soon spend what little money they have – then they take to stealing, and then what are they? They are gone.'

He also referred to the issue of alcohol, declaring himself 'strongly opposed to intemperance'; when the nature of the Baptists' temperance pledge was explained to him, 'he expressed himself very ready to have his name attached to it'.[73]

---

[70] E.g. he refers dismissively to 'medicine men', who combat witchcraft, who 'go in a state of nudity, eat swine's flesh, and are considered by the Mahomedans as a very wicked people': *Biography*, 22–3.

[71] *Ibid.*, 24–5.

[72] *Ibid.*, 32.

[73] Letter of Mrs N. A. L. Judd, 8 Oct. 1847, in *Christian Contributor*, 19 Jan. 1848.

It might perhaps be supposed that in expressing himself thus, Baquaqua was merely seeking to ingratiate himself with the Baptists of the Free Mission, by identifying with their pacifist and pro-temperance views.[74] But an alternative reading would be to suggest that, here again, in linking soldiering and drinking, he had in mind conditions in his African homeland, and his own passage from a Muslim to a non-Muslim context within it. That he saw this, in retrospect, as a wrong turning in his life is also suggested by the fact that, when he initially joined the Judds' household, prior to expressing any interest in actual conversion, he was from the beginning eager to acquire an education, explaining that 'he had a brother older than himself in Africa, who could both read and write'. The implication seems to be that he wished to make up for the opportunity which he had lost by dropping out of Islamic school in Africa.[75]

It seems permissible to conclude that what Baquaqua felt regret and guilt about was his abandonment of the Muslim lifestyle of his family, and his entrance into the hard-drinking world of the professional warrior, which had led him into the personal disaster of his sale into overseas slavery. This is not to suggest that he was not 'really' converted, or that he did not see any difference between Islam and Christianity; indeed, it seems possible that the distinctively Christian doctrine of vicarious salvation through the sacrifice of Jesus might have a special appeal to one who, like Baquaqua, was oppressed by guilt at his personal failure hitherto to live up to the tenets of his religion. The argument is rather that the particular elements in Baptist Christianity by which he was attracted and upon which he focused were ones which were suggested by his Muslim background. In becoming a Baptist he was, if not reverting to Islam, at least putting an Islamic gloss on his new religion.

This is, of course, an exercise in reading into the text rather than out from it, and may perhaps be judged excessively speculative. But it is offered here as an exercise in informed and controlled, rather than arbitrary and undisciplined, hermeneutics; and it is against that claim that it will hopefully be measured.

---

[74] Although pacifism was not, like temperance, a declared principle of the American Baptist Free Mission Society, pacifist sentiments were widespread among its members, partly through the influence of William Lloyd Garrison. The *Biography*, 58–9, records that Baquaqua's departure from Haïti back to the USA in 1849 was accelerated by fears that he might be drafted for military service, and comments that he 'was opposed to the spirit of war as well as was [*sic*] my master and mistress [i.e. the Rev. and Mrs Judd]'.

[75] Letter of Mrs N. A. L. Judd, 8 Oct. 1847, in *Christian Contributor*, 19 Jan. 1848.

Transactions of the RHS 12 (2002), pp. 141–65 © 2002 Royal Historical Society
DOI: 10.1017/S0080440102000051 Printed in the United Kingdom

THE MYTHS OF THE SOUTH SEA BUBBLE

By Julian Hoppit

READ 18 MAY 2001

ABSTRACT. The South Sea Bubble of 1720 looms large in popular depictions of eighteenth-century Britain. But in many respects it is seriously misunderstood. This article begins by exploring mythic 'facts' about the events of 1720, but is also concerned to explore why the Bubble was mythologised long after the event. On several levels, therefore, the Bubble has itself been bubbled.

THERE is something very familiar about the South Sea Bubble of 1720. It is that rare thing, a label given to an eighteenth-century occurrence that has entered reasonably common usage. *The Times*, for example, referred to it twelve times in 2000, the *Guardian* seventeen times and the *Independent* thirteen times.[1] In recent years a facsimile edition of Bubble playing cards from 1720 has been sold on the high street, and the Bubble is on the BBC's web site timeline for British history.[2] In such places the Bubble is obviously employed with reference to the financial crisis of 1720, so brilliantly evoked in Hogarth's famous depiction of frenzied irrationality, economic chaos, religious corruption and sexual dissipation, all in pursuit of lucre and luxury. But so familiar is the Bubble that it is also used as a fanciful allusion or metaphor, as in Noël Coward's *South Sea Bubble: A Comedy in Three Acts* (1956) which is actually about the twilight of the British empire in the Pacific. In short, the Bubble has attained legendary status, at once familiar if distant, to be used confidently and freely. Yet this familiarity has two mythical aspects: the Bubble has suffered from considerable myopia and misunderstanding, such that some of its long-lived evocations often need to be considered mythologically, with their own origins and dynamics.

The Bubble, which was blown and burst in 1720, centred upon the joint-stock South Sea Company which had been founded in 1711 with monopoly trading rights to much of South America, even though the well-established Spanish and Portuguese empires there made the region

[1] Figures produced by searching for 'South Sea Bubble' on the CD editions of these newspapers. The respective figures for 1999 were thirteen, fifteen and sixteen.

[2] www.bbc.co.uk/history.

Plate 1 W. Hogarth, untitled allegory on the South Sea Bubble, 1721. Copyright Guildhall Library, Corporation of London.

largely out-of-bounds. In fact, trade was always of minor importance to the company, for it had been established to help the Tory government organise the national debt and exploit public credit after nearly twenty years of expensive warfare. Its political origins, as a counterweight to the Whiggish Bank of England and East India Company, were fundamental. As such it was a vital part of the 'financial revolution' that took place in the generation after the Glorious Revolution of 1688–9.[3] That revolution centred upon how the government established a permanent and funded national debt by employing parliamentary promises of future tax revenues to repay what had been borrowed. But initially there was much about this that was uncertain and experimental. Some of those problems were mainly administrative and organisational, but some were political, not least because of the potential threat to creditors of a Jacobite restoration. Consequently, very high interest rates often had to be offered in order to attract lenders. After the successful peace of 1713, which reconfirmed the Revolution settlement

[3] P. G. M. Dickson, *The Financial Revolution in England: A Study in the Development of Public Credit, 1688–1756* (1967) is the definitive account. I am very indebted to it.

of 1689 and the Hanoverian succession, and when interest rates were now much lower, governments naturally looked for ways to renegotiate the debts of the 1690s and 1700s so as to lessen their burden.

In 1719, mimicking events in Paris, the South Sea Company submitted a comprehensive scheme to do this, offering its own equity to those public creditors who surrendered their original assets. This provoked a counter-proposal from the Bank of England, with the South Sea Company winning the bidding war with the Treasury by offering £7.5 million, though there was also considerable bribery and treating, both at court and in parliament, to obtain the necessary political backing. Moreover, to get public creditors to exchange their assets for stock, the Company lured them less with the prospect of dividend income, which would have required a profitable trade in goods, than by a rising share price achieved by offering stock on extended terms, by hyperbole and, it is likely, by insider trading.[4] In this it succeeded handsomely and soon its shares began to rise sharply in price. As Figure 1 shows, about the start of 1720 the price stood at 130 but rose to nearly 1,000 in June, a seven-fold rise. Given the modest trading prospects of the Company such a rise was generated largely by the self-fulfilling expectation amongst investors and potential investors that the price would rise, a state of mind that rested on a particular form of confidence or faith. But that confidence waned and slumped in August and September 1720 as more and more investors questioned the Company's medium- and long-term prospects. Quite suddenly it was found that 'all is floating, all falling'.[5] By October the share price was around 200, where it hovered until the full story began to emerge in the spring of 1721 from an investigation by a House of Commons Secret Committee.

At one level that was the South Sea Bubble; it was the spectacular rise and precipitous collapse of one company's share price. But as Figure 1 suggests, the stock market was more generally disordered in 1720. The East India Company share price also surged by over 100 per cent and even that of the Bank rose by about 60 per cent, both then falling back. In fact, speculation took place very widely. Though the details are very hazy, perhaps 190 separate joint-stock projects were launched in 1719 and 1720, with a collective nominal capital of £93.6 million by one report, £300 million by another, an unprecedented level

---

[4] For detailed accounts of the scheme see Dickson, *Financial Revolution*, chapters 5–6; J. Carswell, *The South Sea Bubble* (revised edn, Stroud, 1993). J. G. Sperling, *The South Sea Company: An Historical Essay and Bibliographical Finding List* (Boston, MA, 1962) is an invaluable guide to much of the available literature.

[5] Historical Manuscripts Commission [hereafter HMC], *Calendar of the Manuscripts of the Marquis of Bath*, III (1908), 489.

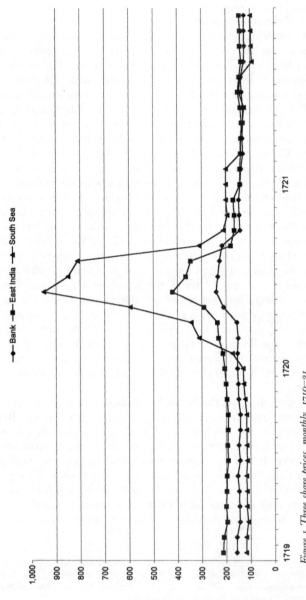

Figure 1 Three share prices, monthly, 1719–21
Source: L. D. Neal, The Rise of Financial Capitalism: International Capital Markets in the Age of Reason (Cambridge, 1990), 234.

of activity.[6] Most were very fanciful, never raised much money and sunk quickly without trace, the passage of the so-called Bubble Act in June 1720 and the issuing of writs against four of them in August effectively putting an end to such a frenzy.[7]

I turn now to consider three commonplace views which show the types of misunderstandings and myopia the Bubble has been prey to: first, that investors came from far and wide, but blindly left behind all reason and prudence, scepticism and caution; second, that it produced considerable social mobility by enriching many and impoverishing more still; and, third, that its collapse led to widespread and profound economic dislocation.

It is not hard to find contemporary expressions of each of these views, views that have proved highly resilient. In March 1720, even before the scheme had been approved, Robert Harley, the earl of Oxford, was told by his daughter that 'The town is quite mad about the South Sea, some losers, many great gainers, one can hear nothing else talked of.'[8] By May his son reported that 'The madness of stock-jobbing is inconceivable. This wildness was beyond my thought' and in the following month that 'The demon of stock-jobbing is the genius of this place. This fills all hearts, tongues, and thoughts, and nothing is so like Bedlam as the present humour which has seized all parties, Whigs, Tories, Jacobites, Papists, and all sects.'[9] The social mobility bemoaned was especially of the accumulation of fortunes by those of lowly and foreign birth and the loss of wealth and place by old families. The *Worcester Post-Man* newspaper, for example, reported that 'a certain Wharfinger ... has gain'd 15,000 l. ... by selling South-Sea', that the Canton of Berne made £1 million by trading in South Sea stock, and that 'Mrs Oldfield and Mrs Porter, the two celebrated Actresses, have quitted the Stage, having made their Fortunes by South-Sea-Stock'.[10] After the event, Sir Gilbert Heathcote, former lord mayor of London and a commercial and financial colossus, 'was sorry to see great Estates acquired by Miscreants, who, twelve Months ago, were not fit to be

---

[6] A. Hammond, *A Modest Apology, Occasion'd by the Late Unhappy Turn of Affairs, with Relation to Publick Credit* (1721), 28; *Historical Register*, 5 (1720), 290–6. Very little evidence about these companies survives. W. R. Scott provides information on the advertised capitalisation of 111 of them, totalling £221,118,000: *The Constitution and Finance of English, Scottish and Irish Joint-Stock Companies to 1720* (3 vols., Cambridge, 1910–12), III, 445–58. Actual amounts raised are unknown, but after most were suppressed by the Bubble Act it was claimed that 'no less than a Million and a half ... will be lost': *Northampton Mercury*, 27 June 1720, 107.

[7] The Bubble Act was, therefore, a cause of the financial crisis not, as is often thought, a consequence.

[8] HMC, *The Manuscripts of His Grace the Duke of Portland*, v (1899), 593.

[9] *Ibid.*, 599.

[10] 25 Mar.–1 Apr. 1720, 2; 24 June–1 July 1720, 3; 30 Sept.–7 Oct. 1720, 5.

Valets to the Gentlemen they have ruin'd'.[11] That the pricking of the Bubble was ruinous to the whole economy is similarly well attested. Contemporaries frequently remarked that the confusions of the corporate economy reverberated across the nation quickly and generally. By one report, for example,

> What I reckon the Evil, which affects the Nation in general, is the Decay and Loss of private Credit; which is absolutely necessary to carry on Commerce, to prevent the Nation's losing Millions every Year, to support the Government, to pay the Proprietor of the Funds his Interest, the Landed-Man his Rent, to set the Manufacturer at work, and clothe and feed the Poor.[12]

If the effects of the stock market collapse crossed different sectors of the economy this was also held to have taken place quickly and to have continued for some months. So, for example, the government was told in October 1720 that 'the scarcity of money is a general complaint' and the earl of Oxford in February 1721 that 'paper credit languishes ... All credit in trade is stopped.'[13]

These powerfully expressed views were, however, sometimes founded on quicksand. The first point, which has often been forgotten, though Dickson made it clear, is that the South Sea scheme was subjected to considerable debate from an early date. Most obviously the Bank of England's counter-proposals gained support in both the Commons and the Lords, such that the South Sea scheme suffered from searching criticism both inside and outside of parliament well *before* it was given statutory form on 7 April 1720. In the Commons there were significant divisions against the proposals, though we lack details of the debates to know just what happened. In the Lords it was complained on 4 April that the South Sea Company's proposal 'was unjust in its nature, and might prove fatal in its consequences; since it seemed calculated for the enriching of a few, and the impoverishing of a great many, and not only made way for, but countenanced and authorised the fraudulent and pernicious practice of Stock-jobbing'.[14] Here Lord North and Grey was repeating a critique that had been well developed by two MPs outside the Commons. The best known of these was by Sir Richard Steele, first in *The Crisis of Property*, then in *A Nation a Family* and lastly in his periodical *The Theatre*, each produced early in 1720. In the last he warned of the risks to public creditors of exchanging their assets for South Sea stock. He doubted that the Company had good

[11] *Historical Register*, 5 (1720), 382.
[12] *Considerations on the Present State of the Nation, as to Publick Credit, Stocks, the Landed and Trading Interests* (1720), 3–4.
[13] Public Record Office, SP 35/23/104; HMC, *Portland*, v, 614.
[14] *The Parliamentary History of England*, ed. W. Cobbett (1714–22), VII (1811), col. 646.

trading prospects and, consequently, believed that 'the Managers of this Stock will be ... like the Bank at a Gaming-Table, who sit in greater Security, and swallow by insensible degrees the Cash of the unfortunate Adventurers round the Board'. He was sure that the whole scheme was nothing but 'a bulky Phantom'.[15] Steele's pen was characteristically powerful, but like as not it rested upon the hard thinking and tireless arithmetic of Archibald Hutcheson, who had for several years made detailed enquiries into the national debt and become a backbencher of considerable knowledge and weight on the subject. At the end of March 1720, for example, he produced a pamphlet attacking the South Sea scheme, concluding that 'there is no real Foundation for the present, much less for the further expected, high Price of South-Sea Stock'.[16] Steele and Hutcheson were far from lone voices, for a number of pamphlets complained that because the Company's trading prospects were poor, public creditors could be tempted to surrender their original rights only by share prices being manipulated upwards, what contemporaries called stock-jobbing. As one concluded on 8 March 1720, 'it is pretty certain the Nation will be deceived if they trust to the *South-Sea* Company's Generosity to the Annuitants'.[17]

Clearly the weaknesses of the South Sea scheme were carefully detailed in February and March 1720, before it gained statutory authority. Those criticisms were powerfully and widely voiced, such that those who embraced the scheme would often have had to set aside such criticisms or been persuaded of the merits of the Company's proposal. Doubtless avarice and dreams of luxury played their part in encouraging people to invest in the scheme, but other motives were surely at work as well. One was that for a time the scheme looked like a legitimate and sensible investment. For *several* months the gradually rising share price drew in investors, and that was fact not fiction. Just as important, the governor of the Company was the king, the scheme had been championed by the chancellor of the Exchequer and endorsed by parliament, and even some 'professional' investors invested in it, including the Bank of England, the East India Company and the Million Bank. With such weighty supporters was it really so foolish of the wider public to embrace it given the information they had? Indeed,

---

[15] *The Theatre*, ed. J. Loftis (Oxford, 1962), 8 Mar. 1720, 89.

[16] 'Some Calculations Relating to the Proposals Made by the South-Sea Company, and the Bank of England, to the House of Commons; Shewing, the Loss to the New Subscribers, at the Several Rates in the Said Computations', in A. Hutcheson, *A Collection of Treatises Relating to the National Debts & Funds ... and also a Collection of Treatises Relating to the South-Sea Stock and Scheme* (1721), 8.

[17] *A Further Examination and Explanation of the South-Sea Company's Scheme*, 2nd edn (1720), 35.

investing in it was partly a patriotic and a constitutional act – one for the good of buoying a scheme to reduce national burdens. For sure other motives were also at work. Lady Pembroke, for example, complained that 'nobody likes the thing yet ... estates are got by it' and so the already financially strapped duke of Portland invested heavily, 'thinking to retrieve himself by the South Sea' but only succeeded in completing his ruin.[18] Yet the perilous basis of the rising share price was appreciated early, with the mob insulting new coaches in the ring at Hyde Park in April with 'the Cry of *South-Sea-Stock, Stock-Jobbers,* & c.'.[19] Moreover, many investors were fully aware that the share price had to peak and, at least, stagnate at some point, so that what was critical was selling at the right time or, more realistically, not selling at the wrong time. As Alexander Pope noted in late September 1720: 'Most people thought the time wou'd come, but no man prepar'd for it; no man consider'd it would come *like a Thief in the night.*'[20] This element of gambling may not only have been widely appreciated but even relished. Indeed, the distinction sometimes drawn between 'rational' investment and 'irrational' gambling is not very robust; buying stock could be undertaken for reasons of consumption as well as of investment.[21] Certainly there is evidence of cautious investors selling up before the slide of share prices set in during August, most notably the duchess of Marlborough, Jacob Tonson the publisher and Thomas Guy the bookseller – though sadly those many public creditors who embraced the scheme and surrendered their annuities were unable to do the same because the Company only issued their stock to trade on 30 December 1720. Investing, therefore, was undertaken for a range of reasons, some of which were credible. Other potential investors, perhaps persuaded by the likes of Steele and Hutcheson, gave the whole affair a wide berth, possibly in significant numbers. There were those who lacked 'Courage or Ability' as one newspaper put it; and perhaps many were like Harley's daughter who was very clear that 'It is being very unfashionable not to be in the South Sea. I am sorry to say, I am out of fashion.'[22]

Looking again at Figure 1, it is clear that if you had invested in the Company in January 1720 and held fast through the Bubble to the end of December then your holdings would have risen in value by 50 per

[18] *The Wentworth Papers 1705–1739, Selected from the Private and Family Correspondence of Thomas Wentworth, Lord Raby,* ed. J. J. Cartwright (1883), 450.

[19] F. Harris, *A Passion for Government: The Life of Sarah Duchess of Marlborough* (Oxford, 1991), 228; *Worcester Post-Man,* no. 564, 8–15 Apr. 1720, 3.

[20] *The Correspondence of Alexander Pope,* ed. G. Sherburn, II: *1719–1728* (Oxford, 1956), 53.

[21] G. Clark, *Betting on Lives: The Culture of Life Insurance in England, 1695–1775* (Manchester, 1999).

[22] *Northampton Mercury,* 27 June 1720, 103; HMC, *Portland,* v, 593.

cent, an excellent rate of return. The effect of the Bubble on stock-holders, in other words, rested heavily upon the specific timing of investment decisions. And here it is reasonable to suppose that few invested heavily after the peak in prices was clearly over, say from early August. Moreover, if the Bubble mainly entailed losses for those who bought or obtained shares in the rise of March to June they were not left asset-less when the Company's share price collapsed in the autumn. A further refinement to this point is that as the Company expanded the number of its shares in the market through the four money subscriptions (or stock offers) so it asked for an initial payment followed by a number of subsequent payments spread over months and years. So, for example, John Gay the poet bought £10,000 of stock in the third subscription in June 1720 by making an immediate payment of £1,000 which was to be followed by nine further payments of £1,000 spread over nearly five years. With the collapse of the scheme in the autumn of 1720 such commitments were cancelled and share owners issued with new stock at no cost. Gay therefore only ever paid for one tenth of his investment, of which he recovered £400. This was a loss to be sure, and though in July his paper worth was said to have been £20,000, his real loss should properly be put at £600. Quite what fraction of his wealth this represented is unknown, but again many investors would have committed only some of their funds to the scheme – much of their wealth was held in other forms. In terms of proportions, though not of absolutes, this is probably the order of magnitude of losses of most investors in the scheme.[23] Obviously such losses did not simply disappear into the ether, they filled the pockets of the well informed, the duplicitous and the lucky, perhaps to be hoarded, more likely to be spent and invested. Inevitably one person's loss was another's gain.

Cases such as Gay's can be multiplied. So, for example, though it is often said that Sir Isaac Newton lost £20,000 in the Bubble the evidence to support this is very inconclusive and certainly he was not immiserated by it.[24] Similarly the Canton of Berne did not make £1 million out of the Bubble, but kept its holding, which dated back to a loan it had made in 1710.[25] Is it, however, possible to get beyond this case-by-case approach to uncover who bought into the company and how much they committed? It is not possible to answer that with any precision, for much evidence has not survived and that which has often looks

---

[23] D. Noakes, *John Gay: A Profession of Friendship* (Oxford, 1995), 311–13.

[24] For an example of the report see J. K. Galbraith, *A Short History of Financial Euphoria* (Harmondsworth, 1994), 44. Its perilous basis is made clear in R. S. Westfall, *Never at Rest: A Biography of Isaac Newton* (Cambridge, 1990), 861–2, and *The Correspondence of Isaac Newton*, VII: *1718–1727*, ed. A. R. Hall and L. Tilling (Cambridge, 1977), 96–7.

[25] Dickson, *Financial Revolution*, 280.

suspect, but early in 1721 the House of Lords received details of the four money subscriptions. We can begin by looking at Table 1.

Table 1 *The South Sea Company's four money subscriptions (stock issues), 1720*

	Stock issued	Total cost, £	Number of subscribers	Average total to pay £	Average first payment, £
1st, 14 April	2,250,000	6,750,000	1,473	4,582	917
2nd, 29 April	1,500,000	6,000,000	1,786	3,359	336
3rd, 17 June	5,000,000	50,000,000	5,135	8,569	857
4th, 24 August	1,250,000	12,500,000	2,590	4,633	927

Sources: House of Lords RO, Parchment Collection, B57–63; P. G. M. Dickson, *The Financial Revolution in England: A Study in the Development of Public Credit, 1688–1756* (1967), 124–5.

A number of points arise from this. The first is that investors in these issues were committing very substantial sums – the averages do not hide a long tail of small subscribers. Consequently, at a time when the annual income of prosperous merchants was reckoned in hundreds not thousands of pounds, when clergymen typically enjoyed incomes of £60 and army and navy officers usually little more, it is clear that initial investors in the subscriptions were from the very wealthiest members of society, rarely from the middling sort and probably never from the base of society. Second it is clear, as has long been recognised, that the scheme was underpinned by massive backing by the political elite – in the first subscription the royal family put down for 40,000 shares, and Stanhope and Sunderland, the leading ministers in the government, 4,000 each. As against that, only 6 per cent of investors in this first subscription were women, well short of the 20 per cent figure for women's holdings in loans of the Bank of England and East India Companies at much the same time.[26] The dominant impression gained by looking at the first three subscriptions is of their political complexion, from the royal family, through the peerage, senior judiciary and MPs to members of the urban and county elites, all translating *some* of their considerable wealth into South Sea stock. As Dickson has shown, around three-quarters of members of the Commons and the Lords were subscribers.[27]

It is worth remembering that the first three subscriptions were directly controlled by lists kept by the Company's twenty-nine directors, by its sub and deputy governor and through a handful of members of the government – just thirty-five individuals for the third and largest subscription. Each of these was given a finite amount of stock to distribute, such that to invest required not only substantial funds, but

[26] *Ibid.*, 282.
[27] *Ibid.*, 107–8.

also connections and introductions, condemning even some high-status individuals to disappointment. Of course, a secondary market in the stock issued by the first three subscriptions developed, but only the fourth was placed on the open market, though even here investors were likely to have been people of considerable substance. Where investors more generally were involved was with the exchange by public creditors of their annuities for lower-bearing South Sea assets. Even so, the direct evidence supports one contemporary view, voiced in October 1720, that 'The loss would fall chiefly on the persons of quality.'[28] Put another way, contemporary reports of the hurly burly of Exchange Alley in 1720 need to be treated sceptically, indeed too many investors pursuing too few shares might cause such bustle. No hard evidence survives of the volume of shares being traded, only of their price.

From this pattern of investment activity there is good reason to question whether the Bubble produced considerable social mobility. Certainly cases of fortunes being made or lost can be found, but like as not this tended to be within a fairly narrow section of society. Again for want of evidence it is unclear how common gains and losses were, though given the close relationship between land and status some indications are provided by considering what was happening to the land market. Looking at land prices there initially seems to have been a significant effect. Clay has pieced together tidbits of information to conclude that in 1720 there was 'an extraordinary explosion of prices' but that 'These unprecedented prices lasted no longer than the speculative boom in South Sea securities', a view confirmed by Habakkuk.[29] Such short-term price variations were caused by increasing demand for land from those who had seen their paper fortunes rise in London, not least amongst directors of the South Sea Company itself, and an unwillingness amongst the landed to sell. That unwillingness was partly socially driven, partly consequent upon the growth of the legal device of strict settlements since the Restoration. This can usefully be put in the context of evidence of transactions implied by deed registrations in Middlesex and the East and West Ridings of Yorkshire, though as this is of numbers of deeds registered rather than the value or acreage of land exchanged, it needs to be interpreted cautiously. In Middlesex, annual deed registrations rose continuously and by 122 per cent between 1715 and 1720. There was a decline of 15 per cent in 1721, but from 1722 the upward march of numbers was resumed. In the Yorkshire, by contrast, a rise of 48 per cent lasted from 1716 to 1719, and was followed

---

[28] HMC, *The Manuscripts of the Earl of Dartmouth* (1887), 326.

[29] C. Clay, 'The Price of Freehold Land in the Later Seventeenth and Early Eighteenth Centuries', *Economic History Review*, 27 (1974), 177; J. Habakkuk, *Marriage, Debt and the Estates System: English Landownership, 1650–1950* (Oxford, 1994), 510–11.

by a fall of 6 per cent in 1720 and two more years of stagnation. In neither Middlesex nor the Yorkshire does the Bubble appear to have led to a collapse of the land market and in the former, where the effects were probably most direct, the consequences were distinctly ephemeral.[30] Such evidence is, of course, quite general but it can be complemented with much more specific evidence. French and Hoyle have recently concluded two detailed studies of all land transactions through the period at Slaidburn in Lancashire and Earls Colne in Essex and in both places the years around 1720 were unremarkable; land transactions were no more and no less frequent than in the early eighteenth century as a whole.[31] The suggestion from all of this is that those estates bought and sold because of the Bubble were few rather than many and, by extrapolation, that social mobility amongst the landed was limited and specific.

I turn now to consider briefly how far the South Sea Bubble disrupted the wider economy. To test this precisely ideally one would want to call upon statistics of investment, output, employment and income either side of 1720. In practice the economic indicators to hand are occasional and often imperfect, such that one is driven to use rough and ready proxies. For example, we have no year-by-year figures of gross domestic product or output, and if historians have compiled yearly indices of industrial output they have clear limitations – though it is interesting to note that neither of the main indices show the Bubble having any impact whatsoever.[32] So where can one turn? Overseas trade is one obvious resort, for the government had since 1696 collected reasonably good data here. Again they show no marked effect in 1721 or 1722, as imports and domestic exports fell by only 3 and 2 per cent respectively from 1720 to 1721 and re-exports grew by nearly 17 per cent. Excise data tell a similar tale of mixed fortunes amongst industries. For example, output of spirits and candles grew between 1720 and 1721, but fell for starch, soap and printed goods.[33] So neither trade nor

[30] F. Sheppard, V. Belcher and P. Cottrell, 'The Middlesex and Yorkshire Deeds Registries and the Study of Building Fluctuations', *London Journal*, 5 (1979), 209.

[31] H. R. French and R. W. Hoyle, 'The Land Market of a Pennine Manor: Slaidburn, 1650–1780', *Continuity and Change*, 14 (1999), 349–83. I am very grateful to Dr French for making available to me as yet unpublished research on Earls Colne.

[32] W. G. Hoffmann, *British Industry, 1700–1950* (Oxford, 1955), Table 54 (between 330–1); N. F. R. Crafts, S. J. Leybourne and T. C. Mills, 'Trends and Cycles in British Industrial Production, 1700–1913', *Journal of the Royal Statistical Society*, 152 (1989), 58. On problems of surviving evidence see J. Hoppit, 'Counting the Industrial Revolution', *Economic History Review*, 43 (1990), 173–93.

[33] E. B. Schumpeter, *English Overseas Trade Statistics 1697–1808* (Oxford, 1960), 15–16, 18; B. Mitchell, *British Historical Statistics* (Cambridge, 1988), 407, 412, 414–15; T. S. Ashton, *An Economic History of England: The Eighteenth Century* (1972), 248.

industry was universally or dramatically upset by the chaos of the summer and autumn of 1720.

For the largest sector of the economy, agriculture, statistical evidence is especially creaky for any year-by-year analysis. That said, there is no reason to suppose that the Bubble would have directly or significantly affected the agricultural economy – the harvest of 1720 was sown prior to the crisis, that of 1721 largely after it and, as ever, the weather took its own course. Hoskins judged that for wheat those harvests were 'average' and 'good' respectively.[34] Certainly prices for agricultural goods, generally low in this period, fell for many products between 1720 and 1721 – by nearly 6 per cent for wheat, 16 per cent for cattle and 22 per cent for hops for example – but whether that was caused by a slump in demand and/or a growth supply is impossible to say.[35] However, other things being equal, such falls would have increased expenditure on non-food items and lowered raw material costs for many industries, both effects helping to stimulate the wider economy.

Some indicators of the effect upon the business and investment environment are also available. For example, there was no overwhelming surge of the number of bankrupts in the wake of the Bubble. Annual totals for the three years 1719, 1720 and 1721 were 193, 206 and 226, a rise to be sure, but hardly a meteoric one. Statistically speaking, for bankruptcy the long-forgotten crises of 1710–11 and 1727–9 were more significant.[36] Similarly, Muldrew's important study of everyday credit and court action over debt provides no evidence of the impact of the Bubble.[37] That said, there is some statistical evidence that domestically liquidity was sought as the Bubble burst, but it is not very compelling. This is most clearly suggested by the rise in the price of gold, the once traditional bolt hole for the nervous investors. In the year prior to the summer of 1720 it was very steady at £3.90 an ounce, but for the last four months of the year was generally 5 per cent higher.[38]

By available statistical data there is reason to doubt the depth and breadth of the economic effect of the Bubble within Britain. Trade, industry and agriculture were their usual medley of success and failure. Some of the qualitative evidence suggests just the same. From complete

---

[34] W. G. Hoskins, 'Harvest Fluctuations and English Economic History, 1620–1759', *Agricultural History Review*, 16 (1968), 30.

[35] P. J. Bowden, 'Statistics', in *Agrarian History of England and Wales*, v, part ii, 1640–1750, *Agrarian Change*, ed. J. Thirsk (Cambridge, 1985), 831, 839.

[36] J. Hoppit, 'Financial Crises in Eighteenth-Century England', *Economic History Review*, 39 (1986), 47–8.

[37] C. Muldrew, *The Economy of Obligation: The Culture of Credit and Social Relations in Early Modern England* (Basingstoke, 1998), 222, 224.

[38] 'An Account of the Market Prices of Standard Gold in Bars', *Parliamentary Papers*, 1810–11, x, 197–8.

runs of the *Northampton Mercury*, *Worcester Post-Man* and *Newcastle Weekly Courant* newspapers for the period, it is clear that though all carried news drawn from the London papers of the crisis, none made note of decay or depression in local industries or trade brought on by that crisis. They reported the Bubble as very much a metropolitan phenomenon, albeit one with links to Paris and Amsterdam, and were preoccupied after October 1720 with how the government and parliament handled the catastrophe. Their silence on the local economy, though in keeping with their usual perspective, is as striking as the absence of evidence ever can be. Elsewhere one occasionally comes across positive evidence that the Bubble's provincial impact was inconsiderable. William Stout, the Lancaster merchant, noted that 'It did not afect this country much, but the Lord Lonsdall lost most of his estate.'[39] He was clear that local floods in October 1720 were much more destructive, though he did note monetary dislocation in the following year.

Apparently powerful evidence of local disruption is provided by eighty-seven petitions, submitted to the House of Commons in the parliamentary session after the Bubble, complaining in some way about the crisis. These came either from counties as a whole or from particular urban centres across Britain, from Caithness in the far north to Southampton in the south, and from Pembrokeshire in the west to Aldeburgh in the east. By the standards of the day this was a significant expression of public opinion. Moreover, the petitioners sang from the same hymn book. Birmingham, for example, complained that 'Trade amongst them is wonderfully decayed ... they want Money to carry it on, and to pay the poor Workmen for their Labour ... wholly owing to the Decay of publick Credit, occasioned by the Mismanagement, Avarice, and fatal Contrivances, of the late Directors of the *South Sea* Company.'[40] Rochester in Kent lamented 'the general Decay of Commerce, Trade, Manufactures, and publick Credit, and from the Misery and Ruin which vast Numbers of his Majesty's faithful and innocent Subjects now labour under; occasioned chiefly by the wicked and detestable Contrivances, Artifices, and Mismanagement of the late Directors of the *South Sea* Company'.[41]

There is no question that these petitions are powerful statements: their language is keen, their positions unequivocal. But they may not be quite what they seem. First, the parliament they were submitted to opened in December 1720 (and closed in July 1721) but seventy-five

---

[39] *The Autobiography of William Stout of Lancaster, 1665–1752*, ed. J. D. Marshall (Manchester, 1967), 180.

[40] *Journals of the House of Commons*, 19 (1718–21), 530.

[41] *Ibid.*, 507.

of the eighty-seven petitions were submitted in just six weeks between mid-April and late May 1721, fully nine months after the Bubble burst. Most of them immediately followed the receipt by the Commons of detailed inventories of the estates of the directors of the South Sea Company and immediately preceded the decisions begun on 26 May of how much of those estates were to be confiscated. Second, many of them employed strikingly similar language (hinting at an organised campaign) and particularly asked for the Company's directors and their cronies to be punished fully. In only two is there meaningful detail about local circumstances. Third, the signatories of the petitions were rarely groups of manufacturers or traders, much more frequently gentlemen and leading citizens, often meeting at assizes, quarter sessions or as corporations. Fourth, of the sixty-three sent by urban centres fifty-nine (94 per cent) came from parliamentary boroughs. Finally, it is interesting to note that no petitions were submitted to the House of Lords or the Privy Council. These points suggest that the petitions were reactions to the political rather than the economic aftermath of the Bubble, especially to the enquiry then underway in the Commons. They were less expressions of actual economic experience than exhortations to MPs to keep on the straight and narrow in their work of retribution and repair. This particular context has often been lost sight of, with the petitions and similar evidence frequently being read simply as statements of economic reality. But the politico-cultural consequences of the Bubble were driven by their own imperatives that were attached to the economy in a very confusing way.

There are good reasons to doubt that the Bubble generally disrupted the British economy in the eighteen months after it burst in the late summer of 1720. Much data suggests that at that general level its effects were relatively modest and that other apparently powerful evidence of disruption was often politically inspired. But undeniably there was a profound crisis that turned some peoples' lives upside down. Some idea of the particular effects is provided by looking three exchange rates in the period (see Figure 2). From this it is clear that the London on Paris rate changed dramatically from late 1719 to mid-1720. Ashton long ago pointed out that sharp shifts in exchange rates often indicated financial crises – in his words 'one of the earliest signs of impending crisis was often ... an adverse movement of the foreign exchanges. Paradoxical as it may appear ... when crisis came there was usually a sudden ... upward, or "favourable" movement', which he explained in terms of the demand for holding sterling in cash.[42] Certainly the graph of exchange rates needs to be put in the context of reports from contemporaries noting the flow of English funds into Paris and the

---

[42] T. S. Ashton, *Economic Fluctuations in England, 1700–1800* (Oxford, 1959), 113.

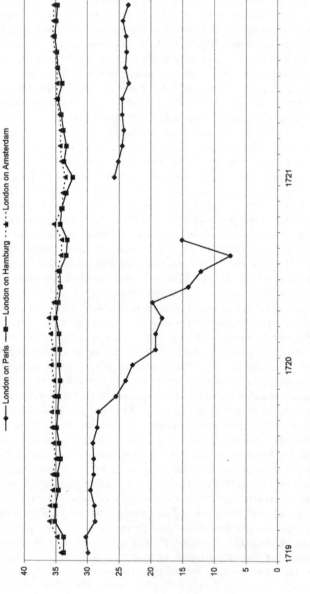

Figure 2 Three exchange rates, monthly, 1719–21 (various denominations)
Source. J. J. McCusker, *Money and Exchange in Europe and America, 1660–1775* (1978), 58, 77, 95.

Mississippi scheme in 1719 and the return of much of those funds and some French capital besides into London and the South Sea scheme in 1720. In June 1720, for example, it was reported that 'Abundance of Mississippians and other Forreigners are come over to Negotiate in Exchange-Alley.'[43] Though this graph apparently shows no particular effects with regards to Amsterdam or Hamburg, with which London was closely connected at the time, this is partly a question of the scale used, for both rates fell by about 7 or 8 per cent through much of 1720 and rose about 6 per cent from January to October 1721. Again, this bears out contemporary comments about the international movement of funds, of the flow of investments into Britain as the South Sea scheme unfolded and a flow out after the Bubble had burst, though there were also reports of some English money being invested in Dutch schemes. Deposits at the Bank of Amsterdam, which we would expect to have been a bolthole for nervous investors seeking solidity, rose from 20 million guilders in 1720 to 29 million in 1721, though of course much of this would have been from domestic Dutch investors.[44] Such international flows would have influenced liquidity within overseas trade and it is interesting to note that within England numbers of merchants going bankrupt did double between 1719 and 1721.[45] If the Bubble did not disrupt general trading patterns, the flow and ebb of funds across the Channel helps to demonstrate, as Neal has shown, one particular form of credit – international settlements between major financial centres – that was deeply disordered in 1720 and 1721.[46] But, of course, such disorder was only partly provoked by events in London. The failure of the Mississippi scheme in Paris is well known, but there was also a rash of speculative insurance flotations in Amsterdam and northern Germany in 1720 that foundered. In part the South Sea Bubble was an international as much as a national phenomenon, to the extent that its label is rather misleading.

Problems within the sphere of international finance were linked to those of domestic high finance. Well-grounded reports can be found of runs on some banks and of others shutting shop, even going bankrupt. In September 1720 it was said that 'four goldsmiths walked off', the South Sea Company's own bank, the Sword Blade Company, closed its doors, in October the bank of Midford and Martins in Cornhill

[43] *Worcester Post-Man*, no. 572, 3–10 June 1720, 3.

[44] J. G. van Dillen, 'De Amsterdamasche Wisselbank, Mede Gedeele Door', *Economisch-Historisch Jaarboek* (1925), 245–8.

[45] Public Record Office, B4/3.

[46] L. D. Neal, *The Rise of Financial Capitalism: International Capital Markets in the Age of Reason* (Cambridge, 1990), chapter 5; E. S. Schubert, 'Innovation, Debts, and Bubbles: International Integration of Financial Markets in Western Europe, 1688–1720', *Journal of Economic History*, 48 (1988), 299–306.

reportedly collapsed, perhaps owing £170,000 to some 400 creditors, and in December Wanley, a banker at Temple Bar, allegedly lost £100,0000 in the chaos.[47] It is certainly notable that numbers of suicides in London were 40 per cent above trend levels in 1721.[48] Collapses of goldsmiths and bankers must have strained liquidity beyond London, but much depended upon the specific connections involved. So, Bishop Nicolson was told (probably wrongly) that Ulster 'sensibly felt' the disruption and that by early December 'Our Trade, of all kinds, is at a stand', and if Cork was affected Dublin was not.[49]

The Bubble's effects were not generally felt across Britain and Ireland partly because of the continued symbolic support for the Bank of England from the king and prince of Wales (via Spencer Compton, speaker of the Commons), partly because in turn the Bank of England made strenuous efforts to support credit and partly because the Treasury raised the interest on Exchequer bills to build confidence in them as financial instruments. Similarly, in Scotland the Bank of Scotland acted early to stop a drain of coin to London, such that the collapse of the Bubble does not appear to have had much impact there.[50]

The argument so far has been three-fold. First, that people invested in the Bubble for a variety of reasons, not mere acquisitiveness, and were often more aware of the perils involved than is usually thought. Second, that probably most purchasers of new South Sea stock came from society's patrician heights in both town and county, such that the social mobility between winners and losers involved a narrow band of society. Finally, that the Bubble's economic effects were more specific yet more international than is often allowed. Undeniably it was a catastrophe, but it was blown by particular people and its bursting hit particular people. Fundamentally the Bubble was about high politics, high finance and high society.

These three points are not especially original, but they have often been lost sight of. They also pose something of a problem, for how is the huge impact that the Bubble had at the time and in subsequent interpretations to be explained? If, so to speak, some of the Bubble's

---

[47] HMC, *Bath*, III, 489; *Northampton Mercury*, 31 Oct. 1720, 320, 12 Dec. 1720, 391.

[48] London *Bills of Mortality*, counts of those said to have 'made away themselves', 'self murder'd' or 'kill'd themselves'. M. Macdonald and T. R. Murphy argue, in *Sleepless Souls: Suicide in Early Modern England* (Oxford, 1990), 276–8, that this surge in numbers of suicides in the wake of the Bubble was a decisive final stage of a very gradual shift in attitudes away from viewing suicide only as self-murder.

[49] F. G. James, 'Derry in the Time of George I: Selections from Bishop Nicolson's Letters, 1718–22', *Ulster Journal of Archaeology*, 3rd series, 16 (1953), 181–2; L. M. Cullen, 'Economic Development, 1691–1750', in *A New History of Ireland*, IV: *Eighteenth Century, 1691–1800*, ed. T. W. Moody and W. E. Vaughan (Oxford, 1986), 144–5. I am grateful to David Hayton for advice on this point.

[50] R. Saville, *Bank of Scotland: A History 1695–1995* (Edinburgh, 1996), 89.

stature has been argued away, why did it make such an impact upon contemporaries and why does it continue to be provide such an alluring reference point? I turn now to consider how this has taken place, to do which it is helpful (if necessarily artificial) to distinguish four phases in the development of perceptions of the South Sea Bubble. These phases differed in scale and significance, but separating them allows the history of the myths of the South Sea Bubble to be sketched.

The first phase constituted the reactions of 1720 and 1721, which, in turn, took two main forms. The first was concerned with the political corruption and ill judgement that had allowed the South Sea Company to win out over the Bank in early 1720 and then manipulate its share price in the spring and summer. The Bubble was in considerable measure caused by a dramatic failure of the political process to act for the public good, thereby providing ammunition for opponents of the Hanoverian succession and Whig one-party rule (the religious credentials of which were already suspect to their opponents because of the recent repeal of the treasured Schism and Occasional Conformity acts, as well as Convocation's suspension).[51] Much of this reaction concentrated upon those human frailties among particular individuals that had allowed the innocent majority to be misled. Corruption and cronyism were blasted, its perpetrators hunted down in a passionate quest for punishment. But the political reaction also involved questions of power and property, for at its heart the Company's scheme aimed to undermine the value and integrity of earlier holdings of the national debt. From one perspective 'The owners ... of this Property, who step out of the Rank of common Subjects, with their Fortunes in their Hands, and gave them to the Faith of the Legislature, are exempt from any Act of Legislature.'[52] But proponents of the scheme had to argue that such property was not sacrosanct: 'There are in England various Properties equally secure with us; and yet we daily see the Legislature breaking in upon them, and giving the Possessors valuable Considerations; as in the Case of making Rivers Navigable, Publick Roads, Erecting of Forts, and other Publick Edifices.'[53] Put most simply, this central part of the South Sea scheme was absolutely about liberty and property and consequently, given their totemic significance, could not but cause a storm. But it also involved profound questions about definitions of 'public' and 'private' interest, about monopolies and individual rights and queried the distinction hitherto all too happily employed between the landed and the monied interest. And if the capacity for share prices to fluctuate markedly was confirmed by the

[51] J. Hoppit, *A Land of Liberty? England 1689–1727* (Oxford, 2000), 235.
[52] R. Steele, *The Crisis of Property* (1720), 18–19.
[53] *The Crisis of Honesty: Being an Answer to the Crisis of Property* (1720), 9.

Bubble, underlining its peculiarity as wealth, ideas that land had an intrinsic value were also shattered by the surge in its price in 1720, it too 'had taken its Frisk with the rest'.[54] In short, the Bubble blurred many traditional categories of political action and expectation, provoking considerable angst in the process.

Political reactions to the Bubble took place alongside what can best be called moral ones (there was no clear distinction between them). A good deal of this was explicitly religious in language and sentiment, with many clergymen blasting the whole affair from the pulpit. Of more lasting significance has been the satiric reaction. It is a commonplace that the period between the Restoration and the second quarter of the eighteenth century was a golden age of satire and, given the commercial basis of publishing at the time, the Bubble provided its practitioners with an irresistible target. Poems and ballads, plays and pamphlets, engravings and woodcuts were all employed. For many nothing better encapsulates the Bubble than Hogarth's famous representation, completed in 1721. It is indeed a compelling, articulate and rich work that has powerfully influenced interpretations of the Bubble. As Plates 2 and 3 show, other remarkable visual satires were also produced, though it is worth noting that domestic productions were numerically dwarfed by those from Holland and might, as in Plate 3, simply translate foreign engravings into an English setting.[55] To literary satirists the Bubble was no less of a godsend, from Thomas d'Urfey's 'Hubble bubble' ballad, to Jonathan Swift's 'The run upon the bankers', John Gay's mock panegyric to the goldsmith Mr Thomas Snow and Alexander Pope's later 'Epistle to Lord Bathurst'.

Considerable ink has been spilt interpreting this outpouring, not merely as art and literature but as windows into public opinion.[56] Undoubtedly this route has achieved much, but there are obvious dangers because satire is both polemic and caricature. It makes no pretence to factual objectivity or principled subjectivity, for it is an argument and a hope: as Defoe baldly put it 'The end of Satyr is reformation.'[57] But what exactly needed reforming? Bishop Berkeley was sure that 'The South-Sea affair ... is not the original evil, or the

---

[54] *A True State of the Contracts Relating to the Third Money-Subscription Taken by the South-Sea Company* (1721), 12–13; J. G. A. Pocock, *Virtue, Commerce and History: Essays on Political Thought and History, Chiefly in the Eighteenth Century* (Cambridge, 1985), chapter 6.

[55] For the Dutch prints see A. H. Cole, *The Great Mirror of Folly (Het Groote Tafereel der Dwaashed): An Economic-Bibliographic Study* (Boston, MA, 1949). The English prints are discussed in M. Hallett, *The Spectacle of Difference: Graphic Satire in the Age of Hogarth* (1999), 57–68.

[56] The best studies are S. Stratmann, *'South Sea's at Best a Mighty* BUBBLE.' *The Literization of a National Trauma* (Trier, 1996), and T. Seymour, 'Literature and the South Sea Bubble' (PhD thesis, University of North Carolina, 1955).

[57] D. Defoe, *The True-Born Englishman and Other Writings*, ed. P. N. Furbank and W. R. Owens (1997), 24.

Plate 2 Anon., 'The Bubblers Medley', 1720. Copyright Guildhall Library, Corporation of London.

great source of our misfortunes; it is but the natural effect of those principles which for many years have been propagated with great industry.'[58] In this analysis, which was made by others, the South Sea

[58] *The Works of George Berkeley Bishop of Cloyne*, ed. T. E. Jessop, IV (1953), 84.

Plate 3 B. Picart, 'A Monument Dedicated to Posterity in Commemoration of Ye Incredible Folly Transacted in the Year 1720', 1720. Copyright Guildhall Library, Corporation of London.

Bubble could be viewed as a symptom of wider problems, where luxury had infected society and atheism was rampant. One sign of that was the alarming rise of highway robberies about London and of masquerades and a debauched stage within – it is ironic that Steele's attacks on the South Sea scheme were in his periodical *The Theatre* that defended the stage from moralisers.[59] It is worth recalling that in March 1721 there was a Privy Council proclamation against the so-called Hell Fire clubs, that in April a bill against blasphemy was introduced into the Lords, though it was not enacted, and that at much the same time a campaign was underway by justices in Westminster to suppress gaming houses.[60] Thus, it might appear providential that the plague broke out in southern France in the autumn of 1720, prompting quarantine measures to keep it and God's wrath at bay. There were, therefore, a range of issues of concern to the socially and religiously nervous in 1720 and 1721 and the Bubble needs to be put in that wider moral-reform context. Contemporary reactions to the Bubble were

---

[59] Hoppit, *A Land of Liberty?*, 449, 485.

[60] *London Gazette*, 25–9 Mar. 1721; *Failed Legislation, 1660–1800: Extracted from the Commons and Lords Journals*, ed. J. Hoppit (1997), 296 (57.025); R. B. Shoemaker, *Prosecution and Punishment: Petty Crime and the Law in London and Rural Middlesex, c. 1660–1725* (Cambridge, 1991), 265.

often less about the Bubble itself than much wider perceived failings in the politico-religious order. That is essential in understanding the force of reactions to it.

The second phase of the development of myths of the Bubble took place in 1771, when the term 'South Sea Bubble' was used for the first time in the original edition of the *Encyclopaedia Britannica* (volume III, p. 632).[61] Until then the main crisis of 1720 was invariably called the South Sea 'scheme' or 'affair' – and through the whole eighteenth century the phrase 'South Sea Bubble' was never used in the title of any published work, including, it would seem, Hogarth's engraving. The bubbles of 1720 – lower case and plural – were those 190 or so joint-stock ventures mentioned earlier. In 1720 and 1721 only very rarely was the South Sea scheme called a bubble at all, and in the many works I have consulted it was *never* called the South Sea Bubble. Consequently, the 'South Sea Bubble' is not in Johnson's *Dictionary*, Smolett's *History* or Postlethwayt's *Universal Dictionary of Trade and Commerce*, all published in the 1750s. What happened in 1771 was that a concept was invented to make sense of the confused events of 1720, but ever since this single label has suggested a unity to what were three different if interrelated events: the South Sea scheme, the 190 joint-stock bubbles and the crisis in international finance that began in Paris. Furthermore, words matter here because of what they hint at. A bubble is all puff, waiting to be pricked whereas a scheme suggests more care, though perhaps no less artifice. Contemporaries were clear that the 190 bubbles were mere ephemera, but that the South Sea scheme was much more substantial and serious. So to speak of the South Sea Bubble involves anachronism and elision, avoiding the care taken at the time to distinguish very different things.

The third phase in the unfolding mythology of the South Sea Bubble took place in the second quarter of the nineteenth century when the events of 1720 became the subject of historical enquiry or reflection. If this partly rested upon earlier work by the likes of Adam Anderson, who had been a clerk of the South Sea Company in 1720, and by Archdeacon Coxe in his study of Walpole, there began in 1825, the powerful tradition of comparing financial crises of the day (1825–6 was very severe) to that of 1720 – a connection encouraged by the repeal of the Bubble Act in that year.[62] In this view there is a long history of

---

[61] Given the Scottish origins of the *Encyclopaedia* it is interesting to note that the Scottish economy was showing distinct signs of over-heating in 1771 and suffered a major collapse in credit in the following year. See H. Hamilton, 'The Failure of the Ayr Bank, 1772', *Economic History Review*, 8 (1955–6), 405–17. I am very grateful to Peter Marshall for this suggestion.

[62] A. Anderson, *An Historical and Chronological Deduction of the Origin of Commerce* (2 vols., 1764); W. Coxe, *Memoirs of the Life and Administration of Sir Robert Walpole, Earl of Orford* (3

crises of which the Bubble was the first British instance (it is invariably linked with the Dutch Tulip mania of 1637 and the French Mississippi debacle of 1719-20). This link between the past and the present was explicitly made in the title of an anonymous book of that year: *The South Sea Bubble, and the Numerous Fraudulent Projects to Which it Gave Rise in 1720, Historically Detailed as a Beacon to the Unwary against Modern Schemes ... Equally Visionary and Nefarious*. This approach reached a climax in Charles Mackay's famous book of 1841, *Extraordinary Popular Delusions and the Madness of Crowds*, a work that has been in print for much of the past 160 years and which has inspired many successors, including J. K. Galbraith.[63] Such an approach is prey to two objections: once again the anachronism and the elision of identifying a single and unitary Bubble; and a certain teleology and de-contextualisation. In such approaches the peculiarities of the South Sea Bubble tend to be passed over, and its modernity and timelessness emphasised. It might almost be said that the Bubble has been a victim of a type of Whig history.

Mackay and the railway mania of the 1840s helped to embed the South Sea Bubble in both dictionaries and a wider literary consciousness. Indeed, it soon began to resonate more widely, and this constituted the final stage in the mythologising of the Bubble. As is well known, concerns to avoid indebtedness and bankruptcy were central to so-called middle-class values in nineteenth-century Britain.[64] In such an environment the South Sea Bubble provided a particular potent and apparently unambiguous negative exemplar in the cultural sphere. In 1847, for example, Matthew Ward completed a major oil painting called 'The South Sea Bubble, a scene at Change Alley in 1720', now owned by the Tate.[65] In 1868 the Bubble was the subject of an historical novel and had become so commonplace that in 1872 the fanciful uses of the term began in earnest with a travel book called *South Sea Bubbles*.[66] The lure of the Pacific, which was in any case very strong at this time, has often proved irresistible in this context, to the extent that the Latin American aspect of the South Sea Bubble is often

---

vols., 1798). For the crisis of 1825–6 see A. D. Gayer, W. W. Rostow and A. Schwartz, *The Growth and Fluctuation of the British Economy, 1790–1850* (2 vols., Oxford, 1953), I, 205–7. The 'Bubble Act' was not the name given to the original statute of 1720 but, once again, a much later invention.

[63] Most recently surveyed in *Great Bubbles: Reactions to the South Sea Bubble, the Mississippi Scheme and the Tulip Mania Affair*, ed. R. B. Emmett (3 vols., 2000).

[64] B. Weiss, *The Hell of the English: Bankruptcy and the Victorian Novel* (Cranbury, NJ, 1986); G. R. Searle, *Morality and the Market in Victorian Britain* (Oxford, 1998).

[65] And so was part of 'the great age of history painting': R. Strong, *And When Did You Last See Your Father? The Victorian Painter and British History* (1978), 42.

[66] W. H. Ainsworth, *The South Sea Bubble* (published in parts in 1868 and as a book in 1871); Earl of Pembroke and G. H. Kingsley, *South Sea Bubbles* (1872).

either overlooked or unknown.[67] Either way, to use the South Sea Bubble in such ways, as in Noël Coward's play, is merely allusive, merely suggestive. That would not matter, but what is being alluded to and suggested melds, often unconsciously, fact and fiction indiscriminately.

Frivolous familiarity is unlikely to be the handmaiden of good history and so it is unsurprising that for many years the South Sea Bubble has been subjected to scholarly rigour. In that sense this paper contributes to a long line of studies, stretching back to W. R. Scott in 1910-12, through Carswell and Dickson and including, since 1990, the highly rationalist accounts of Neal, Garber and Harris.[68] It has emphasised the need to approach the Bubble with an open mind: to use hindsight cautiously; to recognise the biases in contemporary evidence; to appreciate silences as well as noise; to employ appropriate concepts; to pay close attention to specific chronologies; and to place the Bubble in its full context. Too often contemporary lamentations of the Bubble have been taken at face value; too often second- or third-hand gossip has been preferred to first-hand evidence; too often vibrant satires and colourful jeremiads have been isolated from the discipline of counting; too often those aspects of the Bubble which were timeless have cast a dark shadow over its peculiarities.[69] In short, the South Sea Bubble needs to be rid of some of its myths. But such rationalism has its limits, for myths can be so powerful. As has been seen, the Bubble played a major role in the early 1720s in contemplating the consequences of subtle yet profound politico-religious changes; as a label it was invented by 'enlightened' conceptualisation; then (and ever since) it became the benchmark for moments of intense financial speculation, in the process becoming so light and airy as an idea that writers could use it almost unthinkingly. The result is that the South Sea Bubble is a highly potent symbol or mode of communication, too much part of everyday discourse for its meaning to be easily changed by a mere muttering historian.[70] After all, if the myths of the South Sea Bubble were 150 years in the making, so perhaps putting good history back in will take just as long.

---

[67] R. Edmond, *Representing the South Pacific: Colonial Discourse from Cook to Gaugin* (Cambridge, 1997).

[68] Scott, *Constitution and Finance*; Carswell, *The South Sea Bubble*; Dickson, *Financial Revolution*; Neal, *Financial Capitalism*; P. Garber, *Famous First Bubbles* (Cambridge, MA, 2000); R. Harris, 'The Bubble Act: Its Passage and its Effects on Business Organization', *Journal of Economic History*, 54 (1994), 610–27.

[69] My thinking on these issues has been greatly helped by P. U. Bonomi, *The Lord Cornbury Scandal: The Politics of Reputation in British America* (Chapel Hill, 1998).

[70] On these issues see *The Myths We Live By*, ed. R. Samuel and P. Thompson (1990).

Transactions of the RHS 12 (2002), pp. 167–221 © 2002 Royal Historical Society
DOI: 10.1017/S0080440102000063   Printed in the United Kingdom

THE PLACE OF TUDOR ENGLAND IN THE MESSIANIC VISION OF PHILIP II OF SPAIN*

The Prothero Lecture

By Geoffrey Parker

READ 4 JULY 2001

ABSTRACT. Messianic visions burgeoned simultaneously in Judaism, Christianity and Islam in the sixteenth century, directly involving sovereign rulers, and powerfully influencing international relations. This essay examines the propensity of Philip II (1556-98) to frame his policies in messianic terms, with special regard to England. It uses the Ridolfi plot (1570-1) and the Armada (1587-8) to show how the king disregarded strategic concerns, and failed to formulate fall-back strategies, because he expected God to provide a miracle to bridge the gap between means and ends. It also compares his vision with those of his Christian, Jewish and Muslim contemporaries.

MESSIANIC visions form an integral part of Judaism, Christianity and Islam because all three faiths ascribe a crucial role to a messiah (in Islam, to a Mahdi or 'rightly guided one'): a saviour or redeemer sent by God both to establish a new order characterised by justice for all and (often) to herald the end of the world. At certain times, messianic visions have become particularly prevalent; and in the sixteenth century they burgeoned simultaneously in all three faiths, directly involved sovereign rulers and powerfully influenced international relations.[1]

---

*I am very grateful for suggestions, references and corrections to Carter Findley, Matthew Goldish, Jane Hathaway and Matthew Keith at the Ohio State University; to Bethany Aram, Paul Arblaster, Cristina Borreguero Beltrán, Cornell Fleischer, Barbara Flemming, Jan Lechner, Patricia Seed, Sanjay Subrahmanyam and Robert Verdonk, who attended a symposium on 'Messianic Visions' sponsored in October 2000 at Antwerp by the Fundación Duques de Soria; and to Nicholas Canny, Pauline Croft, Wim de Groot, Norman Housley, Ann Jannetta, Santiago Martínez Hernández, John Morrill, Glyn Redworth, Stafford M. Poole, Wendell Smith, Nancy van Deusen and, above all, Juan Tazón. Maurizio Arfaioli provided wonderful assistance in securing and interpreting some Italian sources at short notice. I also learned a lot from the excellent thesis of Luz María Santamarta Lozano, 'Don Guerau de Spes en la Corte Isabelina: La documentación diplomática y el conflicto anglo-español (1568–1571)' (PhD thesis, University of Oviedo, 2001).

[1] A note on terminology is in order. Although 'messiah', from the Hebrew *mashah* (to anoint) and *mashiah* (the anointed one), appears in the Bible, recorded use of the adjective

My name is Shah Isma'il. I am God's mystery.
I am the leader of all these ghazis...
I am the living Khidr, and Jesus, son of Mary.
I am the Alexander of my contemporaries.

The Perfect Guide has arrived. Faith has been brought to all.
All the ghazis are full of joy at the coming of the seal
    of the Prophets.
A man has become a manifestation of the truth.
    Prostrate thyself!
Pander not to Satan! Adam has put on new clothes.
    God has come.[2]

Shah Isma'il, founder of the Safavid dynasty of Iran and author of
these verses, was just one of many Muslims who claimed to be the
'Mahdi' during the tenth century of the Muslim era (1494-1592 CE).
Visitors noted that Isma'il's entourage called him 'neither king nor
prince, but saint and prophet' and the success of his religious propaganda soon alarmed other Muslims, particularly his western neighbour
the Ottoman Sultan Selim, until in 1514 the two rulers clashed in battle.
After his victory, which allowed Selim to add the three holy cities of
Jerusalem, Mecca and Medina to his empire, the sultan used messianic
epithets such as 'shadow of God on earth' and *Sahib-kiran*, or 'world
conqueror', while his courtiers and chroniclers compared him with
Alexander the Great, Genghiz Khan and Tamerlane.[3] Selim's son and

'messianic' only dates from the nineteenth century in English, French and Italian; and
from the twentieth century in Dutch, German and Spanish. For an excellent discussion
of 'apocalyptic' and other terms see the introduction to *Tudor Apocalypse: Sixteenth-Century
Apocalypticism, Millennarianism and the English Reformation from John Bale to John Foxe and
Thomas Brightman*, ed. R. Bauckham (The Courtenay Library of Reformation Classics,
VIII, Abingdon, 1978).

[2] V. Minorsky, 'The poetry of Shâh Ismâ'il I', *Bulletin of the School of Oriental and African
Studies*, 10.4 (1939-42), 1006a-1053a, at pp. 1042a and 1049a, translated from the original
Turkish. The Shah's claims were indeed extreme. 'Khidr' is the mysterious 'green man'
associated by Muslims with Moses, Elijah and Alexander the Great – a sort of leprechaun
of human dimensions associated with ushering in the Mahdi. For Muslims, Jesus was
merely a prophet and not the Son of God; but since Muhammad was the 'Seal of the
Prophets', Ismail's claim to be another would outrage most other Muslims.

[3] See S. Subrahmanyam, 'Du Tage au Gange au XVIe siècle: une conjoncture
millénariste à l'échelle eurasiatique', *Annales: histoire, sciences sociales*, 61 (2001), 51-84, at
57-8; C. Fleischer, 'Mahdi, Messiah and the Last Roman Emperor: Ottoman Sovereignty
and the Intersection of Muslim, Christian and Jewish Apocalyptic' (forthcoming), 35; and
J. Hathaway, *A Tale of Two Factions: Myth, Memory, and Identity in Ottoman Egypt and Yemen*
(forthcoming), ch. 7. Another 'messiah' of this period, Sayyid Muhammed of Jaunpur,
declared himself to be the Mahdi in 900 AH/1494 CE and gained many followers in
north-west India until his death a decade later (Subrahmanyam, 'Du Tage au Gange
au XVIe siècle', 67-8). I am deeply grateful to Professors Fleischer, Hathaway and
Subrahmanyam for sharing their path-breaking work with me in advance of publication.

heir Suleiman likewise used the title *Sahib-kiran*; and in 1532 he began
to wear a special tiara with four crowns, symbolising the rule of the
last world emperor. Suleiman also welcomed histories and prophecies
that compared him with his namesake Solomon and with Alexander
the Great (to ensure the accuracy of the prophecies, Suleiman lent his
geomancer some rare apocalyptic texts from his own library.) Several
Ottoman writers hailed him as *mujaddid* ('renewer'), the eschatalogical
figure who appears in each age to 'renew' the Islamic community.[4]

The Jewish communities of medieval Spain and Portugal also looked
for a messiah, and their expulsion from the peninsula during the 1490s
heightened speculation that his appearance was imminent – both
among those who retained their faith and fled and among those who
converted to Christianity and remained. Thus Isaac Abravanel, who
composed three messianic treatises in exile in Italy, argued that redemption would occur between 1503 and 1573; while Solomon Molcho, a
Portuguese convert to Christianity who returned to Judaism and
circumcised himself, believed he had a messianic mission and went to
Regensburg in 1532 to meet the Habsburg emperor, Charles V. Molcho,
obtained a two-hour audience, during which he displayed the banner,
shield and sword that he proposed to use when he led the Jews against
Sultan Suleiman, then advancing into Hungary. He failed to convince
Charles, however, who imprisoned him, took him back to Italy in a
cage, and had him burnt at the stake.[5]

By then, many contemporaries saw Charles too as a messiah.
Burgundian court tradition, drawing on Byzantine and western imperial
precedents, included accession pageants that displayed the ruler as 'the

[4] Fleischer, 'Mahdi, Messiah', 53; Hathaway, *A Tale*; G. Necipoglu, 'Suleyman the
Magnificent and the Representation of Power in the Context of Ottoman–Hapsburg–
Papal Rivalry', in *Süleymân the Second and his Time*, ed. H. Inalcik and C. Kafadar (Istanbul,
1993), 163–94; and B. Flemming, 'Public Opinion under Sultan Süleymân', in *ibid.*, 49–
57. See also C. Fleischer, 'The Lawgiver as Messiah: The Making of the Imperial Image
in the Reign of Suleiman', in *Soliman le magnifique et son temps*, ed. G. Veinstein (Paris,
1992), 159–77; B. Flemming, 'Sahib-kiran und Mahdi: Türkische Endzeiterwartungen im
ersten Jahrzehnt der Regierung Süleymâns', in *Between the Danube and the Caucasus*, ed. G.
Kara (Budapest, 1987), 43–62; and R. Finlay, 'Prophecy and Politics in Istanbul: Charles
V, Sultan Süleyman, and the Habsburg Embassy of 1533–1534', *Journal of Early Modern
History*, 2.1 (1998), 1–31.

[5] H. Lenowitz, *The Jewish Messiahs, from the Galilee to Crown Heights* (Oxford, 1998), 120–
3, prints several accounts of the meeting between Molcho and Charles. See also M. Idel,
Messianic Mystics (New Haven and London, 1998), 144–52; S. T. Nalle, 'The Millennial
Moment: Revolution and Radical Religion in Sixteenth-Century Spain', in *Toward the
Millennium: Messianic Expectations from the Bible to Waco*, ed. P. Schäfer and M. R. Cohen
(Leiden, 1998), 151–71, at 153–9; and M. Goldish, 'Patterns in Converso Messianism', in
*Millenarianism and Messianism in Early Modern European Culture: Jewish Messianism in the Early
Modern World*, ed. M. Goldish and R. H. Popkin (Dordrecht, 1998), 41–63, at 46–7 and
53–4. Note that Hebrew also renders 'messiah' as 'Ben-David' – or Solomon.

Expected One' and the city he 'entered' as Jerusalem. The first pageant celebrating Charles's entry into Bruges in 1515 resembled the birth of Christ, with three angels presenting the young prince with a crown, a coat of arms and the keys of the city, just as the three Wise Men had brought gifts to the Christ child (see Plate 1). Subsequent tableaux equated Bruges with Jerusalem and displayed the prince's descent from David: they so impressed Charles that he asked to see the whole show again the next day.[6] The following year, Charles became king of Spain, another area rich in messianic imagery, both Christian and Jewish. In particular, legends abounded of *El Encubierto*, a 'hidden king' who would appear unexpectedly and create a benign government that would give everyone what they wanted.[7] In addition, the chroniclers of Charles's grandparents, Ferdinand of Aragon and Isabella of Castile, portrayed the deeds of the 'Catholic Kings' (a title conferred by the papacy) as fulfilling ancient prophecies and claimed that God guided their every step, provided miracles to assist their cause and protected them from all harm. They also saw Ferdinand not only as *El Encubierto* but also as a 'New David' who would emulate the deeds of the Old Testament kings. Charles inherited all this messianic imagery, too, along with the titles 'Catholic King' and 'king of Jerusalem'.[8]

Charles also generated apocalyptic propaganda of his own. Some examples were visual, such as the representations of the young ruler as one of the three Wise Men; while others involved prophecies. A particularly striking prediction foretold that the young prince would conquer the English and the Italians; that he would destroy Rome with

[6] Details from *La tryumphante entrée de Charles, prince des Espagnes, en Bruges*, ed. S. Anglo (facsimile edn of Rémy du Puys's account, published Paris 1515; New York, 1970) – see p. 12 for the 'encore'; G. Kipling, *Enter the King: Theatre, Liturgy and Ritual in Medieval Civic Triumph* (Oxford, 1998); and W. Blockmans and E. Donckers, 'Self-Representation of Court and City in Flanders and Brabant in the 15th and 16th centuries', in *Showing Status*, ed. W. Blockmans and A. Janse (Turnhout, 1999), 79–102. On the medieval precedents, see E. H. Kantorowicz, 'The "King's Advent" and the Enigmatic Panels in the Doors of Santa Sabina', in E. H. Kantorowicz, *Selected Studies* (New York, 1965), 37–75, especially 38–42. I thank Shawn Martin and Edward Tabri for drawing these references to my attention.

[7] For Spain, where a *rey encubierto* actually appeared during the rebellion of Valencia in 1522, see Nalle, 'The Millennial Moment', 159–64; for Portugal, where an *O Encoberto* legend merged after 1580 into Sebastianism, see J. Hermann, *No reino do desejado: a construção do Sebastianismo em Portugal, sécolos XVI e XVII* (São Paolo, 1998).

[8] See J. Cepeda Adán, 'El providencialismo en cronistas de los Reyes Católicos', *Arbor*, 17 (1950), 177–90; W. A. Christian, *Apparitions in Late Medieval and Renaissance Spain* (Princeton, 1981); A. Milhou, 'La chauve-souris, le Nouveau David et le roi caché (trois images de l'empereur des derniers temps dans le monde ibérique: XIIIe–XVIIe siècles)', *Mélanges de la Casa de Velázquez*, 18 (1982), 61–78; J. Bilinkoff, 'A Spanish Prophetess and her Patrons: The Case of María de Santo Domingo', *Sixteenth-Century Journal*, 23 (1992), 21–34; and above all the richly documented study of J. M. Nieto Soria, *Fundamentos ideológicos del poder real en Castilla (siglos XIII–XVI)* (Madrid, 1988).

Plate 1 Charles of Habsburg makes his ceremonial 'entry' to Bruges as count of Flanders
in 1515. (Österreichische Nationalbibliothek, Vienna, Codex 2591: 'Le tryumphante et
solomnelle entrée faicte sur le joyeulx advenement de ... Charles prince des espagnes ... en
la ville de Bruges'.)

fire; that he would capture Jerusalem. 'No one would be able to resist him', the prophecy continued, 'because God's arm would be with him, and he would ... gain the universal dominion of the earth.'[9]

These and other messianic visions of the early sixteenth century – Christian, Jewish and Muslim – shared five common denominators.

- First, all claimed to fulfil prophecies that predicted change, upheaval and the unification of the world.
- Second, all involved a 'founding' or 'refounding' myth (Isma'il established a new dynasty; Selim, Suleiman and Charles dramatically increased the size of the states they inherited).
- Third, all presumed that the end of the world was imminent, since the appearance of the messiah would herald the end of time, so that immediate action was required to fulfil their destiny (something Norman Housley has called the 'eschatalogical imperative').
- Fourth, all assumed that the messiah could both discern God's purpose for the world and pursue appropriate policies to achieve it.
- Finally, at a more practical level, all sought to emulate Solomon; all drew upon the same or related prophecies (such as the Book of Daniel or the visions associated with Daniel); and all placed great emphasis on possession of Jerusalem.

Thanks in part to these shared concepts, the various visions readily crossed cultural boundaries as each leader took careful note of claims advanced by or for the others, and tried to surpass them. Thus the remarkable four-tiara crown made for Suleiman in 1532 was a direct response to the papal coronation of Charles two years before.[10]

Messianic imperialism seldom lasts long, however. Although it gains strength when it runs in harmony with other considerations – dynastic, economic, religious – it proves difficult to sustain when Time perversely

---

[9] O. Marín Cruzado, 'El retrato real en composiciones religiosas de la pintura del siglo XVI: Carlos V y Felipe II', in *El arte en las cortes de Carlos V y Felipe II*, ed. W. Rincón García (Madrid, 1999), 113–26, at 123, notes three distinct representations of Charles V as one of the Three Kings. For the prophecies, see Archivo Municipal de Zaragoza, caja 7775, Pope Leo X to Ferdinand of Aragon, 1 Nov. 1515 (my thanks to Bethany Aram for sharing with me this amazing document); *Theories of Empire, 1450–1800*, ed. D. Armitage (Aldershot, 1998), chs. 3 (by J. M. Headley) and 4 (by F. Bosbach); and A. Chastel, *The Sack of Rome, 1527* (Princeton, 1983), 86. F. Checa Cremades, *Carlos V y la imagen del héroe en el Renacimiento* (Madrid, 1987), 163–71, provides an excellent survey of 'The image of the emperor as the new messiah'.

[10] For more on these common denominators, see Fleischer, 'Mahdi, Messiah', *passim*; S. Subrahmanyam, 'Connected Histories: Notes towards a Reconfiguration of Early Modern Eurasia', in *Beyond Binary History: Re-imagining Eurasia to c. 1830*, ed. V. Lieberman (Ann Arbor, 1999), 289–316; and N. Housley, 'The Eschatalogical Imperative: Messianism and Holy War in Europe, 1260–1556', in *Toward the Millennium*, ed. Schäfer and Cohen, 123–50, especially at 134–5 and 156–7. On the crown with four tiaras, see Necipoglu, 'Suleyman the Magnificent'.

refuses to stop, or when the designated world conqueror fails to achieve his goals. Thus Isma'il's defeat by Selim in 1514 led to considerable moderation in the messianic claims made on his behalf; and although Suleiman and Charles won great victories in the 1520s, leading to ever more extravagant claims, they both faltered in the 1540s. Suleiman thereupon dropped his favoured title of *Sahib-kiran* ('the world conqueror') while, once it became clear that Charles V was not destined to fulfil all the imperialist prophecies, Habsburg supporters began to target his son and heir Philip.

The messianic aura that surrounded Philip II displayed the same five characteristics as the visions of the previous generation – the fulfilment of prophecies; the creation of a founding myth; an apocalyptic eschatology; a direct link to heaven; the emulation of Solomon and the quest for Jerusalem – which encouraged the king to pursue confessionally driven policies both at home and abroad. From early in his reign, supporters hailed Philip as a ruler divinely chosen to reunite Christendom and regain Jerusalem, and they equated his enemies with God's enemies. In 1562, the papal legates at the council of Trent prayed God to 'give Your Majesty victory over your enemies, who are the enemies of Our Lord Jesus Christ and of the well-being of the world'. In 1588, the *Exhortation to the Soldiers and Captains Who Sail on this Campaign to England*, written by Pedro de Ribadeneira (a Jesuit who had worked to restore Catholic worship in England in the 1550s), confidently asserted that 'We are not going on a difficult enterprise, because God our Lord, whose cause and most holy faith we defend, will go ahead; and with such a captain we have nothing to fear.' Ribadeneira portrayed God's cause, Philip's cause and Spain's cause as all one.[11] Ten years later, a chaplain sent to collect testimony from those who had been present at the king's death predicted that 'we can regard His Majesty as a Saint (*podemos contar a Su Magestad por un santo*)'. In 1610, Sebastián de Covarrubias Orozco included among his 'Moral emblems' one that hailed the king as 'Monarch of the world, a sage Solomon, a warrior David' and another that noted his 'resemblance to God (*el rey procura asemejarse a dios*)'.[12] By then, Fray Julián de San Agustín, a Franciscan hailed by many as a saint, had experienced a vision in which the clouds

---

[11] A. M. Rouco Varela, *Staat und Kirche im Spanien des 16. Jahrhunderts* (Munich, 1956), 96n, legates to Philip II, 7 May 1562. Ribadeneira's *Exhortación* quoted, with many other fascinating illustrations of the Jesuit's attempt to 'sacralize' the enterprise, by C. Gómez-Centurión, *La Invencible y la empresa de Inglaterra* (Madrid, 1988), 70.

[12] R. Vargas-Hidalgo, 'Documentos inéditos sobre la muerte de Felipe II y la literatura fúnebre de los sigles XVI y XVII', *Boletín de la Real Academia de la Historia*, 192 (1995), 377–460, at 399, quoting Fray Antonio Cervera de la Torre; S. de Covarrubias Orozco, *Emblemas morales* (Madrid, 1610), centuria I emblema 34 and III emblema 82. A third emblem (I. 36) portrayed the 'sepulcro de Filipo, Rey segundo' – the Escorial – as a miracle.

suddenly lit up like day enabling him to see the soul of King Philip ascend from purgatory into heaven, a revelation later commemorated in a spectacular canvas by Bartolomé Esteban Murillo.[13]

Many works of art produced in his own lifetime portrayed Philip in direct communion with heaven. Some, like Pompeo Leone's larger-than-life-size sculpture beside the High Altar in the Escorial and El Greco's *Dream of Philip II*, showed him at prayer. In Titian's *Gloria* and El Greco's *Burial of the Count of Orgaz* he intercedes for the dead; while in Titian's *Offering of Philip II* he makes an ostentatious sacrifice to God. Other artists portrayed him as one of the Three Kings; and in a Flemish engraving of 1585, Christ directly confers the insignia of power on Philip, while Pope Sixtus V looks on with evident disapproval (Plate 2).[14]

Nevertheless, all these messianic visions originated with others, not with the king, and they were intended for public consumption. The same was true of those involving Charles V, most of his rivals and almost all their predecessors: first-person statements claiming that their purpose coincided with God's purpose remain rare. Philip II and many of his ministers, by contrast, repeatedly asserted in their private correspondence that the king enjoyed a special relationship with heaven. He once even reassured a dispirited minister with the extraordinary boast: 'May God give you life and health, because you are engaged in His service and in mine – which is the same thing.'[15]

Like his medieval forebears, Philip also regularly acted as *rex et sacerdos*: king and priest. In 1556, when Pope Paul IV excommunicated him and declared war, the king and his advisers considered calling a 'national council' of the church, or even a council 'not only for Spain but for all the territories of Your Majesty and of his allies'. Although he stopped short of this extreme step, throughout the first half of his reign Philip continued to follow his own agenda for church reform. He repeatedly ordered public prayers to be said throughout his kingdoms

[13] Details from D. Angulo Iñiguez, 'Miscellanea Murillesca', *Archivo Español del Arte*, 34 (1961), 1–24, and 45 (1972), 55–7. The first article described the painting, one of a series done in the 1640s for the cloister of San Francisco of Seville in the 1640s, but could not identify it; the second provided the missing link and the text of the vision, recorded in 1603 by Fray Julián (who had over 600 miracles to his credit within three years of his death). The painting is today exhibited in the Sterling and Francine Clark Art Institute of Williamstown, Massachusetts. M. Tanner, *The Last Descendant of Aenead: The Hapsburgs and the Mythic Age of the Emperor* (New Haven and London, 1993), 204–5, reproduces and briefly discusses Murillo's painting, done in 1645–8. My thanks to Jonathan Brown for guidance on this topic.
[14] F. Checa Cremades, *Felipe II: mecenas de las artes* (2nd edn, Madrid, 1993), reproduces the items by Leone, Greco and Titian. For an English parallel to the 1585 print, see p. 181 below.
[15] Bibliothèque Publique et Universitaire, Geneva, MS Favre 30/73v, Philip II to Don Luis de Requesens, 20 Oct. 1573, copy of holograph original ('Spero en Dios ... que os dara mucha salud y vida, pues se empleara en su servicio y en el mío, que es lo mismo').

*Plate 2 Christ invests Philip II with royal insignia: an engraving by Hieronymus Wierix,
1585. (Bibliothèque Royale Albert 1er, Brussels, Cabinet des Estampes A.1511.)*

'begging God to re-unite our Holy Christian religion'; and when Pope
Pius IV agreed to reconvene the council of Trent, the king announced
that 'if it could be, and if the state of our affairs would allow, we would
attend the council in person'.[16] He argued with the pope over the form

---

[16] Archivo General de Simancas [hereafter AGS] Estado 112/245–50, 226–9 and 216–
18, Juana, regent of Castile, to Philip II, 25 Sept., 21 Nov. and 14 Dec. 1556, and 114/257
'Memorial de las personas con quien se ha de tratar' (quotation from Estado 114/245–
50); AGS Patronato Real 21/133, Philip II's Instructions to the count of Luna, his envoy
to the council (Oct. 1562), holograph addition, copy. For the 'plegarias por la unión de
la religión cristiana' from 1560 onwards, see AGS Cámara de Castilla: Libros de cédulas
321/248v–9, 272–5, 248–6v. More surprisingly, one of the few works that Philip kept in
his personal library in Madrid was 'A book entitled *The Interim*, in German.' This
document, drawn up by moderate Catholic and Lutheran theologians at the insistence
of Charles V (despite strong papal disapproval), had brought religious peace to the Holy
Roman Empire for a few years after 1548, including the year of Philip's residence in
Germany. Since Philip could not read German, one must assume that he kept a copy of
the text handy lest another opportunity arose to reconcile the dissonant creeds. (See
J. L. Gonzalo Sánchez-Molero, 'Las joyas de la librería personal de Felipe II', in *Felipe
II y su época*, ed. F. J. Campos y Fernández de Sevilla, 1 (El Escorial, 1998), 469–70.) In
1568–9, Philip also showed keen interest in acquiring first a copy and then the original
of the Augsburg confession: see J. and P. Rodríguez, *Don Francés de Álava y Beamonte:
correspondencia inédita de Felipe II con su embajador en París* (San Sebastián, 1991), 286–7 and
316, Zayas to Álava, [late 1568] and 2 Mar. 1569; and *Colección de Documentos Inéditos para*

of the assembly, refusing to forward the bull of convocation to 'his' bishops until it had been amended to state explicitly that this would be a continuation of the earlier sessions at Trent (and not a new gathering as the French desired). As long as the council remained in session, Philip launched a barrage of advice on points that he felt required further attention, and tried unsuccessfully to prolong the assembly until they had been resolved.[17] After the council closed, the king asserted his right to preside over the provincial synods convened to implement the Tridentine decrees throughout his dominions. Having decided that 'our personal attendance is not necessary', he instead sent special commissioners (all of them laymen) and through them provided each synod with detailed instructions. He changed what he did not like ('His Majesty desires that the rules of episcopal residence should be a little looser than those contained in the Tridentine decrees'); he forbade discussion of some decrees (such as Session xxv, *De Reformatio*, chapter 3, which 'seems to authorise ecclesiastical judges to proceed against laymen, confiscating their goods and sequestering their persons, which the laws of this kingdom do not allow and should not allow'); and he prohibited any appeal to Rome against his orders. Such measures, in the graphic phrase of one royal commissioner, 'translated the council of Trent into Spanish'.[18]

Shortly afterwards, the king provided lavish funding and detailed editorial direction for another venture designed to 'reunite our Holy Christian religion': the 'Polyglot Bible'. Arias Montano, the scholar charged with oversight of the venture, worked with Biblical scholars from Lutheran and other 'suspect' creeds, because the king hoped that providing agreed texts in Hebrew, Greek, Aramaic and Latin (Vulgate), with additional Latin versions specially translated from the Greek and Aramaic texts, would appeal to Protestant and Orthodox as well as to Catholic Christians. The motto chosen for the enterprise was PIETATIS

---

la *Historia de España* [hereafter *Co. Do. In.*] (112 vols., Madrid, 1842–95), xxxviii, 56–7 and 94, Alba to Philip II, 4 Apr. and reply 15 May 1569.

[17] M. Ferrandis Torres, *El Concilio de Trento: documentos procedentes del Archivo de Simancas*, ii (Valladolid, 1934: Archivo Histórico Español, vi), 162–6, Philip II to Ambassador Vargas, 17 Jan. 1561; 202–5, Report of the 'junta de teólogos', 26 Feb. 1561; and 218–21, Instructions to Don Juan de Ayala, 13 Mar. 1561. See also J. L. González Novalín, *Historia de la Iglesia de España*, iii-1 (Madrid, 1980), 319–20.

[18] A. Fernández Collado, 'Felipe II y su mentalidad reformadora en el concilio provincial toledano de 1565', *Hispania Sacra*, 50 (1998), 447–66 (quotations at 458–61 and 463: Don Francisco de Toledo, the future 'pacifier' of Peru). A 'rex et sacerdos' link is also suggested by F. Fernández Albaladejo, ' "Imperio de por sí": la reformulación del poder universal en la temprana edad moderna', in *idem, Fragmentos de monarquía: trabajos de historia política* (Madrid, 1992), 168–84; C. Lisón Tolosana, *La imagen del rey: monarquía, realeza y poder ritual en la casa de los Austrias* (Madrid, 1991), 103–6; and J. Martínez Millán and C. J. de Carlos Morales, *Felipe II (1527–1598): la configuración de la monarquía hispana* (Salamanca, 1998), chs. 6–7.

CONCORDIAE and the title page boldly proclaimed that it was 'Intended for the piety and study of the Holy Church by Philip II, the Catholic King.' In case anyone missed the point, the second page displayed a female figure (representing Religion) holding a copy of the new Bible in one hand and a shield bearing Philip's insignia in the other. She stood upon a plinth inscribed with a legend that restated the king's initiative in producing this new tool to unite all Christians (Plates 3 and 4).[19]

Although as his reign progressed the king became somewhat less assertive in ecclesiastical affairs, he continued to feature in numerous messianic prophecies. Thus in 1592, when Philip and his son visited the English College in Valladolid, selected students delivered speeches to him based on verses from Psalm 72. At the outset, the college rector pointed out that the

> Psalme, thoughe it were written properlie and peculiarly of Christ himself, yet by secondarie application and some similitude, it maie also very aptelie be accommodated to this Most Christian King [Philip II] and his son, that are so principall ministers of Christ, and do imitate so manifestlie his kinglie vertues, which in this Psalme are expressed.

Ten scholars then recited a verse in turn and applied it to the policies followed by Philip towards England's Catholics, demonstrating 'how all this prophesied of Christ our Saviour maie also in good sense and reason be verified in the acts of your royall majestie'.[20]

Philip likewise featured in founding myths, as his father had done. The iconography of his ceremonial entry into Lisbon as king of Portugal in 1581 included one triumphal arch that showed Janus surrendering the keys of his temple 'as if to the lord of the world, who holds it securely under his rule', while another bore the legend 'The world, which was divided between your great-grandfather King Ferdinand the Catholic and your grandfather King Manuel of Portugal, is now linked into one, since you are lord of everything in the East and West.' A medal struck in 1583 made the same point more concisely: it showed the king's head with the inscription PHILIPP II HISP ET NOVI ORBIS REX (Philip II, king of Spain and the New World) on one side; and on the other, around a terrestrial globe, the uncompromising legend NON SUFFICIT ORBIS (the world is not enough).[21]

---

[19] *Biblia Sacra, Hebraice, Chaldaice, Graece et Latine* (8 vols., Antwerp, 1569–73.) See also G. Morocho Gayo, 'Felipe II: las ediciones litúrgicas y la Biblia Regia', *Ciudad de Dios*, 211 (1998), 813–81.

[20] See R. Persons, *A Relation of the King of Spaines Receiving in Valladolid, and in the English College of the Same Towne, in August Last Past of This Yere 1592* (Antwerp, 1592: facsimile edition, 1970), 25 and 47 (see also 40–3.).

[21] Checa Cremades, *Felipe II*, 271–2 and 486; G. Parker, *The Grand Strategy of Philip II* (2nd edn, New Haven and London, 1999), 5.

Plates 3 and 4 The first (above) and second (over) title pages of the 'Polyglot Bible', volume 1, printed at Antwerp, 1569. (Courtesy of the Beinecke Library, Yale University.)

Finally, like most sixteenth-century Christians, the king firmly believed that the world was about to end. For example, one day in 1574 he felt 'in a foul mood and fit for nothing': his army in the Netherlands had mutinied and the Turks had taken Tunis. 'Everything seems about to fall apart: how I wish I could die so as not to see what I fear', he complained to his secretary. 'I am enduring the greatest burdens and worries that I believe any man has endured since the creation of the world.' But then he opened more letters and 'when I saw how they started, I read no further … If this is not actually the end of the world, I think we must be very close to it – and, please God, let it be the end of the *whole* world, and not just the end of Christendom.'[22]

This apocalyptic mind-set made Philip II both unrealistic in his strategic plans and inflexible when his subordinates complained about them. Worse, instead of devising contingency plans, he relied on divine intervention to remedy any shortcomings; so when his fortunes received an unexpected boost he would assure his ministers that 'God has done this', whereas news of a setback led him to call on God to save his cause. In 1574, as bad news from abroad poured across his desk, Philip grumbled: 'Unless God performs a miracle, which our sins do not merit, it is no longer possible to maintain ourselves for [more than a few] months, let alone years.' Further reverses simply made him more impatient: 'May God help us with a miracle. I tell you that we need one so much that it seems to me that He *must* choose to give us a miracle, because without one I see everything in the worst situation imaginable.'[23]

Initially, the king's 'eschatological imperative' targeted Muslims. In 1534, aged seven, he already knew by heart a ballad about the exploits of El Cid against the Moors, and in 1541 he wanted to join Charles V's attack on Algiers. That same year, his teacher bought him an Arab grammar and the following year a Koran, and they began to study Arabic and Hebrew together.[24] In 1543, now regent of Spain, the prince acquired numerous books about the Turks: their history, their possessions, their military organisation – and how to defeat them. An emblem prepared for him in 1548, full of allusions to David and Solomon, showed a sun with the name Philip and the motto '*Donec auferatur Luna* [until the moon disappears]: [that is] until he destroys the Turks, the Arabs and all other peoples who use the moon as their emblem.' The following year Nicholas Mameranus offered the prince a presentation copy of a book with a binding that juxtaposed the names of Philip and Christ in gold letters and

---

[22] Archivo y Biblioteca de Zabálburu, Madrid [hereafter ABZ] 144/34, Mateo Vázquez to Philip II and reply, 10 Dec. 1574. On the widespread belief that the world was about to end, see R. B. Barnes, *Prophecy and Gnosis: Apocalypticism in the Wake of the Lutheran Reformation* (Stanford, 1988); D. Crouzet, *Les guerriers de Dieu: la violence au temps des troubles de religion, vers 1525–vers 1610* (2 vols., Paris. 1990), i, chs. 2–3; A. Cunningham and O. P. Grell, *The Four Horsemen of the Apocalypse: Religion, War, Famine and Death in Reformation Europe* (Cambridge, 2001), ch. 1; and Bauckham, *Tudor Apocalypse*, chs. 8–9.

[23] ABZ 166/92 and 100, the king's rescript on Hernando de Vega to Philip II, 9 and 11 Nov. 1586 (upon learning that the annual Indies fleet had arrived safely at Seville); Instituto de Valencia de Don Juan [hereafter IVdeDJ] 53/3/56, Vázquez to Philip II and replies, 13 May 1574, and ABZ 144/36, same to same, 11 Dec. 1574.

[24] B. Alonso Acero and J. L. Gonzalo Sánchez-Molero, 'Alá en la corte de un príncipe cristiano: el horizonte musulmán en la formación de Felipe II (1532–1557)', *Torre de los Lujanes*, 35 (1998), 109–40, at 121–3. They note that 'the Koran' purchased may in fact have been Bernardo Pérez de Chinchón, *Libro llamado Antialcoran* (Valencia, 1532), a collection of twenty-six sermons attacking the Koran.

called upon the prince to bring peace to Christendom, extirpate heresy and wrest Constantinople and Jerusalem from the Turks.[25]

Philip's acquisition of the 'crown matrimonial' of England in 1554 changed this focus dramatically. Tudor kingship had also incorporated Biblical imagery on a grand scale. Writers and artists had portrayed Henry VIII (Philip's father-in-law) as Moses, David and Solomon; while the title page of the Great Bible of 1540 showed the king receiving the Scriptures directly from God. Fourteen years later, Cardinal Reginald Pole delivered a speech at Westminster to Philip and Mary, surrounded by the peers and commons, that drew a slightly different parallel. Charles V had attempted to achieve the reconciliation of Christendom, Pole noted, but he had failed; just as David,

> Thoughe he were a manne elected of God, yet, for that he was contaminate[d] with bloode and war, coulde not builde the temple of Jerusalem, but left the finishynge thereof to Salamon, whiche was *Rex Pacificus*. So may it be thoughte, that the appeasing of controversies of religion in Christianity is not appoynted to this emperour, but rather to his sonne, who shal perfourme the buildyng that his father hath begun.[26]

Philip had long been familiar with this edifying image. In 1540, he acquired a copy of the *Jewish Wars* by Josephus, and three years later St Jerome's commentary on Ezekiel: both works contained detailed descriptions of the Temple in Jerusalem. In 1549, during his progress through the Netherlands, triumphal arches and *tableaux vivants* in almost every city showed Charles and his son Philip as David and Solomon while others portrayed Philip building Solomon's Temple.[27] The parallel

[25] Biblioteca Nacional, Madrid [hereafter BNM], 5938/440–IV, 'divisa' by Gabriel Rincón; N. Mameranus, *Carmen Gratulatorium* [Leuven, 1549], an item still in the Escorial library. Alonso Acero and Gonzalo Sánchez-Molero, 'Alá en la corte de un príncipe cristiano', 134 and 136, discuss these items.

[26] J. N. King, 'Henry VIII as David: The King's Image and Reformation Politics', in *Rethinking the Henrician Era: Essays on Early Tudor Texts and Contexts*, ed. P. C. Herman (Urbana, IL, 1994), 78–91 (plus plates); J. G. Nichols, ed., 'The chronicle of Queen Jane and of Two Years of Queen Mary', *Camden Society*, 1st ser., 48 (1850), 158, as recorded by John Elder, who claimed to have used the notes on the speech taken by a member of parliament who heard it. A Spanish version, written by an anonymous eye-witness, was printed in Seville later that year: A. Muñoz, *Viaje de Felipe II a Inglaterra*, ed. P. de Gayangos (Madrid, 1877), 135.

[27] Many have claimed that Philip was inspired by Solomon's temple, but various works by J. R. de la Cuadra Blanco remind us that Ezekiel visualised how the *new* Temple – to replace the destroyed edifice of Solomon – would one day be built, whereas Josephus provided a detailed description of the Second Temple: see, especially, Cuadro Blanco, 'La *idea* de El Escorial y dos textos históricos hebreos', *El Olivo*, 19 (1995), 41–62, and 'El Escorial y el templo de Salomón: influencia de las fuentes históricas hebreas en la idea y traza del Monasterio de El Escorial', *Anales de arquitectura*, 7 (1996), 4–13bis.

became commonplace after Philip succeeded his father. In 1556, in Antwerp (where the king then resided), Sebastián Fox Morcillo and Felipe de la Torre each published a treatise of government that called on Philip to build a new Temple by renewing the Catholic Church; and his humanist adviser Juan Paéz de Castro urged him to create a library modelled on that of Solomon.[28] The following year, Juan Martín Cordero brought out a Spanish translation of Josephus, with its description of the Temple as Christ had known it, and presented a luxuriously bound copy to Philip. Meanwhile the king himself commissioned a magnificent stained glass window, full of such symbolism, for the church of St John at Gouda in Holland. In the upper section, Solomon prays at the dedication of his Temple, and the voice of God responds: 'I have heard your prayer, and if you walk in my sight as your father did, I shall perpetuate your royal throne for ever' (Plate 5). In the central section, Christ presides at the Last Supper and speaks with his disciple Philip, whose hand rests protectively on the shoulder of his namesake as, beside Queen Mary Tudor, he kneels in reverence (Plate 6).[29]

Philip's five-year experience as ruler of England left a deep impression. He relished not only the role of 'Defender of the Faith' but also the title, conferred by the pope on England's rulers; and he later contemplated reclaiming it.[30] He learned a lot about the governance of England, both

---

[28] S. Fox Morcillo, *De regni, regisque institutione libri III* (Antwerp, 1556); F. de la Torre, *Institutio de un rey christiano* (Antwerp, 1556; ed. R. W. Truman, Exeter, 1979). For a précis of the two texts, see R. W. Truman, *Spanish Treatises on Government, Society and Religion in the time of Philip II* (Leiden, 1999), chs. 3–4. Biblioteca del Real Monasterio de El Escorial [hereafter BSLE] MS &. II–15/190–1: J. Páez de Castro, 'Memorial al Rey Don Felipe II sobre las librerías' (1556: my thanks to Wim de Groot for this reference).

[29] *Los siete libros de Flauio Iosefo, los qvales contienen las guerras de los Iudios, y la destrución de Hierusalem y d'el Templo ... dirigidos a la S. C. y R. M. d'el Rey don Felipe* (Antwerp, 1557: for the de luxe copy, see J. L. Gonzalo Sánchez-Molero, *La 'Librería Rica' de Felipe II: estudio histórico y catalogación* (El Escorial, 1998), 508); *The Seventh Window*, ed. W. de Groot, (Amsterdam, 2002). In 1558, at the funeral service for Charles V held in Brussels, the preacher called upon Philip to act like Solomon after the death of his father and build a new Temple; the following year, a painting commissioned for the chapter of the Golden Fleece held in Ghent portrayed Philip as Solomon. Details on these and similar parallels in J. R. de la Cuadra Blanco, 'El Escorial como nuevo Templo de Salomón en la literatura de los siglos XVI y XVII', *La Ciudad de Dios*, 213 (2000), 449–76). *Un monarca y su época: las tierras y los hombres del rey*, ed. L. A. Ribot García (Valladolid, 1998), 272–4, discusses and reproduces Lucas de Heere's painting.

[30] BSLE MS &. III.12, Lorenzo de San Pedro, *Diálogo llamado Philippino, donde se refieren cien congruencias concernientes al derecho que Su Magestad del rei Don Felippe nuestro señor tiene al reino de Portugal* (1579), fos. clv–clvi: 'the title *Defensor Fidei* belongs to His Majesty ... because our powerful king has destroyed three enemies of the church: heretics, Jews and Muslims'. In 1584, Gabriel de Zayas, who had served Philip in England, objected to a seal made for Philip II that contained the phrase 'Fidei Defensor, which is very bold because, although good and holy, and something that belonged to His Majesty when he was king of England, once he ceased to reign there it is not appropriate' (IVdeDJ 69/279, Zayas to Mateo Vázquez, 13 Dec. 1584).

Plates 5 and 6 The upper and middle sections of the 'Royal Window' in the St Janskerk, Gouda, showing the consecration of Solomon's Temple (above) and the Last Supper (overleaf). (Courtesy of Wim de Groot.)

during his two years of residence and while absent (for he insisted on being consulted on a wide range of issues). He also acquired several books on England (and continued to acquire more throughout the reign) including some describing the seaborne invasions that had repeatedly overthrown or seriously undermined English governments in the five centuries since the Norman Conquest.[31] He also discovered that the Tudor state was both complex and unstable: he survived both a major revolt and an assassination attempt during his first year, and saw for himself the inroads made by Protestantism (especially in the south-east of the country).[32] His personal experience convinced the king

[31] See the list of books on England purchased for the king's collection in the 1550s in Gonzalo Sánchez-Molero, *La 'Librería Rica' de Felipe II*, 859–60. See also G. Redworth, *In Defence of the Church Catholic: The Life of Stephen Gardiner* (Oxford, 1990), xi and 308, on an anonymous 'Machiavellian treatise' written at this time about how to 'tame' England. For Philip's list of invasions, see Archivo Histórico Nacional, Madrid, Órdenes Militares [hereafter AHN OM] 3511/4 and 3512/27–8.

[32] Details in *Calendar of State Papers, Domestic Series: Mary I (1553–1558)*, ed. C. S. Knighton, (1998), 111, 147, and so on, letters to his 'Select Council' in England, and 172, about the assassination attempt (part of the Dudley conspiracy). It is hard to be sure exactly what Philip learned from his experience in England because a ship carrying his archives foundered on the journey back to Spain in 1559 – see G. Parker, *Guide to the Archives of*

that he was the world's foremost expert on English affairs. He therefore could not understand why in February 1570 Pope Pius V excommunicated Elizabeth and called on Catholic rulers to depose her without consulting Philip first. Surely the pope knew 'that I could give him better information and advice on that kingdom, and on its affairs and people, than anyone else'?[33]

In a brilliant essay, María José Rodríguez-Salgado stressed the urgent need for a new analysis of Anglo-Spanish relations in the later sixteenth century. In particular, she noted that 'to achieve a more accurate perspective, we must abandon the current paradigm and, instead of searching for antecedents to the war of 1588, try to explain the *peace* that prevailed until then and that returned soon afterwards'. Rodríguez-Salgado emphasized Philip II's frequent pacific statements concerning England between 1559 and 1585, to his own ministers as well as to Elizabeth, despite repeated pleas by the papacy to overthrow the Tudor state; and she urged historians to take them literally. As long as France retained the power to intervene in England – which is to say, until the collapse of Valois power during the winter of 1584–5 – Rodríguez-Salgado emphasized that Spain could not afford to launch an attack on Elizabeth. But she also noted one significant exception: the Ridolfi plot in 1571, an episode that provides a superb example of the direct and decisive impact of Philip's messianic outlook on his foreign policy.[34]

In the course of 1568, four events well known to Tudor historians refocused the king's attention on English affairs. First, in March, Philip refused to grant further audiences to Ambassador John Man and

---

the Spanish Institutions in or concerned with the Netherlands, 1556–1706 (Brussels, 1971), 26 – but see the brilliant analysis of G. Redworth, 'Felipe II y las soberanas de Inglaterra', *Torre de los Lujanes*, 33 (1997), 103–12.

[33] A. Teulet, *Relations politiques de la France et de l'Espagne avec l'Ecosse*, v (Paris, 1862), 59–60, Philip II to Don Francés de Álava, 26 June 1570. See also M. A. S. Hume, *Calendar of Letters and State Papers relating to English Affairs Preserved in, or Originally Belonging to, the Archives of Simancas: Elizabeth* (4 vols., 1892–9; hereafter *CSPSp*), II, 254, Philip II to Don Guerau de Spes, 30 June 1570: 'my knowledge of English affairs is such that I believe I could give a better opinion upon them and the course that ought to have been adopted under the circumstances than any one else'. The history of Philip's policies towards England strikingly confirm Robert Jervis's observation that first-hand experiences can seriously distort political choices by statesmen: R. Jervis, *Perception and Misperception in International Politics* (Princeton, 1976), 240–52.

[34] M. J. Rodríguez-Salgado, 'Paz ruidosa, guerra sorda: las relaciones de Felipe II e Inglaterra', in *La monarquía de Felipe II a debate*, ed. L. Ribot García (Madrid, 2000), 63–119, quotation at 67. Pauline Croft has also noted the strident and sustained pressure for peace among subjects of both Philip and Elizabeth engaged in commerce: see Croft, 'Trading with the enemy, 1585–1604', *Historical Journal*, 32 (1989), 281–303; and 'English commerce with Spain and the Armada war, 1558–1603', in *England, Spain and the Gran Armada, 1585–1604*, ed. M. J. Rodríguez-Salgado and S. Adams (Edinburgh, 1991), 236–63.

demanded that Elizabeth recall him, virtuously informing the pope that the continued presence of a Protestant cleric at his court might offend God, 'whose service, and the observation of whose holy faith, I place far ahead of my own affairs and actions and above everything in this life, even my own'.[35] Second, two months later, Mary Stuart, queen of Scotland (and, in the eyes of many Catholics, also the rightful queen of England), fled to England where Elizabeth placed her under house arrest. Third, the following November, five ships carrying specie sailing from Spain to the duke of Alba's bankers in the Netherlands took refuge in English ports. Philip's ambassador in London asked Elizabeth to protect the precious cargo – urgently needed to finance Alba's army – if necessary by allowing it to travel overland to Dover. The queen agreed, and the treasure came ashore. There it stayed, because (fourth and finally) news arrived that Spanish forces in the Caribbean had attacked and decimated an English merchant fleet commanded by John Hawkins. Elizabeth was both embarrassed and furious: despite promising Philip's ambassador that she would prevent Hawkins's voyage, she had loaned him two warships from the royal navy; now the Spaniards had sunk one of them and seriously damaged the other.[36]

These diplomatic incidents required careful handling: everything depended on the diplomatic skills of Don Guerau de Spes, the new Spanish ambassador, who arrived in London in September 1568. Virtually nothing is known about Spes – he seems to have held no public office before his appointment as ambassador; no portrait of him has survived; he was murdered by bandits on his way home – and Philip imposed severe restrictions on his freedom of action. Spes had to travel from Spain to England via Brussels, in order to discuss his mission with the duke of Alba, Philip's governor-general in the Netherlands, and 'as long as the duke holds that position, and you serve as my ambassador in England, you must carry out the orders that he gives you just as you carry out mine' since 'he knows what is best for my affairs'. Furthermore, in all Spes's dealings with English Catholics, 'you must inform me of your opinions before acting on them, so that I shall know and can tell you what you must do'.[37]

[35] L. Serrano, *Correspondencia diplomática entre España y la Santa Sede durante el Pontificado de San Pío V* (4 vols., Madrid 1914), II, 360, Philip II to Don Juan de Zúñiga, his ambassador in Rome, 8 Mar. 1568. See the excellent account of this incident in G. M. Bell, 'John Man: The Last Elizabethan Resident Ambassador in Spain', *Sixteenth-Century Journal*, 2.2 (October 1976), 75–93.

[36] For Elizabeth's promises regarding Hawkins, see *Co. Do. In.*, XC, 19–11, 40 and 136 (précis in *CSPSp*, II, I, 17 and 73–4), Guzmán de Silva to Philip II, 3 Jan. and 27 Mar. 1568, and Spes to Philip II, 24 Sept. 1568. For the truth see J. A. Williamson, *Hawkins of Plymouth* (2nd edn, 1969), 100–56.

[37] J. Calvar Gross, J. I. González-Aller Hierro, M. de Dueñas Fontán and M. del C. Mérida Valverde, *La batalla del Mar Océano* (3 vols., Madrid, 1988–93; hereafter *BMO*), I,

Despite these attempts to counteract the new ambassador's inexperience, within a few weeks and almost single-handed, Spes managed to turn the problems he inherited into a trade war. On 21 December 1568, he informed Alba (wrongly) that Elizabeth had confiscated the treasure and urged him to embargo all English property in the Netherlands in retaliation (and to ask the king to do the same in Spain). A few days later Spes called on the French ambassador in London, Bertrand de Salignac, lord of La Mothe Fénélon, 'to discuss with me matters that might concern the common interests of our two masters. [Spes] made two proposals, which he deemed of great importance, indeed almost essential to Christendom: the first was that, according to him, he knew of no greater heretic in this world, nor a greater enemy to the Catholic faith, than Master [William] Cecil.' Spes suggested that the two ambassadors, in the name of their sovereigns, 'should work to make him lose his office, and the favour and credit that he enjoyed with his mistress the queen'. The second suggestion was that the French and Spanish monarchs should warn Elizabeth that they would 'combine to forbid her subjects to undertake any trade with France, the Netherlands and Spain unless they return to the Catholic faith and to the obedience of the Roman church. This will force the queen to do the same, both for herself and for her kingdom.' Spes asserted that the queen and her leading subjects depended so heavily on the yield of exports that they would not be able to withstand an embargo.[38] Unknown to the ambassador, in Brussels the following day the duke of Alba ordered the seizure of all English goods in the Low Countries and a cessation of trade. Elizabeth reciprocated early in January 1569, and also placed Spes under house arrest and threw the captains and some of the crews from the treasure-ships into prison.[39]

Philip now possessed no direct diplomatic channel through which to resolve the dispute, which gave Alba even greater influence over the king's English policy. The duke had resided in England during the

2–3, Instructions of Philip II to Špes, 28 June 1568. Admittedly, the king had imposed a similar restriction on Guzmán de Silva: *Co. Do. In.*, LXXXIX, 3–11, Philip II's Instructions, 19 Jan. 1564.

[38] Kervijn de Lettenhove, *Relations politiques des Pays-Bas et de l'Angleterre sous le règne de Philippe II*, v (Brussels, 1884) [hereafter Kervijn], 198ff, Spes to Alba, 21, 22, 25, 27 and 30 Dec. 1568; C. Purton Cooper, *Recueil des dépêches, rapports, instructions et mémoires des ambassadeurs de France en Angleterre: correspondance de Bertrand de Salignac de la Mothe Fénélon* (7 vols., Paris and London, 1838–42) [hereafter *La Mothe*], I, 69–73, La Mothe to Catherine de Medici, 28 Dec. 1568. La Mothe, like Spes, was new in his post: he arrived in England in late November 1568.

[39] For details see C. Read, 'Queen Elizabeth's Seizure of the Duke of Alva's Pay Ships', *Journal of Modern History*, 5 (1933), 443–64; G. D. Ramsay, *The Queen's Merchants and the Revolt of the Netherlands* (1986), 90–111; and W. T. MacCaffrey, *The Shaping of the Elizabethan Regime: Elizabethan Politics, 1558–1572* (Princeton, 1968), 188–95.

1550s and maintained his own intelligence network there.[40] He also possessed his own agenda. On the one hand, he never saw the point of replacing Elizabeth Tudor with Mary Stuart, brought up at the French court and closely related to the French royal family. On the other hand, since the prosperity of the Netherlands over which he ruled depended on free trade with England, Alba opposed any policy that jeopardised it – even when expressly ordered by the king himself. This fundamental policy difference between Brussels and Madrid constituted perhaps Elizabeth's greatest asset during the trade war with Spain (albeit one of which she seems to have remained unaware).[41]

Initially, outraged by the imprisonment of his ambassador and the confiscation of his treasure, Philip contemplated an outright attack on England. In February 1569, he angrily informed Alba that 'it appears to me that, after my special obligation to maintain my own states in our Holy Faith, I am bound to make every effort to restore and preserve it in England as in former times' and asked the duke to suggest how best to do it. Alba refused: he replied forcefully that open war with England would be a catastrophic mistake. He reminded Philip that he had spent most of the previous year defeating an invasion of the Netherlands by rebel forces, which left his treasury empty so that he lacked 'the ships and many other things necessary for a fresh war'. Moreover, he considered that the situation in France, where the Protestant rebels seemed likely to gain the upper hand, must have the first claim on any spare resources. (Shortly afterwards, a major expeditionary force left the Netherlands and another set out from Spain to fight against the French Protestants.) Instead, the duke sent an informal emissary to Elizabeth to discuss restoring trade and suggested that Philip should write an emollient letter to Elizabeth, asking why she felt aggrieved. The outbreak of rebellion among the Moriscos of Granada, which absorbed an increasing share of Philip's resources, added force to this suggestion and in the autumn the king authorised

---

[40] It is easy to document Alba's numerous envoys sent to England in attempts to get trade restored, starting in January 1569 – before he had received authorisation from the king! (Kervijn, v, 220–6; Alba's Instruction to d'Assonleville). Naturally, it is less easy to trace his clandestine network. See, however, Archivo de la Casa de los duques de Alba [hereafter AA] 44/79, Juan Milio (Alba's agent at Court) to Don Hernando de Toledo, 29 Sept. 1571, passing on news secretly transmitted to Alba by 'un Flamenco' whom he had sent to England.

[41] Ramsay, *The Queen's Merchants*, 200, pointed out that Elizabeth never seems to have realised her advantage: she always assumed that Alba slavishly followed the policies decreed by Philip in Spain, and refused to negotiate with him! (See, for examples, *CSPSp*, II, 203 and 219–20, Chiappino Vitelli to Alba, 23 Oct. and 19 Dec. 1569.) Cf. Archivio di Stato, Florence, Mediceo del Principato [hereafter ASF MP] 4903, unfol., Ambassadors Nobili and Caccia to Prince Francesco, Madrid, 10 May 1571, expressing surprise that Elizabeth insisted on negotiating only in Spain.

Alba to send a formal envoy, Chiappino Vitelli (a Florentine soldier of fortune serving Philip in the Netherlands), to ascertain the terms on which the queen might settle.[42]

By then, however, a new player had come on the scene. Roberto Ridolfi, born in Florence in 1531, had worked in England since 1562 as a banker, and four years later he began to handle the secret funds sent by Pope Pius V to English Catholics. In January 1569, the French ambassador noted that Ridolfi, 'a person of quality', had offered his services to Elizabeth 'to go, as if in his own name, to arrange reconciliation and some accommodation with the duke [of Alba] in this matter'. The arrival of Alba's emissary in England made Ridolfi's mediation seem superfluous, but the following month the Florentine brought a message to Ambassador Spes from the duke of Norfolk and two of Elizabeth's Catholic councillors, Lords Arundel and Lumley, saying that they intended to overthrow Cecil and force the queen to restore close links with both Rome and Spain. Ridolfi also brought a cypher to use in all communications with the English nobles – ensuring that, since Spes remained under house arrest for much of the year, Ridolfi formed the only link between them.[43]

This proved unfortunate, because Ridolfi had an ambitious agenda of his own. In March 1569, he secretly informed Ambassador La Mothe that he held a commission 'from the pope in person to arrange the restoration and re-establishment of the Catholic faith in England, working with the Catholic peers of the country'. He admitted that he used his financial dealings with Arundel and Lumley as a cover for their political discussions and asserted that other peers – above all Thomas Howard, duke of Norfolk – had expressed support for the overthrow of Cecil and the restoration of Catholicism. He planned to go to Rome to obtain papal instruments to permit England and its queen to be reconciled 'which these lords, having by then acquired power, would earnestly press upon her; and in this way they would begin to arrange the re-establishment of the Catholic faith'. Ridolfi urged the French to make common cause with Spain in the trade war

[42] CSPSp, II, 109, Philip II to Alba, 18 Feb. 1569 (see also Archivo Documental Español, XI, 394, Philip II to Mary Stuart, 28 Feb. 1569, promising her assistance); CSPSp, II, 132–3, Alba to Philip II, 10 Mar. 1569, and 150, Philip II to Alba, 15 May 1569; and Co. Do. In., XC, 187–9, Philip II to Elizabeth, undated but probably also 15 May 1569.
[43] La Mothe, I, 115–16, to Charles IX, 17 Jan. 1569; BMO, I, 25, Spes to Alba, 20 Feb. 1569, reporting Ridolfi's visit two days before; Co. Do. In., XC, 242, Spes to Philip II, 14 June 1568 (stating that he had not met the peers before his arrest, and now 'could only deal with them by third parties' – above all Ridolfi). This was not the first attempt of the two Catholic peers to secure aid from the Spanish ambassador: see Co. Do. In., LXXXIX, 264–5, Guzmán de Silva to Philip II, 4 Feb. 1566, with an account of a visit from Arundel and Lumley, asking for direction.

against Elizabeth in order to increase the pressure on her and Cecil.[44] Spes now took matters a stage further, and in late May drew up a plan to depose Elizabeth for which he coined the term 'the Enterprise of England'. Expanding the plan he had outlined to La Mothe, he advised Philip to persuade France, Portugal, the independent states of Italy, Poland and Muscovy to boycott all trade with England; to send financial support to Norfolk and the English Catholic nobles; and to fan the discontent of Irish Catholics with English rule. More radically, Spes suggested that the king should either support Mary Stuart's claim to the English crown or else claim it for himself. Spes smuggled his plan, together with a copy of Ridolfi's proposal, to the duke of Alba, who (despite serious misgivings) forwarded the documents to the king.[45]

The outbreak of a Catholic-led rebellion in northern England in November 1569 seemed to confirm the analysis of Spes and Ridolfi and so, the following month, the king urged Alba to send support. Nevertheless, conscious that he wrote far from events, and worried about the rising cost of the war in Granada, the king concluded with a disclaimer. 'I only mention all this so that you will know what we are thinking here; and so that, with your great prudence, and bearing in mind the state of affairs in all areas, you can consider what would be most appropriate.' The duke's 'great prudence' naturally decreed that he should do nothing.[46]

The following month, in a tortuous twenty-two-page letter, Philip therefore provided Alba with a full account of his dilemma. Elizabeth had confiscated a treasure shipment by his bankers and the goods of his subjects in England; she had welcomed his rebels (including perhaps 30,000 Dutch exiles, many of them declared rebels); she had sponsored and strengthened Hawkins's trading voyage to the Caribbean; and she had licensed attacks on ships sailing through the Channel under Spanish

---

[44] *La Mothe*, I, 258–62, secret memorial to Catherine de Medici, 14 Mar. 1568, 'after getting her to promise that she would talk to no one in this world about this'. Even in his own register copy (the basis of this edition), the ambassador prudently left all names blank and only filled them in later. In the end, Ridolfi sent his proposal to the pope by mail, not in person: an English translation appears in J. H. Pollen, *The English Catholics in the Reign of Queen Elizabeth: A Study of their Politics, Civil Life and Government* (1920), 140–1. A month later, Ridolfi returned to the French embassay to press his scheme: *La Mothe*, I, 332–3, letter of 20 Apr. 1569 (the 'gentilhomme prudent et bien avisé, qui ayde, au nom du pape, de conduyre icy ceste entreprinse' must have been Ridolfi). For Ridolfi's financial dealings with Arundel and Lumley, see Kervijn, VI, 18–19.

[45] AHN OM 3511/4, 'Consideraciones de Don Guerao de Spes sobre la forma que se podría tener para la empressa de Inglaterra', London, 31 May 1569 (this is the original document of which a rather garbled summary appears, in translation, in *CSPSp*, II, 157–9); Kervijn, V, 406–8, Alba to Spes, 21 June 1569. In the same letter, while warning Spes not to meddle in English politics, Alba agreed to send 6,000 escudos to Norfolk, Arundel and Lumley.

[46] *BMO*, I, 38–9, Philip II to Alba, 16 Dec. 1569.

colours. 'By contrast', Philip noted, 'the damage that she, her kingdom
and her subjects have received from us is so little ... that one could
justly say that she has declared war on us, but we are at peace with
her.' Should Spain now retaliate? To justify intervention, Philip resorted
to messianic rhetoric. He declared that God's service 'required' him to
help place Mary queen of Scots on the throne of England and to
restore Catholicism, especially since 'God has already granted that by
my intervention and my hand that kingdom has previously been
restored to the Catholic church once'. Therefore, he continued:

> Although human prudence suggests many inconveniences and diffi-
> culties, and places before us worldly fears, ... the confidence that we
> can justly place in the cause of God will remove them, and will
> inspire and strengthen us to overcome them. Certainly, we could not
> avoid remaining with great guilt in our soul, and great regret, if
> because of some failure on my part that queen [Mary] and those
> Catholics – indeed the [entire Catholic] faith – should suffer.

Philip proceeded to list three possible strategies for achieving these
ends – an outright invasion by his various forces; a joint invasion with
the French; and an assault on Ireland – and ordered Alba to evaluate
them. He also instructed the duke secretly to provide both the English
Catholics and Mary Stuart with money, arms and munitions, and to
send military advisers to help train her supporters. But still the king
shied away from an open declaration of war. He warned Alba: 'I only
wish to become involved in this business in such a way that, should
something come up that might oblige me to change my mind, I would
be free to do so.'[47]

Neither the spiritual blackmail nor the strategic alternatives impressed
the duke. He fired off increasingly rude letters ordering Spes to avoid
any involvement with the English Catholics and he sent the king a
detailed rebuttal of his invasion strategy laced with heavy sarcasm.
'Even though the principal means must come from God, as Your
Majesty very virtuously and piously suggests', Alba began, 'nevertheless
since He normally works through the resources He gives to humans, it
seems necessary to examine what human resources would be needed
to carry out your wishes.' The duke immediately ruled out an invasion,
with or without the French, on the grounds both of cost and of Spain's
strategic commitments elsewhere. He also pointed out that, although
the English Catholics begged for assistance, they had made it very clear
that they did not want deliverance to come by means of a foreign
army. He noted that, since Ireland lay closer to Spain than to the
Netherlands, Philip must organise any operations in that quarter

---

[47] *BMO*, I, 42, Philip II to Alba, 22 Jan. 1570: a most remarkable letter.

himself. Finally, he intercepted and detained the agent sent from Spain with aid and encouragement for the (now defeated) northern rebels.[48]

The king, suitably chastised, passed the initiative for coordinating the English policy of his monarchy back to Alba's non-interventionist hands. He reminded Spes that 'English affairs depend so entirely on those of Flanders, and the duke of Alba is managing them with so much prudence and consideration, to the benefit of my interests, that you will continue to follow the instructions he may give you.' Fatefully, however, and against Alba's advice, he also ordered Spes to maintain contact with Ridolfi.[49]

The Florentine had continued to further the plans of the English Catholic peers. In June 1569 he again offered his services to the Privy Council as an intermediary with the duke of Alba; at the same time, he conveyed their seditious messages to the French and Spanish ambassadors.[50] He also used his banking services to establish a link – soon the only link – between Spes, Alba and Norfolk; and he made contact with Alba's envoy, his fellow Florentine Chiappino Vitelli, before and during his mission to England. Then, in September 1569, he transferred a substantial sum from Spes to the bishop of Ross, Mary Stuart's ambassador at the English court.[51] Not surprisingly, these manifold activities attracted the government's attention and in October, just before the Northern Rebellion, they arrested and imprisoned Ridolfi and 'several other individuals, Italians and English, and some Spaniards'. He faced twenty-five charges, but gained his freedom when news arrived in London six weeks later that the Catholic lords of northern England had risen in rebellion. While under arrest, it seems almost certain that Ridolfi was 'turned': in return for his life and his

---

[48] *BMO*, I, 43–7, Alba to Philip II, 23 and 24 Feb. 1570 (W. S. Maltby, *Alba: A Biography of Fernando Álvarez de Toledo, Third Duke of Alba, 1507–82* (Berkeley, 1982), 200–1, mis-dates these documents to 1571). Alba had already used the same arguments – and the same sarcastic tone – to rebuff a similar suggestion from Puis V: see *BMO*, I, 35, Alba to Don Juan de Zúñiga, Philip's ambassador in Rome, 4 Dec. 1569. For his increasingly rude letters to Ambassador Spes, see Kervijn, v, 421–2, 447 and 455 (letters of 2 July, 24 Aug. and 4 Sept. 1569); for his decision to detain the messenger, see *ibid.*, 603–6, Alba to Spes, 20 Feb. 1570.

[49] *CSPSp*, II, 254–5, Philip II to Spes, 30 June 1570.

[50] *La Mothe*, II, 52–4 and 113–14, memoirs of 21 May and 27 July 1569. Note also *ibid.*, 202–3, memoir of 1 Sept. 1569, in which La Mothe recorded that he and Spes continued 'nostre mutuelle visitation par messaiges'.

[51] Ridolfi maintained his link with both Norfolk and Alba via the money sent by the pope and Philip II to aid English Catholics: see F. Edwards, *The Dangerous Queen* (1964), 298–300, and AGS Estado 826/137, receipt by the bishop of Ross on 22 Sept. 1569 for £2,916 paid by Ridolfi on behalf of Spes. The previous month, Ridolfi also loaned money to Arundel and Lumley, guaranteed by Norfolk and Spes: Kervijn, VI, 19–20. For his contact with Vitelli, see ASF MP 650/110, Vitelli to Secretary of State Concini, 21 July 1569.

freedom, he promised to betray those whose trust he had won.[52]

Spes continued to plot – undaunted by Ridolfi's mysterious release from prison, the failure of the Northern Rebellion, and the imprisonment of most Catholic peers. On 1 January 1570, and again ten days later, he visited the French ambassador 'for a conference on the state of affairs in this kingdom'. They concluded that Elizabeth's success against her Catholic critics might well lead to increased English intervention abroad in support of the Protestant cause, especially in France and the Netherlands 'against the interests of our masters'. Spes therefore proposed that each ambassador should urge his monarch to work together to replace Elizabeth with Mary Stuart, and that both states 'should get their armed forces ready for the hour when we, who are on the spot, will tell them'. Before long, the Catholic peers regained their liberty and resumed relations both with the ambassadors and with Ridolfi. The 'hour' seemed to be fast approaching.[53]

Alba did his best to muzzle both Spes and Ridolfi, but in September 1570, the Florentine sent details to the pope of a new plot hatched (he claimed) by Norfolk and other peers who wished to 'free Mary and restore Religion'.[54] In March 1571, armed with 'instructions, commissions and letters' from Norfolk and Mary, Ridolfi left England to secure foreign support. He first explained his mission to the duke of Alba, who feared his indiscretion as well as the deleterious implications of the plot for the Netherlands, and then to the Grand Duke of Tuscany, who expressed unqualified enthusiasm, before reaching Rome at the end of April. He arrived at a fortunate moment. Although Pius V had anxiously sought a ruler ready to carry out his Bull deposing Elizabeth the previous year, the focus of his attention had subsequently shifted to the creation of a Holy League to oppose the Turks. Now that his efforts in that quarter seemed close to success, he listened intently and enthusiastically to Ridolfi's proposal. On 20 May 1571, the same day that representatives of Spain, Venice and the papacy signed

[52] On the arrests, see *La Mothe*, II 278 and 285, letters to Charles IX, 13 and 18 Oct. 1569. For evidence that Ridolfi was 'turned' during his imprisonment, see the appendix on pp. 215–21 below. Elizabeth and her ministers also suspected that Vitelli had encouraged the Northern Rising, see Kervijn, v, 541–2, Vitelli to Alba, 6 Dec. 1569; and ASF MP 650/167v, Vitelli to Cosimo I, 22 Jan. 1570.

[53] *La Mothe*, III, 29–30 and 102, memoir to Charles IX and Catherine de Medici, 21 Jan. and 27 Mar. 1570; Kervijn, v, 653–57, Ridolfi to Spes, Spes to Alba and Alba to Spes, 13, 15 and 25 May 1570, and 673, Spes to Alba, 3 July 1570, about the Florentine's financial dealings with the Catholic peers.

[54] Kervijn, v, 644–5 and 656–7, Alba to Spes, 3 and 25 May 1570, trying to silence Ridolfi; J. M. Rigg, *Calendar of State Papers relating to English Affairs Preserved Principally at Rome*, I (1916: hereafter *CSPR*), 346–8, Ridolfi to Pius V, 1 Sept. 1570. Shortly afterwards, Ridolfi again offered his services to Walsingham as a mediator with Spain: see p. 216 below and *La Mothe*, III, 364 and 370, reports of 9 and 14 Nov. 1570.

the League, Ridolfi left Rome for Spain, armed with papal letters urging Philip to support the plan.[55]

Initially, he received a cool reception. Even before he left the Netherlands, Elizabeth's agents intercepted a letter from Ridolfi to Mary Stuart's chief adviser revealing full details of his plot – including the participation of the duke of Alba – and, when this became known, many observers concluded that 'the plot would go up in smoke'.[56] Nevertheless, at the behest of the papal nuncio (who pointed out that Ridolfi brought personal messages from the pope), on 3 July Philip granted an audience. The Florentine not only presented his 'design' but also beguiled the king with appeals to his familiarity with English affairs and his clear mandate from God to reclaim the island once more for the Catholic faith. Philip immediately forwarded the documents Ridolfi had brought to his council of state, several of whose members had (like the king) lived in England and played a part in its return to Catholicism in the 1550s.[57]

First the councillors questioned Ridolfi and also Chiappino Vitelli, who happened to be at court, about logistics. Then on 7 July 1571 – citing God's will, the pope's blessing, the plight of England's Catholics and other 'inescapable' religious pressures – they unanimously recommended to Philip a complex strategy to overthrow the Tudor regime. They resolved that Norfolk and his friends should either capture or kill the queen in the autumn while she was on her annual progress through the Home Counties. This, according to Ridolfi, would unleash a general rising of English Catholics that would free Mary Stuart, who would then marry Norfolk. At this point (but not before) ships assembled by

[55] For Alba's misgivings, see Teulet, *Relations politiques*, v, 77–87, Alba to Philip, 7 May 1571. For proof that Ridolfi also revealed his mission in Florence, see ASF MP Minuti di lettere e registri 58/80, Prince Francesco to Concini, 26 Apr. 1571. For Pius's enthusiastic reception, and for the date of Ridolfi's departure, see Serrano, *Correspondencia diplomática*, IV, 258–9 and 338n, Don Juan de Zúñiga to Philip II, 30 Apr. and 22 May 1571. J. I. Tellechea Idígoras, *El Papado y Felipe II*, I (Madrid, 1999), 239, prints a holograph brief of Pius V asking Philip II to read carefully the 'literas nostras' that Ridolfi would give him, but those letters have apparently not survived (English précis in *CSPR*, I, 407).

[56] ASF MP 610/210, Concini to Cosimo I, 12 June 1571; *La Mothe*, IV, 122–3, to Catherine de Medici, 2 June 1571, and 160–1, to Charles IX, 28 June 1571. For Philip's reaction, see *Co. Do. In.*, XC, 473, Philip II to Spes, 20 June 1571. Burghley had the letters in mid-April: F. Edwards, *The Marvellous Chance: Thomas Howard, Fourth Duke of Norfolk, and the Ridolphi Plot 1570–2* (1968), 45–84.

[57] *CSPR*, I, 413–26, prints an English translation of Ridolfi's memorial and exhortation. Serrano, *Correspondencia diplomática*, IV, 380–1, Castagna to Rusticucci, 3 July 1571, reported the audience (précis in *CSPR*, I, 435–6). Perhaps Philip, like Pius, saw the signature of the Holy League as an auspicious omen. The Venetian ambassador in Madrid recorded the king's high spirits at precisely this time: M. Brunetti and E. Vitale, *La corrispondenza da Madrid dell' ambasciatore Leonardo Donà (1570–1573)*, I (Venice and Rome, 1963), 318–23, Donà to Doge and Senate, 3 July 1571.

Alba in the ports of Zealand, reinforced by a flotilla already standing by at Santander, would carry 6,000 troops drawn from the army of Flanders across to England to assist Norfolk. The council called on Philip to send Alba 200,000 ducats specifically to prepare this task force.[58]

When, two days later, the nuncio obtained another audience to urge the king to support Ridolfi's plot, to his surprise,

> His Majesty, contrary to his normal custom [at audiences], spoke at length and entered into great detail about the means, the place and the men [to be involved] ... He ended by saying that he had wanted and waited a long time for an occasion and opportunity to reduce, with God's help, that kingdom to the [Catholic] faith and the obedience of the Apostolic See a second time, and that he believed the time had now come, and that this was the occasion and the opportunity for which he had waited.

The nuncio also noted that 'every day, at all hours, His Majesty asks Ridolfi for various pieces of information, to which he provides excellent answers. So that we have high hopes.' But, he cautioned, 'His Majesty has *not* yet said "Write and tell the pope that I promise to undertake this venture"! Rather, his words signified that he was now inclined to do so, but wished first to take advice on the means and the method.'[59]

Immediately after this audience the king moved from Madrid to El Escorial where, in gratitude for his victory over the French at the battle of St Quentin on 10 August 1557, St Lawrence's day, he had founded a monastery dedicated to that saint because 'he understood that such an illustrious beginning to his reign came through the saint's favour and intercession'.[60] The king intended the Escorial complex to resemble Solomon's Temple and, throughout his reign, he sponsored research on that eminent structure and insisted that his architects incorporate its findings. Like Solomon, Philip therefore used gold, bronze and precious stones as the principal adornments; he attached a royal palace to the shrine erected to honour God; and he placed giant statues of six kings of Israel involved in building the Temple outside the basilica. Even 'the stonecutting technique implemented at the Escorial was

---

[58] F. Mignet, *Histoire de Marie Stuart*, II (5th edn, Paris, 1877), 428–31, consulta of the council of state, 7 July 1571 (a remarkable document which records the substance of each councillor's views at two meetings of the council, and a further interview with Ridolfi, all on the same day). On Vitelli's involvement, see Serrano, *Correspondencia diplomática*, IV, 381–4, Castagna to Ruticucci, 9 July 1571. Feria, Ruy Gómez de Silva, Don Antonio de Toledo and Secretary of State Gabriel de Zayas had all resided in England in the 1550s.

[59] Serrano, *Correspondencia diplomática*, IV, 382, Castagna to Rusticucci, 9 July 1571 (précis in *CSPR*, I, 436–7).

[60] J. de Sigüenza, *La Fundación del Monasterio de El Escorial* (1605: Madrid, 1988), 8.

modelled on the one used in Solomon's quarries'.[61]

In the summer of 1571, the Jeronimites assigned to the new monastery moved from their temporary lodgings and sang mass for the first time in the new building, with the king looking on from a window in his apartment, which overlooked the altar. Shortly afterwards, a group of novices arrived from Madrid, followed by more monks from a neighbouring religious house. This raised the religious complement at the Escorial to forty and Philip delighted in attending their daily services. 'You can well imagine', a minister wrote to his colleague 'the happiness that His Majesty feels when he sees things already in this state.' In this heady atmosphere of exhaustion and exaltation, the king decided to overthrow the Tudor state.[62]

On 13 July 1571, at the Escorial, Philip signed a letter informing Don Guerau de Spes that he had met with Ridolfi and listened to his proposal; that he wanted to participate in the plot; but that it would take time to arrange. Spes must do nothing until he received further orders. The king also instructed his ambassador in Rome to restrain the pope from taking any precipitate action.[63] The following day,

---

[61] A vast literature has grown up on the parallels between the Temple and the Escorial. See, above all, G. Lazure, 'Perceptions of the Temple, Projections of the Divine: Royal Patronage, Biblical Scholarship and Jesuit Imagery in Spain, 1580–1620', *Calamvs Renascens: Revista de Humanismo y tradición clásica*, 1 (2000), 155–88, quotation from 170; J. L. Gonzalo Sánchez-Molero, 'Los orígenes de la imagen salomónica del real Monasterio de San Lorenzo de El Escorial', in *Literatura e imagen en El Escorial: actas del simposium* (El Escorial, 1996), 721–49; and the article by Cuadra Blanco cited in n. 29 above. For the sponsored research, see vol. VIII of the *Biblia Regia* (Antwerp, 1572); J. Prado and J. B. del Villalpando, *In Ezechielem explanationes et apparatus urbi ac Templi Hierosolymitiani* (3 vols., Rome, 1596–1604; Spanish translation, Madrid, 1991); and BNM MS 6035/134–54, 'Relación sumaria del modelo de la antigua Hierusalem', a description of a model of the city and temple sent by Villalpando (along with the first volume of *In Ezecheliem*) in a gilded chest bearing the arms and style of 'Philip II, the Catholic King of Spain and Jerusalem' and presented to Philip in person.

[62] Details from Sigüenza, *Fundación*, 42–3; quotation from AGS Estado 153/77, Velasco to Zayas, 9 Aug. 1571. For the king's involvement in services, and its impact on the transaction of business, see the entry for 25 July, St James's Day, in the 'Diurnal' of Antonio Gracián, who served as the king's private secretary at this point: *Documentos para la historia del monasterio de San Lorenzo El Real de El Escorial*, VIII [hereafter *DE*], ed. G. de Andrés (El Escorial, 1965), 46. See also p. 202 below.

[63] *Co. Do. In.*, XC, 477–8 (précis in *CSPSp*, II, 323), Philip II to Spes, 13 July 1571, enclosing letters from Ridolfi to Norfolk and Mary for Spes to forward; Serrano, *Correspondencia diplomática*, IV, 389–90, Secretary of State Zayas to Don Juan de Zúñiga, 17 July 1571. Although Zayas, in Madrid not the Escorial, told Zúñiga that the contents of the letter to Alba were the same as the one to Spes, he was wrong (note that Zayas did not countersign the letter of 14 July, nor has a copy survived among the *Estado* series in Simancas). As usual, Philip sent the letters via Brussels and, as soon as Alba read them, he forbade Spes to pass on the letters 'or even to say a word, large or small' to the recipients until he received further orders: Kervijn, VI, 157–8, Alba to Spes, 30 July 1571.

however, Philip sent an express courier to the duke of Alba with a secret letter that went much further. It began by stating that Mary Stuart was 'the true and legitimate' heir to the English throne, 'occupied by Elizabeth (*la Isabel*) through tyranny' and asserted that the duke of Norfolk

> Has the resolve, and so many and such prominent friends, that if I provide some help it would be easy for him to kill or capture Elizabeth (*le sería facil matar o prender a la Isabel*) and to place the Scottish queen at liberty and in possession of the throne. Then, if she marries the duke of Norfolk, as they have arranged, they will without difficulty reduce [England] to the obedience of the Holy See, restore the Catholic faith, and renew to my entire satisfaction the ancient treaties of friendship that I and my predecessors have maintained with that crown.

Philip promised to send Alba detailed instructions with another courier 'in a few days' – 'right now I only want to share my plan with you' – but he advised the duke that the conspirators had asked (via Ridolfi) for 6,000 infantry armed with arquebuses for England, 2,000 for Scotland and 2,000 more for Ireland, plus a reserve of 4,000 arquebuses, 2,000 suits of armour and 25 field guns. The duke must have everything ready within six weeks. No doubt realising that this would seem totally unrealistic, Philip assured Alba that, 'since the cause is so much His, God will enlighten, aid and assist us with His mighty hand and arm, so that we will get things right'.[64]

The king's unbounded religious elation amazed even councillors who had worked with him for years. 'It is extraordinary to see the ardour of His Majesty for the Enterprise of England', one of them wrote to a colleague, 'and how little it has been cooled by the news that the queen knows about Ridolfi's plans, and by the mistrust of the duke [of Alba].' 'Certainly, I have never seen, nor would you believe, the ardour of His Majesty in this business.'[65] A few days later the same minister added 'I have never seen the king as animated in any other item of business.' The duke of Feria, who had served as Philip's ambassador in England and thereafter championed the English Catholic exiles at the Spanish court, voiced the same sentiments. 'His Majesty is very ardent in this

[64] AA 7/58, Philip II to Alba, 14 July 1571, cyphered with decrypt, received in record time on 30 July. The king repeated three times that Elizabeth would be 'either killed or captured' (in that order), and in another paragraph 'dispatched' (which, as in English, often meant 'killed'). Pollen, *English Catholics*, 176 n. 2, tries to diminish the menace of these words, but he fails to convince (he also overlooks the threatening use of 'La Isabel' instead of 'the queen' throughout Philip's letter.)

[65] AGS Estado 153/68 and British Library [hereafter BL] Additional 28,336/70, Velasco to Zayas and to Espinosa, both on 27 July 1571.

English business – and rightly so, because if it succeeds it will be the most prestigious and useful thing for him. Otherwise, the Netherlands will always hang by a very thin thread' (a very perceptive strategic observation!).[66]

When on 4 August Philip sent the 'detailed instructions' he had promised Alba he began cautiously by acknowledging that 'we must not undertake or start this venture, either by war or plot; rather it must be started by [Norfolk and his associates]'. He also expressed some doubts about Ridolfi's credibility but urged Alba to operate on the assumption that the plot would unfold as planned: the duke must therefore be ready to intervene the moment Norfolk had proclaimed Mary Stuart as queen of England. Philip also proposed that a fleet at Santander, bearing 1,200 Spanish troops under the command of the Julián Romero (a veteran who had served in England) originally intended to reinforce the army of Flanders, should instead take part in the invasion. Realising that these orders would appal the duke, Philip administered another strong dose of messianic blackmail:

> No one can deny that this venture involves many and great difficulties, and that if it goes wrong we will incur considerable inconveniences (as you have prudently pointed out) ... In spite of all this I desire to achieve this enterprise so much, and I have such complete confidence that God our Lord, to whose service it is dedicated, will guide and direct it (because I have no personal ambition here), and I hold my charge from God to do this to be so explicit, that I am totally determined and resolved to proceed and participate, doing on my side everything possible in this world to promote and assist it.[67]

Philip also casually announced two more changes to the plan: his decision to entrust command of the expeditionary force to Chiappino Vitelli, who would return to Flanders immediately, and the inclusion of yet another group of dubious English conspirators.

In April 1571, George Fitzwilliam, representing John Hawkins, whose fleet Philip's forces had attacked and largely destroyed in the Caribbean over two years before, arrived at the Spanish Court. Hawkins had left Fitzwilliam in Mexico as a hostage and he languished in gaol until, in July 1570, Feria had him set free. Fitzwilliam made his way back to England and reported to Hawkins that twenty more of his men remained in prison in Seville.[68] Hawkins now visited Spes and promised that he would never again sail to American waters if only Philip would

---

[66] AGS Estado 153/72, Velasco to Zayas, 1 Aug. 1571, and 153/102, Feria to Zayas, 2 Aug. 1571.

[67] BMO, I, 57–9, Philip II to Alba, 4 Aug. 1571.

[68] Archivo General de Indias [hereafter AGI], Justicia 902/2/500–1, royal order to release Fitzwilliam, 27 July 1570, received and implemented on 3 Aug.

restore his men and his goods. Even the normally credulous Spes remained unconvinced – 'It just isn't wise to believe these people' he told Alba – and so Hawkins resolved on yet another strategy.[69] In March 1571, the same month that Roberto Ridolfi left England, George Fitzwilliam left for Spain bearing an offer from John Hawkins to place a small fleet at Philip's disposal.

Fitzwilliam boasted excellent connections which improved his credibility. His relatives included both the Irish lord deputy, Henry Sidney, and the Irish treasurer-at-war, Sir William Fitzwilliam; he was thus also kin both to Elizabeth's favourite, the earl of Leicester (whose sister had married Sidney), and to her chief minister, William Cecil (Lord Burghley from 1571, and married to one of Fitzwilliam's cousins). Through the Sidneys, he was also a close relative of Lady Jane Dormer, duchess of Feria.[70] Fitzwilliam brought a letter from Hawkins to the duchess, thanking her for helping to free him (and two of the other hostages) and asking her to help free the rest of his men. After a few days waiting for an answer, Fitzwilliam appeared to become restless and, under the duchess's patient questioning, he confessed that Hawkins had entrusted him with a second mission:

> If [Philip II] should decide to free the queen of Scots and support the Catholic party so that they would place the said queen on the English throne, John Hawkins and his brother would come with twenty-five ships to take part and assist, because they were Catholics and held the queen of Scotland to be their true sovereign.

Feria now stepped in and began to ask Fitzwilliam for more information: who were his Catholic supporters, had he made contact with Mary Stuart, how many ships and guns did he have, how much would it cost to hire them and what recompense did he seek? Failing to receive satisfactory responses, Feria ordered Fitzwilliam to return to England to secure not only answers to eleven specific questions but also a formal letter of authorisation from Hawkins and a letter of credence from Mary. In return, Feria sent a ring to Hawkins, and another to Mary,

---

[69] Kervijn, v, 693–4, Spes to Alba, 21 Aug. 1570. A few days later he said the same to the king: *CSPSp*, II, 274, Spes to Philip II, 2 Sept. 1571. Philip had come across Hawkins before: see his comments on information about him in letters from Guzmán: *Co. Do. In.*, LXXXIX, 21 (31 July 1564), 177–8 (27 Aug. 1565), 264–5 (4 Feb. 1566). He later received a stream of information about Hawkins's third voyage to the Caribbean in 1567–8 and even a copy of the captain's own account of his 'Unfortunate Voyage': Kervijn, v, 384–5, Spes to Alba, 15 May 1569.

[70] The mother of Jane Dormer, duchess of Feria, was Henry Sidney's sister, Mary. For the other connections, see M. E. Finch, *The Wealth of Five Northamptonshire Families, 1540–1640* (Oxford, 1956), 102–7, 112–14, and the Fitzwilliam 'pedigree'. George may have been the son of Brian Fitzwilliam, Sir William's brother.

while the duchess of Feria and Philip sent gifts for the queen of Scots.[71]

As soon as Fitzwilliam arrived back in England, he visited Don Guerau de Spes, explained his mission and asked him to arrange a meeting with Mary. When the ambassador proved unable to oblige, Hawkins asked Lord Burghley 'to obtain him a license to have access unto her, for her letter to the king of Spain, for the better obtaining of our men's liberty: which, otherwise, are not to be released'. Burghley duly arranged the meeting, which took place in early June, and Fitzwilliam delivered the duchess's gifts. In return, he received from the queen a missal in gold letters with a special dedication in Mary's hand for the duchess, and letters for both Feria and Philip II requesting the release of Hawkins's men. Fitzwilliam at once showed the package to Burghley – no doubt as part of the bargain to get him access – and to Hawkins. At this point, if not before, Hawkins also told Burghley of his offer to serve Spain with a fleet and suggested that this might be used to 'discover the practices of the enemies' (Burghley had just got wind of the Ridolfi plot) as well as to secure compensation for his losses.[72]

Fitzwilliam now visited Ambassador Spes again and, with Burghley's open support, requested a passport to return to Spain. He arrived there late in July 1571, bringing with him Mary's package, an ingratiating letter from Hawkins (who claimed to be Feria's servant 'to the end of his days'), and Hawkins's answers to the duke's eleven specific questions. These proved disappointing: Hawkins confessed that he had no contact with English or foreign Catholics, that he had no links with Mary Stuart except via Fitzwilliam, and that he had only sixteen ships.[73]

[71] The documentation in this matter is problematic. Fitzwilliam brought no written offer from Hawkins: he merely wrote it out when requested by the duchess of Feria (AGS Estado 824/26, 'Lo que Jorge Fitzvilliams, gentilhombre inglés embiado por el Capitán Juan Aquines, refiere'). Feria's conversation and his questions are in Estado 824/27 and 28 (copy in BL Additional 26,056B/172), 'Memoria de las cosas que el duque de Feria dixo al criado de Juan Haquines' [Apr. 1571]. AGS Estado 824/29, 'Lo que propone Jorge Fitzwillians', contains a detailed account of the delicate negotiation with Feria and his wife (perhaps written to inform Alba). Feria's 'articles', and the gifts brought back by Fitzwilliam, were later described in a paper written by Hawkins for Burghley: BL Cotton Galba C.V/263–5, 'touchinge his intelligence', Jan. 1577.

[72] On the abortive attempt to arrange a visit through Spes, see BL Cotton Caligula c.III/228–9, bishop of Ross to Burghley, 9 Nov. 1571 (although the meeting must have taken place in May, and not March as the bishop recalled). Interestingly, Ross feared that Fitzwilliam might be a 'practiser'. For Burghley's role, see *An English Garner: Voyages and Travels, Mainly during the Sixteenth and Seventeenth Centuries*, ed. T. Seccombe (Edinburgh, 1902), 127–9, Hawkins to Burghley, 13 May and 7 June 1571. On Fitzwilliam's audience with Mary, see W. K. Boyd, *Calendar of State Papers relating to Scotland and Mary Queen of Scots*, III (Edinburgh, 1903), 595, earl of Shrewsbury to Burghley, 3 June 1571.

[73] *Co. Do. In.*, XC, 471, Spes to Philip II, 15 June 1571, reporting Fitzwilliam's visit (précis in *CSPSp*, II, 317–18); AGS Estado 824/33, Hawkins to Feria, 14 June 1571; AGS Estado 824/25 (copy at BL Additional 26,056B/231–2), 'La respuesta que dió Jorge Fitzwilliams

Nevertheless, as a Spanish minister noted, 'In this matter, His Majesty proceeds in a way that excludes nothing that can help him' and Philip immediately turned the dossier over to his council of state and to Roberto Ridolfi. The former debated the matter on 28 July, 'but without reaching a conclusion'; the latter submitted a paper four days later which, while generally favourable, added an important additional task for Hawkins – to set fire to the royal navy as it lay at anchor.[74] Although some councillors feared deception, the opportunity seemed too good to miss. 'We have discussed and examined this business of the Englishman [sent by] Hawkins and, having heard in detail what he says and the responses he has given to our questions, it seems more substantial than we were led to believe. It also seems that he is more truthful and open than it seemed', wrote the normally suspicious Dr Martin de Velasco. 'We therefore decided [to go ahead], holding this to be one of the most important ways to achieve the goal of this sacred business.'[75] Euphoria at the approach of the patronal festival of the monastery – and the anniversary of the victory at St Quentin – seems to have affected everyone at the Escorial. 'His Majesty is so enthusiastic about these plans for England that he makes me seem indifferent to them!' wrote the duke of Feria.

> The fact that we are going to take the final decision on the eve of St Lawrence's day is no small cause for greater hope, because on the same day we knocked the French for six (*dimos con la casa de Francia patas arriba*) – which is no more than the truth, because they have never raised their heads again. And, please God, so it will be in this business.[76]

Having taken the fateful decision to accept Hawkins's offer to help destroy Elizabeth, the king, his courtiers and the monks together

---

en nombre de Juan Haquins', Madrid, 27 July 1571; and Estado 824/34, 'Memoria de los naves con que Juan Haquins offresce seruir a Su Magestad.' Fitzwilliam also brought some papers written by Hawkins in an execrable mixture of Spanish and Italian (e.g. 'Los navios de I. H., sus portaio y quantos hombres poido levar': AGS Estado 826/74–6) and a holograph letter from Mary Stuart to Philip, dated 3 June 1571: Estado 826/86.

[74] AGS Estado 153/77, Velasco to Zayas, 9 Aug. 1571; *DE*, 48 (entry for 28 July 1571); Estado 824/24, 'Memoriale di Roberto Ridolfi sopra la Petitione d'Achins' (probably the document noted by Gracián in *DE*, 50: entry for 2 Aug. 1571). Thomas Stukeley, another enemy of Elizabeth at the Spanish Court (pp. 217–18 below), had already suggested setting fire to the queen's ships in the Medway (see *CSPR*, I, 374–5, papers of Feb. 1571).

[75] BL Additional 28,336/76, Velasco to Espinosa, 9 Aug. 1571. For discussion of Hawkins's terms see AGS Estado 153/95, Feria to Zayas, 26 July 1571; and *DE*, 51 (8 Aug. 1571). Part of the reluctance to free the English stemmed from worries that it might produce pressure to free French prisoners taken in Florida: Estado 153/48, Gracián to Zayas, 6 Aug. 1571 (copy at BL Egerton 2047/280–1). For fears of a ruse, see the sources in n. 77 below.

[76] AGS Estado 153/103, Feria to Zayas, 9 Aug. 1571.

celebrated a sung mass, solemn vespers and finally matins. 'His Majesty was present at all of them,' Philip's secretary noted, adding slyly: 'although he was writing letters during part of the matins.' He continued: 'The king does not have time to hear the decisions taken by the various councils in the afternoon until after dinner; and then he has to decide how to reply to each minister.' It was not an atmosphere conducive to clear-headed decision-making.[77]

On St Lawrence's day, 10 August 1571, Feria and Fitzwilliam signed their agreement. The latter promised, in Hawkins's name, to serve with his sixteen ships for six weeks at Philip's expense wherever the king (or Alba in his name) should order. In return, the English prisoners still in Seville would gain their freedom and all those involved in the 1568 expedition would get a full pardon, while Hawkins and Fitzwilliam received permission to bring suit in the king's courts for the losses they claimed.[78] Feria thereupon revealed details of the entire Enterprise to Fitzwilliam and sent him back to England with explanatory letters for Hawkins, Spes and Mary. The king also granted Fitzwilliam an audience, presented him with 500 ducats in gold for his expenses, a ring and a beautiful ruby for Mary.[79]

The involvement of Hawkins compromised the 'Enterprise of England' in three ways. First, adding another fleet made the plan dan-

---

[77] AGS Estado 153/54, Gracián to Zayas, 9 Aug. 1571, full of details on the frantic pace of work among the ministers at the Escorial. Gracián served as secretary to the group of councillors of state at the Escorial since Zayas remained in Madrid (DE, 43, entry for 18 July). The correspondence of the two groups, preserved in AGS Estado 153 and BL Additional 28,336, together with Gracián's 'Diurnal', provides a day-by-day account of Philip's decision-making unequalled for any other period of his reign.

[78] T. González, 'Apuntamientos para la historia del rey D. Felipe II', Memorias de la Real Academia de la Historia, 7 (1832), 364–5, 'Lo que se ha tractado' between Feria and Fitzwilliam, 10 Aug. 1571 (original at AGS Estado 824/35; copies at ibid., fos. 37 and 54, and BL Additional 26,056B/241–2; slightly amended copy at ABZ 153/153). Philip's approval is at Estado 824/32 (draft at fo. 33, copy at fo. 36). AGS Estado 824/34, 'Memoria de los nauios con que Juan Aquines offresce seruir a su Magestad' (copy at fo. 37 and IVdeDJ 88/340) is in effect a codicil to this agreement, setting out in detail the ships, crews and guns that Hawkins would provide. See also Feria's draft at Estado 824/184, with ideas on how Hawkins could raise a larger fleet. For the order to free the English prisoners in Seville, see AGS Estado 153/75–8, Velasco to Zayas, 5, 9 and 11 Aug. 1571; and AGI Justicia 908/2/10v–12, royal pardon for Hawkins, Fitzwilliam and others, 10 Aug. 1571 (register copy).

[79] Public Record Office, London, State Papers 70/119/86, Feria to Hawkins, 11 Aug. 1571, holograph, professing himself 'your true friend'. For the audience and gifts, see DE, 52 (entry for 10 Aug.), and BL Additional 28,336/76, Velasco to Espinosa, 9 Aug. 1571. The ruby ring brought out the miserly side of both Philip and Elizabeth. The king did not choose one of his own jewels to give to Mary, but one of those that had belonged to his late son, Don Carlos (ibid.); and when Fitzwilliam showed Elizabeth the stone, she kept it! (BL Cotton Galba C.V/263v, Hawkins's statement of January 1577: 'The kynge sent agayne to quene Mary a fayre rube in a rynge, which the quen's majestie now hath').

gerously unwieldy. Philip intended Hawkins's ships to ferry Alba's troops across the Channel, so that now three different forces – each separated from the others by hundreds miles of sea (in Plymouth, Santander and Zealand) – must unite before the invasion could take place. Second, the long delay in finalising arrangements allowed knowledge of Philip's intentions to spread far and wide. According to the nuncio in Paris, 'this plot of Ridolfi has been revealed in this Court just as in England'; while the Grand Duke of Tuscany observed that it had become 'public knowledge not only in France but also here and in Rome'.[80] Sometimes, of course, the decision to persevere with an obvious strategy, even one that has been talked about for months, can still achieve total surprise; but when major participants betray every move, a successful outcome becomes highly unlikely.[81] For, third and finally, both Fitzwilliam and Hawkins were double agents.

In hindsight, the warning signs seem obvious: the inherent improbability that Hawkins, having been so recently humiliated by Spain, would offer his services; the knowledge that Fitzwilliam had been in frequent contact with Burghley.[82] But Philip, his heart uplifted by the ceremonies at the Escorial, and confident that God would provide, overlooked or ignored all contrary indications. Instead, the day after approving the agreement with Fitzwilliam and granting him an audience, he sent Chiappino Vitelli word of his appointment as commander of the invasion army. The Florentine was appalled: 'Cardinal Espinosa, who is like a second king here, instead of giving me news of some nice reward, told me that His Majesty had decided that I should return to the Netherlands to serve him in the Ridolfi business.' Although flattered that the king and his advisers 'placed more confidence in him than in

[80] Serrano, *Correspondencia diplomática*, IV, 397n, nuncio in France to Rusticucci, 2 Aug. 1571; ASF MP 4905/105v, Grand Duke Cosimo to his ambassadors in Spain, 12 Sept. 1571.

[81] See E. Luttwak, *Strategy: The Logic of War and Peace* (Cambridge, MA, 1987), 7–17, for an illuminating discussion on 'The conscious use of paradox in war.' It is worth remembering that Elizabeth did indeed make a progress through Essex in August and September 1571, where she would have been more vulnerable to assassination: see J. Nichols, *The Progresses and Public Processions of Queen Elizabeth*, I (1823), 279–82.

[82] Philip asked Spes to verify Hawkins's reliability (*Co. Do. In.*, xc, 477, letter of 13 July 1571), but did not wait for his reply before accepting the bargain (*ibid.*, 488, Spes to Philip, 8 Aug. 1571). On 19 July Spes mentioned that Fitzwilliam had 'often' communicated with Burghley (*Co. Do. In.*, xc, 480–1), a fact which Philip duly noted (*ibid.*, 493–5, 30 Aug. 1571). Spes also told the king that although Norfolk was 'ynclinado a la confesión augustana' (!), his Catholic relatives considered that he might convert if the time were right (AHN OM 3511/4, 'Consideraciones de Don Guerao de Spes'). Although several of Philip's councillors feared 'engaño' (a ruse), none seemed to notice these points: see AGS Estado 153/75 and 77, Velasco to Zayas, 5 and 9 Aug. 1571; *ibid.*, fo. 100, Feria to Zayas, 29 July 1571; BL Additional 28,336/78, Velasco to Espinosa, 14 Aug. 1571 ('If this is a ruse, it will not draw much blood from us').

any other Italian', according to the Florentine ambassador in Madrid, 'Chiappino suspected that everything would go up in smoke.'[83]

He was not the only one. Receipt of the king's letter of 4 August provoked a fresh torrent of protest from the duke of Alba.

> I confess to Your Majesty that this letter has placed me in the greatest confusion, because at the beginning Your Majesty says that it is not your intention to take a course of action that would lead to the outbreak of war with our neighbours, and elsewhere Your Majesty tells me that you wish to help the duke of Norfolk ... which, done in the way you describe, is a clear and direct declaration of war.

The duke railed against the reliance placed by the king on the opinions of people like Spes, who 'although a fine gentleman ... has not the experience of public affairs to deal with something as important as this', and Ridolfi, 'who is not a soldier, and has not seen a military operation in his life'.

> [They] think that one can conjure up armies out of thin air or pull them out of one's sleeve, and achieve with them whatever occurs in their imagination. To claim that at the same time one can create one army to capture the queen of England and another to free the queen of Scotland, and that at the same time one can capture the Tower of London and set fire to the galleons in the river [Medway] – well, even if Your Majesty and the queen of England agreed to cooperate to make it happen, even that would not suffice to make it happen at the time they propose.

The duke devoted the next several pages to repeating 'what I have written to you so many times before about the dangers that will arise when Your Majesty makes war on England' and concluded bluntly: 'I have not even begun to make any preparations.'[84]

Devastated by this news, the king responded with more messianic rhetoric. On 14 September, dismissing all Alba's practical objections, he repeated that

[83] ASF MP 650/340, Vitelli to Concini, 11 Aug. 1571; ASF MP 4903 unfol., Leonardo de' Nobili, Florentine ambassador in Madrid, to Prince Francesco, 24 Aug. 1571. It was characteristic of Philip's administrative style to make the announcement through a minister rather than in person; however, Vitelli insisted on a personal briefing from the king, which took place at the Escorial two days later: *DE*, 53 (entry for 13 Aug. 1571); BL Additional 28,336/78, Velasco to Espinosa, 14 Aug. 1571; and AGS Estado 153/83, Velasco to Zayas, 14 Aug. 1571.

[84] *BMO*, I, 59–62, Alba to Philip II, 27 Aug. 1571. The duke's contempt for Spes knew no bounds: see the first paragraph on p. 60 of this letter and the further examples cited in n. 48 above. Some years later Alba stated that only the ambassador's murder on the way back to Spain had saved him from disgrace and imprisonment (Ramsay, *The Queen's Merchants*, 161).

I am so keen to achieve the consummation of this enterprise, I am so attached to it in my heart, and I am so convinced that God our Saviour must embrace it as His own cause, that I cannot be dissuaded, nor can I accept or believe the contrary. This leads me to understand matters differently [from you], and makes me play down the difficulties and problems that spring up; so that all the things that could either divert or stop me from carrying through this business seem less threatening to me.

He reminded Alba that, if Spain did not act, Elizabeth would surely turn on her Catholic subjects and either kill, expel or force them to convert. 'How many greater, more dangerous and more difficult obligations will that create for us? How shall we explain ourselves to God? What shame shall we feel if things come to that pass?'[85]

It no longer mattered. Fitzwilliam reached England on or before 4 September, ten days before Philip wrote his anguished letter, and immediately shared with Hawkins his detailed information on Spain's invasion plans. Hawkins in turn sent them (and Fitzwilliam) straight to Burghley, who ordered Norfolk's arrest and sent a letter 'haste, post haste, haste, haste for life, life, life' instructing Mary's jailer to keep the queen closely confined and to 'provoke her to answer' questions concerning 'her labours and devices to stir up a new rebellion in this realm [of England] and to have the king of Spain assist it'.[86]

The information produced by this and other, harsher, interrogations, marked a turning point for Elizabethan England. At home, the queen's government increased its surveillance of all Catholics and executed those who proved obdurate (including Norfolk); it also kept far closer watch on Mary. Abroad, Elizabeth made haste to sink her differences with France, negotiating a defensive alliance that promised French assistance should England be attacked by a foreign power. 'For the first seven months of the year 1572', wrote Ambassador La Mothe at the end of his embassy, 'the king of France was able to act in England as if it were his own duchy of Brittany.' Although María José Rodríguez-

---

[85] *BMO*, I, 62–4, Philip II to Alba, 14 Sept. 1571. See also two earlier euphoric letters on 30 Aug. 1571: Algemeen Rijksarchief, The Hague, *Staten Generaal* 12548, loketkas 14B/14, to Alba (telling the duke to send money to Mary's supporters in Scotland); and *Co. Do. In.*, XC, 493–5 (précis in *CSPSp*, II, 333–4), to Spes (with news of Hawkins's involvement).

[86] See Williamson, *Hawkins*, 185–6, Hawkins to Burghley, 4 Sept. 1571; P. Collinson, *The English Captivity of Mary Queen of Scots* (Sheffield, 1987), 42–3, Burghley to Lord Shrewsbury, 5 Sept. 1571; and *Co. Do. In.*, XC, 497, Spes to Philip II, 7 Sept. 1571 (on a visit from Fitzwilliam). Note the striking difference in the questions put to Norfolk's servants before and after Fitzwilliam's return: W. Murdin, *Collection of State Papers ... Left by William Cecil*, II (1759), 67–71 (interrogations of Robert Higford, 2, 4 and 17 Sept. 1571) and 87–90 (interrogations of William Barker, 4, 5 and 10 Sept. 1571).

Salgado is right to stress that peace rather than war continued to characterise Anglo-Spanish relations for the next thirteen years, Elizabeth never trusted Spain and her monarch again. In December 1571, she told La Mothe confidentially:

> that since the king of Spain had worked so hard to provoke and create havoc in [her kingdom] – of which she had proof in intercepted letters written with his own hand and by several of his ministers, and in the form of his tokens and rings intended for those who were to lead the said enterprise – she no longer held herself restrained by the consideration she had always shown him until now.[87]

Elizabeth proved as good as her word: henceforth, she openly welcomed and succoured rebels against Philip, whether in the Netherlands, in America or (after the Spanish annexation of 1580) in Portugal. In addition, she tolerated, and sometimes sponsored, privateering activity against Philip's monarchy: a dozen major expeditions left England in the 1570s to plunder Spanish property.

The king soon learned that Elizabeth had arrested Norfolk and discovered his plan to invade; yet, strangely, the dashing of his plans to overthrow the Tudor regime did not affect his messianic vision. For two more months, he continued to hope that either Ridolfi or Hawkins would achieve something. In November 1571, he signed *Instructions* to the duke of Medinaceli, still waiting with a fleet and Julián Romero's Spaniards at Santander, which warned him to be ready to invade England should Alba issue the order while he was at sea. Early in 1572, on reading in a letter from Don Guerau de Spes that Hawkins and Fitzwilliam still stood ready to serve Spain, the king scribbled hopefully in the margin: 'We need to take care that this is not thwarted too, like all the rest.' In 1574, he again laid plans to invade England, using a fleet assembled in Santander, and in 1579-80 he allowed his ships to convey two papal expeditionary forces to Smerwick in Ireland.[88]

How can we explain this persistence since, as Primo Levi once noted, 'few are the men who draw moral strength from failure'? Part of the explanation lies in a series of spectacular events in other theatres that

---

[87] *La Mothe*, I, xxviii, La Mothe's 'Discourse' in July 1575 (in the eighth month of 1572, of course, the Massacre of St Bartholomew caused Elizabeth to draw back from the French alliance); and IV, 315-17, to Charles IX, 22 Dec. 1571, relating a conversation 'tout bas' with Elizabeth at dinner three days before. Five months later she repeated that Philip's plots to overthrow her justified England's aid to the Dutch rebels: *ibid.*, 453-5, to Charles IX, 13 May 1572.

[88] *CSPSp*, II, 349, Instruction to Medinaceli, 11 Nov. 1571; *Co. Do. In.*, XC, 528-9, Philip apostil on a letter from Spes, 12 Dec. 1571. See also, however, his pessimistic assessment noted on p. 221 below. For the invasion projects of 1574 and 1579-80, see Parker, *Grand Strategy*, 164-7.

served to reassure Philip that he still enjoyed God's support. In October 1571, his brother, Don John of Austria, routed the Turks at Lepanto. At the Escorial, the monks attributed the king's success to his veneration of St Lawrence while, in Madrid, a minister compared it with the drowning of Pharaoh's army in the Red Sea and argued that such an indubitable sign of God's special Providence towards Spain 'leaves us with little more to desire but much to expect from His Divine mercy'.[89] Messianic visions concerning Philip now turned from England back to the Mediterranean. Poets and playwrights – led by Tasso and Cervantes – composed works that called for the liberation of Jerusalem; and many speculated that Philip would continue, with God's grace, to lead a new crusade and revive the title 'emperor of the east'.[90] The following year, the massacre of St Bartholomew seemed to end the Protestant menace in both France and the Netherlands, and news of the events in Paris caused Philip 'to laugh, with signs of extreme pleasure and satisfaction'. He told his ambassador in France (the source of the news) that:

> I had one of the greatest moments of satisfaction that I have had in all my life; and I shall feel the same again when you write to tell me what else has happened, and especially what is going on in the other towns and regions of that kingdom. If they do the same as in Paris, it will set the seal on the matter.

Six years later, the death of King Sebastian of Portugal and many of his nobles in battle, which left Philip as heir presumptive to the Portuguese throne, also seemed like the handiwork of God, 'because Divine Providence does not permit an extraordinary event, such as the

[89] P. Levi, *The Drowned and the Saved* (1988), 48; Sigüenza, *Fundación*, 42; BL Additional 28,704/270v–1, Espinosa to Alba and Don Juan de Zúñiga, 4 Dec. 1571, minutes, on the victory, 'la mayor después de la del Vermejo'. Fernando de Herrera's canticle on Lepanto also compared the victory with the drowning of Pharaoh's army in the Red Sea (see J. López de Toro, *Los poetas de Lepanto* (Madrid, 1950), 233–42).

[90] For the poems and plays, see P. García Martín, 'La *Jerusalén libertada*: el discurso cruzado en los autores del Barroco', in *Felipe II y su tiempo: V reunión científica: asociación española de historia moderna*, ed. J. L. Pereira Iglesias, 1 (Cadiz, 1999), 45–52. On the host of prophecies unleashed in Italy by the victory, see C. Ginzburg. 'Due note sul profetismo cinquecentesco', *Rivista storica italiana*, 78 (1966), 184–227, at 207–12; A. Olivieri, 'Il significato escatologico di Lepanto nella storia religiosa del mediterraneo del 500', in *Il Mediterraneo nella seconda metà del '500 alla luce di Lepanto*, ed. G. Benzoni (Civiltà veneziani, studi xxx, Florence, 1974), 257–77; H. Jedin, *Chiesa della Storia* (Bergamo, 1972), 703–22; and E. García Hernán, 'Pío V y el mesianismo profético', *Hispania Sacra*, 45 (1993), 83–102. For the 'emperor of the east' project, see E. García Hernán, *La Armada española en la monarquía de Felipe II y la defensa del Mediterráneo* (Madrid, 1995), 67–8. Nevertheless, papal pressure for Philip to invade England continued intermittently between 1571 and 1585, see Parker, *Grand Strategy*, 164–6, 169 and 179–80.

one that has befallen this land [of Portugal], without great cause'.[91]

The king's enthusiasm for godly causes abroad, and his passionate 'cult of the miracle' to achieve them, therefore persisted; so did his tendency to adopt over-ambitious goals, to expect divine intervention and to eschew contingency plans. In the 1580s, when England returned to the top of Philip's priorities, his plans depended on the same apocalyptic vision. In 1587, when the commander of the Great Armada complained about the danger of leading his ships against England late in the year, the king replied serenely: 'We are fully aware of the risk that is incurred by sending a major fleet in winter through the Channel without a safe harbour, but ... since it is all for His cause, God will send good weather.' In July 1588, after a storm had damaged some Armada vessels, driven others into Corunna and scattered the rest, the king reassured his dispirited commander: 'If this were an unjust war, one could indeed take this storm as a sign from Our Lord to cease offending Him; but being as just as it is, one cannot believe that He will disband it, but rather will grant it more favour than we could hope.'[92]

The Armada's catastrophic failure temporarily punctured the king's euphoria, but not his apocalyptic approach to English affairs. When he first learned the scale of the disaster, in November 1588, Philip confided to his secretary that he longed for death because:

> Very soon we shall find ourselves in such a state that we shall wish that we had never been born ... And if God does not send us a miracle (which is what I hope from Him), I hope to die and go to Him before this happens – which is what I pray for, so as not to see so much misfortune and disgrace.

A few days later, however, he welcomed his councillors' recommendation that the war with England should go on since 'it corresponds perfectly ... to the purpose that has inclined me to this enterprise from the beginning, for the service of our Lord, the defence of His cause, and the benefit of these realms'.[93] In 1590, although Philip expressed his regret for the debts he had incurred in 'the defence of

---

[91] G. Groen van Prinsterer, *Archives ou correspondance de la maison d'Orange-Nassau*, 1st ser., supplement (Leiden, 1847), 125*, St Gouard to Charles IX, 12 Sept. 1572; AGS Estado K 1530/53bis, Philip II to Don Diego de Zúñiga, 18 Sept. 1572; and R. Cueto, '1580 and All That ... Philip II and the Politics of the Portuguese Succession', *Portuguese Studies*, 8 (1992), 150–69, at 156, Cristobal de Moura to Philip II, 25 Nov. 1578.

[92] AGS Estado 165/2–3, Philip II to Archduke Albert, 14 Sept. 1587; E. Herrera Oria, *La Armada Invencible: documentos procedentes del Archivo General de Simancas* (Archivo Histórico Español, II, Valladolid, 1929) 210–14, Philip II to Medina Sidonia, 1 July 1588. For other examples of Philip's spiritual blackmail at this time, see Parker, *Grand Strategy*, 106.

[93] ABZ 145/76, Mateo Vázquez to Philip II and reply, 10 Nov. 1588; AGS Estado 2851, unfol., royal rescript to a consulta of the council of state, 26 Nov. 1588.

our holy faith and the conservation of my kingdoms and lordships', he warned his subjects that they would have to increase further.

I could not – and cannot – neglect the war with England and the events in France, because I have such a special obligation to God and the world to deal with them. Also, if the heretics prevail (which I hope God will not permit), it might open the door to worse damage and danger, and we shall have war at home.

When, the following year, the king's long-serving private secretary (and chaplain), Mateo Vázquez, questioned the need to devote so many of the monarchy's resources to these conflicts, Philip's reply was firm. 'We cannot abandon these matters, because they involve the cause of religion, which must take precedence over everything.' For the rest of his reign, he strove to topple Elizabeth Tudor, sending two more Armadas. In each case, he counted on God to overcome logistical deficiencies with a miracle and dismissed the objections of his admirals with messianic statements such as 'You must execute the order without delay, depart quickly, and trust that God will set everything right.' Neither fleet even reached the Channel.[94]

Nevertheless, after 1588 the king occasionally showed more caution in his policies towards England, looking more carefully for signs of possible Divine disfavour. Thus in May 1589, bowing to intense pressure from his confessor, Philip agreed to authorise a thorough investigation of alleged abuses among the Spanish Jesuits; but the draft of the order landed on his desk just as news arrived of the Anglo-Dutch descent on Corunna and the king immediately saw a connection. 'You will have heard of the report that came today from Corunna', the king informed his secretary. 'The English fleet has arrived there and has put troops ashore; so I am not sure that this is the right time to proceed against the Society of Jesus ... I think that what has already been done must suffice for now.'[95]

Naturally, not everyone in Spain shared the king's blind confidence that God fought on his side. The Cortes of Castile protested on occasion

---

[94] Karpeles Manuscript Library, Santa Barbara, California, Medina Sidonia Papers: Cartas Reales, 6/174, Philip II to Medina Sidonia, 15 Dec. 1590; IVdeDJ 51/1, Vázquez to Philip II and reply, 8 Feb. 1591 (Vázquez's proposal in G. Parker, *Philip II* (4th edn, Chicago, 2001), 181; E. S. Tenace, 'A Case of Strategic Mismanagement: The Armadas of 1596 and 1597 and the Grand Strategy of Philip II' (forthcoming).

[95] IVdeDJ 69/234A, Mateo Vázquez draft of the king's reply to a consulta of the council of the Inquisition, ordering the 'Visita', 10 May 1589, with the king's rescript countermanding it. On the king's efforts to secure a Visita for the Spanish Jesuit Order in the 1580s, see A. Astraín, *Historia de la Compañía de Jesús en la asistencia de España*, III (Madrid, 1909), chs. 11 and 12.

that 'Although the wars against the Dutch, the English and the French are holy and just, we must beg Your Majesty that they may cease.' The king responded, as usual, with assurances that God would provide; but not everyone believed him. 'I do not know whether God will always perform miracles' warned one minister; 'In the end, we cannot do so much with so little, and God will not always produce miracles for us' echoed another.[96] Why did such prudent voices not prevail? Why did failure seem to reinforce rather than reduce the king's messianic imperialism?

In the first place, the 'prudent voices' belonged to a minority. Even the king's critics often adopted the same messianic language. Thus several English and Irish exiles at the court of Spain, desperate to restore Catholicism to their homeland by force, claimed to be God's mouthpiece and accused the king of defaulting on his special relationship with God. 'I do not know how Your Majesty will be able to excuse yourself before God if you fail to assist and support people and groups who with such zeal and such religious conviction ask you for help', an Anglo-Irish exile in Spain told Philip bluntly in 1572.[97] Most of the king's ministers also shared his apocalyptic outlook. Don Francés de Álava, Spanish ambassador in France, protested that if, in the course of his official duties, 'I am [required] to become an instrument that raises human considerations above divine ones, I hope that God removes me from this world.' The scale and significance of the slaughter of Protestants at St Bartholomew seemed evidence of Divine favour even to the pragmatic duke of Alba.

> The events in Paris and France are wonderful [he wrote to a subordinate], and truly show that God has been pleased to change and rearrange matters in the way that He knows will favour the conservation of the true Church and advance His holy service and His glory. And, besides all that, in the present situation, these events could not have come at a better time for the affairs of the king our lord, for which we cannot sufficiently thank God's goodness.[98]

[96] *Actas de las Cortes de Castilla*, XVI (Madrid, 1890), 170 (from one of several papers of protest read out in the Cortes in May 1593); *Correspondance du Cardinal de Granvelle*, ed. C. Piot, XII (Brussels, 1896), 126–7, Granvelle to Margaret of Parma, 15 Nov. 1585; AGS Estado 590/23, Parma to Philip II, 28 Feb. 1586 – and, in another letter of the same day, 'God will grow weary of working miracles for us' (Estado 590/22). For more critics, see F. Bouza, 'Servidumbres de la soberana grandeza: criticar al rey en la corte de Felipe II', in *Imágenes históricas de Felipe II*, ed. A. Alvar Ezquerra (Madrid, 2000), 141–79.

[97] AHN OM 3511/10, Thomas Stukeley to Philip II, 15 Mar. [1572]. See other examples in Parker, *Grand Strategy*, 103.

[98] Rodríguez, *Don Francés de Álava*, 97, Álava to Alba, 17 Mar. 1568; Archives Générales du Royaume, Brussels, Audience 1728/2/77, Alba to Count Bossu, 29 Aug. 1572. When a disgruntled minister, Don Juan de Silva, complained in 1589 that 'Everyone relies on

Naturally, the king's numerous clerical officials expressed similar views. Juan de Ovando, priest, inquisitor and president of the council of the Indies, put it most succinctly. When asked whether appointment as president of the council of finance might fatigue him, Ovando responded: 'This can be overcome with the work and health that I have sacrificed in the service of Your Majesty, because it is the same as God's service.'[99]

The same sublime confidence coloured the accounts written by Spanish conquistadors in America. All of them invoked God with notable frequency: almost three times in every thousand words! God constantly gave them strength, courage, consolation, inspiration, aid, support, victory and health; He delivered, preserved, rewarded, foresaw, forgave, led, saved, wished and directed. The only words that appeared more frequently in their chronicles were 'war', 'the king' and, of course, 'gold'.[100] Some of Philip's subjects believed that they could interpret God's purpose for Spain just as well as the king: the messianic visions of 'Plaza Prophets' like Lucrecia de León, Miguel de Piedrola and Sor María de la Visitación (also known as 'the Nun of Lisbon') gained a widespread following in the 1580s.[101] Others went even further

---

the miracles and supernatural remedies that God visibly provides for His Majesty', he immediately added the qualification: 'and may He continue to do so, because it cannot be denied that the cause is His' (Biblioteca Casanatense, Rome, MS 2417/37–42, Don Juan de Silva to Esteban de Ibarra, 13 Aug. 1589).

[99] IVdeDJ 51/31, Mateo Vázquez to Philip II, 31 May 1574; IVdeDJ 24/38, Ovando to Philip II, 16 Jan. 1574, holograph: 'Ésta se podra vencer con mi trabajo y salud, que yo tengo sacrificado al servicio de vuestra magestad, por serlo también de dios' (an interesting echo of the king's similar claim the year before: see p. 174 above).

[100] B. Grunberg, 'Le vocabulaire de la "conquista": essai de linguistique historique appliquée à la conquête du Mexique d'après les chroniques des conquistadores', *Histoire économique et sociale*, 4 (1985), 3–27. More data may be found in B. Velasco, 'El alma christiana del conquistador de América', *Missionalia hispánica*, 21 (1964), 257–88, 22 (1965), 257–87, and 24 (1966), 129–65; A. Prosperi, 'America e Apocalisse: note sulla "conquista spirituale" del Nuovo Mondo', *Critica storica*, 13 (1976), 1–61; and J. L. Phelan, *The Millenarial Kingdom of the Franciscans in the New World: A Study of the Writings of Gerónimo de Mendieta (1525–1604)* (Berkeley, 1956).

[101] On the Plaza Prophets, see R. L. Kagan, 'Politics, Prophecy and the Inquisition in Late Sixteenth-Century Spain', in *Cultural Encounters: The Impact of the Inquisition in Spain and the New World*, ed. M. E. Perry and A. J. Cruz (Berkeley, 1991), 105–24. On Philip's direct interest in Lucrecia, see R. L. Kagan, *Lucrecia's Dreams: Politics and Prophecy in Sixteenth Century Spain* (Berkeley, 1990), 129, 132; and in Piedrola, see BL Additional 28,263/432, Vázquez to Philip II and reply, 11 Aug. 1587. See also the interesting evidence of a growing religious obsession among Spaniards in the later sixteenth century see C. Eire, *From Madrid to Purgatory: The Art and Craft of Dying in Sixteenth-Century Spain* (Cambridge, 1995), Book I, 'Eager for Heaven'; A. Terry, 'War and Literature in 16th-century Spain', in *War, Literature and the Arts in 16th-Century Europe*, ed. J. R. Mulryne and M. Shewring (1989); and S. T. Nalle, 'Entre la esperanza y el diablo: el tratamiento de los falsos mesías en el mundo ibérico', in *El Hispanismo Anglonorteamericano: aportaciones, problemas y perspectivas sobre Historia, Arte y Literatura españolas*, ed. J. M. de Bernardo Ares (Córdoba, 2001), 1, 643–61.

and claimed that they *were* the messiah, like Bartolomé Sánchez, a wool carder from a village in Castile whose version of the Lord's Prayer in the 1550s began 'My father, who art in Heaven …'; or like Fray Francisco de la Cruz in Peru who in the 1570s claimed in turn to be the new David, pope, king of Peru (later, of Israel) and Christ.[102]

A remarkable ideological consensus thus linked the king with most of his domestic critics, ministers, churchmen, soldiers and ordinary subjects. But was it uniquely Spanish? Among Catholics, many Portuguese believed that King Sebastian, who fell in battle in 1578, would return as the messiah; while numerous French writers compared Louis XIII and his mother, Marie de Medici, with Christ and the Virgin Mary. Among Protestants, many subjects of Elizabeth Tudor equated the cause of their country and of their sovereign with God's cause, just like Philip's subjects. English Puritans may have written of 'special providences' rather than of miracles, and they may have concentrated more on Jerusalem destroyed than on Jerusalem rebuilt, but they searched for supernatural and Biblical warrant for political decisions just as avidly as Spanish Catholics. Finally, as Alexandra Walsham reminds us, 'Early modern England nurtured a sizeable brood of bogus Christs and obscure persons claiming to be Enoch, Elijah or some other ecstatic figure foreshadowed in the Bible.' For every Francisco de la Cruz there was a William 'Frantick' Hacket, who claimed to be both John the Baptist and Daniel (even wrestling with the lions in the Tower Zoo to prove it) before declaring that he was the messiah, that the world was about to end and that Elizabeth had forfeited her throne.[103]

Philip II's extensive correspondence reveals that his apocalyptic vision lay far below this level. It also seems relatively modest when compared with the claims advanced by some adherents of other creeds in the

---

[102] Details in S. T. Nalle, *Mad for God: Bartolomé Sánchez, the Secret Messiah of Cardenete* (Charlottesville, 2001), quotation at p. 77; and J.-P. Tardieu, *Le nouveau David et la réforme du Pérou: l'affaire María Pizarro, Francisco de la Cruz (1571–1596)* (Bordeaux, 1992). A full transcript of the trial is available in V. Abril Castelló and M. J. Abril Stoffels, *Francisco de la Cruz: Inquisición: Actas* (3 vols., Madrid, 1992–6) – see, for example, the sixteen lines of references to 'David' in the index.

[103] On continental Europe, see Hermann, *No reino do desejado*; A. Y. Haran, *Le lys et le globe: messianisme dynastique et rêve impérial en France aux 16e et 17e siècles* (Seyssel, 2000); and Y. Bercé, *Le roi caché: sauveurs et imposteurs: mythes politiques populaires dans l'Europe moderne* (Paris, 1990). On England, see A. Walsham, *Providence in Early Modern England* (Oxford, 1999), 203–18, 226–32 and 310–25; and *idem*, ' "Frantick Hacket": Prophecy, Sorcery, Insanity and the Elizabethan Puritan Movement', *Historical Journal*, 41 (1998), 27–66. Bauckham, *Tudor Apocalypse*, 128–30, notes that although a few zealots hailed Elizabeth as a new Deborah, Judith or Zerubbabel, most English apocalyptic writers ignored her. He also lists Tudor 'messiahs' in ch. 10.

later sixteenth century. Although few knew the remarkable messianic prophecies by Isaac Luria of Safed until much later, Jewish Kabbalistic writers in Italy predicted that both 1575 CE and 1598 CE would be the 'year of redemption'. The Muslim millennium occurred between these dates (1591-2 CE), and in parts of the Ottoman empire and India eschatological agitation rose as many predicted the end of the world and some claimed to be the Mahdi. Although the Mughal emperor Akbar did not share these fears, and rejected the advice of his courtiers that he proclaim himself divine 'like Shah Ismail', from 990 AH (1581 CE) onwards he led Friday prayers in person as *khatib*. He also commissioned a 'Millennial history' of all the Muslim lands since the death of the Prophet that suggested the Mughals would soon reunite them all.[104]

Admittedly, Philip nominated hundreds of bishops and abbots, and dismissed, exiled and punished scores of 'turbulent and scandalous' clerics in his dominions around the globe, and told almost all the popes of his reign what he thought they should do; yet his ecclesiastical powers were far less extensive than those even of Protestant monarchs like Elizabeth, let alone those wielded by Akbar. Nevertheless, his messianic vision possessed two unique features. First, no other Christian ruler so openly equated his or her service with God's service – they were, as Philip memorably stated, 'the same thing'. Moreover, although many sycophants, propagandists and apologists made extravagant claims for their patrons, and although many advisers (especially clerics) believed that God fought on their side, no other monarch of this period regularly framed foreign and domestic policy on the assumption that she or he had divined God's purpose. Fewer still routinely relied on miracles to bridge the gap between ends and means. Second, and no less significant, no other European ruler *needed* a messianic vision as much as Philip II. The king had inherited territories – Spain and parts of Italy, the Americas and the Netherlands – so far flung that they were, in effect, indefensible. The acquisition of the Philippines after 1565 and of the Portuguese empire in 1580-3, although remarkable successes in themselves, gravely exacerbated these problems of 'strategic overstretch' (to use Paul Kennedy's felicitous phrase). A letter written shortly after the king's death by one of his leading diplomats offered a shrewd analysis of the strategic dilemma created by the extent of Philip II's possessions:

---

[104] For Akbar, the *Tārīkh-i Alfī* (literally 'The Thousand-Year History') and the second Mahdi of Jaunpur, see Subrahmanyam, 'Du Tage au Gange', 70–6; on 'Istanbul at the Millennium' see C. Fleischer, *Bureaucrat and Intellectual in the Ottoman Empire: The Historian Mustafa Ali (1541–1600)* (Princeton, 1986), 133–4, 138–42 and 244–5 (Ali also began a millennial history in 1000 AH). On Jewish messianic writings at this time see Idel, *Messianic Mystics*, 158–60, and Lenowitz, *The Jewish Messiahs*, ch. 6.

We are gradually becoming the target at which the whole world wants to shoot its arrows; and you know that no empire, however great, has been able to sustain many wars in different areas for long. If we can think only of defending ourselves, and never manage to contrive a great offensive blow against one of our enemies, so that when that is over we can turn to the others ... I doubt whether we can sustain an empire as scattered as ours.

The *empire* on which the sun never set had thus become the *target* on which the sun never set. Only Providence, which had created the global monarchy, could defend it.[105]

Messianic visions therefore continued to influence Spanish foreign policy. Although Philip III rejected his father's advice on almost every other subject, he pursued the same spiritual politics. At his first meeting with the council of state, he instructed his ministers to do two things: 'First, let the affairs of state that you discuss conform to the precepts of Divine law'; and second, although they should strive to mobilise all available resources for Spain's wars, 'let there also be prayers and supplications to God, so that the world may understand that we do not trust so much in the power of our armies as in the favour of His potent arm'. In 1644, his son Philip IV ordered all his subjects to engage in continuous prayers for the success of his policies, 'since it is by spiritual more than by material means that this monarchy will be reunited, and preserved from its enemies and rebels'. Twelve years later, having just declared war on England, Philip IV observed: 'Everywhere our enemies are preparing against us, and we have little left with which to resist them. But what is most at stake in this war is religion, and therefore I trust that God will provide the means for our defence.'[106]

Rather like their French Bourbon descendants, the Spanish Habsburgs seemed to learn nothing and to forget nothing. Instead, they persevered, unshaken in their confidence that a final miracle would save them, until in 1700 the extinction of their line and the subsequent

---

[105] IVdeDJ 82/444, duke of Sessa to Don Balthasar de Zúñiga, 28 Sept. 1600, minute. For more on Spain's strategic dilemma, see G. Parker, 'David or Goliath? Philip II and his world in the 1580s', in Parker, *Empire, War and Faith in Early Modern Europe* (2002), ch. 1.

[106] G. González Dávila, *Historia de la vida y hechos del ínclito monarca, amado y santo, Don Felipe III* (Madrid, 1771), 44–5; R. A. Stradling, *Philip IV and the Government of Spain, 1621–1665* (Cambridge, 1988), 270, royal proclamation of 28 Oct. 1644; and 276, Philip IV to Sor María de Ágreda, 19 Mar. 1656. For further examples of this strategic vision during the seventeenth century, see *ibid.*, 269–76, and J. H. Elliott, 'Managing Decline: Olivares and the Grand Strategy of Imperial Spain', in *Grand Strategies in Peace and War*, ed. P. M. Kennedy (New Haven and London, 1991), 87–104. See also the continuing concern for spiritual goals among the political writers reviewed in M. D. Gordon, 'Morality, Reform and the Empire in 17th-century Spain', *Il pensiero politico*, II (1978), 3–19.

partition of the monarchy at last solved Spain's strategic dilemma and thus rendered a messianic vision superfluous.

Appendix: who really betrayed the Ridolfi plot?

Some thought that both Ridolfi and Hawkins acted as double agents. Others blamed the duke of Florence. Who was right?

I Ridolfi

1. In February 1569, Ridolfi visited the Spanish ambassador in London, Don Guerau de Spes, with authority from two English Catholic councillors of Elizabeth to seek support for their plan to overthrow the queen's Protestant advisers. The following month, he informed French Ambassador La Mothe that he held a commission 'from the pope in person to arrange the restoration and re-establishment of the Catholic faith in England, working with the Catholic peers of the country' (p. 190 above). He also made contact with Mary Stuart, through her ambassador in London the bishop of Ross, and in September Ridolfi transferred almost £3,000 from Spes to Mary.[107] The English government arrested him in October. By his own account, Ridolfi faced twenty-five separate charges but, 'thanks to God and my friends', obtained his release on 22 November. Three days later he visited the French ambassador in London and informed him that the rebels urgently needed foreign assistance.[108]

It seems highly unlikely that a man who had just spent six weeks in prison would be so rash – unless his captors knew and approved. Evidence that Ridolfi remained on excellent terms with Francis Walsingham (in whose house he had been confined) appears in the latter's account of a meeting in October 1570, in which the two discussed ways of ending the trade war with Spain. They favoured sending a mediator and Ridolfi volunteered his services because 'he thinketh his credyt sooche with the king of Spaynes mynisters as he were able to doe some good in that behalfe, wherein he seamethe not unwyllyng to deale'. Writing to Lord Burghley, Walsingham speculated: 'Surely, Sir, the late experyence that I have dyvers ways had of him makethe me to hope that

---

[107] Late in 1568, Ridolfi may also have been one of the 'Italians' who told Ambassador La Mothe about the plan for a Catholic embargo against England (*La Mothe*, 1, 71, Catherine, 28 Dec. 1568). In spring 1569, he supplied both the French and Spanish ambassadors with detailed information on debates in the English Privy Council (*La Mothe*, 1, 258–63 and 332–3, and Kervijn, v, 307 n. 1 and 333–4.

[108] C. Roth, 'Roberto Ridolfi e la sua congiura', *Revista storica degli archivi Toscani*, 2 (1930), 119–32 (including a transcription of Ridolfi's Memorial setting out details of his 'service' in England; quotation from p. 129); *La Mothe*, II, 350–1, to Charles IX, 25 Nov. 1569.

yf he were imployed in that behalfe he woold deale bothe dyscreatly and
upprightly.' On 25 March 1571 Ridolfi had an audience with Elizabeth
and left for the continent the following day bearing a commission to open
discussions to end the trade war, as well as authorisation from Norfolk
and Mary to secure Spanish aid for their plot.[109]

2. No record exists that, while abroad, Ridolfi ever discussed ending
the trade war; but he dramatically misrepresented Norfolk's strategy
once he left England. The duke had declared himself willing to lead a
rising to seize Elizabeth, as a means of compelling her to free Mary, as
soon as he heard that Spanish troops had landed in England. To Alba,
Pins and Philip, however, Ridolfi claimed that the rising would occur
before the Spaniards landed, and that Norfolk would seize both Elizabeth
and the Tower of London, liberate Mary and then join the invaders
when they landed – quite a difference![110]

3. In the autumn of 1571, Philip sent Ridolfi back to the Netherlands
and Alba subjected him to a thorough interrogation that revealed some
of these discrepancies. 'I find that Ridolfi has no contacts in England.
Instead he told me that the ambassador [Spes] is the one who directs
the business and the one who keeps men with some of the [Catholic]
lords.' To Alba, Ridolfi seemed 'a man of limited understanding ...
who had been told what he had to say, because when I asked him to
repeat what I had seen in dispatches, he did not know what to say'.
The duke realised that 'the plot cannot rest on the foundations that I
had imagined until now'.[111]

4. Whether or not Ridolfi was a double-agent, he certainly betrayed
all the conspirators.

- From the start, Ridolfi, his English contacts and Spes all used the
  same cypher, and later so did the papal nuncios in Spain and Paris.
  Therefore, once Elizabeth acquired the key from one of Ridolfi's
  messengers in mid-April 1571 – apprehended with suspicious ease –
  she could read everybody's mail.
- In any case, Ridolfi also wrote uncyphered letters to Mary as he
  moved from Brussels to Rome and Madrid, keeping her up to date

[109] Kervijn, VI, 18 n. 1, Walsingham to Burghley, 22 Oct. 1570; Pollen, *English Catholics*,
172. Ridolfi had also offered his services to Elizabeth's ministers as a go-between with
Alba in 1569: see pp. 189, 192 above.

[110] Compare these points in Norfolk's 'Commission', in A. Labanoff, *Lettres, instructions
et mémoires de Marie Stuart*, III (Paris, 1848), 242 and 245 (English translation in W. Turnbull,
Letters of Mary Stuart Queen of Scotland (1845), 198–208), with Alba's account in Teulet,
Relations politiques, V, 79–81, Alba to Philip, 7 May 1571. Edwards, *Dangerous Queen*, 395–
402 and 407–10, suggested that Ridolfi also forged Mary's 'Instructions' and her letter
asking Alba for assistance in March 1571.

[111] Duke of Alba, *Epistolario del III duque de Alba* (3 vols., Madrid, 1952), II, 758–60, Alba
to Philip, 19 Oct. 1571.

on the progress of the plot, and thereby (since all Mary's mail was intercepted and read) keeping Elizabeth up to date too.

For a genuine spy, this was the height of imprudence. As Ambassador La Mothe put it, 'His negligence and his [over]confidence, while he was overseas, have ruined the very respectable cause (*très honneste cause*) that he had in hand.'[112]

II Hawkins

1. Although from 13 May 1571 onwards, Hawkins kept Burghley informed of his dealings with the court of Spain via Fitzwilliam, he appears to have concealed several material facts.

- He remained silent about his contacts in 1564, 1565 and 1566 with the Spanish ambassador in London, Guzmán de Silva, in which Hawkins indicated that he might be willing to enter Spanish service (specifically, to fight the Turks in the Mediterranean).
- An account of his direct dealings with Philip II, prepared for Lord Burghley in January 1577, made clear that Hawkins had sent Fitzwilliam on his first mission to Spain without Burghley's knowledge.
- Both in 1571 and in 1577, Hawkins failed to state that he had instructed Fitzwilliam to make contact with Thomas Stukeley, Elizabeth's sworn enemy. At his reluctant interview with the duchess of Feria on his first visit to Spain, Fitzwilliam asserted that Hawkins had heard of Stukeley's welcome in Spain, and wanted to know what Philip might do for him, for Mary and for the Catholics of England. Fitzwilliam even claimed that Hawkins wanted to contribute twenty-five ships to Stukeley's planned attack on Elizabeth 'on account of the great affection that has always united the two'.[113]

---

[112] *CSPSp*, II, 111, Spes to Alba, 20 Feb. 1569; Serrano, *Correspondencia diplomática*, IV, 383, Castagna to Rusticucci, 9 July 1571; *La Mothe*, IV, 123, to Catherine, 2 June 1571, written just after an audience with Elizabeth. Later, La Mothe would protest vehemently that he knew nothing of Ridolfi's plans: *ibid.*, 381 and 385–6, letters of 19 and 24 Feb. 1572. For the suspiciously easy capture of Charles Bailly, see Edwards, *The Marvellous Chance*, ch. 1.

[113] AGS Estado 824/29, 'Lo que propone Jorge Fitzwilliams', a draft account of Fitzwilliam's first mission (by Antonio Gracián?), and fo. 26, 'Lo que Jorge Fitzvilliams ... refiere', article 2. In 1572, Stukeley referred to Hawkins as 'a great friend of mine, and I was the first person to win him and his ships over to the service' of Spain (AHN OM 3511/10, Stukeley's Memorial, 15 Mar. [1572]). On the English government's fear of Stukeley, see Edwards, *Marvellous Chance*, ch. 5, and the forthcoming study of Juan E. Tazón.

- He appears to have revealed his 'practice' to Burghley only after Fitzwilliam had seen Mary in June 1571.[114]
- Hawkins failed to tell Burghley about either his letter to Feria dated 14 June or the holograph documents about his 'practice' delivered by Fitzwilliam on his second visit.

2. The absence of any mention of Stukeley seems particularly surprising and significant. Just possibly, Hawkins (and Fitzwilliam on his behalf) feigned their desire to follow in the footsteps of Stukeley in order to find out what he was up to and, if possible, sabotage it. Letters from Hawkins to Burghley making this clear may have been lost, or are yet to be found; however, his surviving letters seem otherwise complete and refer to no other correspondence.

3. Was Hawkins, then, serious in his initial offer of assistance to Philip II? He must have heard reports of the king's generous treatment of Stukeley – English spies at the Spanish court reported the grant of titles (including 'duke of Ireland') and cash in return for Stukeley's offer to work against Elizabeth – and perhaps Hawkins hoped for something similar. Fitzwilliam soon discovered, however, that Stukeley had received virtually nothing (no titles and only 2,000 ducats) and had even been forced to leave his son as a hostage for good behaviour! Perhaps this information, brought back from Spain by Fitzwilliam in May, coupled with a pessimistic assessment of Philip's invasion strategy, led Hawkins to reveal his hand to Burghley. Even then, Fitzwilliam refused to carry with him a copy of the agreement he had signed in August with Feria, 'fearing it would be a knife [to his throat]' – which confirms the suspicion that Hawkins did not wish to reveal to Burghley all that he had offered in Spain.[115]

4. Hawkins, like Ridolfi and everyone else, realised that Mary Stuart represented the 'reversionary interest' to the English crown because she possessed the strongest title to the English throne should Elizabeth die. Although statutes barred her succession, similar statutes barring the succession of both Mary and Elizabeth Tudor had been overturned after the death of their predecessor: the same might happen should Elizabeth die, since she had no heir. Several other Elizabethans kept in touch with Mary (the earl of Leicester met her twice, while both

[114] See *Co. Do. In.*, LXXXIX, 264–5, 295, 313 and 354–5, Guzmán de Silva to Philip II, 4 Feb., 30 Mar., 4 May and 3 Aug. 1566; BL Cotton Galba C.V/263, holograph paper signed 'I. H.' (although dated 'January 1576', according to *stilo anglice* this would be January 1577); *An English Garner*, ed. Seccombe, 128–9, Hawkins to Burghley, 7 June 1571 (his letter of 13 May, *ibid.*, 127–8, does not mention the 'practice').

[115] *CSPR*, I, 385, Zayas to Stukeley, 8 Feb. 1571 (details on Stukeley's 'reward'); BL Egerton 2047/284, Gracián to Zayas, 12 Aug. 1571, sending the 'capitulation' to be forwarded to the duke of Alba for transmission to Spes. When it arrived, however, Alba deemed it too dangerous to send: see *Epistolario*, II, 758, Alba to Philip II, 19 Oct. 1571.

'took the waters' at Buxton) and some covertly declared their support for her succession should Elizabeth die (like Sir Edward Stafford, England's ambassador in Paris from 1583 to 1591).[116] The Ridolfi plot offered Hawkins a means of keeping his options open: if it somehow succeeded, he could expect a rich reward from Mary, whose messages Fitzwilliam had conveyed to Spain; if it failed, he could expect a reward (albeit somewhat less) from Elizabeth. Much the same was true of Ridolfi. Despite his extreme indiscretion, should the plot succeed he could expect a rich reward from all its supporters (Mary, Norfolk, Philip and the pope); should it fail, he might hope that his 'leaks' would at least produce the restoration of his confiscated property (which he estimated at 14,300 escudos) by a grateful English government. As long as the two sides did not compare notes, Hawkins and Ridolfi might hope to avoid any suspicion of double-dealing.

This would explain the surprising duration of each party's participation in the affair: in November 1571, in Rome, Ridolfi still gushed enthusiasm for the plot; the following month, Fitzwilliam told Spes that he was prepared to return to Spain to receive further orders from the king. Early the following year Hawkins and Fitzwilliam entertained Spes for five weeks before ferrying him to Flanders, and exchanged a common cypher so that they could continue to correspond after they parted company. Spes therefore arrived in Brussels in February 1572 'resolved more than ever to press forward with the Ridolfi affair'. Two years later, marooned in the Netherlands, he still dreamed of using Hawkins and his ships to end the Dutch Revolt.[117]

III Florence

Once they realised that the plot had miscarried, the main participants sought a scapegoat. Ridolfi, well aware that Alba held him in low esteem, blamed the duke, claiming that he had done everything possible to sabotage the venture. Perhaps in response, Philip's private secretary prepared a list of questions to be put to Ridolfi 'in great secrecy'. He was to declare 'who had been instrumental in telling the queen of

---

[116] On the meetings at Buxton, see Collinson, *The English Captivity*, 20; on Stafford, see Parker, *Empire, War and Faith*, ch. 3.

[117] For Ridolfi's continuing enthusiasm for the plot, see Serrano, *Correspondencia diplomática*, IV, 542–3, Zúñiga to Philip II, 27 Nov. 1571; for his bid to recover his confiscated property after Elizabeth's death, see Roth, 'Roberto Ridolfi', 13; and Edwards, *Marvellous Chance*, 373–80. For Spes's delusions, see *Co. Do. In.*, XC, 528–9, Spes to Philip II, 12 Dec. 1571; ASF MP 651/1, Vitelli to Concini, 4 Feb. 1572; and AGS Estado 826/91, 'Información acerca de lo que podría servir Joan Achins ingles a su Magestad, dada por don Guerau d[e] Spes', 19 Mar. 1574, holograph (shorter draft at *ibid.*, fo. 38). For the claim that Fitzwilliam was ready to go to Spain again, see *ibid.*, and Kervijn, VI, 190, Spes to Alba, 21 Oct. 1571.

England about the business that the said Ridolfi proposed to His Majesty', and especially 'that Chiapin Vitelli should go with 2,000 [*sic*] infantry with arquebuses to support the English princes and nobles who were to rebel'. He must also reveal what exactly Alba had said to him when he returned to the Netherlands and what conversations had taken place between Ridolfi and six named individuals in Madrid and Brussels. But by then the Florentine had returned to Italy and gave no answer.[118]

Alba himself thought the leak had come from Florence. In December 1573 he told his successor as governor-general of the Netherlands that it had been a grave error to

> Entrust the enterprise of England to Chiapin Vitelli, who was the servant and confidant of the duke of Florence, and to have sent him from [Spain] trumpeting the details throughout France. He also told and assured me that the duke of Florence was the one who had really revealed the whole plot to the queen, and also made contact with the rebels of the Low Countries, and with those in France and Germany who supported them, so that they would make trouble and embarrass His Majesty, fearing that he wanted to destroy him through resentment at the title of 'Grand Duke' that he had taken.[119]

The king remained unconvinced. When he read the draft of a letter urging Ambassador Spes 'to find out in detail what contacts the duke of Florence may have with that queen and in that court', and hinted at treachery, Philip deleted the passage and noted in the margin: 'It is not good to make accusations like this.' No evidence of a secret correspondence between Florence and London has come to light; rather, the Grand Duke repelled attempts by France to turn him against Spain and instead participated fully in the Lepanto campaign alongside Philip's forces, providing the majority of the papal squadron. In any case, the information provided to Elizabeth's ministers first by Ridolfi and then by Fitzwilliam and Hawkins more than sufficed to thwart the plot. Perhaps because his deep religious faith had led him to trust these men so completely, the king never seems to have grasped that they betrayed him. Nevertheless, he fully realised the significance of the

---

[118] *CSPR*, I, 463–6, Ridolfi to Rusticucci, 8 Oct. 1571, and Roth, 'Roberto Ridolfi', 130; ABZ 136/25, 'Lo que con mucho secreto se ha de preguntar a Ruberto Rodolfi' (undated, in the hand of Mateo Vázquez).

[119] IVdeDJ 67/1, Don Luis de Requesens to Andrés Ponce de León, Jan. 1574, reporting a conversation with Alba. The pope conferred the title 'Grand Duke' in 1570 but Spain, following the lead of the Holy Roman Emperor, refused to recognise it. The Spanish ambassador in Rome, Don Juan de Zúñiga, also blamed the Grand Duke: see Serrano, *Correspondencia diplómatica*, IV, 486, 497, 513 and 542–3, Zúñiga to Philip II, 16 and 28 Oct., 10 and 27 Nov. 1571.

fiasco and where the ultimate responsibility lay. Upon reading Alba's damning report of his interview with Ridolfi in October 1571, the king wrote: 'This is a bad business – and not, I fear, only for the present but also for the future. And if this proves true, any number of victories over the Turks will not console me, because this is worse. I also fear that we ourselves bear the responsibility for the dreadful situation in which we find ourselves.'[120]

Postscript

When I delivered the Prothero lecture, on 4 July 2001, both Roy Porter, who gave the Matthew lecture, and Sir John Plumb, who trained both Roy and me at Christ's College Cambridge, were still alive. Over the past forty years I gained more than I can say from their learning, their example and their friendship, and I grieve over their passing. I therefore dedicate this essay to their memory, in gratitude, admiration and affection.

---

[120] *Co. Do. In.*, xc, 520, Philip II to Spes, 31 Oct. 1571, draft; *Epistolario*, ii, 760, royal apostil on Alba to Philip II, 19 Oct. 1571. Admittedly, Charles IX of France tried to get Florence to join an anti-Spanish league (G. Canestrini and A. Desjardins, *Négociations diplomatiques de la France avec la Toscane*, iii (Paris, 1865), 649–50 and 655–7, Petrucci to Prince Francesco, 8 and 19 Mar. 1571). In time, this became known to Spanish diplomats: Serrano, *Correspondencia diplómatica*, iv, 500, Zúñiga to Philip II, 3 Nov. 1571. My thanks to Maurizio Arfaioli and Juan Tazón for discussing these intricate issues of possible double-dealing with me.

Transactions of the RHS 12 (2002), pp. 223–44 © 2002 Royal Historical Society
DOI: 10.1017/S0080440102000075   Printed in the United Kingdom

THE CHARITY OF EARLY MODERN LONDONERS*

By Ian W. Archer

READ 19 OCTOBER 2001 AT THE UNIVERSITY OF SUNDERLAND

ABSTRACT. This essay explores further the notion associated with W. K. Jordan that a new rational protestant philanthropy emerged after the Reformation. Drawing upon a sample of London wills from the period 1520-1640, it argues that protestants sought to forge an association between protestantism and charity, but suggests that there were rather more continuities with the catholic past than the polemics of the early reformers would leave one to believe. It explores the variety of forms in which voluntary giving was expressed, and argues that although giving was increasingly channelled through public institutions, giving within those institutional frameworks was often mediated through discretionary relationships of patronage and clientage.

IN 1614 Dr Andrew Willet, the moderate puritan minister of Barley in Hertfordshire, dedicated to Sir Thomas Middleton, the lord mayor of London, 'A catalogue of such charitable workes as have been done in the times of the Gospell within the space of 60 yeares, under the happie raignes of King Edward, Queene Elizabeth, King James, our Gratious Soveraigne.' This he appended to the fourth edition of a work he had first published in 1592, the *Synopsis Papismi*, a lucid exposition of the points of controversy between protestants and catholics. The omission of Mary from his list of monarchs was telling for Willet's thesis in his 'golden catalogue' was that 'more charitable works have beene performed in the times of the Gospell then they can shew to have been done in the like time in popery'. It was a remarkable piece of research which enumerated individual bequests and attempted to quantify them. He had enlisted the support of Middleton's predecessor as lord mayor who had instructed the livery companies to give him information, and he drew upon notes of charitable bequests kept by one of the clerks of the prerogative court of Canterbury. Some of the problems he encountered will be familiar to those historians of London who have followed him: he lacked data from the London hospitals between 1567 and 1575; some companies had been 'too nice and scrupulous' about revealing

* I am extremely grateful to Ben Coates, Jennifer Melville and Rosemary Sgroi for their assistance with the work on London wills that lies behind this essay.

the extent of their charitable resources; some of the records he was dealing with were so 'worne and consumed ... that I could but here and there note a sum'. But this representative of the 'stupor mundi clerus Britannicus', as Joseph Hall described him, completed his survey with a bold attempt at quantification, summing the bequests given by Londoners in the previous sixty years at £335,000, adding an estimate of £40,000 for his missing years, and a capitalised value of £240,000 for the annuities he had uncovered, producing a total for London charity of £615,000. 'So then to conclude', he asserted, 'these and many other such charitable workes ... doe glister as pearles, and the workers thereof, doe shine as starres amongst us: their religious acts are as the pomegranates in Aarons priestly garment, and themselves as the tinkling bels hanging thereon, doe sound abroad the praises of the Gospell.'[1]

Willet's methodology and conclusions are remarkably similar to those of that other indefatigable chronicler of London charity, Wilbur K. Jordan, whose book *The Charities of London* appeared forty years ago. Like Willet, Jordan worked from the testamentary records of the prerogative court of Canterbury and calculated the volume of Londoners' benefactions. His figures are not far off those of his seventeenth-century predecessor: between 1550 and 1620 (a slightly longer period than was within Willet's purview) Londoners gave a total of £782,790 in charity. Like Willet, Jordan saw the reformation as marking a decisive break in patterns of charitable giving. The catholic view that almsgiving was meritorious to the salvation of the donor encouraged indiscriminate giving whereas protestants directed their charity in a more rational way: it was increasingly discriminating, channelled through institutional forms like the parish and the hospital, and subject to lay control. More sophisticated mechanisms were devised, for example in the form of loan stocks providing start-up capital to young tradesmen, the interest payments upon which could be used to support some other form of charitable activity. Londoners entrusted their companies with a swelling volume of endowments which supported parish lectureships, schools, and parochial relief throughout England. And there was much more charity around. Jordan calculated that Londoners released approximately £4,200 p.a. in the period 1480–1540 compared to nearly £24,000 p.a. in the period 1600–40.[2]

---

[1] A. Willet, *Synopsis Papsimi* (4th edn, 1614), 1219–43, quotations at 1220, 1224, 1243. The 5th edition (1634) is prefaced by 'The Life and Death of Andrew Willet', from which Hall's remark is taken (p. (b)). See also A. Milton, *Catholic and Reformed: The Roman and Protestant Churches in English Protestant Thought, 1600–1640* (Cambridge, 1995), 13–19.

[2] W. K. Jordan, *The Charities of London, 1480–1660: The Aspirations and Achievements of the Urban Society* (1960); *idem, Philanthropy in England: A Study of the Changing Pattern of English Social Aspirations* (1959).

Jordan's critics were quick off the mark. His figures failed to take account of inflation, and once the six-fold increase in prices over the period under review is taken into account, the scale of that increase in charitable provision (also approximately six-fold) is cast into doubt. The most egregiously erroneous of Jordan's assertions was that public support from rates contributed only 7 per cent of the total charitable expenditures (in other words that the contribution of the voluntary sector hugely outweighed public provision for the poor), for this was based on a comparison of the income from bequests in wills with the rate assessments on *surviving* overseers' accounts which are of course no guide to the actual incidence of rating. But there is a danger of throwing the baby out with the bath water. Jordan calculated the amount released in charity each decade, mixing capital grants and once-for-all payments, rather than calculating income. J. F. Hadwin pointed out that once the yields of previously accumulated endowments are taken into account a rather more impressive picture emerges. The best recent estimates produced by Paul Slack suggest that at the end of the first decade of the seventeenth century, the yield of endowments nationally exceeded that from rating (about £25,000 p.a. as opposed to £10,000 p.a.), but that by 1650 with the more widespread adoption of rating, rates and endowments contributed the same, about £100,000 p.a. each). By the end of the seventeenth century rating had leapt ahead, yielding according to the Board of Trade £400,000 as compared to probably no more than £150,000 from endowments.[3]

I shall return to the knotty question of the size of the voluntary sector in poor relief later, but let us begin with the ideological framework of post-reformation charity. Willet's stress on the contribution of the gospel to the charitable activities of Londoners reflects the acute sensitivity of protestants to the criticisms of the 'carping popelings'.[4] The battle-lines had been drawn early in the reformation as the evangelicals attacked the catholic hierarchy for its waste of resources which might have been directed to charitable uses. But the disappointment of the early reformers' hopes that the monastic resources might be turned to social welfare left them vulnerable to the charges of their adversaries that they had simply lined their own pockets from the spoliation of the church. Stephen Gardiner clashed with Thomas Mowntayne, the protestant minister of St Michael Paternoster Royal at the outset of Mary's reign. The bishop, declaring that protestants

---

[3] W. G. Bittle and R. T. Lane, 'Inflation and Philanthropy in England: A Reassessment of W. K. Jordan's Data', *Economic History Review*, 2nd ser., 29 (1976), 203–10; J. F. Hadwin, 'Deflating Philanthropy', *Economic History Review*, 2nd ser. 31 (1978), 105–17; P. Slack, *Poverty and Policy in Tudor and Stuart England* (1988).

[4] J. White, *Two Sermons the Former Delivered at Pauls Crosse ... the Latter at the Spittle on Monday in Easter Weeke 1613* (1615), 71.

were 'good for nothynge but for the fyere', demanded, 'whate good workes was ther done other yn kynge Hary's dayes, or yn kynge Edward's days?' Mowntayne responded by asserting that the abolition of papal authority, the reform of the universities and the foundation of the London hospitals were 'notable thynges most worthye of perpetuall memory to the ende: are not al these good workes, my lord?'. Gardiner was unimpressed: 'Ser, you have made a greate speke; for wheras yow have set set upe one begarlye howse, yow have pulde downe an C prynsly howses for yt; puttynge owte godly, lernyd, and devoyte men that sarvyd god daye and nyghte, and thruste yn ther plase a sort of scurvye and lowsye boyes.' It was a charge which to some extent stuck. Willet's Cambridge mentor Laurence Chaderton had admitted in a Paul's Cross sermon of 1578 that 'the papistes alwayes cast in our teeth the great and famous hospitalitie of their nobility and cleargie, the buylding of Abbies, Monasteries, and Nunneries, Cathedrall Churches, colledges, with many other outward works which in deede are such as do stoppe our mouthes and put us Protestants to silence'. The satirist Thomas Nashe reported the claims of 'travailers of credit' that 'in London is not gyven the tenth part of that almes in a weeke which in the poorest besieged citty of Fraunce is gyven in a day'. 'Let not our adversaries grind the face of our religion', warned Nathaniel Shute in his funeral sermon for Richard Fishburne in 1626, 'to say Religion and Charitie were at one time thrust out of this kingdome'.[5]

It is perhaps for this reason that the protestant establishment moved so quickly to assert the godly credentials of key donors. Most strikingly Thomas Sutton's Charterhouse foundation with its enormous endowment, presented by Willet as 'the greatest gift that ever was given in England, no abbey at the first foundation thereof excepted', became an exemplar of protestant charity. Sutton was 'the right Phoenix of Charity in our times', 'the Master-piece of Protestant English Charity'.[6] One occasionally detects a degree of re-invention as donors like William Lambe (d. 1580), against whom there had been 'privy whisperings' of papist sympathies, were presented as orthodox models of godly piety and so celebrated in Holinshed's *Chronicles*. It was implausible for the crown to claim in its letters patent founding Wadham College that the

[5] *Narratives of the Days of the Reformation*, ed. J. G. Nichols (Camden Society, o.s., LXXVII, 1859), 181–2; L. Chaderton, *An Excellent and Godly Sermon ... Preached at Paules Crosse the XXVI Daye of October An. 1578* (1580), sig. Ciiiiv; T. Nashe, *Works*, ed. R. B. McKerrow (5 vols., Oxford, 1910), II. 160–1; N. Shute, *Corona Charitatis: The Crowne of Charitie* (1626), 22–3.

[6] *The Charterhouse with the Last Will and Testament of Thomas Sutton Esquire* (1614), 6; T. Fuller, *The Church History of Britain from the Birth of Jesus Christ Untill the Yeare MDCXLVIII* (1656), 64; idem, *The History of the Worthies of England* (1662), part ii, 168; P. Burrell, *Suttons Synagogue or the English Centurion Showing the Unparalleled Bounty of Protestant Charity* (1629); *Commons Journals*, I, 736.

founders sought to promote the pure gospel, for Nicholas and Dorothy Wadham were probable recusants. (Willet recognised the problem pointing out that although they were known to be popish they had provided by statute that the scholars attend Church of England services.)[7] Even Sutton's case had required a certain amount of spin for his will had been contested by disappointed kin and the charity's opponents argued against the concentration of such enormous resources on one project.[8] But the cumulative effect of funeral and commemoration sermons, memorial tablets and monumental epitaphs celebrating the piety and charity of benefactors, the ritual distribution of charity within the parochial framework and the recitation of prayers for benefactors was to inscribe the association of charity and protestantism. The fellows of Pembroke Hall celebrated their Draper benefactors in 1658 for having 'furnished us with more real arguments wherewith to confront the Romish brags of their good works than any Protestant city in the world besides'.[9]

The celebration of benefactors was one strand of the post-reformation discourses about charity; the excoriation of a miserly elite was another powerful theme. Charity 'waxes cold'; 'every man's private devotion is poor'; 'the dead doe give more then those that are alive', 'to despise those whom God has chosen is to swerve from God'; Londoners live in an 'iron age' in which it is hard to persuade men to part with money for charity; 'as this citie is lamentable for the multitude of the poor and wretched men, so it is more to be lamented for the miserable riche men'. Charity was merely token.

Many that have raked a deale of wealth together by fraude and deceit, by usurie, extortion, and oppression, and by other wicked and unlawfull shiftes they perswade themselves, if in their life time they give now and then a penie to the poore, or at their death when they can use their pelfe no longer, if they cloathe then a fewe poore people to attend upon them to their grave, or give sumwhat to set forth their prayse that they dyed the children of God or give sumwhat

---

[7] *New Dictionary of National Biography*, s.n. William Lambe; D. Wootton, 'Reginald Scot/Abraham Fleming/the Family of Love', in *Languages of Witchcraft: Narrative, Ideology, and Meaning in Early Modern Culture*, ed. S. Clark (2001), 124–6; Willet, *Synopsis Papismi*, 1239. I am grateful to Cliff Davies for discussions of the founding of Wadham.

[8] *The Letters and Life of Sir Francis Bacon*, ed. J. F. Spedding (7 vols., 1861–74), IV, 247–54; P. Bearcroft, *An Historical Account of Thomas Sutton Esq. and his Foundation in Charterhouse* (1737), 123–5.

[9] I. W. Archer, 'The Arts and Acts of Memorialisation in Early Modern London', in *Imagining Early Modern London: Perceptions and Portrayals of the City from Strow to Strype, 1598–1720*, ed. J. F. Merritt (Cambridge, 2001), 89–113; A. H. Johnson, *The History of the Worshipful Company of Drapers of London* (5 vols., Oxford, 1914–22), III, 248.

to an hospitall or almeshouse, they perswade themselves to merit some great matter at Gods hands.[10]

The reformers urged the needs of the poor insistently. Although many of their specific prescriptions for the treatment of the poor owed much to humanist social thought, the godly cranked up the rhetoric. In the early stages of the reformation the swarms of beggars on the London streets were taken as evidence of the corruption of the catholic church which had squandered resources on idle clergy; the evangelicals power- fully identified with the needs of the poor, to such an extent that they could be readily depicted as social subversives. The so-called commonwealthmen, though lacking a coherent programme of social reform, nevertheless contributed a sense of evangelical urgency to the proper ordering of social relationships. Hence their bitter attacks on covetousness and the repeated denunciation of the metropolitan evils of usury, rack-renting and conspicuous consumption. They were reluc- tant to press the binary division of the poor into the deserving and undeserving; they did not wish to see the duty to support the poor displaced on to public authorities, and they called for a more inclusive charity which did not discriminate between persons in the giving of alms. Their key text was that of casting the bread upon the waters. It is true, as Felicity Heal has shown, that by 1600 the idea of catholicity in giving was being replaced by a stronger emphasis on discrimination between deserving and undeserving, reinforced by a calvinist emphasis on giving to those who were of the 'household of faith', and by the intervention of the public authorities who banned begging save under licence in 1598. But the moralists continued to urge the duty of domestic support of the poor, and there was continuing anxiety lest the public support of the poor should detract from the practice of charity and face-to-face encounters with the poor. As Samuel Bird put it, 'we must bid the poore to our houses, notwithstanding our money collection'.[11]

To whatever extent attitudes may have been becoming more dis- criminating, there was no letting-up of the pressure for voluntary support for the poor in the early seventeenth century. It is one of the paradoxes of calvinism that while denying that good works were efficacious in achieving salvation, its adherents were nevertheless urged

---

[10] T. Drant, *Two Sermons Preached the One at S Maries Spittle ... the Other at Windsor* (1570), sigs. Hi–Hiiii; H. Smith, *The Poore Mens Teares Opened in a Sermon* (1592), 11; T. White, *A Sermon Preached at Pauls Cross the 17 November 1589* (1589), 39; W. Cupper, *Certaine Sermons concerning Gods Late Visitation in the Citie of London* (1592), 285.

[11] M. Todd, *Christian Humanism and the Puritan Social Order* (Cambridge, 1987), ch. 5; P. Slack, *From Reformation to Improvement: Public Welfare in Early Modern England* (Oxford, 1999), ch. 1; S. Brigden, *London and the Reformation* (Oxford, 1989), 318–19, 470–83; F. Heal, *Hospitality in Early Modern England* (Oxford, 1990), 122–40; S. Bird, *The Lectures ... on the 8th and 9th Chapters of the Second Epistle to the Corinthians* (Cambridge, 1598), 79.

to perform them. The explanation lies in the tension within calvinist theology between 'the absolute confidence in the promise of pre-destination with the deep need for assurance or proof that the promise applied to [its adherents] personally'. The quest of the godly for assurance produced an intensely activist and evangelical piety.[12] The elect were to be distinguished from the reprobate by their good works. Stephen Denison, lecturer at St Katherine Cree summed up the position. 'Faith must be tried by the fruits ... for faith without good works is but a carcass of faith ... For howsoever faith alone doth justify the person, yet works must necessarily justify the faith.' Or as Willet put it, 'we also urge good works as necessary fruits and lively testimonies of our faith'. Another element in the rhetoric of charity was provi-dentialism, the sense that God would punish his people for their flinty-heartedness towards the poor: unmercifulness towards the poor would bring down the wrath of God, warned Adam Hill at Paul's Cross in 1595. Although the call for good works was articulated by the godly within a predestinarian framework, the strongly voluntarist language of the call to charity, particularly in the context of charity sermons, might well have been interpreted by the laity as indicating that their works would assist them in their passage to heaven. Those who listened to the mellifluous words of Daniel Price's 1616 Spital sermon could be forgiven for thinking that their charitable deeds would get them to heaven:

> good men ... are as signets on his finger, starres in his hand, apples of his eye ... they shall flourish as the bay tree, the olive, the myrrh, the palme, the Cedar of Lebanus ... their names shall be in heaven (Luke 10:20); their numbers in his book (Psalm 139:19); their meate commeth from his hand (Psalm 245:15); their bones kept by him (Psalm 34:21); their haires numbred by him (Matthew 10:30); their teares reserved with him (Psalm 56:7).[13]

What do their wills tell us about the impact of these insistent calls to the exercise of charity? I am in the process of surveying changing patterns of charitable giving by Londoners through the sixteenth and seventeenth centuries. All the London wills proved in the prerogative

---

[12] P. Lake, *The Boxmaker's Revenge: 'Orthodoxy', 'Heterodoxy', and the Politics of the Parish in Early Stuart London* (Manchester, 2001), 20–48; R. T. Kendall, *Calvin and English Calvinism to 1649* (Oxford, 1979). I. Green, *Print and Protestantism in Early Modern England* (Oxford, 2000), also sheds much light on the tensions between theological and pastoral priorities within protestant discourse.

[13] Denison is cited by Lake, *Boxmaker's Revenge*, 21; Willet, *Synopsis Papismi*, 1068; A. Hill, *The Crie of England: A Sermon Preached at Paules Crosse in September 1593* (1595), 68; D. Price, *Maries Memoriall: A Sermon Preached at St Maries Spittle on Munday in Easter Week Being Aprill 1 1616* (1617), 60.

court of Canterbury (PCC) in the years 1528-30 (on the eve of the reformation), 1550-3 (the highwater mark of Edwardian protestantism), 1570-3 (as the Elizabethan settlement bedded down), 1594-7 (in the midst of the crisis years of that troubled decade) and 1636-8 (during the Laudian reaction) have been examined. Some of the lesser probate jurisdictions where the wills of people of more modest means were proved have also been analysed for the 1570s, 1590s and the 1630s.[14]

Table 1   *Patterns of charitable giving by Londoners*

	1528–30	*1550–3*	*1570–3*	*1594–7*	*1635–8*
Prerogative Court of Canterbury wills: London testators					
Citizens					
	n = 102	n = 246	n = 218	n = 332	n = 383
Any poor	58%	69%	72%	65%	52%
Hospitals		24%	32%	32%	14%
Prisons	29%	26%	23%	17%	9%
non-London					
Poor	10%	18%	19%	24%	28%
Gentlemen/professional					
	n = 7	n = 39	n = 45	n = 76	n = 115
Any poor	43%	54%	42%	42%	49%
Women					
	n = 13	n = 31	n = 47	n = 82	n = 121
Any poor	77%	71%	64%	52%	46%
Other jurisdictions: all London testators					
Any poor	13%	32%	35%	24%	18%

Sources: as n. 14.

The broad trend lines are clear from the figures for the citizens (on whom this essay concentrates). The proportions giving to the poor on the eve of the reformation are higher than previous estimates, perhaps

[14] Public Records Office [hereafter PRO], PROB 11/22–3, 33–6, 52–5, 83–90, 170–8; Guildhall Library [hereafter GL], MSS 9051/3–5, 8; 9171/15–16, 18; 25626/2–3, 5; London Metropolitan Archives [hereafter LMA], DL/C/358–9; S. Brigden, 'The Early Reformation in London: The Conflict in the Parishes, 1522–1547' (PhD thesis, University of Cambridge, 1979), 358–9, *idem*, 'Religion and Social Obligation in Early Sixteenth-Century London', *Past and Present*, 103 (1984), 104–5. For other treatments of the testamentary evidence from London, see C. Schen, 'Charity in London, 1500–1620: From the "Wealth of Souls" to "Most Need"' (PhD thesis, Brandeis University, 1994); D. J. Hickman, 'From Catholic to Protestant: The Changing Meaning of Testamentary Religious Provisions in Elizabethan London', in *England's Long Reformation, 1500–1800*, ed. N. Tyacke (1998); *idem*, 'Religious Belief and Pious Practice Among London's Elizabethan Elite', *Historical Journal*, 42 (1999), 941–60.

because I have included those cases where the testator left the residue of his estate to vaguely defined works of charity at his executor's discretion.[15] But it is clear that there was an increased level of participation in charitable giving during the reformation period, and that it peaked probably in the 1570s. The reasons for that increase are difficult to disentangle. What was the balance between a perception of greater need resulting from the dissolutions and mounting economic pressures on the one hand and ideological change, whether of the humanist or protestant variety on the other hand? We have underestimated the damage done by the dissolutions, both because the scale of the alms distributed through monasteries and fraternities has been underestimated, and because the fraternities provided an institutional framework within which informal support could also be offered.[16] As we have seen, there was a great deal of evangelical exhortation to increased charity, but by no means all donors were convinced protestants, and for many traditionalists giving to the poor may have been a form of displacement, seeking the intercession of the poor when other forms were denied. It is suggestive that a number of Edwardian testators with so-called 'protestant' preambles nevertheless left money for deeds of charity 'meritorious fore thelthe of my soul', further proof, if it were needed, that the preamble does not provide a window into the soul.[17]

It is clear that after the 1570s levels of participation in charitable support at death declined: the trajectory is still clearer if we include Peter Earle's sample of 181 Londoners of the middle station from 1665 to 1720, only 30 per cent of whom made charitable bequests.[18] This decline might give some support to the moralists' complaints that charity waxed cold, and it may reflect the effects of the introduction of compulsory rating in 1572. A proposal for the reform of charitable provision in the city in c. 1596 shows considerable scepticism about rates 'forasmuche as charitie ought to be free and not forced or compulsory', and suggested that more would be raised by a 'free and voluntary contribution'.[19] Conversely, some donors expressed anxiety

[15] Brigden, 'Early Reformation', 358–9.

[16] M. K. McIntosh, 'Local Responses to the Poor in Late Medieval and Tudor England', *Continuity and Change*, 3 (1988), 209–45; N. S. Rushton, 'Monastic Charitable Provision in Tudor England: Quantifying and Qualifying Poor Relief in the Early Sixteenth Century', *Continuity and Change*, 16 (2001), 1–44.

[17] PRO, PROB 11/34, fos. 258–9; 35, fos. 33v, 114v–6; 36, fos. 79–80. Cf. E. Duffy, *The Stripping of the Altars: Traditional Religion in England, 1400–1580* (1992), 504–23.

[18] P. Earle, *The Making of the English Middle Class: Business, Society, and Family Life in London, 1660–1730* (1989), 316–19. Cf. D. T. Andrew, *Philanthropy and Police in London: Charity in the Eighteenth Century* (Princeton, 1989), 45–9; D. E. Owen, *English Philanthropy, 1660–1960* (1965); C. Wilson, 'The Other Face of Mercantilism', *Transactions of the Royal Historical Society*, 4th ser., 9 (1959), 81–101.

[19] Corporation of London Records Office [hereafter CLRO], Remembrancia, ii, no.

that their charity might be used by recipient communities as an excuse for reducing the volume of public provision.[20] It is also possible that Londoners were being called upon more regularly to support a variety of well-organised fund-raising projects. In particular, the sustained programme of beautification of London's parish churches in the early seventeenth century entailed the mobilisation of lay support, some of it through parochial assessments backed by the coercive apparatus of the church courts, but also often by voluntary donations.[21] There had long been subscriptions among parishioners and companymen for specific projects – financing lawsuits, extending the church yard, buying a hearse cloth, establishing a parochial school – but these subscriptions were becoming more frequent and were more often organised on a city-wide, or even, as with the repair of St Paul's in the 1630s, on a national basis. In the later seventeenth and eighteenth centuries such subscription charities were to become common.[22] Another contributory factor to declining participation levels in testamentary provision may have been changing sensibilities about funerals. As we shall see, many of the more token distributions to the poor had been directed towards securing their attendance at the funeral, and they became less popular with growing reservations about public funerals.[23]

One important change was the degree to which charity came to be channelled through public institutions like hospitals, the livery companies and the civil parish. About a quarter of the wealthier Edwardian citizen testators made bequests to the recently established hospitals; in the 1570s and 1590s about one third did so. Many legacies now went direct to the churchwardens 'for the more discreete bestowing of the same'; in other cases executors were instructed to take the advice of the minister, churchwardens and overseers, sometimes assisted by specified numbers of the 'most sufficient inhabitants' or the 'chief of the parish' or the 'ancients' in making distributions.[24] In some cases

---

87. Cf. J. Walter, 'The Social Economy of Dearth in Early Modern England', in *Famine, Disease and the Social Order in Early Modern England*, ed. R. Schofield and J. Walter (Cambridge, 1989), 111–12.

[20] PRO, PROB 11/171, fos. 11–13.

[21] J. F. Merritt, 'Puritans, Laudians, and the Phenomenon of Church Building in Jacobean London', *Historical Journal*, 41 (1998), 935–60.

[22] GL, MS 6155/2, accts. for 1595–6 and 1596–7; Southwark Archives, St Olave's Vestry Minutes, 1552–1604, fo. 18v; Churchwardens' Accounts, 1546–92, 303–13; I. W. Archer, *The Pursuit of Stability: Social Relations in Elizabethan London* (Cambridge, 1991), 189 n. 138. For the eighteenth century, see references in n. 18.

[23] R. Houlbrooke, *Death, Religion and the Family in England, 1480–1750* (Oxford, 1998), 272–7; D. Cressy, *Birth, Marriage, and Death: Ritual, Religion and the Life Cycle in Tudor and Stuart England* (Oxford, 1997), 412–16, 443–8.

[24] GL, MS 9051/4, fo. 221v; PRO, PROB 11/170, fo. 307v; 171, fos. 307–8v; 172, fos. 1r–v, 94–6, 109v–12v, 169r–v; 173, fos. 420–1; 175, fos. 24v–5v, 336v–8; 176, fos. 49r–v, 183–4v. For the significance of the language, see H. R. French, 'Social Status, Localism

donors targeted their relief on publicly identifiable groups of poor like the parish pensioners ('to the poor of the parish so many as are pensioners', those 'relieved of the common charity of the parish') or company alms men.[25] Thus the lines between public and private provision were blurred. A further consequence was that testators did insist on increasing discrimination in the distribution of their relief. Relief should be confined to the 'godly religious poor', 'the honest godly poor', the 'godlie, aged, and well disposed', 'the godly poor of the church of god', the 'godliest poor', 'poor freemen of best report', 'such as have greate neede indeede and be of honest behavyour and good conversacion and no drunkarde nor swearer', 'labouring and industrious persons of honest life and conversation', 'old people of honest life such as have been willing to take pains for their living formerly'.[26] Some elaborated on the godly theme to explain what they meant: 'only the well ordered poor and those who usually resort to church at other times when they are able and behave themselves reverently there and are respective to the governors and government in the parish', 'such as can saie the lordes prayer, the articles of their belefe and the tenne commaundementes in englishe without the book'.[27]

We should not exaggerate the pace and scale of the shift towards distribution through public channels and increasing discrimination. There remained an insistent desire for the presence of the poor at funerals. This could be achieved either by a traditional dole to the poor, or the clothing of poor, or inviting the children of Christ's Hospital to attend singing psalms over the corpse. In the 1590s 32 per cent of those making some kind of bequest to the poor expected that the poor would be present at the funeral; by the 1630s the proportion had fallen but was still 17 per cent.[28] Some waxed indignant at the practice, 'a popish invitation of such as were desirous after their deaths to have their souls prayed for', but sensibilities of this kind were unusual.[29] Even those of godly persuasion, like Robert Offley (d. 1596), a friend of the puritan lecturer Dr Thomas Crook and the sponsor of a variety of loan stocks, ordered a dole for 1,600 people (£20 at 3d

---

and the "Middle Sort of People" in England, 1620–1750', *Past and Present*, 166 (2000), 66–99.

[25] PRO, PROB 11/52, fo. 197v; 89, fo. 162; 160, fos. 8v–9.

[26] PRO, PROB 11/53, fo. 74; 67, fo. 130; 71, fo. 70; 88, fo. 79; 89, fos. 89v, 310, 438v; 90, fo. 141v; 171, fos. 124v–6v; 172, fos. 202v–4; 174, fos. 202v–4; 175, fos. 80v–2v, 272v, 336v–8; 176, fos. 33v–7.

[27] PROB, PROB 11/55, fo. 207; 84, fo. 248; 175, fo. 378.

[28] FL, MS 9051/4, fos. 150v–1; PRO, PROB 11/171, fos. 207–8v; 174, fos. 332v–3. GL, MS 22682 (the Christ's Hospital burial book) shows that the children were present at an average of thirty-eight funerals a year from 1622 to 1648. Cf. Houlbrooke, *Death, Religion, and the Family*, 266–8, 275–9; Cressy, *Birth, Marriage, and Death*, 443–9.

[29] PRO, PROB 11/173, fos. 99v–100v.

apiece) and asked that sixty poor men in gowns be present at his funeral.[30] Londoners were insistent that their funerals should be without 'pomp and vainglory', 'in a decent and comely manner as becometh a christian of my degree and calling', seeking a mean which would avoid 'all sordid parsimony and vainglorious ostentation'. But though that might entail a hostility to mourning blacks or the 'vaine ostentacion to be made by herauldes or scutchions and ... the excesse of these tymes practized in feasteing at great dynners',[31] it did not extend to the presence of the poor, for those who proscribed feasting and blacks might simultaneously require the presence of the poor.[32] To invite the children of the hospital or to clothe the poor was a surer means of targeting one's relief, but it is striking that demands for doles continued into the 1630s. If doles declined it was less because of their popish associations than because of the problems of crowd control posed by the enormous numbers envisaged, up to 600 in some cases in the 1630s. At Lady Mary Ramsey's funeral some of the poor were crushed to death; one testator left money for the beadles for 'regulating and ordering' the poor 'in a court'; Sir William Craven expressed his hostility to doles 'for avoyding of tumultes'. But even Craven had demanded that his churchwardens distribute money to the poor on the day of his funeral.[33]

Funeral doles, however many people continued to request them, constituted only a tiny minority of the funds released by testators, and many mixed doles with other types of charitable provision. Whether distributed by executors or by parochial officers or by company wardens – and we should bear in mind that there was considerable overlap between these groups given the breadth of experience of office-holding – the growth in charitable activity afforded numerous opportunities for the exercise of discretion towards the needy. The terms on which that discretion was exercised are elusive, but it is clear that charity became part of the currency of patronage. Discussions of the London poor are often clouded by the image of the anonymous pullulating mass that derives from the fulminations of the authorities against uncontrolled immigration, alleys stuffed with poor, beggars swarming on the streets. There undoubtedly were many transients, though perhaps not so many as the rhetoric would have us believe, and many of the poor were not faceless. Testators identified groups or

[30] PRO, PROB 11/87, fo. 230.

[31] PRO, PROB 11/33, fos. 90, 139v–40v, 163r–v; 34, fos. 68–9v, 123r–v; 68, fo. 314; 86, fo. 15; 169, fo. 88; 170, fo. 162v; 171, fos. 221v–3, 340v–1; 172, fos. 127–30; 173, fo. 400; 174, fos. 352v–3; 175, fos. 8ov–2v, 348v–50v.

[32] PRO, PROB 11/84, fo. 127; 171, fos. 124v–6v; 172, fos. 127–30.

[33] PRO, PROB 11/132, fos. 70–3v; 170, fos. 218–21; 172, fos. 109v–12v; 173, fos. 252v–3; *The Letters of John Chamberlain*, ed. N. E. McClure (2 vols., Philadelphia, 1939), I, 135.

individuals with whom they had face-to-face dealings through ties of
service, employment, landlordship and neighbourhood proximity: 'poor
honest men who have done me service', 'poor workmen ... in her
majesty's printing house', 'every one of my poor customers', the porters
in Cheap 'that use to bind marchauntes fardelles', 'poor workmen of
our company edgers and trimmers', 'poor workmen that resort to me
for trade', 'every one of my tenants in Maidenhead alley', the water-
bearers, parish sexton, nurse and so on.[34] The insistence of some
testators that their charity should 'not be given for favour or affection
but where most need shall be' suggests that some worried that these
kind of connections might lead to deserving cases being overlooked.
But others were explicit that charity should go to 'suche poore as my
especial freindes shall speake for'.[35] Female testators in particular might
be very specific about intended recipients and those they wished to
exercise patronage. Thus Joan Wright, the wife of an alderman,
specified in 1634 that as many poor gowns as she was years old should
be distributed, 'Goody Barnes my waterbearer to be one, and Goody
Barrett, and Goody Browne which washes here, and Goody Morley at
Saint Albons; Stanley that looks to her boys to send a woman.' Her
'loving friends', Sir George Crooke, her cousins Richard and Thomas
Bennett, Thomas Hampson and William Brownelowe were each to
have the disposal of two gowns, 'and her husband all the rest'.[36] The
remarkable executors' accounts for the expenditure of the charitable
bequests of Robert Nowell (d. 1568), attorney of the court of wards
demonstrate some of those forms of mediation, as familiar figures from
the London elite sponsor individual recipients. Godly preachers like
Robert Crowley and James Young, city officials like the bridgemasters
and chamberlain, local brokers like the aldermen's deputies, and
members of the deceased's kin nominated recipients in a process of
considerable bureaucratic sophistication, for the accounts refer to
numbered 'bills of commendacion' (letters of recommendation) which
were kept on file.[37]

Although the processes of mediation are less clear in companies and
parishes, there is evidence of the persistence of face-to-face transactions
within these institutional frameworks. When the vestrymen of St Saviour
Southwark built their almshouses in 1580 the first inmates were nominated by individual vestrymen who paid their pensions in return for
an undertaking that the almspeople would look after any people taken

[34] PRO, PROB 11/56, fo. 1; 83, fos. 214v, 223v; 88, fo. 24; 167, fo. 130; 168, fo. 201;
169, fos. 54, 99; GL, MSS 9051/3, fo. 438; 9051/4, fo. 202v; 9171/16, fo. 442.

[35] PRO, PROB 11/52, fo. 23; 55, fo. 210v; 85, fo. 127; 88, fo. 82; 173, fos. 347–8.

[36] PRO, PROB 11/171, fos. 189–91v.

[37] *The Spending of the Money of Robert Nowell of Reade Hall, Lancashire*, ed. A. B. Grosart
(Manchester, 1877).

sick in the houses of their benefactors. Successive Merchant Taylor almshouse projects in London in the 1590s and 1630s involved sponsorship by wealthy company members who nominated the recipients.[38] Although balloting procedures were often used to ensure that loans were not given out for 'affection or friendship', it is clear that one of the perks of being an assistant of a livery company was the right to nominate recipients of charity. The results were not always entirely fortunate, as the Merchant Taylors complained in 1637 that the practice whereby the master and wardens nominated the recipients of Robert Donkyn's clothing charity had resulted in the charity being given to non-freemen and people dwelling out of the city who were ineligible for it.[39] Public authority was shot through with private discretion as individuals took advantage of their institutional power to reinforce personal relationships of patronage and dependency.

Willet and Jordan both emphasise the heroic donors. They were very much in the minority. In the 1590s less than 5 per cent of the PCC testators left money for loan stocks; less than 10 per cent left any kind of endowment (including loan stocks) or annuity, and some of those who did left very modest amounts, often just £20 to be added to the parish stock and used to subsidise the fuel of the poor in winter. In those few cases where we can link testators to their inventoried wealth, very few were leaving more than 2–3 per cent to charity. Those who did leave very large endowments tended to be childless.[40] However, the heroes did make a difference. It has not proved possible in the current state of my research to produce accurate figures for the London yield of endowments over the whole period, though I am reasonably confident that they will be calculable, but the record of individual institutions is quite telling. Expenditure from all endowed charities by the Clothworkers' Company rose three-fold from the 1590s to the 1630s (£143 p.a. to £418 p.a.), by the Grocers' Company four-fold (£72 p.a. to £296 p.a.), and by the Merchant Taylors nearly seven-fold (£240 p.a. to £1,620 p.a.).[41]

Because these endowments involved distributions to communities often remote from London, the capital was becoming more enmeshed with provincial society. There are indications that the charitable hori-

[38] LMA, P92/SAV/449, 162, 163; Merchant Taylors' Company, Court Minutes, 1575–1601, fos. 252v, 262, 266, 310r–v, 315r–v; 1636–54, fos. 40v–1v; Wardens' Accounts, 1638–9.

[39] Merchant Taylors' Company, Court Minutes, 1636–54, fo. 36r–v; PRO, PROB 11/52, fo. 23; 87, fo. 230.

[40] I. W. Archer, *The History of the Haberdashers' Company* (Chichester, 1991), 72–4; R. Grassby, *Kinship and Capitalism: Marriage, Family, and Business in the English Speaking World, 1580–1740* (Cambridge, 2001), 260–2, 399–400.

[41] I. W. Archer, 'The Livery Companies and Charity, 1500–1700', in *Guilds, Society, and Economy in London, 1450–1800*, ed. I. A. Gadd and P. Wallis (Centre for Metropolitan History, 2002).

zons of Londoners broadened over our period, increasingly directed to the provinces: 18 per cent of PCC citizen testators left money to the poor outside London in the 1550s, 24 per cent in the 1590s, and 28 per cent in the 1630s. By the 1630s the Merchant Taylors were distributing annuities to the poor of Marcham (Northamptonshire), Odiham (Hampshire), Brighton (Sussex) and Doddington (Isle of Ely); they paid for schoolmasters in Crosby (Lancashire), Wolverhampton and Great Bloxwich (Staffordshire), Bromfield (Cumberland), Hayfield (Derbyshire) and Burnsall (Yorkshire). Some individual donors spread their charitable interests very widely. Most remarkably Sir Thomas White, in addition to founding St John's College, Oxford, and making major donations to Coventry, established a loan charity which rotated between twenty-four towns from Newcastle to Exeter, and from Shrewsbury to Ipswich. As Joe Ward has suggested, the management of the endowed charities brought Londoners into frequent contact with the localities, appointing schoolmasters, mediating local disputes or finding themselves in dispute with the recipient communities.[42] The Londoners who left money to provincial charities became powerful figures in local memory, legends sometimes developing around them. Sir Rowland Hill, for example, was remembered in the town annals of Shrewsbury as the 'frynd of the wydowe and fatherles'. Around their haberdasher benefactor, William Jones, the townspeople of Monmouth developed a fund of local stories, such as that he had been kicked out of the town as a young lad, not being able to pay ten groats, a powerful lesson in the opportunities for social mobility. Sir Thomas White's benefaction was commemorated in portraits of him in Bristol, Canterbury, Coventry, Exeter, Gloucester, King's Lynn, Leicester, Lincoln, Norwich, Oxford, Reading, Salisbury and Southampton. Works celebrating the charitable endeavours of Londoners like the successive editions of Stow's *Survey* which gradually protestantised the text, provided source material for works with a less local audience. From Fuller's *Worthies* we learn that counties compared their charitable foundations: the natives of Shropshire 'confess and complain of a comparative dearth (in proportion with other shires) of Benefactors to the publick'. Not only was charity a badge of protestant identity; it could be a powerful agent of national integration.[43]

[42] Merchant Taylors' Company, Wardens' Accounts, 1638–9; R. Tittler, 'Sir Thomas White of London: Civic Philanthropy and the Making of the Merchant-Hero', in his *Townspeople and Nation: English Urban Experiences, 1500–1640* (Stanford, 2001), 100–20; J. P. Ward, 'Godliness, Commemoration, and Community: The Management of Provincial Schools by London Trade Guilds', in *Protestant Identities: Religion, Society and Self-Fashioning in Post-Reformation England*, ed. M. C. McClendon, J. P. Ward and M. Macdonald (Stanford, 1999), 141–57, 323–6.

[43] W. A. Leighton, 'Early Chronicles of Shrewsbury', *Transcriptions of the Shropshire Archaeological and Natural History Society*, 1st ser. 3 (1880), 259–60; Fuller, *Worthies*, part III,

But how much of it was there? What was the relationship between the public and private provision? We must return to Jordan and his critics. The problem of all existing work is that is that it limits the voluntary sector to endowed charity and testamentary provision.[44] While the extent of public provision is more easily quantified, particularly at the level of the individual community, estimates of the size of the voluntary sector based on the testamentary evidence are no more than bare minima, because of the variety of ways in which voluntary support was offered. We can make reasonable estimates of the size of the poor rate in early modern London; we can (albeit by laborious means) estimate the yield of endowments and even the contribution of the livery companies to charitable provision, but we can be much less sure about life-time giving. The moralists saw life-time giving as superior to death-bed charity as a life-time gift entailed an immediate sacrifice. Ezechiel had urged that 'a man should give his own bread to the poor' (18.7); Jesus had urged his disciples to sell their possessions and give alms, earning an unfailing treasure in heaven (Luke 12:33). Charles Richardson, following Jeremiah, warned that death-bed charity might lead men to 'turne bread gotten by oppression and usury into a work of mercy'. Life-time charity was secure against corrupt executors: potential donors were warned to 'make their owne eyes their Overseers and their owne hands their executors so their work shall prosper'. Those 'mirrors of charity' like Robert Dowe or Sir Thomas Smith who gave out extensive alms in their life-times were singled out for praise:

> Good done at our end is like a lanterne borne after us that directeth them that come after us, but affordeth us little light; whereas the good done in our life-time is like a light borne before us that both benefiteth them and also us alike, imparting light equally unto either.[45]

10, part IV, 54; Titler, 'Sir Thomas White', 119–20, J. F. Merritt, 'The Reshaping of Stow's Survey: Munday, Strype, and the Protestant City', in her *Imagining the City*, 52–88.

[44] Archer, *Pursuit of Stability*, 163–82; C. S. Evans, ' "An Echo of the Multitude": The Intersection of Governmental and Private Initiatives in Early Modern Exeter', *Albion*, 32 (2000), 408–28. For the longer-term perspective, see J. Innes, 'The "Mixed Economy of Welfare" in Early Modern England: An Assessment of the Options from Hale to Malthus, c. 1683–1863', in *Charity, Self-Interest, and Welfare in the English Past*, ed. M. J. Daunton (1996); I. Ben-Amos, 'Gifts and Favors: Informal Support in Early Modern England', *Journal of Modern History*, 72 (2000), 295–338.

[45] C. Richardson, *A Sermon against Oppression and Fraudulent Dealing Preached at Paules Crosse* (1615), 33; T. Gataker, *Davids Instructor: A Sermon Preached at the Visitation of the Free-Schoole at Tonbridge in Kent* (1620), sig. A3; N. Hardy, *A Divine Prospective: Reporting the Just Mans Peacefull End, in a Funeral Sermon at the Enterrement of Sir John Gayr* (1654), 28; G. Hughes, *The Saintes Losse and Lamentation: A Sermon Preached at the Funerall of the Worshipfull Captaine Henry Waller ...* (1632), 52; Willet, *Synopsis Papismi*, 1121; Houlbrooke, *Death, Religion, and the Family*, 61–2.

Some of this life-time giving is quantifiable. Bequests were supplemented by collections in response to charitable briefs (that is licences from the crown to collect beyond the locality), collections at sermons and communions and donations to the poor box. In St Botolph Aldgate there were regular collections on behalf of individuals bearing letters from figures as diverse as the local preacher, the bishop of London, the alderman of the ward and the lord admiral, as well as by letters patent from the crown or precepts from the lord mayor. These provided support for a variety of groups (including a poor scholar, a wounded soldier, an epileptic and individuals who had suffered losses by fire and suretyship in St Botolph Aldgate 1583–4), and they might raise around £8 in a given year, a figure which compares with £40 in poor rate in the same parish.[46] Collections at sermons in most parishes appear to have added modest amounts (no more than £2–3 p.a.), communicants appear to have offered an average of ½d each at Easter time (no more than £2–3 p.a.), but in some parishes the figures are more startling. In Holy Trinity Minories about £26 p.a. was being collected at the church door from 'the godly congregations that hether resorted to heare the worde of God' in the heady days of the early 1570s when the parish was a refuge for nonconforming ministers, and the resort of the sermon-gadding godly. Likewise, when the puritan Richard Greenham was lecturer at Christ Church Newgate Street from 1591 collections at his sermons amounted to £23 16s 4¾d and at communions to £5 3s 1¼d.[47] Quantifying the full extent of this voluntary charity at a parochial level is difficult because of the inconsistencies and complexities of accounting practices. Although churchwardens' accounts might include expenditure from legacies for the poor, especially when they took the form of annuities, it was common to keep separate accounts of charitable disbursements from the poor box or from collections at communions and sermons. Likewise, the recording in vestry minutes of disbursements from the poor box is usually not consistent enough for us to feel confident that the coverage is comprehensive.[48]

Some parishes, however, have records such that we might feel that we are getting something closer to a full picture. At St Margaret Westminster collections at communions along with legacies are recorded on the accounts of the collectors for the poor. Leading parishioners organised the distribution of their alms through the parochial authorities.

---

[46] GL, MSS 9234/1; 4415/1, 4959, fos. 93–4, provide details of church briefs. See W. A. Bewes, *Church Briefs, or Royal Warrants for Collections for Charitable Objects* (1894); C. Schen, 'Constructing the Poor in Early Seventeenth-Century London', *Albion*, 32 (2000), 450–63.

[47] GL, MSS 4959; 9163; 9234/1 7; LMA, P92/SAV/1385, 1387, 1397; Westminster City Archives [hereafter WCA], E144–9; F304–29; Lambeth Palace Library, Holy Trinity Minories Churchwardens' Accounts, 1566–1686.

[48] GL, MSS 4824; 4959.

Major life-time givers were Lady Winifred Paulet marchioness of Winchester, giving £35 10s p.a. in alms by the time of her death in 1586, and her daughter Lady Anne Dacre (d. 1595) who was paying 12d per week for twenty poor women and making supplementary payments of £46 in the dearth year of 1594–5. From 1572 the dean allowed the parish officers to participate in the distribution of his alms though it took place within the abbey church. Resources available in St Margaret's rose steadily: approximately £170 p.a. in the 1570s, £215 p.a. in the 1590s, £228 p.a. in the period 1598–1608. The proportion coming from voluntary giving was high: 60 per cent in the 1570s, and 81 per cent in the 1590s. Thus the difficulties of raising the rates meant that it was through private charity that the crises of plague and dearth in the 1590s were met: in the plague year of 1593 Lord Treasurer Burghley, the high steward, Gabriel Goodman, the dean of Westminster and Thomas Knyvett, a groom of the privy chamber, were noted as the 'speciall relevers of the poore in this tyme of God his great visitation'. 1598 emerges as a key date in the development of rating: as poor law administration tightened in the wake of the late Elizabethan statutes, rates were raised and the next occasion of plague was met with supplementary rates. The proportion raised through benevolences fell to 55 per cent in the ten years after 1598. There was, of course, no such thing as a typical parish, and St Margaret's was less typical than most: very much a Cecil fief with the abbey constituting a rather conservative ecclesiastical presence, and a number of high profile aristocratic donors potentially distorting the pattern of charitable provision.[49] Perhaps more typical was neighbouring St Martin-in-the-Fields where benevolences and legacies accounted for 38 per cent of poor receipts 1590–7, 24 per cent 1598–1608 and just 13 per cent in 1620–5: total receipts increased eight-fold in that period and the parish's population between three- and four-fold.[50] But voluntary provision was

---

[49] WCA, E144–9. I have studied the Westminster records independently, but there is a fuller account in J. F. Merritt, 'Religion, Government, and Society in Early Modern Westminster, c. 1525–1625' (PhD thesis, University of London, 1992), ch. 6. Dr Merritt's forthcoming monograph on early modern Westminster will add very significantly to the subject. See also J. P. Boulton, 'The Poor Among the Rich: Paupers and the Parish in the West End, 1600–1724', in *Londinopolis: Essays in the Cultural and Social History of Early Modern London*, ed. P. Griffiths and M. Jenner (Manchester, 2001), 197–225; *idem*, ' "Going on the Parish": The Parish Pension and its Meaning in the London Suburbs, 1640–1724', in *Chronicling Poverty: The Voices and Strategies of the English Poor, 1640–1840*, ed. T. Hitchcock, P. King and P. Sharpe (Basingstoke, 1997), 19–46; B. Coates, 'Poor Relief in London during the English Revolution Revisited', *London Journal*, 25 (2000), 13–39; J. F. Merritt, 'The Cradle of Laudianism? Westminster Abbey, 1558–1630', *Journal of Ecclesiastical History*, 52 (2001), 623–46.

[50] WCA, F301, 304–52; R. M. Smuts, 'The Court and its Neighbourhood: Royal Policy and Urban Growth in the Early Stuart West End', *Journal of British Studies*, 30 (1991), 118 n. 3.

significant all over the metropolitan area: in the 1590s a minimum of 47 per cent of parochial resources for relief in St Saviours Southwark, 50 per cent in St Botolph Aldgate and 53 per cent in St Andrew Wardrobe came from voluntary contributions; in St Dunstan in the West in the later 1640s the proportion remained 54 per cent.[51]

A parochial focus on the balance between public and private provision leads one to exaggerate the significance of rating in the overall picture because rates were parochially organised, while the voluntary sector was mobilised through a greater variety of institutions. Well-organised charitable projects with conciliar backing could raise substantial sums: citizens contributed benevolences of £1,045 7s 2d to the repair of St Pauls in 1561-2 (more than was raised through the two city fifteenths granted by common council for the same project); the Nantwich fire disaster fund of 1583-6 raised £600 from the London laity.[52] These are impressive figures when set beside the yield of the poor rate in Elizabethan London which was no more than £2,250 p.a. before 1598. Other notable government sponsored initiatives were the collections for the beleaguered city of Geneva in 1582-3, or for the recovery of the Palatinate in 1620 and 1623, or for religious refugees in 1628 and 1630, the latter being channelled through those paragons of charitable endeavour, the stranger churches. The collections for the Palatinate refugees in 1628 and 1630 raised a minimum of £9,608 nationally.[53] Within the city the aldermen used set piece civic occasions like the sermons at Paul's Cross or the Easter Spital sermons to raise monies for otherwise neglected charitable objects: in the later Elizabethan period, for example, collections at the Easter holiday sermons raised between £70 and £100 a year for redeeming captives.[54] Emergencies like plague and dearth were met by special collections which were

[51] Archer, *Pursuit of Stability*, 188–90; GL, MS 2088/1; LMA, P92/SAV/1397, 1566–9; J. P. Boulton, *Neighbourhood and Society: A London Suburb in the Seventeenth Century* (Cambridge, 1987), 92–7; R. W. Herlan, 'Poor Relief in the London Parish of St Dunstan-in-the-West during the English Revolution', *Guildhall Studies in London History*, 3 (1977), 13–36.

[54] P. Collinson, *Archbishop Grindall, 1519–1583: The Struggle for a Reformed Church* (1979), 157–61; C. J. Kitching, 'Fire Disasters and Fire Relief in Sixteenth-Century England: The Nantwich Fire of 1583', *Bulletin of the Institute of Historical Research*, 54 (1981), 171–87. The national subscriptions for the re-edification of St Paul's raised £82,303 7s 0d between May 1631 and Michaelmas 1638, compared to the total of £5,968 16s 1d raised in 1561–4: GL, MS 25475/1; J. Hayward, *Annals of the First Four Years of the Reign of Queen Elizabeth*, Camden Society, o.s., VII (1840), 88–9. On the themes of this paragraph, cf. D. Underdown, *Fire From Heaven: Life in an English Town in the Seventeenth Century* (1992), 125–8.

[53] P. Collinson, 'England, 1558–1640', in *International Calvinism*, ed. M. Prestwich (Oxford, 1985), 203–10; O. P. Grell, *Dutch Calvinists in Early Stuart London: The Dutch Church in the Austin Friars, 1603–1642* (Leiden, 1989), 176–223.

[54] CLRO, Rep. 18, fo. 197v; Rep. 20, fos. 322v, 420; Rep. 21, fos. 294, 531, 548v; Rep. 22, fo. 53v; Rep. 23, fos. 520v, 534, 563v, 565, 594v–5; *Chamber Accounts of the Sixteenth Century*, ed. B. R. Masters (London Record Society, xx, 1984), 6, 7, 81–2.

increasingly centralised. In July 1596 householders were requested to contribute to special collections for the poor, 'for that it is a woorke of charitie for those whom almightie god has blessed in more plentifull measure to releeve their poor and neadie breatheren'; the monies collected (sufficient for 4,000 2d loaves per week) were handed over to city treasurers and redistributed among the wards according to need.[55]

Other charitable resources flowed through the livery companies and hospitals. The endowments of the companies supplemented by quarterage dues supported poor members to the tune of £1,650 p.a. in the 1590s (compared to a poor rate raising £2,250 at that date) as well as acting as conduits for other charities in London and elsewhere in the kingdom. The three hospitals of Christ's, St Bartholomew's and St Thomas's enjoyed a combined income at the same time of £6,000 p.a. (three-quarters of it from endowments, legacies and benevolences). In assessing the overall contribution of the voluntary sector, it is easy enough to play down the significance of its individual components: the resources of no single institution seemed adequate to its task; no individual collection appeared to raise funds sufficient to meet the problems it purported to address. But if we were able to piece together all the individual items of the puzzle together we might be more impressed. Some years ago I made estimates of the various sources of support for the poor in Elizabethan London, including company pensions, poor rate, city, tolls, endowments, bequests to the poor (but significantly excluding collections at communions and sermons and charitable briefs). Those figures show private charity contributing 52 per cent of resources in the early 1570s and 67 per cent in the mid-1590s (rates and tolls: 41 per cent and 26 per cent respectively; company pensions, steady at 7 per cent). It will be clear from the previous discussion of individual parishes that these proportions shifted markedly in favour of public provision in the early seventeenth century, but the fact remains that the figures for private charity remain minima.[56]

They must be minima, for the greatest obstacle to quantifying the contribution of the voluntary sector is the 'dark figure' of face-to-face charity. We know that in the long run it declined, but we have little sense of the chronology of decline or its significance. There is a tendency to discuss the topic with reference to urban/rural dichotomies – the gentry come to the city to escape the obligations of rural hospitality; hospitality was less common in the supposedly 'anonymous' urban environment – but a variety of neighbourhood studies have called into

[55] CLRO, JCC 24, fos. 141, 143v, 148v, 152, 179. Cf. S. Hindle, 'Dearth, Poverty, and Alms: The Campaign for General Hospitality in Late Elizabethan England', *Past and Present*, 172 (2001), 44–86.

[56] Archer, *Pursuit of Stability*, 149–203.

question the assumption of urban anomie in those arguments, and the testamentary evidence can be used to support the notion of *increasing* generosity by the gentry residents of the capital as they came to identify more closely with the metropolis.[57] Alternatively, there is the literature of complaint – the constant pressure from the moralists for the citizens to show more charity, or the nostalgia of someone like John Stow looking back to the almsgiving of the religious houses – but this material suffers from its immediate rhetorical purposes.[58] Face-to-face giving took a variety of forms, few of them obvious in the records: casual almsgiving, distributions of left-over food to poor neighbours, the regular support of designated poor families. There is still evidence of these practices in the early seventeenth century. John Dorell a gunmaker referred to the poor women 'which used to come weekly to my house for alms', offering them 2s 2d in his will as 'the last benevolence they can expect from me'. Dorothy Leech left money for the twenty poor women of St Margaret Westminster to whom 'she usually gives alms'.[59] Much of this activity would shade into support offered to poorer kin. As John Downame pointed out, 'hee cannot be truly and christianly liberall who neglecteth the poore of his owne family and kindred'. It was one of the features of the upward social mobility of the London elite that its members tended to have poorer kin; the positioning of bequests to kin in wills in the midst of their charitable bequests ('among the poorest sorte of my kyndred in Chesshire', 'to my poor kinsfolk in Shropshire') suggests that testators saw support for kin as the fulfilment of their charitable duties. The mid-sixteenth-century mayor Sir Rowland Hill was celebrated in the county of his birth both because 'he gave yearely to the poore people of the contrey iij C shyrtes and smockes as many frocks and coates to cover them withall' and because of his 'helpinge and preferringe his poore kynsfolkes and servaunts to great lyvings and promotions'. It is at this point, of course, as the definition of charity becomes highly elastic – some might see help of the kind Hill gave his relatives as a species of corruption – that one gives up the effort at quantification.[60]

[57] Heal, *Hospitality*, 114–22, 141–53; A. Bryson, *From Courtesy to Civility: Changing Codes of Conduct in Early Modern England* (Oxford, 1998), 129–40; Archer, *Pursuit of Stability*, ch. 3; Boulton, *Neighbourhood and Society*.

[58] I. W. Archer, 'The Nostalgia of John Stow', in *The Theatrical City: Culture, Theatre, and Politics in London, 1576–1649*, ed. D. M. Smith and R. Strier (Cambridge, 1995), 18–34; L. Manley, *Literature and Culture in Early Modern London* (Cambridge, 1995), ch. 2.

[59] Archer, *Pursuit of Stability*, 178–80; Walter, 'Social Economy of Dearth', 75–128; Ben-Amos, 'Gifts and Favors'; PRO, PROB 11/75, fos. 31v–3; 176, fos. 62v–3.

[60] J. Downame, *The Plea of the Poore: Or a Treatise of Beneficence and Almes-Deeds* (1616), sig. A2; PRO, PROB 11/53, fo. 68; 82, fo. 241; Leighton, 'Early Chronicles of Shrewsbury', 259–60; *Spending of the Money of Robert Nowell*, ed. Grosart; D. Cressy, 'Kin and Kinship Interaction in Early Modern England', *Past and Present*, 113 (1980), 138–69; I. W. Archer,

Voluntary giving took a variety of forms and was in a complex relationship with public provision for the poor. It ranged from casual almsgiving, through personally organised household relief, to donations to the poor box or special collections, from funeral doles to the establishment of endowed charities, and individuals usually mixed these forms in their charitable practice. Donors could exercise discretion among their own contacts with the poor, or they might direct their charity to groups already identified by the authorities. Many of the donors would have had first-hand experience of poor law administration, having served the parochial offices themselves or participated in the decisions about relief in the vestry. Private charity was often distributed through public institutions, but those public institutions often allowed individuals considerable discretion in decisions about who got money, so that the distinction between 'face-to-face' giving and the new rational philanthropy is somewhat blurred. Bureaucratic forms did not fully displace relationships of patronage within the institutional frameworks for the distribution of relief.[61] The transformation of the charitable practice of Londoners was therefore not as pervasive nor as extensive as Jordan suggested. But although the reformation may not have effected quite the changes Willet and Jordan asserted, it had succeeded in forging an association between protestantism and charity.

'Social Networks in Restoration London: The Evidence from Pepys' Diary', in *Communities in Early Modern England*, ed. A. Shepard and P. Withington (Manchester, 2000), 82–4, 87–9.

[61] Cf. S. Hindle, 'Exclusion Crises: Poverty, Migration, and Parochial Responsibility: English Rural Communities, c. 1560–1660', *Rural History*, 7 (1996), 125–49; *idem*, 'Exhortation and Entitlement: Negotiating Inequality in English Rural Communities, 1550–1650', in *Negotiating Power in Early Modern Society: Order, Hierarchy, and Subordination in Britain and Ireland*, ed. M. J. Braddick and J. Walter (Cambridge, 2001), 102–22, 268–72.

Transactions of the RHS 12 (2002), pp. 245–59 © 2002 Royal Historical Society
DOI: 10.1017/S0080440102000087   Printed in the United Kingdom

Professor Roy Porter delivered this paper as the Royal Historical Society's Colin
Matthew Memorial Lecture at St Anthony's Church, Holborn, on the evening of
8 November 2000. In it he drew out of his larger study of the Enlightenment
those aspects of it which he thought particularly significant. Professor Porter died
on 4 March 2002. We are proud to publish this essay as a tribute to his memory.

MATRIX OF MODERNITY?

The Colin Matthew Memorial Lecture

By Roy Porter

READ 8 NOVEMBER 2000

THIS new millennium year has led historians to address moments in
the past which represent epochs in human affairs. The Enlightenment
comprised such a turning-point, since it secularised the world-view and
trained eyes and attention towards the future. British thinkers played
an influential part in this intellectual revolution – though, as I have
maintained in a recent book, *Enlightenment: Britain and the Creation of the
Modern World* (2000), that is a contribution widely ignored or played
down, by contrast to that of France. In that book I tried to explain
that neglect, and I shall not bore you by repeating myself now. Rather
my aim this evening is to set before you some key innovations in
theories and thinking which emerged from eighteenth-century Britain,
in particular ones specially pertinent to Sir Thomas Gresham and his
College, and to the Royal Historical Society. I shall be focusing, in
other words, on enlightened ideas about wealth and economics, science
and history.

Thanks to ideas and attitudes developed in Britain during the long
eighteenth century, attention became focused, perhaps for the first time
ever, on the future rather than the past, and the drive to create a better
future generated a belief in progress. The achievements of scientists
like Isaac Newton and philosophers like John Locke bred new faith in
man's right and power to achieve knowledge of himself and the natural
world, and encouraged practical action in such fields as overseas
exploration, technology, manufactures, social science and legal reform.
Philosophers also became committed to the ending of religious strife,
bigotry, ignorance, prejudice and poverty, and the creation of polite
new social environments and lifestyles.

History is progressive, proclaimed enlightened activists in ever-swelling chorus. 'Rousseau exerts himself to prove that all *was* right originally', commented Mary Wollstonecraft, 'a crowd of authors that all *is* now right: and I, that all *will be* right'. Sights became trained on the future – not the Apocalypse of orthodox Christian eschatology but one continuous with the here-and-now. Indeed, the Enlightenment brought the birth of science fiction – Samuel Madden's futurological *Memoirs of the Twentieth Century* (1733), for instance, or the anonymous and not too chronologically inaccurate *The Reign of George VI, 1900-1925* (1763).

The scent of progress was in the air. The Anglican Edmund Law professed his faith in the 'continual Improvement of the World in general', while the Glasgow Professor John Millar taught that how 'one of the most remarkable differences between man and other animals consists in that wonderful capacity for the improvement of his faculties'. Improvement seemed so visible and tangible. 'Who even at the beginning of this century', asked Richard Price, fired by rational Dissent:

> would have thought, that, in a few years, mankind would acquire the power of subjecting to their wills the dreadful force of lightning, and of flying in aerostatic machines? ... Many similar discoveries may remain to be made ... and it may not be too extravagant to expect that (should civil governments throw no obstacles in the way) the progress of improvement will not cease till it has excluded from the earth most of its worst evils, and restored that Paradisiacal state which, according to the Mosaic History, preceded the present state.

Even 'Parson' Malthus set off his demographic gloom against scientific glory, celebrating 'the great and unlooked for discoveries that have taken place of late years in natural philosophy ... the ardent and unshackled spirit of inquiry that prevails'.

Late Enlightenment belief in progress was, to be sure, a secular theodicy – progress, you could say, was the opium of the Enlightenment – but, as a piece of mythologising, Mary Wollstonecraft's 'all *will be* right' was not complacent in precisely the same way as earlier Leibnizian all-is-for-the-best optimism. The world, as she explained, was not perfect *yet*: rather it was mankind's duty to perfect it, through criticism, reform, education, knowledge, science, industry and sheer energy. The stunning information revolution then in train – compare the World-Wide-Web today – would make all the difference: the dynamo of advancement, proclaimed the psychologist David Hartley, was 'the diffusion of knowledge to all ranks and orders of men, to all nations, kindred, tongues, and peoples', a progress which 'cannot now be stopped, but proceeds ever with an accelerated velocity'. And all this optimism about the future, this overcoming of dark ancestral fears about 'forbidden knowledge', was buoyed up by the conviction, in the thinking of the likes of Hartley, Price and Priestley, that Divine Providence guaranteed such developments, or, as suggested by the Deist, Erasmus Darwin, that social progress was underwritten by the surge of biological evolution at large.

Progress was the abstract form of 'improvement', that ultimate Georgian buzz-word. The idea of novelty was catching. Landscapes, gardens, manufactures, manners, taste, art and literature – all were constantly talked up as 'improving', while advertisers puffed 'modern methods' in manufactures, or the 'latest' in sartorial or culinary elegance, and literary classics were modernised and Englished for the masses.

Traditional historical pessimism was addressed and allayed by Gibbon, a man constitutionally sceptical of facile credos. Would not, as many believed, the calamities which had destroyed Imperial Rome recur in 'this enlightened age'? No: the great 'source of comfort and hope', explained the *Decline and Fall*, was the permanency of improvement. From savagery mankind had 'gradually arisen to command the animals, to fertilise the earth, to traverse the ocean, and to measure the heavens'. Such betterment had no doubt been 'irregular', with 'vicissitudes of light and darkness'. Yet the 'experience of four thousand years should enlarge our hopes', soothed Gibbon, and since technical skills could never be lost, no people 'will relapse into their original barbarism'. At bottom, therefore, mankind could 'acquiesce in the pleasing conclusion that every age of the world has increased, and still increases, the real wealth, the happiness, the knowledge, and perhaps the virtue, of the human race'. Moreover, progress had no foreseeable limits, for once made, gains were irreversible. 'Observations on the Fall of the Empire in the West', the long essay rounding off the first half of Gibbon's history, explained that any new 'Gothic' invaders could succeed only by first assimilating modern achievements, not least military technology: 'before they can conquer they must cease to be barbarians'.

In short, by 1800, progress was the big idea, set to turn into the great panacea, or *ignis fatuus*, of nineteenth-century Whiggery, Macaulay-style – and as such to be sent up by that last of the enlightened, Thomas Love Peacock.

Crucial to the birth of the modern was a rethinking of economics, bringing to a head a remarkable series of long-term transformations in attitudes towards work and wealth. Though for different reasons, Greek philosophy and Christian theology had condemned the love of money. The Churches had deemed lucre filthy, greed evil, profit without labour usurious. The Christian duty to conduct personal economic dealings in a just manner had been mirrored in Tudor commonwealth thinking at large. 'Mercantilism' – the economic outlook which dominated the

Stuart century and beyond – took good housekeeping as its model, projecting the practices of domestic prudence on to the nation at large. Advocates like Sir Thomas Mun, a director of the East India Company and author of *England's Treasure by Forraign Trade* (1664), measured economic well-being principally in terms of a favourable balance of trade generated by export surpluses: being in pocket. Associating wealth with money or gold and silver, mercantilism's advocates approved the hoarding of reserves, the promotion of exports, the limitation of imports and the management of vital national monopolies.

Enlightened thinking mounted a sustained attack on such policies for being unscientific and hence futile. David Hume's essay 'Of the Balance of Trade' thus argued that a nation never need be apprehensive of losing its money so long as it preserved its people and its industry, because an automatic self-adjusting mechanism operated which 'must for ever, in all neighbouring countries, preserve money nearly all proportionable to the art and industry of each nation'. Mercantilist doctrines were thus shortsighted. In place of regulation, labour and consumption – that is, at bottom, desire – were to be set at the heart of the new thinking.

Mercantilism's faith in interference, critics now argued, was superficial, opportunistic and often poisonous. Regulation had made bad worse, especially when that 'insidious and crafty animal, vulgarly called a statesman or politician' – the phrase is Adam Smith's – was pulling the strings. What was needed instead was an informed grasp of the macro-economics of cash transfers, the relations between wealth and bullion, money and commodities, the short and the long term. Economic policy must be grounded on empirical realities not on rulers' wish-lists, and certainly not on the machinations of monopolists.

A profound revaluation of economic activity itself was under way. The old 'moral economy' was coming under fire from a new 'political economy' which laid claim to a scientific grasp of wealth creation and want satisfaction – a purported analysis of actualities rather than aspirations, what really happened and not what statesmen airily decreed.

Distancing themselves from pious precepts, privileges and practices, enlightened analysts insisted that, like it or not, economic activity was inexorably governed by fundamental laws of its own. Ideals such as the just price, the proper reward for labour and other aspects of what E. P. Thompson called the moral economy might all be very admirable, but they were fatally flawed. They did not, for one thing, reflect human nature. Man was, if not nakedly rapacious *à la* Hobbes, at least an accumulating creature, and therein lay the motivation for economic activity, rooted as it was in the constant human desire for self-improvement. To ignore or expect to override such omnipresent motives was pie-in-the-sky.

The moral economy was thus self-defeating, whereas the new political economy prided itself upon being grounded on a proper grasp of motives, ends and means, individual and system, self and social – natural science, in particular, Newtonian physics, often being invoked to prove how economic forces 'gravitated' to an equilibrium: prices were 'continually gravitating, if one may say so', wrote Smith, 'towards the natural price'. Like water, economic activity would find its own level, and regulation was thus futile, indeed utterly counter-productive. 'Trade is in its Nature free, finds its own Channel, and best directeth its own Course', dogmatised Charles Davenant in the 1690s in impeccably liberal hydrostatic tones. Since profit-seeking was only human nature, it was best to leave trade free and let the economic players get on with it. 'The main spur to Trade, or rather to Industry and Ingenuity', opined Davenant's contemporary Dudley North, 'is the exorbitant Appetites of Men, which they will take pains to gratifie, and so be disposed to work, when nothing else will incline them to it; for did Men content themselves with bare Necessaries, we should have a poor World'. Here, as so often, enlightened thinking appealed to 'Nature' against the cobwebbed wisdom of cloistered scholars and pontificating divines.

The pioneering figure amongst the liberal theorists of this school was, predictably, John Locke. Not only private property but exchange and money too were, in his scheme, pre-established in the state of Nature, subject to the laws of Nature and human rationality and industry. Value itself was determined by labour. Hence economic regulation formed no part of the state's day-to-day remit. The new political economy thus repudiated moral or statesmanly policing of wealth. Christian commandments against greed were sidelined, and the pursuit of gain secularised, privatised and valorised.

It was Adam Smith who systematised the new political economy, grounding it in a science of human appetite, 'the desire of bettering our condition'. Given the ceaseless urge to 'self-improvement', 'every man', it followed, 'lives by exchanging ... and the society itself grows to be what is properly a commercial society'. Selfishness made the world go round: 'It is not from the benevolence of the butcher, the brewer, or the baker, that we expect our dinner, but from their regard to their own interest.' His formula – let demand decide – expresses the enlightened inclination to trust in Nature and its resultant play of wants and needs. In so doing, Smith was forced to confront the old civic humanist warnings and worries about private wealth and greed. Could *enrichissez-vous* prove compatible with socio-political stability? Would not the pursuit of affluence compromise virtue, and 'luxury' subvert liberty, set class against class, and corrupt the commonwealth?

Smith was no narrow 'economist' and his *Inquiry into the Wealth of*

Nations (1776) must be assessed in terms of its wider contribution to enlightened discussions about freedom, justice, subject/state relations and the quality of life in commercial society.

In his early student lectures at Glasgow University, Smith proposed 'opulence and freedom' as 'the two greatest blessings men can possess'. That was a pairing which packed some shock value. Two contrasting concepts of liberty had been in circulation since Antiquity. In the Stoic view, freedom was a state of tranquillity in which the cravings of the flesh were curbed by the rational will. There was also the 'civic' view, proposed by Cicero and Livy, for whom liberty lay in political activity and public service. Rejecting both the political passivity of the former and the 'direct action' of the latter, Smith held that the true key to freedom was commerce. Classical thinkers would have condemned modern commercial society as inglorious, but for Smith it chimed with that basic 'propensity to truck, barter and exchange', which achieved its full expression only in a nation of shopkeepers.

Whereas Stoicism disparaged economic activity, Smith read 'selfishness' as everyone's laudable desire to get on. Like Hume, he held that the proper stage for human energies was not honour and glory in the Senate, but private, self-regarding pursuits. For Graeco-Roman thinkers, time spent meeting household needs was beneath the dignity of the true male citizen – was indeed, fit only for inferiors, peasants, artisans, women and slaves; for Smith, by contrast, it was the natural business of humanity. Indeed, it was a public benefit, for economic exchange forged supportive social networks: in a 'civilized and thriving country', even the 'very meanest person' could not be provided with even the shirt on his back without the 'joint labour of a great multitude of workmen'. From such interdependency commercial society derived its unique strength.

For Smith, dependency was of course corrupting – a view central to the influential civic humanist equation of freedom with independence. According to such neo-Harringtonians, however, the chief source of corruption and threat to independence lay in the growth of commerce, paper money, the credit nexus and the public debt. Smith rejected this thinking. While never denying that dependency spelt corruption, he counter-insisted that 'commerce is one great preventive' of its occurrence. Economic activity was thus not pathological but prophylactic, preservative of a sound constitution. For the civic humanists, history had been a descent into decadence; for Smith it was more a path to progress.

Science too was a mighty generator of optimism. In the wake of the great age of Newton, the culture of science spread, percolating through society via popularising institutions such as Gresham College and rippling out into the provinces. While the Royal Society remained the nation's senior scientific society, further bodies were added in the capital, notably the Linnean Society of London (1788) and the Royal Institution (1799). The Royal Society of Edinburgh was set up in 1783, and its counterpart, the Royal Irish Academy, in 1785, while science, Dissent and political reformism joined forces from the 1760s in Literary and Philosophical Societies in Manchester, Newcastle and other industrial centres and ports. Science was acclaimed as vital not just to utility but to the civilising process, the leading light in Manchester, Thomas Henry, pronouncing the pursuit of natural philosophy preferable to 'the tavern, the gaming table, or the brothel'.

The most energetic of such gatherings embodying enlightened faith in science was the Lunar Society. Though still a small market town at the beginning of the century, Birmingham grew rapidly; by 1760, with 30,000 inhabitants, it had already become considerable, and in Matthew Boulton's Soho factory it gained a machine-tool works famed internationally. Born in Derby, William Hutton found there an ethos he had not encountered elsewhere: 'I had been among dreamers, but now I saw men awake.'

From about 1765 a group of friends – leading industrialists, scientists, educators, dissenting ministers and physicians – began to meet at Boulton's home, once a month at full moon, to help light them home, discussing innovations in science and technology and the new industrial order they were helping to create. Through such associations, Paul Langford tells us, 'a nation of Newtons and Lockes became a nation of Boultons and Watts'.

Scientific improvement was a label often applied to the land, serving as a code-word for capitalist farming, notably enclosure. The improving spirit in agriculture was increasingly associated with the application of science. In the 'Introduction' to his 600-page *Phytologia* (1800), Erasmus Darwin for instance expressed his regret that 'AGRICULTURE and GARDENING ... continue to be only Arts, consisting of numerous detached facts and vague opinions, without a true theory to connect them.' This had to change. Agriculture had to be made rational and businesslike, through the teachings of political economy: 'for the invention of arts, and production of tools necessary to agriculture, some must think, and others labour; and as the efforts of some will be crowned with greater success than that of others, an inequality of the ranks of society must succeed'.

Farming became regarded as a form of manufacturing, with Robert Bakewell's fat sheep serving, rather like Newton's prism, as icons of Enlightenment. That distinguished Leicestershire stockrearer explicitly bred sheep, cattle and pigs as meat-producing engines, selected so as to maximise expensive cuts and minimise bones and waste: animals were thus turned into machines.

As this example hints, if agriculture was celebrated as, in Arthur Young's phrase, 'the greatest of all manufactures', it was another field of progress which now received the warmest accolades: manufacturing as such. Progressives had long expressed their fascination with industry in the traditional meaning of skilled work, praising *homo faber*. Remember Daniel Defoe's portrait of his castaway. Overcome with despair, Robinson Crusoe surveyed his predicament: 'I was wet, had no clothes to shift me, nor anything either to eat or drink, to comfort me; neither did I see any prospect before me, but that of perishing with hunger, or being devoured by wild beasts.' Salvation came for Defoe's hero, however, in the implements and weapons he fished out from the wreck: knives and forks, a spade and pickaxe, needles and thread, muskets, gunpowder and shot. Implements formed the basis of civilisation reborn: 'I had never handled a tool in my life; and yet, in time, by labour, application, and contrivance I found at last that I wanted nothing but I could have made, especially if I had the tools.'

Technological innovation was advancing on a broad front. Waterwheel design became a model of experimental efficiency, and the engineer John Smeaton perfected the lighthouse. In 1758 the 'Improved Birmingham Coach' had blazoned on its side, a touch over-optimistically, 'FRICTION ANNIHILATED', and by 1801 Richard Trevithick had put a steam carriage on the road. Above all, textiles technology was transformed and the steam engine revolutionised power.

At the dawn of this stunning transformation, a poem on Whitehaven (1755) carried a telling 'Preface'. It opened with a paean to agriculture:

> When we behold rich improvements of a wild and uncultivated soil, in their state of maturity, without having observed their rise and progress, we are struck with wonder and astonishment, to see the face of Nature totally changed.

and then significantly changed tack:

> But how great and rational soever the pleasure of such a sight may be, it is still surpassed by that arising from the extraordinary increase of a trading Town, and new plantations of Houses and Men. Such was the satisfaction the author felt at the appearance of the town and harbour of Whitehaven, after an absence of somewhat less than thirty years.

Manufacturing's appeal to enlightened minds was potent and many-sided. Technology was in, as the cutting-edge of novelty. 'The people in London, Manchester and Birmingham are *steam mill mad*', Matthew Boulton assured James Watt.

Industry also was a prime instance of disciplined rationality. An experimentalist in his own right, Josiah Wedgwood the potter aimed to 'make such *machines* of *Men* as cannot err', introducing clocking-on to ensure punctuality among his workforce. Surveying the progress so visible across the West Midlands, he declared, 'Industry and the machine have been the parent of this happy change. A well directed and long continued series of industrious exertions, has so changed, for the better, the face of our country, its buildings, lands, roads and the manners and deportment of its inhabitants, too'. Business, in other words, promoted not just wealth but well-being.

Manufacturing, moreover, seemed to be producing a new breed of heroes, principally the 'captain of industry', the self-made man, raising capital for factories, forges and foundries, ploughing back profits, organising productive capacity, recruiting, training and deploying the workforce, calculating market opportunities. The industrialist was trumpeted as a national hero. One of the children's tales in Anna Barbauld's primly improving *Evenings at Home: Or the Juvenile Budget Opened* (1794) celebrated Sir Richard Arkwright's rise to fame and fortune. 'This is what manufacturers can do', explained papa to his children, in an enlightened idiom approaching profanity: 'here man is a kind of creator, and like the great Creator, he may please himself with his work and say it is good.' Showing his youngsters round a factory, the fictional father insisted what fun it all was: there was 'more entertainment to a cultivated mind in seeing a pin made, than in many a fashionable diversion'.

The entrepreneur was thus applauded as the exemplar of modern energy. 'I shall never forget Mr Boulton's expression to me', recalled James Boswell of a visit to the Soho works: ' "I sell here, Sir, what all the world desires to have, – POWER". He had about seven hundred people at work ... he seemed to be a father to this tribe.'

Like Boulton, his friend Josiah Wedgwood was one of a remarkable new breed of men conspicuous for applying enlightened thinking to business. Though of meagre formal education, he displayed a consummate faith in reason, and a passion for measuring, weighing, observing, recording and experimenting: all problems would 'yield to experiment'. His rational outlook extended beyond business to Unitarianism in religion and radicalism in politics – he was hostile to slavery, and a warm supporter of the American colonists and later the French Revolution. He thought big: 'I shall ASTONISH THE WORLD ALL AT ONCE', he declared to his partner, Thomas Bentley, 'for I hate piddling you know.' Becoming 'vase-maker general to the universe', he died worth half a million.

It is Robert Owen, however, who offers the perfect illustration of the application of enlightened ideas to the empire of industry. Born in mid-Wales, Owen got his first employment as an errand-boy; then he moved into drapery, rising to a partnership in a Manchester firm, before, at the turn of the century, becoming partner and manager of the New Lanark Mills on Clydeside. For the next two decades he combined entrepreneurship with social reform. In his *A New View of Society* (1813) – today we would call it his 'mission statement' – Owen urged rational social rebuilding on the basis of universal education. Manufacturing would provide the foundation for happiness, but only once divested of the arbitrariness of the dog-eats-dog market and reorganised according to social utility. Character could be moulded by correct environmental influence. If the labouring classes were ignorant, brutalised and criminal, they were victims and it was society that must shoulder the blame.

Owen gloried in the changes he was helping to bring about. 'Those who were engaged in the trade, manufactures, and commerce of this country thirty or forty years ago formed but a very insignificant portion of the knowledge, wealth, influence or population of the Empire', he explained:

> Prior to that period, Britain was essentially agricultural. But, from that time to the present, the home and foreign trade have increased in a manner so rapid and extraordinary as to have raised commerce to an importance, which it never previously attained in any country possessing so much political power and influence.

But Owen was no Smithian. *Laissez-faire* was useless for ensuring long-term prosperity and welfare – market forces would 'produce the most lamentable and permanent evils', unless there were 'legislative interference and direction'. Though industrialisation held out the promise of untold human benefit, under the competitive system some grew fabulously rich while others were pauperised. Cooperation was needed to effect industry's potential social advantages. Since people were products of circumstances, education would make all the difference, according to Owen's plan for 'a national, well digested, unexclusive system for the formation of character, and general amelioration of the lower orders'. In his New Lanark factory village, the provision of schooling, along with such amenities as a museum, would programme workers for happiness. Here was a veritable social experiment in action, one which

> cannot fail to prove the certain means of renovating the moral and religious principles of the world, by showing whence arise the various opinions, manners, vices and virtues of mankind, and how the best or the worst of them may, with mathematical precision, be taught to the rising generation.

An unbeliever, Owen secularised Christian aspirations in envisaging 'the foretold millennium ... when the slave and the prisoner, the bondman and the bond-woman, and the child and the servant, shall be set free for ever, and oppression of body and mind shall be known no more'.

Owen was thus a logical *terminus ad quem* of certain strands of Enlightenment thought, envisaging comprehensive benevolent control within a scheme of industrialisation, and showing a Helvétius-like concern with education and discipline over his 'human machines'.

Many penned anthems to improvement, uniting science and imagination, poetry and social theory. Working on the model of Lucretius's *De rerum natura*, Richard Payne Knight's *Progress of Civil Society* (1796) was divided into six books whose very titles – 'Of Hunting'; 'Of Pasturage'; 'Of Agriculture'; 'Of Arts, Manufactures, and Commerce'; 'Of Climate and Soil'; and 'Of Government and Conquest' – clearly show that he was setting Enlightenment speculative anthropology to verse, giving a poetic rendition of the lessons of Adam Smith's progressive stages of society.

The most notable and prominent poetic prophet of progress, however, was Erasmus Darwin. Born near Nottingham in 1731, Darwin was the son of an 'honest and industrious' lawyer with a taste for antiquities. In 1750 he went up to St John's College, Cambridge, then crossing the Tweed (like so many others) to complete his medical training in Edinburgh. He set up in medical practice in Lichfield, which proved his home for twenty-five years.

Though, like his friend, Joseph Priestley, a stammerer, the energetic and ebullient Darwin was a domineering talker, becoming noted for his raillery directed against Christianity. From the 1760s he grew familiar with the circle of 'learned insane' which developed into the Lunar Society, already mentioned.

A physician first and foremost, Darwin practised for some forty years, and his *magnum opus, Zoonomia* (1794-6), was essentially a work of medical theory, heavily influenced by David Hartley's materialist physiological psychology. Despite his busy medical practice, he poured his boundless energies into many channels. In 1771 he was dabbling with a speaking-machine or mechanical voicebox; in the next year he had long discussions with Wedgwood and the engineer James Brindley about extending the Grand Trunk Canal; with his friend Brooke Boothby, he founded the Lichfield Botanic Society, which in time brought out translations of Linnaeus's classification system. His gardening interests also blossomed on a site west of Lichfield, where in 1778 he established a botanic garden, the inspiration of his later poem of the same name.

Uniting arts and sciences, medicine, physics and technology, the brisk, business-like and corpulent Darwin was not only a man of the broadest improving interests but the very embodiment of enlightened

values. 'All those who knew him will allow that sympathy and benevolence were the most striking features', wrote Keir: 'He despised the
monkish abstinences and the hypocritical pretensions which so often
impose on the world. The communication of happiness and the relief
of misery were by him held as the only standard of moral merit.'

Darwin embraced a humanitarian benevolence hostile to Christian
values and judgements. From early years, he rejected Christianity in
favour of Deism. Indeed, he found the Christian Almighty quite
repellent: how could a truly loving Father visit terrible diseases upon
innocent children? The notion of a jealous Lord was quite perverse; he
loathed the Churches' fixation upon punishment, guilt and suffering;
and his *Zoonomia* pathologised religious enthusiasm and superstition,
diagnosing such religiosity as symptomatic of madness.

Championing Hartley's philosophy, Darwin was a materialist through
and through. 'Dr Darwin often used to say', remembered the pious
Quaker, Mrs Schimmelpenninck:

> Man is an eating animal, a drinking animal, and a sleeping animal,
> and one placed in a material world, which alone furnishes all the
> human animal can desire. He is gifted besides with knowing faculties,
> practically to explore and to apply the resources of this world to his
> use. These are realities. All else is nothing; conscience and sentiment
> are mere figments of the imagination.

(One suspects that, in front of his male cronies, Darwin used a saltier
phrase than 'a sleeping animal'.)

Anti-Christian materialism shaped his humanitarianism: while bigots
blamed, men of reason would inquire and sympathise. Hearing of an
infanticidal mother, he wrote a commiserating letter to his correspondent:

> The Women that have committed this most unnatural Crime, are
> real Objects of our greatest Pity; their education has produced in
> them so much Modesty, or Sense of Shame, that this artificial Passion
> overturns the very Instincts of Nature! – what Struggles must there
> be in their Minds, what agonies! ...
>
> Hence the Cause of this most horrid Crime is an excess of what
> is really a Virtue, of the Sense of Shame, or Modesty. Such is the
> Condition of human Nature!

Politically Darwin was a dyed in the wool liberal. His books and letters
echo with condemnations of despotism, slavery and bloodshed: 'I hate
war.' 'I have just heard', he raged on one occasion to Josiah Wedgwood,
'that there are muzzles or gags made at Birmingham for the slaves in
our island. If this be true, and such an instrument could be exhibited
by a speaker in the House of Commons, it might have a great effect.'

From its outset he supported the French Revolution, and after the 1791 Birmingham riots he wrote to Joseph Priestley deploring his victimisation by fanatics – while also politely advising him to quit his theological maunderings and get on with something more useful, namely scientific experiments. Darwin's politics were, however, never revolutionary. Law, order and property were essential ingredients for the social progress which would be achieved within the framework of free-market capitalism and industrialisation.

As the summation of his myriad ideas, Darwin developed the first comprehensive theory of biological evolution: 'would it be too bold to imagine, that all warm-blooded animals have arisen from one living filament, which THE GREAT FIRST CAUSE endued with animality?' The endless mutual competition of burgeoning organic forms within the terraqueous globe also resulted in death, destruction and even extinction:

> From Hunger's arm the shafts of Death are hurl'd,
> And one great Slaughter-house the warring world!.

Nevertheless, rather as for Adam Smith, though not for Owen, the law of competition brought about net improvement, and the aggregate rise of population spelt not Malthusian misery but an augmentation of happiness according to a cosmic felicific calculus.

> Shout round the globe, how Reproduction strives
> With vanquish'd Death – and Happiness survives;
> How Life increasing peoples every clime,
> And young renascent Nature conquers Time.

Darwin's evolutionism provided the British Enlightenment's clinching theory of boundless improvement.

The epic of progress, implicit or explicit in most late Enlightenment opinion and given a scientific grounding by Darwin, stands in stark contrast to such earlier visions of the human condition as *Paradise Lost* and Pope's *Essay on Man*. For Milton, what was fundamental was the relationship between God and man: Adam's offence lay in violation of God's command; man's destiny was couched in a transcendental revelation. Pope for his part presented a view of the human amphibian as fixed on a divinely ordained scale:

> Plac'd on this isthmus of a middle state,
> A being darkly wise, and rudely great;

With a static 'Chain of Being' in mind, Pope viewed beings suspended between the divine and the animal, a predicament at once laughable and lamentable,

Created half to rise, and half to fall;
Great lord of all things, yet a prey to all.

Darwin, by contrast, painted a wholly optimistic, naturalistic and this-worldly picture, grounded on evolution, biological and social. Human capacities were the products of biological and physiological development which extended to 'the progress of the Mind'. Not only was there no Miltonic Lucifer and Fall, but neither was there, as for Pope, an irreconcilable conflict between mind and body, man and Nature. Addressing humanity from Nature's viewpoint not God's, Darwin granted a far more elevated position to mankind: man alone had consciousness of the natural order. Whereas Pope scorned pride as hubristic, for Darwin, as for Hume before him, pride and its triumphs had their legitimate basis in Nature. The *homo sapiens* satirised by Pope was celebrated by Darwin.

Progress proved the ultimate Enlightenment gospel. It kindled optimism and pointed to a programme: the promise of a better future would expose and highlight whatever remained wrong in the present. It was a vision of hope, a doctrine of change. If *Paradise Lost* told mankind's tale in terms of disobedience, sin and punishment – and perhaps redemption – so as to justify the ways of God to man; and if the *Essay on Man* offered an enigmatic view of man as a riddle, even if in principle, at least capable of improvement through self-knowledge, Darwin and his peers presented a man-centred view of man making himself – a Promethean vision of infinite possibilities. God had become a distant cause of causes; what counted was man acting in Nature. The theodicy, the master-narrative had become naturalised, even secularised.

Of course, as we know very well, Erasmus Darwin's evolutionary theories were not accepted in his own day – far from it. Evolutionary thinking long lay under a cloud, being condemned as materialistic, brutalising and atheistic and associated with that great abomination, the French Revolution. Therein lay one of the reasons why his grandson, Charles, was so terribly hesitant about publishing his own evolutionary theory, and why, when the *Origin of Species* finally saw the light of day in 1859, it still created such a storm.

Something similar happened with many of the key ideas of the Enlightenment. Original and challenging, they had never met with universal acceptance, and there always remained throughout Georgian England powerful groupings of High-Flying Churchmen, Jacobites, Tories, traditionalists, Methodists and so forth for whom the enlightened accent on critical reason was an absurdity or an obscenity.

Undergoing socio-political growing pains and tensions, and in particular when confronted by the French Revolution, the Revolutionary and Napoleonic Wars, and their backlashes, liberal ideologies began to shiver into fragments. For some libertarian rhetoric led to Jacobin radicalism – witness Tom Paine's very titles: *Common Sense, The Age of Reason* and *The Rights of Man*. Bourgeois liberalism, as endorsed by the Whiggish *Edinburgh Review*, founded in 1802, for its part put a different face upon enlightened ideology: individualism was to obey the iron laws of political economy; social progress demanded time-and-work discipline, penology and scientific poor laws; while humanitarian impulses bled into proto-Victorian sentimentality. Meanwhile, establishment apologists began to draw conclusions of their own from enlightened premises. Malthus in particular put a new gloss on desire, recruiting science to prove how legislative action could not, after all, relieve suffering and starvation. More dramatically, French Revolutionary turmoil led many to change sides: Wordsworth, Southey and Coleridge, for instance.

Yet, in the long run, enlightened ideologies were not discarded: they had bored too deep into the bones. By providing secular legitimation for capitalism, they continued to inform Victorian self-help liberalism and free-market ideology – the road from Smith to Smiles. By touting rational self-help, they promised a meliorist, moralised future which immunised native radicals against Marxist creeds of class war or communitarian socialism. Phrenology, secularism and Fabianism were all, in their own ways, enlightenment legacies. John Stuart Mill could declare at the beginning of the Victorian age that every Englishmen was by implication 'a Benthamite or a Coleridgian': the former were evidently children of the Enlightenment. The famous Halévy thesis perhaps needs modifying: perhaps it was not Methodism but rather the Enlightenment which inoculated the English against the French, indeed, against all subsequent, revolutions.

None of these developments was without the most profound tensions. Enlightened activism always involved clashing interests, and its elastic ideological resources could be deployed for radical ends or equally by sections of the propertied, plutocratic and polite against those they sought to discredit, convert or marginalise. If I have argued that the Enlightenment generated the idea of progress, mine has been no simple tale of 'progress', but of the ongoing war of ideas against ideas.

ENGLISH POLITENESS: CONDUCT, SOCIAL RANK
AND MORAL VIRTUE, c. 1400–1900

A Conference held at the Huntington
Library, San Marino, California, USA,
14–15 September 2001, and the Institute
of Historical Research, University of
London, 24 November 2001

Transactions of the RHS 12 (2002), pp. 263–6 © 2002 Royal Historical Society
DOI: 10.1017/S0080440102000099   Printed in the United Kingdom

INTRODUCTION

By John Tosh

THIS was the first time a Society conference had been hosted by the Huntington. The invitation was issued by Robert Ritchie, Research Director of the Huntington, and the event was organised jointly by Anthony Fletcher and John Tosh. Two days of discussion devoted to the history of English politeness was always going to seem somewhat out of place in the environment of southern California. In the event the choice of theme acquired unanticipated layers of meaning, since it began three days after the terrorist attacks on New York and Washington on September 11. Its content now seemed even more at odds with the world around us, while the decision to proceed with the event became caught up in the 'business as usual' outlook with which so many Americans responded to the tragedy. For a day or two it was not clear whether the conference could be held at all. A substantial proportion of the British contingent was temporarily stranded at the Grand Canyon, while three of the scheduled speakers – Michèle Cohen, Philip Carter and Penny Russell – were prevented from attending altogether by the disruption of air traffic. However, with the strong encouragement of Robert Ritchie, it was decided to proceed with the conference. The first session was preceded by a flag-pole ceremony at which conference participants and Huntington staff could pay their respects to the dead. The size of the audience was inevitably reduced. Some thirty people, mostly from the Los Angeles region, attended, in an atmosphere which was sombre but attentive. Several people made the point that, in these appalling circumstances, it was no bad thing to be reminded of the virtues of politeness, particularly their capacity to transcend their early elitist associations.

Unusually, a second instalment of the conference was held. The Society laid on a one-day follow-up event at the Institute of Historical Research on 24 November 2001, in order to give a hearing to Michèle Cohen and Philip Carter, the two British participants who were prevented from reaching San Marino. Many of the original paper-givers attended; so too did a small but expert audience whose comments have influenced the drafting of several of the papers printed here. The paper by Penny Russell appears here for the first time – and is particularly welcome in giving an extra-European perspective which was lacking at the original conference.

Whereas accessible accounts for the lay reader have tended to deal with a big sweep of history,[1] most of the distinguished work on English politeness over the past twenty years has remained firmly located in comparatively short time spans. The conference was devised with the intention of identifying and exploring both the common traditions and the historically specific features which have characterised politeness in English society over some five centuries, and there was a full range from the earliest courtesy books of the twelfth century to the rhetorical rejection of politeness in the politics of Gladstone and Bright. Participants had also been encouraged to consider the relationship between precept and practice, as well as the implications of politeness beyond the regulation of inter-personal behaviour. Social rank is clearly of fundamental importance here. Until politeness became devalued to mean little more than the etiquette of personal encounter, it always entailed a display of leisure – and thus also acted as a marker excluding the unleisured. The 'polite' were the 'better sort', entitled to respect from the common, and entitled to govern, with moral worth as the clinching justification for class privilege. It may have gone without saying that this political entitlement was confined to men, but codes of polite behaviour made explicit a specific pattern of relations between the sexes. From the medieval period onwards, politeness seems to have combined two ideas: the special protection due to women (not just a man's immediate dependants, but 'women' in general), and the idea that men would remain coarse and brutish unless 'civilised' by social intercourse with women. The gender hierarchy implicit in that formulation is clear, but politeness nevertheless assumed an elite culture which was, in some degree, the common property of men and women – and which could act as a solvent of more polarised notions of sexual difference.

One distinguishing feature of recent historical work on politeness is that it has relied heavily on the evidence of prescriptive literature.[2] There is certainly much still to be gleaned from sensitive readings of didactic texts, as Philip Carter demonstrates. Prescription also looms large in John Tosh's consideration of manliness. All the same, reliance on prescriptive literature was much less in evidence than might have

---

[1] E.g. Harold Nicolson, *Good Behaviour* (1955), and Philip Mason, *The English Gentleman* (1982).

[2] Anna Bryson, *From Courtesy to Civility: Changing Codes of Conduct in Early Modern England* (Oxford, 1998); Fenella Childs, 'Prescriptions for Manners in English Courtesy Literature, 1690-1760 and their Social Implications' (DPhil thesis, Oxford University, 1984); Michael Curtin, *Propriety and Position: A Study of Victorian Manners* (New York, 1987).

been expected in a conference on this theme. An impressive variety of approaches was employed. The primary sources ranged from the medieval romances discussed by John Gillingham, though the urban topographical literature examined by Rosemary Sweet, to the childhood diaries presented by Anthony Fletcher.

Despite the intentions of the organisers, the periodisation of politeness in English history proved elusive. Arguments for continuity were repeatedly asserted over and above notions of change or period specificity. John Gillingham points out that everything in Erasmus's *De Civilitate* is to be found in the courtesy books of the High Middle Ages. At the conference Paul Langford not only conceded that the content of eighteenth-century politeness literature was 'traditional', but also maintained that the Victorian concern with manly simplicity and sincerity was fully anticipated in what he calls 'the *Spectator* mode' of politeness in the early part of the eighteenth century. The contexts of polite behaviour modulated through many forms, but the governing principles appear to have been remarkably stable over a very long time.

Periodisation in fact proved to be the least illuminating theme of the conference. Other, more rewarding issues were thrown open to closer scrutiny. One fundamental question was whether politeness performed a facilitating or constraining role. The codes of behaviour enforced at court were a minefield for the unwary or the accident-prone. In the early eighteenth century politeness was championed as a demonstration of ease and naturalness, in explicit contravention of the rigid artificiality of the royal court. Yet for anyone with less than total confidence in his or her social graces, politeness was likely to become a formula, however unconvincing the resultant persona might be. As Paul Langford shows, from being a means of benevolent intercourse, politeness became 'an instrument of social warfare', as the more confident strove to exclude the newer aspirants from polite society. In Penny Russell's account of nineteenth-century Australia, politeness was ruthlessly policed by the colonial elite as a last bastion against the rising tide of egalitarianism.

Politeness is, of course, centrally a matter of social relationships, but several papers make clear how in practice it was associated with particular spaces. Thus in Nicholas Cooper's account, the gentlemanly status of the prosperous Elizabethan is demonstrated not only through the lay-out of his house, but its ornamentation, with classical flourishes considered an expression of 'good manners'. Rosemary Sweet emphasises the centrality of amenities like coffee-shops and assembly halls when provincial towns were staking out a claim to polite status. Helen Berry offers a novel analysis of shopping in which the conventions of politeness negotiated the potentially impolite activities of browsing and bargaining.

One reason why politeness commends itself to social as well as cultural historians is that it crosses so easily the vexatious divide between public and private. Rosemary Sweet shows that politeness was the nub of the social standing of English provincial towns in the eighteenth century. John Tosh's discussion of the Victorian period is exclusively focused on the public content of politeness and its undermining by a more populist concern with authenticity and directness. On the other hand, in Anthony Fletcher's material on the early nineteenth century politeness was mediated to the elite young through lessons in self-control, courtesy and moral responsibility which were administered within the family, or in enclosed educational institutions. Elizabeth Foyster shows how polite standards were invoked by women to restrain the behaviour of men in the most intimate relationships – as documented in divorce and separation proceedings.

It would be intriguing to speculate on the influence which the setting of the conference had on its deliberations. The Huntington, with its fabulous art collection and its magnificent research resources, may have seemed like a haven of refuge from consumerism and vulgarity. The conference offered many reminders that English politeness has historically provided an uncertain marker of social rank and a precarious bulwark against encroachment by the lower orders.

Transactions of the RHS 12 (2002), pp. 267–89 © 2002 Royal Historical Society
DOI: 10.1017/S0080440102000105   Printed in the United Kingdom

FROM *CIVILITAS* TO CIVILITY: CODES OF
MANNERS IN MEDIEVAL AND EARLY MODERN
ENGLAND

By John Gillingham

ABSTRACT. Argues that to see the contrasts between late medieval 'courtesy books'
and early modern manuals of manners as markers of changing ideals of social
conduct in England is an interpretation too narrowly based on works written in
English. Examination of Latin and Anglo-Norman literature shows that the ideal
of the urbane gentleman can be traced back at least as far as the most
comprehensive of all courtesy books, the twelfth-century *Liber Urbani* of Daniel of
Beccles, and was itself underpinned by the commonplace secular morality of the
much older *Distichs of Cato*.

EVER since the pioneering cultural history of Norbert Elias, the
emergence of the words 'civil' and 'civility' in Western European
languages, English included, in senses pertaining to refined and polished
manners, has been taken to mark a highly significant shift between the
Middle Ages and the Renaissance in the styles and tastes of the upper
classes, a shift neatly encapsulated in the title of Anna Bryson's book:
From Courtesy to Civility.[1] It remains generally agreed that the concept of
civility developed first in Italy, where its association with 'city' meant a
great deal, and that as it spread throughout Europe, so the terms 'civil'
and 'civility' changed their meanings, gradually displacing 'courteous'
and 'courtesy' as the fashionable terms denoting approved conduct.[2]
Bryson, while acknowledging that

> nothing in the courtesy literature of the sixteenth and seventeenth
> centuries supports the notion that 'civility' represents a bourgeois

[1] A. Bryson, *From Courtesy to Civility: Changing Codes of Conduct in Early Modern England*
(Oxford, 1998).

[2] M. B. Becker, *Civility and Society in Western Europe, 1300–1600* (Bloomington, IN, 1988);
P. Burke, 'A Civil Tongue: Language and Politeness in Early Modern Europe', in *Civil
Histories: Essays Presented to Sir Keith Thomas*, ed. P. Burke, B. Harrison and P. Slack (Oxford,
2000), 36; E. Cameron, '"Civilized Religion" from Renaissance to Reformation and
Counter-Reformation', in *ibid.*, 50.

standard of behaviour at odds with the previously established aristocratic ideals of 'courtesy'

none the less elaborates Elias's view that the new term meant a new
concept, a new 'way of seeing' social conduct and social life.[3]

Central to this view is the contrast commonly drawn between
medieval 'courtesy books' and early modern manuals of manners. In
support of this contrast Bryson summarises the style and contents of
the courtesy books composed in English in fifteenth-century England.
They

> are all cast in a simple easily memorizable verse form, running to a
> few hundred lines and addressed to young pages within the noble
> household. Although interspersed with moral exhortations to piety
> and humility, the precepts are largely practical and technical. The
> overwhelming preoccupation of their authors is with table manners,
> ... with the formal dinner as the central ritual of the household, one
> which dramatized both its internal hierarchy and its relation to the
> outside world in the provision of hospitality.[4]

Whereas medieval courtesy had emphasised 'rituals of lordship and
service within the noble household', the equivalent early modern works,
beginning, just as Elias proclaimed, with Erasmus's *De Civilitate Morum
Puerilium*, are said to present ' "civil" behaviour as a technique for the
representation of personal virtue within a broader "civil" community'.
Civility in manners becomes 'an extensive practical science of sociability'
rather than 'a set of rules for use in a limited range of situations'.[5] In
this paper in an attempt to compare like with like I shall for the most

[3] Bryson, *Courtesy to Civility*, 60, 276–7. Many of the contributions to *Civil Histories*, ed.
Burke, Harrison and Slack, reveal the influence of the 1984 DPhil thesis on which this
fine book is based. Although I tend here to cite it only when I disagree, I could not have
written this paper without it, and I have, in any case, only done what she herself had
foreseen in anticipating that 'continuing research on the value of "courtesy" in medieval
society would almost certainly modify the contrast between the two periods which is
posited in this book', *ibid.*, 277–8.

[4] Bryson, *Courtesy to Civility*, 27. What goes unmentioned in the 'practical and technical'
didactic literature, but is clear – at least in the minds of the male authors of romances –
is the impact made by the elegant performance of table service by a handsome and well-
dressed young man: 'no lady seeing him was not deeply affected and troubled by the
pangs of love ... did not want to hold him softly to her under an ermine coverlet', 'The
Romance of Horn', in *The Birth of Romance*, trans. J. Weiss (1992), 11.

[5] Although the contrast is said to lie 'less in the context of particular rules than in the
assumptions and preoccupations which seem to govern the range and form of codification',
and in a new conception of what manners were *for*', Bryson, *Courtesy to Civility*, 60, 68–
71, 107, 277. In working out the contrast Bryson accepts Ariès's notion that a clear
concept of childhood first emerged in the sixteenth century (*ibid.*, 67), an idea explicitly
rejected by recent historians of medieval children, S. Shahar, *Childhood in the Middle Ages*
(1990), 1–6; N. Orme, *Medieval Children* (2001), 3–10.

part confine myself to looking at medieval didactic expositions of gentlemanly manners in the light of what I have learned, thanks very largely to Anna Bryson's guidance, about early modern expositions. (This means that I shall leave to one side the notion that during the sixteenth century the term 'civility' began to take on some of the connotations of 'civilisation' as the opposition between the 'civil' and the 'barbaric' implicit in classical writings was allegedly developed in response to the challenge presented by the discovery of the 'savage' inhabitants of the New World, and then applied in a contrast between English civility and Irish barbarity.[6] I do so since I have elsewhere discussed the notion of a civilising process in medieval and early modern England.[7])

To base the contrast between medieval and early modern on works written in English is understandable since nearly all modern studies of medieval conduct books focus on them, and are written by scholars specialising in English literature,[8] but it is not without its dangers. The late development of English as a language of elite culture and politics in post-1066 England means that concepts existed and were expressed in Latin and in French (Anglo-Norman) long before the equivalent English words were coined. So far as extant writings go, courtesy literature is a genre which emerged in the twelfth century – together with such other new arrivals relevant to the self-perception of the English elite as heraldry, tournaments, vernacular romances (in which women were given central roles), non-monastic schools and universities. Twelfth-century courtesy literature was written in Latin, part of an elite culture common to all Western Europe.[9] From the thirteenth century onwards we have courtesy poems written in Anglo-Norman, often used

---

[6] 'One of the meanings of "civil" was the opposite of "wild", "rude" or "barbarous"', *Civil Histories*, ed. Burke, Harrison and Slack, v. See Bryson, *Courtesy to Civility*, 51–2, 72–4, 107, 277, and D. Knox, '*Disciplina*: The Monastic and Clerical Origins of European Civility', in *Renaissance Society and Culture*, ed. J. Monfasini and R. G. Musto (New York, 1991), 129–32.

[7] J. Gillingham, 'Civilising the English? The English Histories of William of Malmesbury and David Hume', *Historical Research*, 74 (2001), 17–43. It is clear that the contrast between English civility and Irish barbarism took root in the twelfth century.

[8] For a recent example see all the essays on England in *Medieval Conduct*, ed. K. Ashley and R. L. A. Clark (Minneapolis, 2001). A helpful guide to the ways in which a number of genres in both vernaculars deal with the subject is D. Burnley, *Courtliness and Literature in Medieval England* (1998).

[9] By far the most helpful study of the genre in English is J. W. Nicholls, *The Matter of Courtesy: Medieval Courtesy Books and the Gawain Poet* (Woodbridge, 1985). Even Nicholls, however, decided that table manners were so central to medieval courtesy literature that he omitted one twelfth-century poem, the *Facetus: moribus et vita*, from his list of poems (pp. 146, 181–2) on the grounds that it did not deal with the 'kind of material associated with courtesy books' – and this despite the fact that it began 'Whoever wishes to be courtly (*facetus*) in manners and life, let him read me.' For text and translation see A. G. Elliott, 'The *Facetus*: Or, The Art of Courtly Living', *Allegorica*, 2 (1977), 27–57.

as texts in the acquisition of the language of polite society. Indeed one of the attractions of the word *courteis* was that it could be rhymed with *franceis*, as in these lines from the thirteenth-century *Urbain* (also known as *Urbain le Courtois*): 'Be debonair and courteise, and see that you know how to speak franceys', which the poet immediately identifies as the language 'de gentil home'.[10] There are thirteenth-century examples of the Anglicised form 'gentleman' and although the OED cites Chaucer as the earliest author to use the word 'gentleman' in the sense of 'a man of gentle birth who possessed the fine feelings appropriate to his rank', the notion that men of rank should be more refined than those of lower status is a much older one. So although it is arguable that in the twelfth and thirteenth centuries the words *gentilhommes* and 'gentlemen' may have meant primarily 'men of gentle birth entitled to bear arms' there is no doubt that this status also implied a claim to superior culture – a culture common to the whole 'gentle' class, from princes and earls downwards.[11]

Two of the five extant Anglo-Norman texts bear a close resemblance to fifteenth-century English courtesy books.[12] The other three, including *Urbain*, much the most widely disseminated of the five, are not so preoccupied with table manners or service at table. Rather they are general treatises on the manners and morals thought appropriate to a social elite, 'traités de savoir-vivre', to use the apt term used by modern French students of the genre.[13] They contain plenty of good advice for budding gentlemen such as: do not boast about your mistress. If you do, you will find that all the decent women (*tutes les gentils femmes del monde*) will avoid you. Or: when choosing a wife, do not choose one either for her beauty or for her learning.[14] In early modern England the vocabulary of politeness was dominated by words imported from Italy and France; in twelfth-and thirteenth-century England courtesy literature was composed in Latin and French. Copies of these Latin

---

[10] H. Rosamund Parsons, 'Anglo-Norman Books of Courtesy and Nurture', *Publications of the Modern Language Association of America*, 44 (1929), 399, 410. See also such lines as 'Se tu veulx estre bien courtois / Regardes ces reigles en françoys', F. J. Furnivall, *Manners and Meals in Olden Time* (1868), II, 3, 8, 16.

[11] At all levels aristocracy and gentry had in common 'a distinctive life-style and a self-conscious adherence to a set of courtly and chivalric values', C. Dyer, *Standards of Living in the Later Middle Ages* (Cambridge, 1989), 19. Hence the genre of Mirrors of Princes aimed at a much wider audience than princes. Cf. D. A. L. Morgan, 'The Individual Style of the English Gentleman', in *Gentry and Lesser Nobility in Late Medieval Europe*, ed. M. Jones (1986), and P. Coss, *The Knight in Medieval England 1000–1400* (Stroud, 1993), ch. 5.

[12] They are *L'Apprise de Nurture* and the *Petit Traitise*, both known only in a single fifteenth-century manuscript, Parsons, 'Anglo-Norman Books', 430–1, 451.

[13] *Pour une histoire des traités de savoir-vivre en Europe*, ed. A. Montandon (Clermont-Ferrand, 1994).

[14] Parsons, 'Anglo-Norman Books', 404, 413.

and Anglo-Norman works continued to circulate during the fifteenth century, so even for fifteenth-century England it is misleading to focus exclusively on courtesy literature written in English. Moreover, if the form and approach of Erasmus's *De Civilitate* 'suggest not so much the training of boys in noble households but the environment of the school',[15] it follows that in the first instance we should compare it with medieval works from a similar environment. Whereas the works written in Anglo-Norman and in English seem to have been widely used in households, both aristocratic and mercantile, the Latin poems were primarily for use in schools.[16] In any case, before claiming, as many do, that the *De Civilitate* of Erasmus marked a new departure, it would seem sensible to compare Erasmus's Latin not only with fifteenth-century courtesy literature in a vernacular, as many do, but also with earlier literature in Latin.

One of the shortest and most widely diffused twelfth-century courtesy poems in Latin was the text now known as *Facetus*.[17] It was loosely constructed in the gnomic form of its model, the third-century *Distichs of Cato*, of which it claimed to be a supplement (and on which see below p. 279). *Facetus* had become a set text in English schools by 1300 and remained in use until swept out by the humanists in the 1520s.[18] In addition to giving advice on table manners, it dealt with conversation, dress, deportment and social relationships. Such universally cynical advice as: 'whatever you do, do not tell your secrets to your wife', went hand in hand with 'He who speaks badly of women is a boor (*rusticus*), for truly we are all born of women.'[19] *Rusticus* and *rusticitas* are key words in courtesy literature, indicative of its claims to teach socially superior behaviour.[20] Another extremely popular work, surviving in

---

[15] Bryson, *Courtesy to Civility*, 29.

[16] Nicholls, *Matter of Courtesy*, 73–4. Naturally the 'bourgeois' wished to be as well mannered as the 'noble', and this was a genre that was read by both. On the urban household's reading matter see F. Riddy, 'Mother Knows Best: Reading Social Change in a Courtesy Text', *Speculum*, 71 (1996), 66–86, especially 77 for the point that it was more acceptable for a businessman's son to try to be Sir Gawain than it was for his daughter to pass herself off as a lady.

[17] Or *Facetus: cum nihil utilius* to distinguish it from another *Facetus* poem (see above n. 9). Edited in J. Morawski, *Le facet en françoys* (Poznan, 1923). In one MS it is called *liber facetie*, in another *liber urbani*, Nicholls *Matter of Courtesy*, 10 n. 10.

[18] N. Orme, *English Schools in the Middle Ages* (1973), 104–6; Nicholls, *Matter of Courtesy*, 62–5, Bryson, *Courtesy to Civility*, 26–7. For the fifty-eight early printed editions see S. Gieben, 'Robert Grosseteste and Medieval Courtesy-Books', *Vivarium*, 5 (1967), 51.

[19] Morawski, *Le facet*, 11. 45 bis, 73–4. Book Two of the mid-fifteenth century Sloane Courtesy Book makes extensive use of the *Facetus*, Nicholls, *Matter of Courtesy*, 166–7.

[20] In the 1240s John of Garland placed the *Septem Rusticitates* in opposition to the *Septem Curialitates*, *Morale Scolarium of John of Garland*, ed. L. J. Pactow (Berkeley, 1927), chs. 20 and 21. Chapter 9 on table manners entitled *De curialitatibus* begins by saying 'I defend courtliness and criticize rusticity.' See also Gieben, 'Grosseteste', 54–5, for the seven *rusticitates* opposed to the seven *urbanitates*.

many English manuscripts from the twelfth to the sixteenth centuries, was the *Disciplina clericalis* written by Petrus Alfonsi, a converted Spanish Jew deeply versed in Arabic literature.[21] This includes a description of the qualities of the ideal counsellor. He should be well instructed in the seven liberal arts, in the seven rules of good conduct (do not eat or drink too much, do not harm anyone, lie to anyone, be dissolute or envious, keep bad company or conversation – all very conventional); and in the seven knightly skills (*probitates*): riding, swimming, archery, combat, falconry, chess and song-writing. It also contains sections on how to reply to invitations, how to behave as a guest and on good table manners, including 'do not grab the tastiest morsels, or you will be reproached for your *rusticitas*'.[22] Petrus Alfonsi practised medicine at Henry I's court[23] – a court which was certainly perceived as a school of good manners by those close to it. One of the nobles brought up there became King David I of Scotland and was congratulated by William of Malmesbury for his policy of offering tax rebates to any Scotsmen who would learn 'to live in a more civilised style, dress with more elegance and eat with more refinement'. David did this, in William's view, because 'the rust of his native barbarism had been polished away by his upbringing among us'.[24]

The most substantial courtesy poem in any language is the work usually known as *Urbanus Magnus* – although *Liber Urbani*, translated by Robert Bartlett as 'The Book of the Civilized Man', is the more accurate title. On palaeographical grounds the bulk of the treatise can be dated to the twelfth century. Its author was an Englishman, Daniel of Beccles, who hoped to attract the attention of 'Old King Henry' – probably Henry II (though Henry I has also been suggested).[25] It takes the form, characteristic of both medieval and early modern courtesy literature, of a father's advice to his son, but closes with lines indicating that Daniel hoped to have female as well as male readers, laymen as well as clerks.[26] It has some specifically English features, notably mentions of 'Was hail' and 'drinc hail' as traditional toasts.[27] In the full

---

[21] J. Tolan, *Petrus Alfonsi and his Medieval Readers* (Gainesville, 1993), Appendix 3, for a list of manuscripts.

[22] Cc. 4 and 26, in *The 'Disciplina Clericalis' of Petrus Alfonsi*, ed. E. Hermes, (1977) 114–15, 150–1.

[23] C. Burnett, 'The Works of Petrus Alfonsi', *Medium Aevum*, 66 (1997), 44.

[24] William of Malmesbury, *Gesta Regum Anglorum*, I, ed. and trans. R. A. B. Mynors, R. M. Thomson and M. Winterbottom (Oxford, 1998), c. 400.

[25] *Urbanus Magnus Danielis Becclesiensis*, ed. J. G. Smyly (Dublin, 1939). It ends 'Explicit liber Urbani Danielis Becclesiensis', after stating that it was 'Old King Henry' who first gave this teaching to the uncourtly (*illepidis*). It has become conventional to add the word *magnus* to its title to distinguish it from other poems called *Urbanus*.

[26] *Urbanus*, ll. 2834–5.

[27] *Urbanus*, ll. 944, 1073.

version it comprises 2,839 lines of Latin verse, roughly ten times longer than *Facetus: cum nihil utilius*. Although in very general terms its importance was recognised earlier, its contents remained unexploited until Bartlett gave it half a dozen pages in his volume in the New Oxford History of England.[28] It is a difficult work to use, inadequately edited, so episodic as to be a jumble, full of digressions, with wild swings of subject matter and tone which make the (probably) often humorous or ironic intentions of the author (or even authors) hard to assess.[29] Even so, it is clearly dangerous to generalise about the characteristics of medieval courtesy literature while neglecting – as medievalists did until very recently – precisely that work which Nicholls described as 'the most comprehensive courtesy poem in any language, covering every aspect of life'. And all the more so since, as Nicholls himself showed, it had a considerable influence on later works in the genre.[30]

Daniel's book begins: 'Reader, read and re-read me if you wish to be adorned with good manners, if you wish to be respected and to lead a civilised life (*urbanam ducere vitam*) as a noble householder (*nobilis heros*).' A dozen lines later it uses the phrase which sums up one of its main themes: elegance of manners (*gracia morum*).[31] There follow some 200 lines on how to behave in church, but the poem's ethos was far from being religious. It ends with over 300 lines of advice on how to live a long, healthy and happy life, on what to drink and eat, with some recipes thrown in, on when to take baths, how much exercise to take, how often to have sex and so on. Moderation in all things, of course, seasonally adjusted. In summer cut back on both hot baths and sex.

---

[28] R. Bartlett, *England under the Norman and Angevin Kings 1075–1225* (Oxford, 2000), 579, 582–8. There are some useful comments in T. Zotz, 'Urbanitas: Zur Bedeutung und Funktion einer antiken Wertvorstellung innerhalb der höfischen Kultur des hohen Mittelalters', in *Curialitas: Studien zu Grundfragen der höfischritterlichen Kultur*, ed. J. Fleckenstein (Göttingen, 1990), an article to which I am much indebted.

[29] How, for example, should we read the warning against striking an enemy while he is squatting to defecate? *Urbanus*, ll. 1094–7.

[30] Nicholls, *The Matter of Courtesy*, 162–6, 185. The subject of Daniel's influence on subsequent works, particularly in Anglo-Norman, is one which has been taken further by Frédérique Lachaud in 'Littérature de civilité et "processus de civilisation" à la fin du XIIe siècle: le cas anglais d'après l'*Urbanus magnus*', in *Les échanges culturels: actes du congrès des médiévistes français, Boulogne-sur-Mer 2001*, ed. D. Courtemanche and A.-M. Helvétius (Paris, 2002). I owe much to Frédérique Lachaud's kindness in letting me see in advance of publication both this and another paper, 'L'enseignement des bonnes manières en milieu de cour en Angleterre d'après l'*Urbanus magnus* attribué à Daniel de Beccles', to be published in *Erziehung und Bildung am Hofe. 7. Symposium der Residenzen-Kommission in Celle*, ed. H. Kruse and W. Paravicini (Sigmaringen, 2002).

[31] *Urbanus*, ll. 1–2, 14. For other examples of the phrase *gracia morum* see C. S. Jaeger, *The Origins of Courtliness – Civilizing Trends and the Formation of Courtly Ideals, 939–1210* (Philadelphia, 1985), 33, 95–6, 140.

Cheerful songs will keep you in a good mood. Cultivate entertaining conversation, avoid quarrels, getting some new clothes is often a good idea.[32] There is certainly a good deal on table manners and on the duties of those servants who perform honourable services, both political services as envoys and personal services, at table, in the bedchamber and in the privy, the kinds of services which, well done, led either to promotion or to love and marriage.[33] There is advice on how to eat and drink politely, both in the company of social superiors and inferiors.[34] One of its main themes was the importance of control of the body, the kind of subject dear to Norbert Elias.[35] When, where and how you can urinate, defecate, spit, belch and fart politely; for example, when you belch remember to look up at the ceiling; guidelines such as that only the head of household was entitled to urinate in the hall.[36] There are nearly 400 lines on household management: house and garden, entertaining, sleeping arrangements, children, guests, the endless worries of the house of household, the servant problem.[37] You are advised to build a beautiful house with ornate chambers and decent privies, situated so as to keep unpleasant smells to a minimum.[38] At times Daniel was thinking, as Bartlett puts it, 'of the country gentleman who wishes to make it clear that the stress is on the "gentleman" rather than the "country"'.[39] Time and again Daniel condemns certain actions

---

[32] *Urbanus*, ll. 2524–833. A version of this section of the poem was printed in Furnivall, *Manners and Meals*, II, 34–57. The text is close to the well-known Salernitan Regimen of Health (itself addressed to a king of the English), so dating this section of *Urbanus* to either the twelfth or thirteenth century, depends partly upon what view is taken of the difficult question of the chronology of composition of the Regimen, a later version of which Sir John Harrington translated as *The School of Salernum*. See P. W. Cummins, 'A Salernitan Regimen of Health', *Allegorica*, 1 (1976) 78–81.

[33] *Urbanus*, ll. 1116–220, 1266–92, 1326–39. Technical precepts were intermixed with advice on how to make the best of the time (possibly a lifetime) spent in service.

[34] Including the injunction not to attack one's food *more canino*, *Urbanus*, ll. 1398–9. I am not inclined to make much of the greater frequency with which Erasmus compared behaviour of which he disapproved with that of animals. But for a different view see Bryson, *Courtesy to Chivalry*, 278, and Knox, '*Disciplina*', 107, 117, 126. In the short fifteenth-century poem, *Ut te geras ad mensam*, you were advised not to scratch yourself like a mole, Furnivall, *Meals and manners*, II, 26.

[35] Elias believed that 'courtois verses say little on this subject', *Civilizing Process*, 110, but he did not know of Daniel's work.

[36] *Urbanus*, ll. 1047–9, 1083–103.

[37] *Urbanus*, ll. 2144–524.

[38] *Urbanus*, ll. 1290–2, 2203–5. Cf. T. A. Heslop, 'Orford Castle: Nostalgia and Sophisticated Living', *Architectural History*, 34 (1991), 44, for the careful attention paid to the ventilation of privies in a twelfth-century castle.

[39] In this section 'a major preoccupation is the continuous and difficult attempt to segregate the working life of an agrarian community from the civilized enclave of the semi-public household space', Bartlett, *England under the Norman and Angevin Kings*, 587–8.

as boorish.[40] When plied with questions, 'reply with courteous words (*verba faceta*) as befits a nobleman'.[41] But this gentleman is not above efficient estate management. On the contrary, Daniel quotes Ovid – pauperis est numerare pecus – only to disagree. It is not low class to count your flocks, to keep a sharp eye on your property, to work to improve the yields of fields and livestock. If you do this you can afford to be generous.[42]

If we say that everything I have mentioned so far is focused on the household, it still only comes to about a half of the whole poem. There are additionally some 400 lines on the duties and problems of a wide range of vocations: judges, officials, advocates, knights, teachers, students, citizens, merchants, sailors, singers, thieves, doctors, religious, princes. It is an awkward text for those who think that the life of the secular elite was dominated by war since there are only a dozen lines on soldierly activity (less than 0.5 per cent of the total number). As a genre, indeed, courtesy books of all periods have little to say about war. There are ten times as many lines on the role of the judge, grumbling about lawyers and lamenting the corruption of the times. There are almost three times as many lines on the temptations and problems of holding administrative office. There are at least 670 lines of general advice, practical wisdom of the *Distichs of Cato* type, on such matters as how to hold a conversation, how to deal with friends and with enemies, how to choose a patron or a wife.[43] There are more than 250 lines on how to deal with women. If your wife is unfaithful (and she is bound to be, given female sexual appetites which make it virtually impossible for them to say no to any well-endowed male), pretend not to notice. 'It is better to conceal your shame as a husband than disclose the evil that brings a blush to your face and grief to your heart.'[44] If your lord's wife makes a pass at you, pretend to be ill – and don't say a word to her husband.[45] As is commonplace in courtesy literature we hear not only about controlling emotions, but also about concealing

---

[40] E.g. *Urbanus*, ll. 888, 1047–9, 1105, 1107–9

[41] *Ibid.*, ll. 1414–15.

[42] *Urbanus*, ll. 2182–200. In lines 1141–6 Daniel refers to the work of clerks in keeping accounts and drawing up legal documents. The thirteenth-century 'managerial revolution' in the administration of manors should be borne in mind here. See S. L. Waugh, 'Tenure to Contract: Lordship and Clientage in Thirteenth-Century England', *English Historical Review* 101 (1986), 811–39.

[43] In conversation comport yourself *more Catonis, Urbanus*, l. 102.

[44] *Urbanus*, ll. 2002–12. Nor indeed should you either beat or desert your wife, 1997–9, 2013–26. There is also some succinct advice on best practice when with a prostitute, 2103–6. It seems likely that much of what Daniel wrote about sexual relations between the sexes was intended to amuse. See Bartlett, *England under the Norman and Angevin Kings*, 586–7.

[45] *Urbanus*, ll. 1896–922.

them.[46] The *Liber Urbani* gives advice on proper and urbane conduct in what has been called 'a dizzying range of situations'.[47] Not just in the country, but also in towns.[48] Daniel emphasises the importance of *pax in urbe*, of living at peace with neighbours and fellow-citizens (*concives*).[49] We do not have to wait until the sixteenth century to find a courtesy manual with 'ambitious claims to define good behaviour at all times and in all companies'.[50]

The fact that Daniel of Beccles was thinking of a gentleman's lifestyle and that he wrote in quite difficult Latin verse does, of course, raise unanswerable questions about lay literacy. Michael Clanchy points out that 'ideally ladies (and gentlemen) in twelfth-and thirteenth-century England should be able to read in three languages at least: Latin, French and English'. By 1300 the ability to read some Latin was, he suggests, 'common among the gentry' since 'bureaucratic demands in Latin were sufficiently common to make it useful to any landowner to be able to understand them'. Moreover, 'literacy for recreation or self-improvement' was increasing as more was being written down in the vernacular languages.[51] What is clear is that heroes of romance could read. For example in the late twelfth-century romance *Ipomedon* written by Hue of Roteland, the young hero had a tutor who was 'mult bien lettrez' and who ensured that he was literate too.[52] In the later English versions of *Ipomedon* the interest in the hero's upbringing and education was retained and further developed.[53] It is noticeable how much space Caxton's courtesy book gives to the authors whose works should be read: Gower, Chaucer, Lydgate, Hoccleve.[54]

Throughout the *Liber Urbani* a principal theme is restraint. Watch

---

[46] And not just as in the commonplace advice to hide grief under a smile, but also in the recommendation that you pretend not to hear unkind words, *ibid.*, 398–9, 820–4, 858–62. According to the twelfth-century *Historia Gaufridi ducis*, Henry II's father, Geoffrey le Bel, was praised because 'he bore injuries patiently and clemently; if he heard abuse heaped on him he pretended not to hear it', *Chroniques des comtes d'Anjou*, ed. L. Halphen and R. Poupardin (Paris, 1913), 177.

[47] Bartlett, *England under the Norman and Angevin Kings*, 582.

[48] *Urbanus*, ll. 1354–7, 1748–56.

[49] *Urbanus*, ll. 449–73. In this short passage the word *concives* is used five times. See also p. 281. It is not easy to see how later authors could make a clearer connection than Daniel does 'between good manners and other virtues perceived to promote social harmony and peace in the community', Bryson, *Courtesy to Civility*, 70.

[50] Bryson, *Courtesy to Civility*, 68.

[51] M. T. Clanchy, *From Memory to Written Record* (2nd edn, Oxford, 1993), 194, 198–200, 246–7.

[52] *Ipomedon: Poème de Hue de Rotelande*, ed. A. J. Holden (Paris, 1979), ll. 203–7, 325–6, 1160.

[53] C. Meale, 'The Middle English Romance of *Ipomedon*: A Late Medieval "Mirror" for Princes and Merchants', *Reading Medieval Studies*, 10 (1984), 136–83, esp. 150–6.

[54] *Caxton's Book of Courtesy*, ed. F. J. Furnivall (1868), 32–7. In a poem of just 532 lines, fifty-six are on the subject of reading these four authors.

your tongue, say little, avoid giving offence, make sure your words are cheerful, courteous and polished, *iocosa, faceta, polita*.[55] Do not lose your temper, for example when losing at chess; do not mock, do not threaten, do not react violently to threats, do not take precipitate revenge, do not harbour resentments.[56] Do not always insist on your rights – for if you do, you will have few friends. Love moderation if you wish to be courtly (*Dilige temperiem, si diligis esse facetus*).[57] If this theme is treated only in passing in fifteenth-century English courtesy works, it is not because it was regarded as of little importance in an essentially violent, honour-based society, but because it was a familiar commonplace. As with the *Distichs of Cato*, much of it was proverbial.[58] The most basic rule throughout courtesy literature in all languages is: do not do or say anything that might offend or humiliate others.[59] If you do, you will pay in the end. There is no room here for the notion, central to Elias's interpretation of courtesy and civility, that Renaissance civility reflected 'a new tendency to assert a general rule of consideration towards one's fellows'.[60] According to Erasmus, the essence of civility (*maxima civilitatis pars*; in Robert Whittinton's translation 'the chief part of gentyll maner') was 'gentilly' to pardon the shortcomings of others; if you advised them where they went wrong, it was good manners to do so in private and 'with gentill fashion' (*solum ac blande monere civilitatis est*).[61] Elias's comment on this passage was that compared with earlier courtly literature 'the change of tone, the increased sensitivity, the heightened human observation and the sharper understanding of what is going on in

---

[55] *Urbanus*, ll. 664–5, 847–8; cf. 'Le bel teisir est curteisie', *Ipomedon*, l. 2630.

[56] *Urbanus*, ll. 398–9, 642–87, 833–6, 845–6. Cf. 'Vos ne prendrez la venjaunce, De espeye ne de launce, Mais autrement purrez conquere, Amendement par lay de terre, Ne seez pas trope hastif, Ceo vous prie, moun chere fiz', in *Urbain le Courtois*, Parsons, 'Anglo-Norman Books', 404.

[57] *Urbanus*, ll. 845, 923.

[58] Extracts from the *Liber Urbani* in the earliest manuscript (Oxford, Bodley, Rawlinson, C.552) are headed *Proverbia Urbani*, Nicholls, *Matter of Courtesy*, 162.

[59] In 'How the Good Wife Taught her Daughter' she was advised to be courteous to all; for example, no matter how unacceptable a proposal of marriage might be, not to pour scorn on the man who made it, Furnivall, *Manners and Meals*, i, 37. For a few other examples of this ubiquitous theme see *ibid.*, i, 15, 55–6, ii, 28, 30. The young men at Edward IV's court were to be taught 'temperate behaving and patience', A. R. Myers, *The Household of Edward IV* (Manchester, 1959), 126–7.

[60] Bryson, *Courtesy to Chivalry*, 110. For example Elias argued that a comment on farting made by Erasmus showed 'the old unconcern in referrring to bodily functions that was characteristic of medieval people, but enriched by observation, by consideration of what others *might* think', *Civilizing Process*, 66. But Daniel's views on this subject, including his disapproval of farting noisily for fun, were equally based on what others might think, *Urbanus*, ll. 1090–103.

[61] Erasmus, *De civilitate morum puerilium* in *Opera Omnia* (Leiden, 1540), tom. i, 870; Robert Whittinton's bi-lingual version in the 1554 edition, sig. Diii–iv; modern English in *Complete Works of Erasmus*, xxv, ed. J. K. Sowards (Toronto, 1985), 289.

others are unmistakable. This sensitivity showed how little Erasmus identified with the code of the courtly upper class of the time.'[62] But in his *Liber Urbani* Daniel wrote, 'do not ridicule your fellow if he makes a mistake; if you know the right way, correct him politely (*urbane*)'. According to the Anglo-Norman *L'Apprise de Nurture* 'Reprove no one in public, but wait to say your piece until you are in a place where you can say it to him well and privately.'[63] In essence the ideas in *De Civilitate* were medieval commonplaces.[64] What can, however, be said is that with Erasmus 'what oft was thought, was ne'er so well expressed' – had never before been so effectively put into classicising schoolbook Latin.[65]

As Stephen Jaeger has emphasised, gentleness of spirit (*mansuetudo*) came to be 'one of the dominant themes of medieval ethical writings'. This was, in his view, because patience, affability and gentleness, whether natural or acquired, were politically astute strategies if one were to survive in the competitive hothouse of court society. He argued that clerics attached to royal and princely courts in the tenth and eleventh centuries were the first to see the value of this quality, and claimed that as this idea filtered through the ranks of the lay nobility, it marked 'nothing less than the civilising of Europe'.[66] Certainly this gentleness was, according to the eleventh-century author of the *Life of King Edward*, one of the qualities possessed in abundance by Earls Godwin and Harold Godwinsson and which helped to explain their dominance of the English court.[67] In view of all this – the entirely

[62] Elias, *Civilizing Process*, 64–5.

[63] *Urbanus*, ll. 159–60; Parsons, 'Anglo-Norman', 437.

[64] C. Roussel, 'Le legs de la Rose: modèles et préceptes de la sociabilité médiévale', in *Pour une histoire des traités de savoir-vivre en Europe*, ed. A. Montandon (Clermont-Ferrand, 1994), 1. Erasmus was 'a monk versed in medieval tradition' whose achievement was to give 'coherence and orderly arrangement to the medieval body of precepts', M. T. Brentano, *Relationship of the Latin* Facetus *Literature to the Medieval English Courtesy Poems* (Lawrence, KA, 1935), 105–6. To this I would add that he seasoned his commonplaces with an occasional phrase in Greek.

[65] Its success was due to 'the eminence of its author, the elegance and pedagogic utility of its language (Renaissance Latin adapted to the level of a well-schooled boy of ten), and its systematic treatment', M. Ingram, 'Sexual Manners: The Other Face of Civility in Early Modern England', in *Civil Histories*, ed. Burke, Harrison and Slack, 92.

[66] Jaeger, *The Origins of Courtliness*, 36–7. I am more inclined to believe that laymen and secular-minded clerics always shared values which clerics then first expressed in written form.

[67] Godwin 'took infinite trouble in all his dealings with inferiors and among equals to cultivate the gentleness (*mansuetudo*) he had learnt from boyhood', *Life of King Edward*, ed. F. Barlow (2nd edn, Oxford, 1992), 8–9. Cf. J. Gillingham, 'Thegns and Knights in Eleventh-Century England: Who Was Then the Gentleman?', *TRHS*, 6th ser., 5 (1995), repr. in *idem*, *The English in the Twelfth Century* (Woodbridge, 2000), 163–85, esp. 180–2. In Gerald de Barri's *De instructione principis*, *mansuetudo* is the first virtue a ruler needs, *Giraldi Cambrensis Opera Omnia*, VIII, ed. G. F. Warner (Rolls Series, 1891), 9–12.

conventional emphasis upon restraint and gentleness, upon consideration for others – it is impossible to take seriously the notion that Obadiah Walker was both summing up 'the new ideal of civility' and rejecting an 'earlier honour-based system', when he asserted in the 1670s that civility consisted of doing kindness to others, and of neither committing honour-threatening acts against others nor resenting or over-reacting to threats or insults by others.[68] Walker himself, for whom the rules of civility were 'founded upon Prudence and Charity', remarked that many of them 'seem plain and obvious, such as are fit to be insinuated into the practice of children'.[69]

Indeed the basic ideas of the prudential morality underlying courtesy can already be found in a work which was read by all those children who learned Latin, at least from the ninth century and very probably from much earlier: the *Distichs of Cato*. Composed in the third century AD by an unknown author, this was a work of practical morality in the Stoic tradition which taught that cultivation of certain personal qualities would win public esteem.[70] With the one exception of one *Distich* (III.19),[71] the work lacks the distinctive vocabulary of courtesy; hence it has never been classified as a courtesy book. But countless echoes of it in courtesy literature make its influence plain. The sententious practical wisdom contained in the *Distichs* stands in the same relationship to 'courtesy' as do Obadiah Walker's plain and obvious rules to civility.[72] The wisdom of the *Distichs* was that of the worldly and the practical, based on a cynical and calculating view of human motives. The reader, 'if he had followed to the letter the precepts given him, would have cultivated patience, prudence, temperance and fortitude'; in a world in which Fortune was active in the affairs of men, he would have done so out of self-interest, not out of any 'higher' motive. The religious-minded were often troubled by those *Distichs* in which 'Cato', like courtesy books, recommended dissimulation or concealment. None the less it remained well known throughout the

[68] Burke, 'A Civil Tongue', 37.

[69] O. Walker, *Of Education, Especially of Young Gentlemen* (3rd impression, 1677), 219.

[70] The unknown author explained that he had written *maxime ut gloriose viverent et ad honorem contingerent*, T. Hunt, *Le Livre de Catun* (Anglo-Norman Text Society, Plain Texts Series 11, 1994), 9.

[71] Speak modestly and with restraint at dinner parties 'if you wish to be thought well-mannered (*dum vis urbanus haberi*)'. In one of the three Anglo-Norman translations, dated by Tony Hunt to the thirteenth century, it is at this point – and only at this point – that the word *curtais* was used, Hunt, *Livre de Catun*, 34. The word does not occur in the other two Anglo-Norman versions printed in *Maître Elies Überarbeitung der ältesten französischen Übertragung von Ovids Ars Amatoria nebst Elies de Wincestre, eines Anonymus und Everarts Übertragungen der Disticha Catonis*, ed. E. Stengel (Marburg, 1886), 110–45.

[72] Hunt, *Livre de Catun*, 1. It was not a work on *savoir-vivre*, but on *savoir-vivre*'s indispensable moral underpinning, Roussel, 'Le legs de la Rose', 4.

Middle Ages, 'the first full-length literary piece the student read', was edited by Erasmus and continued to be printed up to c. 1600.[73] One of the paradoxes of a supposedly Christian and clerical medieval culture is that throughout this period the standard primary schoolbook was a pagan and secular one. Its effect was 'to indoctrinate the medieval world with the principles of ancient morality'[74] – the morality of the courtesy book.

If the terms 'civil' and 'civility' contained so little that was new, then what should we make of their introduction?[75] Probably when English schoolboys read *De Civilitate* in Latin (as in bilingual editions such as those of Robert Whittinton in 1532, 1540 and 1554), it may well have been the first time they came across the words *civilis* and *civilitas* – but then that would have been true of any number of Erasmus's words since, as Knox has made abundantly clear, *De Civilitate* was a drill-book for lower forms.[76] In fact the words *civilis* and *civilitas* with the meaning of 'refined' had been commonly used many centuries earlier by English authors who knew their classics: by Bede and Alcuin in the eighth century;[77] by William of Malmesbury,[78] John of Salisbury, Herbert of Bosham and Gerald de Barri in the twelfth.[79] John of Salisbury used 'civil' in senses embracing the aesthetic criterion of good taste, the moral standards of self-restraint and the political values of good lordship. To feed 5,000 with five loaves was the act of a 'most liberal, most civil (*civilissimus*) and most courtly (*facetissimus*) paterfamilias'.[80] In a passage

[73] *Distichs* 1.14; 1.26; II.7; II.18; III.3; IV.20. See R. Hazelton, 'The Christianization of "Cato"; The *Disticha Catonis* in the Light of Late Medieval Commentaries', *Medieval Studies*, 19 (1957), 157–73.

[74] R. R. Bolgar, *The Classical Heritage and its Beneficiaries* (Cambridge, 1958), 125.

[75] It may be that the connotations of 'ordered political life' contained in the word *civilitas* helped to strengthen the connection 'between good manners and other virtues perceived to promote social harmony and peace in the community'. See n. 49 for this in Daniel of Beccles.

[76] D. Knox, 'Erasmus' *De Civilitate* and the Religious Origins of Civility in Protestant Europe', *Archiv für Reformationsgeschichte*, 86 (1995), 7–55. According to my count, Erasmus used forms of *(in)civilis* twenty times, *(in)decorum* fifteen times, *(in)urbanus* eleven times, *rusticus* eight times.

[77] Bede describes Oswine of Northumbria as 'pleasant of speech, courteous in manner' (*affatu iucundus et moribus civilis*), *Historia Ecclesiastica*, III.14. In *De Rhetorica*, Alcuin advised those who wanted to learn *civiles mores* to read his book; cited in C. S. Jaeger, *The Envy of Angels: Cathedral Schools and Social Ideals in Medieval Europe, 950–1200* (Philadelphia, 1994), 30–1.

[78] William described Wihtred of Kent as *domi enim civilis* (translated by Mynors as 'civilized at home'), and said that after brutal beginnings Cnut settled down to behave *magna civilitate*, Malmesbury, *Gesta Regum*, cc. 15, 181.

[79] According to Gerald, the Emperor Augustus, famed for his patronage of architecture and letters, lived *civilissime*, *Giraldi Cambrensis Opera*, VIII, ed. G. F. Warner (Rolls Series, 1891), 51.

[80] H. Liebeschütz, *Medieval Humanism in the Life and Writings of John of Salisbury* (1950), 92–3. John distinguished three types of dinner parties: plebeian, philosophical and the

on Thomas Becket's care and responsibility for the education of young men in his household, Herbert of Bosham used the word 'civil' no less than seven times, including the claim that although Becket himself did not enjoy the feasting, he pretended to enjoy it *civili dissimulatione*.[81] But in the literary ferment of the twelfth and early thirteenth centuries a 'new' Latin was created and *civilis/civilitas* fell out of fashion, although Matthew Paris used it on occasion.[82] Even an author such as John of Garland who defended classical learning preferred to use *urbanitas* and *curialitas*. In consequence later medieval Latin was less classical than twelfth-century Latin, but none the worse for that – except, of course, by the somewhat curious standards of humanists of all ages.[83] While it is true that the words 'civil' and 'civility' gradually became fashionable English usage thanks first to Erasmus[84] and then to Italian and French authors of early modern courtesy books, it is worth noting that sixteenth-century English readers would have come across the Latin forms in some of the historians most familiar to them: Bede, William of Malmesbury and Matthew Paris.[85] Where readers, however, would not have found the words 'civil' and 'civility' in senses relating to refined conduct was in pre-Erasmus Latin courtesy literature. Daniel of Beccles used the word 'civil' but only in an explicitly urban context. The good citizen should act *civili more* and ensure that he did not violate *pacem civilem*.[86]

In medieval Latin courtesy literature the three key adjectives are *urbanus*, *facetus* and *curialis*. In the mid-twelfth-century *Liber Derivationum* of Osbern of Gloucester the words are treated as equivalents, meaning

---

civil. The plebeian is characterised by its excesses, so far removed from urbanity as to be closer to barbaric vice than to the civil life (*ab omni urbanitate adeo procul est ut barbariei vitiis familiarius sit quam vitae civili*); the philosophical by its sober solemnity; the civil by its moderation, rationality and witty good cheer, *Policratici sive de nugis curialium et vestigiis philosophorum libri VIII*, ed. C. C. J. Webb (Oxford, 1929), II, 253–7, 279–84.

[81] According to Herbert, Thomas possessed *civilis gratia ... urbana, benigna, socialis*. The well-born youth sent to serve at his court was *tam civiliter eruditam et tam urbane edoctam* thanks to the care (*civilem et domesticam custodiam*) taken by *urbanus novus hic noster paterfamilias*, a man who added *civilitas* to his moderation, *Vita Sancti Thomae*, in *Materials for the History of Thomas Becket*, III, ed. J. C. Robertson (Rolls Series, 1877), 227–33. The passage is discussed in Zotz, 'Urbanitas', 428–30, and Jaeger, *Envy of Angels*, 297–308. Cf. Erasmus: if someone behaved boorishly at table *civiliter dissimulandum* (*Opera Omnia*, I, 868).

[82] Matthew Paris described Robert Grosseteste as *in mensa refectionis corporalis dapsilis, copiosus et civilis, hilaris et affabilis, Chronica Majora*, v, ed. H. R. Luard (Rolls Series, 1880), 407. Southern translated *civilis* here as 'urbane'. According to Aquinas, Orpheus *homines bestiales et solitarios reduceret ad civilitatem*, cited by J. Fisch, 'Zivilisation, Kultur', in *Geschichtliche Grundbegriffe*, ed. O. Brunner *et al.*, VII (Stuttgart, 1992), 694.

[83] On the legacy of the humanists see Clanchy, *Memory to Written Record*, 14–16.

[84] Whittinton translated *civilitati morum* as 'civilitie and nurture', sig. Aii (1554 edn).

[85] M. McKisack, *Medieval History in the Tudor Age* (Oxford, 1971).

[86] *Urbanus*, ll. 471, 1748.

in the vernacular *curteis* (according to a Hereford gloss of c. 1200).[87] *Urbanus* is so common that it is unlikely that there was anything distinctively 'urban' in Erasmus's use of the word.[88] The second key word in this genre is *facetus*, which could mean refined and courtly in general, though it was more commonly used of speech, in its Ciceronian sense of witty, as indeed *urbanus* sometimes was too.[89] Surprisingly perhaps, the Latin words closest to the vernacular 'courteous' and 'courtesy', i.e. *curialis* and *curialitas*, are more rarely found in this didactic genre. *Curialitas* was a new word coined in the late eleventh century, after the classical words *curia* and *curialis* (originally referring to the Roman Senate) had recently come back into fashion as synonyms for *aula/palatium*. It is a neologism which reflects both a classicising trend, and an independent development of that trend.[90] *Curialis* and *curialitas* are commonly used in narrative and other literary sources from the twelfth century onwards, including the Parisian *De Amore* of Andrew the Chaplain,[91] but more rarely in didactic courtesy literature. In this genre we find *curialitas* only, I think, in the *Morale Scolarium* written in Paris in the 1240s by an Oxford-educated Englishman, John of Garland, where it is very prominent indeed,[92] and in the fifteenth-century Eton poem *Castrianus*.[93] In Daniel of Beccles, the most comprehensive of all guides to 'elegance of manners' the key words are the Ciceronian ones: *urbanus* and *facetus*.[94]

What these three key words had in common is that, unlike *civilis*, they were sometimes used in pejorative ways. Lanfranc showed where his priorities lay when he wrote that he would rather be *rusticus et idiota* as a good Catholic than *curialis atque facetus* as a heretic.[95] William of St Thierry criticised *urbanitas* which he associated with 'the wisdom of the flesh'; St Bernard wanted priests to avoid talking in a way that others thought of as *facetum* and *urbanum*.[96] 'What shall we say about the many knights who foul their lives by imitating the damnable courtliness

---

[87] Entry 'facetus' in *Dictionary of Medieval Latin from British Sources*, 1 (1975); T. Hunt, *Teaching and Learning Latin in Thirteenth-Century England* (Cambridge, 1991), 1, 177.

[88] *Pace* Bryson, *Courtesy to Civility*, 113.

[89] In *De Civilitate* Erasmus never uses *facetus* – but then his style in this work is, as its translator Brian McGregor observed, 'dry, pedantic, and somewhat repetitious', *Complete Works*, xxv, 272.

[90] Jaeger, *Courtliness*, 122, 127, 154–61; Zotz, 'Urbanitas', 409–11.

[91] *Andreas Capellanus on Love*, ed. and trans. P. G. Walsh (1982), 80, 116, 160, 270, 272. According to the Lanercost Chronicle, Grosseteste possessed *tanta curialitas*, cited Gieben, 'Grosseteste', 47–8.

[92] Indeed it ends with a chapter on the *curialitas* of the Virgin Mary, *Morale Scolarium*, c. 36.

[93] Printed by Gieben, 'Grosseteste', 71.

[94] Extracts from his text were, however, called *Liber curialis* and *curialitates ecclesiasticorum*, Gieben, 'Grosseteste', 49, 70.

[95] Lanfranc, 'Liber de corpore et sanguine', *Patrologia Latina*, 150, 414.

[96] Zotz, 'Urbanitas', 393, 406.

curialitatem – or rather *scurrilitatem* – of courtiers', wrote the English abbot, Alexander Neckam.[97] These monks were in the tradition of St Augustine and Gregory the Great for whom *urbanitas* was *perversio mentis*. But other clerics, court clergy, used precisely these same words in a positive sense.[98] The key words of the new genre drew attention to behaviour that was attractive and charming, which drew admiration, not to behaviour which satisfied Christian morality. Where the *Distichs* advocated worldly wisdom, courtly literature added elegance and refinement. This suggests that the impetus for the genre came, precisely as Jaeger argued, from courts, not from monasteries. The court was a school, as it always had been, for example in King Alfred's day as described by Asser.[99] Becket's household was a school of conduct not because Thomas was so religious but because he was so civilised; he possessed, wrote Herbert of Bosham, *gratia civilis et urbana*.[100] A famous passage in the Black Book of the Household of Edward IV lays down that the master of the boys being brought up at court was to teach them to ride, to joust, 'to have all courtesy in words, deeds and degrees, the rules of goings and sittings, various languages and other virtuous learning, to play the harp, pipe, sing and dance, and with other honest and temperate behaving and patience'.[101] It has been argued that although the 'ability to make a charming and memorable social impression ... must always have been of importance in the courts of kings or magnates', it was not until the later sixteenth century that 'it became enshrined in literature as a major element in the self-image of the aristocracy'.[102] But it was precisely this ability to charm, *gracia morum*, which centuries earlier had shaped both language and genre, the establishment of a new genre and the creation of a new word, *curialitas* – 'courtoisie' in the new vernacular of the Francophone elite of England.

The fact that a cluster of key-words disliked by monks was dominant in the new genre undercuts Dilwyn Knox's argument that the inspiration for secular codes of comportment, beginning with the twelfth-century *Facetus* poems, came from the rules of disciplined behaviour cultivated

---

[97] Alexander Neckam, *De naturis rerum*, ed. T. Wright (Rolls Series, 1863), 312.

[98] Zotz, 'Urbanitas', 396–406.

[99] Asser, c. 75. Cf. Jaeger, *Envy of Angels*, 113, for Hincmar's description of Louis the German's court as a school dealing with dress, deportment, speech and gesture (*habitu, incessu, verbo et actu*).

[100] 'He pleased the world as well as God. His table was more like Caesar's than a prelate's.' *Vita Sancti Thomae*, 230–1.

[101] He was also to supervise them at table 'how mannerly they eat and drink, and to their communication and other forms curial, after the book of urbanitie'. All this was to be according to 'the schools of urbanitie and nurture of England', Myers, *The Household of Edward IV*, 126–7.

[102] Bryson, *Courtesy to Civility*, 121.

in monasteries.[103] His argument seems to have won approval from early modern historians, and I can only suppose that this is because, as Knox himself pointed out, it is an argument in tune with the belief that 'the dominant cultural development of the thirteenth to sixteenth centuries' was 'the transition from a culture and religion sustained primarily by clerics and religious institutions to one more secular in organization, transmission and content'.[104] It might more plausibly be argued that Erasmus's preference for *civilitas* was in part an attempt to free good manners from courtly ambiguities. In that case Erasmus's 'Renaissance' code was more influenced by religious values than the codes produced by his medieval clerical predecessors had been. If such had been his intent, then he failed. As Martin Ingram has emphasised, the key texts of six-teenth-century civility, imbued as they were with aristocratic ideals of honour and with scorn for 'clownish' or 'rude' behaviour, inevitably stood in an ambiguous relationship to Christian morality.[105] That is to say they contained precisely the same ambiguities as the earliest extant courtesy literature, and which had been central to its development and its values.

Someone who took on board Daniel's advice and who was able to stand up to the domineering women of Daniel's imagination – the women he called *matrone testiculate*[106] – would certainly match up to the model seventeenth-century English gentleman: 'at his best he could combine political leadership and intelligent financial management with courtesy, magnanimity and cultural sophistication in daily living'.[107] At this level of generality and optimism such a description could well apply to the gentleman of England five or six hundred years earlier.[108] There were, after all, some important continuities throughout the pre-

---

[103] Knox, '*Disciplina*', 107–35. Part of the problem is that in this article Knox consistently writes as though 'monastic' and 'clerical' were one and the same thing, a sleight of hand which elides the gulf between two very different sorts of clerics, the courtly and the austerely religious. Nicholls had earlier made a case for monastic influence on the origins of courtesy, pointing to similarities between provisions about table manners and spitting in courtesy books and monastic rules and customaries. But on Nicholls's evidence, it is only in provisions for receiving guests – when the outside world comes in – that we get phrases such as *iocundus, facetus*, Nicholls, *The Matter of Courtesy*, 27.

[104] Knox, '*Disciplina*', 117; see Cameron, ' "Civilized Religion" ', 49, and Ingram, 'Sexual Manners', 93.

[105] Ingram, 'Sexual Manners', 91–3. The suggestion that there was 'a new conception of manners which by implying a separation between good manners and morality allowed the first to be judged by the standards of the second', Bryson, *Courtesy to Civility*, 199, is to ignore the monastic attacks on courtly manners.

[106] *Urbanus*, l. 1948.

[107] F. Heal and C. Holmes, *The Gentry in England and Wales 1500–1700* (1994), 276.

[108] On the material culture of the late Anglo-Saxon aristocracy and gentry see R. Fleming, 'The New Wealth, the New Rich and the New Political Style in Late Anglo-Saxon England', *Anglo-Norman Studies*, 23 (2000), 1–22; and on their close involvement with towns, *eadem*, 'Rural Elites and Urban Communities in Late-Saxon England', *Past and Present*, 141 (1993).

industrial period. 'The portfolio of ideas, attitudes and policies regarding wages, work, workers, subsistence, consumption, leisure and charity proved exceptionally durable, as did the behaviour of the labouring poor.'[109] The English kingdom was geographically no larger in the sixteenth than in the eleventh century and some fundamentals of government remained constant: 'a more or less centralised monarchy lacking a large bureaucracy, standing army or police force, with an absence of modern technology to transmit and enforce orders on the ground'.[110] The belief that towns and markets were essential to a civilised life-style was just as powerful in the twelfth and early thirteenth centuries (when new towns were founded at a faster rate than at any other period of English history) as in later times.[111]

There were, of course, changes, especially marked during the seventeenth century, which had an impact on the 'gentle' life-style. New fashions in dress and in house design (though in 'upstairs' and 'downstairs' the new houses still retained the basic division into master's side and servants' side).[112] Gentlemen and their families were able to enjoy more privacy, as the trend for provision of more private rooms visible since Anglo-Saxon times continued to unfold.[113] More gentlemen, accompanied by their wives, spent more time in London than had their medieval counterparts.[114] They may have taken baths less often.[115]

---

[109] J. Hatcher, 'Labour, Leisure and Economic Thought before the Nineteenth Century', *Past and Present*, 160 (1998).

[110] C. Carpenter, 'Who Ruled the Midlands in the Later Middle Ages?', *Midland History*, 19 (1994), 5. Cf. A. McFarlane, 'Civility and the Decline of Magic', in *Civil Histories*, ed. Burke, Harrison and Slack, 156–7.

[111] Gillingham, 'Civilizing the English?', 38–9. See also P. Nightingale, 'Knights and Merchants: Trade, Politics and the Gentry in Late Medieval England', *Past and Present*, 169 (2000), 36–62, on the long history of the appeal of commercial profit to nobility and gentry.

[112] D. Starkey, 'The Age of the Household', in *The Later Middle Ages*, ed. S. Medcalf (1981), 244. See also N. Tadmor, 'The Concept of the Household-Family in Eighteenth-Century England', *Past and Present*, 151 (1996).

[113] For earlier re-buildings involving a tendency to create more and smaller, more private, more functionally defined rooms, C. M. Woolgar, *The Great Household in Late Medieval England* (1999), 59–68. For similar fashions in religious houses where the monks wished to live like gentlemen, B. Harvey, *Living and Dying in England 1100–1540* (1993), 78n, 130–3. For Daniel's awareness of the head of the house's private space, *Urbanus*, ll. 1360–5.

[114] Heal and Holmes, *Gentry 1500–1700*, 312–15. We should not, however, underestimate the amount of time the late medieval gentry spent in London, often leaving their wives to look after their country estates, C. Richmond, 'The Pastons and London', in *Courts and Regions in Medieval Europe*, ed. S. R. Jones, R. Marks and A. J. Minnis (York, 2000), 213. By then the aristocracy tended to move, in a 'modern pattern', between a London house and just one or two major country houses, Dyer, *Standards of Living*, 99–100. See also C. Barron, 'Centres of Conspicuous Consumption: The Aristocratic Town House in London 1200–1550', *London Journal*, 20 (1995).

[115] K. Thomas, 'Cleanliness and Godliness in Early Modern England', in *Religion, Culture and Society in Early Modern Britain*, ed. A. Fletcher and P. Roberts (1994), 58, 61.

Some of these changes had an impact on what was expected of the accomplished gentleman. The new rules of chess help to explain the game's decline as a gentlemanly pastime.[116] Gentlemen were expected to appreciate music, but stunning virtuosity was no longer an aristocratic ideal as it had been in the twelfth century.[117] Technological changes in armour and weaponry led to the end of the tournament and to the precipitate decline in falconry.[118] More importantly they changed the nature of war. Whether gentlemen could expect to go to war more or less often is another question altogether, and one on which courtesy literature throws no light, though many of them continued to learn how to fight.[119] Most important of all was the 'decline of the great noble household', particularly marked in the later seventeenth century.[120] As the great household declined as a place of education a higher proportion of the gentry attended school and university, and this clearly meant that service in the hall and at table no longer played the prominent role in codes of manners that it once had done. By unduly emphasising the service aspect of courtesy, historians have focused attention on the area of significant change and rather tended to assume that everything else changed with it.

Above all, the notion that there were fundamental changes in socio-political values seems to me to be based on generalisations which are always far too sweeping and often misconceived. I remain struck by how often I read even in very recent works statements such as: the Tudors turned chivalry to the service of the state;[121] or: in the sixteenth century an honour cult of lineage and violence declined in the face of increasing opposition from the 'humanist' concept of a 'nobility of virtue'.[122] Such views are essentially paraphrases of Lawrence Stone's statement that 'the medieval system of values placed obedience to the public authority and devotion to the common good below individual

[116] R. Eales, *Chess: The History of a Game* (1985), 71–9.

[117] C. Page, *Voices and Instruments of the Middle Ages* (1987), ch. 1.

[118] R. Grassby, 'The Decline of Falconry in Early Modern England', *Past and Present*, 157 (1997), 37–62. A. Young, *Tudor and Jacobean Tournaments* (1987), 40–2. On fishing see R. C. Hoffmann, 'Fishing for Sport in Medieval Europe: New Evidence', *Speculum*, 60 (1985), 877–902.

[119] S. Anglo, *The Martial Arts of Renaissance Europe* (2000).

[120] F. Heal, *Hospitality in Early Modern England* (Oxford, 1990), esp. 91, 147–52, 165–6. K. Mertes, *The English Noble Household 1250–1600* (Oxford, 1988) for the lack of change prior to 1600.

[121] T. Meron, *Bloody Constraint: War and Chivalry in Shakespeare* (Oxford, 1998), 109.

[122] Most such statements reflect the influential views of M. E. James, e.g. *Society, Politics and Culture: Studies in Early Modern England* (Cambridge, 1986). However, his belief that ancient ideas on virtuous and noble conduct had little or no influence until they appeared in print is founded upon the usual assumptions about the scale and ubiquity of violence in medieval English politics. See Bryson, *Courtesy to Civility*, 237, for another qualification of his theory of a seventeenth-century attenuation of honour.

loyalty ... Under such circumstances disruption of public order by private violence was inevitable.'[123] Here we remain in the thought-world of Norbert Elias, according to whom a 'permanent readiness to fight, weapon in hand, was a vital necessity in medieval society'.[124] Most historians of early modern England write as though the political patterns of the Wars of the Roses were typical of the medieval centuries, whereas in fact they are highly atypical. I know of no evidence that the secular elite of twelfth- or thirteenth-century England was more prone to violence than the secular elite of the sixteenth and seventeenth centuries. Even in the twelfth century, the heyday of the castle, castles were more about image and display, powerhouses in that sense, than they were places primarily designed to withstand siege.[125] The notion that with every passing century even the English gentleman became more peaceful than before is just one of those 'grand evolutionary narratives that we need to get away from'.[126] Recent work by landscape historians and archaeologists is showing that once we get away from the Scottish and Welsh marches then designed landscapes, ornamental fishponds and gardens, dovecotes, viewing pavilions, roof walks, a concern for comfort rather than defence, were all there in medieval England – it is just that, above ground, they barely survive, and certainly make less impression than ruined walls which appear to speak of war.[127]

While it is the case that with the decline of the crusading ideal, with the end of the tournament in the 1620s and with new architectural fashions, the *image* of aristocracy was less martial than in previous centuries, I am not sure that the reality was. Consider the evidence of household accounts and inventories. Christopher Dyer has pointed to 'the lack of much household expenditure on weapons, except in the unusual circumstances of the Scottish border'; 'inventories and the bequest made in gentry wills show that silver plate, bedding and clothes figured among their most valuable possessions, followed by kitchen and farming equipment. Valuable armour and weapons tended to be owned by a minority.' In 1397 Thomas duke of Gloucester's armour was valued at £103, his books at £124, and both items were far outweighed by

[123] L. Stone, *The Crisis of the Aristocracy 1558–1641* (Oxford, 1967), 96–7.

[124] Elias's belief that 'the knight's life is divided between war, tournaments, hunts and love', *Civilizing Process*, 176, would have surprised Daniel of Beccles.

[125] Heslop, 'Orford Castle'; C. Coulson, Cultural Realities and Reappraisals in English Castle-Study', *Journal of Medieval Hisory*, 22 (1996), 171–208; *idem*, 'Peaceable Power in English Castles', *Anglo-Norman Studies*, 23 (2000/1), 69–95.

[126] M. S. R. Jenner, 'Civilization and Deodorization? Smell in Early Modern English Culture', in *Civil Histories*, ed. Burke, Harrison and Slack, 143.

[127] C. Taylor, 'Medieval Ornamental Landscapes', *Landscapes*, 1 (2000), 38–55; R. Liddiard, 'Castle Rising, Norfolk: A "Landscape of Lordship"?', *Anglo-Norman Studies*, 22 (1999/2000).

what he spent on tapestries, beds, chapel vestments and silver plate.[128] Taking up arms against the crown was always regarded as treason in law, and although it was occasionally risked, it was risked no more often in thirteenth-and fourteenth-century England than in sixteenth-and seventeenth-century England. Stone himself provided plenty of evidence for the physical violence with which aristocratic disputes were still being pursued in the second half of sixteenth century. Indeed in the rapier and the duel the gentleman-swordsman of the sixteenth and later centuries found ways of shedding blood which had escaped his medieval ancestors. No wonder Lodowick Bryskett in his *A Discourse of Civil Life* written in the 1580s called the recent emergence of the duel 'barbarous ... and contrary to all honest and civil conversation'.[129] In the sixteenth and seventeenth centuries the gentlemanly elite were more likely to kill one another in pursuit of political ends than they had been in the twelfth and thirteenth centuries, when the gentle values of chivalrous compassion towards the defeated so much emphasised in contemporary didactic and romantic literature were also practised in real political life – hence the astonishment of an early Stuart historian, Samuel Daniel, at the lack of bloodshed during the so-called 'Anarchy' of Stephen's reign.[130] On the one hand, the image of gentleman as politician and magistrate goes back to Daniel of Beccles and the twelfth century; on the other, the image of gentleman as officer and swordsman survived into the seventeenth century and beyond.[131]

Even if we were to accept the case for a relatively high level of elite literacy in medieval England, it would be absurd not to insist that the printing press enabled readers to obtain infinitely more reading matter than before, to become, in short, more bookish. What difference would this make? It is, for example, true that they could now read books on dancing, but it is not immediately obvious that this would either have made them better dancers or have added to the pleasure they took in dancing.[132] But one effect of the print revolution was to deliver

---

[128] Dyer, *Standards of Living*, 53, 76–7.

[129] L. Bryskett, *Literary Works*, ed. J. H. P. Pafford (1972), 65–85, esp. 70–1.

[130] S. Daniel, *The Collection of the Historie of England* (1618), 67. By basing his views on the high level of aristocratic bloodshed in medieval England on ducal statistics, T. H. Hollingsworth, 'A Demographic Study of the British Ducal Families', *Population Studies*, 11 (1957), 8, Becker took no account of anything before 1337 when the first English dukedom was created, *Civility and Society*, 5.

[131] Daniel of Beccles would have had no difficulty in agreeing with John Aubrey's view (cited by Heal and Holmes, *Gentry 1500–1700*, 276), of the educated gentleman: 'the management of his estates will take up most of his time, besides visits and returns of visits'.

[132] For the spread of the earliest treatises on dancing, composed in mid-fifteenth-century Italy, via France to England, N. Orme, *From Childhood to Chivalry: The Education of the English Kings and Aristocracy 1066–1530* (1984), 173–4.

gentleman-readers into the hands of the humanists who came to dominate the curriculum and enjoy a monopoly of the press. Humanists did not refer to medieval authors even when they were merely repeating or echoing them, nor did they look to medieval figures as models of good conduct.[133] All their models of good conduct and good style were drawn from antiquity. One side effect of Erasmus's *De Civilitate* or of, for example, Sir Thomas Elyot's *Governor* was to dump everything that had been done or thought between 400 and 1500 into a black hole. In this paper I hope to have shown that the basic ideals of gentlemanly conduct are several centuries older and hence more deeply entrenched than is sometimes supposed; I hope also to have rescued some of the fairly commonplace and trite thoughts of some medieval authors from the oblivion to which they had been consigned by humanists, anxious to make their own fairly commonplace and trite thoughts seem deeply significant.

---

[133] Contrast the references to Roland and Oliver, to Gawain, to Horn and Ipomedon as models of good conduct in the Anglo-Norman *Urbain*, Parsons, 'Anglo-Norman Books', 411.

Transactions of the RHS 12 (2002), pp. 291–310 © 2002 Royal Historical Society
DOI: 10.1017/S0080440102000117   Printed in the United Kingdom

RANK, MANNERS AND DISPLAY: THE
GENTLEMANLY HOUSE, 1500–1750

By Nicholas Cooper

ABSTRACT. In the early modern period the amenities of the upper-class house provided for approved modes of polite behaviour, while the initial, piecemeal display of antique ornament in the sixteenth century expressed the status and the education of the governing class. In the seventeenth century a more classically correct architecture would spread in a climate of opinion in which approved behaviour was increasingly internalised and external display less favoured. The revolution of the seventeenth and eighteenth centuries was in superseding architectural languages that had lent themselves to the expression of status with a national style that did not.

THE last few years have seen the rapid growth of what may be called 'country house studies'. There has been an increasing synthesis of a number of discrete study areas – architectural history, studies of power structures, of estate management and the economics of landowning, of family relations and upper-class recruitment, of household evolution, of education and of the concept of privacy, and country house literature. However, the architectural, economic and social dimensions of the country house are perhaps better established than the ways in which houses express their owners' aspirations and education, and the image of themselves as members of a elite that owners wished to project. While the culture of the class evolved as the corollary of its wealth and responsibilities, its expression in the country house paralleled other displays of manners in advertising the possessors' education, refinement and social distinction. While the appearance of the house was the public expression of its owner's status and culture, its plan evolved in response to the evolving demands of privacy, to the changing needs of household, community and peer-group relations, and to its owner's wish for cultural self-expression in the house's furnishing and decoration. The house was not only the scene where ideals of gentility and manners could be realised: it provided an essential display of gentility in itself.

The earliest printed plan of an English house is not in any architectural publication but in Gervase Markham's *The English Husbandman*

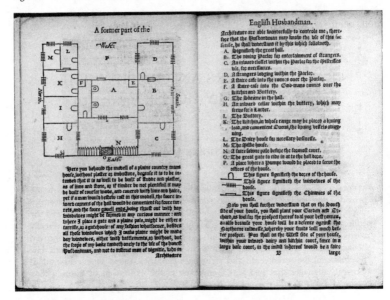

Plate 1 'A Plain Man's Country House', *from Gervase Markham,* The English Husbandman *(1613). Reproduced by permission of the British Library.*

of 1613 (Plate 1).[1] It shows a house with which his readers will have been very familiar and which remains widespread. One wing has polite rooms for entertaining, and the other, rooms for everyday functions and services; the layout is essentially hierarchical, and at the centre is a hall which mediates between the house's two ends. The rooms are those one would have found in any house of a rich yeoman farmer or of the lesser gentry, but in the accompanying text Markham carefully distinguishes between the two classes. He calls his plan 'the model of a plain man's country house', but describes in some detail how the outside might be embellished with turrets and decorative gables and other architectural ornament. 'But the scope of my book' he concludes 'tendeth only to the use of the honest husbandman, and not to instruct men of dignity.' It is clear that what is significant for Markham is that gentlemen's houses are distinguished visually from those of the lesser ranks of society, however prosperous individuals might be.

Architectural display based on rank is in any case well documented in the era when Markham was writing. Some Lancashire gentry have ornamental gables to their houses while their farming neighbours do

---

[1] Gervase Markham, *The English Husbandman* (1613), sig. A4–B.

not.[2] In areas of timber building, gentry houses are often marked by
an excess of structural ornament – itself a form of conspicuous consumption, and as such a display of rank that was the right and even
the duty of the governing class in a well-ordered society. On the
southern edge of the Cotswolds, the houses of village gentry have been
noted as having stone window mullions, while yeomen's houses have
mullions of wood.[3] The widespread occurrence of such examples
demonstrates the widespread acceptance of the principles of class-based
display that Markham implied.

Concurrent with the growth in the numbers of the governing classes
in sixteenth-century England was the increasing recognition on the part
of the members of these classes of their duties as well as of their powers.
Concern with the duties and privileges of rank and with recruitment
to its higher echelons was of course pervasive, and if in the course of
the seventeenth century social mobility came to be seen as less of a
threat to civil order, there was no lessening of concern for the manners,
behaviour and modes of display that were seen as appropriate to the
classes of society. And while medieval codes of courtliness were gradually
superseded by a humanist ethos of civility, ultimately civility would
itself become frozen as rules of politeness and good breeding. What the
owners of grand houses wished to express externally, and to realise in
the internal arrangements of these houses, was their membership of a
class that was distinguished by its behaviour, its growing responsibilities,
its increasing education and its members' awareness of belonging to a
recognisable and exclusive elite.

The desire for architectural display was not new. Under the Yorkists
and the first Tudors, architectural display had reached formidable levels
of excess. Such display implies recognition that political status demanded
visible expression, whether through squads of liveried retainers or
through the impressiveness of the magnate's seat of power, and was
justified by a sense of the magnificence appropriate to the great man.[4]
Both in England and abroad, the greatest houses of the late fifteenth
century were inspired by chivalry as they recalled the genuinely fortified
castle. But in the course of the sixteenth century, a growing concern
for the character of display followed from the changing character of
the ruling class itself – from one in which power was the consequence
of military might or feudal lordship, to one in which power comprised

---

[2] Royal Commission on the Historical Monuments of England, *Rural Houses of the
Lancashire Pennines, 1560–1760* (1985), 46–9.

[3] Linda Hall, 'Yeoman or Gentleman? Problems in Defining Social Status in Seventeenth-Century and Eighteenth-Century Gloucestershire', *Vernacular Architecture*, 22 (1991),
2–19.

[4] Simon Thurley, *The Royal Palaces of Tudor England* [hereafter Thurley] (New Haven
and London, 1993), 11–13.

the wise exercise of responsibilities and privileges bestowed by the state. Such exercise still deserved visible distinction, but rather a display of the qualities appropriate to the possessors of these powers. And in such a display, the introduction of classical ornament played a significant part.

'Antic' ornament was appearing on luxury goods, in interior decoration, on coats of arms and on tombs from the 1520s onward, in contexts where it was immediately associated with the individual concerned. In the furnishing and decoration of the house, its expense and its association with alien products and craftsmen linked it clearly with wealth, with comfort and hence with elite status.[5] It is tempting to see the English use of classical ornament on a par with other types of intellectual symbol: with the heraldry that proclaimed lineage and gentility, and with *imprese*, the personal and often cryptic devices expressive of private circumstances and values, the very reconditeness of which could be seen to increase their value. When classical architectural details first appear in England, they seem to be seen as cultural statements, not as architectural forms. Not infrequently, classical and more personal symbols are combined, as at Lyveden New Build where the triglyphs of a Doric frieze alternate with the instruments of the passion, placed there by the recusant owner, Sir Robert Tresham; or at Moreton Corbett in Shropshire where a riotous conjunction of classical, heraldic and personal emblems in part defies analysis.

With the demand for an educated ruling class, it is tempting to believe that classical ornament was seen as appropriate to the sophisticated ruler who could not only afford to keep up with fashion but had studied the exemplars of society, of public duty and statesmanship to be derived from Plato and Cicero, and modern writers such as Castiglione and Sir Thomas Elyott. No contemporary English statement explicitly identifies classical ornament with the house of the governor, but it is at least implicit in the introduction to John Shute's *First and Chief Groundes of Architecture* of 1554. Recounting how he had been sent to Italy by the duke of Northumberland to study architecture there, Shute describes how in doing so he was 'as it were stirred forward to do my dutie unto my Countrie wherein I live and am a member'.[6] The sentiment of duty to the commonwealth is conventional, but none the less real; the introduction of classical forms drawn from the fountainhead is here presented as a patriotic service. John Shute died with little to show from his visit, but sources of such ornament were coming to be available, both through the recruitment of foreign craftsmen – a very few Italians, more French – and through continental engravings and such writers

---

[5] Maurice Howard, *The Early Tudor Country House* (1987), 120–35; Thurley, 207–46.
[6] John Shute, *The First and Chief Groundes of Architecture* (1554), sig. Aiii.

as Alberti and the commentators on Vitruvius that only the rich and the educated could either afford or understand. When comparing the elaboration of late Elizabethan houses to the austere correctness of Palladian, it is perhaps difficult to see both as manifestations of an essentially classical culture. But on the portico of Hardwick Hall, of the 1590s, two lines from Ovid appear in contemporary graffiti, by which the house is compared to a heavenly palace,[7] and one must see Hardwick against a background where even grammar school boys will have known great chunks of Ovid by heart.

In the sixteenth century, polite attitudes towards the building craft were ambivalent. It is clear that too close a knowledge of the skills of the artisan was considered inappropriate for members of the upper classes.[8] Yet from the middle years of the century onwards, increasing numbers of the aristocracy were taking an active interest in the form and detail of their houses, and it is significant that those at the forefront of such interest were among the most highly educated and the most prominent of their time: men such as Sir John Thynne of Longleat, the most revolutionary house of its age; William Cecil, the creator of the barrel-vaulted, stone stair at Burghley, without English precedent or parallels and possibly imported ready-made; Cecil's brother-in-law the diplomatist Sir Thomas Hoby who placed a line of precocious, pedimented windows along the front of his brother's medieval house at Bisham; travellers such as Sir Robert Corbet of Moreton Corbet, whom Dugdale described as 'carried away by the affectionate delight of architecture';[9] and Sir Thomas Smith who owned six editions of Vitruvius. Smith's nephew described his uncle's house, built in the 1560s and among the most architecturally advanced of its day, as having been 'answerable to that honourable estate and calling wherein he served under the Queene's most excellent majesty'.[10] It was proper that the house of the governor should be suited to his place in the commonwealth, and that its ornament should satisfy the ideas he had derived from his learning. The Vitruvian rules for the hierarchical composition of the classical orders were a paradigm of other ideals of civic virtue and civil order, while for those who could master Pythagorean proportional systems, architecture was assimilated to the harmonies of the universe.

---

[7] 'Hic locus est quem si verbis audacia detur / haud timeam magni dixisse palatia caeli', Ovid, *Metamorphoses*, Bk 1 lines 175–6.

[8] Nicholas Cooper, *Houses of the Gentry, 1480–1680* [hereafter Cooper] (New Haven and London, 1999), 27–51.

[9] William Camden, *Britain ... Translated into English by Philemon Holland* (1637), 594.

[10] Quoted in Paul Drury, 'A Fayre House, Buylt by Sir Thomas Smith: The Development of Hill Hall, Essex, 1557–81', *British Archaeological Association Journal*, 146 (1983), 116.

Neither Vitruvius nor foreign renaissance models had any great impact on the overall form of the house until the seventeenth century; Gervase Markham's house is still traditional in its layout, with the hall mediating between the high and the low ends. Neverthless, the period between 1520 and 1580 saw a fundamental change in what upper-class houses looked like which was to have the most profound consequences for architectural development thereafter. The late medieval house was essentially an accretive one, which expressed externally the relative importance of each of its parts. By 1580 the most modern upper-class house was wholly symmetrical, and its internal arrangements undetectable by the outside viewer. The reason for this repudiation of external distinctions was not in itself stylistic, but rather lay in the image of its owner and of a changing household community that the house was intended to project. The late medieval household had been one of structured grades of service and dependency, and it may seem paradoxical that the rapid decline of external marks of status in the appearance of the house should coincide with Tudor sumptuary legislation and with other attempts to define the privileges of different ranks of society. But whereas the house had once expressed by its disparate parts the structure of the community it served, the whole building was now coming to express the status and cultivation of its owner in a way comparable to the use of classical ornament. The layout of the medieval, hierachical house can be read from the outside; the undifferentiated house could not be. The solution to this paradox is another paradox: that the symmetrical, undifferentiated house can be seen as expressing the cultivation of its owner by making a public display of privacy and exclusivity. And in a society that made extensive use of symbolic languages, the integrated, visually balanced house can itself be seen as a species of device, a symbol of harmony. External marks of differentiation could be sacrificed for the sake of an alternative image of gentility.

By the achievement of symmetry and the abandonment of the principal of hierarchical distinction as a basis for design, the appearance of the house could now be determined by purely formal and archi-tectural considerations. And while the requirements of knowledgeable owners were increasing, the craft-based expertise of masons was declin-ing with the collapse of gothic church building, further contributing to a shift in craftsman–client relationships, while novel requirements both in the layout and in the ornament of the house made demands on craftsmanship that traditionally trained workmen were less able to supply. The example of prominent builders, and Vitruvian claims for the standing of architecture that linked it expressly with mathematics and the classics rather than being the province merely of the artisan, were increasingly licensing a knowledge of it on the part of a class whose education was advancing in both areas. The huge amount of new house building from the middle years of the sixteenth century – remarked on by contemporaries and clear in any analysis – was the result of the rapid increase in the numbers and wealth of the gentry class, but the inevitable prominence of these new houses itself drew attention to them, and must in itself have provoked thought about the form and appearance of the house on the part of a competitive and increasingly educated group. A further incentive for a reconsideration of the form of the house was the need to accommodate rooms and relationships between social spaces that were themselves the consequence of evolving manners.

Within the house, evolving civility showed itself in the desire for greater privacy and in the need for more rooms – in other words, in the provision of rooms with more specialist uses, and in developments in the plan that made for a clearer distinction betwen private and public spheres.[11] Such distinction was in any case explicitly prescribed by Vitruvius.[12] In a sample of some 200 sixteenth- and seventeenth-century inventories, Figure 1 shows the first occurrence of some of these rooms and, equally important ly, of other cultural goods such as books and pictures. The sample is not large enough to take account of significant regional differences, or those of wealth within the ranks of the upper classes, but sixteenth-century innovations that it shows include the progressive removal of beds from rooms of entertainment, and the appearance of rooms described as studies. In the seventeenth century the process continues, and both great chamber and dining parlour are superseded by dining rooms, so called, as names change to correspond to changing functions. The different functions of chambers would themselves become distinguished and their occupants' privacy further provided for, with the provision in the seven teenth century of separate dressing rooms.

The figure does not show how the decline of the hall both as a functional and as a symbolic space made it the more acceptable to reduce its height to a single storey only and to place chambers – most frequently the great chamber, the principal room of polite entertainment – above it, in order to meet the demands of entertainment and hospitality by which the growing numbers of the gentry consolidated their position and their alliances. Nor does it show the process whereby the hall itself would become purely a room for formal entrance into the house or a saloon for the polite entertainment of visitors of equal rank with the owner, while servants' eating would be removed into a separate servants' hall. Indeed, in some seventeenth-century great houses there would be separate halls for upper and lower servants.

[11] Cooper, 273–316.
[12] Vitruvius, *Ten Books on Architecture*, Bk 6, ch. 5.

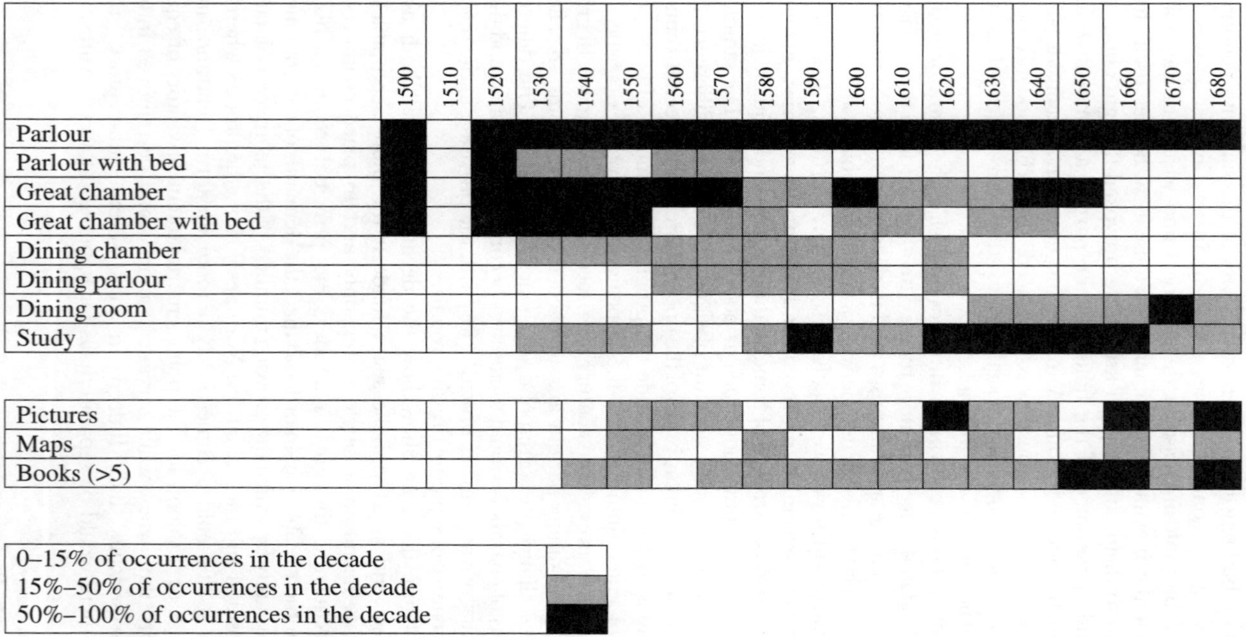

	1500	1510	1520	1530	1540	1550	1560	1570	1580	1590	1600	1610	1620	1630	1640	1650	1660	1670	1680
Parlour																			
Parlour with bed																			
Great chamber																			
Great chamber with bed																			
Dining chamber																			
Dining parlour																			
Dining room																			
Study																			

Pictures																			
Maps																			
Books (>5)																			

0–15% of occurrences in the decade
15%–50% of occurrences in the decade
50%–100% of occurrences in the decade

Figure 1 Selected entries in 200 upper-class inventories, 1500–1680

Until well into the seventeenth century the upper-class house still retained essentially the traditional, hierarchical layout shown by Gervase Markham, its appearance regularised almost as a species of intellectual conceit, enhanced by classical detail that expresses the credentials of its owner, and its plan progressively elaborated by comparable demands for more specialised and private space. However, demands for additional rooms and novel functional relationships were difficult to meet within the layout and the form of the traditional, hierarchical plan. The increase in rooms for entertainment could be met by building upward, as at Chatsworth, Worksop and Hardwick where the grandest rooms were on the second floor. The elaboration of the plan that was the result of these demands for more specialised spaces had been among the reasons for such vast, sprawling, late Elizabethan and Jacobean prodigy houses as Burghley, Holdenby, Theobalds, Hatfield and Audley End. These aristocratic houses retained tall, great halls; the wealth and status of their builders led them to perpetuate a form that had a traditional association with lordship, but the great hall was ceasing to be useful even as a symbol. The fact that after Audley End there were no more of these monstrous houses was not only because of their ruinous cost and because in inflating the traditional, hierarchical house to so huge a size it had expanded beyond what was practical; two of the greatest, Theobalds, Holdenby and half of Audley End were pulled down less than a century after they were built. Behind these demolitions lay not only economics and the obsolescence of the layout; underlying them also was an evolving attitude to display. Both the layout and the appearance of the house continued to reflect the need for accommodation commensurate with the status, manners and way of life of the owner and for a house that appeared suitable to his rank; however, both the form and appearance of the house would change with a decline of the old-fashioned, hierarchical household of graded ranks of service, and with changes in the sense of what it was right to display.

The revolution of the seventeenth century was the appearance of novel, more compact forms of plan, and of simple silhouettes that made a total contrast with the extravagant outlines that had characterised the most ostentatious of Jacobean houses. Although the expense of these prodigy houses was one reason for their abandonment, and the fact that there were no longer statesmen like the Cecils to build them was another, it is clear that from the 1620s there was a change in attitudes away from the demands of Aristotelian magnificence, towards a greater reticence. Whereas Serlio in the mid-sixteenth century would praise 'a middle-class person who is generous in spirit and who spends most of his money on his house',[13] Henry Peacham in 1622 would quote

[13] Myra Nan Rosenfeld, *Serlio on Domestic Architecture* (Mineola, 1996), 50.

with approval Macchiavelli on Cosimo de Medici, whose 'buildings ... were princely ... yet so governed by wisdom that he never excelled the bounds of civil modesty'.[14] While Hatton and Burghley had commiserated with each other about the huge sums they were both spending on their houses, Fuller's injunction of the 1650s is well known – that it was better to build a house that was too small for a day than one too large for a year.

The social credentials of the house with an unconventional hall had already been established in the aristocratic lodge, essentially a house for polite recreation away from the large and structured household of the principal seat. The most significant model for the new, compact house was, however, in the polite houses of London, the acknowledged centre of fashion and civility. London households were very different from those of the country estate, where the household was larger and where there was a constant fluidity at its edges where it interacted with the broader community. The upper-class, London house was less concerned with community – which did not exist in the sense of the rural estate – and more concerned with polite entertainment. Here, plan forms had already been developed that accommodated different patterns of social behaviour and a more sharply polarised household than that which had been accommodated by the hierarchical layout of the country house. The town house that made the most of a constricted site by having a plan of two rooms deep and in which the hall was no longer at the centre of a hierarchical layout provided a model for a house with a deep, rectangular plan without wings, a form that could be readily transplanted from the town to the suburbs and then to the country beyond.[15] The rapid growth in the numbers of the upper classes frequenting the capital, which led James and Charles I to issue increasingly frantic and largely futile proclamations ordering their return to their estates and duties in the provinces, had exposed ever more of them to the allurements of the City and to the architectural innovations of the inner suburbs – to the conveniences, both social and physical, of the compact, rectangular house that was being evolved there.[16] And in admiring aspects of London houses and in due course reproducing them in the countryside, those who did so would adopt the setting for novel modes of elite behaviour.

The London house provided a formula which could be expanded to almost any size. The deep, compact plan is known to architectural historians as a 'double pile', a term derived from Sir Roger Pratt who around 1660 summed up its practical advantages as economy and regularity.[17] Pratt's arguments in its favour have sometimes been taken as explaining how it originated; that is not the case, but they were a powerful recommendation once London had established its acceptability for the houses of the upper classes. Aesthetically, too, the rectangular plan had much to recommend it. Already by 1580 a form of house had emerged that had a strictly symmetrical façade, but whereas the emergence of the symmetrical house may have been prompted by symbolism, once achieved, regularity had rapidly become a basic design formula, capable of almost infinite variation. Symmetry was a principle as easy to grasp as a rectangular plan. By the end of the seventeenth century, Roger North could write that 'uniformity ... is what all expect to find, and blame if not observed ... I add that the most knowing enjoys no more.'[18]

In style as well as in planning these innovations were metropolitan. From the confusion of styles that Sir John Summerson so well named 'artisan mannerism' there was emerging by the 1630s, under the influence of Inigo Jones and of the Commission on New Buildings of which Jones was a member, a plainer style of house building that was characterised by hipped roofs, by simple, repetitive decorative elements or else which lacked any ornament at all. These stylistic characteristics would gradually spread from London and the home counties to become perhaps the first national style of architecture since the middle ages, and by their association with the new plan forms evolving at the same time and in the same area, new layouts and the new building style would spread together.

Among these houses is John Aubrey's house, Easton Piers (Plate 2), probably built in the late 1650s, and perhaps the first English house to have been described as a villa, a term and a concept familiar to contemporaries as the ancient Roman house of cultivated retirement.[19] The taste for architectural simplicity is an aspect of a broader and deeper change in the mental climate of the seventeenth century. Underpinning the evident extravagance of the Elizabethan prodigy houses had been a humanist ideal that laid stress on the nobility of public service and that justified a display of magnificence as the duty of the suitably qualified public servant. The notion would persist, but it was also in profound contrast to a very different notion of virtue that would develop in the course of the seventeenth century and which also found its inspiration in the classics: the idea that virtue resided not in

[17] R, T, Gunther, *The Architecture of Sir Roger Pratt* (Oxford, 1928), 24.

[18] Roger North, *Of Building: Roger North's Writing on Architecture* [hereafter North], ed. Howard Colvin and John Newman (Oxford, 1981), 149.

[19] Oxford, Bodleian Library, MS Aubrey 17f.2.

Plate 2 John Aubrey's house at Easton Piers in Wiltshire. Bodleian Library, University of Oxford, MS Aubrey 17 f.5r.

a wise engagement with the world but in a contemplative withdrawal from it, and that the vanity of display and the turmoil of public affairs were a detraction from the inner peace whose attainment was the proper goal of the wise man. Abraham Cowley put it explicitly: for him the most enviable class of people was

> the men placed in the Countrey by their Fortune above an High-Constable, and yet beneath the trouble of a Justice of the Peace, in a moderate plenty ... and with so much knowledge and love of Piety and Philosophy (that is of the study of God's Laws, and of his Creatures) as may afford him matter enough never to be Idle without Business, and never to be Melancholy though without Sin or Vanity.[20]

There is any amount of literary and anecdotal evidence for this greater taste for retirement. Take, for instance, the great earl of Arundel, in the 1630s increasingly preferring what he called his 'darling cottage' at Albury to the life of town or even that of his lodge at Highgate, and whose grandson Charles, probably in the 1650s, went still further to build at the Deepdene what John Aubrey called 'his cottage of retirement, where in the troublesome Times, he withdrew from this wicked World, and enjoy'd himself here, where he had only one Floor, his

[20] Abraham Cowley, *Essays and Other Prose Writings* [hereafter Cowley], ed. A. B. Gough (1915), 121.

little Dining Room, a Kitchen, a Chapel and a Laboratory'.[21] Hollar's elegiac engravings of Albury and the country around capture the mood perfectly.[22]

Just as the involvement in public affairs advocated in the previous century is in the clearest possible contrast to the philosophy of withdrawal advocated by Cowley, there is an equally obvious difference between the well-known 'country house' poems of the early seventeenth century and the poetry of retirement and privacy that rapidly grew in popularity from the second quarter of the century onwards. Poems such as Jonson's *Penshurst* had invoked a stratified, hierarchical and beneficent community of lords and dependants which is idealised and backward-looking in defiance of all the trends of the times. But Jonson also translated Martial's *Epigram 47* of his Tenth Book – a text which has been described as 'the key poem of English literary classicism'.[23] Jonson's translation begins

> The things that make the happier life, are these,
> Most pleasant Martial; Substance got with ease,
> Not labour'd for, but left thee by thy sire;
> A soyle not barren; a continewall fire;
> Never at Law; seldom in office gown'd;
> A quiet mind; free powers; and body sound;
> A wise simplicity; freindes alike-stated;
> Thy table without art, and easy-rated.

In other words, a life of modest retirement on ancestral acres.

Perhaps the clearest illustration of the new taste is the extraordinary outburst of English translations of the works of the most important of classical writers on the theme of retirement, virtually from a standing start. Table 1 shows some of these, while retirement themes occur with increasing frequency in original poetry.[24] These include a Horatian idealisation of the simple husbandman, a neo-Stoic idealisation of a Christian disengagement from the world, an increasingly naturalistic description of the real countryside in place of the artificial conventions of Elizabethan pastoral poetry and the contemplation of the ordered world of nature as a reflection of the Divine purpose, evolving with the Restoration into an Epicurean enjoyment of the delights of country life for their own sake.

One may associate this taste for retirement with an increasing interest in local topography, with a growing personal involvement by landowners

---

[21] John Aubrey, *Brief Lives*, ed. Oliver Lawson Dick (1949), lxxviii.
[22] Repr. in John Harris, *The Artist and the Country House* (1979), 30–1.
[23] Maren-Sofie Rostvig, *The Happy Man: Studies in the Metamorphoses of a Classical Ideal, 1600–1700* [hereafter Rostvig] (Oslo, 1954), 82.
[24] The table derives from Rostvig.

Decade	Horace (13)	Virgil (12)	Martial (13)	Claudian (5)
1620	1621 John Ashmore 1625 Thomas Hawkins	1620 J. Brinsley 1628 William Lisle 1628 Thomas May	16xx Jonson† 1621 John Ashmore† 1629 Thomas May	1629 Sir John Beaumont
1630	1631 *Hawkins* 1635 *Hawkins* 1637 Wye Saltonstall 1638 *Hawkins* 1638 Henry Rider	1633 *Brinsley* 1634 John Biddle	1633 Abraham Cowley† 1635 *Cowley†* 1638 Thomas Randolph†	1638 Thomas Randolph
1640	1649 John Smith	1649 John Ogilby	1648 Mildmay Fane†	1648 Mildmay Fane
1650	1652 Richard Fanshaw 1653 Holyday	1650 *Ogilby* 1654 *Ogilby*	1656 R. Fletcher	
1660	1666 A. Brome	1665 *Ogilby* 1668 *Ogilby*	1661 Owen Felltham†	1663 Abraham Cowley
1670				1678 Henry Vaughan
1680	1684 Thomas Creech 1684 John Harington	1684 *Ogilby*	1689 Thomas Cotton† 1689 Henry Killigrew	
1690		1697 Dryden	1691 Thomas Heyrick† 1695 *Killigrew*	

Table 1 *English translations of Horace, Virgil (Eclogues and/or Georgics), Martial and Claudian, 1620–1700.*
†Translations of Martial: Bk x, *Epigram 47*. New editions in italics.

in estate management and improvement, with the taste for gardening, and in painting, with the growing taste for actual landscape and the depiction of real houses in their setting. These varied concerns can be explicity linked. William Habington, one of the most severely moral of the neo-Stoic poets, recommended that one should make oneself expert in what he called 'home cosmography' rather than reading about the wider world, and himself wrote the first history of Worcestershire, his native county.[25] John Evelyn included a chapter on the villa (now lost) in his great unpublished work on gardening, *Elysium Britanniae*. Roger North, writing of the ideal house in around 1690, noted that 'it is no unseemly object to an English gentleman to see his servants and buissness passing at ordinary times'.[26] It is certainly tempting to see a connection between such mental attitudes and the growing acceptance of an architecture that was more restrained than that of earlier generations, and of houses which, if not actually smaller than their predecessors of a generation before, appeared from their compact outline to be so. Of houses, in fact, that were less ostentatious. To quote Cowley again: he writes 'I never had any desire so strong ... that I might be master at last of a small house and a large garden, and there dedicate the remainder of my life only to them and the study of Nature.'[27] Elsewhere he is explicit about what he has in mind: not 'a stately Palace, nor guilt rooms, or the costliest sorts of Tapestry; but a convenient brick house, with decent Wainscot, and pretty Forest-work hangings',[28] together with, he says, an income of £500 a year which would have placed him comfortably within the ranks of the gentry class.

Cowley has a clear picture in his mind of the kind of house that he wants: it is one like John Aubrey's. A type of house had emerged and was spreading from the London area that would satisfy the ethos of the age as well as meeting the exigencies of a time that was not propitious for extravagant building. The plain, rectangular house, refined by successive architectural fashions, would be the accepted model for the gentry house for the next hundred and fifty years. By introducing into the layout new spatial and functional relationships, and in rejecting the ancient, hierarchical sequence of low end and high end, it opened up new possibilities of planning. However, the form did not provide a wholly satisfactory model for the houses of men of higher rank. The appearance of the house had been in a sense democratised by the plain, rectangular model. Though at an earlier date the symbolism of

[25] William Habington, *Observations upon History* (1641), quoted in Rostvig, 126.
[26] North, 129.
[27] Cowley, 121.
[28] Cowley, 183.

heraldry and classical ornament had identified its owner with membership of an elite, the plain house without external decoration no
longer distinguished its occupant save by its size and setting, and in the
later seventeenth century it becomes easier to find explicit demands for
architectural display suitable to rank. Thus Lord Wentworth considered
that Sir William Savile's houses were 'not suitable for [his] quality';[29]
William Woolley condemned the house of Godfrey Clerk of Chilcot as
'not equal to his estate and quality, being Knight of the County',[30]
while Celia Fiennes found that at Shuckburgh 'in general all things
were very well as any private Gentleman has whatever'.[31] By implication,
the nobleman's house should be further distinguished.

Around 1660 Roger Pratt had written that 'as there are three sorts
of persons for whom houses are built of any consideration, viz.
gentlemen, noblemen and princes, so are there so many kinds of
buildings, which are to be formed according to the usual estates of men
of such condition'.[32] Pratt's prescriptions were largely theoretical, but
they included progressively richer architectural decoration. The political
stability that followed the settlements of 1660 and 1688 was the
background to a new period of architectural extravagance that climaxed
in the grand gestures of the baroque, Chatsworth, Castle Howard and
Blenheim. At the end of the century, Roger North condemned Melton
Constable, one of the largest houses of the rectangular, hipped-roof
type, as 'suburbian'. North considered its form inappropriate as the
country seat of a baronet who was one of the largest landowners in the
county. The earl of Carlisle, Castle Howard's builder, copied into his
account book a passage from Leoni's translation of Palladio: 'an
Architecte must chiefly observe, what Vitruvius recommends ... that
when he builds for persons of quality, and more particularly those that
are in public employment, he must Build their Palaces with Portico's,
Galleries and large stately Halls richly adorn'd'.[33] In strong contrast to
the mid-century poems of retirement are verses such as Thomas
Shipman's lines on Belvoir of 1679 which strike a new note in the
approval of aristocratic consumption. 'See the rich furniture in all the
rooms ! / Floors spread with carpets, weaved in Turkey looms ! / Beds
soft, and costly, they may vie / With those whereon luxurious Asian
princes lie!'[34] The epitaph no less than the figures themselves on John

[29] Quoted in J. T. Cliffe, *The Yorkshire Gentry from the Reformation to the Civil War* (1969),
103.
[30] William Woolley, *William Woolley's History of Derbyshire*, ed. C. Glover and P. Riden,
Derbyshire Record Society VI (1981), 137.
[31] Celia Fiennes, *The Journal of Celia Fiennes*, ed. Christopher Morris (1947), 117.
[32] Gunther, *The Architecture of Sir Roger Pratt*, 29.
[33] Charles Saumarez Smith, *The Building of Castle Howard* (1990), 26.
[34] Alastair Fowler, *The Country House Poem* (Edinburgh 1994), 359.

Nost's monument to the earl of Bristol strikes precisely the approved
Epicurean note of retirement combined with distinction:

> He was naturally inclined to avoid the hurry of a public life,
>   yet careful to keep up the port of his quality;
>   was willing to be at ease, yet scorned obscurity:
> and therefore never made his retirement a pretence to draw
> himself within a narrower compass, or to shun such expense
>   as charity, hospitality, and his honour called for.[35]

Yet the baroque in England was always a half-hearted affair by
comparison with Italy, Germany or France. The earl of Shaftesbury
had in mind baroque extravagances when early in the new century he
condemned 'edifices and gardens unknown to our ancestors and unnat-
ural to such a state and climate as Great Britain' and called them 'the
sacrifices made to wrong pride and ignorant self-esteem by one whose
inward character must necessarily ... become as mean and ignorant as
his outward behaviour insolent and intolerable'.[36] Shaftesbury, pupil of
Locke and philosopher of the Revolution of 1688, made express
connections between patriotism, the aristocratic principle, reason, morality and aesthetics. Properly ordered, houses and their surroundings
were models of a higher mind set, connecting appropriate architectural
display to both morality and manners. Though worked out by Shaftesbury, such an equation of aesthetics, morals and politeness was of
course long established. The language of earlier writers is loaded with
terms of moral opprobrium. Evelyn had written that 'it is from the
asymmetrie of our buildings, want of decorum and proportion in our
Houses, that the irregularity of our humours and affections may be
shrewdly discern'd'.[37] The themes of retirement that characterised the
poetry of the mid-seventeenth century are repeated by Pope, and in
the Palladian revival of the early eighteenth century and the widespread
adoption of the villa model for the country house one can see a parallel
revival and reinforcement of architectural restraint. In Shaftesbury such
restraint is allied with manners and with the proper political interests
of the landed order.

In the seventeenth century the image of the landed elite was being
underpinned in a variety of ways. Pride of possession, and consciousness of place in the local community, underlies the origins in the mid-
seventeenth century of written county histories, concerned largely with

---

[35] John Hutchins, *The History and Antiquities of the County of Dorset* (1774), ii, 381; Royal
Commission on the Historical Monuments of England, *West Dorset* (1952), plates 169–72.
[36] Anthony Ashley Cooper, 3rd earl of Shaftesbury, *Characteristics of Men, Manners,
Opinions, Times*, ed. Lawrence E. Klein (Cambridge, 1999), 412.
[37] John Evelyn, *A Parallel of Architecture, both Ancient and Modern, by Roland Freart de Chambray*
(1664), sig. b.(1).

celebrating the lineage and confirming the standing of leading families. The increasing inclusion of views of houses in published books, culminating with Jan Kip and Leonard Knyff's great national conspectus of 1707, are a visual confirmation of the centrality of the house to the estate, not only in a physical but in an ideological sense. Significantly, the title of their work is *Britannia Illustrata*; the nation is depicted in terms of the architectural decorum of its political leaders – a view which Shaftesbury would have applauded. Engravings of houses continued to be an integral element of published county histories throughout the eighteenth century, but in 1715 appeared the first volume of what was for England a new kind of architectural publication, Colin Campbell's *Vitruvius Britannicus*. Campbell's moral condemnation of un-English baroque echoed Evelyn and Shaftesbury in his evocation of the pathetic fallacy: 'How affected and licentious are the Works of Bernini and Fontana?' he wrote; 'How wildly extravagant are the Designs of Boromini, who has endeavoured to debauch Mankind.'[38] And whereas earlier views had shown houses in their settings, *Vitruvius Britannicus* comprised plans and elevations – purely architectural representations that presupposed an ability and a willingness to understand this kind of formalised representation on the part of a lay public.

The renewed building boom of the late seventeenth century had already seen the emergence of a group of individuals best described as gentleman designers – Hooke, May, North, Pratt, Samwell, Talman, Vanburgh himself, Winde and Wren. In the sixteenth century, the intellectual credentials of architecture had prevented its dismissal as the exclusive province of the artisan but at the same time had created a gulf between theory and practice. Early in the seventeenth century, Inigo Jones's Baconian understanding of both had conformed to the scientific spirit of the time, while his role as a royal arbiter of taste had done much to establish the social credentials of his art. In the mid-century, exiles such as Pratt and Evelyn were acquiring architectural connoisseurship on their foreign travels, while those who retired to their estates at home were increasingly focused on their improvement. By its end, knowledge of architecture, of the theory of the classical orders, of a range of modern exemplars and enough practical knowledge to be able to produce finished designs that could be realised on the ground, was the province of a number of men of education, gentry by birth, with no background in the building trades. And just as the gentlemanly status of the early members of the Royal Society had given credibility to their researches, the architectural involvement of such men – including members of the Society itself – not only gave authority to their own work but must itself have enhanced the standing of

[38] Colin Campbell, *Vitruvius Britannicus, or, The British Architect* (1717), I, sig. B.

architecture and increased the demands for gentlemanly houses from those who, if they lacked such extensive knowledge themselves, were concerned that the architecture of their houses should do them justice.[39]

Vitruvius Britannicus was the primary text of neo-Palladian formalism, the codification of architectural correctness which was the development of a concern for classicism that had begun in the eclectic architectural symbolism of the sixteenth century. The subscription lists of *Vitruvius Britannicus* and of other folios include practising craftsmen as well as connoisseurs and the owners of houses illustrated, and the eighteenth century saw a host of cheaper books aimed at the practising artisan. The original reason for the adoption of classicism as a language of culture has gone, to be succeeded by pattern books that make architectural good manners available to anyone whose joiner had William Halfpenny's or Batty Langley's books in his tool bag.[40]

Perhaps this marks a further parallel between architectural style and manners. The way in which artisans' pattern books like these diffused the Palladian rules is not unlike the way in which new fashions too were welcomed – the tendency that the diarist John Byng would deplore towards the end of the century when in his travels he would see country milkmaids aping West-End fashions. And no doubt the easy and universal availability of superficial architectural correctness was in part, at least, responsible for the snobbishness of Lord Chesterfield's recommendation to his son, in Italy in 1749:

> If you read about one-third of Palladio's Book of Architecture, with some skilful person, and then, with that person, examine the best buildings by those rules ... you may soon be acquainted with the considerable parts of Civil Architecture; and as for the mechanical parts of it, leave them to masons, bricklayers, and Lord Burlington, who has, to a certain extent, lessened himself by knowing them too well.[41]

Pattern books confirmed the democratisatisation of architecture that had initially been made possible by the simpler, architectural styles of the seventeenth century; and with the codification of architectural rules, architectural expertise would become increasingly the province of the professional rather than of the connoisseur.

But Chesterfield himself used architecture as a metaphor of good manners. Reminding his son of the plainness of the Tuscan order, he

---

[39] See Steven Shapin, *A Social History of Truth: Civility and Science in Seventeenth-Century England* (Chicago, 1994).
[40] Peter Borsay, *The English Urban Renaissance* (Oxford, 1989), 41–59; Eileen Harris, *English Architectural Books and Writers, 1556–1775* (Cambridge, 1990), 32–7.
[41] *Letters of Philip, Earl of Chesterfield*, ed. John Bradshaw (1892), I, 259.

went on

> If upon the solid Tuscan foundation, the Doric, the Ionic, and the
> Corinthian Orders rise gradually with all their beauty, proportions
> and ornaments, the fabric seizes the most incurious eye, and stops
> the most careless passenger ... Just so it will fair with your little
> fabric, which at present, I fear, has more of the Tuscan than of the
> Corinthian Order ... The several parts which must compose this
> new front, are elegant, easy, natural, superior good breeding; and
> engaging address; genteel motions; an insinuating softness in your
> looks, words and actions; a spruce, lively air, fashionable dress; and
> all the glitter that a young fellow should have.[42]

Just as civility itself began as morality and tended in time to lose its
ideological force and become frozen as rules of behaviour and etiquette,
so creative styles can begin as experiment or inspiration and finish up
as a set of rules. In the achievement between the sixteenth and
eighteenth centuries of a universal classicism, one may perhaps see this
happening. Over the space of two hundred and fifty years, architectural
expression has evolved from ideology to manners; from the Vitruvian
man, the measure of the Renaissance scholars' universe, into Lord
Chesterfield's model of formal correctness.

[42] *Ibid.*, 273.

Transactions of the RHS 12 (2002), pp. 311–31 © 2002 Royal Historical Society
DOI: 10.1017/S0080440102000129   Printed in the United Kingdom

THE USES OF EIGHTEENTH-CENTURY POLITENESS

By Paul Langford

ABSTRACT. Politeness is a 'key word' for historians of eighteenth-century Britain. It implied a distinguishing vision of wider social concerns and less constricted cultural tastes than was attributed to earlier ages. What part it played in identifiable shifts of behaviour is harder to judge. Among people who served the growing commercial and professional needs of the day, its influence seems well attested. More problematic was its impact on plebeian life. Yet even here, there is evidence to suggest some degree of 'polishing' in line with contemporary expectations, to the extent that politeness itself ceased to describe social aspirations and became synonymous with basic standards of civil behaviour.

A THOUGHT that must occur to all of us in these proceedings is that the word with which we are most concerned is a difficult one to pin down. This is partly because 'politeness' as we use it today has such a bland superficiality about it. Not only is this true of common, everyday usage. It is equally true of much of the formal study of human manners. Social anthropologists have admittedly generated a body of jargon on the subject, including such acronyms as MPs (not Members of Parliament, but Model Persons), and FTAs (Face Threatening Actions), and requiring the ranking of priorities such as D, P and R (Social Distance, Social Power and Rating of Imposition).[1] But methodology aside, even they employ 'politeness' as an unproblematic term connoting the deference which individuals display when confronting other individuals in everyday situations.

Here eighteenth-century historians encounter a difficulty. For us 'politeness' has more significance. It is what might be considered, to employ Raymond Williams's term, a key word, with a meaning and implications that open doors into the mentality of a period.[2] This is less true, if true at all, for other periods. Historians more generally

[1] Penelope Brown and Stephen C. Levinson, *Politeness: Some Universals in Language Usage* (Cambridge, 1994).
[2] *Keywords: A Vocabulary of Culture and Society* (rev. edn, 1983). Williams did not use 'polite' or 'politeness' though his introductory example of a key-word, 'sentimental', is supported by a text which happens to include the word 'polite'.

might well regard 'polite' as a synonym for terms such as 'civil', 'courteous', 'well-mannered' and so on. For those of us seeking to navigate the polite eighteenth century, such semantic assimilation would be confusing and misleading.

As a term of art, politeness in its eighteenth-century sense has two connotations of particular relevance to us here. One might be called the 'Spectator' mode, to be found famously in Addison and Steele, but widely imitated elsewhere, in all kinds of didactic literature, and in the works of fiction which sought both to mirror and to mould contemporary manners. The appeal of the politeness thus paraded, described, characterised, applauded but rarely very precisely defined was its enabling capacity, permitting people who lacked the traditional components of social status – inherited rank, formal education and a place in the political hierarchy – to achieve it by adopting a looser, supposedly more 'natural' code of behaviour. (It also had implications for the relative roles of men and women, which have given rise to a flourishing historical literature, but here my concern is with social status rather than gender.)[3] The second might be called the 'Shaftesbury' mode, after the third earl of Shaftesbury, whose writings were once the preserve of philosophers but are nowadays of wider interest to those pursuing cultural studies.[4] Shaftesbury was read and imitated by enlightened authors who found in his work notions of virtue and taste that challenged the assumptions of an older intellectual order, and in principle made polite culture open to all suitably enquiring minds.

In both of these respects the social effects were potentially wide-ranging, and capable of combining with other forces for change, political as well as economic. The new money and new mobility that benefited by the emergence after 1688 of a parliamentary polity could also be viewed as being legitimised by the manners and tastes of a similarly inclusive politeness. Moreover, this lowering of barriers between the elite and numbers of its inferiors was envisaged as proceeding without subverting social stability and authority.

We need to be aware, though, that politeness also had other functions which might conflict with these attractively enhancing missions. In fact in origin it almost certainly had a less consensual purpose. Its appeal, after all, lay in the desire of relatively well-placed people to enable, enfranchise or empower only themselves. The politesse of the turn of the seventeenth and eighteenth centuries helped provide a means of

---

[3] Notable contributions to the debate include: Larry Klein, 'Gender, Conversation and the Public Sphere in Early Eighteenth-Century England', in *Textuality and Sexuality: Reading Theories and Practices*, ed. J. Still and M. Worton (Manchester, 1993); P. Carter, *Men and the Emergence of Polite Society in Britain 1660–1800* (2001); M. Cohen, *Fashioning Masculinity: National Identity and Language in the Eighteenth Century* (1996).

[4] Larry Klein, *Shaftesbury and the Culture of Politeness* (Cambridge, 1984).

escape on the part of the well-born from the trammels of the even better-born. Much has been made of its function in France in validating an aristocratic revolt against the social stranglehold of the French court. This was arguably the first and not the least damaging of all revolts against the monarchy of the Bourbons, which gave to Paris rather than Versailles the role of setting 'the tone in manners'.[5] The analysis can be plausibly carried over to England. The early Hanoverian court even lost its power to inflict social oblivion on the nobility. The famous story of the duchess of Queensberry's insulting defiance when forbidden to attend court by George II struck even a French observer as an astonishing example of aristocratic emancipation.[6] On the other hand under George III royalty managed a successful rearguard action when it reasserted its role as the provider of a much-valued if somewhat colourless form of approved status. Polite society did not depend on monarchy in the late eighteenth century, but it did grant the king and queen the right of conferring social respectability through its levees, formal festivities and mourning regimes.

In any case the revolt against the court was only one and by no means the most appealing cause for which politeness could be hoisted as a banner calling the less than deprived to arms. The formality against which many protested most vociferously was not so much that of the court as that of the great aristocratic families who mimicked the monarchy with their own lesser but elaborate hierarchies. The traditions that in the early eighteenth century still had the sons of the gentry serving their apprenticeship with blue-blooded cousins and neighbours, still had younger sons and their families enmeshed in the household arrangements of their elders, still found the great families with regional hegemonies enfolding layers of county society in their embrace, were perhaps the most objectionable of all. Arguably it was the dependants and semi-dependants of the higher nobility who might benefit most from Spectator-like informality. It is often said that the parliamentary politics of the eighteenth century represented a modest empowerment of the younger sons of aristocratic England. Something of the same might be said of what happened in polite society.

In all social warfare of this kind caricature versions of the enemy are essential. Who provided them mattered little but in England one of the most quoted examples was presented by the Percy family, who for decades beyond their own lives offered a pattern of oppressive gentility that stood for an older, decaying and finally ruined order. The tenth earl of Northumberland, who died in 1668, was described by Clarendon

[5] Nicole Castan, 'The Public and the Private', in *A History of Private Life*, III: *Passions of the Renaissance*, ed. Roger Chartier (Cambridge, MA, 1989), 424.

[6] Madam du Bocage, *Letters concerning England, Holland and Italy* (2 vols., 1770), I 62.

as the 'proudest man alive'.[7] His widow, who died in 1705, left behind her a reputation for haughtiness on a scale impressive even for ladies of her rank. Her grandson the sixth duke of Somerset, who married the last heiress of the Percies, passed into history as the 'Proud Duke'. Between them this trio generated an extraordinary wealth of anecdotes about their brutal treatment of less fortunate members of their own families and many others. The brutality concerned what might seem rather trivial matters. The sufferings of gentlemen kept waiting for hours by a duke, of ladies not permitted to sit until requested to do so by a countess, or of a duchess prohibited from kissing her husband without being invited, do not tug at the heartstrings of the reader today but their currency suggests something of their symbolic significance at the time.[8]   Whether very much of it was true, we cannot know, of course. Its function was to help validate and justify a social adjustment taking place in aristocratic families throughout the land. The beneficiaries doubtless subscribed to the Addisonian orthodoxy, but they are unlikely to have had much concern with the application of the creed behind their own cousinhood. It was sufficient that pride and Percy went together as identifiable enemies in a rhetoric of social progress. It should be added that this did not prevent at least one sycophantic student of manners taking advantage of the aristocratic status of the Percies while advancing doctrines of which they were widely regarded as living antitheses.[9]

There was also the obvious and awkward fact that while in theory politeness was available to anyone of natural virtue, in practice it required a degree of leisure and wealth, albeit on a lesser scale than older notions of gentility laid down. Moreover, the boundaries between the polite and impolite could vary to reflect localised patterns of wealth. What was polite in Berkeley Square was not necessarily what was polite in Finsbury or Hammersmith, let alone in Shadwell or Wapping. In the provinces still more diversity prevailed. Deciding who to exclude from a polite circle was as important as ensuring that it included the right people. Countless tiny elites throughout the land exercised this exclusive power, themselves arranged in hierarchies that might be mutually exclusive or at least only partially overlapping. The tensions were always implicit in the code of politeness but there came a point when they could not be contained within the structure that had generated them. Indeed, by the late eighteenth century politeness as

[7] *The History of the Rebellion and Civil Wars in England Begun in the Year 1641*, ed. William Dunn Macray (1888), VI, 398.
[8] *Horace Walpole's Correspondence*, ed. Wilmarth Sheldon Lewis (48 vols., 1937–83), XLII, 378; *Horace Walpole's Miscellany 1786–1795*, ed. Lars E. Troide (New Haven, 1978), 112.
[9] Stephen Philpot, *An Essay on the Advantage of a Polite Education Joined with a Learned One* (1747), dedicated to the duchess of Somerset.

an instrument of social warfare rather than a tool of benevolent intercourse was close to superseding earlier usages, as the unashamed snobbery and exclusiveness of portions of the aristocratic elite set an example which petty imitators further down the scale could mimic.

It must also be recognised that the utility of politeness as a contemporary catchword did not necessarily depend on its didactic originality. To the extent that it emphasised the outer self – behaviour that contributed to social ease, and taste that chimed with cultural correctness – rather than the inner self of moral or religious virtue, it certainly broke with the past.[10] But in some other respects it marked no radical departure from the older courtesy codes and literature. In fact those codes and literature went on developing steadily, to some extent along rather traditional lines in the course of the eighteenth century. The term 'polite' did increasingly come to be used more and more but its effective incorporation was relatively slow and often superficial. Moreover, the actual advice offered in courtesy literature was often a modulated version of what had been offered in earlier decades if not centuries. Most celebrated of all eighteenth-century contributions to this genre was Chesterfield's *Letters of his Son.* Its debt to the Castiglione tradition is obvious. So is its continuing legacy in the nineteenth and twentieth centuries in rather sanitised form. What many people thereby acquired from Chesterfield accordingly diverged significantly from the values that were commonly associated with it by most eighteenth-century enthusiasts for politeness.

With all these qualifications, however, the fact is that the language of politeness had enormous power in its day. At the very least it provided a lowest common denominator of social intercourse that drew the most snobbish of people into some recognition of those immediately below them in the social scale. And the power of politeness as a rhetoric was precisely that it could reconcile or conceal conflicting purposes. Above all, if there was one key feature of what was meant by being polite that came to be considered axiomatic in the eighteenth century, it was its emphasis on avoiding constraint and ceremony, in favour of ease and informality, even in arcane rituals of daily intercourse.[11] The ease that came from personal self-assurance was not new. But the ease that came from an assumption of social equality with others was. So entrenched did this assumption in the rhetoric of manners become that even when, in the early nineteenth century, politeness was reduced to a rigid set of rules for repetition in etiquette books, it continued to be

[10] Fenela Ann Childs, 'Prescriptions for Manners in English Courtesy Literature, 1690–1760, and their Social Implications' (DPhil thesis, Oxford University, 1984), ch. 3.
[11] See, for instance, Penelope J. Corfield, 'Dress for Deference and Dissent: Hats and the Decline of Hat Honour', *Costume*, 23 (1989), 64–79.

insisted that 'palpable attention to form' was 'always to be avoided'.[12]

In short, politeness had to be accessible, attainable. If it was not within the reach of all then it had no claim to recognition. Not only did this mean rejecting the inherited tyranny of the Percies and their like, it also meant accepting that the manners that made a gentleman and a lady could be possessed by those who had no such status by birth. More importantly it left space for less hypocritical recognition of the effects of appearances and the material wealth they implied as determinants of status. That is not to say that it did not come with a good many moralising assumptions and arguments, but in scrutinising them one should not be distracted from the central fact that its appeal lay primarily in its apparent endorsement of all kinds of self-aggrandisement. 'Levelling up' has always had the rhetorical advantage of enlisting social parvenus as well as egalitarian ideologues in its cause.

It is not difficult to see a variety of purposes in what was proposed as politeness. But granted that those who thought themselves polite in principle subscribed to the socially enlightened principle of access to all who could behave politely, a harder task is to assess the extent to which manners did in fact change among those who were supposed to benefit by them. There is a temptation to avoid the question altogether and take refuge in the analysis of discourse for its own sake, as something that represents interests and ideas rather than something that might actually have had an impact on social behaviour. Yet the question is surely worth asking. What can we say, if anything, about the actual effect of this great body of argument and instruction in favour of a less forbidding and restrictive code of manners, which gave the supposedly impolite the chance of achieving their much heralded apotheosis?

For the kind of upwardly mobile, modestly middle-class society that throve on the new commerce and commercialism of the post-Revolution world the question may seem superfluous, so large is the body of evidence amassed by those tracking its activities. Without a certain flexibility of manners implied by the notion of an accessible politeness, numerous of the material and cultural transformations recorded by historians would make no sense. The 'urban renaissance' of Britain's Georgian towns and cities is one such.[13] Another is the richness of the ordinary London town house as a European phenomenon.[14] Middle-class consumerism as a matter of 'social, as well as economic factors'

---

[12] *Etiquette for Gentlemen* (2nd edn, 1838), 63.
[13] P. Borsay, *The English Urban Renaissance: Culture and Society in the Provincial Town 1660–1770* (Oxford, 1989).
[14] Dan Cruikshank and Neil Burton, *Life in the Georgian City* (1990), 51–73.

assumes it.[15] So does the confidence of provincial women below 'the quality' that they were 'polite' and 'genteel',[16] and the self-conscious 'sensibility' that revised both men's and women's views of relations between the sexes.[17] Nor would the hedonism that created the 'pleasure-loving grandparents' of the Victorian[18] or the educational revolution that made high culture 'the property of a larger public'[19] be plausible without such an enfranchising lowering of social boundaries. One could go on. A large proportion of what has been uncovered about Georgian society in recent years reinforces the role of politeness as a force that radically revised notions of social acceptability and status.

The precise effects in terms of what is today called social inclusiveness is harder to gauge. Much of the evidence must be anecdotal. On the other hand, when it comes from sceptical witnesses it is at least more plausible. One of the most sceptical witnesses was surely Horace Walpole, who lived through the hey-day of the new politeness and whose jibes at the vulgarity of his own class did not make him necessarily more sympathetic with the classes below. Yet on the admittedly rare occasions when circumstance compelled him to mix with the latter, he was reluctantly impressed. At King's Lynn for example when he became its MP in 1754, he met precisely that class of municipal semi-gentlemen and ladies whose conversion to polite manners was apparently at the centre of the Addisonian mission. Walpole remembered what they had been like in his father's day. He was also ready to be patronising about the prospect of hearing 'misses play on the harpsichord', and seeing 'an alderman's copies of Rubens and Carlo Marat. Yet to do the folks justice, they are sensible and reasonable, and civilized; their very language is polished since I lived among them.'[20]

It is possible to go further and argue that social mores had more far-reaching effects on behaviour than the relatively superficial gloss that Walpole was describing. Laurence Stone claimed that the early eighteenth century witnessed a pronounced 'softening of manners', representing the influence exerted by an increasingly market-oriented middle class.[21] Stone's approach to these matters tended to be rather

---

[15] Lorna Weatherill, *Consumer Behaviour and Material Culture in Britain 1660–1760* (2nd edn, 1996), 200.

[16] Amanda Vickery, *The Gentleman's Daughter: Women's Lives in Georgian England* (New Haven, 1998), 13.

[17] G. J. Barker-Benfield, *The Culture of Sensibility* (Chicago, 1992).

[18] Roy Porter, 'Material Pleasures in the Consumer Society', in *Pleasure in the Eighteenth Century*, ed. Roy Porter and Marie Mulvey Roberts (1996), 35.

[19] John Brewer, *The Pleasures of the Imagination: English Culture in the Eighteenth Century* (1997), xvii.

[20] *Horace Walpole's Correspondence*, IX, 350.

[21] Lawrence Stone, in *Past and Present*, 108 (1985), 219, 222, defending his 'Interpersonal Violence in English Society, 1300–1980', *Past and Present*, 101 (1983), 22–33.

impressionistic, and not necessarily the worse for that. But there is quantifiable evidence to hand in studies of litigation concerning inter-personal relations. Christopher Brooks finds a significant decline in civil litigation, marked from the 1680s onwards, and quite dramatic in the 1730s and 1740s.[22] Violent crime generally may have followed the same trajectory and in the case of homicide certainly did.[23] Whether these developments are to be attributed to the progress of urbanity is debatable but the chronological correlation is at least suggestive.

The eighteenth century's conception of economic development and social virtue assumed such a correlation. As Pocock summarises it, 'it was preeminently the function of commerce to refine the passions and polish the manners'.[24] In some cases the consequences were quite predictable. The professions that serviced propertied society were naturally influenced by changing fashions and values. They also had the strongest possible interest in making themselves amenable to their potential employers, regardless of the purely social advantages that they might thereby obtain. Lawyers and physicians were the obvious examples. Viewed in a commercial light, the clergy were another instance of the polish that derived from social contact brought about by the provision of services.[25] But beyond that, contemporaries thought that they could identify still more striking instances of the polishing effect of commerce on middle-class manners, notably the innkeeper and the shopkeeper. Each came into continual contact with strangers; each demonstrated the beneficent effect of trade; each lacked the predictable breeding of people of rank or people used to consorting with people of rank.

English inns, at least on the great highways, possessed the undisputed supremacy in their trade. But when every allowance had been made for their material comfort it was the quality of their personal service that was most impressive. From the innkeeper and his wife to that uniquely English institution, 'boots', a pleasing manner was said to be the rule. Foreigners were startled to find the innkeeper helping them out of their carriage, his wife at the door to show the ladies to their rooms.[26] English travellers, hoping for 'the alacrity of an English waiter,

---

[22] Christopher Brooks, 'Interpersonal Conflict and Social Tension: Civil Litigation in England, 1640–1830', in *The First Modern Society: Essays in English History in Honour of Lawrence Stone*, ed. A. L. Beier, David Cannadine and James M. Rosenheim (Cambridge, 1989), 357–99.

[23] J. M. Beattie, *Crime and the Courts in England 1600–1800* (Princeton, 1986), ch. 3; R. B. Shoemaker, 'Male Honour and the Decline of Public Violence in Eighteenth-Century London', *Social History*, 26 (2001), 190–208; R. B. Shoemaker, 'The Decline of Public Insults in London, 1660–1800', *Past and Present*, 169 (2000), 97–131.

[24] J. G. A. Pocock, *Virtue, Commerce, and History* (Cambridge, 1985), 49.

[25] Penelope J. Corfield, *Power and the Professions in Britain 1700–1850* (1995).

[26] Johanna Schopenhauer, *Reise durch England und Schottland* (2 vols., Leipzig, 1818), I, 254.

or the civility of an English landlord', professed to find nothing comparable abroad.[27] German innkeepers were welcoming only to people of noble rank, and then with manners that were better described as obsequious than polite. In France they did not even trouble to present themselves, leaving the social graces on these occasions to servants. Elsewhere they were best considered as glorified tradesmen, whose idea of hospitality was what they would have bestowed on the lowliest commercial traveller. In America the innkeeper was a nuisance, not a host but a hectoring busybody. Evidently, even Anglo-Saxon stock returned to its primitive rusticity in a new country.[28] Americans did not disagree; they were astounded by the superiority of an English inn.[29] Of course, the artificiality of all this civility made its mercenary quality obvious at least to those who poked beneath the surface. Pedestrian travellers, who, it was assumed in England, must possess neither gentility nor money, complained of the grossest rudeness and ill treatment both from landlords and their servants.[30]

Shopkeepers were not less modern in their manners. Satirists as diverse as Ned Ward and Robert Southey derided 'counter-coxcombs' for their pretentious behaviour with customers.[31] The polite establishment of the ordinary shopkeeper generated criticism of his wife with 'her tea, her card-parties, and her dressing-room' and even of his apprentice who 'has climbed from the kitchen-fire to the front-boxes at the play-house'.[32] Foreigners were surprised that even Parisian shopkeepers could not compete. As the émigré vicomte Walsh remarked, whereas people of rank everywhere had learned their manners from the salons of Paris, the shopkeepers of France had had to learn the 'bon ton du comptoir', and the 'bonnes manières des magasins' from England.[33]

Innkeepers and shopkeepers were polite because they sold commodities which in England were in ready supply, which were the subject of intense competition, and the sale of which could be maximised by skilful merchandising. They came to embody one of the most noted features of English life, its supposed indifference to rank. The ease of such men in relating to all classes, including the highest, provided a notable contrast with what occurred elsewhere. They 'receive their

[27] Ann Radcliffe, A Joiurney made in the Summer of 1794 (1795), 158.
[28] Monthly Review, 97 (1822), 254.
[29] Mordecai M. Noah, Travels in England, France, Spain, and the Barbary States, in the Years 1813–14 and 15 (New York, 1819), 25.
[30] Carl Philipp Moritz, Journeys of a German in England in 1782, trans. and ed. Reginald Nettel (1965), 113, 132.
[31] Edward Ward, The London Spy (3rd edn, 1702), VII, 7; Robert Southey, Letters from England: By Don Manuel Alvarez Espriella (3 vols., 1807), I, 119.
[32] London Magazine (1767), 668.
[33] Joseph Alexis, vicomte Walsh, Lettres sur l'Angleterre ou voyage dans la Grande-Bretagne en 1829 (Paris, 1830), 323.

customers of rank', it was observed, 'as if they were equals, and the transactions between them mutually beneficial'.[34] The contrast with France, where the genteel and pseudo genteel of the *ancien régime* strenuously resisted such familiarity, seemed very striking. 'Thus an upstart lady of quality (an imitator of the old school) would not deign to speak to a milliner while fitting on her dress, but gave her orders to her waiting-women to tell her what to do. Can we wonder at twenty *reigns of terror* to efface such a feeling.'[35]

That commerce was indeed the key seemed undeniable. Confronting some particularly offensive ferrymen on the Severn in 1798 Richard Warner reflected that it was their possession of a commercial monopoly that made them so objectionable.

> There are no separate interests; no competitions; no struggle to deserve preference by particular attention, or superior courtesy; no endeavour to engage the future custom of the passenger by consulting his present ease, convenience, or pleasure; no stimulus to ensure civility; no check to prevent insolence; and the consequence is what we may naturally expect it to be, the mariners engaged in the business are as rude, turbulent, and violent, as the estuary they navigate.[36]

Commerce must be liberated to ensure its efficacy.

The downward transmission of manners as successive layers of society were brought within the refining field of commercial gravity could be seen as a natural progression. But bringing commercial politeness to bear on all classes seemed an ambitious goal. William Tremayne, who conceived a scheme for the reform of English grammar, was confident that what he called 'the spirit of vanity' would alone achieve the desired effect. 'Many would adopt the improvements from true taste; infinitely more from mere affectation and love of novelty. It would now become "quite the thing," "the ton"; and, by descending even to the lower ranks, in half a century it would prevail throughout the kingdom.'[37] Suggestive examples could be cited, such as the consumption of tea and the self-conscious female sociability which went with it.

Tremayne's confidence that even the 'lower ranks' would respond to treatment begged an awkward question about the limits of politeness. The notorious unsociability of the ordinary Englishman amounted to a national stereotype, and in some unregenerate circles was almost a

---

[34] Oloff Napea, *Letters from London: Observations of a Russian, during a Residence in England of Ten Months* (1816), 249. See Paul Langford, *Englishness Identified: Manners and Character, 1650–1850* (Oxford, 2000), pp. 226ff.

[35] *Complete Works of William Hazlitt* (21 vols., 1930–4), XVII, 358.

[36] Richard Warner, *A Walk through Wales, in August 1797* (Bath, 1798), 9.

[37] *The Literary Correspondence of John Pinkerton, Esq.* (2 vols., 1830), 83, Tremayne to Pinkerton, 16 Sept. 1785.

matter for pride rather than the national disgrace that champions of politeness considered it. Foreigners were notoriously the worst sufferers by the much described and much discussed barbarism of London's lower orders, as numerous anecdotes testify. There is little point in dwelling on them. They fuelled a mass of European prejudices and presumptions about the English, contributing to generalisations about national character as well as national mores that had implications beyond the merely picturesque. In his Shandean satire, *Another Traveller*, of 1767, Samuel Paterson offered 'suppositions' concerning European countries, which the traveller could take for granted without bothering to check for himself. The 'mob full of insolence' formed part of his characterisation of London.[38] Pierre Grosley, who was in England in 1765, remarked that the streets of a London made perfect sense of the state of nature conceived by the Englishman Thomas Hobbes.[39]

Here was a particular challenge for the new manners, one which it behove London, as the commercial capital of Europe, in F. W. Taube's phrase, to accept.[40] Among the great urban centres of Europe only Amsterdam, where 'Holländische Höflichkeit' was notoriously brutish and offensive, had a comparable reputation.[41] Received wisdom taught that the city was the natural home of civility, and capital cities in particular had high standards to live up to. Indeed, the modern social psychologist assumes that city streets 'even in times that defame them, provide a setting where mutual trust is routinely displayed between strangers'.[42] He had numerous co-believers in the eighteenth century, at least in point of aspiration. If any lower-class Englishmen were capable of breaking the class barrier of eighteenth-century civility it must be Londoners. In fact doing so came to be seen as a duty. The anti-social Londoner must be made aware that he was betraying the commercial interest of his country, especially where foreign visitors were concerned. Alienated tourists would make bad customers themselves and discourage still more who had never set foot in London from becoming customers too. 'How can our nation reconcile its proper interest with uncivil and shocking manners?'[43] The literature devoted to this aspect of politeness emphasised the discipline rather than the liberation, the duty rather than the ease, the formality rather than the informality.

---

[38] Samuel Paterson, *Another Traveller! Or Cursory Remarks and Tritical Observations Made upon a Journey through Part of the Netherlands in the Latter End of the Year 1766, By Coriat Junior* (2 vols., 1767–9), I, 460.

[39] Pierre Grosley, *A Tour to London; Or, New Observations on England, and its Inhabitants*, trans. Thomas Nugent (1772), 84.

[40] *Deutsches Museum*, Leipzig, II (1776), 630.

[41] *Johann Bernoulli's Summlung kurzer Reisebeschreibungen* (Berlin, 1781), I, 110.

[42] Erving Goffman, *Behaviour in Public* (1971), 17.

[43] *Lettres d'une Angloise écrites à une de ses amies* (Brentford, 1769), 23.

But however ambivalent, the underlying aim was the same, to show that a nation could be civilised.

One observer, Georg Forster, son of Captain Cook's naturalist, philosophical writer, and participant in the Rhineland's French-imposed revolution in the 1790s, indeed selected one decade as crucial in this respect. In 1790 he visited England after an absence of twelve years. Recording his impressions of the changes which had occurred during this period he described a 'real revolution in manners'. One of its manifestations was the improved demeanour of 'the common people'.[44] They were, he decided, more polite than he could recall them, and especially so to foreigners.

Forster's claim was not unique, though the precise timing might be debated. In 1770 Joseph Baretti, the friend of Johnson, Reynolds and Burke, thought he saw sufficient signs of change among plebeian Englishmen to predict that 'in about twenty years more they will become quite as civil to strangers as the French and Italians'.[45] Baretti's trial for murder in a street brawl may or may not add weight to his testimony, but in retrospect it certainly looks prophetic. Numerous other witnesses can be cited to the effect that ordinary people were more considerate, more respectful, more decorous than had not long before been the case.[46] This was not just a matter of the way foreigners were treated. Residents as well as visitors were aware that a change had taken place. The American painter Benjamin West told his compatriot Benjamin Silliman in 1805 that 'he had traced a growing refinement and humanity in the manners of the people. Formerly, every young gentleman was obliged to learn boxing to defend himself against the insults of the mob, which he was sure to receive in walking the streets; but now, there is universal decorum and civility in the manners of the lower ranks.'[47] As for Londoners themselves, there seems to have been a lessening of concern on the subject. By the 1820s the principal encroachers on what was described as 'the laws of civil society in pedestrian excursions through a crowded Metropolis' were said to be not boorish plebeians but tradesmen whose barrows, drays, pots, pails and trays sometimes made progress difficult.[48]

This was not achieved without much campaigning. It was precisely

---

[44] 'Ansichten vom Niederrhein, von Brabant, Flandern, Holland, England und Frankreich', in *Georg Forster's sämmtliche Schriften* (9 vols., Leipzig, 1843), III, 381.

[45] Joseph Baretti, *A Journey from London to Genoa, through England, Portugal, Spain, and France* (4 vols., 1770), I, 63.

[46] Louis Dutens, *L'ami des étrangers qui voyagent en Angleterre* (1787), 3–4; *Briefe zur Charakteristik von England gohörig; geschrieben auf einer Reise im Jahre 1784 von Heinrich von Watzdorf* (Leipzig, 1786), 159.

[47] Benjamin Silliman, *A Journal of Travels in England, Holland and Scotland, and of Two Passages over the Atlantic, in the Years 1805 and 1806* (2 vols., New York, 1810), I, 163.

[48] *Real Life in London* (2 vols., 1821), I, 645–8.

the object of much contemporary instruction to lessen the public displays of animosity that so disfigured the life of London compared with other European capitals. For instance, *Rules for Behaviour, of General Use, though much Disregarded in this Populous City*, in 1780, were specifically directed at the belligerence of life on the streets. These rules covered quite a range of things, from the way to carry a cane without turning it into a weapon, to approved laws of precedence when passing people on the pavement, to discrete behaviour when meeting strangers. 'Not to fasten your eyes upon any person entering into a publick room, for fear (by such a broadside) of shocking his modesty, and dismounting his assurance.'[49] The fact that accessible spaces other than streets were giving rise to concerns about the gap between polite and impolite behaviour was telling. 'Publick rooms' both in London and the provinces were multiplying, as recreational facilities improved. Those in principle open to all, from coffee houses to art exhibitions, were particularly vulnerable in this respect. Much concern was expressed at signs of strain, such as Sir Ashton Lever's decision in 1773 to restrict the admission of the 'lower class' to his celebrated natural history collection on account of the 'insolence of the common People'.[50] Improving the behaviour seemed to many far superior to excluding them.

If there was a significant shift, it may have had as much to do with context as conduct books. In the newly fashionable parts of the metropolis, whole new neighbourhoods appealing to the well-off, if not the very rich, were springing up. Any encounter on foot in their streets was likely to be either with people who lived in such households or with those who serviced and supplied them. Even the slums which grew up alongside the West End were defined by their proximity.[51] Squalid courts, alleys and back streets were rarely glimpsed in the 'prospects' displayed in contemporary prints, yet they were close at hand in reality.[52] The most genteel neighbourhoods had pockets of vulgarity. One such sordid court full of poor Irish off Portman Square attracted notoriety that resulted in the formation of a charitable society specifically for its relief.[53] Such positioning made the manners of their inhabitants somewhat different from those of manufacturing or maritime

---

[49] *London Magazine* (1780), 197.

[50] D. Ripley, *The Sacred Grove: Essays on Museums* (1970), 32.

[51] L. D. Schwarz, 'Social Class and Social Geography: The Middle Classes in London at the End of the Eighteenth Century', in Peter Borsay, ed., *The Eighteenth-Century Town: A Reader in English Urban History* (1990), 328–30, and more broadly, L. D. Schwarz, *London in the Age of Industrialisation: Entrepreneurs, Labour Force and Living Conditions, 1700–1850* (Cambridge, 1992), ch. 3.

[52] Sir Walter Besant, *London in the Eighteenth Century* (1902), 338.

[53] Louis Simond, *Journal of a Tour and Residence in Great Britain, during the Years 1810 and 1811, by a French Traveller* (2 vols., Edinburgh, 1815), II, 259; Dorothy George, *London Life in the Eighteenth Century* (1966), 122–3.

districts. Holborn and Soho might be as wretched as Spitalfields or Wapping, but they were less likely to impress the stranger unfavourably. The East End that so repelled and fascinated the late nineteenth century already had a distinctive identity in this respect, one which strengthened steadily in the early nineteenth century as the contrast with politer slums grew more marked. As Cornelius Webbe pointed out in his *Glances at Life in City and Suburbs* in 1836, this had nothing to do with poverty, degradation and crime which were to be found equally in pockets of central London. Rather it was a matter of different customs, values and manners. In Whitechapel 'their total habits, tastes, language, idioms, houses, streets, etc. etc., are at least forty years behind those of any other part of the "wen" '.[54]

Certain features of the emerging social geography would readily fit with Forster's impression of a new attitude on the streets. One was the prominence of household servants. Treasury ministers are not a bad guide to changing indexes of consumable wealth, and it was during this period that they first subjected servants to taxation, manservants in 1777 and maidservants in 1785. Estimates of the numbers are mostly guesswork, though all agree that service played a still more significant role in the economy of the capital than it did elsewhere. The impression is supported by the hard evidence that does exist, for male servants in 1780. London, with a tenth of the population, had a quarter of registered manservants.[55] A quite disproportionate number of these was employed in Westminster. Significantly for the transmission of genteel manners, Westminster also possessed a uniquely high proportion of households with two or more servants.[56] Servants, male or female, were well placed to transmit changing norms of conduct.[57] The conventional anxiety was precisely that they might contaminate the poor with ideas above their station, at a time, moreover, when new sensibilities were imperilling the hierarchies of family life.[58] Alternatively, and especially in the case of female servants, this could be viewed more positively as spreading a web of superficial politeness through the families from which they sprang, and which in due course they would multiply.

The streets themselves bore a novel appearance. During the early

---

[54] (1836), 154.

[55] 13,608 out of a national total of 52,004; the figures come from a complete survey for that year now at PRO, T47.8. It should be added that evasion rendered them at best partial, and was probably easier in country districts than in the capital.

[56] Westminster had 6,159 compared with 1,897 in the City and 5,552 in Middlesex parishes. Westminster's households with at least two servants numbered 1,117, against 848 with one; the City and indeed every county in England and Wales registered more households with one than with two.

[57] J. Jean Hecht, *The Domestic Servant Class in Eighteenth-Century England* (1956), 203ff.

[58] G. J. Barker-Benfield, *The Culture of Sensibility: Sex and Society in Eighteenth-Century Britain* (Chicago, 1992), 179.

years of George III numerous local improvement acts were passed, providing for street-paving, lighting and adornment.[59] Scotch granite, initially denounced for what it suggested about the all-pervading influence of Lord Bute, put Londoners literally on a new footing. Paving itself constituted a polite zone invading areas otherwise of lowly standing. London was unrivalled in this respect. The Russian Karamzin reckoned that 'no other city in the world is so delightful for the pedestrian' and even the patriotic duc de Lévis conceded that while one must live in Paris one could only walk in London.[60] The political implications were explained in Mercier's *Tableau de Paris*. Parisian streets revealed that it was not the pedestrian people who made laws in France. Londoners would never tolerate the disrespect and even brutality displayed by the rich and their coachmen, not to say the carnage caused by the resulting traffic accidents.[61]

Navigating the metropolis became a matter of locating these avenues of assured security and respectability. Travel guides took care to explain the advantages of the evolving grid of paved streets.[62] They kept traffic away from pedestrians, pedestrians away from houses, imposing order even as one walked them.[63] They were not, however, identified as 'promenades', like the boulevards and ramparts of continental cities, licensed for polite display and often policed by troops whose duty it was to keep the impolite away. In its royal parks London had such 'theatres where beauty and nobility might be rendered conspicuous and familiarized to the publick', in the words of the architect John Gwynn, but the newly paved thoroughfares were not of this kind.[64] They were open to all and used by all; whatever civilities they engendered must accommodate every kind of Londoner. Additional encouragement was provided by devising new street names to substitute modern gentility for ancient vulgarity. Some of these, for example the attempt to rename 'Poultry' as 'Mansion House Street', were controversial.[65]

---

[59] Dan Cruickshank and Neil Burton, *Life in the Georgian City* (1990), 13ff. I count thirteen such acts passed for parishes in London under George II, twenty-seven in the first two decades of George III's reign and twenty-one in the decade 1780–90; in the bumper year of 1783 there were no less than seven. These figures exclude statutes solely concerned with the watch.

[60] N. M. Karamzin, *Letters of a Russian Traveller 1789–1790*, trans. and abridged by Florence Jones (New York, 1957), 275; Pierre-Marc-Gaston, duc de Lévis, *L'Angleterre au commencement du dix-neuvième siècle* (Paris, 1814), 51.

[61] Louis-Sébastien Mercier, *Tableau de Paris* (8 vols., Amsterdam, 1783), I, 32.

[62] *Letters Written during a Residence in England Translated from the French of Henry Meister* (1799), 182.

[63] *An Essay on the Many Advantages Accruing to the Community, from the Superior Neatness, Conveniences, Decorations and Embellishments of Great and Capital Cities* (1734), 43–5.

[64] John Gwynn, *London and Westminster Improved, Illustrated by Plans* (1766), 88.

[65] *Caledonian Mercury*, 27 Jan. 1776.

If metropolitan growth was in some measure promoting the polite manners which contemporaries connected with commercial advance, metropolitan politics looked less promising. The Wilkesite disturbances, the Keppel Riots and above all the Gordon Riots suggest an intensification rather than a reduction of popular violence. Westminster was becoming more vulnerable than the City, as radical politics moved out of the bailliwick of the corporation into the less predictable parishes beyond its walls. The notorious Westminster election of 1784 did not on the face of it suggest a more disciplined approach to London's politics.

One possibility is that such extremes of violence were in the nature of the last flow of a tide that was about to ebb. Considering the strains of the 1790s it is remarkable in retrospect that the capital remained as orderly as it did. The peaceful nature of the enormous demonstration in St George's Fields in June 1795 astonished contemporaries.[66] Writing in 1810, J. P. Malcolm remarked that the Gordon Riots might be considered to have closed 'the article of popular tumult' and constituted the 'last scene of the Drama'.[67] A recent judgement that the riots were the final expression of 'an older, ceremonial order, not the new dawn of Liberty' would seem to have the support of those who lived through this period.[68]

We also need to exercise care in defining what constitutes reformed behaviour. As I have emphasised, one advantage of the term 'politeness' was precisely that it was sufficiently vague to embrace a great variety of values, attitudes and ideas. The improvement might be of a superficial kind or more fundamental, but there were certainly those who thought it the latter. Francis Place is a much quoted but not negligible source of information on this point. In matters such as drinking, swearing, common decency and decorum, he claimed to have witnessed a considerable revolution among his own class of people between the 1770s and the 1820.[69] This general improvement in what was called refinement of manners was about far more than implicit agreement not to be offensive to foreigners.

Numerous forces at work perhaps contributed to this shift in behaviour. Various circumstances were rendering propertied opinion increasingly suspicious of the use that the ordinary Englishman might make of his liberty. Perhaps the very unrest of London between the accession of George III and the end of the America War had made all concerned more sensitive to the dangers. After 1780 radical politicians seem to

[66] Albert Goodwin, *The Friends of Liberty* (1979), 372–3.

[67] J. P. Malcolm, *Anecdotes of the Manners and Customs of London during the Eighteenth Century* (2nd edn, 1810), II, 106.

[68] Nicholas Rogers, *Whigs and Cities* (Oxford, 1989), 389.

[69] British Library, Add. MS 27827, fo. 144; George, *London Life*, 17–18.

have been even less ready than government supporters to invoke the crowd.[70] Certainly there was no shortage of anxious comment and advice, on subjects as diverse as 'Robin Hood' debating societies, the obscene and seditious cartoons on view in print-shop windows and the tide of criminality that followed peace and demobilisation in 1783. In the resulting initiatives, some statutory, such as the repression of Sunday assemblies and debating clubs in 1781, others extra-parliamentary, such as the Sunday School movement and the campaigns against vice and immorality, London and Middlesex figured prominently.

These campaigns tend to be treated as events in the history of the Evangelical Revival, but it is also possible to locate them in the wider context of late Enlightenment sensibilities. Historians of philanthropy and moral reformation have characterised the 1780s in England as a 'decade of crisis and hope' which saw a determined 'attempt to reform society through a redemptive police'.[71] The most influential ventures launched at this time, including the anti-slavery campaign, the 'reformation of manners' movement and the Philanthropic Society, certainly had an Evangelical tinge, but their concerns were also broadly humanitarian in a way that can be as readily related to Leopold's Tuscany, Pombal's Lisbon, Voght's Hamburg, as to Wilberforce's 'Purity of Manners'. In the manifold projects of the 1780s for better schooling, less restricted medical services, more effective poor relief and superior public morals, it is difficult to disentangle moral from utilitarian objectives. But whatever the perspective adopted, there were implications for plebeian behaviour.

The treatment of strangers was itself one of the matters raised. Fifty years earlier venomous xenophobia had been a commonplace of conventional discourse. London had then been the place where the entire world's 'Scum and Filth' washed up, where 'the Foreigner finds Food and Footing, grows Great, forgets his Nakedness, and the Natives'.[72] Such language had no place in the humanitarian, even cosmopolitan vocabulary of the 1780s. Educationists directed their attention to the elimination of 'national prejudices' and 'unreasonable aversions'.[73] The Strangers' Friend Societies, commencing in London in 1784, were designed to assist people who could not claim entitlement

---

[70] Nicholas Rogers, 'Crowd and People in the Gordon Riots', in *The Transformation of Political Culture: England and Germany in the Late Eighteenth Century*, ed. Eckhart Hellmuth (Oxford, 1990), 54; E. P. Thompson, *The Making of the English Working Class* (1968 edn), 78.

[71] Joanna Innes, 'Politics and Morals: The Reformation of Manners Movement in Later Eighteenth-Century England', in *The Transformation of Political Culture*, ed. Hellmuth, 57; Donna T. Andrew, *Philanthropy and Police: London Charity in the Eighteenth Century* (Princeton, 1989), 165.

[72] *A Trip through London* (1728), 1.

[73] Joseph Priestley, *Lectures on History and General Policy* (Birmingham, 1788), 9.

to relief under the poor law.[74] When Leopold Berchtold published his schedule of questions with which the enquiring tourist might assess the advantages of the places he visited he included one on this subject: 'What regulations has the police made in favour of foreign travellers?'[75]

It was at this time that the word 'police' came commonly to be used in English to mean what it means today, without the contaminating associations which French and Scottish usage had formerly given it.[76] The Gordon Riots made public order a keynote of the 1780s, and did so in the context of a conflict of polite and plebeian opinion.[77] There was intense debate about suitable punishment for the rioters, and then about the best means of preventing a recurrence. Numerous proposals for metropolitan policing, some of which were eventually taken up by parliament, were put before the public. Perhaps the most concrete immediate outcome of all this anxiety was the coordinated sentencing strategy of the judges, which produced a marked increase in the rate of executions.[78]

It would be strange if these preoccupations did not have some effect on the general tenor of metropolitan life and indeed beyond, seeping into the mentality of people who might not consciously have shared them. On the other hand an analysis that gives compulsion and a coercive climate of opinion the main emphasis is not convincing. Contemporaries did not find the Londoner cowed, especially when compared with his counterparts in Vienna and Paris, where the atmosphere of the 1780s seemed notably more oppressive. In terms both of visible and invisible policing London continued to look relaxed. Vigorous though the debate about law and order was, it produced little of consequence before the Stipendiary Justices Act of 1792, itself a modest measure, especially when compared with the radical restructuring that took place in Dublin.[79] The main law enforcer remained the parish watchman, the London 'Charley', his duties regulated by a statute of 1774 and numerous local acts, but essentially unchanged since the reign of Charles II. How was it, visitors asked, that nearly a million

[74] George, London Life, 310.

[75] Leopold Berchtold, An Essay to Direct and Extend the Inquiries of Patriotic Travellers (2 vols., 1789), I, 383.

[76] Leon Radzinowicz, A History of English Criminal Law and its Administration from 1750 (4 vols., 1948–68), IV, 5; Policing and Prosecution in Britain 1750–1850, ed. Douglas Hay and Francis Snyder (Oxford, 1989), 5.

[77] Colin Haydon, Anti-Catholicism in Eighteenth-Century England: A Political and Social Study (1993), 222ff.

[78] Beattie, Crime and the Courts in England, 583ff.

[79] R. Paley, 'The Middlesex Justices Act of 1792: Its Origins and Effects' (PhD thesis, Reading University, 1983); Stanley H. Palmer, Police and Protest in England and Ireland 1780–1850 (Cambridge, 1988), 84–92.

people could be held in check by a few hundred watchmen who would merely have appeared comical elsewhere?[80] If lower-class Londoners were compelled to be more considerate and polite it must have been by a subtle form of compulsion.

There is another consideration. Theories of social control are prone to force an unrealistic dichotomy between brute coercion on the one hand, and voluntary action on the other.[81] Treating the impolite as subjects for treatment, blanks for imprinting with the commands of those above, seems far-fetched, given the wealth of evidence adduced for the vigour of plebeian culture at this time. Moreover, while it may have been possible to drive football, bull-baiting and other recreations from streets which had customarily been thought of as 'legitimate playing places by the common people', it was less easy to regiment the display of demeanour, gesture and bodily bearing that impressed Forster.[82] Is it not possible that improved manners were a spontaneous response to altered circumstances rather than a submissive assent to altered instructions?

Two elements in the concerns of polite society at this time might suggest something on these lines. One was the growing preoccupation with the power of example. The responsibility of people of rank to conduct themselves decently in public was a feature of even the most reactionary polemic and much emphasised by the moral reformers. Secondly, the unspoken discipline of the streets could work in both directions. Perhaps the genteel were not above being schooled into compliance with respectful manners just as the vulgar were.

Forster himself was intrigued by the sartorial novelties that he found on his return, suggesting as they did a growing conformity on the part of fashionable people to the standards of their inferiors. His compatriot Wendeborn remarked that it had become virtually impossible to determine social status on the streets of London.[83] The theme was not an entirely new one. The English upper class had long had a reputation for 'dressing down', which could either be disparagingly described as making a gentleman look like his coachman or alternatively suggest a refreshing taste for simplicity and equality. But the 1780s do seem to have been crucial in this respect, if only in a new appreciation of the

---

[80] Adolphe Blanqui, *Voyage d'un jeune français en Angleterre et en Ecosse pendant l'automne de 1823* (Paris, 1824), 326.

[81] See the telling critique by Allan Silver, 'The Demand for Order in Civil Society: A Review of Some Themes in the History of Urban Crime, Police, and Riot', in *The Police: Six Sociological Essays*, ed. David J. Bordua (New York, 1967), 1–24.

[82] Robert W. Malcolmson, *Popular Recreations in English Society 1700–1850* (Cambridge, 1973), 140.

[83] F. A. Wendeborn, *A View of England towards the Close of the Eighteenth Century* (2 vols., 1791), I, 265.

significance of the trend. Writing in 1789, the philologist Philip Withers observed, 'In former Ages, a Gentleman was easily distinguished from the Multitude by his DRESS. In the present Period, all external Evidence of Rank among Men is destroyed. Every outward Distinction is also lost in the Female World.'[84]

Self-conscious sartorial egalitarianism is often attributed to the influence of the French Revolution, but as the Anglomaniacs of Paris were well aware, it had its origins in England.[85] Englishmen could take pride in it without avowing excessively democratic sentiments. The universal blue or black coat, the hair worn without wig or powder, the boots tolerated indoors as well as outdoors, all indicated a readiness to sacrifice social superiority to uniform understatement. To the contemporary historian of London, Sir Richard Phillips, this 'approach to equality' revealed the 'modesty and good sense of the gentry'. He suggested a telling contrast with other countries: 'An English gentleman carries himself toward his inferior with real attention and civility; a foreigner of that class, either with absolute neglect, as if an inferior could no more occupy his thoughts than his post-horses, or with the still greater insult of an openly affected condescension.'[86] He might have cited other innovations that suggest a desire to minimise the overt discrimination implicit in social encounters. These included the growing tendency to address relatively humble men and women as Mr and Mrs, the dropping of titles of rank in common discourse, the adoption of less ceremonious modes of salutation. Forster selected one change as particularly significant, the disappearance of swords, suggesting at once the inappropriateness of displaying weapons in public and the unwisdom of flaunting gentility. Canes and umbrellas were emblems of the new, pacific street manners.

Exhibitionism was discouraged. Henri Decremps, who published a well-informed guide for French visitors in 1789, and also testified to the new-found politeness of the ordinary Londoner, none the less warned of the risks of offending his sense of propriety. Manners in England were dictated by the general will. A foreigner who dressed flamboyantly was violating English law just as an Englishman who criticised the sovereign in Paris or Vienna would be violating French or Austrian law. The difference was that in London the people was sovereign, not the king. Decremps helpfully provided details of the shops in which English-looking dress could be purchased by foreigners. He gave similar warnings on the subject of street manners. In England gentlemen not only did not think it demeaning to 'give the

---

[84] Philip Withers, *Aristarchus, or The Principles of Composition* (2nd edn, [1789]), 169.
[85] Aileen Ribeiro, *Fashion in the French Revolution* (1988), 39–44.
[86] Sir Richard Phillips, *Modern London* (1804), 138.

wall' to people of lower rank, they considered it a matter of politeness to do so.[87]

In short, Forster may have been registering the settling of a lower common denominator of public conduct rather than the enforcement of a hegemonic code on a subjugated class. There was a price, however. Increasingly, while observers agreed that a rather monochrome civility had been achieved by quite diverse classes, they found it by no means as attractive as it should have been. Fenimore Cooper expressed a common view with uncommon precision when he observed that the cost of mass politeness had been the loss of that ease and liberty of manners so much desired and the substitution of a highly formulaic code.

> As one descends in the social scale, I think the English get to be much the most artificial people I know. Instead of recognising great and governing rules for deportment, that are obviously founded in reason and propriety, and trusting to nature for the rest, having heard that simplicity is a test of breeding, they are even elaborate and studied in its display. The mass of the people behave in society like children who have had their hair combed and faces washed, to be exhibited in the drawing-room, or with a staid simplicity that reminds you always how little they are at their ease, and of the lectures of the nurse.[88]

Cooper's lifetime coincided with a whole new genre of conduct books, that reflected the development he was observing. The 'etiquette' guides of the early nineteenth century lacked both the moral foundations of the old 'courtesy' tradition and the social mission of the new 'politeness', reducing manners to a universal standard of outward civility.[89] The corollary was that 'politeness' itself lost the cluster of meanings which it had carried since the days of Addison and Shaftesbury, ceasing to describe a vision of accessible gentility and becoming synonymous with what it has since remained, an indication of commonplace civility. Superficial success carried with it the extinction of its distinctive character.

---

[87] Henri Decremps, *Le parisien à Londres, ou avis aux français qui vont en Angleterre* (2 vols., Amsterdam, 1789), I, 90 1, 94; II, 13.

[88] Fenimore Cooper, *England* (3 vols., 1837), I, 117–18.

[89] Marjorie Morgan, *Manners, Morals and Class in England, 1774–1858* (1994), ch. 1.

Transactions of the RHS 12 (2002), pp. 333–54 © 2002 Royal Historical Society
DOI: 10.1017/S0080440102000130   Printed in the United Kingdom

POLITE 'PERSONS': CHARACTER, BIOGRAPHY AND THE GENTLEMAN

By Philip Carter

ABSTRACT. Attempts to distinguish modern theories of refinement led eighteenth-century writers to highlight the moral integrity of a new code – politeness – in which outward civilities could be read as the manifestation of inner social virtues. To sponsors of polite culture this assurance was indicative of the superiority of modern manners manifest in the Lockean polite 'person'. Yet the possibility and validity of synthesis remained a subject for debate; partly because of the difficulty of communicating character, partly because of the potential exploitation of a supposed congruity between outer expression and inner motive. In response, late century theorists sought to reinvigorate aspects of Locke's ideal through a culture of sensibility which both developed and criticised the existing polite code. But prone to similar weaknesses, sensibility was itself abandoned in the nineteenth century as writing on morals and manners diverged, and the distinctive, enlightened concept of politeness gave way to etiquette and a modern regimen of social dos and don'ts.

TO START with a couple of pieces of good advice, the first from *Some Thoughts concerning Education*, John Locke's 1693 guide on gentry upbringing.

> He that is a good, a vertuous and able Man, must be made so within. And therefore, what he is to receive from Education, what is to sway and influence his Life, must be something put into him betimes; Habits woven into the very Principles of his Nature; and not counterfeit Carriage, and dissembled Out-side, put on by Fear, only to avoid the present Anger of a Father, who perhaps may disinherit him.[1]

Several pages later, Locke turns to the issue of '*Manners*, as they call it', and offers the following:

> Never trouble your self about those Faults in them, which you know Age will cure. And therefore want of well-fashion'd Civility in the

[1] John Locke, *Some Thoughts concerning Education* (1693), ed. John W. and Jean S. Yolton (Oxford, 1989), 110.

Carriage, whilst *Civility* is not wanting in the Mind (for there you must take care to plant it early) should be the Parent's least care ... Be sure to keep up in him the Principles of good Nature and Kindness ... and when they have taken root in his Mind ... fear not, the Ornaments of Conversation and the outside of fashionable Manners, will come in their due time.[2]

The second piece of good advice comes courtesy of Philip Dormer Stanhope, fourth earl of Chesterfield, in a letter to his son written in October 1748:

The height of abilities is ... a frank, open and ingenuous exterior, with a prudent and reserved interior; to be on your own guard, and yet, by a seeming natural openness, to put people off theirs ... A prudent reserve is therefore as necessary as a seeming openness is prudent ... In order to know people's real sentiments, I trust much more to my eyes than to my ears; for they can say whatever they have a mind I should hear; but they can seldom help looking what they have no intention that I should know.'[3]

Here somewhat on the defensive, in a letter sent a month before Chesterfield had urged his son to take the initiative in social encounters:

When you go into good company ... observe carefully their turn, their manners, their address; and conform your own to them ... observe their characters, and pry, as far as you can, into both their predominant passions, or their prevailing weakness; and you will then know what to bait your hook with to catch them.[4]

In several respects Locke's and Chesterfield's advice share common features: both take the form of, or originated as, correspondence; both are written for young men from the gentry; both demonstrate an understanding of a concept of self-identity dependent on internal and external qualities, in each case open to development for the individual's promotion within society. Equally, however, and as these excerpts suggest, the nature of this relationship and its implications for conceptions of the sociable self are also potentially quite different. For Locke, civility requires a combination of inner and outer values, both of which are directed towards a shared purpose: the display of a natural good nature in a polished and pleasing form. Yet for Chesterfield a reputation for civility (since 'reputation' is all that is required) demands no such synthesis between inner will and outer display. Externalities are sufficient, not just to be seen as civilised but also to deceive those

---

[2] *Ibid.*, 124–5.
[3] *Lord Chesterfield's Letters*, ed. David Roberts (Oxford, 1992), 105.
[4] *Ibid.*, 89.

with whom one socialises by disguising ungenerous thoughts under a show of manners. Where Locke expects congruity and morality, Chesterfield requests distortion and the possible deception of one's audience. Where Locke seeks to reveal inner motives so as to enhance the quality of sociability, Chesterfield calls for their disguise for personal benefit.

Awareness of this relationship between internal and external civilities was not, of course, new to the eighteenth century. As Lionel Trilling suggests, that acts of seemingly generous civility could be motivated by less worthy aims was an increasingly important issue for sixteenth-century English moralists alarmed at the growing popularity of continental court literature. Anna Bryson has recently explored some of the manifestations of this tension during the seventeenth century. Initially a serious problem, Bryson argues that by the late seventeenth century concern over dissonance between inner and outer was in decline as a post-Puritan generation, more accustomed to life in civil society, learned the wider social benefits of a little dissembling. Such views, it is suggested, gained ground in the eighteenth century, ensuring that by the 1720s and 1730s the then fashionable term – 'politeness' – had come to be equated merely with the external proprieties of civility.[5]

This paper, by contrast, proposes an alternative picture of later debates on refinement, and in particular over the features by which its advocates distinguished 'politeness' from existing standards of civilised behaviour: to argue, in short, that the eighteenth century witnessed a rather more energetic attempt, if not to reject external civilities, then certainly to bind them, as Locke proposed, into a synthesis of inner and outer refinement. As a result, an eighteenth-century gentleman's civilities were less relegated to acts of social lubrication than elevated and encouraged as a positive indication of the superiority, moral and physical, of modern modes of social interaction. Eighteenth-century writers identified this form of refinement as distinctive and gave to it a precise label – 'politeness' – by which to distinguish it from earlier codes. The essence of the Lockean gentleman and his successors was to be his integrity, a quality which Locke identified as being, through education, the transition from the status of 'man' to that of 'person': rounded, moral, responsible and 'polite' in the true sense of the word.

High ideals, however, were ever vulnerable to misinterpretation or conscious distortion. Proponents spent much time shoring up the polite

---

[5] Lionel Trilling, *Sincerity and Authenticity* (1974); Anna Bryson, *From Courtesy to Civility: Changing Codes of Conduct in Early Modern England* (Oxford, 1998); Fenela Childs, 'Prescriptions for Manners in English Courtesy Literature, 1690–1760, and their Social Implications' (DPhil thesis, Oxford University, 1984), 102–28; Jorge Arditi, *A Genealogy of Manners: Transformations of Social Relations in France and England from the Fourteenth to the Eighteenth Century* (Chicago, IL, 1998).

person in the face of corrupting alternatives, of which Lord Chesterfield's provided one of the most glaring but also beguiling examples. Defending politeness took a number of forms over the period – spiritual and secular, moral and satirical – and included by mid-century its gradual redefinition as an alternative and, to its advocates, superior concept of social refinement – sensibility – which sought to reinject integrity into a 'polite' system whose historical legacy and contemporary value were exposed by episodes like the posthumous publication of Chesterfield's correspondence in the mid-1770s. Two points are made in conclusion. First, that the efforts of several generations to blend morality and manners requires us to look at the blueprint of eighteenth-century gentlemanhood in a somewhat more positive light than subsequent observers have been wont to do. And, second, that the exposure of sensibility itself by the 1790s brought an end to Lockean attempts at blending morals and manners, prompting a final and enduring sep-aration with some rather beneficial implications for Lord Chesterfield's legacy.

The connection between manners and moral virtue, though gaining unprecedented importance in this period, was not a distinctly eight-eenth-century invention. Writers like Locke drew on two existing literary traditions with a similar understanding of the value of inner and outer civilities and the required synchronicity between the two. The first of these, a sixteenth-century humanist tradition, built principally on the work of Erasmus, found its way to England through translations of his work on the conduct of boys and via adaptations such as William Fiston's *The Schoole of Good Manners* (1609) – subtitled 'a New Schoole of Vertue' – which promoted an image of the civilised individual as a product of manners grounded as much in humanist learning as lineage: 'by the Manners', wrote Fiston, 'are lively represented the habit of the Minde and disposition of Man'.[6] The potential, proposed in such work, for developing a concept of gentlemanliness based as much on personality as birth appears to have been taken up by a substantial number of later seventeenth-century writers who at least tolerated the idea of merchants and traders appropriating gentility. Locke, too, clearly followed this line in a study which, while written specifically for a member of the gentry, purposefully attracted a far wider audience via its focus less on gentlemanly than moral education, and its stress on the potentially universal development of the unsocialised 'individual' to

---

[6] William Fiston, *The Schoole of Good Manners* (1609), n.p. For an alternative discussion of the interaction of manners and morals see Martin Ingram, 'Sexual manners: The Other Face of Civility in Early Modern England', in *Civil Histories: Essays Presented to Sir Keith Thomas*, ed. Peter Burke, Brian Harrison and Paul Slack (Oxford, 2000).

the civilised, sociable 'person'. A second English tradition, of which Richard Allestree's *The Whole Duty of Man* (1660) is a leading example, sought to blend notions of gentlemanliness with that of the good Christian. Echoing medieval concepts of noble courtesy, these writers emphasised the value of men who valued practical acts of charity over courtly polish. Again, in forming his own concept of morality, itself based on natural or God's laws, Locke drew on familiar Christian ethics as a basis for the truly civilised person.

Yet it is on the question of the nature of the internal, moral origins of civility that Locke and his successors also made a significant contribution to the eighteenth-century equation between virtue and manners. Thus, while Christian ethics remain integral to Locke's advice, his was a distinctly human and humane concept of virtue in which civility derived less from an imposed moral obligation than the natural pleasure that man – that 'Sociable Animal'[7] – gained from socialising and communicating with others of like temperament. That civility was both the result and the means to express what Locke described as inner 'good nature' or 'kindness' proved to be a powerful argument by which early eighteenth-century commentators sought to establish the integrity of their new model of social interaction – to which they gave a precise name 'politeness' – as a pragmatic but morally grounded code befitting and derived from recent advances in urban society.[8]

Nowhere was this combination of factors more evident than in the most influential and imitated promotion of these new standards of sociability, Joseph Addison's and Richard Steele's *Spectator* project. In promoting its cause the *Spectator* pursued two lines of argument. The first was to reveal the true corruption of earlier systems of civility and, in particular, that of the Renaissance court. Courtiers came in for special condemnation, typically depicted as impeccable and inscrutable and therefore inferior to the open, kind and moral modern polite gentleman of the town. Self-proclaimed 'worthies', claimed Steele, distinguished only for their 'cold and repeated Civilities' and a 'meer conformity of Looks and gestures'.[9] 'Apes of a King' who offered 'false

---

[7] The term, of course, is Addison's, see No. 9 (10 Mar. 1711), *The Spectator*, ed. Donald F. Bond (5 vols., Oxford, 1965), I, 39.

[8] On this transition see Lawrence E. Klein, *Shaftesbury and the Culture of Politeness: Moral Discourse and Cultural Politics in Early Eighteenth-Century England* (Cambridge, 1994), and his 'Coffee-House Civility, 1660–1714: An Aspect of Post-Courtly Culture in England', *Huntington Library Quarterly*, 59 (1997), 30–52; Philip Carter, *Men and the Emergence of Polite Society, Britain 1660–1800* (2001), ch. 1; Peter Burke, 'A Civil Tongue: Language and Politeness in Early Modern Europe', in *Civil Histories*, ed. Burke, Harrison and Slack. An important statement on earlier Tory concepts of politeness is Hannah Smith, 'English "Feminist" Writings and Judith Drake's *An Essay in Defence of the Female Sex* (1696)', *Historical Journal*, 44 (2001), 727–48.

[9] *Spectator*, No. 193 (11 Oct. 1711), II, 257; No. 394 (2 June 1712), III, 478.

Friendship' and, like marble, were 'well Polished but very hard' was the opinion of a contemporary.[10] A second, more positive, strategy demanded the education of these would-be town gentlemen in correct forms of refinement. Following Locke, the *Spectator* described how 'true politeness' was the product of man's desire for and enjoyment of genuine sociability. It was, as Addison put, a quality 'born within us' – and hence distinct from acquired manners – without which there could be 'no Society or Conversation ... kept up in the World'.[11] In highlighting the naturalness of good sociability, the *Spectator* again distinguished between modern politeness and earlier Renaissance modes. Seemingly accommodating and relaxed, court civility had been conditioned by the Castiglionean concept of *sprezzatura* or the art of appearing sociable. Courtiers were to learn the appearance of nonchalance and to apply their skills in courtly competition either to ingratiate or intimidate with seeming ease. New polite gentlemen, by contrast, were less concerned with competition than with the pleasure of socialising conveyed principally through, on the one hand, entertaining and informative speech and, on the other, a generous tolerance to listen to others without interruption. Addison's desired blend materialised in individuals like the fictional Manilius, modelled on the then lord chancellor, William, first Baron Cowper, from whom there came 'a thousand obliging Things ... upon every Occasion ... always so just and natural, that it is impossible to think he was at least Pains to look for them'. The result was a man of 'engaging Softness' who 'commands your Respect, whilst he gains your Heart'. 'Nothing can equal the Pleasure ... taken in hearing him speak, but the Satisfaction one receives in the Civility and Attention he pays to the Discourse of others.'[12]

Through the work of Locke and Addison the bond between inner and outer, between moral virtue and manners became a commonplace for later adherents to and promoters of *Spectatorial* politeness. And nor, it is worth noting, were these discussions the preserve of what we might describe as urban lifestyle commentators, being equally those of sections of the clergy; a valuable theme for a subject typically identified with a secular tea-table but in which the minister as conduct educator proved an enduring feature. Men like the Revd Edward Alanson whose essay on the *The Man of Integrity's Character* (1734) described a subject dedicated to the social good, 'to the Ease, the Benefit, and Comfort of all around him', which he conveyed by 'innocent, sincere and agreeable speech': 'His words are the interpreters of his Thoughts. He detests

[10] Abel Boyer, *The English Theophrastus; or Manners of the Age* (1702), 114–19.
[11] *Spectator*, No. 169 (13 Sept. 1711), II, 165–6.
[12] No. 467 (26 Aug. 1712), IV, 153.

Flattery, and ... that destructive Civility which suffers an unhappy Neighbour ... to walk into Ruin.'[13] For Samuel Johnson, writing in the early 1750s, 'genuine politeness' was likewise 'sincerity and affection', rather than 'diverting elegance and outward Address'. Twenty years on, *The Polite Academy* taught its youthful charges to view 'Politeness as the Influence of natural Refinement ... the happy Mixture of Greatness with Benignty', at odds with a courtly civility which 'though often falsely thought the same', was in fact 'mostly Surface without Depth ... a Gloss over the Outside even of Vice and Meanspiritedness'. To a contemporary, John Harris, it was a quality 'more easily felt than understood', based on 'sympathetic and generous feelings of the heart', with external manners the 'polish of this most virtuous and noble sentiment'.[14]

In view of this focus on the moral origins of politeness it is worth dwelling briefly on Harris's reminder that such qualities were ultimately apparent to one's company only through good manners. Locke had himself welcomed what he described as a 'Civil carriage' or 'outer fashionable Manners' as long as they came after a young man's development of inner civilities. To be benevolent but boorish was just as much a failing of his ideal as to be cold and polite. Mr Spectator had similarly cast manners, or what he and many imitators termed 'good breeding', as the only means of conveying good nature and therefore of establishing true politeness. 'Exterior Shows and Appearances of Humanity', declared Addison, 'render a Man wonderfully popular and beloved when they are founded upon a real Good-nature.'[15] Where Locke had seen externalities as a later facet of the civilised gentleman, Addison proposed a more interactive relationship between good breeding and the moral qualities that such manners served to express. The result was an effortless yet highly effective display of social civilities by another model *Spectator* citizen, Ignotus, who being 'firmly established in all Matters of Importance', ensured that the 'certain Inattention which makes Mens Actions look easie', appeared 'in him with greater Beauty', so bestowing that much sought-after quality, 'Gentleman-like Ease'.[16] Such theoretical validations of external good

[13] Edward Alanson, *The Man of Integrity's Character* (1734), 16.

[14] Samuel Johnson, No. 98 (23 Feb. 1751), in *The Rambler* (1750–2), ed. W. J. Bate and Albrecht B. Strauss, in *The Yale Edition of the Works of Samuel Johnson* (16 vols, New Haven, CT, and London, 1958–90), IV, 161–2; *The Polite Academy; or School of Behaviour for Young Gentlemen and Ladies* (5th edn, 1771), p. 1; John Harris, *An Essay on Politeness* (1775, 3rd edn, 1820), 33.

[15] *Spectator*, No. 169 (13 Sept. 1711), II, 165.

[16] *Ibid.*, No. 75 (26 May 1711), I, 325. In addition to manners, the *Spectator* stressed the value of clothing as communicator of natural sociability; to role models like Manilius the synchronicity was flawless, 'his outward Garb' being 'but the Emblem of his Mind ... genteel, plain and unaffected'. To those who relied on outer appearance alone the effect

breeding were also of considerable importance to a host of eighteenth-century writers, among them the Oxford dancing master Matthew Towle, who made their living either instructing or writing about the finer points of deportment, posture and movement. Towle's guide, published in 1771, was typical of the genre in providing exhaustive rules for genteel behaviour in all conceivable circumstances, even what to do on meeting royalty. Yet it is interesting to note that, just as theorists of politeness highlighted the value of manners, so Towle made clear that his instructions, at least, were also motivated by natural virtue. His aim, he claimed, was to fuse 'moral and social duties', the result being that 'Actions, such as walking, standing, sitting, kneeling, speaking' were undertaken 'in a Manner as to Sympathise with thy Soul.'[17]

This, at least, was the theory. Yet, turning now to the redefinition of politeness, a gradual process which arguably reached maturity in the 1770s, it is also necessary to appreciate the concern that many advocates felt over its potential for distortion or corruption – even within a discourse so firmly rooted in moral virtue. To an extent, politeness was a code ever on the defensive, hindered by an internal weakness born of its on-going identification and criticism of inferior forms, like the court, which none the less endured as rival, and sometimes easier and more useful systems. That generations of polite sponsors felt it necessary to define their subject in contrast to 'mere flattery', 'destructive Civility' or 'diverting elegance' suggests the durability of these anachronistic and apparently immoral codes, not least while English gentlemen enjoyed ready access to the continent, and especially France, where in a sympathetic political climate affectation was thought to flourish unchecked.

Alongside these rival temptations, polite theorists were also aware of the practical difficulties of behaving in ways which conveyed a suitable balance of moral virtue and manners. Being polite, despite the *Spectatorial* emphasis on relaxed sociability, could prove burdensome, as readers of Towle's dos and don'ts might find, as well as difficult to enact in the cut and thrust of a supposedly polite, but also highly competitive, society. There were, moreover, additional factors. Writing in the *Rambler*, Samuel Johnson pursued a popular theme when he drew attention to the influence of occupation on the capacity for polite expression. Naturally, men like dancing masters who spent time educating others, or tailors and mercers who mixed with genteel female company, would gain through their employment a proficiency for refinement. But there were others, notably academics and authors, whose careers provided

---

was less impressive: 'When a Gentleman speaks Coarsly, he has dressed himself Clean to no purpose', Nos. 467, IV, 153; 75, I, 324.

[17] Matthew Towle, *The Young Gentleman and Lady's Private Tutor* (Oxford, 1771), 86.

little instruction on how to socialise in person, regardless of the fluency of their written work. Rare examples of the sociable scholar were held up as remarkable figures, described by Oliver Goldsmith as 'true men of taste' situated in that difficult middle ground 'between the world and the cell'.[18] Yet, as Johnson pointed out, the majority failed to make the transition having spent 'in the privacies of study, that season of life in which the manners are to be softened into ease, and polished into elegance'. The result often came as a shock to readers when they encountered a favoured author. But this, in Johnson's opinion, was to overlook the fact that 'the graces of writing and conversation are of different kinds', and that a man 'wholly accustomed to works of study, may be without that readiness of conception, and affluence of language, always necessary to colloquial entertainment'.[19]

In such circumstances, there was a tendency, especially when mixing with one's social superiors, to overemphasise the mannered element of politeness. The result was not politeness but 'ceremoniousness', a fastidious, superficial and hence incomplete form of conduct, suitable for earlier, less sophisticated societies, but inadequate for the modern, civilised moralist. One who regularly fell into this trap was Oliver Goldsmith, the subject of bemused conversations for associates such as Johnson, James Boswell and Joshua Reynolds. Reynolds spoke for many when he described Goldsmith's habit of abandoning his true personality – what Reynolds labelled 'character' – 'as a man of observation' in favour of that by 'which nobody is afraid of being humiliated in his presence'. At times reprimanded by his friends Goldsmith sought to improve, as Reynolds put it, by carrying 'his character about with him in society', only to fail and revert to type. Observers debated Goldsmith's slippage between 'being' and 'expressing', and variously traced his bad habits to a boorish Anglo-Irish upbringing or, more simply, to his boundless desire to be liked.[20]

Regardless of the inconsistency of Goldsmith's social performance, his true, sober, 'writerly' character was thought essentially stable. Yet a growing awareness of the quality of self-identity – assisted by influential studies like Locke's *Some Thoughts concerning Education* and *Essay on Human Understanding* (1690) – also stimulated interest in a concept of personality now turned less to the religious purposes of earlier Puritan memoirists than to the social ends of the would-be polite. To those who encouraged such enquiries as a source of personal development, writing and in particular self-writing in the form of diaries, journals, day books and

---

[18] Oliver Goldsmith, *An Enquiry into the Present State of Polite Learning* (1759), in *Collected Works of Oliver Goldsmith*, ed. Arthur Friedman (5 vols., Oxford, 1965), I, 306.

[19] *Rambler*, No. 14 (5 May 1750), IV, 79.

[20] Joshua Reynolds, 'Reynolds on Goldsmith', in Reynolds, *Portraits*, ed. Frederick W. Hillies (1952), 42–3.

memoranda became a valuable mechanism for the detailing of character and, more importantly, for its alteration by way of self-regulation, reflection and improvement. Yet here too there were problems, evident in more candid autobiographical texts which highlighted the quotidian variations and inconsistencies of personality and its role in explaining the gaps between proscribed, desired and actual modes of social interaction.

If autobiography pointed up, and to some extent served to explain, the dissonance between one's own inner and outer personality, then a concomitant interest in biography – the search for the true personality in or by a third party – demonstrated a further area of antagonism now prompted by the biographer's scrutiny of the character of another, and the often impolite social performance required of an author to achieve such insight. It did not have to be this way, of course. Richard Holmes suggests a closer synchronicity between biography and politeness when he traces the genre's appeal and popularity to a specific early eighteenth-century cultural network – typified by the sociable, and often civilised, coffee-house – where gossip and hearsay flourished, and so gave life to a literary form dedicated to what Holmes terms 'inventing the truth'.[21] Samuel Johnson likewise saw the modern pre-occupation with biography as the welcome product of his society's capacity for social intimacy and perception by authors and readers who rejected 'vulgar greatness' in favour of 'domestic privacies, and ... the minute details of daily life, where exterior appendages are cast aside, and men excel each other by only prudence and by virtue'.[22] For Johnson's contemporary, Andrew Kippis, editor of the *Biographia Britannica* (1747–66), 'Biographical knowledge' was well suited for 'enlarging our acquaintance with Human Nature ... in correcting our prejudices, in refining our sentiments, and in regulating our conduct.' Central to Kippis's *Biographia* project was the publicising and celebration of the inner qualities of great men. In doing so, biography, like Locke's 'outer civilities', served to communicate moral values and so ensured not just the emulation of readers, but also the preservation of virtue in a potential subject 'sensible that his labours will not be buried in oblivion.'[23]

Yet others remained wary of a form which they viewed as potentially disruptive of polite society. First came the possible dangers of reading biography. Early eighteenth-century commentators proved particularly

---

[21] Richard Holmes, 'Biography: Inventing the Truth', in *The Art of Literary Biography*, ed. John Batchelor (Oxford, 1995).

[22] *Rambler*, No. 60 (13 Oct. 1750), IV, 321; Paula R. Backscheider, *Reflections on Biography* (Oxford, 1999), 188.

[23] Quoted in Isabel Rivers, 'Biographical Dictionaries and their Uses from Bayle to Chalmers', in Rivers, ed., *Books and their Readers in Eighteenth-Century England: New Essays* (Leicester, 2001), 157, 153.

sensitive to a genre based on the exceptional and singular, and thus at odds with the shared civilised assumptions which underpinned a would-be polite society.[24] More specifically, Augustan observers expressed alarm at the salacious tone of a fledgling biography market which already appeared to be the preserve of Grub Street hacks. Thus, where Johnson predicted studies displaying prudence and virtue, others saw the pursuit of true character leading to the corrosion of sociability, tolerance and respect. Eager to privilege reserve, privacy and benevolence as foundations of politeness, Joseph Addison criticised what he saw as a new fashion for intrusion in the name of biographical verisimilitude. The result was believed to be destructive both for writers who hunted after scandalous details to undermine the great, and for readers since 'our Admiration of a famous Man lessens upon our nearer Acquaintance with him ... and decays upon growing familiar with its Object'.[25]

The importance of private life as a route to true character also carried implications for a research methodology now directed towards capturing a subject's unguarded, domestic moments. In theory, at least, such concentration was essential for innovative and interesting biography. As Johnson reminded would-be students of the form: 'More knowledge may be gained of a man's real character, by a short conversation with one of his servants, than from a formal and studied narrative, begun with his pedigree, and ended with his funeral.'[26] 'Nobody', he later told Boswell, 'can write the life of man, but those who have eat and drunk and lived in social intercourse with him.'[27] This said, the actual pursuit of such a course could prove more troublesome, as Boswell himself discovered on publishing his *Life of Johnson* in 1791. Actively researching Johnson's biography for more than a decade before his subject's death, Boswell used his journal as a means of recording Johnson's pronouncements, before replaying these comments back into the biography. Boswell's justification, that it is through conversation that a man 'will best display his character', was a truism of eighteenth-century politeness. Yet, to shared friends, Boswell's habit of lurking with a note book to record private comment – while capturing Johnson's character for posterity – simultaneously threatened the rules of civil sociability by recasting intimate speech as public and so inhibiting free conversation once Boswell's methods became known. Only fully disclosed on publication of the biography, Boswell's approach prompted a closing down of social circles by former

[24] On the tensions between politeness and the singularity born of biography see Paul Langford, *Englishness Identified: Manners and Character, 1650–1850* (Oxford, 2000), 292.

[25] *Spectator*, No. 256 (24 Dec. 1711), II, 495–6.

[26] *Rambler*, No. 60, IV, 322.

[27] James Boswell, *Life of Johnson*, ed. Pat Rogers (Oxford, 1980), 474.

associates tricked by an absence of what has since become the necessity of comments made 'on' and 'off the record'. Writing after publication of the *Life*, one member of Johnson's circle made clear to Boswell his new found reluctance to invite gentlemen 'more shy and delicate than I' to gatherings which might 'excite sentiments of unease or apprehension' founded on Boswell's practice of 'publishing without consent that which has been thrown out in the freedom of private conversation'. According to Thomas Percy, another of Johnson's early biographers, Boswell had himself been 'studiously excluded from all decent and good company' for 'violating the primary law of civil society in publishing ... men's unreserved correspondence and unguarded conversation.'[28] It had been John Arbuthnot's view that an early eighteenth-century fashion for biography brought with it a new terror to death; arguably with Boswell and his kind, such chills also now accompanied the sociability and polite conversation of the living.

Faced with a series of potential slippages between inner and outer personality, promoters of politeness had at their disposal various strategies by which either to assert the genuineness of their social expressions, or to ridicule those who persisted in inferior styles. Among the former we might include the positive example set by men like the exemplary Manilius. Or Keith Thomas's intriguing identification of the eighteenth-century shift away from signing letters 'your humble servant' – a form now deemed excessively supplicatory and potentially duplicitous – in favour of 'yours sincerely' or 'yours truly' as statements of the congruence between sentiment and action in a type of communication where moral virtue and genteel prose could be stretched with little hope of detection.[29] A third, satirical device involved the use of that very popular eighteenth-century genre, character literature, to provide would-be polite gentlemen with vignettes on how not to behave. Popular among these was the fop type, a figure committed to fashionable manners but ever lonely in a sociable world whose pleasures he was denied by a moral vapidness promoted by his irrepressible narcisism.[30]

Yet by the mid-eighteenth century there was a growing suspicion that such strategies might not be adequate to resolve these tensions. Central

---

[28] Quoted in Adam Sisman, *Boswell's Presumptuous Task* (2000), 285–6. On Boswell's impolite intrusion as biographer see also Richard Wendorff, *The Elements of Life: Biography and Portrait-Painting in Stuart and Georgian England* (Oxford, 1990), 12–13; James L. Clifford, 'How Much Should a Biographer Tell?', in his *From Puzzles to Portraits: Problems of a Literary Biographer* (Chapel Hill, NC, 1970).

[29] Keith Thomas, 'Yours', in *The State of the Language*, ed. Christopher Ricks and Leonard Michaels (1990).

[30] See Carter, *Men and the Emergence of Polite Society*, 137–55; Michele Cohen, *Fashioning Masculinity: Nationalism and Language in the Eighteenth Century* (1996), 37–41.

to this thinking was the emergence of what can be conceived of as an alternative system of social refinement – sensibility – better equipped to re-establish and maintain the Lockean synthesis of manners with moral virtue. In proposing a shift from politeness to sensibility, we should be cautious of overplaying the degree of change. Certainly both discourses had points of overlap. Many of the linguistic and conceptual components of sensibility – for example, benevolence, tenderness and moral sense – were common to politeness, even if they differed in terms of their extent and manifestation in presentations of refined gentlemen across the period. Likewise, the language of politeness continued to be used during the 1760s, 1770s and 1780s – the high point of sentimental culture – and was often applicable to this new, enhanced attention on moral virtue. In defining politeness as something 'more easily felt than understood' based on 'sympathetic and generous feeling of the heart', John Harris evoked the key aspects of sensibility in the name of a now increasingly ques-tionable ideal. Harris's contemporary, Hester Chapone, similarly retained the language of 'politeness' to describe what she, like Harris, identified as a new standard of social interaction based not on 'modes and ceremonies but in entering into the feelings of our companions'.[31] Sensibility is there-fore best seen less as a break with politeness than as a phase within a broader eighteenth-century civilising process dedicated to the bonding of manners and moral virtue.

But in doing so, sentimental theorists also reacted against established practice, seeking both to reinvigorate Lockean first-principles and to offer a timely corrective to polite distortions of this ideal. In thinking about differences, we do well to return to Hester Chapone's awareness of a new mode of sociability dependent on 'entering into the feelings of our companions'. It was this emphasis on communing with others' emotions, rather than acting with good breeding, which most clearly distinguished sentimental from polite sociability. Two underlying intel-lectual influences are particularly noteworthy. The first centred on attempts by Scottish moral philosophers to develop the *Spectatorial* model of politeness, and in particular its equation between refinement and a new urban social context, into a more advanced thesis of human progress – no less than a science of man – within developing social and economic environments over time. Man's ability to progress owed much to his innate inclination towards benevolent and sociable acts grounded in what David Hume described as 'mutual sympathy'.[32] Key to this new perspective on sociability, sympathy was broadly identified as the quality by which one person reproduced and came to experience

[31] Hester Chapone, 'On Conversation', in *Miscellanies in Prose and Verse* (1775), 29.
[32] David Hume, 'Of the Rise and Progress of the Arts and Sciences' (1742), in *Essays, Moral, Political and Literary (1742/52)*, ed. Eugene F. Miller (Indianapolis, IN, 1985), 131.

the feelings of another by observation. Communication of these feelings owed much to a second substantive development – this in attitudes to human anatomy – which saw the transition from an early modern understanding of a physiology based on static humours to one characterised by a wire-like system of nerves, along which feelings or sensations stimulated by sympathy were conveyed in and out of the body to equally sympathetic observers.[33] Both lines of enquiry gained a wider appeal from their dissemination in popular mid-eighteenth-century literary forms, most notably the novel and the magazine essay in which complex moral philosophical and medical theories were made accessible by comparison of the body with finely tuned musical instruments or barometers, with sympathy described as the activation of a nervous physiology through sensory perceptions of daily life shared via readily identifiable social signs: among them tears, facial gestures and that 'tender look of fellow feeling'.[34] Hume's equation of behaviour and social environment ensured that, once generated, an individual's capacity to experience sensibility was likely to improve. Increased opportunity to fulfil naturally sociable urges in the modern world necessarily stimulated the flow of sympathy between its members, enabling what Hume identified as a greater appreciation of 'those fine emotions, in which true virtue consists'. This increased fineness or delicacy of emotion in turn enhanced the quality of sociability by providing what he went on to describe as 'a greater sensibility of all the decencies and duties of life'.[35] Thus, for Hume, as for other academic and mid-century popular analysts, sensibility indicated not just quickness of perception or feeling but the application of this perception for moral ends: a system of social interaction rooted in man's natural tendency to sympathise, and dedicated to the relief of others through the physical and practical expression of this sympathy.

Such thinking had implications for later eighteenth-century discussions of the appearance and conduct of the refined individual. Moral feeling, it was claimed, could and should not be restrained by the levels of decorum deemed appropriate by an earlier generation of behavioural writers; a view prompting, in effect, a shift from the polite to the sentimental gentleman. As before, there were points of interaction between the two discourses and, as with politeness, so the physical body remained a principal means of displaying sensibility. But again there

[33] G. J. Barker-Benfield, *The Culture of Sensibility: Sex and Society in Eighteenth-Century Britain* (Chicago, IL, 1992), esp. ch. 1; John Mullan, *Sentiment and Sociability: The Language of Feeling in the Eighteenth Century* (Oxford, 1988), ch. 5; G. S. Rousseau, 'Towards a Semiotics of the Nerve: The Social History of Language in a New Key', in *Language, Self, and Society: A Social History of Language*, ed. Peter Burke and Roy Porter (Cambridge, 1991).

[34] James Fordyce, *Addresses to Young Men* (2 vols., 1777), II, 92.

[35] Hume, 'Of National Characteristics', in *Essays*, ed. Miller, 202.

were distinctions. Whereas polite writers emphasised the body through detailed instruction on deportment, the nature of sensibility demanded more encompassing, less precise, or mannered form of communication. Released from existing codes of good breeding now thought incapable of conveying sympathy, sensibility encouraged less regulated and more expressive actions – among them sighing, trembling and weeping – as evidence of refined inner feeling. One consequence of this development was a suggestion that the sentimental gentleman might be not just unwilling but also unable to conform to universal standards of civility, despite a surfeit of inner moral virtue lurking under what polite observers would have formerly criticised as a boorish exterior. An earlier generation had certainly appreciated that displays of good breeding were to be adapted to fit circumstances and, indeed, might have to be abandoned should manners threaten the true purpose of sociability. In the words of Edward Alanson, 'He would rather be thought so impertinently rude than to be so courtly as to let his Friend be oppressed with ignorance.' The mid-century poet, William Shenstone, likewise appreciated that certain social situations required a choice between what he called the '*Rules* of Politeness, or (what are more sacred with men) the *Laws* of Sincerity'.[36]

Yet Alanson's or Shenstone's careful decisions were not the same as the sentimental man's inability to conform to a mannered code which few writers now held in such high regard. Moreover, in view of the proposed declining contribution of good breeding to sociability, sentimental authors urged, if not praise, then at least tolerance and understanding for these less polished individuals. 'Under a negligent and seemingly rough manner', claimed the Scottish theologian, Hugh Blair, 'there lies a tender and feeling heart.' Friends of Samuel Johnson used just this line as a means to explain away the great man's legendary brutishness: 'To be sure', wrote Oliver Goldsmith, 'Johnson has a roughness in his manner; but no man alive has a more tender heart.'[37]

If outward civilities of good breeding were thought increasingly marginal to social exchange then, the argument ran, should one not be suspicious of those who continued to characterise their refinement in terms of external, and hence potentially more corruptible, forms of mannered display? It was in such a climate that politeness suffered its most dramatic exposure following the posthumous publication of Lord Chesterfield's correspondence to his son and godson in 1774. In view of the hostility which greeted the letters, it is worth remembering that

---

[36] Alanson, *Man of Integrity's Character*, 16; Shenstone quoted in Gerald Newman, *The Rise of English Nationalism: A Cultural History, 1740–1830* (New York, 1987), 132.

[37] Hugh Blair, 'On Sensibility' (1790), in *Sermons* (5 vols., Edinburgh, 1777–1801), III, 26; Boswell, *Life of Johnson*, 400.

some did look favourably on what the *London Magazine*'s reviewer identified as advice 'well calculated to form the man', with 'many valuable articles for private and public life'.[38] This said, the majority view proved less accommodating. Never intended for publication, and conveniently dating from an earlier, pre-sentimental era, Chesterfield's letters gave readers an unprecedented glimpse into an outmoded, immoral code which disguised self-advancement under a veneer of well-bred civilities. For the *Westminster Magazine*, Chesterfield's advice was characterised by a conflation of true refinement with a mere show of good breeding devoid of feeling or even an older *Spectatorial* notion of complaisance. To recall a phrase from Paul Langford's essay in this volume, the effect reduced politeness to 'polish', what in his own assessment of Chesterfield Boswell termed the 'perpetual attention to external elegance of manners'.[39] Combining 'politeness and insincerity together' the letters transferred refinement from a moral virtue to the 'outside recommendations of the glittering suit of cloaths', and the refined gentleman from a 'wise, accomplished Man' to 'a pretty, painted, lacified popinjay'.[40] At last, claimed the poet William Cowper, had their author been exposed as a 'Polish'd and highfinish'd Foe to Truth', a 'Greybeard Corrupter of our list'ning youth'.[41]

In the light of this reaction, we should note that Chesterfield was certainly not the first to show how external manners might exist independent of inner virtue. Even the revered figure of Manilius, for example, had combined sociable virtues with an awareness of 'how to *appear* free and open without danger of Intrusion, and to be cautious without *seeming* reserved'.[42] 'Politeness', claimed a well-meaning contemporary, 'does not always inspire a Man with Humanity' despite its providing 'him in appearance what he should be in reality'.[43] For Samuel Johnson, politeness required one to be 'pleased with a man's work', though only when 'he is present'.[44] What exonerated such commentators was that their advice could be seen (perhaps somewhat generously) as having a wider social purpose, either by steering men away from these misguided notions or by promoting the benefits of well-intentioned, pleasing, if not always truthful conversation. Crucially what set Chesterfield apart, and what prompted much of the criticism of his advice, was what his critics saw not just as an awareness, but his

---

[38] *London Magazine*, 43 (1774), 193.

[39] Boswell, *Life of Johnson*, 188.

[40] *Westminster Magazine*, 5 (1777), 22–3, 69.

[41] *The Letters and Prose of William Cowper*, ed. James King and Charles Ryskamp (5 vols., Oxford, 1979–86), I, 435.

[42] *Spectator*, No. 467, IV, 154 (my emphasis).

[43] Boyer, *English Theophrastus*, 10.

[44] Boswell, *Life of Johnson*, 844.

ready exploitation, of the supposed congruity between external polish and moral virtue (a congruity to which the earl expected those with whom he socialised to continue to adhere). To his detractors, Chesterfieldian manners were motivated not by the now all-important sensitivity or sympathy for others but by a duplicitous bid for personal advancement: the art of being on one's own guard while, by affecting a natural openness, putting people off theirs.

That Chesterfield's advice provoked such alarm undoubtedly owed much to its appearance at a time of mounting mistrust of politeness, and the development of an alternative, corrective sentimental code which itself certainly gained momentum as a now necessary purge of corrupt polite practices. Yet, it remains a strong possibility that Chesterfield's letters would have provoked consternation had they become public at the time of writing. What Chesterfield claimed to offer in his correspondence was, of course, an education for his son, the very activity that Locke prized so highly as the means for nurturing natural inner civilities and transforming the innocent 'individual' child into the socialised moral 'person'. It was precisely this aspect of the letters on which a series of sentimental educators focused, alarmed at what they saw not just as the earl's negligence of his own child, but also the potential allure of his advice to another generation of innocents. Chesterfield, according to the Tonbridge School headmaster, Vicesimus Knox, had presented an 'ornamental education' that led men to adopt 'varnished qualities' and the 'mean motives of self-interest'.[45] James Fordyce, the popular preacher and sermon writer, expressed a similar view, rejecting 'a wretched system of education' intended to make a vulnerable young man 'vain ... and smooth rather than polite'.[46]

It came as little consolation to these writers to learn that Chesterfield's attempt at education, performed in a bullying, hectoring, belligerent and hence far from polite correspondence, failed in its aims: young Philip Stanhope, who lived only to his mid-thirties, grew to be a shy, graceless and awkward adult – a 'mere booby pedantic booby' was Fanny Burney's verdict, 'a perfect Tony Lumpkin' that of another whose failure in the externalities of breeding ironically suggests a diffidence and sensitivity closer to the Lockean ideal of 'inner civility'.[47] More troubling was evidence that Chesterfield's legacy lived on in the second recipient of his advice, his godson the fifth earl, whom Horace

---

[45] Vicesimus Knox, 'On the Superior Value of Solid Accomplishment' (1782), in *The Works of Vicesimus Knox* (7 vols., 1824), II, 202.

[46] Fordyce, *Addresses*, II, 175.

[47] Fanny Burney, *The Early Journals and Letters of Fanny Burney*, ed. Lars E. Troide (3 vols., Oxford, 1988–94), II, 62; *The Manuscripts and Correspondence of James, First Earl of Charlemont*, HMC 28 (2 vols., 1891–4), I, 324. For Boswell's kinder assessment see *Life of Johnson*, 188.

Walpole described as a 'worthless young man, universally despised', not least for his infamous stance against the Revd William Dodd in summer 1777. Dodd, the fifth earl's former tutor, was accused of forgery by his employer, was tried, imprisoned and hanged despite appeals for clemency which passed unheeded by this new Chesterfieldian corrupter. Dodd, by contrast, was depicted as the archetypal sentimental gentleman: sensitive, morally upstanding and prone to sudden emotional outbursts; an embodiment of new refinement sacrificed by the inhumanity of an elite system wedded to the old.

The aim of this paper has been to highlight the centrality of moral virtue to eighteenth-century definitions of social refinement. Building on the equation of inner and outer civility proposed by John Locke, later writers sought to validate their chosen discourse by highlighting its origins in the generosity, benevolence and genuine sociability in each protagonist. That these efforts came in the second half of the eighteenth century to demand the restyling of politeness as sensibility ultimately proved less important than the maintenance of the link between the moral and the well mannered, however conceptions of the latter developed over time. Moral virtue, in short, mattered greatly to eighteenth-century advocates of social refinement eager, as befitted a self-consciously modern and enlightened society, to distinguish their experiments in social improvement from what they saw as earlier, inadequate forms of refinement.

This is a point worth emphasising if we are to view, as is surely correct, the eighteenth-century gentleman as an essentially social and sociable individual. For in characterising him thus there is a temptation, certainly within academic studies of the concept of gentlemanliness, to treat the Hanoverian gentleman as something of a poor relation to his nineteenth-century incarnation identified by the likes of John Burrow, Stefan Collini and Sheldon Rothblatt as the 'man of character'.[48]

Such a personality cuts an impressive figure: dedicated, on the one hand, to scrupulous moral vigour, self-improvement and 'cultivated individuality'[49] and, on the other, to a flight from the dependency and stagnation which many nineteenth-century observers identified as an inevitable drawback of creeping civilisation. In so doing, the argument runs, the man of character also sought to escape his predecessor, the sociable and socially constructed eighteenth-century gentleman. By

---

[48] J. W. Burrow, *Whigs and Liberals: Continuity and Change in English Political Thought* (Oxford, 1988), ch. 4; Stefan Collini, 'The idea of character in Victorian literature', *TRHS*, 5th ser., 35 (1985), 29–50, and *idem, Public Moralists: Political Thought and Intellectual Life in Britain, 1850–1930* (Oxford, 1990); Sheldon Rothblatt, *Tradition and Change in English Liberal Education* (1976).

[49] Burrow, *Whigs and Liberals*, 82.

default, the Hanoverian ideal compares rather poorly. At best a dedicated social conformist, for the polite gentleman success and self-worth remained in the gift of others, a pursuit of esteem which led to the cultivation of associations for personal ends replicated endlessly in his willing investment in the patronage network which distinguished eighteenth-century whiggery from nineteenth-century liberalism.[50] Resistance to this distinction between Hanoverian and Victorian archetypes is grounded not with its principal object of focus – the nineteenth-century man of character – but with its implications for representations of his sociable predecessor who, as this paper suggests, is perhaps himself deserving of a reputation as a man of integrity, self-scrutiny and adaptability: in short, not just a 'man of character' in his own right, but one whose character was largely determined by, and shaped, the refined sociability which later critics came to regard as his very weakness.

That the eighteenth-century gentleman has suffered such a poor reputation perhaps owes something to the ultimate failure of his attempts – sentimental as well as polite – to reconcile and stabilise the relationship between manners and moral virtue. Taking the story of the sentimental gentleman beyond its high point of the 1770s reveals several decades of decline during which his own value system was exposed as equally vulnerable to the duplicities and corruptions from which he had sought to rescue the polite. Typically, sensibility's end is seen as a consequence of the French Revolution in which its values were found wanting both by radical and by conservative observers. Yet, like politeness, sensibility's weaknesses were inherent and long running – though events of the 1790s undoubtedly sharpened these tensions. Thus, as politeness was thought vulnerable to and promotive of deceit, so sensibility, despite its emphasis on emotion above studied good breeding, was also open to exploitation from the outside by cool Chesterfieldian cynics and from within by those affecting tears and trembles for personal gain. And, like politeness, which suffered following the discovery of Chesterfield's duplicity, so sensibility's reputation dwindled once the affectation of leading sponsors was revealed: men like James Fordyce and William Dodd, whose clerical and literary careers had been dedicated to reinjecting moral virtue into refined conduct. For critics, it was this professionalisation which lay at the heart of the decline. Fordyce and his kind were motivated less by sentiment than self-interest, and have been duly recorded: Fordyce, for example, as

---

[50] See, for example, the changing tone in biographies of the Bath impresario Richard 'Beau' Nash from complimentary eighteenth-century studies of his sociability to nineteenth-century criticism of his triviality and lack of 'character', Peter Borsay, *The Image of Georgian Bath, 1700–2000* (Oxford, 2000), 110–11.

Mary Wollstonecraft's puffer of 'sentimental rant' and 'pumped up passions';[51] Dodd meanwhile has gone down in history as the fashionable 'Macaroni Parson', calling for benevolence and philanthropy on the one hand, while sporting fine white gloves and rings on the other.

If we can speak of a victor in the battle over politeness during the 1770s then it is, somewhat surprisingly, the fourth earl of Chesterfield. Alongside the decline of his own value system, the sentimental gentleman had to suffer the popularity of the earl's *Letters to his Son*, which ran to five editions in the initial year and eleven by 1800, as well as via numerous spin-offs and compilations both in Britain and pre- and post-revolutionary America.[52] That his advice proved such a good seller was certainly in part due to its controversial reputation. But it is also the case that much of Chesterfield's advice on dress, self-regulation, moderation and the attainment of knowledge was not only useful for the daily 'cut and thrust' of being polite, but also proved much closer to the *Spectatorial* model than many of his critics cared to admit.

It was not, however, this rounded Lockean or Addisonian ideal which resurfaced at the close of the eighteenth century. Rather, the exposure of sensibility brought to an end attempts to reconcile moral virtue and manners which now followed distinctive trajectories. For moralists a new home was to be found not at the assembly or dinner table but within an emerging evangelical religious movement whose exponents chose to convey this quality with little recourse to outward shows of good breeding. As one 1815 study, *The Character of a Renewed or Regenerate Man*, put it: 'His politeness is a continual self-forgetfulness, and a perpetual sacrifice of his own will ... It consists not in outward forms, and demonstrations of civility, but in a sweetness of soul that makes him please without adulation, falsehood or affectation.'[53] This is not to imply an equation between evangelicalism and boorishness, but rather a redefinition of the meaning of good behaviour away from eighteenth-century gentilities towards what might be described as a more 'early modern' concept of civility through self-regulation: less knife and fork politeness, more (clean) body and soul. Later pictures of gentlemanliness appear to have accommodated this enduring moral ideal in, for example, the spirituality of Cardinal Newman's archetype – 'he who never inflicts pain' – or even, a century on, in the gentle anti-militarism of George Orwell's cheery, revolverless policeman.[54]

[51] Mary Wollstonecraft, *A Vindication of the Rights of Woman* (1792), in *Political Writings*, ed. Janet Todd (Oxford, 1994), 167–8.

[52] On Chesterfield's contribution to nineteenth-century transatlantic concepts of refined conduct see C. Dallett Hemphill, *Bowing to Necessities: A History of Manners in America, 1620–1860* (New York, 1999), esp. ch. 4.

[53] *The Character of a Renewed or Regenerate Man* (2nd edn, 1815), 7.

[54] Henry Newman, *The Idea of a University* (1852), quoted in Roger Scruton, *England: An*

Manners, by contrast, took a different turn, bolstered at the close of the century by the re-emergence of the aristocracy as a driving force in standards of refined conduct. The result was a shift from politeness to 'etiquette', a term coined by Chesterfield in 1750, and a system dedicated less to the earlier equation with sociability than to social interaction centred on a precise code of social dos and don'ts defining civilised visiting, dining and greeting. Unlike moral refinement, etiquette permitted no opportunity for the regenerate man's 'self-forgetfulness' or 'perpetual sacrifice', owing instead its popularity to a conscious emphasis on excluding (inferior) individuals who failed to understand or enact the detailed rules by which breeding was now evaluated.[55] Polite 'persons' were, in effect, becoming polite 'personas'.

It would underplay the complexity of Chesterfield's advice to suggest that it found its logical outcome in this new system of etiquette. Nevertheless, the early nineteenth-century separation of morals and manners – a legacy with which to some extent we still live[56] – did provide Chesterfield with what might have been described as the 'last laugh' were not the earl's letters so critical of displays of open mirth as evidence of vulgarity. Dr Johnson, while famously critical of Chesterfield's lack of moral integrity, also claimed that were the 'immorality' removed the earl's letters would have made a 'very pretty book ... [to] be put into the hands of every young gentleman'.[57] To a sentimental generation, of course, this proved impossible. However, a later separation of morals and manners meant that, while the scent of immorality might linger (and in some quarters continue to offend), it now became increasingly incidental to the instruction of manners via re-editions untainted by scandal and packaged as acceptable, useful

---

Elegy (2000), 158; George Orwell, *The Lion and the Unicorn: The Genius of English Socialism* (1941; repr. 1982), 41.

[55] Michael Curtin, 'A Question of Manners: Status and Gender in Etiquette and Courtesy', *Journal of Modern History*, 57 (1985), 395–423; Leonore Davidoff, *The Best Circles: Society, Etiquette and the Season* (1973); Marjorie Morgan, *Manners, Morals and Class in England, 1774–1858* (Basingstoke, 1994).

[56] None the less, generations of commentators have drawn attention to the deterioration of even these basic standards of social interaction. Recent statements, which equate the decline of manners with the rise of a hedonistic pleasure principle, include Daniel Bell, *The Cultural Contradictions of Capitalism* (1976), and Richard Putnam, *Bowling Alone: The Collapse and Revival of American Community* (2000), while the British implications of these changes, together with that of post-war decolonisation, are considered by Michael Elliott, 'Rude Britannia', *Prospect* (May 2001). Nor does a recent trend for confessional journalism indicate a revival of the inner self as the marker of true sociability; rather, motives remain closer to Chesterfieldian self-promotion (albeit via distinctly un-Chesterfieldian means), censured by the novelist Philip Roth as 'hyperdramatization of the merest emotion', *The Human Stain* (2000).

[57] Boswell, *Life of Johnson*, 754.

social advice.[58] To the modern reader, as indeed to many of his later eighteenth- and nineteenth-century book-buying contemporaries, Chesterfield's advice is sound and pragmatic and, if perhaps not in name, has continued to influence subsequent English patterns of gentlemanliness and social interaction.

Thus Chesterfield's maxims – self-observation, reserve, circumspection, the need to conform to the prevailing tone of a society and the horror of being seen to blow one's own trumpet – were certainly not out of place in the nineteenth-century man of character as he developed to emphasise the value of self-worth and individualism, not least in his self-reliant and accommodating role as a domestic and imperial civil servant. Likewise the twenty-first century reader, if critical of Chesterfield's attitudes to women, is surely more at home with his concept of multiple and constructed selves than with the sober morality of the sentimental gentleman. Moreover, in his emphasis on self-presentation, on the importance of first impressions and on the correct deportment in new company, Chesterfield spoke on topics which are staples of modern advice literature on social interaction. Thus, shorn of the 'morals of the whore', Chesterfield's erstwhile 'manners of the dancing-master' have since been transformed, though not considerably, to become those of the aspiring politician, the first dating couple or the prospective job interviewee.

---

[58] For example: *The Accomplished Gentleman; or, the Principles of Politeness* (1806); *The New Chesterfield: Containing Principles of Politeness* (1830), and the *Encyclopaedia of Manners and Etiquette: Comprising Chesterfield's Advice to his Son on Men and Manners* (1850), part of George Henry Bohn's miniature classics series.

Transactions of the RHS 12 (2002), pp. 355–74 © 2002 Royal Historical Society
DOI: 10.1017/S0080440102000142   Printed in the United Kingdom

TOPOGRAPHIES OF POLITENESS

By R. H. Sweet

ABSTRACT. Politeness was a quintessentially urban concept; the formulation of a
code of polite behaviour was a response to the pressures of urban living and the
cultivation and display of polite manners took place in the social spaces of the
urban locale. Not all towns were equally polite, however, and the degree of
politeness on display in a town became another yardstick by which to categorise
and judge provincial society. London was often presented as the centre of true
politeness, in contrast to provincial vulgarity, but other towns were quick to
appropriate the concept and its rhetoric as a means of self-promotion. In so doing
politeness underwent modification as it was reinvented as a virtue of provincial,
middling urban society.

For it is certain that the asperity of man's manners is sooner overcome
in towns than in the country.[1]

THIS comment by Alexander Hay, an eighteenth-century historian of
Chichester, expresses something of a truism in the historiography of
eighteenth-century culture. Whereas earlier notions of civility or gentility
were primarily associated with courtly culture, or developed within the
context of the gentry household, politeness has always been located
within the urban environment; indeed, the very concept could not have
been developed without the concomitant growth of urban society.[2] The
decisive shift towards a more heavily urbanised population which
occurred over the course of the eighteenth century created, it has
been argued, both the demand for a new cultural paradigm and the
environment in which it could be encouraged. That paradigm has often
been identified with the cult of politeness.[3]

Contemporary theorists of politeness and subsequent historians have
sought to elucidate the reciprocity of the relationship between urbanisation and the spread of politeness; as a preliminary starting point one

[1] Alexander Hay, *History of Chichester* (Chichester, 1804), 331.
[2] Anna Bryson, *From Courtesy to Civility: Changing Codes of Conduct in Early Modern England* (Oxford, 1998), 149–50.
[3] Lawrence E. Klein, *Shaftesbury and the Culture of Politeness: Moral Discourse and Cultural Politics in Early Eighteenth-Century England* (Cambridge, 1994), 11.

may identify three major variants on this theme. The earl of Shaftesbury's vision of politeness was above all the art of pleasing in company. The continual process of interaction with others smoothed the roughness of manners and developed the proper qualities of complaisance and civility. 'We polish one another and rub off our corners and rough sides by a sort of amicable collision.'[4] Good company and sociability were to be found, not in the court, but in the society of the town, in the increasingly commercialised settings for leisure and recreation such as the theatre and the assembly.

Shaftesbury's view of politeness was unequivocally 'gentlemanly'. Addison and Steele offered a more explicitly commercial view of politeness in the pages of the *Spectator* which was less closely identified with the post-courtly gentlemanly elite: it was generated in the coffee house; it eased the day-to-day contacts necessitated in the transactions of urban living and created a harmonious and cultivated society. Politeness went hand in hand with the political liberty of a Whig regime which was explicitly connected with the flourishing commercial, urban society. It lent itself easily to consumption by the literate town dwellers of metropolis and provinces for whom complaisance and the art of pleasing were an essential part of commercial life.[5]

The third strand is that of the Scottish Enlightenment, particularly the work of David Hume and Adam Smith, whose philosophical and sociological analysis drew on the Addisonian language of politeness and tied the nation's progress towards civilisation to the rise of a commercial and urban society.[6] Human society moved from gothic barbarism and ignorance in step with the growth of urban society; the rise of towns broke the bonds of feudalism and allowed liberty, refinement and the arts to flourish by encouraging social interaction and stimulating creativity. People, wrote Hume 'flock into cities' and 'love to receive and communicate knowledge; to show their wit or their breeding; their taste in conversation or living, in clothes or furniture'.[7]

The urban world was thus the prime location of polite society, and the connection between a 'polite and commercial people' which was

---

[4] Anthony Ashley Cooper, third earl of Shaftesbury, *Characteristics of Men, Manners, Opinions, Times*, ed. Lawrence E. Klein, (Cambridge, 1999), 31.

[5] Lawrence E. Klein, 'Politeness for Plebes: Consumption and Social Identity in Early Eighteenth-Century England', in *The Culture of Consumption: Image, Object, Text*, ed. John Brewer and Ann Bermingham (1995), and *idem*, 'Coffee-House Civility, 1660–1714: An Aspect of Post-Courtly Culture in England', *Huntington Library Quarterly*, 59 (1997).

[6] Nicholas Phillipson, 'The Scottish Enlightenment', in *The Enlightenment in National Context*, ed. Roy Porter and Mikulas Teich (Cambridge, 1981); *idem*, 'Politics, Politeness and the Anglicisation of Early Eighteenth-Century Scottish Culture', in *Scotland and England, 1280–1815*, ed. Roger Mason (Edinburgh, 1987).

[7] David Hume, 'Of Refinement in the Arts', in *Essays Moral, Political and Literary*, ed. Eugene F. Miller (Indianapolis, 1985).

drawn by Blackstone was readily made by others.[8] Addison's and Steele's deliberately comic creation of Sir Roger de Coverley exemplified the rural and unpolished world to which politeness had not yet spread. His traditional values of country living, whilst equipping him for the life of the country squire, left him helpless in the complexities of modern urban living. The spaces in which polite sociability could take place: squares, assemblies, walks, theatres, racecourses, were all necessarily urban. The print culture through which polite manners were disseminated and through which a community of polite and cultivated readers was discussed was an urban creation. Peter Borsay's definitive study, *The English Urban Renaissance*, which delineates the growth of urban cultural and social provision through some of the leading provincial towns of eighteenth-century England, elegantly demonstrated the relationship between the growth of provincial towns and the spread of polite culture through eighteenth-century Britain (not just England) as a whole.[9]

The concept of a polite urban renaissance has been an immensely fruitful one, but there is always a danger of over-simplification and uncritical usage of the term, not least because of the equally promiscuous manner in which it was deployed in the eighteenth century. Politeness properly considered was a model of behaviour, 'an Art of life' as the *Polite Companion* put it, but it lent itself as a descriptor to institutions, publications and patterns of consumption.[10] George Whitefield's sermon on the polite and fashionable diversions of the age reduced polite behaviour to the pursuit of fashion and the taste for assemblies, playhouses and racecourses.[11] Hence it is tempting to make the additional step of equating coffee house and assembly room with a common polite culture, and to chart the dissemination of a uniform set of polite values through Britain as a whole. This approach does not do much to help us understand why the term was being used or exactly what sense its usage was intended to convey. The significance of using the label 'polite' lay as much in its rhetorical force as in its purely descriptive qualities. As one cynical visitor to Shrewsbury, John Macky, noted, the so-called coffee houses were nothing more than alehouses 'only they think that the Name of Coffee House gives them a better Air'. Macky clearly did not consider that Shrewsbury was as polite as it would like to think itself, yet the proprietors of the coffee houses were equally laying claim to a notion of fashionable politeness which they and the

---

[8] William Blackstone, *Commentaries on the Laws of England* (4 vols., 1765–9), III, 326. See Paul Langford, *A Polite and Commercial People* (Oxford, 1989), 1–2.

[9] Peter Borsay, *The English Urban Renaissance* (Oxford, 1989).

[10] *The Polite Companion* (2 vols., Birmingham, 1749), I, iii.

[11] George Whitefield, *The Polite and Fashionable Diversions of the Day Destructive to Soul and Body* (1740).

citizens of Shrewsbury would have understood, even if it did not conform to the expectations of the London visitor.[12] For the historian, the interest lies in both the innkeepers' appropriation of the term and Macky's disgusted reaction.

It is the intention of this paper to explore this connection between politeness and urban society outside the world of the West End of London, or that other centre of polite activity, Bath. Consideration will also be given to how the concept of urban politeness developed over the century and the contexts in which it was used. The distinction made in the earlier part of the century between the 'polite society' found in some towns, which was located in coffee houses, assemblies and cultivated by good company, and its antithesis in rural, or even barbaric society was less frequently made; rather attempts were made to distinguish the vulgar from the truly polite as the institutions and social activities through which 'politeness' was generated became rather more widespread. By the end of the century the term polite had lost some of its exclusivity and rhetorical power and was in fact being used with less frequency; in its place we find a range of alternative key words, of which the concepts of 'good taste' and respectablility were perhaps the most important.

The basis of this analysis comes from contemporary topographical literature, both published and unpublished, produced by travellers or travel writers, and local guides and histories written both for the visitor and the local market. This type of topographical writing was in itself a polite activity: travel was fashionable, and visiting towns was one of the major objectives of the polite itinerary. Tourists would see the visible evidence of the nation's progress towards civilisation in the growth and prosperity of provincial urban England. Writing down their reactions and comments was a means of rationally engaging with what they had seen, and provided material for reflection and conversation in polite discourse.[13] The material is of course flawed: visitors saw only what they wanted to see. Or, in some cases they simply wrote down what others had seen before them. Local writers also had a clear agenda of self-promotion or vindication. However, the material does allow us to explore some of the tensions which were set up by the growth of urban society and the dissemination of politeness beyond the gentlemanly elite.

Eighteenth-century travellers invariably had a set of criteria by which to judge a town: the intelligent tourist and the man of taste would wish to be informed as to the history, government, parliamentary

---

[12] J. Macky, *A Journey through England* (1724), 154.
[13] The major study of travel writing as a literary genre in the eighteenth century remains Charles Batten, *Pleasurable Instruction: Form and Convention in Eighteenth-Century Travel Literature* (Berkeley and Los Angeles, 1978).

representation, principal manufactures and trade, poor relief, and also the degree to which politeness had taken hold. Most tour writers were London based, or writing for a primarily London-oriented readership, for whom London, or at least the West End, was the centre of politeness. Only Bath, 'the theatre of the polite World', could truly be said to rank with London; between them they set a standard by which the provincial centres would be compared and found more or less wanting.[14] Politeness was the creation of 'the Town' but for London-centric commentators (both then and now) 'Town' was synonymous with London, and all else was but a pale and deficient reflection. The 'Town' referred to a social elite rather than the phenomenon of urbanisation, but the abstraction of the language allowed for ambiguity in its usage.

There was a predisposition in fashionable travellers to find the society of provincial towns inferior and lacking in politeness in order to confirm the superiority of London life and the taste of the traveller. As ever, travel serves as much to confirm prejudices as it does to broaden the mind. However, there was a hierarchy of politeness beyond the metropolis: at the most basic level there was a crude assumption that the further from London one travelled the more backward the society in which one would find oneself: the antithesis to politeness here being rusticity. Travellers were therefore wont to profess considerable surprise when they found evidence of what they recognised as politeness or refinement in the more distant corners of the land. Mere distance could be counteracted by the quality of the communications with London and with the volume of traffic passing through a town. The opening of roads to London was held to be the end of gothic barbarism.[15] Sophia Ward, touring Wales in 1791, found that Haverford West had become infinitely more civilised since the mail coach had run from Bristol to Milford Haven.[16] Even in the early nineteenth century, Aeneas Mackenzie, seeking to account for the elegance of the couture of Newcastle ladies and the tasteful window displays in the shops explained it in terms of the 'constant and extensive intercourse that exists between Newcastle and London'. There were, he suggested, 'more people in proportion in Newcastle, who have visited the metropolis, than in many towns two hundred miles nearer to it'.[17]

---

[14] Peter Borsay, 'The London Connection: Cultural Diffusion and the Eighteenth-Century Provincial Town', *London Journal*, 19: 1 (1994).

[15] Charles Heath, 'Former and Present State of Monmouth', in *Historical and Descriptive Accounts of the Ancient and Present State of the Town of Monmouth* (Monmouth, 1804), no pagination.

[16] National Library of Wales, Ward MS 19758A, 'A Tour through South Wales and the Western and Southern Counties of England', fo. 21.

[17] Aeneas Mackenzie, *Descriptive and Historical Account of the Town and County of Newcastle upon Tyne* (Newcastle, 1827), 731–2.

Politeness was bred by conversation and discussion; it flourished in the context of social interaction and exchange. It demanded a breadth of outlook rather than narrow selfish interests, which was encouraged by frequent dealings with a wide range of people. Thus, those towns through which much traffic passed and which could attract significant numbers of visitors were assumed to be more polite. Nathaniel Spencer was favourably impressed by Northamptonshire towns finding the inhabitants extremely polite, 'which', he wrote, 'is not to be wondered at, when we consider the great numbers of nobility and gentry that reside among them, and the many publick roads that pass through the different towns, by which they have an opportunity of conversing with strangers in every part of the kingdom'. The inhabitants of Oxford were said to be particularly polite because of the frequent opportunities they had for conversing with the undergraduates and scholars of the University. These towns were therefore deemed to have achieved a higher level of politeness than centres which were more isolated, and through which fewer fashionable travellers passed, and which received less in the way of the printed media through which polite tastes and values were disseminated. In Shropshire, Spencer found 'those in the principal towns nearly resembling the most polite people in England'; however, the inhabitants of Welsh towns 'and other remote parts' were 'too much addicted to that selfish motive' which, he pointed out, had already been noted as the distinguishing feature of the ancient Britons. The relative politeness of any centre could thus be predetermined to a certain extent by a perusal of a road book; a tactic which, if one should chose to be cynical, was not overlooked by a number of the more prolific travel writers.[18]

A closer inspection of the town would reveal additional materials for assessing its politeness, the most important of which was the number of gentry or nobility residing in or near the town. For all the subtle refinements in the theoretical understanding of politeness and its relationship to education, manners and taste, for most purposes there was a simple equation between social status and politeness. The gentry and nobility were polite by virtue of their birth and breeding, others were not. Time after time the quality of a town's society was apprised in terms of the resident gentry presence. It was assumed, particularly in the first half of the century, that the institutional manifestations of politeness, from bowling green to assembly room, owed their existence entirely to gentry patronage. A hinterland well filled with gentry families, as enjoyed by Bury St Edmunds or Kentish towns such as Maidstone, was bound to encourage the kind of polite society for which

[18] Nathaniel Spencer, *The Complete English Traveller; or a New Survey and Description of England and Wales* (1771), 281, 464, 440.

travellers such as John Macky were always on the look out. Road books followed the pattern set by John Ogilby, and listed the gentry seats along the route as one travelled towards a town; the countryside through which one passed was viewed as a composite of estates and gentlemen's seats.[19] The town was the *location* for politeness, but what rendered one town more polite than another was the nature of its relationship to its hinterland and the gentry living there.

On arrival at a town, its physical appearance was an extremely important clue to the levels of refinement reached. There was a close correlation between dark and narrow streets, filled with gothic and medieval structures and the extent to which the spirit of politeness and improvement had penetrated. As one historian noted of Beverley: 'It being partly the business of these pages to record the advancement of the inhabitants in the arts of life, it may be here remarked, that a more convincing proof of their progress towards a state of civilisation cannot be given, than in the repairing of the road and streets within the borough.'[20] Newcastle never enjoyed much of a reputation as a beacon of politeness in the north – and this was matched by the generally critical reactions to its narrow, dark and unimproved streets: 'The town is irregular and in general illy built' commented the American visitor Jabez Maude Fisher.[21] Spencer found that 'it is far from being either regular or agreeable' and has 'a most forbidding appearance' – especially to those not used to living in a town dependent upon commerce. The confined spaces, irregularity, gloom and dirt were the physical manifestations of all that was contrary to the polite ethos: they were the equivalent to pedantry, superstition and that narrowness of mind which betrayed ignorance of the ideals of improvement and a complete lack of taste, the aesthetic expression of true politeness. One traveller found the assembly room ill contrived and tellingly, 'too *narrow* a place for *polite* company to enjoy public diversions', whilst Mrs Lybbe Powys professed herself surprised at the quality of the assemblies at Chesterfield, given the otherwise poor appearance of the town.[22]

Coffee houses, bookshops, libraries and schools were particularly worthy of note as evidence of politeness. These were the institutions

[19] John Ogilby, *Britannia: By a Geographical and Historical Description of the Principal Roads Thereof* (1675).

[20] George Poulson, *Beverlac: The Antiquities and History of the Town of Beverley in the County of York* (1829), 68; cf. William Hutton, *A History of Birmingham* (2nd edn, Birmingham, 1783), 260: 'According as a country is improved in her roads, so will she stand in the scale of civilization ... The manners and the roads of the English, have been refining together for about 1700 years.'

[21] *An American Quaker in the British Isles: The Travel Journals fo Jabez Maude Fisher, 1775–1779*, ed. K. Morgan (Oxford, 1992), 50.

[22] Spencer, *Complete English Traveller*, 537; *Passages from the Diaries of Mrs Philip Lybbe Powys, 1756–1805*, ed. C. J. Climenson (1899), 25.

which offered the facilities for education and rational discourse without which the cultivation of politeness was impossible. Bookshops functioned also as meeting places for discussion, and, like coffee houses, were often the places where conversation was to be found. It was the quality of the conversation which one met with which provided the easiest indicator of polite company. John Macky remarked of York 'that you seldom want for good Conversation' on account of the presence of nobility and gentry, whilst Nathaniel Spencer found the men of Totnes 'very polite and courteous to strangers' which he explained by virtue of the fact that there were many gentlemen 'who have had the benefit of a liberal education, constantly residing in the town'. The lower orders, by contrast, were confined to one particular place and had little education, and therefore 'not having an opportunity of seeing the world, their ideas are contracted, and their minds and temper selfish'.[23] The provision for education in any town, as much as its assembly room and playhouse, was therefore a crucial indicator of its politeness and one which inquiring visitors made careful note of. Tiverton and Bury St Edmunds were both towns whose appeal to the gentry was explained in terms of their grammar schools.[24] The number of educational establishments in a town might be taken as a rough index of its 'politeness' as much as assembly rooms or the per capita distribution of hairdressers. Thus, Samuel Simpson described the grammar school at Tiverton as its beauty and the 'chief nursery of almost all the young Gentlemen of these Western parts'.[25]

The popularity of travel literature ensured that towns rapidly acquired a reputation for being either polite, or lacking in those civilising qualities; the comments of visitors consequently assume a somewhat tautologous nature. The diligent traveller would read his guide before embarking on a journey and would therefore have certain expectations of the towns being visited. Few travellers on a tour conventionally spent more than a day or two in most of the towns through which they passed; their impressions were therefore hastily made, perhaps in the interval whilst the horses were changed, and were often entirely dependent upon the reception they met with at the inn, the quality of the company they found there and information supplied by the landlord. The assumption that politeness was contingent upon good company discouraged the traveller from seeking it or acknowledging it in towns where gentry exercised a less obvious influence, such as port and manufacturing towns.

---

[23] Macky, *Journey through England*, 238; Spencer, *Complete English Traveller*, 25–6.

[24] Edmund Gillingwater, *Historical and Descriptive Account of St Edmund's Bury in the County of Suffolk* (St Edmund's Bury, 1804), 2.

[25] Samuel Simpson, *The Agreeable Historian: Or, the Compleat English Traveller* (1746), 291.

Certain towns did attract rather more sustained commentary, in particular those which showed most rapid growth and greatest wealth, such as Bristol, Liverpool, Manchester or Birmingham. These urban commercial centres were powerful reminders of the changes which British society was undergoing and their evident wealth and prosperity challenged the easy superiority of the metropolis and its cultural dominance. Of all of these Bristol, perhaps, featured the most frequently in discussions of politeness, particularly in the first half of the century. There is a simple explanation for this: first, its focal position in the communications network of the south-west and its growing trade, which sent it temporarily to second position after London in the urban league table, made it the object of curiosity.[26] More importantly, however, it was only a matter of twelve miles from Bath, and therefore an easy excursion for the convalescent in search of what the guide books termed 'valetudinary exercitation'.[27] Bath was polite society at play: Bristol was a busy commercial port. The contrast was not lost on visitors. Coming from the regular, uniform spaces of Bath and dazzled by the extent of new building, they found themselves in a town where some of the streets were too narrow to take carts, where lighting was often inadequate, where sheer density of population and volume of traffic exacerbated the normal problems of street cleansing and repair, and where trade and commerce, rather than leisured consumption, provided the mainstay of the economy.

The unfamiliarity of the Bristolian scene obviously discomfited many of the genteel and polite visitors. Thomas Cox, author of *Magna Britannia*, warned his readers that 'nothing of the politeness and gaiety of Bath is to be seen here'.[28] Other writers were considerably more forthright: Pope dismissed it as 'a very unpleasant place and no civilised company in it'; the author of the *Narrative of the Journey of an Irish Gentlemen* was disgusted at the total want of politeness, it was 'a thing banished from their republic as a contagious distemper'.[29] Deane Swift, in a letter to Sanderson Miller, was damning with faint praise: 'they endeavour to be polite and 'tis then and only that they are eternally ridiculous: you might as successfully fish for turbot in a draw-well as for a rational Companion in the whole City'.[30] Such politeness as they

---

[26] Norwich, Bristol's rival for second position for the first half of the century, never attracted as much comment, due, one may assume, to its rather more remote location and the less obvious extremes of wealth generated there.

[27] For a survey of different travellers' reactions to Bristol, see Peter T. Marcy, 'Eighteenth-Century Views of Bristol and Bristolians', in *Bristol in the Eighteenth Century*, ed. Patrick McGrath (Newton Abbot, 1972), 11–40.

[28] Thomas Cox, *Magna Britannia et Hibernia, Antiqua et Nova: Or a New Survey of Great Britain* (6 vols., 1720–31), IV, 744.

[29] Cited by Marcy, 'Eighteenth-Century Views of Bristol', 20.

[30] *An Eighteenth Century Correspondence: Letters to Sanderson Miller*, ed. Lilian Dickins and Mary Stanton (1910), 20.

had was a mere veneer – the drinking of sherry before dinner – but the effect was ruined by playing only quadrille and breaking up their Assemblies at ten.

The problem with Bristol was that the merchants were too successful: their souls were engrossed by lucre, the pursuit of which had made them so wealthy that they could afford to be insolent to strangers. Business consumed all their time and energies, leaving them little leisure for the pursuit of the polite arts. 'The very parsons at Bristol talk of nothing but trade, and how to turn the Penny.' R. H. Sulivan complained that the inhabitants were too mean to rebuild their houses in a modern and pleasant style.[31] The French visitor La Rochefoucauld recorded in his journal that his friend Mr Walpole warned him against going to Bristol and recommended Bury St Edmunds instead as being more congenial – and also drier.[32] Visitors were wont to laugh at the Bristol merchants who had built themselves a fine Exchange Building, but did not use it, preferring to continue to conduct their business in the traditional manner, standing outside. The anonymous author of a *New Present State of England* (1750) hoped that with the building of an assembly room and other accoutrements of civility, the minds of Bristollians would 'take a happier turn and would be convinced that Politeness is no way incompatible with trade and commerce'.[33]

Just as the tradesmen and nouveau riche merchants become stereo-typical figures of vulgarity in the literature of the age, the external perception of commercial and manufacturing towns was undoubtedly influenced by this image.[34] The literate public was accustomed to assume that new wealth would be spent without taste and that the society of tradesmen and merchants could only be covered with what Samuel Johnson described as the fine varnish of low politeness.[35] Visitors were always surprised to find gentility and good company combined with trade and business in centres such as Maidstone and Exeter. The extent to which such characterisations became orthodoxy is revealed by Mrs Lybbe Powys's comment upon Bristol that it was not 'near so bad a place as report has taught me to expect it'.[36]

[31] Macky, *Journey through England*, 149; R. H. Sulivan, *Observations Made during a Tour through Parts of England, Scotland and Wales* (1778), 92.

[32] *A Frenchman in England 1784: Being the Mélanges sur l'Angleterre of François de la Rochefoucauld*, ed. Jean Marchand, trans. S. C. Roberts (1995), 21.

[33] Marcy, 'Eighteenth-Century Views of Bristol', 34.

[34] Klein, 'Politeness and Plebes', notes that the antonyms to 'politeness' shifted from rusticity and barbarism towards more frequent use of 'vulgarity' over the eighteenth century.

[35] This was Samuel Johnson's verdict on the character of Mr Smith in Fanny Burney's *Evelina*. Quoted in James Raven, *Judging New Wealth: Popular Publishing and Responses to Commerce in England, 1750–1800* (Oxford, 1992), 135.

[36] Climenson, *Passages from the Diaries of Mrs Philip Lybbe Powys*, 49.

In the later eighteenth century the debate over this supposed incompatibility between the commercial and manufacturing functions of a town and its claims to politeness was extended to other centres whose size and wealth were forcing themselves on to the public consciousness. Richard Pococke, later to become bishop of Ossory, was greatly impressed by not just the industry but the civility and obliging behaviour which he encountered amongst the people of Stoke.[37] It must be said that many of his fellow travellers at that time did not share such a positive view of the potteries – or indeed any of the other major commercial and manufacturing centres such as Liverpool, Manchester or Sheffield. The same assumption which led visitors to find fault with Bristol society coloured their view of these other towns too. Travel literature was used to rehearse the stock anxieties of the age: the impact of luxury, new money and commerce on the manners and morals of society; and it was the impact of luxury, rather than an acknowledgement of the growth of politeness, which preoccupied many travellers. Too much wealth, too much business actually inhibited the development of the finer arts of life: 'Few commercial towns' it was said 'have in any considerable degree united a taste for literature with the pursuit of wealth.'[38] Liverpool was singled out by one author to be the only town in England of any pre-eminencey 'that has not a single erection or endowment for the advancement of science, the cultivation of the arts, or the promotion of useful knowledge'.[39] Chetham's Library was little used, noted Sir Richard Colt Hoare in the 1790s, although it was open every day for the use of the inhabitants, 'but in a town where trade engrosses the minds of man, women and child the library cannot be much frequented'.[40] True politeness could not exist in a place where money was quickly gained and lavishly spent: 'what a dog hole is Manchester', wrote the avowedly anti-urban Viscount Torrington.[41]

These towns became something of a rhetorical anti-type. Their politeness or otherwise was not seriously assessed, rather their inhabitants were characterised as money makers, illiberal and impolite in order to validate the arguments that to be truly polite one needed the leisure and education of a gentleman. Politeness or lack of it became increasingly important as a means to translate anxiety about new

[37] *The Travels through England of Dr Richard Pococke*, ed. J. J. Cartwright (Camden Society, 42, 1887), 8.

[38] J. Aikin, *A Description of the Country from Thirty to Forty Miles around Manchester* (1795), 353.

[39] James Wallace, *A General and Descriptive History of the Ancient and Present State of the Town of Liverpool* (2nd edn, Liverpool, 1797), 268.

[40] *The Journeys of Sir Richard Colt Hoare through Wales and England 1793–1810*, ed. M. W. Thompson (Gloucester, 1983), 156.

[41] *The Torrington Diaries*, ed. C. Bruyn Andrews (4 vols., repr. 1970), III, 116.

wealth, social instability and the fragmentation of traditional certainties. Judith Milbanke visiting Newcastle was determined to find the company something less than polite: 'I have had Mrs Mayoress & divers Aldermens Wives to visit me, more vulgar than any thing you can conceive!'[42] Sir Richard Colt Hoare would have been profoundly disturbed had he found the 'blunt tradesmen' transformed into 'the modern fine gentleman'. To admit otherwise would be to undermine his own sense of superiority and in broader terms the cultural hegemony of the ruling elite. True politeness, by definition, was beyond the reach of those who were not born to it. Late eighteenth-century travellers tended now to define politeness against the vulgarity of Fanny Burney's Branghtons, rather than Sir Roger de Coverley's rusticity, to the extent that some professed to find true politeness in those areas most remote from populous centres, which, in their pure and primitive state, were undefiled by the vices, social emulation and corruption of urban life.[43]

However, it is far from being the case that all the topographical literature produced in the eighteenth century was written for or by the *bon ton* of London or a genteel readership. Provincial urban society was quick to exploit the medium of print to promote the town and to provide information for travellers and business. Politeness was not just a criterion by which the country beyond London could be judged and found wanting: the inhabitants of provincial England had internalised it themselves and deployed it equally in their own characterisation and assessment of towns.[44] Politeness was a concept which could be readily exploited in a local context: elite observers might dismiss claims to politeness, but for middling society, politeness was a concept which eased and stabilised the demands of urban living; it could be used to denote a desirable cachet of quality and fashion, and it offered a means by which to achieve social betterment. In the second half of the century, as the provincial presses gathered strength and diversified their publications from newspapers and tradesmen's cards to miscellanies, histories, poems and novels, a clearer expression of provincial politeness can be heard.

---

[42] *The Noels and the Milbankes*, ed. M. Elwin (1967), 108.

[43] This view is recurrently expressed by Byng in all his tours through Britain, but see also, for example, Sir John Cullum's entry for 6 Aug. on his tour through the west of England in 1779: 'I am much pleased with this Excursion to this extreem western Part – for all extreem Parts exhibit Mankind in a more plain and primitive Character, than where they approach large and populous Cities – and I was also pleased to find that my Fellow Creatures, even in these Remote Regions, which we are apt to suppose the scenes of excessive Misery and Degredation, had the appearance of as much Comfort and Civilization as in the more populous and opulent parts.' West Suffolk Record Office, E33/2/2. This MS is unfoliated.

[44] Jonathan Barry, 'Civility and Civic Culture in Early Modern England: The Meanings of Urban Freedom', in *Civil Histories: Essays Presented to Sir Keith Thomas*, ed. Peter Burke, Brian Harrison and Paul Slack (Oxford, 2000), esp. 181–2, 195–6.

It was a matter of some pride to demonstrate membership of that polite society which was the culmination of the progress of civilisation and proof of that liberty and commercial strength upon which Britons preened themselves. Politeness could feed both civic and national sentiment. To claim politeness made economic sense: it was a means of attracting visitors and custom – those gentlemen who gave the town that polite patina in the eyes of visitors had first to be attracted by the promise of some polite society to entertain them. Politeness offered a comparator by which to assert superiority over other towns: a town might be described as exceeding any other in some desirable quality – outside London. Thomas Hinderwell's *History of Scarborough*, a volume aimed at both a local and a visitor readership, cast some serious aspersions on the neighbouring town of Whitby, which might have been seen as a rival to Scarborough's charms; whereas Scarborough exhibited all the 'refined amusements of polished life', with elegant assembly rooms and a neat theatre, Whitby was 'closely and irregularly built', the streets were 'in general inconvenient' whilst the town hall 'is a heavy pile, of the Tuscan Order, and did no great credit to the taste of the architect'. Definitely not of the same order of politeness.[45]

Politeness did not have to be valued against a gold standard set in London. By the end of the eighteenth century the inhabitants of a town such as Manchester or Sheffield could look back over a century of rapid growth, during which the nature of urban society had changed almost beyond recognition.[46] The perennially misanthropic Viscount Torrington might sniff and grumble but the native inhabitant knew that he or she was living in a town which had demonstrably more to offer in terms of leisure, entertainment and 'culture', in which greater order and regulation had been introduced and which appeared to present striking proof of the forward march of civilisation. John Wood had suggested that with the building of the assembly rooms in Bath in 1708 'balls, plays and cards' had usurped 'those rude athletic sports, or gross sensual amusements',[47] But he was far from being the only local historian who delighted in drawing the contrast between the 'rude barbarism' of former ages and the proofs of politeness and civilisation which proliferated in the theatres, libraries, book clubs, assembly rooms and coffee houses. These were the result of the town's rise to prosperity and the improved taste of the inhabitants – not just a cultural implant

[45] Thomas Hinderwell, *The History and Antiquities of Scarborough and the Vicinity* (Scarborough, 1798), 270, 40 per cent of subscribers were locally based, of the remaining 60 per cent around 5 per cent came from London. See Rosemary Sweet, *The Writing of Urban Histories in Eighteenth-Century England* (Oxford, 1997).

[46] See, for example, Joseph Hunter, *Hallamshire: The History and Topography of the Parish of Sheffield in the County of York* (1819), 122–5.

[47] Richard Warner, *The History of Bath* (1801), 349.

by the gentry. In provincial terms, the key antithesis was, perhaps, the opposition with past barbarity.

The negative relationship between the pursuit of wealth and the politer arts did not command a consensus. As the 1810 history of Liverpool declared, in defiance of earlier views: 'Wealth is indeed, equally the nurse of Taste and Commerce.'[48] By this time Liverpool had begun to acquire more of the outward trappings of a cultivated city, but the view that the pursuit of wealth precluded the possibility of participation in the culture of politeness and was doomed to vulgarity was always one which was projected on to the mercantile and manu-facturing sector rather than being fully espoused by it. A poem published in the *Liverpool Chronicle* in 1803, did not shy away from making the connection between the theoretical principal that commerce and trade produced politeness and the practical experience of Liverpool:

> Hence social life her polish'd manners drew
> Hence every art and every science grew;
> For science still on cultur'd life attends,
> And art improves where opulence befriends.[49]

In similar terms, the Nottingham printer John Blackner argued in his history of the town that trade had brushed off the rust of barbarism and brought politeness, social harmony and freedom to society.[50]

There was therefore a non-metropolitan view of politeness. Shaf-tesbury's imagery of the roughness of barbarism being smoothed away by the daily contact of social intercourse and the historical sociology of the Scottish theorists lent itself easily to a literature which celebrated the rapid growth of towns, their wealth and their identity. Shaftesbury might not have recognised in William Hutton, a self-made business man from Birmingham who started life in the silk mills of Derby, a fellow accolyte in the cult of politeness, but he could not have disputed Hutton's meditative comment on Birmingham society that 'Man is evidently formed for society; the intercourse of one with another, like two blocks of marble in friction, reduces the rough prominences of behaviour, and gives a polish to the manners.'[51]

But Hutton was not a devotee of Stoicism, and his reading in classical literature was limited to translations. We should not press the Shaftesburian resonances too far. Hutton was confident that Bir-mingham, his adopted town, was polite, if not genteel. 'Gentlemen' he famously wrote 'as well as buttons have been stamped here, but like

[48] Anon., *History of Liverpool* (Liverpool, 1810), v–vi.
[49] Anon., *The Picture of Liverpool or Stranger's Guide* (Liverpool, 1808), 195.
[50] John Blackner, *The History of Nottingham* (Nottingham, 1815), 194–5.
[51] Hutton, *History of Birmingham*, 259.

them, when finished, are moved off' but Birmingham had no need of the gentry in order to lay claim to politeness.[52] Hutton pointed to signs of politeness throughout Birmingham society: the theatre, the suppression of bull baiting, the opening of pleasure gardens and the growth of the library. But these were just isolated examples of a much more general equation which he drew between a modern commercial town and civility – 'The prosperity of a town depends upon its commerce; as that increases knowledge, freedom, taste, luxury, power and civilization increase.'[53] For Hutton, politeness lay as much in religious toleration, morality, education and good order as in the trappings of leisure and consumption.

The proximity of London and London fashions or the residence of gentlemen and their families was therefore immaterial to the politeness of Birmingham or Derby. Few other writers match Hutton's eloquent celebration of the commercial urban lifestyle, but neither is it true to say that the middling inhabitants of provincial towns accepted the view that they lacked polish and refinement and lived a life of unrelieved vulgarity. Hutton, and other provincial authors like him, argued for an expansion of culture, the arts, learning, and the progressive refinement of society, which might plausibly be called polite and which owed little or nothing to the influence of a non-mercantile, gentry presence. Indeed, the politeness of merchants and professionals was even presented as being more genuine than that of the self-consciously superior gentleman: the merchants and even the better sort of tradesmen of Hull, it was claimed, 'are indeed generally distinguished by a manliness of demeanour, and openness of disposition; equally free from flimsy politeness and arrogant disdain'.[54] Their true politeness was demonstrated in the real attention and civility which they paid to all descriptions of persons; it was a reflection of their education, their independence and their wealth. It was not a question of fashionable manners, of knowing when to drink sherry or not. Similarly the physician William Moss argued that the commercial intercourse of the inhabitants of Liverpool had induced a general harmony and sociability which was 'unclouded by those ceremonies and distinctions that are met with in more polished life'.[55] The conscientious application to trade and the sober approach to spending which it bred amongst the urban classes was celebrated in Andrew Brice's description of polite company amongst the tradesmen of Exeter. Their diversions were 'polite enough'

[52] *Ibid.*, 26.

[53] William Hutton, *The History of Derby* (1791), 186.

[54] Anon., *A Modern Delineation of the Town and Port of Kingston upon Hull: Being an Accurate Guide to All the Various Objects of Public Interest or Importance, Curiosity or Amusement in Hull and its Environs* (Hull, 1805), 39.

[55] William Moss, *The Liverpool Guide* (2nd edn, Liverpool, 1797), 144.

but free from affectation – ladies played cards (for sociable purposes only) but ruinous games of Hazard and Dice were shunned; bowling, music and the theatre offered recreation, but only after dispatch of business. The 'good taste, good sense, true Rationality and Politeness' of Exeter society was demonstrated in their preference for morally improving comedies or affecting tragedies rather than a farce or pantomime – entertainments which only served to kill time.[56]

Brice's comments on the stage and on gambling are illustrative of another strong theme in the middling version of politeness which stressed its links with morality. Shaftesbury had twinned politeness with virtue and an understanding of patriotism and public spirit derived from his reading of Stoic philosophy; middling politeness was much more pragmatically rooted in a code of morality which was suspicious of extravagance, idleness and irreligion. Towns had long since prided themselves on their civility and courteousness to strangers.[57] The traditional values of charity and philanthropy which contributed greatly to the cohesion of the urban community lent themselves easily to being reinvented as the humane benevolence which was the expression of true politeness.[58] Nottingham, it was said in 1807, was more noted for charity than for entertainment, and histories and guide books showed as much pride in listing their charitable institutions as their assemblies and theatres. Politeness could be reinterpreted to suit the needs of the urban community.[59]

Fashion and conspicuous consumption had always formed a part of the 'polite' lifestyle, but rising consumption and 'luxury' in the later eighteenth century had rendered fashion increasingly suspect. Popular literature and periodicals increasingly twinned fashion with vice and located it in the metropolis. There was therefore considerable opportunity for provincial writers to assert the credentials of their own town to a purer form of politeness, uncorrupted by the evils of fashion. Provincial commentators were ready to question the value of institutions such as the assembly room, theatre or racecourse, and as the critique of fashion and aristocratic corruption began to gather force in the later eighteenth century, activities traditionally associated with the patronage of the landed elite lost some of their polish of politeness. Paul Dunvan, a historian of Lewes with radical sympathies, described the racecourse as the place 'where pitched battles, gambling among all ranks, and the other public vices and disorders that commonly disgrace our turf

---

[56] Andrew Brice, *The Grand Gazeteer or Topographical Dictionary* (Exeter, 1759), 550.

[57] Henry Manship, *The History of Great Yarmouth, c. 1619*, ed. C. J. Palmer (1854), 118: 'This town is in regard of the people, civil; for entertainment of strangers, courteous.'

[58] John Harris, *An Essay on Politeness* (1775).

[59] Anon., *The History and Antiquities and Present State of the Town of Nottingham* (Nottingham, 1807), 18.

meetings, have long been annually practised with impunity'.[60] Lewes did, however, have a library society, founded in 1785.

Libraries, book clubs and reading societies offered sounder evidence of the superior taste and good sense of the town. As an anonymous historian of Liverpool commented: 'A community must arrive at a high degree of refinement to relish the beauties or cherish the benign gifts of literature.'[61] Libraries lent themselves to the quantitative listing so popular amongst eighteenth-century travellers: lists of members or subscribers could be reeled off and tallies of books could be counted. According to William Dyde, printer and author of a guide to Tewkesbury, 'that which, above all, evinces the superior Taste and good sense of the town and neighbourhood is the establishment of a Reading Society; a certain criterion of elegant refinement'.[62] Evidence of reading had the additional advantage that it could also be represented as morally improving (with the exception of novels from circulating libraries), and was therefore less morally equivocal than assemblies, racecourses or the theatre. Towns from Uxbridge to Leeds could boast reading societies or libraries; their historians wrote of these as proof of the progress of civilisation and the potential for all ranks to participate in the culture of improvement and enlightenment; so much so that the historian of Lincoln in 1810 expressed positive embarrassment at the town's apparent inability to support a library.[63] The evidence for the spread of literacy and education through schools, libraries and societies offered a means by which the middling sort could lay claim to membership of 'polite society' without falling foul of accusations of false taste.

Areas of typically middling concern came to be taken as marks of politeness: the suppression of animal sports such as bear baiting and cockfighting (an activity to which many members of the gentry were not at all averse of course) was proof of greater civility. The manners of the lower orders offered another index: those of Pontefract were

---

[60] [Paul Dunvan], *Ancient and Modern History of Lewes and Brighthelmston* (Lewes, 1795), 359.

[61] Anon., *The History of Liverpool from the Earliest Authenticated Period to the Present Time* (Liverpool, 1810), 236.

[62] William Dyde, *The History and Antiquities of Tewkesbury* (2nd edn, Tewkesbury, 1798), 81. Dyde was also the publisher of a miscellany called *Farrago* (Tewkesbury, 1792), which included an essay on politeness, defining it as: 'the assimilation of our behaviour to the practice of all those qualities that form the most refined pleasures of social intercourse, the appearance of universal benevolence, generosity, modesty, and of making our own happiness spring from the accommodation of others' (p 96).

[63] G. Redford and G. H. Riches, *The History of the Ancient Town and Borough of Uxbridge* (Uxbridge, 1818), 134–5; R. J. Morris, 'Middle Class Culture 1700–1914', in *A History of Modern Leeds*, ed. D. Fraser (1980), 204–5; A. Stark, *The History of Lincoln* (Lincoln, 1810), 275.

'more refined and polished than in some larger commercial towns; and even more sober and temperate' whilst the lower class of people in Norwich were much less inclined to be dissolute than in other populous cities.[64] For Valentine Green the politeness of the lower class of inhabitants of Worcester was exemplified in their courteousness to strangers and their failure to be addicted to vice of an enormous kind.[65] Too much politeness – the result of excessive wealth and excessive leisure – bred the dangers of dissipation, luxury, effeminacy and threatened a servile dependency. Politeness was therefore linked to that other defining attribute on which the urban middling sort prided themselves, a manly independence. The manners of the people of Hartlepool were 'courteous and civil' and 'their mode of life and thinking' was 'characterised by stern and unbending independence'.[66]

The proliferation of cheap guides to politeness, based upon the grooming programme which Chesterfield devised for his son, had made politeness accessible and theoretically attainable for the non-gentry as never before. His letters were utilised more as a benchmarking document for etiquette rather than as a theoretical exposition of the principles of politeness.[67] John Trusler's *Principles of Politeness* promised to teach the reader all that was necessary to complete the gentleman and man of fashion and make him well received in all companies, but it was patently aimed at those who made their living from trade, with special hints on how to avoid being mistaken for a 'mechanick' (the length of one's fingernails being crucial) or a domestic servant.[68] The fluidity between the upper levels of the middling sort and the gentry classes which marked the period is undoubtedly one of the reasons for the popularity of the 'how to be polite' genre of literature, of which Trusler was such a master.[69] Social distinctions, as so many moralists observed, were becoming harder to sustain, thereby putting additional strain upon the correlation between politeness and the presence of gentry; in many towns tradesmen had traditionally been excluded from participation in assemblies, but in a number of places such as Derby, Stamford, Bury St Edmunds, Southampton or Hull, the tradesmen

---

[64] B. Boothroyd, *The History of the Ancient Borough of Pontefract* (Pontefract, 1807), 495; P. Brown, *The History of Norwich from the Earliest Records to the Present Time* (Norwich, 1814), 98.

[65] John Chambers, *A General History of Worcester* (Worcester, 1819), I, quoting a comment made by Valentine Green in 1795.

[66] C. Sharp, *History of Hartlepool* (1816), 145.

[67] On this issue see Philip Carter, *Men and the Emergence of Polite Society in Britain 1660–1800* (2000), 78–80, 89–90.

[68] John Trusler, *The Principles of Politeness and of Knowing the World, in Two Parts* (16th edn, 1800).

[69] Penelope J. Corfield, 'The Rivals: Landed and Other Gentlemen', in *Land and Society in Britain, 1700–1914: Essays in Honour of F. M. L. Thompson*, ed. Negley Harte and Roland Quinault (Manchester, 1996).

themselves established their own assembly rooms with rules and rituals to match those of the gentry.[70] The presence of gentry, the assembly room, bowling green or coffee house – all those features which had made it easy for travellers in the earlier eighteenth century to assess a town's politeness – were no longer such reliable indicators.

For Daniel Defoe, the most widely read of all eighteenth-century travel writers, the primary interest had always tended towards the commercial and economic aspect of urban life and he was anything but hostile to the commercial spirit which he encountered in the towns of Britain, but in the original version of the *Tour*, the quality of the company to be found in the towns which he visited was equally a source of comment, and that quality of company – and by extension the politeness of the town – was wholly determined by the strength of the gentry presence. Richardson's 1778 edition, the last to be published in the eighteenth century, continued to make the association between the presence of gentry and politeness, as at Brighton for example, but whereas in 1726 politeness was a quality which was dependent upon good company, by 1778 it had become a generic quality of urban living. Thus Birmingham was described as gay and lively, with hackney coaches and Vauxhall gardens complete with orchestra, whilst literature and genteel educations were much cultivated in Bristol.[71] By the turn of the century in most towns theatres and assembly rooms were vying for notice with church and chapel. Book clubs, philanthropic societies and mechanics institutions offered new criteria by which to judge a town. The sharp distinctions between those towns which were marked by politeness and those which could be characterised as backward, old-fashioned and unimproved were becoming blurred.

By the late eighteenth and early nineteenth centuries, the gentry themselves were deserting the county towns, such as York, for the metropolis as the improvement in communications rendered the passage to London both cheaper and easier and the Season ever more attractive.[72] Defoe had thought Lichfield the best place in Staffordshire for 'good conversation and good company' and it had a flourishing theatre, music society, race meetings and balls, as well as library, booksellers and shows of auricula and polyanthus. But by the early nineteenth

---

[70] *Strother's Journal: Written by a Tradesman of York and Hull 1784–5*, ed. Caesar Caine (1912), 50–1, entry for 5 Nov.: 'yesterday was an assembly for tradesmen at Cresswell's Coffee Rooms. So opulent are the middling rank of tradesmen as to vie with the first of the gentry.'

[71] Daniel Defoe, *Tour through the Whole Island of Great Britain* (4 vols., 1778), I 165: 'Brighthelmstone is now become a polite place by the annual resort of gentry in the summer season'; II, 239 (Bristol) and 372 (Birmingham).

[72] J. Jefferson Loony, 'Cultural Life in the Provinces: Leeds and York, 1720–1820', in *The First Modern Society: Essays in English History in Honour of Laurence Stone*, ed. A. C. Beier, D. Cannadine and J. M. Rosenheim (Cambridge, 1989).

century the Cecilian society had dropped all pretensions to music, plays were enjoying runs of a mere fourteen rather than sixty nights at the theatres and the balls were deserted by the neighbouring gentry and nobility.[73] 'Oh what a falling off is there' lamented Tate Wilkinson as he contemplated the decline in subscriptions to his theatre in York; John Byng complained that Warwick, that archetypal town of the Urban Renaissance, was very dull with very little company.[74] Across the country the popularity of the assembly and the bowling green was in a general retreat and the politeness of coffee house sociability was proving transient. Even Bath was becoming declassé and had lost some of its aura of sophistication.

Politeness was a constantly evolving concept, which could encompass a wide range of values, with varying degrees of emphasis, and was as much aspirational as performative. By the early nineteenth century the semantics of politeness were shifting towards the narrower ideal of etiquette; the activities and institutions which had been particularly associated with the development and cultivation of politeness had become more widespread, considerably more common place and had lost their exclusivity. They were still the subject of much pride in the towns in which they were established and taken as proof of the taste, refinement, wealth of the inhabitants, but they were now as much a part of the middling culture as that of the gentry. A library or a racecourse was as likely to be described in terms of respectability as of politeness.[75] The soubriquet of politeness was less frequently attached in order to commend a town and its use as a descriptor in the language of topography was on the wane.

---

[73] Defoe, *Tour through Great Britain* (1778), II, 336; *VCH Staffordshire*, XIV (Oxford, 1990), 161–80.

[74] Tate Wilkinson, *Memoirs of his Own Life* (4 vols., York, 1790), IV, 19; *Torrington Diaries*, ed. Bruyn Andrews I, 227; *Passages from the Diaries*, ed. Climenson, 134.

[75] Anon., *A Picture of Carlisle, and Directory; Containing an Historical and Topographical Account of that City* (Carlisle, 1810), 87–8, 109.

Transactions of the RHS 12 (2002), pp. 375–94 © 2002 Royal Historical Society
DOI: 10.1017/S0080440102000154   Printed in the United Kingdom

POLITE CONSUMPTION: SHOPPING IN EIGHTEENTH-CENTURY ENGLAND*

By Helen Berry

ABSTRACT. Shopping was increasingly seen as a potentially pleasurable activity for middling and upper sorts in Hanoverian England, a distinctive yet everyday part of life, especially in London. This survey considers the emergence of a polite shopping culture at this time, and presents a 'browse-bargain' model as a framework for considering contemporary references to shopping in written records and literary texts. The decline of polite shopping is charted with reference to the rise of cash-only businesses at the end of the century, and the shift towards a more hurried and impersonal form of shopping noted by early nineteenth-century shopkeepers, assistants and customers.

RECENT years have witnessed the rise of a flourishing historiography of consumption for the period 1700–1800. Seminal works by historians such as Paul Langford, John Brewer and Peter Borsay from the late 1980s onwards have posited the role of the middling sorts in generating new patterns of acquisition and leisure in Georgian England.[1] In the early 1990s, a highly influential collection of essays, edited by John Brewer and Roy Porter, and another by Brewer and Ann Bermingham, established the subject of consumption in eighteenth-century studies.[2] These succeeded in incorporating the perspectives of economic historians, together with insights from historians of literary and material culture. More recently, the historiography has diversified to consider other nuanced aspects of consumerism, such as the personal use and meaning of material possessions to Georgian consumers, gender and consumption, contemporary ideas about luxury and the significance of

*I should like to thank Scott Ashley, Jeremy Boulton, Anthony Fletcher, Elizabeth Foyster, Andrew Kaye, Peter Rushton and Roey Sweet for their generous help with additional comments and references.

[1] Paul Langford, *A Polite and Commercial People: England 1727–1783* (Oxford 1989); John Brewer, *The Pleasures of the Imagination: English Culture in the Eighteenth Century* (1997); Peter Borsay, *Urban Renaissance: Culture and Society in the Provincial Town, 1660–1770* (Oxford, 1989).

[2] *Consumption and the World of Goods*, ed. John Brewer and Roy Porter (1993); *The Consumption of Culture, 1660–1800: Image, Object, Text*, ed. John Brewer and Ann Bermingham (1995).

'hidden' second-hand markets.[3] Many have welcomed this trend as an important counterpoint to the over-emphasis on the supply side of eighteenth-century markets, which to a large extent resulted from a pressing concern to anatomise the origins of the Industrial Revolution. It is no doubt symptomatic of the vastness of the subject, however, and the many different approaches to its study, that the historiography of consumption, and the historiography of politeness, have often experienced a failure of communication. In one corner, we find historians quantifying wage-rates, while in another, we find them re-reading Shaftesbury.[4] The controversies generated by such differences of approach to the study of politics, culture and economics in eighteenth-century historiography are frequently animated.[5]

One significant omission in the increasingly well-worked area of eighteenth-century 'consumer studies' is the almost total failure on the part of historians to consider *how* goods were acquired. Material things transport themselves from shops into people's homes and are mysteriously described as part of the process of the 'flow of goods', or attention is given to their display and use, with little attention paid to

---

[3] The re-orientation towards the consumer was anticipated by Ben Fine and Ellen Leopold in 'Consumerism and the Industrial Revolution', *Social History*, 15 (1990), 151–79; for new directions, see Amanda Vickery, 'Women and the World of Goods: A Lancashire Consumer and her Possessions, 1751–81', in *Consumption and the World of Goods*, ed. Brewer and Porter, 274–301; Beverley Lemire, *Fashion's Favourite: The Cotton Trade and the Consumer in Britain, 1660–1800* (Oxford, 1991); see also *idem*, 'Consumerism in Pre-Industrial and Early Industrial England: The Trade in Secondhand Clothes', *Journal of British Studies*, 27 (1988), 1–24; Stana Nenadic, 'Print Collecting and Popular Culture in Eighteenth-Century Scotland', *History*, 82 (1997), 203–22.

[4] The vast literature on the economic history of eighteenth-century England in a global perspective may be no more than represented here; see for example J. Thirsk, *Economic Policy and Projects: The Development of a Consumer Society in Early Modern England* (1978); Carole Shammas, *The Pre-Industrial Consumer in England and America* (Oxford, 1990); Jan de Vries, 'Between Purchasing Power and the World of Goods: Understanding the Household Economy in Early Modern Europe', in *Consumption and the World of Goods*, ed. Brewer and Porter, 85–132; Nuala Zahedieh, 'London and the Colonial Consumer in the Late Seventeenth Century', *Economic History Review*, 47, 2 (1994), 239–61. Influential in studying the Shaftesbury model of politeness is the work of Lawrence Klein; see his 'The Third Earl of Shaftesbury and the Progress of Politeness', *Eighteenth-Century Studies*, 8 (1974), 186–214; and *idem*, 'Politeness for Plebes: Consumption and Social Identity in Early Eighteenth-Century England', in *Consumption of Culture*, ed. Brewer and Bermingham, 362–82. A useful over-view of the recent historiography is Sara Pennell, 'Consumption and Consumerism in Early Modern England', *Historical Journal*, 42, 2 (1999), 549–64.

[5] As witnessed, for example, by the criticism levied against the work of Neil McKendrick by economic historians Ben Fine and Ellen Leopold for his 'trickle-down' theory of cultural emulation. McKendrick's hypothesis was that the dissemination of genteel taste was a stimulant to the rise of commercial culture, whereas Fine and Leopold's preference is for a more precise study of the incomes that made consumer spending possible. See Ben Fine and Ellen Leopold, *The World of Consumption* (1993), 120–3; *The Birth of a Consumer Society*, ed. Neil McKendrick, John Brewer and J. H. Plumb (1982).

the social interactions (in addition to the economic means and processes) which were required to procure them. Yet it is here, at the moment of purchase, that the exercise of politeness interacted with the complex forces of economic opportunity and choice. The expectations of polite society, and motivation to better oneself socially, did not *cause* people to buy things: as the work of Lorna Weatherill has shown, the idea of social emulation is an insufficient model to explain the distinctive spending habits of the middling sort.[6] In any case, the impulse to acquisition was in itself as variable as the individual consumer, and proscribed according to a range of factors such as financial means, degree of access to local markets and awareness of the variety of goods on offer.

However, if we pause to consider the influence of prevailing social norms, beyond trying to uncover an elusive causal relationship, we may see how a vital component of the routine lives of eighteenth-century people who were among, or who aspired to join, the ranks of what was known at the time as 'polite society' has been largely overlooked. Shopping, unlike assembly-going, parading in pleasure gardens, conversing in coffee houses or dancing at balls, is seldom described by historians of the eighteenth century as a distinctively 'polite' activity, yet it was a constituent element of, and of itself produced, a polite lifestyle. In other words, for a certain section of society at this time, polite shopping rituals framed the social experience of consumption as an everyday activity. Like assemblies and pleasure gardens, shops aimed at the middling and upper sorts (especially those in London) were crucial features of the urban landscape, the venues for the interaction of social relationships, leisure and commerce. The unwritten social rules of encounter in shops constituted a form of polite deportment, encompassing gesture, verbal exchange and a ritualised pattern of behaviour as the customer engaged with the shopkeeper. For an increasing number of middling-sort consumers with polite aspirations, the rituals of shopping could thus in themselves become a pleasurable pursuit, associated with sociability, display and the exercise of discerning taste – in sum, the performance of the Addisonian model of politeness.[7] What follows is an investigation into a different perspective on consumption: the process of developing a specifically polite 'shopping culture' in eighteenth-century towns, including the exceptional case of

---

[6] Lorna Weatherill, *Consumer Behaviour and Material Culture, 1660–1760* (London and New York, 1988); see also *idem*, 'Consumer Behaviour and Social Status in England, 1660–1750', *Continuity and Change*, 2 (1986), 191–216.

[7] See in this volume, Paul Langford, 'The Uses of Eighteenth-Century Politeness', *passim*. Another useful survey of middling-sort consumers is Stana Nenadic, 'Middle-Rank Consumers and Domestic Culture in Edinburgh and Glasgow, 1720–1840', *Past and Present*, 145 (1994), 122–56.

London. This survey pursues an ethnographic approach, drawing upon a wide range of contemporary sources (diaries, correspondence, didactic literature, newspapers, periodicals, plays and novels) in order to piece together something of the experience of polite shopping in eighteenth-century England.

There were more places to shop, and an ever-growing range of goods to purchase, as the century progressed. Since the early medieval period, the main centres of consumption in England, outside of London, had been local markets.[8] However, these underwent a crucial transformation during the period 1690–1801, when trade 'passed into the hands of shopkeepers'.[9] In the capital, and in provincial urban locations – whether spa towns such as Bath, or proto-industrial centres such as Newcastle upon Tyne, shops were increasing in number and in specialisation. While on her country-wide tour at the end of the seventeenth century, Celia Fiennes noted that in Newcastle, 'their shops are good and are of distinct trades, not selling many things of one shop as is the custom in most country towns and cittys'.[10] In smaller towns, fewer shops served a broad spectrum of social classes with a wider range of goods under one roof, such as Abraham Dent's shop in Kirkby Stephen, which sold candles and soap to workmen and artisans, and luxury goods, books and stationery to local doctors and clerics.[11] The increase in the number and range of goods in shops (even in rural areas), and signs of rapid expansion in trading activity, were thus prominent features of economic growth in England at this time.[12] But who went shopping in the eighteenth century? The subject of consumption may be approached through the identity of the shopper,

[8] Richard Hodges, *Primitive and Peasant Markets* (Oxford, 1988). Religious houses were also significant centres of consumption before the Reformation. See Derek Keene, 'Shops and Shopping in Medieval London', in *Medieval Art, Architecture and Archaeology in London*, ed. L. M. Grant (British Archaeological Association, London, 1990).

[9] Julian Hoppit, *A Land of Liberty? England 1689–1727* (Oxford, 2000), 331. Hoh-Cheung Mui and Lorna H. Mui, *Shops and Shopkeeping in Eighteenth-Century England* (Montreal and London, 1987), *passim*, observe this trend nationally, focusing chiefly upon the trade in tea.

[10] *The Journeys of Celia Fiennes*, ed. Christopher Morris (1949), 210–11. On the development of English towns, see Penelope Corfield, *The Impact of English Towns, 1700–1800* (Oxford, 1982); *The Eighteenth Century Town: A Reader in English Urban History, 1688–1820*, ed. Peter Borsay (London and New York, 1990); *Cambridge Urban History of Britain*, II: *1540–1840*, ed. Peter Clark (Cambridge, 2000).

[11] T. S. Willan, *An Eighteenth-Century Shopkeeper: Abraham Dent of Kirkby Stephen* (Manchester, 1970), 19.

[12] Craig Muldrew has calculated that trade tokens, which served as change when small coins were scarce, were issued in over 1,500 places between 1649 and 1672, almost double the number of market towns then in existence. In, *The Economy of Obligation: The Culture of Credit and Social Relations in Early Modern England* (1998) 54. See also by the same author 'Hard Food for Midas: Cash and its Social Value in Early Modern EngLand', *Past and Present*, 170 (2001), 78–120.

purpose of the trip and nature of the goods purchased. There is a distinction (a somewhat ill-defined one then and now) between 'luxury' and 'essential' items: consumables which are purchased rarely, as a special event, involving pleasure in the exercise of choice, and those repeat-buys which are mundane, for which those of sufficient means in the eighteenth century could have despatched a servant.[13] There is shopping in person and shopping by proxy, shopping for pleasure, and of necessity. For the purposes of this study, we shall be focusing our attention exclusively upon the shopping trips made by middling or higher-ranking individuals in person, rather than by their servants. The emphasis here is thus upon polite conduct in shops, rather than the sorts of material goods purchased. This approach is useful in that it allows us to consider even small purchases of relatively mundane items (of miscellaneous haberdashery, for example). By concentrating upon the social groups who comprised, or who aimed to join, polite society, we shall be able to undertake a closer study of the factors that made eighteenth-century shopping distinctive in their social milieu.

Who, then, was likely to fall within this group of shoppers? It was usual for unmarried women of a higher social status to be chaperoned on shopping trips by a relative, governess or servant, but, as the female characters of Fanny Burney's and Jane Austen's novels illustrate, evidently even single girls could make short visits to shops unaccompanied. The shops they visited were prescribed by the nature of the establishment, and the degree of respectability held by the shopping district. The heroine in *Cecilia* passed her time 'greatly to her own satisfaction' in London buying books, thereby furnishing herself with 'the mind's first luxury'.[14] This fictional gentlewoman was also portrayed making philanthropic and solitary visits to a haberdasher's shop in Fetter Lane, near the booksellers' quarter in St Paul's churchyard.[15] Jane Austen uses the public streets and shops of Bath as the setting for encounters between the main characters in *Persuasion* (published in 1818). In Bath, high-class retailers were originally to be found in the south-east corner of the city, around the Orange Grove, the Terrace Walk and the Abbey churchyard.[16] By the 1790s, as Peter Borsay's extensive study of Georgian Bath has shown, the focus was shifting northwards to where the exclusive Milsom Street was 'developing its

---

[13] Lorna Weatherill, 'The Meaning of Consumer Behaviour in Late Seventeenth and Early Eighteenth-Century England', in *Consumption and the World of Goods*, ed. Brewer and Porter, 207–8.

[14] Frances 'Fanny' Burney, *Cecilia, or Memoirs of an Heiress* (1782), ed. Peter Sabor and Margaret Anne Doody (Oxford, 1998), 103.

[15] *Ibid.*, 200–1.

[16] Peter Borsay, *The Image of Georgian Bath, 1700–2000* (Oxford, 2000), 30.

legendary reputation as a shopping mall'.[17] An anonymous contemporary poet described how, after breakfast in Bath, 'You may stroll for an hour up and down Milsom-street, / Where misses so smart, at ev'ry fine shop / (Like rabbits in burrows) just in and out pop.'[18]

For ladies in the metropolis, and in provincial towns, going shopping was a familiar part of the rhythm of their day, an activity undertaken in the morning after breakfast while men went about their business. Their afternoons were then occupied with social visits, followed by dinner at approximately four o'clock. This was a synchronised pattern to the day, followed by the wives and daughters of polite families around the country. Fanny Burney's fictional gentlewomen found their mornings 'all spent in gossiping, shopping and dressing'.[19] There is much evidence in gentlewomen's diaries and correspondence that art imitated life: like other young women of their rank across the country, Annabella and Harriet Carr stepped out on morning shopping trips from their house in Charlotte Square, Newcastle, and headed for fashionable Westgate Road.[20] In this, as in many other customs, English women were thought by other Europeans to have considerable freedom. Johanna Schopenhauer (mother of the philosopher) recorded that in her youth in Danzig, 'No woman of the upper classes would have gone ever so short a distance in the streets unattended by her manservant ... no lady went to the shops to make her purchases.'[21] Solitary shopping trips by Englishwomen were thus not uncommon, but in general, company cemented the social pleasures of shopping, and it is instructive how many fictitious and real-life trips are described with two or more companions, friends who may or may not have been related. Groups of women on shopping expeditions were so commonplace as to attract little contemporary comment. Visitors, rather than those for whom it was a routine, were more inclined to comment on their shopping trips in English towns. In September 1786, Sophie La Roche, from Augsburg in southern Germany, went on a trip with a female friend to Leicesterfields in London. As rather starry-eyed tourists, Sophie and her companion marvelled at a pastry-cook's shop, 'surrounded, like a large and spacious room, by glass cases, in which all kinds of preserved fruits and jellies are exhibited in handsome glass jars'. 'What we women liked best of all', Sophie enthused to her family, 'was a large but delightful

---

[17] *Ibid.*

[18] *Ibid.*

[19] Burney, *Cecilia*, 52.

[20] A. W. Purdue, *Merchants and Gentry in North-East England, 1650–1830* (Sunderland, 1999), 192–4.

[21] 'E. W.', *Youthful Life, and Pictures of Travel: Being the Autobiography of Madam Schopenhauer: Translated from the German*, 1 (1847), 243.

covering made of gauze which ... kept the flies off [the pastries].'[22]

Where incidences of men going shopping are recorded, either in diaries or in surviving bills and account books, it is tempting to conclude that the only type of shopping that men did was for high-value, high-prestige, one-off purchases. An example of this was James Boswell's triumphant and detailed account of how he convinced Mr Jefferys of the Strand, 'sword cutter to his Majesty', to sell him on credit a silver-hilted sword worth five guineas, even though he was a stranger to the shopkeeper: 'This I think was a good adventure', recorded Boswell, 'and much to my honour.'[23] (We shall return to look more closely at this purchase later.) The horse-loving menfolk of the Baker family from county Durham were typical of provincial gentry in their preference for shopping for luxury items in London, as an extensive collection of eighteenth-century bills testifies. The main focus of their attention, however, was the trade in horseflesh (hardly 'shopping' in the strict sense we have defined it).[24] Historian Margot Finn has shown how it was a common pattern for unmarried men or widowers to rely upon female relatives to shop for their material comforts and necessities, but also how some men were highly adaptable (if not acquisitive), and preferred to shop for themselves.[25] Other evidence suggests that within families men did not conserve their energies for 'luxury' purchases, but were sent on short errands to buy small items for their households. Edward, Jane Austen's brother, was sent to buy necessities for his family, newly arrived in Bath ('I trust the bustle of sending for tea, coffee, and sugar &c., and going out to taste a cheese himself, will do him good', observed Jane).[26] As with servants sent on errands, when men went shopping, the female organising principle was often still in evidence. Male customers appeared in all manner of shops, even those selling women's consumer items. The shoplifter Charles Speckman recorded in his confession from the gallows that it was not his gender,

[22] *Sophie in London, 1786, Being the Diary of Sophie V. La Roche*, trans. and ed. Clare Williams (1933), 111–12.

[23] *Boswell's London Journal, 1762–1763*, ed. F. A. Pottle (New Haven, 1950), entry for 1 Dec. 1762, 59–60.

[24] Helen Berry, 'The Metropolitan Tastes of Judith Baker, Durham Gentlewoman', in *On the Town: Women and Urban Life in Eighteenth-Century Britain*, ed. Penelope Lane and Rosemary Sweet (Ashgate, forthcoming, 2002).

[25] Margot Finn, 'Men's Things: Masculine Possession in the Consumer Revolution', *Social History*, 25, 2 (2000), 135. Other gender-specific accounts are Elizabeth Kowaleski-Wallace, *Consuming Subjects: Women, Shopping and Business in the Eighteenth Century* (New York, 1997); Lorna Weatherill, 'A Possession of One's Own: Women and Consumer Behaviour in England, 1660–1760', *Journal of British Studies*, 25 (1986), 131–56; Vickery, 'Women and the World of Goods', 274–301.

[26] Jane Austen to Cassandra Austen (17 May 1799). *Jane Austen's Letters to her Sister Cassandra and Others*, ed. R. W. Chapman, 1 (Oxford, 1932), 61.

but his youth, that had provoked comment when he asked to see some lace in a milliner's shop.[27]

As by far the largest and most diverse commercial centre in England, London was a magnet for polite society from all corners of Britain and abroad to spend their money. Cesar de Saussure, a young French Protestant from Switzerland, described London's four main shopping streets in the 1720s – the Strand, Fleet Street, Cheapside and Cornhill – as 'the finest in Europe'.[28] Cheapside had been the hub of shopping activity in the late sixteenth and seventeenth centuries, although from the Restoration period onwards, the central business district for retailing shifted north and westwards, to Covent Garden, the Strand and (later) Oxford Street and Regent Street. Although London streets for passing traffic were still filled with mud, wide and handsome pavements now made leisurely browsing a more civilised and leisurely pastime. The cleanliness and convenience of the environment, and civil sociability of shopkeepers, helped to make browsing a polite activity. Sophie La Roche enthused about London's streets, 'pedestrians need dread neither dirt nor danger here', a pleasure which was lacking in other European capital cities (such as Paris) at this time.[29] To this convenience was added the extra pleasure of sensory stimulation. In Oxford Street, for example, artificial lighting was used to allow shoppers (who could pass by six-deep upon the broad pavements) to gaze at the brightly lit silver, china or glass within, long into the night.[30] Watchmakers and glassmakers eclipsed even goldsmiths' and jewellers' shops with their displays of 'fanciful clocks set in alabaster ... gold and silver, and the richest cut glass lighted by patent lamps at night'.[31] The booksellers placed the most expensive books in their windows, the printsellers their most eyecatching artists, while the undertaker, not to be outdone, covered his window panes with 'escutcheons, crowns and coronets, and the lid of a little velvet coffin'.[32] Visitors to London also commented upon the elaborately decorated street signs outside of shops, some dangerously large and heavy, which were known to cause accidents

[27] Charles Speckman, *The Life, Travels, Exploits, Frauds and Robberies of Charles Speckman, Alias Brown* (1763), reprinted in Philip Rawlings, *Drunks, Whores and Idle Apprentices: Criminal Biographies of the Eighteenth Century* (1992), 189.

[28] *A Foreign View of England in 1725–29: The Letters of Monsieur Cesar de Saussure to His Family*, trans. and ed. Mme Van Muyden (1995), 50.

[29] *Sophie in London*, 111–12. For a European perspective see Roy Porter, 'Material Pleasures in the Consumer Society', in *Pleasure in the Eighteenth Century*, ed. Roy Porter and Marie Mulvey Roberts (Basingstoke, 1996), 219 n. 21.

[30] *Sophie in London*, 141–2.

[31] J. P. Malcolm, *Anecdotes of the Manners and Customs of London during the Eighteenth Century* (2 vols., 1808), II, 473.

[32] *Ibid.*

and even fatalities if they fell from their moorings.[33] In provincial towns such as Chester, a similar process of modernisation, specialisation and competition was taking place in the retailing trades, with modern brick or plaster replacing medieval, half-timber shop fronts, accompanied by environmental improvements such as pavement cleaning and refuse collection.[34]

The imposing bow-fronted shop windows that appeared towards the end of the eighteenth century were no doubt as much a deterrent to those who could not afford the goods within as a magnet to those who could. Francis Place recorded that in April 1801, his new tailor's shop at Charing Cross had a frontage 'as elegant as the place would permit', with each of the panes of glass in the window alone costing him the grand sum of three pounds. 'I think mine were the largest plate-glass windows in London', he later recalled proudly, 'if indeed they were not the first.'[35] Retailers in London, where the market exhibited the widest range of specialist shops, became extremely adept at attracting wealthy customers. This was evident not only in the quality of goods in stock, and the manner of their display, but also in the location of the retail outlet, and the language used to advertise the shop in trade cards and newspaper advertisements. It became fashionable, for example, to describe shops as 'warehouses' from the 1760s onwards, a semantic distinction maintained by Josiah Wedgwood, who encouraged the snobbish illusion of exclusivity among his customers by such singular measures as not issuing trade cards, and choosing smart locations for his exhibition rooms.[36] Polite shoppers from among the nobility and gentry, reflected Wedgwood, 'will not mix with the rest of the World any further than their amusements or conveniencys make it necessary'.[37] Another innovation made by shopkeepers by the end of the Hanoverian period was the practice of placing large and brightly coloured 'by appointment' crests above the doorways of their shops if they were patronised by royalty, a highly visible endorsement of the quality of the goods contained therein.[38] As customers crossed the threshold of a shop, the royal crest over the door fostered the illusion that they were entering temporarily into a space favoured by the ruling elite, even if the latter never went there in person.

[33] David Garrioch, 'House Names, Shop Signs and Social Organisation in Western European Cities, 1500–1900', *Urban History*, 21 (1994), 20–48; see also Ambrose Heal, *Sign Boards of Old London Shops* (1957), 2 and *passim*.

[34] Jon Stobart, 'Shopping Streets as Social Space: Leisure, Consumerism and Improvement in an Eighteenth-Century County Town', *Urban History*, 21, 1 (1998), 3–21.

[35] *The Life of Francis Place, 1771–1854*, ed. Graham Wallas 1898), 34.

[36] Eliza Meteyard, *The Life of Josiah Wedgwood from his Private Correspondence and Family Papers*, II (1866), 31–2.

[37] *Ibid.*

[38] Malcolm, *Anecdotes*, II, 473.

The interiors of shops, particularly those where higher value and status goods were sold, were no less alluring, and, for many, intimidating. The study of the spatial organisation of the exterior and interior of shops is a burgeoning field of historical inquiry in its own right. Clare Walsh, for example, has shown how eighteenth-century goldsmiths and jewellers were highly sophisticated in their strategies of display, exhibiting high-quality and high-value specimens of their craft in long, glass-fronted cabinets.[39] One contemporary observer likened shops on Ludgate Hill to 'perfectly gilded theatres' for their 'variety of wrought silks' and 'so many changes of fine scenes'.[40] Just as today, when window-shoppers may look from the street but not cross the sacred thresholds of designer emporia, there were unwritten, though widely understood, rules about who could enter these eighteenth-century theatres of consumption. These rules are by their nature extremely difficult to reconstruct in history, but are alluded to in the fictional works of contemporary writers such as Daniel Defoe, who had first-hand knowledge of retailing as a former tradesman himself. Our modern notion, for example, that a shop is either open for business or closed and the front door locked was anachronistic in this context. It was not unusual for shopkeepers to leave their premises to visit customers in their homes, or on other short errands. Usually an apprentice or servant was left in charge, but there were potential hazards in this method, as the sharp rise in shoplifting at the start of the eighteenth century testifies.[41] In *Moll Flanders* (1722), Moll finds a silversmith's shop unlocked, with no one in attendance on the valuable goods in the shop window.[42] She is witnessed by a neighbour (described as 'an officious Fellow in a House, not a Shop, on the other side of the Way') who catches her just as she is about to steal a piece of plate. Her subsequent actions are suggestive of the normal conduct that was expected when a passer-by entered a shop and found it unattended: 'I had so much presence of Mind as to knock very hard with my Foot on the Floor of the House, and was just calling out too, when the Fellow laid hands on me.'[43] Caution was required on the part of the shopper in order to avoid suspicion, particularly if he or she entered a place where valuable goods were displayed. In this scenario, the

[39] See Clare Walsh 'The Design of London Goldsmiths' Shops in the Early Eighteenth Century', in *Goldsmiths, Silversmiths and Bankers: Innovation and the Transfer of Skill, 1550–1750*, ed. D. Mitchell (Stroud, 1995), 96–111.

[40] Malcolm, *Anecdotes*, II, 132.

[41] J. M. Beattie, *Policing and Punishment in London, 1660–1750: Urban Crime and the Limits of Terror* (Oxford, 2001), 328–30. Beattie cites the appearance of pamphlets with titles such as *Hanging Not Punishment Enough* a 'Case of Traders relating to Shoplifters ... &c.' (1701).

[42] Daniel Defoe, *The Fortunes and Misfortunes of the Famous Moll Flanders*, ed. G. A. Starr (Oxford, 1981), 269.

[43] *Ibid.*

silversmith responded to Moll's protestations of innocence thus: 'Mistress, you might come into the Shop with a good Design for ought I know, but it seem'd a dangerous thing for you to come into such a Shop as mine is, when you see no Body there.'[44]

The rules of conduct varied according to location and type of shop. It was especially important to be aware of these rules when shopping in the metropolis: a telling part of Moll Flanders's defence against the accusation of shoplifting was that she claimed to be a 'Stranger in *London* ... newly come out of the *North*.'[45] The observation of difference between social mores in different parts of England is well documented in contemporary travellers' diaries, and suggests that Moll's plea of ignorance as a 'northerner' was more than a literary conceit. While the elucidation of these cultural differences is an intricate task (and beyond the scope of the current survey) one example will suffice. The Cambridge clergyman James Plumptre, visiting the north of England in 1799, thought it worthy to record 'the civility of a young man, apprentice to Mr Wilkinson the Chemist', in the market town of Morpeth.[46] The youth advised him upon the cure for a headache, and then resisted any attempt at payment. Plumptre insisted upon giving him something, but reported that the apprentice 'seemed scarcely to be pleased when I left an acknowledgement upon the [shop] counter'. This southern English visitor thus encountered unusually polite generosity from a northern shop assistant, but an equally unfamiliar surliness.

It is surprising, given the expansion and diversification of metropolitan and provincial shops, that little was written on the subject of the art of selling in late seventeenth-and eighteenth-century tradesmen's manuals. There was little notion of specialisation in marketing or sales techniques in the early modern period. *The Compleat Tradesman: Or, the Exact Dealer's Daily Companion* (1684), for example, contains advice 'For all Merchants, Whole-sale men, shop-keepers, Retailers, Young Tradesmen, Countrey-chapmen, Industrious Yeomen Traders in Petty Villages', but consists substantively of guidance on the use of weights and measures, property and quality of goods, how to avoid bankruptcy, etc., but nothing specific on how to sell to customers.[47] 'Merely selling', argues the historian of shopping, Dorothy Davis, was considered 'child's play, and very often children, or at least young apprentices were left to do it'.[48] As the

---

[44] *Ibid.*, 270
[45] *Ibid.*
[46] *James Plumptre's Britain: The Journals of a Tourist in the 1790s*, ed. Jan Ousby (1992) (entry for 24 May 1799), 101.
[47] 'N. H.', *The Compleat Tradesman: Or, the Exact Dealer's Daily Companion* (1684). For a survey of the genre, see Natasha Glaisyer, 'The Culture of Commerce in England, 1660–1720' (PhD dissertation, University of Cambridge, 1998).
[48] Dorothy Davis, *A History of Shopping* (1966), 155.

eighteenth century progressed, this changed, so that shop owners became increasingly aware of salesmanship as a vital ingredient to their prosperity, less the provenance of child employees, and more in need of careful stage-management. Josiah Wedgwood explained in 1767 that he needed a '*Large* room' to display his various wares in their most visually appealing manner, since he anticipated that this would give him space to '*do the needfull* with the Ladys in the neatest, genteelest, and best method'.[49] We have already seen how Wedgwood judged that his gentry customers preferred not to rub shoulders with the lower ranks on shopping expeditions. That he enticed them into his warehouse at all was a considerable achievement. A traditional mark of gentility and noble status was the ability to summon shopkeepers to a private residence or carriage parked outside a shop. In Fanny Burney's play, *The Witlings* (1778), set in a milliner's establishment, the proprietor Mrs Wheedle is summoned by Lady Bab Vertigo's footman to wait upon his mistress in her coach outside. This convenient theatrical device for introducing off-stage action was also plausible in that a titled lady would not have condescended to inspect 'trimmings' within the shop itself. To do so would have entailed rubbing shoulders with the likes of Mrs Voluble, the wife of a prosperous merchant who (as her name implied) had few polite graces.[50]

When well-off customers of the middling sort like Mrs Voluble entered a shop, they would first have been invited to take a seat at the counter, and perhaps to take refreshment.[51] Many illustrated trade cards and shop floor plans indicate the presence of ante-rooms, in which polite customers were invited to take tea before making their purchases. An advertisement for John Gibson's warehouse 'at the Shop lately possessed by Mess. Hodgson and Ormston, the Door above the Flesh-market, Newcastle', boasted 'The Tea Kettle will be always boiling. Gentlemen and Ladies may try the Teas.'[52] A subsequent advertisement for the same establishment developed an even more politely worded invitation from Mr Gibson to prospective customers: not only would he have the kettle on, but 'every Gentleman and Lady that please to favour him with their Custom, may depend upon being well served'.[53] Customers were often invited to take refreshment in a side room or parlour within shops, a custom which was later continued in the earliest nineteenth-century department stores.[54]

[49] Wedgwood, *Life*, 32–3.
[50] Fanny Burney, *The Witlings* (1778) Act 1, in *The Complete Plays of Frances Burney*, 1, ed. Peter Sabor (1995), 9–10.
[51] *Ibid.*
[52] *Newcastle Courant* (15 Aug. 1752).
[53] *Ibid.* (14 Oct. 1752).
[54] Clare Walsh, 'The Newness of the Department Store: A View from the Eighteenth

Once tea and conversation had been dispensed with, the customer would move to browsing in the shop. In an era before quality control and extensive use of brand names, the expectation was that browsing would be a visual and tactile experience, with proper scrutiny and inspection of the goods on sale.[55] Here, the polite shopper combined the exercise of discerning taste in selecting an item that was aesthetically pleasing and suitable with a pragmatic evaluation of its merits. This was not always easy: some customers even suspected that shopkeepers deliberately kept their premises dark so that the true quality of the goods on offer would not be revealed.[56] Jane Austen, ever a prudent shopper, wrote to her sister Cassandra in June 1799 to express her vexation that she had wasted half a guinea on a muslin veil, bought as a present for their future sister-in-law, which turned out when she got it home to be 'thick, dirty and ragged'.[57] The experience of shopping then, even more than today, was bound up with sensory discernment: sight, touch and even smell were important means of gauging first hand the quality of the goods on offer. Some eighteenth-century women turned browsing into an art form, and a distinctive pleasure in its own right. The appearance of new language and social stereotypes to describe women who shopped as a form of recreation is powerfully suggestive that this was more than just a satirical play upon a pre-existing phenomenon, but a new and observable social development. Mr Spectator in August 1712 reported his discovery among the 'fraternity' of Hackney-coachmen, that there was a 'Cant' or slang phrase for women 'who ramble twice or thrice a Week from Shop to Shop, to turn over all the Goods in Town without buying any thing'.[58] These women were known as 'Silk-Worms', by virtue of their habit of unravelling yard upon yard of cloth for inspection. Favoured by the coachmen as their best customers, the 'Silk-Worms' were also indulged by shop assistants, 'for 'tho they never buy' explained the *Spectator*, 'they are ever talking of new Silks, Laces and Ribbands, and serve the Owners in getting them Customers'.[59]

On the other side of the counter, shop assistants had to be skilful in the art of flattery and reassurance, and display a considerable knowledge of their stock. The polite attendant who laboured over elaborate

Century', in *Cathedrals of Consumption: The European Department Store, 1850–1939*, ed. G. Crossick and S. Janmain (Aldershot, 1999), 62; see also Bill Lancaster, *The Department Store: A Social History* (Leicester, 1995).

[55] On the increasing use of brand names for medicines, and product standardisation in the ready-to-wear clothes trade, see John Styles, 'Product Innovation in Early Modern London', *Past and Present*, 168 (2000), 148–64.

[56] Malcolm, *Anecdotes*, II, 473.

[57] Austin, *Letters*, I, 68.

[58] *Spectator*, no. 454 (11 Aug. 1712).

[59] *Ibid.*

deportment and dress, and lapsed into obsequiousness towards his customers, was fertile ground for satire. As early as 1709, the male shop assistants on Ludgate Hill were described as 'the sweetest, fairest, nicest, dished-out creatures' who 'by their elegant address and soft speeches you would guess ... to be Italians'.[60] 'These fellows' were seemingly 'the greatest fops in the kingdom; they have their toilets and their fine night-gowns, their *chocolate in the morning* and their *green tea two hours after*; Turkey polts for their dinner; and their perfumes, washes, and clean linen, equip them for the Parade.' Although this account was evidently satirical, it is instructive to note the carefully calibrated response on the part of the foppish shop assistant to different 'degrees' of customer; an usher (whom we would now recognise as a modern 'greeter') waits at the door to bow to passing coaches and hand ladies in and out of the shop with 'an obliging smile and a pretty mouth made'. Once inside, 'ladies' are shown the most expensive fabrics: Italian silks, brocades, tissues, English velvet embossed'. By contrast, the 'meaner sort' are presented with 'fine thread satins, both striped and plain ... Norwich crapes ... gentlemen's night gowns ready made, shalloons, durances and ... Scotch plaids'.[61] Successful eighteenth-century shop assistants would have been highly skilled at 'reading' their customers' needs, and judging creditworthiness according to outward appearance. Let us return to the incident involving James Boswell and his purchase of a sword on credit, and scrutinise the exact transaction between Boswell and Mr Jefferys, the shopkeeper, more closely. Boswell records:

> I ... looked at a number of his swords, and at last picked out a very handsome one at five guineas. 'Mr Jefferys,' said I, 'I have not money here to pay for it. Will you trust me?' 'Upon my word, Sir,' said he, 'you must excuse me. It is a thing we never do to a stranger.' I bowed genteelly and said, 'Indeed, Sir, I believe it is not right.' However, I stood and looked at him, and he looked at me. 'Come, Sir', cried he, 'I will trust you.' 'Sir,' said I, 'if you had not trusted me, I should not have bought it from you.'[62]

The rituals of polite browsing had the advantage in that it gave the shop assistant time to evaluate the customer's status and credit through his or her outward dress and deportment, if they were not personally acquainted. The early modern economy, as the work of Craig Muldrew and Keith Wrightson has shown, was largely based upon credit networks, with cash only used upon certain specific occasions, such as the posthumous settling of debts by the executors of a will, or when a

---

[60] Malcolm, *Anecdotes*, II, 132–4.
[61] *Ibid.*
[62] Boswell, *London Journal* (1 Dec. 1762), 60.

traveller made purchases on a journey.[63] An individual's capacity to acquire goods was thus to a large extent determined by their ability to establish a personal relationship with the shopkeeper, and to convince him or her to part with them on account. The mutual return of a steady gaze, and a 'genteel' deportment was crucial to Boswell's success. The diarist was gratified to have tested his own credibility as a polite gentleman, which successfully secured for him a degree of credit that was not his by right as a stranger. Returning to pay his bill the following day, Boswell thanked Jefferys ('You paid me a very great compliment. I am much obliged to you') but warned the shopkeeper 'pray don't do such a thing again. It is dangerous.'[64]

Contrary to the idea that there was no such thing as salesmanship in the early eighteenth century, J. P. Malcolm recalled a vivid account from this period of a sales assistant actively courting a female customer with the following patter: 'This Madam is wonderfully charming. This, Madam, is so diverting a silk. This, Madam – my stars! How cool it looks. But this Madam – Ye Gods! would I had 10,000 yards of it!'[65] The tactile nature of the encounter, and unusual degree of licensed handling of the customer's person, is emphasised here. Loose fabric is gathered into a sleeve and set upon the shoulders of the customer with a: 'It suits your Ladyship's face wonderfully well.' Through familiarity and general chit-chat, the shop assistant forges a social bond with the customer in a diverting conversation which masks the underlying commercial purpose of the encounter ('Was you at the Park last night, Madam? Your ladyship shall abate me sixpence. Have you read the Tatler today?').[66] What we are hearing in a distant voice is the flattering tone of polite browsing in action.

There was clearly a gendered dimension to the art of salesmanship, and a long-standing notion by the end of the eighteenth century that the female shopper required cajoling and flattery. References in the popular print culture from as early as the 1690s suggest that it was recognised that male shop assistants could use their sexual allure to court women's custom. One letter to the coffee house periodical, the *Athenian Gazette, or Casuistical Mercury* in 1692 was from a young tradesman at the Royal Exchange who feared that if he were to marry, it would be the ruin of his business. He was probably a haberdasher, a business

---

[63] Craig Muldrew, *The Economy of Obligation: The Culture of Credit and Social Relations in Early Modern England* (1998), 68–101; see also his 'Hard Food for Midas: Cash and its Social Value in Early Modern England', *Past and Present*, 170 (2001), 78–120; Keith Wrightson, *Earthly Necessities: Economic Lives in Early Modern Britain* (London and New Haven, 2000), 289–306.

[64] Boswell, *London Journal* (1 Dec. 1762), 60.

[65] Malcolm, *Anecdotes*, II, 133–4.

[66] *Ibid.*

'chiefly relating to the Female Sex', and his trade was reliant upon his personal charm, for as he explained 'I have many Visitants purely to view my Person, with the pretence of buying some trifle.'[67] His sales technique was to court each female customer equally, thus 'by my fair and impartial Behaviour most have deem'd themselves the absolute Mistress of my Affections'. Whether or not this entertaining first-person account was 'real' is largely irrelevant for our purposes: it is one of the earliest representations of a man using his sexuality to increase his retail trade among female consumers. It is also significant that the *Athenian Mercury* was prompted by this scenario to mock salesmen in general for their vanity, a trait which was thought to belong more properly to the female sex.[68]

For all the rituals of flattery, and indeed flirtation, that went with sales patter, the moment came when dissembling ceased, and the customer moved to find out the price of the goods on offer. The fact that prices were not displayed had two effects upon the experience of polite shopping. First, when a person of 'quality' entered a shop, the immediate social exchange, mirrored in the hospitality, cordiality and deference of the shop assistant, made no reference to the express purpose of the customer's visit: the exchange of goods or services for money. The parameters of these social interactions were framed by the social requirements of polite, 'feminine' sensibilities and ritual courtesy, from 'small talk' to the taking of tea. The goods for sale could be scrutinised and handled without mention of price – free from any commercial connotations, and discussed politely on their merits and suitability alone. Indeed, as the historian of consumption in classical Athens, James Davidson, has suggested, it is a phenomenon common to both ancient and modern civilisations that the lack of a price tag serves to increase the desire on the part of the consumer.[69]

The first stage of shopping, the browse, was facilitated essentially by social interaction. The second stage, however, the bargain, unmasked the illusion that this was a purely social encounter. It was expected that at some stage the price of the goods would be negotiated, adjusted according to the status, and skill, of the customer, and flexibility of the shop assistant. (There were certain exceptions: many eighteenth-century books, pamphlets and news-sheets had the prices printed on the frontispiece or header, although these too could be open to negotiation

---

[67] *Athenian Gazette or Casuistical Mercury* [hereafter *Athenian Mercury*], ed. John Dunton, undated [Mar.–Apr. 1692].

[68] *Ibid.* The Athenian Society's exact retort was: 'Sweet sir, The Character you have given of your Self denotes [what] great Humility and low Esteem you have of your self.'

[69] James Davidson, *Courtesans and Fishcakes: The Consuming Passions of Classical Athens* (2000), 110–11. Davidson uses the example of hetaeras (courtesans) and their skill at masking 'fees for service'.

at the point of sale.)[70] Bargaining was integral to the experience of polite consumption, and was bound up with the notion that the higher the status of the consumer, the greater discount he or she could expect, and the easier it would be for them to obtain credit with the retailer. It was up to the customer to decide when the conversation should move to discussing actual price. Following the shop assistant's elaborate flattery, the shopper made a bid for a price: 'When we had pleased ourselves [looking at the goods, we] ... bid him ten shillings a-yard for what he asked fifteen.' The shop assistant protested 'Fan me, ye winds, your ladyship rallies me! Should I part with it at such a price, the Weavers would rise upon the very shop.'[71] Quaker shopkeepers were exceptional in their refusal to take part in such haggling, since it was part of their religious conviction that they would never overcharge for goods, but offer only the lowest price they could take for them. The fact that they attracted comment for doing so is indicative that this was an anomalous practice. Cesar de Saussure told an anecdote about a man who swore that he would not pay for a piece of cloth after a Quaker merchant refused to lower his price. The man later sheepishly returned once he realised he could not obtain a cheaper one elsewhere, but the Quaker refused to serve him, since he was on oath. 'Few merchants', observed Saussure, 'would have had the delicacy of feeling this Quaker merchant had.'[72]

Polite shopping of the browse/bargain model here described belongs to an era when ties of sociability and mutual obligation, mediated through the operation of credit networks, were a prevalent and meaningful form of consumption for a particular sector of society, but this was soon to change. By the early to mid-nineteenth century, the rise of industrial production, economic expansion and the efforts of successive governments to rationalise the currency and encourage free trade were transforming the English economy into a modern capitalist system.[73]

---

[70] For auction sales 'by the candle' in coffee houses, see Brian W. Cowan, 'The Social Life of Coffee: Commercial Culture and Metropolitan Society in Early Modern England, 1600–1720' (PhD dissertation, Princeton, 2000).

[71] Malcolm, *Anecdotes*, II, 133–4. Another literary example of enthusiastic salesmanship, followed by a cavil upon the price, made by 'the first architectural upholsterer of the age', Mr Soho, in Maria Edgeworth's *The Absentee*, 1812 (1904), 101–4. The upholsterer finishes his elaborate plans for his customer's apartment thus: 'And, of course, you'd have the *sphinx candelabras*, and the Phoenix argands. Oh! nothing else lights now, ma'am. Expense! Expense of the whole! Impossible to calculate here on the spot – but nothing at all worth your ladyship's consideration!' I am extremely grateful to Nicholas Cooper for drawing my attention to this reference.

[72] Saussure, *Foreign View*, 201–2.

[73] *The Economic History of Britain since 1700*, ed. Roderick Floud and Donald McCloskey (2 vols., Cambridge, 1981); D. E. C. Eversley, 'The Home Market and Economic Growth in England, 1750–1800', in *Land, Labour and Population in the Industrial Revolution*, ed. E. L. Jones and G. E. Mingay (1967). For Jan de Vries's influential theory of an 'industrious

Towards the end of the eighteenth century, new forms of shopping emerged. On the initiative of shop owners, many realised that there were ways of making larger profits than the old credit system had allowed. Those who witnessed a change in attitudes and practices commented upon the erosion of polite shopping rituals. One pioneer of new retailing practices in the last quarter of the eighteenth century was the bookseller James Lackington, whose novel plan was for a 'ready-money business' that denied credit to all customers: '*no exception was … made, not even in favour of Nobility*'.[74] Universal cash-based transactions in shops required a sea-change in attitudes among shop assistants and customers alike. Lackington recorded, 'I was much laughed at and ridiculed, and it was thought that I might as well attempt to rebuild the tower of Babel, as to establish a large business without giving credit.' Responses from the public were at first highly unfavourable: 'Many unacquainted with my plan of business were very much offended', Lackington recalled, while others actually became angry and abusive.[75] These reactions were indicative of the way in which the ability to shop had hitherto been intimately bound up with individual reputation: refusal of credit would have been highly insulting to a polite customer.

The young Robert Owen also contrasted polite shopping with this new form of retailing. In his first job, working at McGuffog's haberdashery in Stamford, Lincolnshire, during the 1780s, he had served only county gentry. Owen later reflected that there had been 'a well-established routine of politeness' at the Stamford shop, 'and nothing had been done in a hurry'. Flint and Palmer's, his next employers, on the other hand, was a cash business, which Owen thought perhaps was the first 'to sell at a small profit for ready money only'.[76] Here, Owen observed the contrast between the old and new approaches to retailing:

> The customers were of an inferior class, they were treated differently. Not much time was allowed for bargaining, a price being fixed for everything, and, compared with other houses, cheap. If any demur was made or much hesitation, the article asked for was withdrawn, and, as the shop was generally full from morning till late in the evening, another customer was attended to.[77]

---

revolution', see 'Understanding the Household Economy', in *Consumption and the World of Goods*, ed. Brewer and Porter, 108, 113–15 and *passim*.

[74] James Lackington, *Memoirs of the First Forty-Five Years of the Life of James Lackington* (1791), 214–15.

[75] *Ibid.*

[76] E. D. H. Cole, *The Life of Robert Owen*, (1930), 50–1.

[77] *Ibid.*

In part, Owen's observations reflected upon the contrast between two separate worlds: one, that of the provincial gentry, locked into older patterns of consumption and credit; the second, a rapidly changing metropolitan environment, where an increasing sector of middle-class society had the means to acquire more consumer goods for 'ready money'. However, as the cash nexus became more firmly entrenched, and the language of 'sorts' gave way to what we would recognise as class awareness, one of the signs of social change was a secretly militant objection on the part of those whose position it was to serve that their performance of politeness was both artificial and humiliating. Francis Place, himself a student of Rousseau and Godwin, resented the fact that his trade as a tailor was 'all a matter of taste, that is, of folly and caprice', and regarded the social expectations upon him with a degree of considerable bitterness: 'The most profitable part for me to follow was to dance attendance on silly people, to make myself acceptable to coxcombs, to please their whims, to have no opinion of my own, but to take special care that my customers should be pleased with theirs.'[78] For Place, the polite show of manners that his customers expected was a source of loathing to him, a subservient self-denial of his own individualism and identity. His observations went to the heart of the problem that an increasing number of people had noticed with politeness from mid-century onwards. Originally, as Philip Carter has shown, it had been equated with 'relaxed and genuine sociability' as an 'essential means of establishing the originality and merits of new modes of social refinement', a reaction against the 'stiff formality' of social manners that preceded it.[79] Politeness had offered the illusion of a civil society based upon quasi-democratic principles of civic humanism and mutual respect, accessible to anyone who studied and adopted its precepts. By the end of the eighteenth century, artisans and tradesmen were increasingly political in their awareness that politeness could not gloss over the social and economic inequalities upon which society was based.

Shopping in the eighteenth century was neither as straightforward nor as familiar an activity as one might assume; it required a considerable amount of social skill and economic nous on the part of the consumer. Viewed in this light, the endless modest purchases and prices chronicled by gentlewomen in their private correspondence and personal accounts read less as proof of their inclination to luxury, nor the 'triviality' of their lives, than a proud record of their almost daily ability to negotiate the rules of polite consumption to their own social and economic advantage. The moment when shopkeepers started to

[78] Place, *Life*, 34.
[79] Philip Carter, *Men and the Emergence of Polite Society: Britain 1660–1800* (2000), 125 and *passim*.

use royal crests as marketing devices was emblematic of the social and economic transformation that took place in England during the eighteenth century. To shop at the same retail outlets as illustrious patrons represented a mark of one's own discernment, but paradoxically, this illusion was only sustained through commodifying, and thus opening up to a wider purchasing public the very 'quality' which was associated with social exclusivity. It was some decades before this symbolic move towards the 'democratisation of luxury'[80] was truly made possible with the arrival of the department store from the 1830s onwards. Vestiges of eighteenth-century forms of polite shopping survive today only in specific minority situations, such as the invitation to take a seat when one enters a high-class jeweller's shop, the personal service offered by the most expensive bespoke tailors or the habits of the current queen of England, whose personal credit is so well established that she famously carries no cash.

We have seen how the application of politeness to social behaviour in shops had a dimension of staged flattery from its earliest stages. Within the context of a society where personal acquaintance and credit still had some purchase, the illusion that this was underpinned by mutual loyalty could have gone some way to authenticating polite interaction between shop assistant and customer as a genuine mark of esteem. In the transition to a cash-based economy, however, and as the nineteenth century progressed, a persistent suspicion emerged among hard-pressed shopkeepers and employees that they were merely exhibiting a sham courtesy in order to obtain the customer's cash in the least possible time. Resistance to customary deference was a contributory factor to the class antagonism that found expression in campaigns for political reform among tradesmen and artisans of the late eighteenth and early nineteenth centuries. Not only this, but the civilising vision of eighteenth-century urban life was eroded, as an overriding respect for the pound gradually replaced a polite regard for the person as society's consuming passion.

[80] Lancaster, *Department Store*, 16–44.

Transactions of the RHS 12 (2002), pp. 395–415 © 2002 Royal Historical Society
DOI: 10.1017/S0080440102000166   Printed in the United Kingdom

CREATING A VEIL OF SILENCE? POLITENESS AND MARITAL VIOLENCE IN THE ENGLISH HOUSEHOLD*

By Elizabeth Foyster

ABSTRACT. This paper explores the impact of polite codes of manners within the home and in marriage. It focuses on marital violence as a manifestation of impolite behaviour, and argues that codes of politeness could offer benefits for wives faced with violent husbands. Instead of silencing discussion of marital violence, ideas about polite behaviour enabled women to define unacceptable male behaviour in marriage, and to find new ways of responding to violence. A case study of one marriage breakdown shows how within the culture of polite manners and sensibility, nervous illnesses became a powerful way for genteel women to signal violent or sexual abuse.

POLITENESS has become a convenient historical category and tool for those studying the eighteenth century. It is a useful descriptor applied to the particular codes of manners prescribed in this period for all those who aspired to social refinement and gentility. Sometimes it has been employed as the term that best summarises the social and cultural characteristics, attitudes and values of specific groups, hence there are accounts of 'polite circles' or 'polite society'. For contemporaries and subsequent historians, 'polite' is the shorthand for the most significant social changes that accompanied the economic and political upheavals of an era.[1] More recently, explorations into how a reputation for politeness could be acquired have allowed historians to

---

*I should like to thank Jonathan Andrews, Helen Berry, Anthony Fletcher, Bob Harris, Steve King, Paul Langford and David Turner for their generous help and advice upon earlier drafts of this paper.

[1] For example, Paul Langford explains how William Blackstone used the phrase 'a polite and commercial people' to describe the English in his influential *Commentaries on the Laws of England* (1765–9), in *A Polite and Commercial People: England 1727–1783* (Oxford, 1989), 1.

describe how this code of manners continued to enable differences in gender to be asserted and displayed.[2]

Politeness has also served a function as an explanatory device for historians. Most notably, it has been historians of violent crime who have used politeness in this way. The eighteenth century has been interpreted as a period of significant change in the levels and degrees of violence that were experienced. The number of recorded violent crimes fell markedly at this time, and a change of attitudes towards violence is attributed as both the cause and consequence of this decline. For Lawrence Stone, the explanation lies with a 'transformation of values during the eighteenth century', which resulted in a 'cultural softening of manners' and 'a greater sensitivity to cruelty and violence'.[3] Before the eighteenth century, J. M. Beattie believes that there was 'less politeness in ordinary human relationships than today ... less patience and control over temper, more aggressiveness, more willingness to seek a violent physical solution to conflicts'. In contrast, over the course of the eighteenth century, there was a 'developing civility, expressed perhaps in a more highly developed politeness of manner', so that individuals sought to resolve their conflicts through non-violent means.[4] In these accounts the filtration of polite manners through society heralds the origins of a less violent and hence more 'civilised', and recognisably 'modern' world. Politeness assumes a new degree of historical importance in this context. Rather than simply a category describing change, politeness itself is a force for change. The polite code of manners becomes more than a list of ideals, but is suggested as a trigger for changes in actual behaviour.

Yet there has been remarkably little academic exchange or debate between historians of crime and those of politeness. It appears that historians of violent crime, faced with quantifying change over time, and explaining complex legal procedures, have found in the concept of politeness an all too convenient solution for interpreting the difficult

---

[2] See for example, L. E. Klein, 'Gender, Conversation and the Public Sphere in Early Eighteenth-Century England', in *Textuality and Sexuality: Reading Theories and Practices*, ed. J. Still and M. Worton (Manchester, 1993), 100–15; M. Cohen, *Fashioning Masculinity: National Identity and Language in the Eighteenth Century* (1996); and P. Carter, *Men and the Emergence of Polite Society in Britain 1660–1800* (2001).

[3] L. Stone, 'A Rejoinder', *Past and Present*, 108 (1985), 219, 220. The rejoinder was to the criticisms aired by J. A. Sharpe, 'The History of Violence in England: Some Observations', *Past and Present*, 108 (1985), 206–15. The debate had been triggered by Stone's article, 'Interpersonal Violence in English Society 1300–1980', *Past and Present*, 101 (1983), 22–33.

[4] J. M. Beattie, 'Violence and Society in Early-Modern England', in *Perspectives in Criminal Law: Essays in Honour of John L. J. Edwards*, ed. A. N. Doob and E. L. Greenspan (Ontario, 1985), 45, and *idem, Crime and the Courts in England 1660–1800* (Princeton, 1986), 112.

historical problems that they have uncovered. These historians do not engage with the studies that have been conducted into politeness and fail to define what they mean by this term. More importantly, they do not show *how* codes of polite manners were transformed into behaviour. Certainly, recent studies of violent crime and interpersonal disputes have suggested that factors in addition to cultural phenomena such as politeness explain changes in the numbers of recorded offences.[5] But while no historian has firmly rejected cultural change from their analysis, the relationship between attitudes and behaviour remains under explored.

As the nature of academic specialism has kept historians apart, neither those examining politeness nor those studying violent crime have paid sufficient attention to the domestic arena. Recorded levels of domestic homicide have remained remarkably steady over time, so that the proportion of killings committed within the family in the eighteenth century is very close to that of today.[6] Why the beneficial effects of the diffusion of polite manners stopped short at the door to the family home is unclear. Meanwhile, family relationships and marriage have attracted little attention from historians interested in politeness. Such an omission would have been surprising to contemporary thinkers and writers on polite conduct who assumed that good manners began in the home. While we have learnt much from historians about the impact of politeness upon ideal notions of masculinity and femininity, the focus of these studies has been upon the practice and display of polite manners in the coffee shops, clubs, assemblies, theatres and pleasure gardens of a burgeoning civil society. The relations between the sexes have been central to many of these studies of politeness, and the roles which women played in 'polishing' and 'refining' male manners, and so fashioning the polite gentleman, have received particular emphasis. But even though mixed sex sociability has sometimes led historians to an examination of politeness in the home, at occasions around the dinner, tea or card table, generally it is the non-familial relationships between hosts and their guests which are studied. Our understanding of how politeness affected the daily patterns of relationships within the family and household, and marriage as the most intimate bond between men and women, is limited.

One important exception to this trend in historical writing has been

---

[5] C. W. Brooks, 'Interpersonal Conflict and Social Tension: Civil Litigation in England, 1640–1830', in *The First Modern Society: Essays in English History in Honour of Lawrence Stone*, ed. A. L. Beier, D. Cannadine and J. M. Rosenheim (Cambridge, 1989), 384–5, 396–7; J. S. Cockburn, 'Patterns of Violence in English Society. Homicide in Kent 1560–1985', *Past and Present*, 130 (1991), 103–4; P. King, 'Punishing Assault: The Transformation of Attitudes in the English Courts', *Journal of Interdisciplinary History*, 27 (1996), 57–62, 72–4.

[6] Cockburn, 'Patterns of Violence', 96, 105.

the work by Margaret Hunt on wife-beating in London in the years 1711 to 1713. Using records of marriage separation from the London consistory court, Hunt examined the causes and consequences of marital violence. Hunt uses the term 'civility', rather than politeness, and argues that this was to have a profound and long-lasting impact on the attitudes and responses to marital violence. In her words, 'the cult of civility' helped to 'create that veil of silence around respectable families that has proved such an obstacle to dealing with domestic violence right up to the present day'. According to Hunt, by 'demonizing' the wife-beater, polite writers such as Addison and Steele rendered marital violence 'unspeakable' in civil society. Far from eliminating marital violence, Hunt believes that its condemnation drove it underground, so that it became an activity shrouded in secrecy and shame. The result was that the battered woman became isolated from support, for, as Hunt explains, 'it is very difficult to intervene in the unspeakable'. Wife-beating was something so 'repellent' and 'deviant' that the middle classes refused to recognise it within their own social group, but instead displaced it upon the working classes, as another vice belonging to the vulgar poor. Following this line of argument, politeness, as the later incarnation of civility, created a collective denial of the existence of marital violence within middle-class homes, protected violent men and muted women's cries for help.[7]

Taking the lead from Hunt's model, this paper suggests that studying marital violence provides us with a new way of understanding the meanings and impact of the codes of manners labelled as politeness. The records of marriage separation cases heard in the church courts are ideal sources for tracing how far polite manners translated into social practice. Those who fought these disputes in the eighteenth century were mainly drawn from the middling to upper social ranks, precisely those for whom a reputation for politeness was thought to hold the greatest appeal. From the detail about relationships within the family and household that was supplied in the course of giving libels and depositions to the church courts, it is possible to highlight the tension points which were created if, and when, individuals applied the ideals of politeness to their daily lives.

Since using physical correction against an unruly wife was popularly thought to be a husband's right, and many marital disputes would have

---

[7] M. Hunt, 'Wife Beating, Domesticity and Women's Independence in Eighteenth-Century London', *Gender and History*, 4, 1 (1992), 10–33; A. J. Hammerton follows this line of argument in *Cruelty and Companionship: Conflict in Nineteenth-Century Married Life* (1992), and believes that it was only in the late nineteenth century that the middle classes recognised that there was a problem of marital violence in their own social rank. A good introduction to the history of marital violence is provided in M. E. Doggett, *Marriage, Wife-Beating and the Law in Victorian England* (Columbia, 1993).

been resolved without recourse to law, a reading of separation cases will never give us a full picture of the extent of marital violence in the past. Hence this paper can make no claim that the codes of politeness made an impact on the incidence of marital violence. Nevertheless, the disputes fought in the church courts do provide a more representative picture of the part that violence took in everyday life than the exceptional incident of homicide. The records reveal that the codes of politeness did bring about changing expectations of male behaviour within marriage. As we will see, in some marriages these expectations were not met, and within these relationships women's experiences of male violence remained essentially unaltered. However, this paper will argue that we can find clearer evidence of how polite manners brought about changes in marital behaviour if we turn our attention away from the perpetrators to the targets of violence. Women's responses to male violence were significantly different from the mid-eighteenth century than in previous periods, and the explanation for this mainly stems from the diffusion of the concept of politeness and the practice of polite manners among the middling orders.

Instead of the essentially negative position assumed by Hunt, this paper will show that codes of politeness could yield positive benefits for married women in violent marriages. Politeness did not leave middle-class women vulnerable and helpless in the face of abusive husbands. Based on a reading of cases of marriage separation brought to the English church courts on the grounds of cruelty in the eighteenth and early nineteenth centuries, this will be shown in three ways. First, it will be demonstrated that marital violence continued to be a talking point within polite society. Secondly, it will be argued that codes of politeness allowed women to define new parameters of acceptable and unacceptable male behaviour in marriage. And finally, it will be shown that through codes of politeness women found and shaped new strategies for expressing discontent and resisting abuse in marriage. Of these strategies, nervous illness, and, in particular, hysteria, was to play a central role. It is contended that for women, far from being a form of paralysis, codes of politeness could provide new tools of empowerment.

I

It is irrefutable that over the course of the eighteenth and nineteenth centuries, the middle classes sought to distance themselves from phys-ically violent behaviour within marriage. Physical violence was popularly believed to be more widely practised and generally tolerated within the working classes. However, this did not create a conspiracy of silence about the subject of marital violence. Indeed, even a brief search into contemporary literature reveals that a considerable quantity of print was devoted to the subject. In the daily newspapers read by the middle classes in their homes and in coffee shops, reports selected from the quarter sessions and from the later London-based police courts told in lurid and bloody details of husbands who had attacked and injured their wives. By the late eighteenth century, through such newspaper reportage, marital violence had become a matter for public consumption and morbid fascination. As Helen Berry has persuasively argued, it was one of the ironies of the period that an interest in impolite behaviour should emerge from a society preoccupied with good manners.[8]

Such violence was not something which the social elite could simply put to one side and disregard once their newspapers had been read. Instead, it was these groups who fulfilled the offices of judges, magistrates, poor law administrators and clergy and so were confronted with the consequences of marital violence as part of their working lives. Large numbers of mainly working-class women made complaints about abusive husbands to these middle-class officials. One estimate puts the number of assault charges brought by wives against their husbands before the Middlesex Justices as at least one per week in the 1780s and 1790s.[9] By 1824 one London mayor, in the context of hearing another case of wife-beating, wearily remarked that 'almost every day brought before him instances of the grossest violations of manly spirit'.[10] Pressure to respond to what was perceived to be a mounting problem of violence within the expanding urban centres of early nineteenth-century England led to the introduction of bills into parliament, and eventually to legislation such as the 1828 Offences Against the Person Act, and an 1853 Act concerned with aggravated assaults, both of which had implications for battered women. Violence within marriage was being discussed within the very highest circles of polite society.

But we should not see this legislation as simply the culmination of elite attempts to control a rough and unruly working class, and politeness as one of the discourses through which those in power sought to distinguish themselves from the masses beneath them. Distancing themselves from the behaviour of the lower orders did not amount to a denial by the middling and upper classes of marital violence within their own social ranks. Denial was hardly feasible when it was largely women from the elite ranks who could afford to obtain a legal exit from violent marriages, and whose pleas for separation were frequently

[8] H. Berry, 'Rethinking Politeness in Eighteenth-Century England: Moll King's Coffee House and the Significance of "Flash Talk"', *Transactions of the Royal Historical Society*, 6th ser., 11 (2001), 65–81.

[9] A. Clark, 'Humanity or Justice? Wifebeating and the Law in the Eighteenth and Nineteenth Centuries', in *Regulating Womanhood: Historical Essays on Marriage, Motherhood and Sexuality*, ed. C. Smart (1992), 192.

[10] *Times*, 7 Oct. 1824, 3c.

heard in the church courts. In contrast to those cases brought by women in the sessions or police courts who wanted to bind their husbands over to keep the peace, successfully obtaining a marriage separation on the grounds of cruelty could require lengthy, detailed accusations, and the examination of numerous witnesses in a process which could last for months, sometimes years. Such cases exposed the painful truth that violence in marriage was to be found in all social ranks.

How then did politeness help women resist violence in marriage? The social elite were acutely aware that the price of increasing privacy within their homes could be the concealment of domestic abuse. But crucially, politeness helped to nurture an intolerance for hypocrisy. Defenders of politeness repeatedly stressed that this was a code of manners which was concerned with more than just surface appearances but had its basis in moral virtues. Within the domestic sphere, polite writers condemned those who were 'most polite in the company of strangers' but 'consider it quite unnecessary to be so at home', where they 'throw aside their good manners, as they do their best clothes'.[11] 'A deception which is extremely culpable and blameable', and which considerably rankled these writers, was 'of man and wife manifesting an inordinate fondness and attachment to each other when in public, whilst their home is made a scene of misery and unhappiness by continual strife and wrangling'.[12]

Sensitive to the differences between public and private behaviour, those concerned about discord in marriage could be determined in their efforts to expose the realities of a marital relationship. When Sarah Petersdorff accused her son-in-law of mistreating her daughter at a dinner party in August 1817, he defended himself by asking all those present whether they knew of any occasion when he had been unkind to his wife. But Sarah was not so easily fooled, 'it is not what you have done to her that they have seen, it is what you have done to her when they were not present', she retaliated.[13] That men could exercise a degree of control over their violent tempers when they were in polite company was a point which was not missed by a judge such as Sir John Nicholl. He ruled in the separation case for cruelty brought by the countess of Westmeath against her husband that the observations of witnesses such as Lord Arthur Hill and Lady Glengall who had met

[11] Mrs Marshall, *The Child's Guide to Good-Breeding, Founded on Christian Principles; Or, Seven Chapters on Politeness* (1839), 27; see also, *Spectator*, no. 149 (21 Aug. 1711), ed. D. F. Bond (5 vols., Oxford, 1965), II, 87.

[12] *The Etiquette of Love, Courtship, and Marriage* (Halifax, 1859), 122.

[13] Lambeth Palace Library, Court of Arches [hereafter CA], Case 7828 (1817), H272/27; for ease of comprehension, all spellings and punctuation from court records have been modernised.

the couple 'in society' were 'of little weight'. 'It is much to be feared', he explained, that 'husband and wife, particularly among the higher ranks, who, from education and habit, have more command over their external behaviour, often appear to the world to be mutually civil and kind, when at home by their own fire-side, they are ill at ease with each other.'[14] Experience taught contemporaries that polite breeding could feed deception, but most were far from being willing agents by supporting that duplicity. The test of the truly polite gentleman was one who displayed an integrity in his conduct at home as well as abroad.[15]

Marital violence formed part of public discourse, and polite society did not naively believe that their homes were havens against its practice. But determining how individuals should respond to the knowledge that domestic violence was being directed to others within their social circle was far from straightforward. Manuals on politeness advised their readers not to talk of domestic matters in polite company, and to refrain from gossiping about the family concerns of others. An essential characteristic of politeness, according to commentators, was the 'art of pleasing others', so the polite were taught to refrain from contradicting others, and in this way avoid potential situations of conflict.[16] But when confronted with the ugly realities of a husband who punched or kicked his wife, politeness did not act as a barrier to intervention. Not to react in such a situation was pushing politeness beyond reasonable limits; 'never carry your complaisance so far as to do, or permit anything improper or unjust', warned one treatise.[17] Since an essential feature of the ideas concerned with sensibility, prevailing from the mid-eighteenth century, was compassion for the sentiments of others, appearing unsympathetic to the plight of battered women would have betrayed a lack of feeling or pity.

There is little evidence that polite manners fostered social embarrassment at becoming involved in the affairs of others. Certainly, there were rare cases when the 'private' relationship of the husband and wife was seen as an unsuitable matter for 'public' intervention. But such a justification for inactivity was used at all social levels, across time, and hence owed little to any new code of manners. Two examples, separated

[14] *Westmeath* v. *Westmeath* (1827), in *English Reports* (187 vols., 1900–30), CLXII, 1026.

[15] P. Carter, 'Polite "Persons": Character, Biography and the Gentleman', in this volume.

[16] See, for example, J. Harris, *An Essay on Politeness* (1775), 23; J. Trusler, *Principles of Politeness* (1775), 102; and *A Treatise on Politeness, Intended for the Use of the Youth of Both Sexes* (1812), 44–5, 50, 192–6; Carter also notes that guides to politeness offered little advice to men on how to manage their domestic affairs 'in company', *Men and the Emergence of Polite Society*, 98–9.

[17] *Treatise on Politeness*, 102.

by nearly two hundred years, illustrate this point. James Shott, a Middlesex constable, refused to intervene when he was asked in 1662 to break up a violent quarrel, 'because they were man and wife'. In the mid-nineteenth century, as Hannah Gray was reprimanded for not calling the police when she heard her female neighbour being beaten to death by her husband, she responded that 'she did not consider it her business to interfere with other people's affairs'.[18] The reasons for such non-intervention in cases of known abuse were more likely to have been because of popular ambiguity over the legal right of husbands to chastise their wives, or fears of retaliation, than because of any sense that it was inappropriately intrusive or socially improper.

II

Instead of acting to limit intervention, the increasing influence of polite standards of conduct provided women and their witnesses with the opportunity to widen the range of incidents that could be labelled as occasions of marital cruelty. There was no question that physical violence in marriage represented a display of a lack of restraint and disregard for the sensibilities of others which was the very antithesis of polite behaviour. But importantly, because politeness extended the number of qualities expected of the ideal gentleman beyond the exercise of reason and self-control, which had been the traditional markers of seventeenth-century manhood, women were able to insist upon new standards of behaviour from their husbands within marriage.[19] Most judges stuck hard and fast to the belief that it was only actual or threatened physical violence endangering life that was permissible as a ground for marriage separation. However, they were interested in determining the marital and familial context in which violence had occurred, and it is the stories which women and their witnesses chose to tell to provide that information which reveal the most evidence of changing codes of manners over time.

Sociability and conversation were the watchwords of politeness. In a cultural context where social participation was crucial to refinement, confinement of a wife within the marital home became an enlarged issue for complaint in the courts. Women were able to represent confinement as cruel behaviour because polite codes of behaviour placed so much importance on sociability both at home, as hospitality, and outside it. It is revealing of contemporary concerns that whether a

[18] CA, Case 1127 (1663), Feet, fo. 80v; *Times*, 9 June 1853, fo. 6.
[19] For discussion of the 'traditional' qualities of manhood, see E. A. Foyster, *Manhood in Early Modern England: Honour, Sex and Marriage* (1999), ch. 2; and for the new requirements of politeness, see Carter, *Men and the Emergence of Polite Society*, ch. 2.

husband had a legal right physically to restrain his wife, and so prevent her from leaving the marital home, was subject to almost as much debate in this period as to whether he could beat her.[20] Many wives included complaints of domestic confinement when they attempted to gain marriage separation in the church courts. Occasionally there were accounts of husbands who took their perceived rights to extremes. John Dineley, a landowner in Cropthorne, Worcestershire, admitted in 1732 to chaining his wife to the floor when he confined her in a garret for three days in his home. Such stories have provided excellent material for the sensational accounts of marriage and divorce written by Lawrence Stone.[21] But more frequently, complaints of domestic confinement focused upon how it prevented women from participating in the social world of polite society. The relative freedoms which were thought to be afforded to women in an urban setting allowed them to object if they believed their husbands were deliberately keeping them from the pleasures of town life. In 1750 when Mary Viscountess Coke accused her husband of cruelty, for example, she said that he had left her confined and in isolation in his Norfolk house for over a year while he resided in London, and had boasted that he would 'keep her in the country for he could not bear to see her about town'. 'It was much cheaper for him' to keep his wife in Norfolk, he had argued, perhaps because this would prevent him from having to meet the costs of his wife's more expensive urban-based leisure pursuits.[22] Other husbands were denounced by their wives in the course of cruelty suits for threatening to 'send them to the country'. Such were the attractions of town life, that the countryside could be regarded as a place of exile or even punishment.[23] Away from their polite neighbours, who could be relied upon to intervene, women feared that they risked being mistreated

---

[20] E. Foyster, 'At the Limits of Liberty: Married Women and Confinement in Eighteenth-Century England', *Continuity and Change*, 17, 1 (2002), 39–62.

[21] CA, Case 2771 (1732), Ee9, fos. 199–201; L. Stone tells his version of the Dineley marriage in *Uncertain Unions and Broken Lives: Intimate and Revealing Accounts of Marriage and Divorce in England* (Oxford, 1995), 348–82.

[22] CA, Case 2068 (1750), D435, fos. 86r, 120r; in the early eighteenth century the Verney women looked forward to their visits to London, believing that the 'dull country affords no diversion', but the male members of the family complained of the costs of such trips, see S. E. Whyman, *Sociability and Power in Late-Stuart England: The Cultural World of the Verneys 1660–1720* (Oxford, 1999), 58; for the attractions which urban living held for women, see J. Ellis, ' "On the town": Women in Augustan England', *History Today*, 45 (1995), 20–7. The disputes which could arise between elite couples when women wished to relinquish the restrictions of life in a country house for urban living were longstanding, see A. T. Friedman, 'Inside/Out: Women, Domesticity, and the Pleasures of the City', in *Material London ca. 1600*, ed. L. Cowen Orlin (Philadelphia, 2000), 232–50.

[23] See, for example, Public Record Office, High Court of Delegates [hereafter DEL] 1/361 (1722), fo. 50v; London Metropolitan Archives, London Consistory Court [hereafter DL/C] 179 (1783), fo. 148v.

with impunity. Thus it was the popular perception that it would be easier for husbands to conceal the abuse of their wives in the 'country' than in the urban centres.

But codes of politeness meant that women complained about confinement for more than pragmatic reasons. In addition, domestic confinement could be shown to be depriving women of the daily rituals of paying visits and receiving guests which had become such an essential part of confirming polite and hence elite status.[24] Elizabeth Heathcote sought sympathy from the courts when she related that after her marriage in 1820 her husband would not allow her 'to receive any visitors at the house, or to visit any of the neighbouring families, and would not permit her to go to the parish church, in order to prevent her from becoming acquainted with the neighbouring families'.[25] A witness in the Dysart household said that the earl 'did debar Lady Dysart of society; I heard him tell her ladyship that he would not have a pack of people coming there after her', and described how the earl would order the servants to say that his wife was 'not at home' if anyone visited.[26] It was only in polite circles that the significance of this denial of sociability would have been fully understood, and so could have been included in accusations of marital cruelty.

Good conversation was what was intended to make sociability pleasurable, and was believed to be a key measure of politeness. But the complaints that wives made to the courts show that a man was expected to apply standards of conversation within as outside the home to be thought polite. A husband who traded the compliments of politeness for insults against his wife could face fierce condemnation. In particular, marriage separation cases reveal that codes of politeness had come to shape notions of appropriate language for husbands to use towards their wives. Thus women who complained of verbal abuse in the eighteenth and early nineteenth centuries did so in a cultural context which was markedly different from the seventeenth century. In the earlier period, stories of marriage breakdown were full of references to occasions when husbands called their wives whores. The term 'whore' was used freely by all social groups, often with little attempt to link the insult with actual behaviour, and neither women nor the justiciary appeared to have had difficulty in naming the offence.[27] However, during the eighteenth century the manner in which this accusation was made altered. Two cases heard in the London consistory

[24] Whyman, *Sociability and Power*, ch. 4; A. Vickery, *The Gentleman's Daughter: Women's Lives in Georgian England* (1998), ch. 6.

[25] Public Record Office, Judicial Committee of the Privy Council, 3/1 (1834), fo. 213v.

[26] *Dysart v. Dysart* (1847) in *English Reports*, CLXIII, 1118.

[27] L. Gowing, *Domestic Dangers: Women, Words, and Sex in Early Modern London* (Oxford, 1996), *passim*; Foyster, *Manhood in Early Modern England*, 181–2.

court, both dated 1783, illustrate this point. Jane Prescott, the daughter of a 'respectable clergyman', complained to the court that her husband had used the type of language to her 'as the vilest of men only use to the most abandoned women'. Similarly, Sarah Terry, the daughter of a London silversmith, 'a very respectable citizen', said that her husband had 'daily reviled her' with 'language as the worst of men use to the most abandoned women'.[28]

By the time these two wives came to seek marriage separation, important changes had taken place which gave their accusations of verbal abuse new meanings. The definition of the term 'whore' had altered so that the 'private' whore was distinguished from the 'public' whore or prostitute. Whore was a term of abuse which had become inextricably associated with whom the two wives labelled as 'abandoned women', in other words, the professional prostitute.[29] Furthermore, and significantly, both the prostitutes and the men who used such language ('the vilest of men' or the 'worst of men') were perceived to be from the lower sorts. Patterns of public insult appeared to confirm this view, as by the end of the eighteenth century there had been a significant decline in the social status of those fighting defamation suits for sexual slander in the church courts.[30] Within the marriages of the middling sorts women could not be expected to tolerate the insult of whore because of its new class and sexual meanings. Hence judges in the church courts condemned men who used the term against their wives. This was even to the point reached in 1823 when James Best, convinced that his wife was adulterous, was still criticised for being cruel by addressing his wife using 'reproofs abounding in epithets always ungrateful to female ears'.[31]

Neither the name of whore nor its utterance were fitting for polite society. The courts could resort to drawing upon a list of stock phrases to describe abusive language which avoided an explicit repetition of what had been said. But this did not amount to a silencing of the issue. The alternative language recorded by court personnel was a shorthand understood by all. Politeness increased intolerance of abusive language within the middling sorts and may have encouraged more wives to include references to verbal abuse in their accusations of cruelty. The

[28] DL/C/179 (1783), fo. 409v; DL/C/179 (1783), fo. 514r.

[29] F. N. Dabhoiwala, 'Prostitution and Police in London, c. 1660–c. 1760' (DPhil thesis, Oxford University, 1995), part I.

[30] A. Clark, 'Whores and Gossips: Sexual Reputation in London 1770–1825', in *Current Issues in Women's History*, ed. A. Angerman, G. Binnema, A. Keunen, V. Poels and J. Zirkzee (1989), 239–40; P. Morris shows how the polite sensibilities of court officials and government commissioners were offended by the sexual nature of defamation cases brought by the lower orders by this period in 'Defamation and Sexual Reputation in Somerset, 1733–1850' (PhD thesis, Warwick University, 1985), 13, 233, 236–42, 438–40.

[31] *Best* v. *Best* (1823) in *English Reports*, CLXII, 154.

power of words to cause harm was recognised by the legal profession who argued over whether language that was threatening could alone justify a separation.[32] In contrast to the seventeenth-century concern with female speech, when women were liable to be labelled as scolds or gossips, as a result of polite codes of manners, the angry words of men in a domestic context had become problematised.[33] As Robert Shoemaker has shown, in the public arena the nature and perhaps even the incidence of offensive and defamatory language changed over the course of the eighteenth century. But what cases of marriage breakdown demonstrate is that through their matrimonial business, the church courts continued to be concerned with the damage that middle-class men could inflict with their words.[34]

III

Codes of politeness held ideals for feminine as well as masculine behaviour and these shaped the ways in which women were expected to respond to marital violence. At first sight, the requirements for the polite lady were a reiteration of some well-rehearsed themes; she should be sexually virtuous, obedient and subservient to her husband. But there were also new emphases. When conversation with the opposite sex was so necessary to male refinement, the expectation that women should be silent could no longer be universally applied.[35] Needless to say, retaliatory female verbal abuse or physical violence, even when it could be presented as self-defence, could never be conceived as an appropriate response. But politeness did not require that women should suffer in silence. Certainly, wives could emphasise to the courts how they patiently endured violence from their husbands, and some told stories of how they tried to conceal their husband's cruelty. Mary Strudwick was said to 'wear a cloth hanging over her eyes' to hide the bruises caused by her husband's cruelty, and in 1758 the London consistory court heard that Anne Marie Brogden, the wife of a surgeon and manmidwife, had worn gloves for several days to hide the evidence of her husband's beatings 'from her acquaintance'.[36] These actions could too readily be interpreted only as evidence of women colluding in the concealment of domestic violence. Their behaviour spoke volumes

---

[32] For conflicting judgements see, for example, *Holmes* v. *Holmes* (1755) in *English Reports*, CLXI, 284, and *Hulme* v. *Hulme* (1823) in *English Reports*, CLXII, 206.

[33] E. Foyster, 'Boys Will Be Boys? Manhood and Aggression, 1660–1800', in *English Masculinities 1660–1800*, ed. T. Hitchcock and M. Cohen (1999), 151–66.

[34] R. B. Shoemaker, 'The Decline of Public Insult in London 1660–1800', *Past and Present*, 169 (2000), 97–131.

[35] Cohen, *Fashioning Masculinity*, 25.

[36] DEL 1/361 (1722), fo. 106r; DL/C/173 (1758), fo. 297r.

to the contrary. It notified those living around them, and the courts, that these women had acted as dutiful wives with a concern to preserve their husband's reputations from the shame of being labelled wife-beaters. Thus, their accounts highlighted the contrast between the polite wife and the impolite husband. More importantly, covering up cuts and bruises was a powerful, non-verbal way of signalling to others that abuse had been committed, which could attract attention rather than deflect it (why did Mary have a cloth hanging over her eyes, why was Anne Marie wearing gloves all the time?). Wearing the early modern equivalents of dark glasses allowed these women to continue socialising and mixing in polite company while sending messages about what they had suffered. That it was witnesses who often remembered such actions shows that their intent had been successfully communicated. Finally, as these women's pleas for marriage separation in the church courts made clear, verbal silence was understood to have a time limit.

The cries and screams of women continued to bring notice to those who were subject to physical abuse, but as politeness contributed to a widening of the notion of marital cruelty, so also it allowed women to signal their distress in novel ways. From the mid-eighteenth century a new discourse of refinement, the culture of sensibility, developed as a response to politeness. With the concept of sensibility, popular attention shifted to the ways in which the human anatomy, in particular the nerves, affected manners and conduct. Those with highly developed, but also more sensitive and vulnerable, nervous systems were thought to have a keener sense of good manners. Significantly, the causes for nervous afflictions were given a gendered basis. The male version of nervous complaint, 'hypochondriasis', was often blamed on the excesses of the polite lifestyle. A surplus of commercial wealth, demanding leisure pursuits and the pressures of consumption and sociability could produce nervous exhaustion for those men who were spending 'life in the fast lane'.[37] In contrast, the legal records of marriage separation reveal that the causes of nervous illnesses for women were thought to be found much closer to home. It was within their personal relationships, and as a result of marital cruelty, that women explained their nervous maladies.

Nervous illnesses became a fashionable avenue for women's complaints in the eighteenth century. This was a female form of expression and reaction to abuse in marriage which was hardly recorded in

---

[37] J. Oppenheim, 'Shattered Nerves': Doctors, Patients, and Depression in Victorian England (Oxford, 1991), ch. 5; G. S. Rousseau, '"A Strange Pathology": Hysteria in the Early Modern World, 1500–1800', in S. L. Gilman et al., Hysteria beyond Freud (Berkeley, 1993), p. 164.

seventeenth-century records. Litigants in marital disputes in the eighteenth and nineteenth centuries sometimes referred in general terms to women's 'agitated nerves' or 'nervous afflictions', but others provided more detailed descriptions of nervous debility. As a result of their husband's treatment women were said to be affected by 'hysterics', 'fits', 'freaks', 'vapours', fainting and 'swooning', a 'want of appetite and spirits', crying and 'deep melancholy'.[38] Women were described as being afflicted by a single disorder, or sometimes by a combination of disorders. For example, Mary Viscountess Coke, who had been confined in her husband's Norfolk house, was alleged to be suffering from a catalogue of nervous illness; 'hysteric fits', cold hands and arms, 'her pulse extremely languid, her appetite very little, her sleep little, a frequent nervous cough'.[39] All of these reactions were understandable to contemporaries immersed in a culture of nervousness. The popular belief that women had more sensitive, delicate or weaker nerves than men, meant that nervous illnesses could be conceived as peculiarly feminine ways of responding to marital unhappiness. Furthermore, the social elite convinced themselves that a greater susceptibility to nervous illness was a sign of refinement and class superiority. Thus nervousness became a form of behaviour to which the genteel woman was thought prone. A heady cultural cocktail of sensibility mixed with politeness came to leave those who consumed it reeling in nervousness. But it was precisely because nervous disorders derived from a culture and code of manners which were pertinent to their gender and class that they could confirm rather than challenge a woman's politeness.[40]

A fit which was labelled as 'hysterical' was, as we shall see, the most dramatic of nervous incidents. The medical causes for fits of hysteria were to elude doctors for much of the eighteenth and nineteenth centuries. Demonological theories concerned with women's magical powers were firmly rejected in this 'age of reason', but while neurological models had been introduced by Thomas Willis and Thomas Sydenham, the idea that hysteria was a uterine disorder proved stubbornly resilient. Of course, whether the nerves or the uterus caused hysteria, both were somatic pathologies which were a far cry from the psychological theories developed under Freud at the end of the nineteenth century.[41] But

---

[38] For examples, see CA, Case 3058 (1703), Ee8/96; CA, Case 7468 (1739), Ee10/66; DL/C/184 (1794), fo. 524v; CA, Case 3366 (1811), D757, fos. 25, 29, 37, 182; and CA, Case 3926 (1846), H736/6, 7.

[39] CA, Case 2068 (1750), D435, fo. 138v.

[40] G. S. Rousseau, 'Towards a Semiotics of the Nerve: The Social History of Language in a New Key', in *Language, Self and Society*, ed. P. Burke and R. Porter (Oxford, 1991), 214–75; G. J. Barker-Benfield, *The Culture of Sensibility: Sex and Society in Eighteenth-Century Britain* (Chicago, 1992), 23–36.

[41] K. E. Williams, 'Hysteria in Seventeenth-Century Case Records and Unpublished

while hysteria remained a medical mystery, evidence from records of marriage breakdown shows that it obtained significance and meaning for lay women and men which was beyond the physician's casebook. To them, abusive husbands were guilty of being the source of the emotional shocks or crises which served as the triggers to women's fits of hysteria or nervous illness.

Women were reported as suffering from hysterical fits after physical and verbal abuse, and in response to domestic confinement. But crucially for women, hysteria also allowed them a vehicle of expression after sexual abuse. Sexual abuse in marriage was the form of violence which was most liable to being shielded behind a wall of silence. By its nature it was normally a silent activity, usually carried out in the bedroom, a zone which the march of the 'civilizing process' had rendered increasingly private and secret.[42] Since shame and humiliation often play a central part in sexual abuse, its victims may have to overcome a formidable degree of self-doubt, disgust and loathing before they can even begin to voice resistance. In this period there was no legal concept of marital rape, and as women were constructed as ideally sexually modest and pure at this time, articulating the details of sexual violence had become highly problematic for them.[43] It was unquestionably impolite for women to talk about sex, even when they had been harmed by its practice.

A case study of the Roper marriage, in which a fit of hysteria played a central role, illustrates how hysteria enabled women to display distress after sexual abuse without jeopardising their feminine or polite status. Sophia, the daughter of a foreign fur merchant, left Francis Roper, her husband, in August 1817 after just three months of marriage, and began separation proceedings on the grounds of cruelty. The testimony of her father, Christian, indicated that he had a premonition of the nature of problems which would beset his daughter's marriage. Since Francis was 'a large weighty man', and his daughter, 'a thin delicate woman', Christian had spoken to Francis before their marriage, 'in a kind of half joking way requesting him to be kind and tender to her, and in particular alluding to the carnal connection between man and wife, expressed a hope that he would not use her too roughly'. But when Francis spoke to Christian a month after the marriage, he boasted, 'indeed I used no ceremony I broke her leading strings pretty well, you must know I am an Englishman and you are a foreigner and have no

Manuscripts', *History of Psychiatry*, 1 (1990), 383–401; M. S. Micale, *Approaching Hysteria: Disease and its Interpretations* (Princeton, 1995), 19–29.

[42] N. Elias, *The Civilizing Process: The History of Manners*, trans. E. Jephcott (Oxford, 1978), especially 190.

[43] A. Clark, *Women's Silence Men's Violence: Sexual Assault in England 1770–1845* (1987), 2, 8, 47, 59–60, 63–5, 75.

spirit', leading Christian to conclude that Francis had behaved 'in a tyrannical and brutal manner rather than with delicacy and tenderness'. Meanwhile, Sophia's mother had become her confidante. Initially, when her daughter complained to her that 'she was so ill and in such pain from her husband having had such repeated and almost continual carnal connection with her', she considered that this was 'what every new married woman must of necessity endure'. But after hearing screams from her daughter during the night, and upon helping her daughter make the bed when a servant was ill, she found the sheets covered in blood. Sophia, crying, told her mother that her husband had told her that 'her situation was nothing to that of his first wife who he said had bled like a pig'. Sophia claimed that Francis would 'compel her to submit' to his sexual demands, and that he insisted upon having sex with her during her menstruation. When Sophia complained of 'pain and soreness in and about her private parts', her mother was 'shocked' to see the extent of bruises on her thighs.

Until Sophia publicly fell into hysterics her parents were powerless to act. This moment came on 3 August 1817 when they, and other family members, were invited to dinner at Sophia and Francis's home. After dinner, as was the tradition in polite circles, the ladies withdrew from the dining table and went to sit in an adjoining room. Moments later, alarmed by the noise of a woman screaming, the gentlemen rushed in to find Sophia 'sitting in a great chair, screaming and making a noise like a person in hysterics'. With numerous witnesses surrounding them, Sophia's parents could now confront their son-in-law. Her father declared to Sophia, 'damn it, if you have anything on your mind speak it out, and if anyone ill uses you by G[o]d I will kill him', raising his fists to Francis. Significantly, Sophia did not speak, but threw a glass of water in Francis's face, and left her mother to be her spokesperson. Her daughter was 'very unhappy and a prisoner in ... [his] house and ... all his neighbours knew it ... you have injured my daughter', she said. When Francis began 'in a most indecent way' to 'expose his wife' by 'tearing away the pins and fastenings of her dress' and verbally abusing her, 'all the persons then present intreating ... [him] to desist', his nephew declared that his conduct 'was not only unlike a gentleman but unlike a man'.[44]

Although the abuse alleged in this case was extreme, it shows how

---

[44] CA, Case 7828 (1817), H272/26–7, 35; the statement '29 November 1819 Party dismissed' is written on the outside of the papers for this case. It is impossible to know from this whether the court rejected Sophia's accusations, she voluntarily withdrew them, or if the couple came to an out of courtroom 'private' separation agreement. The involvement of parents in their children's marriages was not unusual, see E. Foyster, 'Parenting Was for Life, not just for Childhood: The Role of Parents in the Married Lives of their Children in Early Modern England', *History*, 86 (2001), 313–27.

hysteria was a means of bringing sexual abuse into the open. A hysterical incident created a crisis situation which demanded a response, and provided evidence of harm to married women which was as visible as the cuts and bruises of physical blows. During a fit of hysterics women could behave in ways which would in other circumstances be labelled as impolite. They could break free from the restraints of bodily control and propriety, which played such an important part in polite education.[45] Screaming or shouting, flinging limbs one direction and another, reacting violently against anyone who tried to hold them still, this was an invigorating and cathartic release from the strict manners governing feminine politeness.

Undoubtedly some women did endure terrible abuse from their husbands, and genuinely suffered mentally and physically as a result. Women were able to turn 'the gendering of nerves to their own purposes' on such occasions.[46] Nervous illnesses allowed women such as Sophia a moral platform from which they could declare that wrongs had been committed. As a result, nervous disorders had a habit of reversing the usual gender roles of those affected. Just as nervous men could be left enfeebled and passive, and so 'perilously close to the feminine condition', a fit of hysteria temporarily gave women an authority normally confined to men. Hysteria could even bring women a measure of control in a relationship which had hitherto left them apparently powerless.[47] Some early feminist writers on hysteria interpreted it as an illness that was used by Victorian women to protest against their restrictive gender roles.[48] However, the women they studied were assuming a bed-ridden, long-term sick role which bears little resemblance to the experiences of married women who detailed hysteria in eighteenth-and early nineteenth-century marriage separation suits. For these wives, the hysterical fit acted as the catalyst for an exit to marriage, rather than the beginnings of a recovery from illness within the marital home. For these women hysteria bore the potential to be a liberating experience rather than a confining one.

Nervous illness and hysteria offered no straightforward solution to marital distress. In line with critics of other aspects of polite behaviour, men frequently dismissed fits of hysterics as nothing but 'affectation';

[45] A. Fletcher, 'Courses in Politeness: The Upbringing and Experiences of Five Teenage Diarists, 1671–1860', in this volume; see also Rousseau, ' "A Strange Pathology" ', and R. Porter, 'The Body and the Mind, the Doctor and the Patient: Negotiating Hysteria', both in Gilman *et al.*, *Hysteria beyond Freud*, 161, 243.

[46] Barker-Benfield, *The Culture of Sensibility*, xviii.

[47] For the effeminising effects of nervous illness upon men see Oppenheim, *'Shattered Nerves'*, 141, 143.

[48] See, for example, C. Smith-Rosenberg, 'The Hysterical Woman: Sex Roles and Role Conflict in 19th-Century America', *Social Research*, 39 (1972), 652–78.

Sophia was described by her husband as only '*like* a person in hysterics'.[49] Women's talents for practising what Henry Fielding called 'the arts of counterfeiting illness' were satirised in the novels of sensibility.[50] By the time Jane Austen came to write *Pride and Prejudice* (1813), she could be sure that her readers would sympathise with Mr Bennett, who was well accustomed to his wife using her nerves to get her own way. 'You delight in vexing me', she accused him, and 'have no compassion for my poor nerves'. 'I have high respect for your nerves', he replied, 'They are my old friends. I have heard you mention them with consideration these twenty years at least.'[51] In the courtroom, the suspicion that women could sham illness to manipulate others gave further opportunity for scrutinising the honesty and morality of the women making accusations of cruelty. Furthermore, while the exact medical causes of nervous illnesses such as hysteria remained unclear, husbands could easily argue that they were not to blame for their cause. In their defence, their wives' own angry passions or their drunkenness were represented as what had tipped the balance towards hysteria.[52]

Most seriously, the similarities between the behaviour of a woman in a fit of hysterics and the insane could be too close for comfort; even Sophia was described by a doctor who examined her as '*almost* frantic'.[53] Nervous illness could not be fashionable or polite if it became tinged with associations of long-term mental illness. It is important to stress that contemporaries were able to distinguish between a fit of hysteria and insanity. Hence in 1829 when a rape victim 'went into hysterics' in a courtroom, it was reported that 'it was understood that only her feelings, not her reason, were affected'.[54] But because nervous illnesses have always been regarded as 'borderline mental states',[55] women and their supporters in the courtroom needed to ensure that they presented the hysterical fit as only a temporary loss of control, and a disorder to which all members of the weaker sex were subject. The hysterical fit

---

[49] CA, Case 7828 (1817), H272/27, my italics; for other examples of hysterical fits being dismissed as 'affectation', see CA, Case 3058 (1703), Ee8/96; and CA, Case 2068 (1750), D435, fo. 127v.

[50] Barker-Benfield, *The Culture of Sensibility*, 32–4.

[51] As cited in Oppenheim, '*Shattered Nerves*', 209.

[52] Francis Roper said that if Sophia had been in a 'stupor and delirium' it was because of 'her own ungovernable passions', CA, Case 7828, (1817), H272/27; for husbands accused who said that their wives suffered from nervous afflictions because of drunkenness, see, for example, CA, Case 4407 (1737), D997, fos. 46v–7r; and CA, Case 7468 (1739), Ee10/66.

[53] CA, Case 7828 (1817), H272/35, my italics.

[54] As cited in Clark, *Women's Silence*, 66.

[55] Oppenheim, '*Shattered Nerves*', 6.

was an expedient intended to gain attention to a wider marital not a personal mental problem.

Until the period when hysteria became firmly labelled as a disease of the mind which could be 'cured' by a new brand of medical professionals, complaining that cruel husbands had aggravated nervous dispositions was an effective tactic for women to employ. This was not least because it suggested to the courts that granting women's pleas for marriage separation was the best option. For this would allow women to be removed from what they alleged to be their source of stress, and so avoid a repetition of hysterical incidents.

IV

Polite manners did not silence the issue of marital violence in the eighteenth or early nineteenth century. Marital violence was a problem that was widely discussed, and although politeness offered no practical solutions or means of preventing male violence, it did not create an atmosphere of social embarrassment which prevented intervention when it occurred in genteel homes. Politeness codified and provided a common reference point to manners which could be expected in marriage. This was especially important for women when there was no agreed legal definition of what constituted marital cruelty, and it allowed them in the eighteenth century to subject a wider spectrum of men's behaviour in marriage to public scrutiny.

It is impossible to tell how far codes of politeness acted as control mechanisms upon violent male behaviour. The full extent of violence within marital relationships will always remain hidden from the his- torian's view. But just as an excessive devotion to polite manners could render a man effeminate, and to the ridicule of the character of the 'fop', so also a man who displayed a total disregard for polite conduct could risk his manliness. Francis Roper was so violent to his wife that in the eyes of others he 'was not only unlike a gentleman but unlike a man'. Tellingly, men who acted violently against their wives were most frequently described in the courts not as impolite, but as 'barbarous' or 'brutes'.[56] Such men were so uncivilised, so animal-like, that they were without any manners at all. Codes of politeness added a new social unacceptability to a form of behaviour that was already widely condemned by the eighteenth century.

A number of gender historians who have examined the impact of changing codes of manners upon the roles of men and women have shown how ideas of politeness cast women in a new light. In this system

---

[56] For example, see DEL 1/551 (1749), fo. 178; CA, Case 2068 (1750), D435, fos. 50–1; *Dysart* v. *Dysart* (1847) in *English Reports*, CLXIII, 1119.

of manners women were constructed as the ideal promoters of moral standards, whose company and conversation was sought by men who wished to attain a reputation for elegant and sophisticated conduct. In other words, women were viewed more positively by writers of treatises on politeness because of their potential to affect and reform male behaviour. But this paper has shown that codes of politeness could also act as a force to allow women to bring about change and direct the outcomes of their own lives. Rather than simply being a concern for social presentation, codes of manners could be adopted and adapted by women so that they became mechanisms for self-preservation. Clearly women, as well as men, were the beneficiaries of this system of manners.

Polite codes of manners could be the source of marital conflict, as well as offer opportunities for its resolution. As the number and range of occasions for polite sociability increased, especially in the burgeoning towns of eighteenth-century England, questions of hospitality, paying social visits and engaging in leisure pursuits were highlighted as points of tension in some marriages. Wives and husbands certainly did not always agree upon the levels of politeness they expected from each other, as Amanda Vickery has shown in her account of the Shackleton marriage. Elizabeth Shackleton vented her frustrations at her 'unmannerly', violent and drunken second husband by writing extensively in her diary.[57] But this paper has suggested that the ideas of sensibility, which developed alongside those of politeness, offered genteel women, through nervous illness, a less passive and more confrontational, if riskier, way of responding to violent and impolite men.

[57] Vickery, *The Gentleman's Daughter*, 214–22.

Transactions of the RHS 12 (2002), pp. 417–30 © 2002 Royal Historical Society
DOI: 10.1017/S0080440102000178   Printed in the United Kingdom

COURSES IN POLITENESS: THE UPBRINGING
AND EXPERIENCES OF FIVE TEENAGE DIARISTS,
1671–1860

By Anthony Fletcher

ABSTRACT. The paper examines the upbringing of five teenagers between 1671 and 1860. It is based on close reading of their diaries. It deals with the relationship between these teenagers and their parents, siblings, friends and tutors or governesses. Politeness, it is argued, was a framework of behaviour which, learnt and observed, made sense of social life. For boys it was rooted in a training in the classics; for girls it meant a training in manners and the social accomplishments which were believed to guarantee a good marriage. English politeness was inculcated across the board in the higher social ranks. The paper considers a few of the human stories that lay behind this inculcation.

OUR conference is concerned with conduct and manners, fashion and accomplishments, with integrity, inner virtue and its underpinning in faith and worship. Debate was huge, prescriptions were massive, attitudes changed and developed across the 200 years and more that my paper covers. The first of my five subjects was born in the faltering days of Oliver Cromwell's Protectorate; the last when Queen Victoria had been on the throne for five years. But what they have in common in social status is probably more important than what divides them in time. For them all politeness was not an enabling mode but rather the source, in the way they were trained, of confirmation of inherited social rank. Parents recognised the crucial importance of the teenage years in the formation of personal and social identity, as years when a child was old enough to imbibe patterns of behaviour and learn the polite accomplishments that would stand them in good stead in adult life. But politeness of course was deeply gendered. For upper-class boys it was the accompaniment of a style of life which expressed authority and command; gentility was founded first and foremost on a classical education and the view that this formed of the world.

I will begin with my two boys and this training in the classics. Tom Isham, heir to a fine estate in Northamptonshire, was tutored at home and for almost two years kept a diary in Latin. It was begun on

1 November 1671 'by his father's command', at the age of fourteen; it can be seen as a very prolonged piece of homework. Tom was predictably deferential, writing to his father, Sir Justinian, on 4 June 1670 'we have almost conquered half the first Iliad, in which although we proceed slowly we do it with delight and perfectness'. 'Pray sir', he continued, 'please to send us some good books which may be helpful to us for making verses', explaining that Tully's *Epistles* and Aesop's *Fables* 'begin not to be so pleasant to us as they have been', after they had been read repeatedly.[1] William Gladstone, son of a successful merchant trading in the West Indies, went to Eton at the age of eleven. He recalled later that 'there was not in me any desire to know or excel. My first pursuits were football and cricket.' It was the encouragement of a new tutor in 1822 and 1823 that persuaded him to immerse himself in the serious business of his classical education and his diary thereafter records his relentless pursuit of it.[2]

Not that either of these boys was prepared for their adult role on a narrowly classical basis. Enthusiastic about geometry, Sir Justinian ensured that Tom received a thorough grounding in Euclid. He insisted that music and dancing were proper gentlemanly pursuits and encouraged a wide range of field sports, while forbidding Tom to engage in the popular local activity of cock fighting. The diary finds him netting carp, hare coursing and playing bowls with visitors; he was in his element at the prime social events in the county, the races at Harleston and Rothwell.[3] The estate round included inspection of hedges and ditches and oversight of planting apple trees in the sycamore walk; family expeditions took the Ishams to local notables and on acts of noblesse oblige, like viewing the new almshouses at Clipston where Sir Justinian was a trustee.[4] The diary for August 1673 records an illuminating incident: returning from Althorp, 'my sword fell out of the carriage'. Realising the loss, Tom sent his newly acquired manservant back to look. It was recovered, and Tom's amour propre with it, three days later, after the Northampton town crier proclaimed the loss and a baker following the carriage admitted picking up the sword.[5]

One is constantly aware, reading this diary, of a less polite world round the corner. Tom heard with some awe of a bull baiting in a nearby village and how, afterwards, 'the men who had assembled to watch had wrestling bouts till five o'clock'. He related the tale of Anthony Cable, a drunken villager nearly felled to the ground by his

[1] *The Diary of Thomas Isham of Lamport*, ed. Sir Gyles Isham (1971), 15.
[2] J. Morley, *The Life of William Ewart Gladstone* (2 vols., 1903), I, 26–32.
[3] *Diary of Thomas Isham*, ed. Isham, 61, 93, 99, 115, 127, 131, 143, 147, 159, 165, 195, 201, 203, 209.
[4] *Ibid.*, 63, 99, 105, 163, 167, 197, 213.
[5] *Ibid.*, 225.

wife's fist. There was talk of a charivari, that clamorous epitome of impolite society, but, learning a lesson of the gentry's social control, Tom noted that his landlord 'would not permit it on account of Cable's loyalty to him which had many times been put to test'. But his most signal experience of the clash of polite and impolite worlds came on his trip in July 1673 to Oxford, 'the very workshop of eloquence', as he called it. Attending Commemoration in the Sheldonian, Tom saw the gownsmen notice the notorious alewife Mother Louse as she sat there among the 'matrons, maids, countywomen and gentlewomen ... a disgrace to her sex': 'as soon as she was observed she sent the whole theatre into a roar of laughter'.[6]

Sensitive to behaviour that was inappropriate to so refined a household as the Isham one, Tom systematically recorded a series of incidents which seemed to him to cross the boundary between politeness and boorish or rude conduct. In November 1671, a local guest at dinner 'striking up a conversation with mother and officiously doffing his hat' spilled his beer and splashed a more distinguished visitor. In March 1672, Tom noted, Dr Curtius, a visiting Lithuanian refugee patronised by Sir Justinian, 'was very angry with Mr Greene's servant for turning his behind towards him'. In December, a visitor 'got so merry that he fell down from the table in the midst of the ladies so that no one could help laughing'. The next June, another neighbour 'came here drunk and talked rashly and imprudently'. When the family could not get rid of him, a servant was deputed to take him away.[7] This record of growing up on a Northamptonshire estate shows a youngster evolving the standards of morality and behaviour which would mark out his gentlemanly status.

Gladstone's Eton diary provides remarkable insights into how he taught himself the rigid self-discipline that marked his adult personality. A series of laconic entries, back at Eton for a new term in September 1825, encapsulate a pattern of life: on the 16th starting work, 'a good beginning to enure one. Wrote home and began to get settled'; on the 20th sculling on the Thames 'source of exercise and pleasure'; on the 24th 'notes on Juvenal and Theocritus'; on the 25th and the 26th his weekly Latin essay. He drove himself, yet a week into the term he was reflecting, on the 27th, 'today as every day I have wasted much of the time committed to me'.[8] In the holidays too he chid himself. In December 1825 he was reading Boswell's *Life of Johnson* but struggling with himself to get up in the morning the week after term ended: on the 10th 'resolutions to amend in getting up'; on the 13th he failed and

[6] *Ibid.*, 155, 165, 220–2.
[7] *Ibid.*, 63, 93, 177, 213.
[8] *The Gladstone Diaries*, ed. M. R. D. Foot (6 vols., Oxford, 1968), I, 8–10.

on the 14th he noted 'great need of new getting up regulations'. Back for the next summer term, it was the lure of his boat not laziness in bed that he was berating himself about. His 18 April summary read 'holiday ... out in boat ... fourth canto of Darwin ... begun verses ... this will not do'.[9] The diary is a monument to the breadth and depth of Gladstone's teenage academic interests, which ranged from the classics and the bible to history, drama and literature.[10] His appetite for knowledge was immense; he understood knowledge to be the core of gentlemanly standing and reputation.

But it was the Eton debating society that allowed Gladstone's personality to flourish and his mind to take wing. 'Made my first or maiden speech at the society', ran the entry for 29 October 1825, 'funked less than I thought I would by much'. Gladstone rapidly became a leading figure in the society.[11] Contemporary politics were out of order, but every historical, moral, philosophical and academic issue that he and his friends could think up got debated through and through. In the process his skill in oratory, his love of it, its place in his character matured.[12] In his later Eton years, Gladstone's life was built around a series of intense friendships and it was through these that his education in manly politeness blossomed, since these were friendships that expressed high seriousness and that enabled a settled view of moral conduct and personal integrity to evolve in these young men's minds. Adult encomiums summarise the idealism that held the group together. There was George Selwyn, later bishop of Lichfield, 'a man whose character', said Gladstone, 'is summed up, from alpha to omega, in the single word noble'. There was Francis Doyle, 'whose genial character', as Gladstone put it, 'supplied a most pleasant introduction for his unquestionable poetic genius'. There was the political James Gaskell, of whom Doyle said that his nurse must have lulled him to sleep by parliamentary reports and whose first cries on awaking in his cradle must have been 'hear, hear'. Gladstone's bosom companion, of course, was the ineffable Arthur Hallam. They breakfasted together and took walks together; Gladstone would scull the weaker youth up the Thames. Hallam presented the model of male virtue, an epitome of goodness, which remained an inspiration to him long after Hallam's early death at the age of twenty-two. 'His temper was as sweet as his manners were winning', wrote Gladstone later, 'his conduct was without a spot or even a speck. He was that rare and blessed creature, *anima naturaliter Christiana*. He read largely, and though not

[9] *Ibid.*, 23, 43–4.
[10] Morley, *Gladstone*, 33.
[11] Gladstone, *Diaries*, ed. Foot, I, 15, 31.
[12] Morley, *Gladstone*, 34–7.

superficial, yet with an extraordinary speed. He had no high or exclusive ways.' This admiration was reciprocated, Hallam had said, 'since the time when I first knew you'. On 23 June 1830, when Gladstone was only twenty years old, Hallam told him he had always loved and respected Gladstone's character: 'it will be my proudest thought that I may henceforth act worthily of their affection who, like yourself, have influenced my mind for good in the earliest season of its development ... the stamp of each of our minds is on the other'.[13] Manners, behaviour, politeness in this male context are seen as the business of the heart, but a heart to be ruled by a mind set on the path of righteousness.

For upper-class girls, the single imperative was a good marriage. Upbringing was wholly devoted to imposing the manners and accomplishments which would be sure to obtain this.[14] The schoolroom years were a curiously awkward stage of life, when much depended on good relations with governesses and a mother who involved herself in her daughter's development. Three schoolroom diaries, for 1793–7, 1854–8 and 1856–60, will be used here as case studies to analyse patterns of daily activity and the emotional responses of teenagers living on the edge of the adult social world. These were truly formative years for our subjects: journalising was favoured as a form of constructive introspection but could become a refuge and solace in emotional distress.

Sophia Baker's pocket book diaries were gifts, as she recorded, from her mother and they record loving parental care in a family with six children resident in the fine mansion of Brayfordbury in Hertfordshire, with a London home as well. Sophia was only eleven years old when she started her first diary and what emerges is how thoroughly her course in politeness was being pursued even at this age. She was going to child's balls, attending Montem at Eton, taken on visits to Somerset House, to an exhibition of 'birds and beasts' at Exeter House and to the Tower. 'I began to dine with Mama and Papa for good', noted Sophia on 16 June 1793. But the centre of her world then, till she left eight months later, was Miss Laborde. She scribbled her thoughts before bed on 25 February 1794: 'she was a good governess, minded her duty very particularly and never spake but the truth. She was likewise ... a remarkably nice workwoman and was very anxious for our going on well ... walked out with us in all weathers when Mama wished us and gave us all the little comforts she could think of. I am much grieved that Mama can bring herself to part with her.' Miss Laborde's regime was about to be reinforced by lessons in London with a series of dancing and music masters: 'Oh dear!', wrote Sophia after a six-hour day of new lessons.[15]

After a missing diary for 1796, we find Sophia at the age of fifteen facing and faithfully recording the crisis of her teenage years in the first half of 1797 with a new governess, Miss Allen, in charge. The demands upon her were now clearly considerable. Visitors were expecting a display of accomplishments. On 12 January she showed some of them her drawings; on the 16th she 'played on the piano and danced to the organ' for visitors to tea. From February to June there were the major stresses of dancing lessons, London balls and her confirmation. Seeing the tension mount, Mama cancelled lessons in April to give priority to spiritual preparation. Twice things came to a climax. 7 May: 'In disgrace all day: breakfast, dinner and supper by myself for my bad, bad lesson and justifying it to Mama.' 23 June: 'Behaved shockingly to Miss Allen, my best friend. Accused her of severity, very idle in learning my task, upstairs from tea time, very unhappy.' So what was this all about? Sophia was at odds with everyone, pushing and shoving brothers and sisters, answering back adults, kicking against the pricks. There was trouble over performance: her governess had 'found fault for not practising before breakfast again'; 'cried and not quick making my tucker which Miss Allen was so good as to finish'; 'Mama found fault with my reading.' There was non-cooperation: pins were not put ready at dressing time, two days later Nanny again told Sophia off for not being ready to be dressed. There was pique: 'out of temper because Miss Allen would not let me take off my collar to play'; because she 'made me wait to put on new shoes'. There was passion: 'bad day', noted Sophia on 30 March. Her governess had said she was 'susceptible of heat'; next month she confessed to the diary she had again been 'rather pert' to her. The 1797 diary is a litany of the confusions of a teenager struggling to come to terms with herself and the demands upon her. 'I really behave ill for such trifles that I fear I shall never get the better of this horrid temper', she wrote on 18 January; 'oh when shall I be good' was the cry after difficulty with doing her sums on 18 March; 'oh may I be deserving of so great an indulgence', Sophia concluded after a 'tete-a tete' dinner with Mama about her confirmation; 'did not behave well to anybody but gloomy and out of temper all day, sincerely sorry for it' ran the 6 September entry. We are a long way here from the prescriptions about becoming a polite young lady that had poured from the presses through the eighteenth century. Sophia Baker's diary shows how, for some at least, learning them was no bed of roses. Here, for one particular teenager, is the personal cost of the

[15] West Sussex Record Office, Additional MS [hereafter WSRO, Add. MS] 7462, especially 2, 5 Jan., 11, 21 May, 7 June 1793; 7463, 19, 22 Feb. 1794.

obligations of social rank, of awareness of what virtue required, of the demands of politeness.[16]

Lucy Lyttleton's diary, started at almost thirteen years of age, is the largest, the most moving and the most compelling of the intimate memoirs with which I am concerned. Second born to Lord Lyttleton, in a family of twelve, she grew up at Hagley, that vast and white mansion beneath Clent Hill, a home she adored. The security of her upbringing; the inner strength she learnt young; a sense of the rituals of polite behaviour as a required function of station and background; the noblesse oblige of a teenage Sunday school teacher; the grasp of national destiny in the ups and downs of the Crimea: the diary is redolent of all these themes. Life was structured by a mother who was a beacon of rectitude and love and a series of governesses who won Lucy's respect. Miss Pearson was strict, ending Lucy's heedless tomboy years when in her own account she was the 'worry of servants and the ruthless destroyer of frocks'; Mademoiselle was teasable but, as a diary entry on her arrival read, 'Fatty does the lessons very very properly I suppose'; Miss Smith, who quickly followed, was 'most pleasant, useful, nice and satisfactory'.[17] On 18 September 1854, Lucy listed her weekday pattern of life hour by hour: she normally wrote her journal before breakfast at 8.00, music practice was then followed by 'bible with Papa' at 9.00 and exercises till 11.30, when these lessons were repeated to the governess. An Italian lesson came before dinner and some reading in French or English after, before time outside till tea. 'Any lessons not done' took the half hour from 6.30 till dressing for dinner and time 'with the grown-ups'. Miss Smith, we gather, introduced a rather different regime in September 1856: 'our week divided into Monday and Thursday for Italian, Tuesday and Friday for French, Wednesday and Saturday for English'. Lucy, remarking 'she has begun us so well', thoroughly approved of the regularity of this scheme.[18]

Vibrant and energetic, Lucy took her course in the politeness that her station required in her stride. 'Oh ecstacy', ran her account of her introduction, not yet fourteen years old, to Queen Victoria at her first Queen's Ball on 1 May 1855, 'she shook hands with me! imagine my feelings and my curtsey; I kept hold of her dear hand as long as I dared'. But even she blenched at the extreme physical manifestations of the standard regime. 'I groan under fearful inquisitory exercises for the wrenching my shoulder blades into shape' she wrote on 9 January 1857. She was an intellectual girl, quite at ease with her Uncle, William

---

[16] WSRO, Add. MS 7465, passim.
[17] The Diary of Lady Frederick Cavendish, ed. J. Bailey (2 vols., 1927), I, 10–12; Chatsworth House, diary of Lucy Lyttleton, 1 Oct. 1855, 8 Dec. 1856.
[18] Diary of Lady Frederick Cavendish, ed. Bailey, I, 36–7.

Gladstone, riding out at Hawarden. Her reading was catholic, including *Childe Harold*, Macaulay, Hume and *The History of the Christian Church in its First Three Centuries*, Wordsworth, Byron and Longfellow.[19]

Lucy's sensibilities developed with her cultural experience. 'It is capital', was her comment on Sheridan's *The Rivals*, read by Granny after dinner when she was twelve. At fourteen, she was ecstatic at her first Hallelujah Chorus and was immersed in Shakespeare, finding *Lear* 'beautiful', *As You Like It* 'great fun' and *Othello* 'very fine'. Papa's public lecture on the bard at Stourbridge enhanced her hero worship: 'it was so beautiful ... such quotations ... he read them so grandly too'. She loved the dance and scenery in a London production of *The Winter's Tale*, but she found the Keans' acting vulgar. She responded to the 'still, holy, high beauty and grand services' of Westminster Abbey as an oasis of calm in the midst of what she called the 'dissipations ... of this whirling, busy, happy, London life', in the years when she was still a schoolroom girl briefly experiencing visits to the capital. She went home, she recorded, 'thrilling from head to foot' after a lecture there by 'the great Trench', the dean of Westminster, on Political Geography, quoting John of Gaunt's moving paean to England from *Richard II*.[20] Her spiritual strength was growing apace. 'I trust every year may bring her Nearer', she reflected on her elder sister Meriel's birthday. In August 1856, her aunt gave her a blue enamel locket engraved with the word Excelsior: 'such grand thoughts are connected with the beautiful idea', she wrote in her diary, 'it shall be my motto through life'. Ecstatic after her confirmation the next June, Lucy wrote of it as follows: the waiting 'breathlessly for my turn, with the longing for it to be safe done ... I shall never forget the touch of the hand on my head ... I went back ... the crying came then ... the new Life has begun.'[21] Loyalist and monarchist to the hilt, she abhorred Oliver Cromwell and later campaigned against the Westminster statue. Lucy Lyttleton would have seen not a hair's breadth between the ideals of conduct in which she was reared, her social rank and the inner moral virtue for which she strove. Politeness, turning to etiquette, was the very heart of the world she knew.

Louisa Bowater, an only child and the daughter of a groom-in-waiting in Queen Victoria's household, grew up at Thatched House Lodge at Richmond. Born in 1841, she recalled in 1908 that Agnes

---

[19] *Ibid.*, 1, 23, 25–7, 44; Chatsworth, Lyttleton diary, 16 Mar. 1856, 21 Apr. 1856, 9 Jan. 1857.

[20] *Diary of Lady Frederick Cavendish*, ed. Bailey, 1, 22, 29, 34; Chatsworth, Lyttleton diary, 2 Sept. 1854, 20 Oct. 1855, 30 May 1856. Dean Trench is the great great grandfather of the author of this paper.

[21] Chatsworth, Lyttleton diary, 17 June 1856, 8 Aug. 1856; *Diary of Lady Frederick Cavendish*, ed. Bailey, 1, xxix, 45, 55–6.

Lentz, her young German governess, had been her 'chief companion' between the ages of thirteen and eighteen, 'to whom I owe not only the knowledge of German which has been so useful to me all through my life but the strong moral and religious principles which she never ceased to impress upon my youthful mind'.[22] Her diary reveals the breadth of Louisa's curriculum within current assumptions about female upbringing. Sums with her father and scripture with her mother supplemented the German conversation that Agnes loved to inculcate. There was needlework, knitting, pasting, mythology and geography. In January 1857 Louisa embarked upon a 'historical plan'; the next month she wrote: 'I mean to have a book of natural history if I can, prints, drawings of birds, flowers, insects etc.'[23] The social aspect of her polite education, meanwhile, was in full swing, with regular trips to London and Kingston for drawing and dancing lessons. 14 July 1856, she noted, had included, as well as some West End shopping, 'a capital lesson especially a splendid lancers and waltz'. The round of cultural visits took in art exhibitions, the Windsor state apartments, Hampton Court, a panorama of Sebastopol which she noted particularly enjoying, and seeing Kean as Richard II.[24]

Louisa's papers include an account on a single sheet of the signal events on the road to coming out, her first play, first household visits, first wedding and first concert, but pride of place goes to her first juvenile Queen's Ball at Buckingham Plalace. The day, 28 April 1856, was engraven on her memory, since it was the day that she started her journal with an account of the 'intense pleasure' it gave her. We know what she wore: 'my frock was white tarlatan over silk with a silver band and a streamer of flowers on the upper skirt and I wore a white acacia wreath in my hair'. The diary account, interestingly, excludes the gaffe which she twice wrote of in later life:

> At supper I made a dreadful mistake. I went up to the top of the table where the Queen was going not knowing it was the top. The Queen asked me who I was and what I would like ... I can still see my father's face of dismay as he watched our proceedings.[25]

Much less dramatic in terms of public exposure, but equally disconcerting, was an incident, memorialised both at once in the diary and then in later life, concerning an invitation to an outdoor party by

[22] *The Journals of Lady Knightley of Fawsley*, ed. Julia Cartwright (1915), 1–4.

[23] Northamptonshire Record Office [hereafter NRO], K2879, *passim*, especially 11 Jan., 6, 8, 18 Feb., 21 June, 2 July 1856.

[24] *Ibid.*, 26 Apr., 29 May, 13, 28 June, 14, 15, 18 July 1856; *Knightley Journals*, ed. Cartwright, 8.

[25] NRO, K2826, K2879, 28 Apr. 1856; *Knightley Journals*, ed. Cartwright, 3–4.

some neighbours. It rained early in the day on 19 June 1856, so Louisa and her cousin and boom companion Edith, who was staying, were forbidden to attend and sent out in the carriage on some errands with the French governess. But the weather then cleared, so they went to the party, against parental orders, 'just as we were' as the diary account puts it. There were games and country dances, then, as a quadrille was starting, Louisa was handed a note from her mother telling them to 'come away directly'. Reaching home in a dreadful state, 'Papa sent us a message not to appear at dessert ... he would talk to us tomorrow.' Agnes intervened and the storm passed, but the incident indicates the tight demands of Victorian formality and etiquette and the pressure teenagers were under not to challenge these.[26]

Louisa's diary for her fourteenth year reveals the rituals through which she was put in her early social paces. Politesse ran riot during the visit of the daughter of a socially acquainted neighbour, only thirteen and taller, Louisa noted, than herself: 'She plays most admirably, a great great deal better than I do. Between speaking English and German together and French to the governess we ended by not knowing which language we were speaking.' The 1 August 1856 entry recounts a ride with Papa, schoolroom tea and a dinner party starting downstairs: 'I am going to dessert.' Next week, Louisa read to the assembled company in the drawing room, as a set-piece performance, 'a letter in the French courier descriptive of Sydenham Palace'. On 26 October, after an 'excellent sermon' and doing her Sunday lessons, Louisa 'dressed to go out visiting on my own in the little carriage' with her maid. Attending a churching and baptism, she reflected 'I felt rather shy about it but was most kindly received.' Joining a house party for the first time from 29 January 1857 to 2 February was overawing: the second morning a retreat to her room, 'where I laid down for some time', preceded a schoolroom performance on the piano for the hostess with another guest providing accompaniment on the concertina. But, when it was all over, ' I was very sorry to go.'[27]

Agnes Lentz had a huge influence on the teenage Louisa: indeed the first page of the diary records her intention of using it as a 'receptacle for interesting conversations with Agnes'. We may attribute the fact that Louisa's inner life never took the bumpy road that Sophia Baker had travelled to her having a governess who was, as a moral mentor, like a rock. The diary is nevertheless revealing about how, even before the dizzyness of her coming out, Louisa felt the tensions of public attention and performance and pondered the dangers of pride and vanity. 'I had a long conversation which humbled me much. I must

[26] NRO, K2879, 19 June 1856; *Knightley Journals*, ed. Cartwright, 5–6.
[27] NRO, K2879, 30 July, 1, 6 Aug., 26 Oct. 1856, 29 Jan.–2 Feb. 1857.

not forget it', she wrote after one of her walks with Agnes on 30 April 1856. Arranging her room for the summer holiday in Suffolk, she noted her resolutions: 'never neglect my prayers ... to make it a place for serious reflection and to make self examination a regular habit'. She hoped, she declared on 26 October, that 'recollection of yesterday's naughtiness' and thoughts about the baptism she had attended and her own confirmation would 'tend, through God's grace, to bring me nearer salvation'. After what she called 'a fit of perverseness' on 11 December, Agnes advised more use of the journal for spiritual reflection, but, though Louisa wrote 'I am determined to follow this advice', there is little evidence that she did so systematically. Agnes had warned her, and Louisa acknowledged it, 'that I do not think and feel half as much as with the opportunities I enjoy I might about religion'. Her governess, it seems, was quite ready to press high moral conduct as the imperative of social privilege on one who had all before her on the edge of a dazzling social world.[28]

The metaphor used again and again for a girl's launching into the adult world, Leonore Davidoff has noted, was a butterfly emerging from a chrysalis.[29] All of a sudden hair was put up, skirts came down, the destiny that the teenage girl had prepared for was real. The full performance in the Victorian theatre of status and privilege has been well described. Analysis of diaries ranging from the 1790s to the 1850s allows us entry to individual experience and provides a long chronological perspective on these social rituals. Leaving the schoolroom finds no mention in Sophia Baker's account of her later teenage years, yet her diary entries for February to July 1800 do read very like an account of the process that the Victorians called coming out. Her entry for 13 February, the only one that ever mentioned her clothes, significantly longer than any others, described how she was 'presented by Mama': 'I was dressed in white with a festoon of roses, three yellow feathers and gold chain in my hair, a set of topaz earings, clasp and locket, all kind presents ... The Queen was very gracious and good humoured.'

Thereafter life in London became a social whirl for Sophia, with balls and assemblies hard on each other's heels, visits to the opera and an oratorio, her first masquerade when she with her mother and aunt went as nuns in white veils, her first time at Ranelagh and at Vauxhall. Sophia's 1800 season at the very least represents a dramatic change of pace. Twice she was back at court, including the king's sixty-second birthday assembly which she found 'very crowded and brilliant'. This was a real launching, when all the training we have observed was put

[28] NRO, K2879, 25, 30 Apr., 23 Aug., 26 Oct., 11 Dec. 1856.
[29] Davidoff, *Best Circles*, 52.

to the test of public exposure, formality and a multitude of unknown faces.[30]

Lucy Lyttleton's coming out was carefully orchestrated. In May and June 1858, a short London visit, she felt on the edge of the stage. An episcopal consecration service in Westminster Abbey, a day at Crystal Palace and Kean's performance in *Lear* were highlights, but her mind was on the autumn. 9 May, 'we met the three eldest Miss Fortescues ... the third is just out'; at a party at the Gladstones on the 26th, 'I appeared *en qualite* of child, not of grown-up young lady, in which capacity was Meriel'; when Meriel was unwell a fortnight later, Lucy went out to dinner with her father, 'where for the first time I was bowed at to leave the room ... I didn't know if I was on my head or my heals.' Back at Hagley in July, 'I ordered dinner for the very first time in my life. Oh dear!' On 15 August, she realised that there was one month till she left the schoolroom on her seventeenth birthday: 'Oh, the deep sadnesss of the flying years', she wrote, ending a reflective diary entry.[31]

Within a fortnight of her birthday, Lucy began the next piece of dress rehearsal, a round of house party visits. 'I am exhausted with behaving properly and feel as if we had been away from home a week', she wrote after the first of two days away with Papa. The lesson was that it was not all fun: 'I am amused at everything, dulness and all, and in part it has been very pleasant' was her summary. The next longer trip, with Meriel to north Yorkshire, found her thrilled by Rievaulx, learning how to receive compliments and concluding it had been 'a very happy launch into the world'. Yet there is a predictable hint of her nervous tension. 'I have enjoyed it greatly and kept quite clear of all scrapes.' On a longer trip to Cornwall, Lucy seems to have found her social feet as a newly arrived adult. Powerful emotions focused more on events than the people she had to relate to politely. She was 'awestruck' at going on board the *Royal Albert* and astonished by the landscape around Tintagel. But Christmas at home, blowing soap bubbles with the boys, draughts, whist and backgammon were clearly bliss after the rigours of this social induction.[32]

'I have little breathing time to spare from accounts of our perpetual dissipations', wrote Lucy in the midst of her first London season from mid-May to late July 1858. Her training in politeness had become the passport to a series of romantic encounters, lovingly chronicled, through which she indulged her romantic enchantment with the French royal family. It all began on 26 May: 'I was introduced to the Duc d'Aumale,

[30] WSRO, Add. MS 7468, *passim*.
[31] *Diary of Lady Frederick Cavendish*, ed. Bailey, 1, 65, 69–71.
[32] *Ibid.*, 1, 72–9.

the descendant of the old race of French kings. Low was my curtsey, most gracious was his bow, and oh! he spoke to me and I said "oui, monsieur!" I thrilled.'

On 6 June, at the family's 'home ball', she met and danced with the young prince de Conde, 'a gentle, grave and most courteous boy of fourteen'. The overwhelming experiences were two nights of encounters with the comte de Paris on 8 and 9 July. Her hopes of a quadrille with him the first night did not come off but their passages of French conversation were enough. Lucy was entranced with his 'beautiful old French courtesy': 'what with awe, respect, compassion, and gratitude I was nearly out of my mind'. Her course in politeness reached its predictable climax on 11 June with presentation at court. Lyttletons and Gladstones had a special word for one's state of mind in a formidable undertaking; Lucy's diary records 'frightful bathing-feel and awestruck anticipation' at coming up to the queen. 'The way she gave her hand to me to be kissed filled me with pleasure that I can't describe and that I wasn't prepared for ... I feel as if I could do anything for her!'[33]

So spirited a girl was likely to find the demands of properness and etiquette in a first season trying. Lucy clearly did so. Lady Derby's ball on 3 June was 'very dull': 'hot crowds of chaperones and old gentlemen and the dancing a fierce struggle with all-surrounding petticoat and I only danced once'. 20 June was a frustrating night. She had no partners till 2 o'clock, then she missed a quadrille and the cottillons came on which she hated. An 'eventless ball', Lucy concluded. The waltz, imported from Vienna, had caught on by this time but aristocratic families like the Lyttletons could not yet stomach its physical contact and hint of sexuality. In the cause of her inviolability and chastity, Lucy was strictly forbidden to waltz. It would not have occurred to her to challenge this, but one can sense her pangs on a night like 21 June, when 'of the four dances that took place while I was present, I danced one and was asked for three, two being valses and the third we were going'.[34]

Louisa Bowater's account of presentation at court, expressing her satisfaction at her father's apparent gratification at 'the reception I met with and the way I got through it', replicates Lucy's in recording nerves at the key moment. She began to feel 'very pit-a-pat' as we 'began to make our way into the Presence'. But if Lucy Lyttleton worried about what she called the dissipations of high society life in general, Louisa's preoccupation was with the inner sins that her governess, as we have seen, had taught her to beware. Her account of her feelings about her

[33] Ibid., I, 84–5, 87, 92, 97–100; II, 336.
[34] Ibid., I, 86, 92–3.

behaviour at her first adult ball at Norwich at seventeen and a half, was reflective:

> Three days after a ball one can judge of one's feelings calmly and dispassionately, one can tell oneself that one is a little goose for thinking any more of the attention paid one or imagining that one has anything personally to do with the success one has had (for I certainly consider it a success to dance all night at one's first ball). It is always pleasant to be good natured ... But I did forget rather and it has taken me three days to find out that I was vain. The thought Agnes would say it was all fudge did cross my mind ... but it was as she said ... in that brilliant scene it all seemed true and her words distant and faint.

A wildly enthusiastic account followed of her second ball six weeks later. Listing her partners, Louisa recorded dancing fourteen times, and only sitting down once. She continued

> And now for the serious side of it. I know I was vain this time ... it was about my waltzing. I was complimented and sought after ... Oh, fie, am I as singlehearted, as simple and earnest as I ought to be? I fear not ... I did not pray so anxiously beforehand. Agnes's words sounded fainter than before ... However I enjoyed it tremendously and would fain be thankful for the granted pleasure.[35]

Teenage diaries provide insight into the human stories that lay behind the inculcation and practice of English politeness. For an individual, the nuances were all important: how much it meant that Louisa could waltz but Lucy was not allowed to. What we see overall is that politeness gave youngsters a framework of behaviour that, learnt and observed, made sense of social life. As historians, taking the long view, we can trace its conceptualisation in changing terms which moved from courtesy to civility and on to etiquette. The rules of the game were constantly evolving, but the game itself mattered hugely and was not on any account to be treated lightly. Hence our interest in it as historians and its importance in that wider project of understanding the past rituals of English social life.

---

[35] *Knightley Journals*, ed. Cartwright, 19; NRO, K2883, 18 Oct., 1 Dec. 1859.

Transactions of the RHS 12 (2002), pp. 431–53 © 2002 Royal Historical Society
DOI: 10.1017/S008044010200018x   Printed in the United Kingdom

THE BRASH COLONIAL: CLASS AND COMPORTMENT IN NINETEENTH-CENTURY AUSTRALIA

By Penny Russell

ABSTRACT. In colonial Australia, the meanings of politeness were continually contested. The urban centres held a world of strangers of dubious origin. Social edifices erected to deal with the question of who was 'in Society' became ever more elaborate and unstable. To the elite, English manners represented a last bastion of civilisation in a wilderness of social disintegration. To self-made Australians, seeking acceptance rather than exclusion, they were absurd remnants of a class-ridden 'Old World'. Important issues of class, gender, social organisation and identity clustered around the problem of comportment and shaped a redefinition of politeness in a colonial world.

Prologue: Dr Hobson's snigger

IN APRIL 1839 an English lady, splendidly out of place in the Australian bush, watched as an Aboriginal man whom she knew only as 'Joe' demonstrated his hunting skills. For the benefit of his white audience, he climbed several tall eucalyptus trees, showing how he would search in the hollows of the tree for a lurking opossum, pull it from its hiding place and descend with his prize. He displayed little enthusiasm for the hunt. The coming of whites to the Murray River region had devalued Joe's hunting skills and threatened his livelihood. He now lived on the fringe of a white police station and begged for the 'refuse victuals' of passing travellers, trading in exchange a hollow performance of skills which no longer sustained his family or his masculine pride.[1]

Jane, Lady Franklin wrote a detailed account of the scene to her husband, the governor of Tasmania. Her interest in Joe's performance was in part 'scientific', in part the habitual curiosity of a seasoned traveller. But she was not the only recorder of the scene. Beside her

[1] Letter, Jane Franklin to Sir John Franklin, 20 Apr. 1839, in Sir John Franklin, diaries and letters, National Library of Australia MS 114. The various accounts of this scene, and a more detailed discussion of Lady Franklin's colonial travels, may be found in *This Errant Lady: Jane Franklin's Overland Journey to Port Phillip and Sydney, 1839*, ed. P. Russell (Canberra, 2002).

stood a keen young naturalist, Dr Hobson, whose observing gaze fell not only on the young Aboriginal man but also on Lady Franklin herself, enthusiastically watching. One detail of the scene before him, which Lady Franklin had not recorded, struck him as irresistibly humorous. In his diary he wrote that the 'man was clothed in a shirt and jacket only!!!'. He was in fact – 'in Lady Franklin's presence' – naked from the waist down.[2]

In this small incident in the wilderness, modes of civilised behaviour were both tested and starkly revealed. Joe, donning the shirt and jacket that to him perhaps represented the white man's power, but leaving off the trousers that were less obvious symbols of status, and no doubt a downright nuisance when climbing a tree, betrayed his imperfect access to white 'civilisation'. Lady Franklin, loftily failing to notice the bare bottom that ascended and descended the trees before her, displayed her own perfected civility. It was through such enactments of social blindness, such undisturbed comportment, that a lady demonstrated moral virtue, impeccable social conduct and – implicitly – rank. But the implied snigger of the white man who observed the scene mocked both the savage and the lady. The ridiculous appearance of the one, clad in the incomplete trappings of white culture, marked him as unworthy of the civilisation apparently offered him in compensation for his lost land, livelihood and identity. The other's stable identity as a lady, with all its requirements of manner, dress and propriety, made her an equally absurd figure amidst the boundless liberties of the wilderness. Only white men, it seemed, could move freely and without loss of dignity between the urbane centres of civilisation and the social wilderness of the frontier. Yet Dr Hobson's laughter may also betray discomfort – the discomfort intrinsic to colonisers who in their own identities had to 'reconcile the civility and values of home with the raw novelty of sites of settlements'.[3]

I begin with this comedy of manners in the Australian bush not because I can hope to disentangle all its layers of significance in this paper, but rather because the story insisted on being told. The scene has tugged at my mind as I research and write, teasing me with its ambiguous resonances. On the one hand, the place of Lady Franklin in the scene captures much of my central argument, that women in the Australian colonies bore the weight of responsibility for the moral virtue and social conduct that both preserved links with British culture and sustained and solidified class relations within colonial society. They

[2] Edmund Charles Hobson, diary of a journey, with Lady Franklin's party, overland from Melbourne to the Hume River, 20 Apr. 1839, La Trobe Library MS (State Library of Victoria) Box 25/1, M 383/09.

[3] Nicholas Thomas, *Colonialism's Culture: Anthropology, Travel and Government* (1994), 3.

not only did the work, but bore both blame and ridicule – equally for their successes and their failures. On the other hand, the figure of Joe is a discomforting reminder that the interplay of manners and social distinctions at the heart of white society was essentially one aspect of a colonising ethos which aimed to extend white civilisation, and thus crucially underpinned the violent dispossession of indigenous people from Australian lands. A feminist analysis of the scene stumbles against, and must ultimately be reconciled with, a postcolonial assessment of the white woman's privileged position and her complicity in the imperial project. But moments like these, when the English lady and the dispossessed Aborigine confronted each other directly, were relatively rare. To draw the links that hold the two together through the powerful figure of the white colonising male would require a sweeping, complex analysis of the history of manners in Australia, one that saw nineteenth-century civility and colonialism as mutually constitutive.[4] Such a history has yet to be written, and it has begun to seem increasingly important to me that it should be.[5] For today, however, I intend to focus principally on the problems of gender and class in the colonies. In particular I want to listen for the resonances of Dr Hobson's nervous laughter as it echoed through Australian society in the nineteenth century, mocking the paradoxical absurdities of the colonial lady.

Australian etiquette?

If 'politeness' was in eighteenth-century England a 'mode of cultural discourse', of prescription and description, which *organised* social and cultural life,[6] the same could not be claimed of nineteenth-century Australia, where the term was scarcely used. Still, manners mattered, as contested currency in the organisation of a society where the growing fluidities of the English class system were reproduced and intensified.

In 1839, the winds of change blew across the drought-stricken colony of New South Wales through which Lady Franklin travelled *en route* to Sydney. The rapid expansion of pastoralism, which had had such devastating impact on Aboriginal life and culture, had also helped unsettle the social structures of a penal colony. The hegemony of an older landholding class, who had once hoped their estates would emulate the ordered communities of rural England, had been challenged

[4] As Ann Laura Stoler suggests in her 'Cultivating Bourgeois Bodies and Racial Selves', in *Cultures of Empire*, ed. Catherine Hall (Manchester, 2000), esp. 89–95.

[5] Examples of valuable approaches, which transcend national frameworks, can be found in Thomas, *Colonialism*, and in the overview offered by John Darwin, 'Civility and Empire', in *Civil Histories: Essays Presented to Sir Keith Thomas*, ed. P. Burke *et al.* (Oxford, 2000), 321–36.

[6] Lawrence E. Klein, *Shaftesbury and the Culture of Politeness* (Cambridge, 1994), 7.

by the squatters' easy access to free land and convict labour. Now, squatters and landowners, their differences merging, shared a common cause. They fought to secure their monopoly over land and (with growing urgency during the 1840s, as depression deepened) to maintain the supply of cheap convict labour from England. They still dreamed of a future as a landed gentry, perhaps with hereditary powers. But within the decade, such dreams would be laughed to scorn as the delusions of a 'bunyip aristocracy' by the new political interests arising in the towns. A sturdy alliance of radicals and liberals, arguing that the social and economic development of the colony depended on commercial interests and free immigration, demanded the abolition of transportation.[7] In 1842 transportation to New South Wales ceased, and it was clear the future of the colony lay elsewhere.[8]

With the 1850s the forces of change became even more apparent. The announcement of the discovery of gold in New South Wales and Victoria stimulated a rush of free immigration. The injection of funds and people that flowed from the gold rushes diminished the relative significance of pastoralism to the economy. The modern industrialising city was built in Australia by thousands of immigrants, many from the middle class, who brought with them their trade skills, political ideals, religious beliefs, domestic ideology and above all their social aspirations, hoping to 'better themselves' in this new world. Inevitably, the hopes and expectations of many were disappointed. Poverty, disease, slums and malnutrition were features of the colonial cities from the beginning and were never eradicated. But the growing diversity of the economy and immigrants ensured that the Australian colonies, in the second half of the century, were characterised principally by social fluidity. Dreams of exclusiveness, caste and inherited social position were forced to give way before the material and social realities of a brash, democratic, colonial world.[9]

---

[7] It was an argument that found its echoes in England, where colonisation was beginning to be celebrated as 'the mark of a special British genius for building new societies'. Darwin, 'Civility and Empire', 328.

[8] See, among others, Alan Atkinson, *Camden* (Melbourne, 1988); A. Atkinson, 'Towards Independence: Recipes for Self-Government in Colonial New South Wales', in *Pastiche I: Reflections on 19th Century Australia*, ed. P. Russell and R. White (Sydney, 1994); C. M. H. Clark, *A History of Australia*, III (Melbourne, 1973), chs. 7 and 8; Jan Kociumbas, *The Oxford History of Australia*, II: *1770–1860* (Melbourne, 1992); J. B. Hirst, *Convict Society and its Enemies: A History of Early New South Wales* (Sydney, 1983); J. B. Hirst, *The Strange Birth of Colonial Democracy: New South Wales 1848–1884* (Sydney, 1988); Ged Martin, *Bunyip Aristocracy: The New South Wales Constitution Debate of 1853 and Hereditary Institutions in the British Colonies* (Sydney, 1986).

[9] The impact of free immigration on nineteenth-century society has been widely discussed by Australian historians. For examples of various approaches, see David Goodman, *Gold Seeking: Victoria and California in the 1850s* (Sydney, 1994); Kociumbas, *Oxford*

Dreams of an ordered and orderly society continued, reworked to suit the political climate. The form that order should take was perhaps one of the most contested elements in colonial society. Squatters in the growing luxury of rural mansions still thought that power should depend on land. In the cities, doctors, lawyers and merchants established comfortable suburban villas overlooking the sea, but viewed with alarm the still more ostentatious mansions being built by wealthy retailers. Meanwhile the securing of manhood suffrage and some early successes by the skilled trades unions, such as the eight-hour day, promoted the hope that leisure, education and political representation might belong by rights to all men. At every level, luck and hard work seemed as important to success as birth, merit or education, creating some uneasiness about how and where proper standards of culture, civilisation and manners might be set. Where a wealthy leisured class was lacking, Edward Gibbon Wakefield had warned, 'tastes and habits, as well as modes and manners, must necessarily proceed from the lowest class'.[10]

In a climate of uncertainty about who constituted the leaders of society, distinctions of manners assumed marked importance. A culture of gentility flourished, as contesting groups vied to justify and legitimate their authority and to 'elevate' the civilised standards of colonial society by a display of 'socially meritorious attributes'.[11] But almost everyone who sought a place in the 'best' society bore the secret, uneasy awareness that their claims to social merit were in one way or another suspect. Against rigorous 'English' criteria of selection, few would have measured up. There was too much new money, too much taint of trade or industrialism. Even those who could claim links to the highest pedigree of English society knew that they belonged to cadet branches, often descended from wastrel or impoverished younger sons who had given up their English social credentials to make fortunes through means of dubious respectability. Colonists, suppressing their own backgrounds, assessed each other as 'respectable', 'presentable', 'scarcely humanised' or 'vulgar'. They endeavoured to identify an elite group: not a 'polite society' but – often with tongue firmly in cheek – 'the best society', the 'cream' or, most ironic of all, the 'Crème'. This ironic mode, redolent of both competitiveness and insecurity, supports Ann Stoler's argument that in nineteenth-century colonies middle-class 'strategies of identity-

History, 294–319; John Rickard, *Australia: A Cultural History* (2nd edn, London and New York, 1996), esp. 28–35, 100–4; Geoffrey Sherington, *Australia's Immigrants* (Sydney, 1980).

[10] E. G. Wakefield, *A Letter from Sydney*, cited in Darwin, 'Civility and Empire', 332.

[11] The phrase is from Archibald Forbes, 'Some social characteristics of Australia', *Contemporary Review*, 44 (Oct. 1883), 604. Forbes observed that each newcomer to colonial society 'must make himself individually pleasant and meritorious, in a social sense, or rather, to speak more categorically, in some one or more details of the abstract social eligibility'.

making and self-affirmation were unstable and in flux'.[12] In Australia, this insecurity was most apparent in the difficulty of marking status within the broad range of middle-class/ruling-class colonists and in constant, anxious reference to the standards of the metropolis. Manners *mattered* in this society, both as reassurance that the colonies would not slide into barbarity or mediocrity, and as a way of marking, and limiting, the social ascent of individuals.[13]

What standards of conduct, of manners, of social exchange, could be laid down in this shifting world? Between the Scylla of Old World subservience and pretension and the Charybdis of New World philistinism, the concept of colonial manners, of 'Australian etiquette', became contested terrain, marked more by anxiety than prescription. It is next to impossible to study 'Australian politeness' in the nineteenth century, either as an ideal or as a practice,[14] because politeness was not conceived of within such national bounds. Most of the prescriptive literature on manners was unashamedly borrowed from English or European works. Even a volume published in 1886 under the proud title *Australian Etiquette: Rules and Usages of the Best Society in the Australasian Colonies* made no effort to address the specific problems of politeness in a colonial setting. It was a self-avowed 'compilation from all the best and latest authorities', and repeatedly betrays its European origins through such discussions as what to do with your overcoat on a 'New Year's call' – not often a vexing issue on a January day in Australia.[15] The reproduction in such texts of social rules largely irrelevant to Australian social circumstances has been taken as evidence of the 'slavish' imitation of English conduct by Australian colonists,[16] but should perhaps rather be seen as denoting the assumption – more

---

[12] Stoler, 'Bourgeois Bodies', 98.

[13] On manners, gentility, pedigree and distinction in Australian society see P. de Serville, *Port Phillip Gentlemen and Good Society in Melbourne before the Gold Rushes* (Melbourne, 1980), and *idem, Pounds and Pedigrees: The Upper Class in Victoria 1850–1880* (Melbourne, 1991); John Hirst, 'Egalitarianism', in *Australian Cultural History*, ed. F. B. Smith and S. L. Goldberg (Cambridge, 1988); P. Russell, *A Wish of Distinction: Colonial Gentility and Femininity* (Melbourne, 1994); Elizabeth Windschuttle, 'The New Science of Etiquette', *Push from the Bush*, 7 (Sept. 1980), 58–80.

[14] Cf. Anna Bryson, who describes her study of the emergence of 'civility' in early modern England as 'more an exploration of ideals and norms than a history of practice, but there can be no coherent approach to practice without an understanding of ideals and norms'. A. Bryson, *From Courtesy to Civility: Changing Codes of Conduct in Early Modern England* (Oxford, 1998), 6.

[15] *Australian Etiquette: Rules and Usages of the Best Society in the Australasian Colonies* (Melbourne, 1886; facsimile edn, Melbourne, 1980), Preface and 71. On the ubiquity of conduct manuals in early modern English culture and the 'suspiciously long periods of time' over which they remained unchanged, see Bryson, *Courtesy*, 5. The same holds true of nineteenth-century etiquette books.

[16] R. Waterhouse, *Private Pleasures, Public Leisure* (Melbourne, 1995), 106–7.

apparent in ideology than in practice – that politeness and the etiquette of social exchange were grounded not in local societies but in an imperial culture of civility. For many, the greatest danger to colonial development was that colonists should forget the larger civilisation to which they belonged.

Numerous historians of civility, politeness and gentility have pointed out that these concepts served both to define and to divide particular societies, to establish recognised modes of association that also served as standards for exclusion.[17] Anna Bryson suggests that notions of the 'polite' and the 'rude' were used strategically by groups and individuals to mark out the social position of themselves and others.[18] Politeness, with all its implications of self-regulation, sociability and good taste, thus also becomes entangled with spatial metaphors of positioning. In a colonial world, these spatial metaphors took on particular resonance and could become very confused. Metaphors of social position, generally expressed as concentric circles or as pyramids, demanded agreement as to where, precisely, lay the centre or apex. But such agreement was not to be found. In strategic terms, did colonists seek to improve their position on an already existing British pyramid, or were they building their own pyramid, its apex up for grabs by the boldest? Did the governor and his wife, representing English social standards, define the elite of colonial society through the power of their invitation lists, or did those lists simply reflect the social hierarchies that they found already in place in the colonies? Behind such practical questions lay deeper anxieties. Should colonists continue to define themselves, to play their parts, as a 'fragment' of British society, or was their primary responsibility to nurture the differences that marked this new society, and might suggest an embryonic nation? Should they, as exiles from Britain, endeavour to preserve unchanged the standards of conduct they brought with them, or did new circumstances and new social relationships demand a new code of politeness? Was the performance of English politeness a hollow sham in the colonial world, or, conversely, did departures from it reveal a society descending into barbarism? These issues were debated but remained unresolved throughout the nineteenth century, allowing for fluidity and social contest, but also generating specifically colonial anxieties.

Pursuing refinement, Australian colonists often 'found the capital of their culture in another place',[19] and were dogged by the fear of failure to measure up to pre-existing standards. But persistent colonial anxiety

---

[17] See, for example, R. L. Bushman, *The Refinement of America: Persons, Houses, Cities* (New York, 1992), xv. I have borrowed Bushman's terminology here.

[18] Bryson, *Courtesy*, 17–18.

[19] Bushman, *Refinement*, 222.

about English standards of conduct and social merit should not blind us to the ways in which those standards themselves became negotiable currency in the colonial society.[20] While social relationships formed and lived within immediate social circumstances were flavoured by implicit and explicit allusions to the standards of 'Home', every colonist's 'Home' was different. England was frequently evoked as the 'other' against which the emerging 'Australian' society, for good or ill, could be measured. But as Richard White has convincingly argued, 'Australia' was never a completed social reality, but an invention, an 'imagined community' susceptible to frequent reinvention.[21] The same can be said of the shadowy 'England' that was so often sketched in order to throw the characteristics of the new society into relief. Immigrants and colonists, inventing Australia, continually reinvented England. Along the way, they reinvented English manners, to such a degree that to return Home was often a shock.[22]

[20] The colonial context draws attention to the limitations of any model that assumes a 'discourse' of politeness developing according to its own autonomous logic. In the colonial setting, new and contested patterns of authority and hierarchy fundamentally reconstrue the logic of politeness, manners and presentability. The language of politeness in Australia is a language of distinction, which is employed strategically to establish not only position but framework. Pierre Bourdieu's notion of the strategic use of 'cultural capital' in the transformations of social space and his discussion of the relationship between classes and classifications provide useful introductory points for understanding the importance of both 'Englishness' and 'politeness' in this context. See P. Bourdieu, *Distinction: A Social Critique of the Judgement of Taste*, trans. R. Nice (Cambridge, MA, 1984). I am indebted here to Anna Bryson's illuminating discussion of the implications of the theoretical work of Bourdieu, Michel Foucault and others for the study of politeness, *Courtesy*, 15–18.

[21] 'So we will never arrive at the "real" Australia. From the attempts of others to get there, we can learn much about the travellers and the journey itself, but nothing about the destination. There is none.' Richard White, *Inventing Australia* (Sydney, 1981), x. The term 'imagined community' was coined by Benedict Anderson, *Imagined Communities: Reflections on the Origin and Spread of Nationalism* (1983).

[22] Those who did return Home, whether on a visit or for life, confronted the relationship between the England of their imagination and the society they encountered. A rich field for the investigation of 'colonial manners' lies in accounts of such journeys home. On cultural imaginings and personal experiences of England, in the nineteenth and twentieth centuries, see de Serville, *Pounds and Pedigrees*, 222–45; Andrew Hassam, *Through Australian Eyes: Colonial Impressions of Imperial Britain* (Melbourne, 2000); T. F. Pagliaro, 'An Australian Family Abroad, the Rowe Letters, 1873–4' (MA thesis, Monash University, 1981); Ros Pesman, *Duty Free: Australian Women Abroad* (Melbourne, 1996), 158–77; Sherington, *Australia's Immigrants*, 59–87; Angela Woollacot, ' "All This Is the Empire, I Told Myself": Australian Women's Voyages "Home" and the Articulation of Colonial Whiteness', *American Historical Review*, 102(4) (1997), 1003–29. See also the Langton novels of Martin Boyd: *The Cardboard Crown* (1952), *A Difficult Young Man* (1955), *Outbreak of Love* (1957) and *When Blackbirds Sing* (1962).

The wives of Henry Parkes

In July 1839, one week after Lady Franklin had said farewell to Sydney and departed, by sea, for Hobart, an emigrant ship dropped anchor in Port Jackson. On board, amongst the assisted emigrants, a woman of undistinguished origin clutched her two-day-old infant daughter in her arms as she prepared to disembark. Unlike Lady Franklin, who within a few years would return to the drama of her English existence, Clarinda Parkes would make the colony of New South Wales her home for life. The daughter of a Nonconformist butcher of Birmingham, she had been married for three years to the young Henry Parkes, a dispossessed farmer's son from Stoneleigh, near Coventry, who had recently completed his apprenticeship as a bone and ivory turner. Early in 1839 the young couple, bitterly convinced that they could never make an adequate living in their own country, had sought an assisted passage to Australia. Parkes willingly turned his back on England, his heart filled with resentment for past wrongs and hope for future betterment in a more equal society. His wife hoped more modestly that 'if things should turn out well', other members of the family might join them.[23]

Henry Parkes's erratic colonial career often serves as an emblem for social mobility in nineteenth-century Australia. His rapid rise from unemployed to labourer to toyshop owner, newspaper editor and at last successful politician was marred by successive bankruptcies. But for four decades he was in the thick of factional politics, skilfully cobbling together fragile alliances and showing a flair for power in the unstable political climate. Five times premier, he was acknowledged by the time of his death in 1896 as the 'Grand Old Man' of New South Wales politics, and secured a lasting place in Australian history by presiding over early moves towards Federation, lending a picturesque touch to proceedings by the splendour of his patriarchal beard.[24]

Parkes was never allowed to forget just how far he had 'bettered himself'. His 'toyshop' was never forgotten, his constant financial anxieties limited his enjoyment of his political success, and though his powers as a public speaker were frequently acknowledged, few could comment on his oratory without some reference to his mangled aspirates. But the marks of his success were equally tangible. He was appointed KCMG in 1877 and GCMG in 1888 – the first Australian

[23] This brief account draws principally on A. W. Martin 'Parkes, Sir Henry', *Australian Dictionary of Biography*, v (Melbourne, 1974), 399–406, and Clark, *History of Australia*, 167–8. Quotation from Clarinda Parkes's letter is cited in A. W. Martin, *Henry Parkes* (Melbourne, 1980), 23.

[24] As Geoffrey Bolton observes in his entry on Parkes in *The Oxford Companion to Australian History*, ed. G. Davison, J. Hirst and S. Macintyre (Melbourne, 1998), 494.

to achieve the latter honour.[25] On a visit to England in 1882 he had the delight of addressing the children at his home village of Stoneleigh, encouraging them to look towards 'a position of power, honour, influence and responsibility such as that I now fill'.[26] The man who had fled his native land in anger but had then, at every downturn of his colonial fortunes, ached with nostalgic yearning to return, ultimately found the greatest sweets of success in enacting his triumph to an English audience.

Clarinda, Lady Parkes died in 1888. She had not participated fully in her husband's social success: rather, she had helped to define its limits. Although she could share in Sir Henry's title, he could not secure for her a place in the elite society of Sydney. This had been demonstrated most explicitly in 1867, when His Royal Highness the duke of Edinburgh visited the Australian colonies, the first member of the English royal family to do so. The visit threw colonial society into a frenzy of anxiety about who would, or would not, be included on invitation lists. In October 1867 Judge Francis wrote to a friend in Melbourne of his amusement at the 'social rows' and 'petty jealousy' he witnessed. 'All the Sydney Press' – with the exception of the establishment paper – had 'chorussed an indignant howl' at the exclusion of Mrs Parkes from the Ladies' Ball Committee, when her husband was colonial secretary. But Francis had no sympathy. All he knew of her, he wrote, was that 'she was the daughter of the pew-opener at a Little-Bethel in Birmingham, and married a toymaker, who became afterwards a fraudulent Bankrupt, and *by a natural law of colonial development, Colonial Secretary*'. He added sternly, 'People here cannot, or will not, see that a man's political status cannot make his wife socially presentable'.[27]

It is not clear how much value Clarinda Parkes herself placed on such social distinction. By 1870 she was in ill health, worn out by bearing twelve children, and spent most of her time in rural tranquillity. For ten years before her death in 1888 she was a confirmed invalid. Twelve months after her death Sir Henry, then in his seventies, threw down another challenge to social tolerance by marrying the handsome thirty-one-year-old Eleanor Dixon, who had been his mistress for the past eight years and was the mother of several of his children. Government House reacted swiftly. Although the governor, Lord Carrington, was on terms of personal friendship with Parkes himself, the new Lady Parkes was 'pointedly omitted from the list of guests for the Government House Queen's Birthday dinner'.[28] Parkes wrote stiffly to

[25] On the value colonists placed on such honours, see Hirst, 'Egalitarianism'.
[26] Martin, 'Parkes', 403.
[27] Samuel Curtis Candler, diary, 6 Oct. 1867, La Trobe Library MS 9502.
[28] Martin, *Henry Parkes*, 379.

decline his own invitation, saying:

> He owes it to his wife, whatever the occasion, not to enter the door
> that is closed against her, but he desires at the same time to be
> understood as not seeking a reversal of her exclusion, while he insists
> upon sharing any indignity to which she is subjected.[29]

When Carrington was replaced by Lord Jersey, and especially when
Lady Jersey arrived in the colony early in 1891, Sydney society watched
with intense curiosity to see how the new regime would act. Though
the interest was muted in most of the press, that irreverent and avowedly
nationalist paper, the *Bulletin*, was delighted to encourage speculation.
'It will take all Lady Jersey's tact to arrange the matter of Lady -- ...
How Her Excellency ought to act in the "difficult case" is the most
discussed question of Sydney society.'[30]

Lady Jersey was – perhaps to an uncomfortable degree – familiar with
Sir Henry Parkes's social origins. His childhood village of Stoneleigh was
on her grandmother's estate, and she showed a tendency to patronise
him as something like an old family retainer, writing of him as 'a
remarkable character in his way', a man 'undoubtedly able and
tenacious, ... [who] did a great deal for his growing country' but had
'a certain difficulty with his "h's" '.[31] But as governor's wife she did
extend to him the recognition and respect warranted by his age, dignity
and political status. She consulted him on charitable proposals and
such colonial matters as she could take an interest in, and on one
occasion offered to lend him her copy of the *Fortnightly Review*, which
contained an article worth his perusal.[32] Moreover, she shared with
him a liking for florid sentiment and a habit of producing second-rate
poetry. He had coined the phrase 'One People, One Destiny' as a
motto for federation, and soon after her arrival in Sydney she turned
the theme into platitudinous verse.[33]

But she would not acknowledge his wife. In April 1891 a mutual
acquaintance, Henry Gullett, wrote to Lord Carrington that a quarrel

[29] Cited in M. D. McLaurin, *Sir Henry* (Melbourne, n.d.), 101.

[30] *Bulletin*, 21 Feb. 1891, 14.

[31] Margaret Jersey, *Fifty One Years of Victorian Life* (1922), 249.

[32] Letters, Lady Jersey to Sir Henry Parkes, Parkes correspondence, Mitchell Library
MS (State Library of New South Wales), 18 Feb. 1891 (A923); 10 Apr. 1891 (A923); 10
Apr. 1891 (A889).

[33] The poem appeared in the *Sydney Morning Herald* on 11 Mar. 1891. Ten days later the
Bulletin commented: 'The chief moral attaching to the publication of Lady Jersey's verse
is this: as with pills so with poetry – advertising is the chief element of success. If the
noble authoress wishes to find out the market (Heaven forbid that we should say the
true) value of her poetical works, let her write on odd scraps of paper, append the name
of some unadvertised governess, drop the poem into the Herald editor's box and await
the results ere she feeds her hungry Pegasus', *Bulletin*, 21 Mar. 1891, 14.

had arisen between Parkes and the Jerseys, 'All along of Lady P of course.' Not only had she been excluded from Government House, but Parkes had been outraged by a report that Lady Jersey's brother had declared that 'if it was necessary he would protect his sister from the contact of such a &c., &c.'[34] The *Bulletin* reported that Parkes was 'incensed' at his treatment by Government House 'in its social capacity', and had resolved to attend no functions there unless compelled to do so by duty.[35] It suggested that Lady Jersey avoided parties where Lady Parkes might be seen, adding that 'some people are again saying that Lady J. is too hostile altogether'.[36] When opportunity offered, it seems Parkes hit back as best he could. In July 1891 a story circulated that 'some young ladies of Sydney society' had taken too much champagne one evening at Government House, and had acted 'very wildly in consequence'. When Lord Jersey spoke of the affair to Parkes, telling him how shocked he and Lady Jersey had been by it, 'the old politician [was] said to have replied, "Now, Lord J, you see how it is that I can't bring Lady P. to Government House." '[37]

The Jersey List

The problem of Sir Henry Parkes's wives was largely one of gender: the world of men seemed inherently more fluid than the world of women. As Beverley Kingston has put it: 'As the sirs proliferated, so did their ladies, but while the sirs were treated with circumspection according to their place in the political system, their ladies could be snubbed or ridiculed if their behaviour was unacceptable to the select inner circle of the governor's wife and her friends.'[38] But this visible demarcation on the lines of sex served to mark out a division more muted in colonial society: between a world of business and politics, in which wealth and electoral success meant power and therefore earned their possessors a certain measure of social consideration, and a world of manners in which social consideration depended on birth, education,

---

[34] Letter, Henry Gullet to Lord Carrington, 10 Apr. 1891, Carrington papers – correspondence, Australian Joint Copying Project M928 [hereinafter Carrington papers].

[35] *Bulletin*, 4 Apr. 1891, 14.

[36] *Bulletin*, 6 June 1891, 20.

[37] Henry Gullet to Lord Carrington, 20 July 1891, Carrington papers. In other contexts, Parkes expressed a sentimental sorrow rather than wit. A sonnet 'To Eleanor' began: 'And thou hast suffer'd bravely, tender heart! / But well thou know'st the world is not for them – / The social non-conformists who contemn / Or disobey the whitened laws, that part / The saints from sinners, in this painted mart.' Cited in McLaurin, *Sir Henry*, 100.

[38] B. Kingston, 'The Lady and the Australian Girl: Some Thoughts on Nationalism and Class', in *Australian Women: New Feminist Perspectives*. ed. N. Grieve and A. Burns (Melbourne, 1986), 31.

comportment and propriety. The uncertain line that Sir Henry Parkes – like so many other male colonists – trod between success and repeated humiliation was drawn more swiftly, more surely and more impassably for women, to whom the sort of economic or political power that could force social recognition remained virtually unattainable throughout the nineteenth century.

Kingston captures a fundamental difference in the ways men and women related to the problem of English manners in the colonies. She suggests that while the idea of a gentleman in the nineteenth century was so watered down that it 'adapted easily to colonial conditions', the qualities of a lady were more problematic. The elusive ideal of the lady was associated much more firmly with role models of 'real ladies' – English ladies, especially governors' wives, whose association with royalty guaranteed their status.[39]

But Kingston's assertion that for men the ideal transposed easily and that political status ensured social acceptance perhaps overstates the case, or at least overlooks the deeper anxieties of caste that were necessarily masked in this 'egalitarian' world. Again and again, public and private writings by and about men in mid-nineteenth-century Australia emphasised the need for men born and bred as gentlemen to repress and deny their susceptibility to manner, accent and comportment. Clara Aspinall, herself a temporary visitor to the colonies, advised 'fastidious and too-sensitive gentlemen, who cannot bear the jostling of the world and the mixing with many classes', to stay away from the colony.

> Many a gentleman have I seen apparently writhing in agony when some well-to-do architect of his own fortunes has gone up to him and given him a friendly blow on the shoulder, at the same time gaily and familiarly addressing him by his surname alone; I have felt for the suffering inflicted by this rude contact.[40]

'Vulgarity, when supported by wealth, is always obtrusive', wrote the squatter J. H. Kerr tersely, 'and forces itself upon the notice of a superficial observer.' Only the discriminating, such accounts implied, would discover the 'better class' of colonists who shrank from mixing – let alone competing – with the ostentatious vulgarity of the new rich.[41]

When Judge Francis wrote to his friend Curtis Candler of the exclusion of Clarinda Parkes from the Ladies' Ball Committee before

[39] Kingston, 'The Lady', 28–9.

[40] C. Aspinall, *Three Years in Melbourne* (1862), 228–9.

[41] [J. H. Kerr] *Glimpses of Life in Victoria, by a Resident* (Edinburgh, 1872), 406. It has been suggested that Kerr's wife was a joint or perhaps the principal author of this work.

the duke of Edinburgh's visit, he was sure of a receptive audience. Candler, the city coroner in Melbourne, was to all appearances a curmudgeonly old bachelor,[42] a permanent resident at the exclusive Melbourne Club. He was also an inveterate gossip. At around this time, he kept a diary crammed with his observations, anecdotes and reminiscences of the social absurdities of the day. He presented himself throughout as a cynical observer of a society filled with persons of no distinction but much pretension, and dominated by the social ambitions of women. Celebrating his masculine freedom from conventions of status and propriety, he yet observed the processes of social distinction in his world with absorbed, almost obsessive interest.

Candler belittled the drawing of social distinctions as a preoccupation at once provincial and feminine. He was never more pleased than when he could ally himself with a 'metropolitan' standard of gentility by a stance of ironic distance from colonial pretension. The duke of Edinburgh's visit gave him one such opportunity. To be sure, his own naive and incoherent delight when 'HRH' first spoke to him fractured for a time the urbane self-image that he rigorously maintained elsewhere in his diary. But he swiftly recovered and thereafter presented a smooth picture of his lighthearted alliance with the duke and his suite in their frequent bids to escape the stuffiness of vice-regal society and descend into Melbourne's lowlife in search of sex, gambling and adventure. He also sought to instruct them on the provincial pretensions and absurdities of colonial society: an act which of course reflected his own desire to ally himself with the confident superiority of these young English aristocrats. No aristocrat himself, he yet presented himself as a 'man of the world', whose worldly wisdom and self-confidence set him above the petty anxieties of a second-rate society.

In a letter to one of the duke's companions he commented on the current turmoil of Sydney society, and propounded the principles he believed any new governor and his wife should follow. The letter mocked the alarm and anguish of the 'Ancien Régime' witnessing the 'fearful bouleversement of the old Social System' – but Candler's own uneasy sense that indeed new depths of social chaos threatened could not be entirely suppressed. His letter strongly suggests that the disturbance was caused by the admission of particular women, rather than men, to Government House circles. His first piece of advice to new governors was 'carefully to distinguish between what may be called *"State"* or *"Official"* entertainments and *private parties*' – and he explained

---

[42] He was in fact married, to a woman who now lived in Rhodesia – a fact which did not appear until after his death. He also had three children by his mistress. De Serville, *Pounds and Pedigrees*, 282; R. McNicoll, *Number 36 Collins Street: Melbourne Club 1838–1988* (Sydney, 1988), 144.

his rule specifically in terms of the difference between the sexes.

[I]n these colonies, as you have probably seen, a very curious lot come to the surface as Mayors, Ministers and what not. The old residents, of good social position, are fast elbowed out of all public places in a democratic community. The incomers are a sturdy, battling, fighting, set, and their manners don't accord with the tastes and feelings of the former race. The two are as oil and water. In time however they begin to amalgamate; they soften down by degrees and would mix tolerably well – but in steps Madam. Now men may overlook the accidents of birth and education in each other – but women never. They have an everlasting recollection of *that* Mrs Tomkins when she kept the toy-shop in George St. ... Lovely woman is hard on her 'sect', and keeps alive the social distinctions no matter to what height the husband may rise. If then, the wife of a Governor makes the fearful mistake of collecting these turbulent elements in one room, she will, sooner or later, have cause to regret it.

Candler warned that the new Sydney governor and his wife needed to be more on their guard, and quoted from another of his correspondents who had observed that the governor had ' "made up his private parties ... not only with ministers *but their wives*; several of them not in humanised society at all, and others scarcely admitted"!'. Then, perhaps fearing that his pose of ironic distance was beginning to falter, Candler hastened to reinstate it, underlining yet again that these were specifically female concerns. 'I can laugh at this and rather enjoy the fun of seeing the "Bosom" in hysteria. You see I have no wives or daughters to preserve from contamination, and find perhaps a secret, selfish satisfaction in the horror and consternation of the respectable world.' For all this large and masculine indifference, however, he continued to insist that the most important advice for the governor and his wife, the 'Golden Rule', was to '*Exclude everybody that can possibly be excluded from Government House*'.[43]

Candler's performance here was a complex compendium of prejudices and half truths. He upheld the social distinctions even while, mocking them, he scrambled for a position of absolute social superiority over those to whom they mattered. From a reference point at once metropolitan and masculine, he simultaneously endorsed the distinctions and blamed women for them, suggesting they were faintly ridiculous for caring. His take on colonial society was in the final analysis conservative, elitist and English referenced, as well as thoroughly masculinist. But his analysis of the processes of social distinction and

[43] Letter, S. C. Candler to Lord Newry, 9 Feb. 1868, copy in Candler, diary.

their gender dimension shows remarkable similarities with that expressed more publicly during the 1890s by a radical nationalist, republican journal that made its name by ridiculing conservatism, elitism and English manners. This was the *Bulletin*, the journal that reported with such delight on the question of whether or not Lady Jersey would condescend to invite the new Lady Parkes to share her board at Government House.

For the *Bulletin*, the social circles defined by Government House offered boundless fodder for satirical comment. As the representatives of imperial government, and in particular of the 'straight-laced' Queen Victoria, herself a constant target for republican satire, the governor and his wife were under perpetual scrutiny. The most biting commentary came from the 'Woman's Letter', in which Alexina Wildman, under the pen name 'Sappho Smith', made it her especial task to satirise femininity and 'vice regality'. Wildman, it has been suggested, had so exhausted her 'rebellious energy' in fighting her way into the patriarchal world of the *Bulletin* that she had 'none left to fight the larger battle of principle'.[44] Her writing encapsulated an ambivalence similar to that noted by Bushman in America, where the old regime continued to assert its hold on the imagination of an egalitarian society.[45] Sappho Smith simultaneously parodied and pandered to a fascination with fashion, tea parties, social ritual and all the parade of ruling-class society – and in doing so, helped establish a lasting trend in Australian journalism that firmly equated 'women's interests' with this obsession with the elite.[46] Her descriptions of Lady Jersey – 'our social apex' – reflected that ambivalence. She praised her 'kind, clever face beautifully devoid of cosmetics', her youthful carriage and simple hairstyle, but was delighted to note any faults in taste, condemning a hat 'trimmed in a wet-chicken sort of way', or an outfit that defied 'the law of chromatics'.[47]

The chief target of the *Bulletin*'s satire, however, was not the governor's wife but the women of Sydney society who flocked about her, fawned upon her and imitated her. The paper hoped that Lady Jersey's 'good and much-needed example' might discourage the frizzy bangs and heavy make-up of 'many fashionable Sydney Works of Art'.[48] But the Jersey influence was not all good. Sappho wrote gleefully:

It is as I feared – that portion of society which imitates vice-regality from the shoe-latchet to the top-curl, has taken violently to what

[44] Sylvia Lawson, *The Archibald Paradox* (2nd edn, Ringwood, 1987), 203–4.
[45] Bushman, *Refinement*, xix.
[46] Lawson, *Archibald Paradox*, 203.
[47] *Bulletin*, 20 June 1891, 20; 7 Mar. 1891, 8; 4 Apr. 1891, 8; 18 Apr. 1891, 17.
[48] *Bulletin*, 28 Mar. 1891, 14.

may be called the Lady Jersey twitch. It consists of a – er – sniffling movement of the nostrils accompanied by a slight wag of the head, and now Sydney society has got hold of it.[49]

The ladies of Sydney who fawned upon the governor's wife, the *Bulletin* seemed to suggest, represented a palpable barrier to republican nationalism and an egalitarian society. Slavishly attuned to the social distinctions and manners of Britain, wedded to the possibilities of social glory offered by association with the hierarchical 'Old World', they nursed social ambitions that representatives of British sovereignty would not and could not gratify. In so doing, they kept alive an obsession with sexual propriety that the Bohemian *Bulletin* loved to ridicule.

But nowhere did the paper defend Lady Parkes's right to be invited to Goverment House. Instead, it suggested that such exclusions were an inevitable aspect of colonial society. Lady Jersey was acting not on her own judgement, but as the queen's representative. It might be 'christianlike to say that Lady J. ought to be on calmer terms with our ex-impropriety' (the *Bulletin*'s preferred way of referring to the second Lady Parkes):

> but yet one cannot see where she is to get her precedent from. Lady J. is the chosen representative of a straight-laced old lady who won't allow a woman to enter her presence with whom the breath of scandal has had anything to do, so it is hardly likely that Lady Jersey is going to encourage people of the X brand to run tame about Government House![50]

On Lady Parkes's death in 1895, the *Bulletin* offered its most unreserved praise, remarking acidly on the way ' "society" cold-shouldered her from the gilded circle to which she never willingly aspired, and to which her homely virtues gave constant rebuke'.[51] But its ironic distancing from the preoccupations of the 'gilded circle', and its equation of the exclusion with a pandering to the imperial sovereignty of Victoria, allowed it neatly to sidestep the more confronting question of what, then, were the appropriate moral standards for the emergent Australian society. Elsewhere in its columns, it repeatedly betrayed its answer to that question by colourfully endorsing a double standard of sexual morality.

The *Bulletin* parodied the 'fat Sydney Government 'Ouse haunter in the nodding bonnet and handbag'[52] because her thirst for social distinction was antithetical to the republican cause. But one of the easiest ways to parody such pretensions was to hint at the light in which they must appear to the governor and his wife, fresh from the

[49] *Bulletin*, 11 Apr. 1891, 17.
[50] *Bulletin*, 6 June 1891, 20.
[51] Cited in Martin, *Henry Parkes*, 419.
[52] *Bulletin*, 14 Mar. 1891, 17.

aristocratic society of the metropolis. Thus, ironically, the *Bulletin* sometimes echoed the elitism of Curtis Candler. After Lady Jersey's first reception at Government House one columnist noted the vulgarity of her visitors, and wondered how the governor's wife had 'managed the corners of her mouth ... for, unlike most women, Lady Jersey seems to have a keen sense of the comical'.[53]

So while the broader framework was a critique of Australia's colonial dependence, much of the *Bulletin*'s satire drew more directly on a masculinist, Bohemian rejection of middle-class respectability, embodied in the aspiring, prudish figure of the 'Govt 'Ouse haunter'. There was nothing distinctively colonial about this satire, and little to distinguish it from the jokes of that metropolitan man of the world, Curtis Candler. Both owed much, directly or indirectly, to the style of humour made famous by London's *Punch* – favourite reading for Candler, and indubitably a model for aspects of the *Bulletin*'s journalism. Far from proposing that Government House should endorse the social position of those who had achieved success on Australian terms, the *Bulletin* seemed as delighted as Candler could have been by reports of exclusions. In a poem headed 'The Jersey List' it mocked the shudders and anger of all those 'aspirants to *ton*' who had found themselves excluded from viceregal entertainments by a ruthless Lady Jersey with a 'darkened brow'.

> List, list, list – a lot of larky dames
> Have got the Jersey cross against their fashionable names.
> List, list, list – she's adding one or two,
> But, now and then, she takes her pen and strikes a dozen through.[54]

Stuck up as on a pinacle alone

The theme pressed so frequently by Candler and the *Bulletin*, that social distinctions had particular, compelling significance for women, and that women policed origins, manners and sexual behaviour, was borne out in women's own writing. The lives of elite women were devoted – to quite a remarkable degree – to enacting rituals of inclusion and exclusion, to appearing in the best company and the most tasteful clothes at social occasions, to paying calls and investigating the social background of new arrivals, to establishing, to their own satisfaction at least, their own social or moral superiority to other women who moved in intersecting social circles. But where masculinist satire emphasised the social snobbery of this process, and the obsessive, sometimes prurient concern with the background and behaviour of others, women's personal

---

[53] *Bulletin*, 14 Mar. 1891, 17.
[54] *Bulletin*, 5 Mar. 1892, 14.

writings suggest strongly that their most prevailing anxiety was about the security of their *own* identity as 'ladies'.

The nature of gentility is performative.[55] And the nature of the required performance was such that the men of the urban gentry, whose daily lives were fully occupied in parliaments, law courts, hospitals, civil offices and financial institutions of the city, could only play their parts for specific social occasions. Not only did they lack leisure, but too great a display of social exclusiveness could jeopardise profitable business partnerships and political alliances. It was on women that the weight of responsibility for conspicuous taste, conspicuous leisure and conspicuous propriety fell.

The highly urbanised, industrialising societies of the nineteenth century were worlds of strangers, where claims to social acceptance depended on behaviour and appearance. As Karen Halttunen has brilliantly argued with reference to American society, this situation generated profound social anxieties about the false pretences of 'confidence men and painted women'.[56] In colonial society, 'newcomers' were strangers indeed, far removed from the communities in which their original position and character might be known. They were, moreover, acutely conscious of the tenuousness of their own claims to status. It was inevitable that in this context the performance of gentility should appear particularly like a masquerade.

Halttunen suggests that such anxieties were countered by an intense emphasis on ideas of 'sincerity'. In colonial society, sincerity – genuine gentility – was associated with a lack of ostentation, an avoidance of display. This was demonstrated in the complex, unwritten rules governing social conduct in Melbourne in the years immediately following the gold rushes, when the threat of social 'chaos' seemed to be at its height. In a society in which it was all too easy to be satirised along with the tradesmen's wives who jostled each other in the urgency of their desire for an invitation to the Queen's Birthday Ball, who paraded their finery with ostentation and boasted of their familiar association with the governor's wife, those who considered themselves, or wished to be considered, 'ladies' had to eschew any appearance of grasping at position. Instead they endeavoured to establish position and entitlement by a conscious display of unostentatious gentility. This, of course, meant the genteel performance was inherently paradoxical.[57]

When Mrs Cole of Brighton found herself seated alone at the high table at a party, on an elevated platform above the rest of the company,

---

[55] Bushman, *Refinement*, xiv; Russell, *Wish of Distinction*, 58–91.

[56] Karen Halttunen, *Confidence Men and Painted Women: A Study of Middle-Class Culture in America, 1830–1870* (New Haven, 1982).

[57] The argument summarised here is developed more fully in my study of genteel femininity in colonial Melbourne. Russell, *Wish of Distinction*.

she was very anxious for someone to join her in this isolated situation, as 'it is not pleasant to be stuck up as on a Pinacle for a lady alone'.[58] A lady might hope to be distinguished, but she would be distinguished for her modesty, her reserve, her propriety of manner. To be exposed, as an individual, to public notice was less desirable altogether, bearing too many connotations of 'notoriety'. There were a number of layers to this fear of notoriety. First, display in itself was destructive to the image of the lady. Secondly, the anxiety stemmed from colonists' awareness of their own tenuous claims to status – public scrutiny might well reveal a breach of etiquette or failure of taste, which would in turn betray a lack of breeding or of familiarity with social usage. Thirdly, public scrutiny was particularly hazardous for women because of the acute ambivalence about femininity that lay at the heart of Victorian society, and was certainly not confined to colonial settings.

Feminist historians and social theorists[59] have repeatedly drawn attention to the polarities and instability of nineteenth-century representations of femininity, as on the one hand the bearer of propriety and modesty, the acme of civilised behaviour, but on the other hand associated with nature, the body, with degraded sexuality. Though this duality was generally represented in terms of class, or two distinct types of womanhood – the 'damned whores and god's police', as Anne Summers termed it in the Australian context[60] – the dangers of too close an association with nature, with sexuality, was constant for all women. Colonial ladies certainly could not distance themselves altogether from dirt, labour, bodily function. Shortages of servants and the day-to-day demands of domestic life saw them frequently performing household drudgery, caring for the sick, tending women in their confinements. And the most virtuous wife and mother could scarcely help but betray, through pregnancy, that she had some knowledge of sex.

Since the sexualised woman represented to an extraordinary degree the 'degraded feminine', in Cora Kaplan's term,[61] that was the dangerous obverse of the image of the lady, any association with nature and sexuality destabilised the self-image and social reputation of any woman, however respectable her social position. Ladies had to be particularly careful not to reveal any sexual knowledge – a difficult feat to accomplish when their philanthropic work saw them making

[58] Thomas Anne Ward Cole, diary, 5 Nov. 1872, La Trobe Library MS, Boxes 1472–87. Brighton is a prestigious bayside suburb of Melbourne.

[59] See, for example, Cora Kaplan, *Sea Changes: Culture and Feminism* (1986); Carole Pateman, *The Disorder of Women: Democracy, Feminism and Political Theory* (Cambridge, 1989); Mary Poovey, *Uneven Developments: The Ideological Work of Gender in Mid-Victorian England* (1989); Janet Wolff, *Feminine Sentence: Essays on Women and Culture* (Cambridge, 1990).

[60] Anne Summers, *Damned Whores and God's Police* (Ringwood, 1975).

[61] Kaplan, *Sea Changes*, 166–8.

judgements about the 'deservingness' or otherwise of, for example, the poor, pregnant and usually unmarried girls who sought admission to the Lying-in Hospital.[62]

Men like Curtis Candler took a perverse delight in endeavouring to force women to betray – through a blush, a conscious look, or a chance remark – their own sexual knowledge, knowing that this tarnished the image of respectable femininity. A masculine coded language of sexuality, full of double entendre and insinuation, was spoken at public parties, and a woman who betrayed in any way that she understood what was being hinted at would be written up in Candler's diary as evidence of the 'fastness' of Melbourne's female society. Even an innocent remark, surely expressed with the utmost propriety, about the need to 'marry' cucumbers before they would fruit, found a place in his dossier of 'fast' remarks by Melbourne ladies.[63] The remarks that men made in front of women, delighting almost equally in their betrayed comprehension or lack of it, were considerably more offensive, and etiquette manuals even found it necessary to guard ladies against the problem.

> A well-bred person always refuses to understand a phrase of doubtful meaning ... The prudery which sits in solemn and severe rebuke at a *double entendre* is only second in indelicacy to the indecency which grows hilarious over it, since both must recognize the evil intent. It is sufficient to let it pass unrecognized ... Not so when one hears an indelicate word or expression, which allows of no possible harmless interpretation ... Either complete silence should be preserved in return, or the words, 'I do not understand you,' be spoken. A lady will always fail to hear that which she should not hear, or, having unmistakably heard, she will not understand.[64]

The path of a lady as she made her way through the streets and parks, and even the society parties of Melbourne, was strewn with things she must not see, must not hear, must not understand, or having 'unmistakably' seen, heard and understood, must not speak of. Women's private diaries echoed with resounding silences: 'suffered an annoyance the nature of which I think better not to enter in my diary' – 'met with a man who introduced them to more than I should have liked to have seen'.[65]

The social blindness that took them, precariously secure in the mantle of propriety, through a world that sometimes seemed to seethe with

---

[62] Russell, *Wish of Distinction*, 188–92.
[63] Candler, diary, 23 and 24 Sept. 1867.
[64] *Australian Etiquette*, 102.
[65] Cole, diary, 13 Apr. 1867; Annie Maria Baxter Dawbin, diary, 28 Feb. 1864, La Trobe Library MS 7648, MF 35–38.

sexual references, was closely allied to a selective social vision whereby they recognised the existence only of people in their own limited social world. Melbourne's 'gentry' was sustained not only by middle-class women's role as custodians of morality, not only by their insistent monitoring of their own and each other's social behaviour and the attention to the 'trivial' details of calls and invitation lists, but by their capacity to walk down fashionable Collins Street – which to Candler was thronged with roughs and prostitutes – and see only a few elite friends. 'Did not see a soul in town' wrote young Annie Carre Riddell cheerfully after a shopping spree. Her sister Bessie, recognising the absurdity of the remark, made an editorial amendment which drew attention to, but ultimately reinforced, its narrow social vision. 'Did not see a sole in town', the entry finally read, with amended spelling – 'plenty of flatheads'.[66] The ladies of Melbourne lived in a social world largely of their own invention, their own making – but they paid the price incessantly, because that sharply defined social world continued to hold meaning only through the internalised restrictions those ladies bore in their understanding, their comportment and their relationships to human society. Candler thought that women saw too much, and forgot too little, about each other's character and antecedents, but in contrast the constitution of a genteel feminine subjectivity seemed to demand that they see and know nothing. The fundamental paradox was evident in a case like that of Eleanor, Lady Parkes, where those who refused to know her could not help but reveal that they knew why they should not. It was all too easy to satirise ladies for their prurience or their prudery. It was not so easy to be ladies, invested with a disproportionate responsibility for the morals of a community, and held accountable for its failures.

Conclusion

The masculine world of colonial society could not afford to be exclusive. A myth of egalitarianism was indispensable to its processes of accommodation. It was, as Kingston argues, 'by relegating some of the essential responsibility for differentiating status and maintaining social distances to women that male-dominated Australian society was able to project itself as egalitarian'.[67] The ultimate security for a gentleman who had to endure the hearty blows on the shoulder, the hideous familiarity of self-made men, was to know that his wife would not visit theirs.

[66] Annie and Bessie Carre Riddell, diary, 13 May 1872, Carre Riddell family papers, University of Melbourne Archives.
[67] Kingston, 'The Lady', 40.

The penalty for the wives was ridicule: ridicule for adhering to social standards and conduct that seemed out of place in this new world. But the ridicule, though a vital component in the egalitarian myth, was largely insincere. The comportment of a lady – such a preoccupying concern for women, and so readily mocked and trivialised by men – was a vital element in the composition of colonial society, for it seemed to draw a reassuring boundary around the limits of 'good' society. A fluid world with a diverse population, shifting economic base and the inevitable ambivalences of a varying commitment to liberal democracy clung to status distinctions which might define merit, exclusiveness and a proper basis for authority. Manners, conduct, moral virtue and social rank were of vital importance in this democratic society. A culture of gentility permeated the social fabric of colonial life. Far from being an anachronistic piece of cultural baggage, it was 'cultural capital' vital to social relations in the present. It was rendered less visible, but not less significant, by being relegated to the feminine sphere.

But there was a further anxiety – a still more specifically colonial anxiety – that could likewise be allayed by projecting responsibility for manners on to women. I want to return, finally, to the image I sketched at the beginning of this paper, of Lady Franklin and Joe facing each other, from opposite but equally absurd positions. I want to suggest that Dr Hobson's snigger, far from expressing delight at his own comparative dignity, reflected a nervous apprehension that the elements of both absurdities inhabited the identity of the white colonising male. On the one hand lay a fear of being ridiculous, or simply wrong, for bringing into this new world of boundless possibility – which demanded enterprise, rewarded effort and appeared to condone sexual freedom, at least for men – those social rules of manners, conduct and comportment that were appropriate only to an 'old world' riddled with hierarchical distinctions. On the other hand lurked the fear that the colonist who made his way through the physical and social wilderness of this unfamiliar world, far from the centres of that 'civilisation' that underpinned and justified conquest, forced to invent new rules of social conduct to fit unprecedented situations, might himself prove nothing but a barbarian. To rework English standards of conduct into new rules for a new society *might* be a sign of a dawning national confidence. But perhaps in taking some aspects of English manners while ignoring others the colonist rendered himself ridiculous in the eyes of the metropolis, exposing vital gaps in his imperfect clothing of civilisation. Satires on the provincialism of colonial ladies, absurd at once for their excess of propriety and their lack of true cultivation, displaced on to women an uncertainty of standards that lay deep at the heart of colonial society.

Transactions of the RHS 12 (2002), pp. 455–72 © 2002 Royal Historical Society
DOI: 10.1017/S0080440102000191   Printed in the United Kingdom

GENTLEMANLY POLITENESS AND MANLY
SIMPLICITY IN VICTORIAN ENGLAND*

By John Tosh

ABSTRACT. Between the late eighteenth century and the mid-nineteenth century
the notion of the 'polite gentleman' lost its political purchase. 'Manliness' became
the identifying code of both the business class and the 'respectable' working class.
The virtues of rugged individualism and personal integrity were emphasised at
the expense of sociability and ease of manner. In the political sphere debates
about who should be included in the franchise were permeated by the language
of manliness, and the politicians with the greatest popular following were hailed
as 'plain men' possessing a 'simple manliness'.

POLITENESS is not a quality we readily associate with Victorian men.
In the light of the received picture of sober, dutiful earnestness, it strikes
a trivial and anachronistic note. If Gladstone or Mill can be counted
as 'polite' we feel that this was a superficial accomplishment, revealing
little of the individual or the cultural values he espoused. Unlike the
Georgians, the Victorians had little invested in the social virtues of
politeness. The first casualty of the new seriousness was that paragon
of Regency fashion, the dandy – the man who lived for appearances.[1]
Fenimore Cooper reported in 1837 that the English dandy was no
more: 'the men, as a whole, are simple, masculine in manner and
mind'.[2] The second casualty was the conduct book – the dominant
genre of advice literature in the late eighteenth and early nineteenth
centuries – now supplanted by the etiquette manual. Whereas the
conduct book had taught manners in a fundamentally moral framework,
the etiquette book reduced the perplexities of behaviour in company
to strict conformity to fashion. Viewed through the lens of etiquette,
politeness was no more than a mask to facilitate and conceal the

---

*For helpful comment I am most grateful to Michèle Cohen, Paul Langford and
Matthew McCormack.
[1] Robin Gilmour, *The Idea of the Gentleman in the Victorian Novel* (1981); Ellen Moers, *The
Dandy: Brummell to Beerbohm* (1960).
[2] J. Fenimore Cooper, *England* (1837), 195.

ambition of the social climber.[3] The idea of polite society, it appeared, had lost its power to civilise.

This contrast between Georgians and Victorians is so familiar that we may lose sight of there being something to explain. But it is not immediately obvious why politeness should have been so little esteemed by the Victorians. Those with a 'position' in society certainly valued progress in manners and refinement, while at the same time being disturbed by social climbing on an unprecedented scale. But beyond the ranks of 'polite society' politeness had diminishing leverage. Its place as a marker of social and political virtue was taken by 'manliness', defined in terms which emphasised the departure from polite standards. My purpose in this paper is to analyse this process, in a necessarily somewhat schematic way, given the lack of detailed research in this area. My aim is to suggest a way forward by juxtaposing the consensus which has begun to emerge on eighteenth-century politeness with the very uneven literature on manliness during the early and mid-Victorian period.

The most familiar approach to the decline of politeness is to treat it as a shift in the culture of the governing elite. Lord Ashley (later the seventh earl of Shaftesbury) succinctly identified the trend in 1844. Visiting Rugby School with his son's future in mind, he reflected on the poor light in which it placed Eton, the obvious choice for a man of his rank:

> I fear Eton ... It makes admirable gentlemen and finished scholars – fits a man, beyond all competition, for the dining-room, the Club, St James's Street, and all the mysteries of social elegance; but it does not make the man required for the coming generation. We must have nobler, deeper, and sterner stuff; less of refinement and more of truth; more of the inward, not so much of the outward, gentleman.[4]

While Eton had changed little over the previous half-century, Rugby had experienced a transformation. Thomas Arnold (who had died two years earlier) had placed Rugby at the forefront of the reforming movement in the public schools. The school was now a by-word for 'serious' education, in which moral tone and a sense of demanding vocation in life were the preeminent goals. In short, Rugby promised that attention to the 'inward gentleman' which Ashley was looking for.

Of course the contrast with Eton expressed much more than a choice

---

[3] Michael Curtin, *Propriety and Position: A Study of Victorian Manners* (New York, 1987).

[4] Lord Ashley, diary for 21 Nov. 1844, quoted in Edwin Hodder, *The Life and Work of the Seventh Earl of Shaftesbury* (2 vols., 1886), II, 77.

of schools. Arnold's achievement at Rugby represented one of the most significant fruits of the reform of manners since it began to impinge seriously on the propertied classes in the 1790s. And like the Evangelicals, Arnold had little time for the niceties of refined society. He had more weighty things on his mind. 'Gentlemanly conduct' featured second among Arnold's goals (after 'religious and moral principles' and before 'intellectual ability'), but he meant by that the translation of sound religion into action, not the perpetuation of a social code.[5] For Arnold the sense of pressing tasks to be accomplished allowed no time for leisure or sociability. One of his most devoted followers, Arthur Penrhyn Stanley, confessed to an impatience with those who did not 'take life in earnest'; 'I want a sign, which one catches as by a sort of masonry, that a man knows what he is about in life – whither tending, and in what cause he is engaged.'[6] The implication was that he would not find it in polite society. This was the new gentlemanliness: extending far beyond the Evangelical circles in which it had begun, it became the characteristic mind-set of many in public service and political life. It might be described as the moral rearmament of the Victorian governing classes.

The limitation of this line of analysis is that it relates to only a tiny elite. In Arnold's time there were nine recognised public schools. The appearance of a further thirty-two schools between 1840 and 1860 represented a crucial phase in the development of the modern public school.[7] But this growth in absolute terms has masked the fact that the public schools continued to draw upon a very constricted social base. There was significant recruitment from the ranks of the professions, in addition to the traditional landed and clerical classes, but in this period the public schools made virtually no impact on manufacturing and commerce which accounted for the majority of the middle class, including its 'coming men'. In order to register their concerns, we must turn to the alternative models of masculinity current among the non-gentle classes. These occasioned less debate at the time, and have attracted correspondingly less attention from modern historians, but their social reach was considerably greater.

A striking illustration comes from Elizabeth Gaskell's novel, *North and South*, of 1855. During an exchange between the vicar's daughter, Margaret Hale, and the mill-owner, John Thornton, Margaret remarks that to her mind the term 'gentleman' subsumes what John appears to mean by a 'true man'. John turns her proposition on its head:

[5] A. P. Stanley, *The Life and Correspondence of Thomas Arnold* (8th edn, 2 vols, 1858), I, 100.

[6] A. P. Stanley, quoted in James Eli Adams, *Dandies and Desert Saints: Styles of Victorian Masculinity* (Ithaca, 1995), 61.

[7] Figures from J. A. Banks, *Prosperity and Parenthood* (1954), 228–9.

I take it that 'gentleman' is a term that only describes a person in his relation to others; but when we speak of him as 'a man,' we consider him not merely with regard to his fellow-men, but in relation to himself – to life – to time – to eternity.

For John Thornton gentlemanliness is other-related in the negative sense of being caught up in considerations of status and appearance, whereas manliness has to do with interiority and authenticity; he applauds what he calls 'the full simplicity of the noun "man"'.[8] There is a resonance here with Ashley's inner man, defined by 'character' rather than the siren call of worldly reputation. There is also a comparable weight given to work. However, what drives John Thornton is not the elevated calling of the Evangelicals, but the single-minded attention to making money which has brought him from inauspicious beginnings as the son of a bankrupt and suicide, to be a prominent Manchester manufacturer. He speaks for the new entrepreneurial class of early Victorian England who neither claimed nor received the title of 'gentleman'. The standard by which they asked to be judged was 'manliness'.

My contention in this paper is that manliness and gentlemanliness were sharply distinguished in the early and mid-Victorian period, and that much of this distinction turned on their relation to politeness. While 'gentlemen' continued to value a certain refinement and sociability, manliness spoke to the virtues of rugged individualism, and this style of masculinity gained in social and political weight as the century proceeded. Politeness was a critical fault-line between the gentlemanly and manly ideals. It summed up the exclusiveness and affluence of the former, in contrast to the open and unhierarchical character of the latter. One could be born a gentleman – in fact gentle birth gave one a clear edge in status over other brands of gentleman.[9] Manliness, on the other hand, was socially inclusive. Birth, breeding and education were secondary, compared with the moral qualities which marked the truly manly character. Manliness had to be earned, by mastering the circumstances of life and thus securing the respect of one's peers. It lay within the grasp of every man who practised self-help with single-minded discipline.

The association between politeness and gentlemanly status remained close. An exception was often made in the case of country squires who were said to make up in moral sturdiness what they lacked in polish –

---

[8] Elizabeth Gaskell, *North and South* (1855), ch. 20 ('Men and Gentlemen').
[9] 'A gentleman by birth remained a cut above other gentlemen': Mark Girouard, *The Return to Camelot* (1981), 263.

a social type that was certainly not new to the Victorians.[10] Otherwise 'politeness' continued to be synonymous with 'breeding' and leisure: polite behaviour remained the surest indicator of breeding and the indispensable lubricant of sociability. Opinions differed about how much weight should be attached to politeness, just as they differed with regard to the salience of birth or morality in the gentlemanly ideal. The advice books tended to claim more for politeness than daily experience was likely to bear out: to assert, in the words of one didactic writer, that politeness was 'the result of the combined action of all the moral and social feelings, guided by judgment and refined by taste',[11] went well beyond common understanding of the word. James Fitzjames Stephen took a more cynical view: 'when we speak of a gentleman', he remarked, 'we do not mean either a good man, or a wise man, but a man socially pleasant'.[12] But whether merely pleasant or intimating moral worth, politeness was the hall-mark of the gentleman.

Manliness is an even more slippery concept. In nineteenth-century England the word was used in an extraordinary variety of contexts and it was repeatedly pushed in fresh directions by religious writers and social theorists, often in mutually inconsistent ways. In the name of manliness Victorian men were urged to work, to pray, to stand up for their rights, to turn the other cheek, to sow wild oats, to be chaste and so on. It is clear that the idea of manliness exercised a powerful hold over the Victorians, but the nature of that hold has been obscured by recent scholarship. One strand treats manliness as the special province of the public schools, with headmasters cast in the role of expert.[13] The other dominant approach, by resurrecting some of the more eccentric versions of the Tractarians, the Evangelicals and the muscular Christians, has created the misleading impression that manliness was a matter of applied theology.[14] But manliness was more than a subject of learned disputation, more even than an educational tool; it was a guide to life, deeply rooted in popular culture, and often resistant to the redefinitions proposed by didactic writers.

Viewed as an aspect of the 'common sense' of social relations, manliness comprised a set of core values which had characterised masculine culture long before the Victorians. The main thrust is

[10] Anthony Fletcher, *Gender, Sex and Subordination in England 1500–1800* (1995), 325–9.

[11] Charles Duncan, *The Gentleman's Book of Manners or Etiquette* (1875), 7.

[12] [James Fitzjames Stephen], 'Gentlemen', *Cornhill Magazine*, 5 (1862), 331.

[13] David Newsome, *Godliness and Good Learning* (1961), 195–227; J. R. de S. Honey, *Tom Brown's Universe: The Development of the Victorian Public School* (1977).

[14] Norman Vance, *The Sinews of the Spirit: The Ideal of Christian Manliness in Victorian Literature and Religious Thought* (Cambridge, 1985); Boyd Hilton, 'Manliness, Masculinity and the Mid-Victorian Temperament', in *The Blind Victorian: Henry Fawcett and British Liberalism*, ed. L. Goldman (Cambridge, 1989), 60–70; David Alderson, *Mansex Fine: Religion, Manliness and Imperialism in Nineteenth-Century British Culture* (Manchester, 1998).

accurately conveyed by the *Oxford English Dictionary* which gives 'the possession of manly vigour' before 'those virtues characteristic of a man'. Manly vigour included energy, virility, strength – all the attributes which equipped a man to place his physical stamp on the world. Next came the moral qualities which enabled men to attain their physical potential – decisiveness, courage and endurance. These virtues had traditionally had a strong military resonance; now they were considered applicable as much to the struggle of life as to the battlefield. These qualities of physique and character – what Carlyle called 'toughness of muscle' and 'toughness of heart'[15] – were in turn yoked to some notion of social responsibility – whether loyalty to one's peers or chivalry towards women. The desired outcome was the 'independent man' – one who was beholden to no one, who kept his own counsel and who ruled his own household. These were the English characteristics which Hippolyte Taine summarised in the 1860s as 'the need for independence, the capacity for initiative, the active and obstinate will'.[16]

One other attribute was critically important in distinguishing manliness from gentlemanliness: frank straightforwardness, not only in action (about which there could be no disagreement in principle), but also in speech. The touchstone of polite conversation was the anticipated impression made on the listener. The manly man was someone who paid more attention to the promptings of his inner self than to the dictates of social expectation. Manly speech was therefore direct, honest and succinct. Its purpose was not to please, or to shield listeners from the disagreeable, but to convey meaning without equivocation. The result might not be 'socially pleasant'. It came from the heart, unbridled by fear of reprisal or ridicule. What James Fitzjames Stephen called 'plain, downright, frank simplicity' was 'the outward and visible sign of the two great cognate virtues – truth and courage'.[17] It was also the outward sign of 'independence', since conformity in speech was the most telling indication of subservience or deference. Directness and sincerity might well cross the boundary of propriety and appear brusque or even rude. When a man had nothing to say from the heart, the right course was silence. Hence, in complete distinction from the conventions of politeness, manliness often meant taciturnity. Here again it is hard to avoid quoting Carlyle. Manliness was for him exemplified by the man of action, the man of few words: he hailed 'the silent English'[18] and Oliver Cromwell as the 'emblem of the dumb English'.[19]

---

[15] Thomas Carlyle, *Past and Present* (Oxford, 1934), 144.
[16] Hippolyte Taine, *Notes on England*, trans. E. Hyams (1957), 268.
[17] Stephen, 'Gentlemen', 336.
[18] Carlyle, *Past and Present*, 142.
[19] Quoted in Raphael Samuel, *Island Stories: Unravelling Britain* (1998), 286.

No question here of allowing one's conversation to be moulded by ladies.

Robin Gilmour has written of manliness as 'a key Victorian concept', connoting 'a new openness and directness, a new sincerity in social relations'.[20] He overestimates its novelty. Since the days of Addison and Steele objections to the artificiality inherent in polite manners had been cast in terms of an appeal to honesty and authenticity. Taciturnity verging on the brusque had long been considered by foreign visitors to be an English trait.[21] The virtues of 'sincerity' had been a major theme of social moralists in the closing decades of the eighteenth century. With different emphases, both Gerald Newman and Michèle Cohen have shown how the rise of sincerity was a reaction against the indiscriminate imitation of fine manners by social climbers in mid-eighteenth-century urban society, and how it became subsumed in a redefinition of Englishness.[22] What was new in the mid-nineteenth century was the consolidation of sincerity into the dominant gender ideal for middle-class men. This was the ideal of 'manly simplicity', continuously reinforced by general precept and commended in the lives of individual men.[23] Here was the very antithesis of the refinement and artifice of polite society.

Reporting on a visit she had received in 1853 from Charles Kingsley, the proponent of muscular Christianity, Elizabeth Barrett Browning found herself pleasantly surprised: she had steeled herself to receive a manly person of the type she detested, but instead encountered geniality and 'almost tender kindliness'. Barrett Browning was measuring Kingsley not against his own rarified vision of divine manhood, but by the standards of manliness as commonly understood.[24] Energy, assertiveness, independence, directness and simplicity were its core attributes. They were manifest less in formal treatises than in the texture of social existence. They were certainly much older than the nineteenth century. Interestingly, in a recent attempt to distill the essence of manliness as a Western cultural tradition, Harvey Mansfield stresses its individual quality, biased in favour of action, and characterised by struggle, Stoicism and independence.[25] These characteristics can be confirmed

[20] Gilmour, *Idea of the Gentleman*, 18.

[21] Paul Langford, *Englishness Identified: Manners and Character, 1650–1850* (Oxford, 2000), 306–9.

[22] Gerald Newman, *The Rise of English Nationalism: A Cultural History 1740–1830* (New York, 1997), 128–55; Michèle Cohen, 'Manliness, Effeminacy and the French: Gender and the Construction of National Character in Eighteenth-Century England', in *English Masculinities, 1660–1800*, ed. T. Hitchcock and M. Cohen (1999), 44–61.

[23] David Newsome, *The Parting of Friends* (1966), 59; Newsome, *Godliness and Good Learning*, 195–6; Gilmour, *Idea of the Gentleman*, 58, 69.

[24] *Letters of Elizabeth Barrett Browning*, ed. F. G. Kenyon (2 vols., 1897), II, 134.

[25] Harvey Mansfield, 'The Partial Eclipse of Manliness', *TLS*, 17 July 1998.

again and again in the best-selling novelists of the Victorian period, Trollope and Wilkie Collins being perhaps the clearest guides.[26]

The cultural prestige of these manly ideals must be seen in the context of the increasing irrelevance of politeness. In several crucial respects, it had become redundant. Eighteenth-century politeness had expressed a faith in the improving effects of leisure, sociability and social mixing between the sexes. But each of these was downplayed in the social perspective of the Victorians. Leisure was the most fundamental pre-condition of politeness, the mark of the gentleman being either a man living on private means, or someone on whom business did not weigh too heavily. The squire drawing rent from his tenant farmers, the rentier living off investments, the man of letters and the professional with some private capital behind him – all could be accommodated to the traditional model of the leisured gentleman who valued sociability both for its own sake and as a means of contributing to the public good. The emphasis among the Victorian middle class was different. For men who had built up a business from small beginnings or had made their way up a professional ladder, the demands of work loomed much larger. Leisure often amounted to no more than a few snatched moments away from factory or counting-house. Lives were disfigured by excessive attention to business. The mill-owner Isaac Holden was continually distracted from the company of his wife and from the claims of the Methodist community by his 'dear old combing machines'; he appears to have taken all too literally the newly minted motto of the town of Bradford, *Labor vincit omnia* (work overcomes everything).[27] Edward Benson, the first head of Wellington College, filled every hour of the day with work: any time left over from his official duties was devoted to a lifelong scholarly study of the Early Church father, St Cyprian.[28] In their different ways both men shared the profound belief that self-realisation comes from purposeful work, not from the enjoyment of society.

The conditions for men's sociability had also altered. The rationale of eighteenth-century politeness had been to counter social and sectarian division through the civilising effects of company: hence the high value placed on the arts of conversation, guided by restraint of the self and

---

[26] On Trollope, see Gilmour, *Idea of the Gentleman*; on Collins, see Bruce Haley, *The Healthy Body and Victorian Culture* (Cambridge, MA, 1978), 223–6; Alderson, *Mansex Fine*, 62–4.
[27] John Tosh, *A Man's Place: Masculinity and the Middle-Class Home in Victorian England* (1999), 76–7.
[28] David Newsome, *History of Wellington College* (1959), 92, 151.

respect for others.[29] In Victorian society, on the other hand, individualism counted for more than sociability. This was partly a reflection of the competitive conditions in which businessmen and professional men worked. Self-improvement, instead of depending on the leavening effect of polite society, was seen as a solitary endeavour. Not surprisingly the institutions of male sociability were at a low ebb during this period. There were fewer clubs in London than there had been in the eighteenth century, or than there would be after about 1870, and in other cities clubs were slow to develop.[30]

Judged against the requirements of politeness, these clubs offered a problematic form of sociability, in that their membership was confined to men. The civilising properties of women had been especially valued in the hey-day of politeness. Assembly rooms, public balls and theatres had encouraged relations of easy informality between the sexes, allowing the rough edges of masculine behaviour to be smoothed down. By the 1830s the assembly rooms were in decline. The associational life of men and women tended to run in separate grooves – for example in philanthropy where men and women staked out their distinctive responsibilities, with their own organising committees.[31] The only context in which easy relations between the sexes were applauded without qualification was the family, where the demands of domesticity on men were pitched at a higher level during the early and mid-Victorian period than at any time before or since. Domesticity is commonly associated with the Evangelicals, who redefined the home as the site of spiritual exercises and the shrine of angelic womanhood.[32] In fact only a minority fully subscribed to the views of Hannah More and John Angell James, but the Evangelicals were nevertheless running with the spirit of the times rather than against it. Shorn of its religious hyperbole, their notion of domesticity became the accepted wisdom of the respectable classes. Home was experienced as a vital refuge from the alienation of the market and from the degradation of urban life; or in James Anthony Froude's words, as a respite from 'the struggle in the race of the world'.[33]

Yet the sociability offered by domesticity was essentially private. Social intercourse with neighbours was not casual and spontaneous,

[29] John Brewer, *The Pleasures of the Imagination: English Culture in the Eighteenth Century* (1997), 99–112.

[30] Peter Clark, *British Clubs and Societies, 1580–1800* (Oxford, 2000); Brian Harrison, *Separate Spheres: The Opposition to Women's Suffrage in Britain* (1978), ch. 5.

[31] Leonore Davidoff and Catherine Hall, *Family Fortunes: Men and Women of the English Middle Class, 1780–1850* (Oxford, 1986), 436–45; F. K. Prochaska, *Women and Philanthropy in Nineteenth-Century England* (Oxford, 1980).

[32] See Davidoff and Hall, *Family Fortunes*, chs. 1–2; and Tosh, *A Man's Place*, 34–9.

[33] [J. A. Froude], *The Nemesis of Faith* (1849), 113.

but increasingly regulated by invitation and calling rituals. Home offered middle-class men not so much a route into neighbourhood society as a substitute for it. Moreover, the authority vested in the head of the household – and the priority accorded to his needs – meant that his interaction with wife and children was not likely to be easy or equal. All too often growing boys were given by their parents a very discouraging model of intellectual companionship. For that growing proportion of middle-class boys who were sent away to boarding school, this negative impression was intensified by exposure to the casual misogyny of all-male institutions.[34] The ability to relate to members of the opposite sex on terms of equality was much less common among the Victorian middle class than their Georgian predecessors.[35]

Whereas politeness was increasingly redundant and irrelevant, the core values of manliness directly addressed the middle-class life experience. This was true in three respects particularly. Manliness exemplified the polarised conception of sexual character which underpinned the tendency of Victorian men and women to seek the company of their own sex; it fully validated the work ethic; and it set standards of self-discipline for men who faced life as embattled individuals.

Victorian manliness was premised on a powerful sense of the feminine 'other', with each sex being defined by negative stereotypes of the other. The separation of the sexes was not of course just an over-literal reflection of natural difference; it was the outcome of a powerful discursive trend over the previous century which is familiar from the work of Thomas Laqueur. According to his book *Making Sex* a transformation in biological thought occurred in the late eighteenth and early nineteenth centuries, from sexual difference understood in incremental terms, to a two-sex model which exaggerated the anatomical differences between the two sexes. Women were now typecast as sexually passive, men as consumed by an all-powerful libido.[36] Whatever objections to Laqueur's thesis in relation to the seventeenth and eighteenth centuries, there is little dispute that early nineteenth-century medicine emphasised the biological differences between men and women to a greater extent than ever before. With this came an exaggeration of secondary differences, particularly as regards sexual character. Manly independence was dramatised by feminine dependence, manly action by feminine passivity, and so on. Both body and

---

[34] This point was repeatedly made by women didactic writers. See for example: Sarah Lewis, *Woman's Mission* (7th edn, 1840), 32, and Sarah Ellis, *The Mothers of England* (1843), 77.

[35] Tosh, *A Man's Place*, 107–10.

[36] Thomas Laqueur, *Making Sex: Body and Gender from the Greeks to Freud* (Cambridge, MA, 1990).

mind were now sexed.[37] As the educational reformer Emily Davies sadly noted, 'whatever is manly must be unwomanly, and vice versa', leading to 'the double moral code, with its masculine and feminine virtues'.[38] Manliness claimed the active virtues for men, naturalising the privilege by dwelling on their female opposites: dependence, caprice, emotionality and timorousness. All too many of both sexes were fully convinced that the attributes of manliness were either natural or God-given. Hence the charge of effeminacy was more damaging than ever, and for this reason it was perhaps less often levelled than in the past.

Logically the implication of this must be that manliness was exclusive to men. In actual fact women were occasionally described as 'manly', suggesting some confusion between what was human and what was specific to the male sex. Yet, applied to women, 'manly' was a rare complement, and they were doomed always to fall short of total achievement. Thus when Samuel Smiles addressed the writer Eliza Lynn Linton as 'beloved woman, most manly of your sex', he meant that she had surpassed the capacities of women, not that she equalled those of men.[39] The only exponents of manliness who believed that women were on an equal footing with men were writers from the Evangelical camp: the subsuming of manliness in the Christian virtues clearly had androgynous implications, as Claudia Nelson has demonstrated.[40] But common usage respected the assumed polarity between male and female. Manliness was as much to do with separating from the feminine as with affirming the masculine. This sense of a yawning gender divide was reinforced by education: while the promise of intellectual achievement was always extended to middle-class boys (however patchy the actual provision), their sisters were all too likely to be trained in 'accomplishments' which confirmed their inferior standing. The outcome was a significant increase in the cultural obstacles to easy social intercourse between the sexes. Victorian men frequently assumed that female company would be unimproving and unstimulating. The young Mandell Creighton admitted: 'I find ladies in general are very unsatisfactory mental food: they seem to have no particular thoughts or ideas, and though for a time it is flattering to one's vanity to think one may teach them some, it palls after a while.'[41] That remained his view until, three years later, he met his future wife in the intellectually

---

[37] On these dichotomies, see Mary Poovey, *Uneven Developments: The Ideological Work of Gender in Mid-Victorian England* (1988).

[38] Quoted in Claudia Nelson, 'Sex and the Single Boy: Ideals of Manliness and Sexuality in Victorian Literature for Boys', *Victorian Studies*, 32 (1989), 530.

[39] Quoted in A. Smiles, *Samuel Smiles and his Surroundings* (1956), 67.

[40] Claudia Nelson, *Boys Will Be Girls: The Feminine Ethic and British Children's Fiction, 1857–1917* (New Brunswick, NJ, 1991).

[41] Quoted in Louise Creighton, *Life and Letters of Mandell Creighton* (2 vols., 1904), I, 33.

bracing atmosphere of a lecture by Ruskin. It was hardly an auspicious frame of mind in which to cultivate the society of the opposite sex.

Secondly, Victorian manliness was closely identified with work. 'It is by work, work, work – constant, never-ceasing work – work well and faithfully done ... that you are to rise out of things into men' declared William Landels in 1859.[42] Such passages can be read as a somewhat crude attempt to socialise young men in the habits of discipline. But the work ethic was much more deeply inscribed in middle-class masculinity than that. It not only served to keep men at a punishing pitch of self-discipline; it also justified the priority they attached to money-making and personal advancement by elevating work as a good in itself. No one conveyed this message with more rhetorical force than Thomas Carlyle (and no one made less effort to master the niceties of polite behaviour). His own compulsion to keep despair at bay by ceaseless activity produced a secular gospel of work, in which salvation lay in the spirit in which the work was undertaken rather than its outcome, and in which idleness represented a threat to the self. 'Consider how, even in the meanest sorts of Labour, the whole soul of man is composed into a kind of real harmony, the instant he sets himself to work! ... The man is now a man.'[43] The immense popular success of *Past and Present* (1843) testifies to the deep resonance these ideas had with men making their way in life.[44] From this perspective, the gentleman's material ease was corrupting rather than empowering. What had been seen in the eighteenth century as the prerequisite for public life was now thought to undermine moral vigour. It was not unknown for a middle-class man to reject a gentlemanly suitor for his daughter precisely *because* he enjoyed 'prospects', lest she should find herself yoked to a man without energy or self-reliance.[45] Manliness upheld the work ethic; gentlemanliness had a distinctly ambivalent relationship with it.

Thirdly, manliness represented the quintessence of individualism. This is something of a paradox. In one sense Victorian manliness was no different from other models of masculinity in requiring the young male to conform to the expectations of the peer group by adjusting his behaviour and self-image to the approved model of manhood. But in commercial and professional society individualism *was* the approved model. Some of that approval emanated from religious sources. Confronted by what they regarded as the scandalous state of youthful morality, Evangelical writers in the earlier part of the century had

[42] William Landels, *How Men Are Made* (1859), 43.

[43] Carlyle, *Past and Present*, 177.

[44] Walter Houghton, *The Victorian Frame of Mind, 1833–70* (New Haven, CT, 1957), 242–62.

[45] See, for example, John Heaton to Helen Heaton, 17 May 1874, Heaton MSS, private collection, Cornhill-on-Tweed.

aimed to moralise manliness as a vital part of their programme of social regeneration. In their view the problem with manliness lay in its undue respect for the worldly standards subsumed in the notion of 'reputation'; in its place they strove to establish 'character', by which they meant the internal urgings of a man's conscience.[46] The voluminous religious advice literature addressed to young men at this time represents the achievement of manhood almost entirely as a solitary quest, with other men regarded as a temptation to idleness or worse.[47]

But the material underpinning for this individualism was also very strong. The Victorian bourgeois world was highly competitive, and it placed a premium on the virtues of self-reliance and personal autonomy. The strongest metaphors of manliness were drawn from the battlefield (life was 'a battle and a march', insisted Carlyle);[48] it therefore fitted the uphill struggle of outsiders far more closely than the life of those with an assured social position. Success was viewed as a personal achievement, and adversity could only be overcome by calling on personal reserves of character. As Stefan Collini has put it, 'the classic scenes of character-testing are essentially private – facing the discouragement of an empty order-book, coping with the failure of one's inventions and projects, studying deep into the night to acquire by hard labour what seemed to come so easily to the expensively-educated'.[49] Ordeals of that kind were more likely to produce a prickly autonomy than a complaisant ease of manner. Indeed the drive to self-reliance almost eclipsed the idea of sociability. Far from being honed in society, manliness was regarded as a personal possession, achieved and maintained through adversity: in Charles Kingsley's phrase, 'all true manhood consists in the defiance of circumstances'.[50] Growing up to manhood was less about cultivating easy relationships with one's peers than about learning to stand on one's own two feet – and stay standing amid the buffets of fortune. At the age of twenty the future publisher Daniel Macmillan told his brother: 'I do not feel bound to follow in the footsteps of any of my relations. I am here to act for myself ... The most important things must be done by myself – alone.'[51]

---

[46] Marjorie Morgan, *Manners, Morals and Class in England 1774–1858* (1994), 63–71, 100–3, 107–8.

[47] For example: H. S. Brown, *Manliness* (1858); J. B. Figgis, *Manliness, Womanliness, Godliness* (1861); Thomas Hughes, *The Manliness of Christ* (1879).

[48] Quoted in Houghton, *Victorian Frame of Mind*, 206.

[49] Stefan Collini, 'The Idea of "Character" in Victorian Political Thought', *Transactions of the Royal Historical Society*, 5th ser. 35 (1985), 40.

[50] Quoted in Adams, *Dandies and Desert Saints*, 110.

[51] Daniel Macmillan to Malcolm Macmillan, 15 June 1833, quoted in Thomas Hughes, *Memoir of Daniel Macmillan* (1882), 17.

Thus far I have presented manliness as essentially the code of middle-class men. A case can be made for the proposition that manliness was merely the gendered face of class consciousness. Davidoff and Hall, for example, analyse a form of manliness which proved highly functional in bourgeois terms, and since they give scant consideration to other class forms, it is reasonable to conclude from their work that gender, while undoubtedly the subject of a distinctive social language, was subordinate to other forms of status.[52] But there is an important sense in which manliness transcended class, owing its discursive power precisely to its detachment from the strongest social divisions of the day. In common culture manliness stood for those qualities which were respected by men without regard to class − by men *as men*. It provided a language for commending (or disparaging) one's fellows across the boundaries of class. In order to gauge the strength of the reaction against politeness, it is necessary to recognise that many of the manly values which prevailed among the bourgeoisie also had a purchase on the upper reaches of the working class. (The same could hardly be said of politeness; as one working-class writer put it in 1861, the word was rarely used and was taken to mean 'some supposed affectation of "fine" behaviour'.)[53]

Significant differences of emphasis were to be found between working-class and middle-class versions of manliness. The lives of most working men made much heavier calls on their physical strength than was the case in the middle class, and bodily vigour was thus even more at a premium. The manly way to settle a dispute or defend one's honour was with the fists − a convention which did not persist much beyond the schooldays of the middle-class boy. Working-class independence meant not freedom from patronage, but security against penury and the associated indignities of charity and the workhouse. Given the prevalence of women's wage-earning, polarised notions of sexual difference carried less weight among workers than among the bourgeoisie. Equally, middle-class values of individualism were less relevant to a working-class culture permeated by the fraternalism of friendly societies, working men's clubs and trade unions.

But the common ground of manliness was important. One vital element was a strong masculine investment in work. Partly this was because diligence and self-discipline seemed to hold out to working men the promise of upward social mobility (of the kind which Samuel Smiles provided so many invigorating anecdotes). Partly also intense commitment to work was for most workers a precondition of main-

[52] Davidoff and Hall, *Family Fortunes*, *passim*.
[53] J. Shepherd, in *Social Science: Being Selections from John Cassell's Prize Essays by Working Men* (1861), 187.

taining a household: this was the period when the word 'breadwinner' entered the language, and when the 'family wage' became a key objective of organised labour.[54] But in the upper reaches of the working class there existed a version of the 'work-for-its-own-sake' ethos in the valorisation of skill. Masculine self-respect was bound up with apprenticeship and the successful practice of hard-won skill thereafter – as is demonstrated by the craft pride of a community such as the carpet-weavers of Kidderminster described by Sonya Rose.[55] Above all, respect for physical vigour, courage and independence were manly values which transcended class, and which informed the standards by which one man judged another, whatever class he belonged to.

This convergence of gender ideals had considerable political significance. Manly discourse was socially inclusive, uncluttered by class baggage. It elevated attributes which all men admired, which were potentially within the grasp of every man and which therefore served to diminish the moral gulf between classes. Thackeray saluted the person 'who can look the world honestly in the face with an equal manly sympathy for the great and the small'.[56] There was a decided implication of social levelling. In the final analysis manliness was more than an indicator of social mores; it had potentially democratic implications, pointing to a politics of social inclusion.

It was John Vincent who first observed that manliness was 'the great moral idea of liberalism'.[57] By this he meant that Liberalism stood for a rejection of all forms of patronage – in other words it elevated manly independence to be a vital prerequisite of responsible political agency. Liberalism's image of the citizen was someone who stood on his own two feet, responsible for his opinions and answerable to no one. Such a person could safely be entrusted with the franchise because his freedom from obligation would ensure that he would not be susceptible to pressure. Indeed, his resistance against pressure was proof of his political virtue, which helps to explain why many liberals were reluctant to legislate for the secret ballot.[58] The rhetoric of independence was an important dimension of the debates on parliamentary reform prior to 1832,[59] and as the focus of debate about the franchise shifted to the working man, independence became an even more critical determinant

[54] Wally Seccombe, 'Patriarchy Stabilized: The Construction of the Male Bread-Winner Norm in Nineteenth-Century Britain', *Social History*, 11 (1986), 53–76.

[55] Sonya Rose, *Limited Livelihoods: Gender and Class in Nineteenth-Century England* (1992), 128–30.

[56] W. M. Thackeray, *Vanity Fair*, ch. 62, quoted in Gilmour, *Idea of the Gentleman*, 69.

[57] John Vincent, *The Formation of the Liberal Party* (1966), 14.

[58] James Vernon, *Politics and the People: A Study in English Political Culture, c. 1815–1867* (Cambridge, 1993), 102, 158, 314.

[59] Work in progress by Matthew McCormack.

of political virtue, especially during the run-up to the 1867 Reform Act. The most effective working-class political organisations did not demand manhood suffrage, since that would have extended the vote to many categories of men who lacked either the moral or the material resources to cast their vote responsibly. The nub of the reformers' case was that the 'independent working man' met the essential criteria for admission to full citizenship; he came within the pale of the constitution no less than those sections of the middle class granted the vote in 1832. The discourse of reform was, as Keith McClelland has put it, characterised by 'the play of independence and dependence'.[60]

But the political purchase of manliness extended well beyond the benchmark of independence. It also served as a marker to distinguish the broad mass of citizens from the privileged and idle. What 'the people' had in common was what made them socially useful – the dignity of labour. In popular culture this was the foundation of true manliness, and it distinguished the people from the aristocracy. In answer to the question 'In what does manhood consist?', one working-class campaigner responded in 1873, 'Well, certainly not in walking the streets with a cigar and a silver-headed cane.' The men who possessed the rights of citizenship, he continued, were 'the men who swept the streets or shaped the wood, or hammered the iron, or hewed the coal' – a telling indication of the potential scope of manly discourse.[61] One explanation for the high profile of manliness, then, is that its values corresponded with the individualism and the suspicion of privilege which were widespread in popular political culture between the first and third Reform Acts. Manliness worked well as the common profession of a masculine representative democracy whose members, even before 1867, included a great swathe of voters who could never have claimed the name of 'gentleman' or sought admission to polite society.

The seal was set on the decline of politeness as a political reference point by the emergence of 'the plain man' as the ideal citizen. This was not an entirely original conceit, but it was advanced with an entirely new intensity and conviction by the most acclaimed leaders of the Liberal party. John Bright came from a wealthy factory-owning family, but in speech and dress he played up to the image of a man of the people, and the simplicity of his family life at home in Oldham was widely commended.[62] When he retired from politics in 1870 –

[60] Keith McClelland, ' "England's Greatness, the Working Man" ', in C. Hall, K. McClelland and J. Rendall, *Defining the Victorian Nation: Class, Race, Gender and the British Reform Act of 1867* (Cambridge, 2000), 97–101.

[61] Thomas Beckwith, quoted in Eugenio Biagini, *Liberty, Retrenchment and Reform: Popular Liberalism in the Age of Gladstone, 1860–80* (Cambridge, 1992), 286.

[62] Patrick Joyce, *Democratic Subjects: The Self and the Social in Nineteenth-Century England* (Cambridge, 1994), 116–24.

ironically from a nervous disorder which his robustness of manner belied – Walter Bagehot remarked, 'There is an evident sincerity and bluff *bona fides* about him, which goes straight to the hearts of Englishmen.'[63] An even more striking reinvention was achieved by W. E. Gladstone. His education at Eton and Christchurch had been designed to turn him into the consummate polite gentleman. It has been said of Gladstone that 'he accepted the manners of the landed class, not merely without demur, but with enthusiasm' on account of the Welsh estates he acquired through marriage.[64] By the 1860s, however, Gladstone was 'the people's William', and later the 'Grand Old Man'. His honest manliness was symbolised by his much publicised tree-felling at Hawarden – the perfect symbol of full masculine vigour.[65] His career can stand for the triumph of manliness over politeness in English political culture. Manliness provided a major discursive resource against the exclusive pretensions of gentlemanly status by suggesting that all that was needed to make a good citizen was to be a good man. In that sense it was well suited to a political discourse which spoke with increasing authority in terms of 'the people'.[66]

What then was the relationship between gentlemanly politeness and manly simplicity during the high Victorian era? The discussion between Margaret Hale and John Thornton turned on the issue of which could be subsumed in the other. Margaret accepted the ascription of all worthy qualities to the gentleman, including what passed for manly ones. John dismissed gentlemanliness as no more than a code for ordering social relations, which did not touch the inner man. Given the inclusive character of manliness, it would be surprising if there were not substantial convergence. Michael Curtin has observed, for example, that the manly independence and rejection of patronage which were valued so highly by the middle and working classes 'were easily compatible with the characteristics of the ideal gentleman'.[67] Respect for martial fitness and athletic prowess were also shared. The moral qualities of courage and Stoicism were common to both. Independence mattered to the gentleman no less than the businessman or professional man, though it was measured in rents rather than profits or fees. Even the inner integrity in which Thornton took such pride was also

---

[63] Walter Bagehot, 'Mr Bright's Retirement' (1870), repr. in *Historical Essays*, ed. N. St J. Stevas (1971), 226.

[64] Vincent, *Formation of the Liberal Party*, 212–13.

[65] On Gladstone's tree-felling, see Biagini, *Liberty, Retrenchment and Reform*, 396–400.

[66] It would be interesting to evaluate Conservative politicians from the same perspective. Matthew McCormack has pointed out to me that Disraeli, of course, was a vivid throwback to the dandy tradition.

[67] Curtin, *Propriety and Position*, 290.

appropriated by definitions of gentlemanliness. Writing in the *Contemporary Review* in 1869, J. R. Vernon commented: 'A gentleman is a MAN. And he realizes what is contained in that word – the high descent, the magnificent destiny. So in the presence of his God and of his fellowmen he is never abject; he is always manly, always keeps self-respect.'[68] But this was special pleading. The difference between gentlemanliness and manliness was critical, and it turned on the dichotomy between politeness and authenticity. This was the nub of John Thornton's hostility towards the fine gentleman. His views were matched from the other side of the social divide by Thomas Hughes through the character of Tom Brown's father. When Squire Brown declares his belief that 'a man is to be valued wholly and solely for that which he is in himself, for that which stands up in the four fleshly walls of him', he is identifying with 'manly' values and distancing himself from the birth and fine breeding habitually associated with men of his class.[69] The practical force of this distinction was accurately conveyed by the Revd Harvey Newcomb: a growing boy, he counselled, should strive to be 'both a man and a gentleman'. By aiming for the latter he would gain courtesy and propriety; by the former he would acquire courage, energy and perseverance. The desired outcome was 'a solid, energetic, manly character, combined with true gentility of manners'.[70] Manliness represented the common aspiration of men in all walks of life; gentlemanliness was a refinement which marked the boy out as one of a social elite.

Gentlemen had traditionally prided themselves on their refined manners, which served the double purpose of easing interpersonal relations and putting down a marker of social exclusiveness. That rationale still counted for something in the mid-Victorian era, but in a world where the basis of economic and political power was being steadily expanded, gentlemen were compelled to place much greater emphasis than in the past on their moral claims to preeminence, appealing to values which were shared throughout 'respectable' society and beyond. The notions of polite society and of polite conduct were increasingly devalued. James Fitzjames Stephen fairly summed up the meaning of politeness in a phrase which reflects its marginal status in Victorian culture: gentlemen, he said, were 'only picked and polished specimens of the material of which the nation at large is composed'.[71]

---

[68] J. R. Vernon, 'The Grand Old Name of Gentleman', *Contemporary Review*, II (1869), 564.

[69] Thomas Hughes, *Tom Brown's Schooldays* (1857; repr. Oxford, 1989), 52.

[70] Harvey Newcomb, *Youth and its Duties: A Book for Young Gentlemen, Containing Useful Hints on the Formation of Character* (1873), 11.

[71] Stephen, 'Gentlemen', 340.

ROYAL HISTORICAL SOCIETY:
REPORT OF COUNCIL
Session 2001–2002

Officers and Council

- At the Anniversary Meeting on 23 November 2001, Professor J. Hoppit succeeded Professor K. Burk as Honorary Treasurer; the remaining Officers of the Society were re-elected.
- The Vice-Presidents retiring under By-law XVII were Professor A.J. Fletcher and Professor C.J. Wrigley. Professor P.J. Corfield and Professor L.J. Jordanova were elected to replace them.
- The Members of Council retiring under By-law XX were Dr. I.W. Archer, Dr. G.W. Bernard, Professor J.C.G. Binfield and Professor R.H. Trainor. In accordance with By-law XXI, amended, Dr. S.R. Ditchfield, Dr. M. Finn and Professor F. O'Gorman were elected in their place.
- The Election of Officers Subcommittee convened during the year proposed that Dr. Kenneth Fincham succeed Dr. Peter Mandler as Honorary Secretary. Dr. Fincham consented to Council's request that his name be put forward to the Society's Anniversary Meeting on 22 November 2002 to take office with effect from that date.
- Amy Warner was appointed Administrative Assistant to the Executive Secretary in April 2002.
- MacIntyre and Company were appointed auditors for the year 2001–2002 under By-law XXXIX.
- CrippsPortfolio, formerly Cripps Harries Hall, continue to manage the Society's investment funds.

Activities of the Society during the Year

The Society continued to take an ever more active role in representing the interests of the historical profession and of historical research to government, the nation's major research institutions, funding councils and other scholarly bodies.

- The Society contributed to the British Library's consultation on its New Strategic Directions document. Concerns were raised about the ability of the British Library to function as the core provider of scholarly materials, especially in foreign languages, at current

473

funding levels. Regular meetings were held with officials of the British Library and, partly as a result of these meetings, a roundtable of representatives from a wide range of scholarly disciplines was convened by the Arts and Humanities Research Board to broaden the discussions.

- The Society contributed to the government's quinquennial review of the Historical Manuscripts Commission, arguing strongly for the retention of the HMC's functions as a central clearing-house for information on archives and their preservation. This review by Sir Geoffrey Chipperfield concluded with a recommendation that these functions be retained but incorporated in a larger institution. At the end of the year government announced its intention to bring the HMC and the Public Record Office together into a National Archives service, a resolution with which Council was satisfied and towards which it intends to contribute.

- The Society has taken a growing interest in the position of history in the schools, on which subject it always seeks to work in cooperation with the Historical Association. Council welcomed and has agreed to assist with an initiative by the Council for British Archaeology to develop plans for a GCSE in Medieval History. Dr W Childs represented the Society on a Qualifications and Curriculum Agency working group on history and geography in the curriculum. Professor R McKitterick represented the Society on the QCA's History Subject Association's group.

- Closer relations with the History at the Universities Defence Group were established. Council heard regular reports from the HUDG steering committee and the President and Honorary Secretary held a series of meetings with the co-convenors of HUDG which have helped the two bodies pursue a common agenda.

- Council welcomed the results of the British Academy's Review of Graduate Studies in the Humanities and Social Sciences.

- The President and Professor F. O'Gorman on behalf of Council visited the newly-opened British Empire and Commonwealth Museum in Bristol, and Council authorized a donation to the museum of £500 as a token of its support for the venture.

- The Society continued to have representation on all the English Regional Archives Councils, and to consult its representatives – augmented by Fellows active in other sectors of the archives world, including in Scotland, Wales, and Northern Island – through an e-mail list 'Archives Group'.

- The Society continued to administer the British National Committee of the International Committee of Historical Sciences. The 20th Quinquennial Congress will be held in Sydney on 4–11 July 2005, and the President welcomes suggestions for themes and sub-themes.

It was also hoped that grants could be made available for British historians to attend.

One of the high points of the year came on 5 July 2002, at the Anglo-American Conference of Historians in London, when the Society launched its free on-line Bibliography of British and Irish History (www.rhs.ac.uk/bibwel.html). Council expressed its great indebtedness to Dr Ian Archer, General Editor, and to Peter Salt, Project Editor, for the tremendous success of this stage of the project. A new application was in preparation for submission to the Arts and Humanities Research Board which would permit enhancement of the Bibliography by integrating it with other bibliographical projects.

The Society sought to improve its communication with postgraduate students in history by circulating a newsletter to all 3,500 students registered for postgraduate degrees in the United Kingdom. Council agreed to make this an annual publication.

As a result of an initiative from the German History Society, the Society agreed to administer a new prize for a book in German history.

On the recommendation of the Society's Accountants, haysmacintyre, the Society undertook a review of risk assessment, in accordance with the Statement of Recommended Practice: Accounting and Reporting by Charities (SORP).

Mindful of the rapidly changing environment in higher education, of the Society's improved ties to the growing numbers of historians working outside of higher education, and of the need to keep up-to-date the Society's structures and commitments, Council resolved to devote itself at an extended meeting in September 2002 to a review of the Society's governance and activities. Results of this review will be reported in the Society's newsletters and in the next Annual Report.

Meetings of the Society

- Five papers were given in London this year and two papers were read at locations outside London. Welcome invitations were extended to the Society to visit the history departments at the Universities of Sunderland and Manchester. The trip to Sunderland included a tour of a Victorian lighthouse preserved by the National Trust and the visit to Manchester included a guided tour of Chetham's Library. Members of Council met with the departments to discuss issues of interest to historians before the paper was delivered. As always, the Society received a warm welcome and generous hospitality from the universities concerned and is very grateful to them for their kindness. Future visits will include the University of Wales at Aberystwyth and Lampeter on 18 October 2002, the University of Greenwich on 14 February 2003, Oxford Brookes University on 4 April 2003 and the University of Newcastle upon Tyne on 24 October 2003.

- The Colin Matthew Memorial Lecture for the Public Understanding of History – previously known as the Gresham Lecture – was given to a very large and appreciative audience by Professor Peter Hennessy at Staple Inn Hall, High Holborn, London on ' "Tony wants": The Blair Premiership in historical perspective'. These lectures are given in memory of the late Professor Colin Matthew, a former Literary Director and Vice-President of the Society. The lecture in 2002 was on Thursday 7 November by Professor Marianne Elliott on 'Robert Emmet: The Making of a Legend'. The lecture in 2003 will be on Thursday 6 November by Professor Brian Harrison, Editor of the *New Dictionary of National Biography*.

- The Society participated in an international conference 'Locating the Victorians', held at Imperial College, London on 12–15 July 2001, to mark the 100th anniversary of the death of Queen Victoria and the 150th anniversary of the Great Exhibition.

- A conference on 'English Politeness: Conduct, Social Rank and Moral Vitrue, c.1400–c.1900' was held at The Huntington Library, San Marino, California, U.S.A., on 14–15 September 2001. A hastily-prepared follow-up one-day conference, where the two papers were read by contributors unable to attend because of the events of 11 September, was held at the Institute of Historical Research, London, on 24 November 2001. The papers read at both parts of the conference will be published in *Transactions*, Sixth Series, Volume 12, to be published in November 2002.

- A one-day Colloquium on 'Conflicting Loyalties: The Responsibilities of the Historian' was held at the School of Oriental and African Studies, University of London on 16 February 2002. Approximately 100 people attended.

- A two-day conference, 'Architecture and History', held jointly with the Society of the Architectural Historians of Great Britain, took place at the University of Sheffield on 5–7 April 2002. Approximately 70 delegates took part.

- Future conferences would include: i) a joint conference with The National Maritime Museum on the 'Age of Exploration' to be held in September 2003; ii) an annual seminar and an annual conference, held in alternate years in York and London, to commemorate the Society's former President Professor Gerald Aylmer; iii) a joint conference was planned with the North American Conference on British Studies and the British Association for American Studies,

'Crosstown Traffic: Anglo-American Cultural Exchange since 1865', to be held July 2004; iv) a joint conference with the Centre for English Local History, University of Leicester and the Victoria County History to mark the 50 Anniversary of W.G. Hoskins' *Making of the English Landscape* would be held in 2005; v) a conference to mark the Tercentenary of the Union with Scotland would be held in 2007.

Prizes

The Society's annual prizes were awarded as follows:

- The Alexander Prize was awarded to Quintin Colville, BA, MA, for his essay 'Jack Tar and the gentleman officer: the role of uniform in shaping the class- and gender-related identities of British naval personnel, 1930–1939'.

    The judges' citation read:

    'This was an original and ambitious topic, handled with such skill and sensitivity that not only were the 'identities' of the title illuminated but the wider context of social change and tension was brought into firm focus. Exceptionally well-structured and enlivened with well-chosen illustrations, this persuasive exercise in cultural history gripped the readers from start to finish.'

- The David Berry Prize for 2001, for an essay on Scottish history, was awarded to Elizabeth Buettner for her essay 'Haggis in the Raj: Private and Public Celebrations of Scottishness in Late Imperial India'. The judge's citation read:

    'This essay is a fine and innovative study of a constructed national identity. For Scots in India the St Andrew's day dinner became an important annual ritual: a celebration of the Scottish contribution to imperial endeavour as well as a playful evocation of the (often invented) traditions of the homeland. This text draws out the political, social and cultural importance of these events in a subtle and thoughtful analysis that adds much to our understanding of the Anglo-Indian community and the values that infused their working lives.'

- The Whitfield Prize for a first book on British history attracted 19 entries. The generally high quality of the entries was again commended by the assessors.

    The prize for 2001 was awarded jointly to:

    John Goodall, *God's House at Ewelme: Life, Devotion and Architecture in a Fifteenth-Century Almshouse* [Ashgate] and

Frank Salmon, *Building on Ruins: The Rediscovery of Rome and English Architecture* [Ashgate]

The judges wrote:

'The assessors were unanimous in their praise and admiration for these two books, which have much in common, and, coincidentally, were both published by Ashgate. They were looking for the highest possible standards in all aspects of the books. The judges were especially struck by the depth and originality of their research, by their elegant, clear and enthusiastic expression, and by their integration of a wide range of evidence to produce a satisfying and coherent whole.

Goodall has produced a compelling holistic study, a detailed account of an institution, God's House at Ewelme in Oxfordshire, looking at the period of its foundation in the 15 century in particular, but also bringing its story up to date. He shows how it is possible to use the rich records of a single institution to shed light on a wide range of issues and practices from art, architecture and music to politics, charity and religion. He is attentive to the textures of daily life, possible because of the survival of an unusually complete body of medieval material. The founders of God's House lived in times of high drama, in which they fully participated, murder, deception, overweening ambition and intense anxiety about the afterlife.

Salmon's book is organised around a neglected theme, the continuing importance of ancient Rome in the minds of British elites in the first half of the nineteenth century. He traces the activities of British architects between 1740 and 1840 in engaging with ruins and antiquities connected with Rome and Herculaneum. This is then put to work in a series of compelling case studies of major public building projects of the 1830s, in Birmingham, Cambridge, London and Liverpool. He thus attempts, in a spirit of revisionism, to put the far better known Greek revivalism and the enthusiasm for Gothic designs, into a fresh context, and thereby to give the attention to a number of important buildings of which they have hitherto been deprived.'

- Thanks to the continuing generous donation from The Gladstone Memorial Trust, the third Gladstone History Book Prize for a first book on a subject outside British history was awarded. The number of entries increased considerably this year to 30.

The prize for 2001 was awarded to Nora Berend for her book *At the Gate of Christendom, Jews, Muslims, and 'Pagans' in Medieval Hungary, c.1000–c.1300* [Cambridge University Press]. *Proxime accessit* was Dan Healey for his book *Homosexual Desire in Revolutionary Russia. The Regulation of Sexual and Gender Dissent* [University of Chicago Press].

The judges wrote:

'The judges were impressed by the high quality of much of the work read. There was however substantial agreement as to those regarded as the best.

In the light of reading and discussion the committee proposes a prize list comprising three works. All three authors show they have the scholarly skills to go on to be major players within the historical profession in this country and internationally. We wish the authors well in the future.

An Honourable Mention should be awarded Rana Mitter's *The Manchurian Myth: Nationalism, Resistance and Collaboration in Modern China* (University of California Press). The judges commend the way in which the author illuminated an important incident in twentieth-century history through utilisation of both Chinese and Japanese sources, and provided a thoughtful, scholarly and impartial account which makes a major contribution to our understanding of the contentious historiographies of both modern Japan and China. Despite the tragedy involved, Dr Mitter writes with wit and an enviable lightness of touch. The judges liked that.

The place of *proxime accessit* should be awarded to Dan Healey, *Homosexual Desire in Revolutionary Russia. The Regulation of Sexual and Gender Dissent* (University of Chicago Press). The judges were most impressed by the choice of topic – pathbreaking in terms of contemporary Russian history – the prodigious amount of dedicated archival research which lay behind the work, and the theoretical reflection which informed the writing. The result is a genuinely original piece of scholarship which adds, often very movingly, a much concealed human dimension to our understanding of Russian society in the first half of the 20th century. By its exploration of the lives of ordinary men and women, the sometimes bizarre combinations of restriction and liberty emerge in frequently unexpected fashion.

The judges were unanimous in selecting as the winner of this year's Gladstone Prize Nora Berend, *At the Gate of Christendom. Jews, Muslims, and 'Pagans' in Medieval Hungary, c.1000–c.1300* (Cambridge University Press). This is a superb study of marginality – social, ethnic, religious and geographical – in medieval Europe, but is anything but a marginal work. The topic seems narrow, the treatment is emphatically not. The author handles a dauntingly demanding source base with enormous grace, and shows an extremely wide range of linguistic and technical skills. The book begins with a fascinating consideration of her topic in the light of the frontier hypothesis in North American history, and we look forward with excited anticipation to the moment when our Americanist colleagues will be citing Dr Berend's work on medieval Hungary as an important contribution to their own studies of the frontier. She presents a picture which will confound casual readers who believe that "medieval" necessarily connotes bigotry and persecution. The world she describes is certainly an uneasy frontier which is becoming but has not yet become fully Christian but it is also one on which "non-Christians" have both space and rights and one in which intolerance and co-operation mixed in frequently surprising ways.

The judges were particularly impressed by the way in which Dr Berend triumphed over the difficulties of her sources to provide a lucid, poised, scholarly and humane account. She demonstrates dazzlingly that the apparently marginal can provide insight into the most central of historical preoccupations. We hope that this is only, for her, the first of many glittering prizes.'

- In order to recognise the high quality of work now being produced at undergraduate level in the form of third-year dissertations, the Society has instituted, in association with *History Today* magazine, an annual prize for the best undergraduate dissertation. Departments are asked to nominate annually their best dissertation and a joint committee of the Society and *History Today* select in the autumn the national prizewinner from among these nominations. The prize also recognizes the Society's close relations with *History Today* and the important role the magazine has played in disseminating scholarly research to a wider audience.

First prize was awarded to Jeanette Lucraft from the University of Huddersfield for her essay: 'Missing From History: A reinstatement of Katherine Swynford's identity'.

Second prize was awarded to Michael Finn from the University of Liverpool for his essay: 'Mythology of war: civilian perceptions of war in Liverpool, 1914–1938'.

Third prize was awarded to Timothy Leon Grady from the University of Keele for his essay: 'Academic Anti-Semitism: the Friedrich-Alexander University of Erlangen and the Jews, 1929–1938'.

At the kind invitation of the Keeper, all entrants and their institutional contacts were invited to a celebratory lunch and a behind the scenes visit to the Public Record Office in January 2002. Over twenty five candidates and tutors attended.

Articles by all three prize-winners presenting their research have appeared in *History Today* in 2002.

- Frampton and Beazley Prizes for A-level performances were awarded following nominations from the examining bodies:

Frampton Prizes:
- o   Assessment and Qualifications Alliance, formerly AEB and NEAB:
     Gemma Hayward, Ludlow College, Shropshire

- ○ Edexcel Foundation incorporating the London Examination Board:
  Eliza Sydney Kate Coleman, Wycombe Abbey School
- ○ Oxford, Cambridge and RSA Board:
  Elizabeth Osborne, Oxford High School
- ○ Welsh Joint Education Committee:
  Mari Lewis, Ysgol Caereinion, Welshpool

Beazley Prizes:
- ○ Northern Ireland Council for the Curriculum Examinations and Assessment: Charles Edward Kitson, Wallace High School, Lisburn
- ○ Scottish Examination Board:
  Lesley Jackson, Fraserburgh Academy

Publications

- *Transactions,* Sixth Series, Volume 11 was published during the session, and *Transactions,* Sixth Series, Volume 12 went to press, to be published in November 2002.
- In the *Camden, Fifth Series, The Times and Appeasement; The Journals of A.L. Kennedy, 1932–1939,* ed. Gordon Martel (Vol. 17), *The Remembrances of Elizabeth Freke, 1671–1714,* ed. Raymond A. Anselment (Vol. 18) were published during the year. *Travel, Trade and Power in the Atlantic, 1765–1884,* ed. W.A. Speck/B. Wood and M. Lynn (Vol. 19), *Letters from Arnold Stephenson Rowntree to Mary Katherine Rowntree, 1910–1918,* ed. I. Packer (vol. 20) and *British Envoys to Germany, 1816–1866, Vol. II: 1830–1847,* ed. M. Moesslang, S. Freitag and P. Wende (Vol. 21) went to press for publication in 2001–2002.
- The Society's *Annual Bibliography of British and Irish History, Publications of 2000,* was published by Oxford University Press during the session, and the *Annual Bibliography of British and Irish History, Publications of 2001* went to press, to be published in 2002. In addition, the *Bibliography of Imperial, Colonial and Commonwealth History since 1600,* edited by Andrew Porter, was published by Oxford University Press with the assistance of a grant from the AHRB.
- The *Studies in History* second series continued to produce exciting volumes. As scheduled, the following volumes were published during the session:

  - ○ *The Great War, Memory and Ritual: Commemoration in the City and East London, 1916–1939* by Mark Connelly;
  - ○ *The Moravian Church and the Missionary Awakening in England, 1760–1800* by John Cecil Strickland Mason;

- ○ *Lloyd George, Liberalism and the Land: The Land Issue and Party Politics in England, 1906–1914*, by Ian Packer;
- ○ *Power and Border Lordship in Medieval France: The County of Perche, 1000–1226*, by Kathleen Thompson;
- ○ *Henry VIII, the League of Schmalkalden and the English Reformation* by Rory McEntergart.

- These latter volumes will all feature in a launch to be held after the Anniversary Meeting and Presidential Address on 22 November 2002. As in previous years, the membership of the Society will be invited to attend.
- As in the two previous subscription years, volumes in Studies in History series were offered to the membership at a favourably discounted price. 202 accepted the offer for volumes published during the year, and a further 230 copies of the volumes to be published in the year 2002–2003 were ordered. We look forward to the number of Fellows purchasing these volumes continuing to increase as the scheme becomes more established.

The Society was delighted that the Economic History Society agreed to make a most generous subvension to the series, in the sum of £2,000 per annum for five years. It was also pleased to agree to a Member of the EHS, Dr. J. Hunter, being co-opted on to the series Editorial Board.

The Society was investigating the possible re-publication of former Presidential lectures, particularly those of Sir Richard Southern.

Papers Read

- At the ordinary meetings of the Society the following papers were read:

  - ○ 'The place of Tudor England in the Messianic Vision of Philip II of Spain'
    Professor Geoffrey Parker (4 July 2001: Prothero Lecture)
  - ○ 'The Charity of Early Modern Londoners'
    Dr. Ian Archer (19 October 2001 at the University of Sunderland)
  - ○ ' "According to Ancient Custom": The Restoration of Altars in the Restoration Church of England'
    Dr. Kenneth Fincham (18 January 2002)
  - ○ 'Einhardt: The Sinner and the Saints'
    Dr. Julia M.H. Smith (16 March 2002)
  - ○ 'Migrants, Immigrants and Welfare from the Old Poor Law to the Welfare State'

Dr. David Feldman (19 April 2002 at the University of Manchester)
The Alexander Essay Prize reading
'Jack Tar and the Gentleman Officer: The Role of Uniform in Shaping the Class- and Gender-related Identities of British Naval Personnel, 1930–1939'
Quintin Colville (17 May 2002)

- At the Anniversary meeting on 23 November 2001, the President, Professor Janet L. Nelson, delivered an address on 'England the Continent in the Ninth Century: I, Ends and Beginnings'.
- At the Conference entitled 'English Politeness: Conduct, Social Rank and Moral Vitrue, c.1400–c.1900' held at The Huntington Library, San Marino, California, USA on 14–15 September 2001 and at the Institute of Historical Research, London, at the IHR, on 24 November 2001, the following papers were read:

  - 'Gentlemanly Conduct in Medieval England' John Gillingham
  - 'The Gentlemanly House, 1500–1750' Nicholas Cooper
  - 'The Functions of Eighteenth-Century Politeness' Paul Langford
  - 'Politeness Exposed: Character and the Sentimental Gentleman' Philip Carter
  - 'Topographies of Politeness: Polite Culture in Eighteenth-Century Towns' Rosemary Sweet
  - 'Consuming Passions: Shopping, Politeness and Taste' Helen Berry
  - 'Creating a Veil of Silence: Politeness and Marital Violence in the English Household, c.1750–c.1850' Elizabeth Foyster
  - 'Courses in Politeness: The Upbringing and Experience of Six Teenage Diarists, 1671–1890' Anthony Fletcher
  - 'The Puritan and the Polite: The Virtuous Youth in Eighteenth-Century New England' Richard Bushman
  - 'The Brash Colonial: Class and Comportment in nineteenth-century Australia' Penelope Russell
  - 'Masculinity and the End of Politeness' Michele Cohen
  - 'Gentlemanly Politeness and Manly Simplicity in Victorian England' John Tosh.

Finance

- Significant falls in global financial markets since 2000 have put the Society's finances under strain (about half of its income comes from its investments). Between July 2001 and June 2002 the value of its investments fell by £238,606 or 10.43 per cent, from £2,250,106 to

£2,011.500. Expert advice has been taken on how to maintain the long-term value of the Society's portfolio and in response a very cautious attitude towards expenditure has been adopted and an increase in subscriptions has been recommended by Council (to £30 per annum for Fellows, £20 per annum for most other categories). The Society this year had an operating deficit of £20,040, compared with an operating deficit for last year of £32,545, a decrease of £12,505.

- Council records with gratitude the benefactions made to the Society by:

  - Mr. L.C. Alexander
  - The Reverend David Berry
  - Professor Andrew Browning
  - Professor C.D. Chandaman
  - Professor G. Donaldson
  - Professor Sir Geoffrey Elton
  - Mr. E.J. Erith
  - Mrs. W.M. Frampton
  - Mr. A.E.J. Hollaender
  - Professor C.J. Holdsworth
  - Professor P.J. Marshall
  - Mr. E.L.C. Mullins
  - Sir George Prothero
  - Professor T.F. Reddaway
  - Miss E.M. Robinson
  - Professor A.S. Whitfield

Membership

- Council was delighted to acknowledge the awards in the Honours' Lists during the year, to Professor P.J. Marshall [CBE], former President and current Honorary Vice-President, and also to Fellows; Mr. M.M. Hastings, Professor I. Kershaw and Professor C.R. Lucas [Knighthoods] and Sir Michael Howard [CH].
- The procedure for election to the Fellowship was revised during the year. In order to simplify applications without reducing the level of scrutiny, a new form of application was devised consisting of a single sheet of paper, and a single referee's report on the reverse. Referees are specifically directed to testify to the quality of the applicant's contribution to historical scholarship, and further, additional references are sought where appropriate.
- Council was advised and recorded with regret the deaths of 2 Honorary Vice-Presidents, 18 Fellows, 2 Life Fellows, 13 Retired

Fellows, 1 Corresponding Fellow and 3 Associates. These included

Dr. J. Addy – Associate
Professor G.P. Akrigg – Retired Fellow
Professor D.W.R. Bahlman – Fellow
Professor T.C. Barker – Fellow
Professor F. Bédarida – Corresponding Fellow
Dr. E.G.W. Bill – Retired Fellow
The Revd. G.T. Brake – Fellow
Mr. J.D. Brown – Fellow
Professor D.A. Bullough – Retired Fellow
Dr. D. Carrington – Retired Fellow
Miss A.C. de la Mare – Retired Fellow
Mr. B. Denton – Fellow
Professor A.G. Dickens – Honorary Vice-President
Miss E. Drus – Life Fellow
Dr. W. Frohlich – Fellow
Dr. J.L. Gillespie – Fellow
Professor R.J. Harrison – Retired Fellow
Professor F.J. Haskell – Fellow
Professor M.J. Havran – Fellow
Professor R.H. Hilton – Retired Fellow
Mr. K.E. Jermy – Associate
Professor T.K. Keefe – Fellow
Major-General J.D. Lunt – Fellow
Professor O. MacDonagh – Retired Fellow
Professor T.H.D. Mahoney – Fellow
Professor D.C. Moore – Retired Fellow
Sir Dimitri Obolensky – Retired Fellow
Dr. D.M. Owen – Fellow
Professor R.A.C. Parker – Retired Fellow
Professor P.J. Parish – Fellow
Sir John Plumb – Fellow
Professor R.S. Porter – Fellow
Professor D.B. Quinn – Honorary Vice-President
Professor M.A. Reed – Retired Fellow
Mr. F. Sainsbury – Associate
Professor G.N. Sanderson – Retired Fellow
Professor Emeritus R.B. Sheridan – Fellow
Professor V.F. Snow – Fellow and
Mrs. J. Varley – Life Fellow.

- 96 Fellows and 23 Members were elected. 6 new Honorary Vice-Presidents and 6 Corresponding Fellows were invited to accept election. The membership of the Society on 30 June 2002 numbered 2588, comprising 1754 Fellows, 503 Retired Fellows, 19 Life Fellows, 13 Honorary Vice-Presidents, 95 Corresponding Fellows, 88 Associates and 116 Members.

- The Society exchanged publications with 15 Societies, British and Foreign.

Representatives of the Society

- Dr. Julia Crick was asked to succeed Mr. M. Roper, Professor P.H. Sawyer and Mr. C.P. Wormald on the Joint Committee of the Society and the British Academy established to prepare an edition of Anglo-Saxon charters;

- Mr. P.M.H. Bell agreed to succeed Professor M.R.D. Foot on the Editorial Advisory Board of the *Annual Register.*

- The representation of the Society upon various bodies was as follows:

  o Mr. M. Roper, Professor P.H. Sawyer and Mr. C.P. Wormald on the Joint Committee of the Society and the British Academy established to prepare an edition of Anglo-Saxon charters;
  o Professor N.P. Brooks on a committee to promote the publication of photographic records of the more significant collections of British Coins;
  o Professor G.H. Martin on the Council of the British Records Association;
  o Dr. G.W. Bernard on the History at the Universities Defence Group;
  o Professor C.J. Holdsworth on the Court of the University of Exeter;
  o Professor D. d'Avray on the Anthony Panizzi Foundation;
  o Professor M.C. Cross on the Council of the British Association for Local History; and on the British Sub-Commission of the Commission International d'Histoire Ecclesiastique Comparée;
  o Miss V. Cromwell on the Advisory Board of the Computers in Teaching Initiative Centre for History; and on the Advisory Committee of the TLTP History Courseware Consortium;
  o Professor L.J. Jordanova on the Advisory Council of the reviewing committee on the of the Export of Works of Art;
  o Professor R.A. Griffiths on the Court of Governors of the University of Wales, Swansea;

○ Professor W. Davies on the Court of the University of Birmingham;
○ Professor R.D. McKitterick on a committee to regulate British co-operation in the preparation of a new repertory of medieval sources to replace Potthast's *Bibliotheca Historica Medii Aevi*;
○ Professor J. Breuilly on the steering committee of the proposed British Centre for Historical Research in Germany;
○ Dr. W.R. Childs at the Court at the University of Sheffield;
○ Dr. J. Winters on the History Data Service Advisory Committee;
○ Dr. R.A. Burns on the user panel of the RSLP Revelation project 'Unlocking research sources for 19 and 20 century church history and Christian theology';
○ Professor J.A. Tosh on the History Advisory Panel of the Subject Centre for History, Classics and Archaeology.

● Council received reports from its representatives.

Grants

● The Royal Historical Society Centenary Fellowship for the academic year 2001–2002 was awarded to Jonathan Spangler studying for a doctorate at Oxford and working on a thesis entitled 'Princes Etrangers at the Court of Louis XIV: the House of Lorraine and maintenance of Family Fortune and Influence'.
● The Society's Peter Marshall Fellowship was awarded during the year jointly to John Stuart working on a PhD at King's College London, on a thesis entitled 'Race, Politics and Evangelisation: British Protestant Missionaries and African Colonial Affairs, 1945–1963' and Wendy Toon, working for a PhD at Keele University, on a thesis entitled 'U.S. Re-education and the Occupations of Germany and Japan, 1944–1946: Perception and Practice'.
● A grant of £2,500 to the Historical Association was made during the year. This was towards the publication of their Careers in History leaflet circulated to school and college students who take GCSE and A-level examinations.
○ The Society's Research Support Committee continued to provide grants to postgraduate students for attendance at short-term training courses or conferences, funding towards research within and outside the United Kingdom and to assist the financing of small specialized historical conferences, especially where there is substantial involvement of junior researchers. Grants during the year were made to the following:

Training Bursaries:

○ Felicitas Maria BECKER, St John's College, Cambridge
African Studies Association 44th Annual Conference held in Houston, Texas, USA, 15–18 November 2001.

○ Erin Alison BELL, University of York
14th Biennial Conference of Quaker Historians and Archivists held at Haverford College, USA, 20–22 June 2002.

○ Wai Keung CHAN, SOAS, University of London
Annual conference of the Association for Asian Studies, held in Washington DC 4–7 April 2002.

○ Andrew Christopher EDWARDS, University of Wales, Bangor
North American Association for the Study of Welsh Culture and History Conference, held in Syracuse, New York, USA, 19–22 June 2002.

○ Rebekah Frances HIGGITT, Imperial College, London
Conference, 'The Poetics of Biography in Science, Technology and Medicine' held in Copenhagen, on 22–25 May 2002.

○ Elizabeth Ann MATCHETTE, University of Sussex
Conference 'The Circulation of Second-hand Goods', held at the European University Institute, Florence, Italy, 13–14 October 2002.

○ Jennifer McDONALD, University of Aberdeen
37th International Congress on Medieval Studies Conference, held at Western Michigan University, USA, on 2–5 May 2002.

○ Kimberly PERKINS, University of Glasgow
Kalamazoo International Medieval Congress, held in Michigan, USA, on 2–5 May 2002.

○ Roland PIETSCH, Queen Mary College, University of London
'Maritime History Beyond 2000: Visions of Sea and Shore' held in Freemantle, Australia, 11–14 December 2001.

○ Shira Danielle SCHNITZER, University of Oxford
American Academy for Jewish Research Annual Graduate Seminar, 'The Comparative Method in Jewish Studies', held in Philadelphia, USA, 9–13 June 2002.

○ Elizabeth Ann Louisa VLOSSAK, University of Cambridge
48th Annual Meeting of The Society for French Historical Studies, held in Toronto, Canada, on 11–13 April 2002.

○ Raymond William WESTPHAL, University of Exeter
Conference 'War, Virtual War and the Challenges to Communities', held at the University of Oxford, 16–18 July 2002.

Training Bursaries to attend a Royal Historical Society Conference

○ Caroline HARDING-EDGAR, University of Cambridge

Conference, 'Architecture and History', held at the University of Sheffield, 5–7 April 2002.

○ Fleur Louise Warden RICHARDS, University of Oxford
Conference, 'Architecture and History', held at the University of Sheffield, 5–7 April 2002.

○ Kathryn Jane WITHERSBY-LENCH, Liverpool John Moores University
Conference, 'Architecture and History', held at the University of Sheffield, 5–7 April 2002.

Research Fund: Research within the United Kingdom

○ John George BECKERSON, University of East Anglia
Visits to the Isle of Man National Archive, Douglas, and to the Public Record Office, Kew, April–June 2002.

○ Andrea BENVENUTI, University of Oxford
Visits to the Public Record Office, Kew.

○ Janet Elizabeth DICKINSON, University of Southampton
Visits to the British Library, London.

○ Anastasia FILIPPOUPOLITI, University of Leicester
Visits to various libraries in London, Oxford and Aylesbury, May–December 2002.

○ Victor Pedro MADEIRA, University of Cambridge
Visits to various archives in London and Oxford.

○ Sean Joseph MURPHY, University of Essex
Visits to the Public Record Office, Kew.

○ Alexander Mackenzie SUTHERLAND, University of Aberdeen
Visits to archives in Scotland.

○ Benedikta VON SEHERR-THOSS, University of Oxford
Visits to the Public Record Office, Kew.

○ Janice WALLACE, University of Exeter
Visit to the Public Record Office, Kew.

○ Robert WATSON, University of Dundee
Visit to various archives in Scotland.

○ Samuel Bruce Adlam WILLIS, University of Exeter
Visits to the National Maritime Museum.

Research Fund: Research outside the United Kingdom

○ Ama Barbara BINEY, School of Oriental and African Studies, University of London
Visits to archives in Ghana, 22 July–3 September 2002.

○ Sara Anne BONADIO, Southampton University
Visit to archives in Boston, USA.

○ Isobel BROOKS, Royal Holloway, University of London
Visits to archives in Paris, 22 July–6 August 2002.

○ Tatjana BUKLIJAS, University of Cambridge
Visits to archives in Vienna, Austria.

○ Nancy COLLINS, Courtauld Institute of Art
Visits to archives in Paris, France.

○ Mark Paul FELTON, University of Essex
Visits to archives in North America and to the Public Record Office, Kew.

○ Lars FISCHER, University College, London
Visits to archives in Germany and the Netherlands.

○ Nicola Claire FOOTE, University College London
Visit to archives in Texas, USA and in Ecuador.

○ Gregor HOPF, London School of Economics
Visits to archives in Singapore.

○ Christopher JONES, University of Durham
Visit to archives in France.

○ Stefania LONGO, University College London
Visits to archives in Rome, 1 to 31 July 2002.

○ Pawel MACIEJKO, St Hugh's College, Oxford
Visits to archives in Germany.

○ Sloan Courtney MAHONE, University of Oxford
Visits to various archives in Tanzania, Zanzibar, Kenya and Uganda, mid July–September 2002.

○ Martin McELROY, Queen's University, Belfast
Visits to various archives in the Republic of Ireland, Monday 29 May–Wednesday 5 June 2002.

○ Vanessa Anne MIEVILLE, Royal Holloway, University of London
Visits to various archives in France.

○ James MORRISON, University of Birmingham
Visit to the National Archives of Canada, Ottawa.

○ Jason Abram NICE, University of York
Visits to archives in Rennes and Paris, France, 27 June 2002–28 July 2002.

○ Izabela Anna ORLOWSKA, School of Oriental and African Studies, University of London
Visits to archives in Addis Ababa and fieldwork in Northern Ethiopia.

○ Georgios PLAKOTOS, University of Glasgow
Visits to archives in Italy.

○ Katherine Elizabeth QUINN, University College, London
Visits to archives in United States, Cuba and Guyana.

○ Emma ROBERTSON, University of York

Visits to various archives in Nigeria and conducting interviews in Nigeria.
○ Ayako SAKURAI, University of Cambridge
  Visits to various archives in Germany.
○ Paula Regina STILES, University of St. Andrews
  Visit to archives in Barcelona, Spain.
○ Mathilde Ulrike VON BULOW, University of Cambridge
  Visits to archives in Paris, France.
○ Heather WARDLAW, University College London
  Visits to archives in France.
○ William Burgess WOMACK, SOAS, University of London
  Visits to archives in Burma.

Workshop Fund

○ 'Reformulating the Reformation – A. G. Dickens, his work and influence', conference to be held at the University of Hull, 1–2 November 2002 (R. W. AMBLER and P. G. BURGESS).
○ 'The 1630s: Interdisciplinary Approaches' conference held at Keele University, 18–19 May 2002 (Ian ATHERTON).
○ 'Treason, Riot and Heresy': Instability in Britain and Western Europe, 1200–1550, conference held at the University of Durham, 22–24 August 2002 (Jeffrey BECKER, Jonathan BONIFACE, Christopher CANDY).
○ Postgraduate workshop, 'Recent Research in the History of Retailing and Distribution', held at the University of Wolverhampton, on 22 May 2002 (John BENSON).
○ 'Towards a Comparative History of Coalfield Societies' conference held at the University of Glamorgan, 12–14 April 2002 (Stefan BERGER).
○ 'Affluent Britain?' conference held at the University of Bristol, 24–25 May 2002 (Lawrence BLACK).
○ 'Brides of Christ: Towards a History of Women Religious', conference, to be held at St. Mary's College, Strawberry Hill, Twickenham, 12 October 2002 (Caroline BOWDEN).
○ Conference, 'Sir Winston Churchill and Australia', held at the Churchill Archives Centre, Cambridge, 1 and 2 July 2002 (Carl BRIDGE).
○ 'King in Heaven and on Earth: A Symposium on Royal Saints' held at the University of St Andrews, 17–18 November 2001 (Brian BRIGGS).
○ Conference 'A Career in History' held at the Institute of Historical Research, London, 12 December 2001 (K BURK).
○ Annual Fifteenth-Century Conference, held at New Hall, Cam-

bridge, on 5–7 September 2002 (Christine CARPENTER).

o   Conference, 'The Contours of Legitimacy in Central Europe: New Approaches in Graduate Studies', held at St. Antony's College, Oxford, 24–26 May 2002 (Larissa DOUGLASS).

o   Postgraduate workshop on 'New Approaches to the City: 1700–1990' held at the Centre for Urban History, University of Leicester, 14 November 2001 (Shane EWEN).

o   'Subversion in History', Institute of Historical Research Postgraduate Conference, held at the Institute of Historical Research, London, 9 July 2002 (Kate FERRIS).

o   Conference, 'A Critical Condition? Class and the Practice of History in the Twenty-First Century', held at the University of Essex, 15 June 2002 (Sakis GEKAS).

o   Conference 'Re-writing Irish Histories' held at University College, London, 4–6 April 2002 (C M HALL).

o   'The Domestic Interior: 1400 to the Present', Postgraduate Research Day, to be held at the Victoria and Albert Museum, London, 22 November 2002 (Karen HARVEY).

o   'Poverty a multidisciplinary cross-period colloquium III', held at UCL on Monday 29 April 2002 (Elena ISAYEV).

o   Ninth York Manuscripts Conference, 'The Book in the Town', held at King's Manor, York, 19–21 July 2002 (Claire JONES).

o   71st Anglo-American Conference of Historians – 'Re-Writing the Past', held at the Institute of Historical Research, London, 3–5 July 2002 (Mark MAZOWER).

o   European Reformation Research Group Annual Conference, held at the University of Reading, 5–7 September 2002 (Helen PARISH).

o   Conference, 'The religious and the laity: Europe, 1000–1300', to be held at the University of Leicester, 31 July–3 August 2003 (Dave POSTLES).

o   Conference, 'Post Imperial Britain', held at Senate House, University of London, 8–10 July 2002 (Virginia PRESTON).

o   'Gender, Memory and Identity, 900–1300' conference held at the University of Liverpool, 11–13 April 2002 (Holly RICKETTS and Kirsten McMILLAN).

o   'German History from the Margins: Minorities in German History' conference held at the University of Southampton, 13–15 September, 2002 (Mark ROSEMAN).

o   Day Seminar on Medieval English Chantries, held at Goodenough College, London, on Saturday 9 March 2002 (Marie-Helene ROUSSEAU).

o   Conference, 'Defining the Holy: Sacred Space in Medieval and Early Modern Europe', to be held at the University of Exeter, 10–12 April 2003 (Andrew SPICER).

o   Conference 'The Poles in Britain, 1940–2000: New Research' held at the University of Stirling, 2 March 2002 (Peter STACHURA).

o   Conference, 'Controlling Bodies. The Regulation of Conduct, 1650–2000', held at the University of Glamorgan, 24–26 June 2002 (David M. TURNER).

o   'Conscience and the Early Modern World, 1500–1800' conference held at the University of Sheffield, 7–9 July 2002 (Edward VALLANCE).

o   Society for the Study of French History, Annual Conference, held at the University of Newcastle, 4–6 April, 2002 (Timothy WATSON).

o   International colloquium, 'Shaping Understanding: Form and Order in the Anglo-Saxon World, 400–1100', held at The British Museum on 7–9 March 2002 (Mrs. Leslie WEBSTER).

ORS Awards

o   Izabella ORLOWSKA, SOAS, London.
    11 September, 2002

THE ROYAL HISTORICAL SOCIETY
FINANCIAL ACCOUNTS
FOR THE YEAR ENDED 30 JUNE 2002

haysmacintyre
Chartered Accountants
Registered Auditors
London

THE ROYAL HISTORICAL SOCIETY
REPORT OF THE COUNCIL OF TRUSTEES
FOR THE YEAR ENDED 30 JUNE 2002

The members of Council present their report and audited accounts for the year ended 30 June 2002.

PRINCIPAL ACTIVITIES AND REVIEW OF THE YEAR

The Society exists for the promotion and support of historical scholarship and its dissemination to historians and a wider public. This year, as in previous years, it has pursued this objective by an ambitious programme of publications – a volume of Transactions, two volumes of edited texts in the Camden Series and further volumes in the Studies in History Series have appeared, by the holding of meetings in London and at universities outside London at which papers are delivered, by the sponsoring of the joint lecture for a wider public with Gresham College, by distributing over £20,000 in research support grants to 83 individuals, and by frequent representations to various official bodies where the interests of historical scholarship are involved. It is Council's intention that these activities should be sustained to the fullest extent in the future.

RESULTS

The Society experienced a difficult year with total funds decreasing from £2,336,292 in June 2001 to £2,077,185 in June 2002, a decrease of £259,107. This was largely due to a down turn in the stockmarket. Membership subscriptions income increased by 5% mainly due to an increase in the number of Retired Fellows.

Income from royalties/book-sales and the associated publications costs were reduced significantly. This reflects the changeover to the new profit-share arrangement with Cambridge University Press.

FIXED ASSETS

Information relating to changes in fixed assets is given in notes 2 and 3 to the accounts.

INVESTMENTS

The Society has adopted a "total return" approach to its investment policy. This means that the funds are invested solely on the basis of seeking to secure the best total level of economic return compatible with the duty to make safe investments, but regardless of the form the return takes.

The Society has adopted this approach to ensure even-handedness between current and future beneficiaries, as the focus of many investments moves away from producing income to maximising capital values. In the current investments climate, to maintain the level of income needed to fund the charity, would require an investment portfolio which would not achieve the optimal overall return, so effectively penalising future beneficiaries.

The total return strategy does not make distinctions between income and capital returns. It lumps together all forms of return on investment – dividends, interest, and capital gains etc, to produce a "total return". Some of the total return is then used to meet the needs of present beneficiaries, while the remainder is added to the existing capital to help meet the needs of future beneficiaries.

The Society's investments are managed by Cripps Portfolio, who report all transactions to the Honorary Treasurer and provide six monthly reports on the portfolio, which are considered by the Society's Finance Committee which meets three times a year. In turn the Finance Committee reports to Council.

The Society closely monitors its investments, with its main portfolio being assessed against a bespoke benchmark and its smaller Whitfield and Robinson portfolios against the standard APCIMS balanced benchmark.

RISK ASSESSMENT

The trustees are satisfied that they have considered the major risks to which the charity is exposed, that they have taken action to mitigate or manage those risks and that they have systems in place to monitor any change to those risks.

GRANT MAKING

The Society awards funds to assist advanced historical research. It operates several separate schemes, for each of which there is an application form. The Society's Research Support Committee considers applications at meetings held 4 times a year. In turn the Research Support Committee reports to Council. A list of awards made is provided in the Society's Annual Report.

RESERVES POLICY

The Council have reviewed the Society's need for reserves in line with the guidance issued by the Charity Commission. They believe that the Society requires approximately the current level of unrestricted general funds to generate sufficient total return, both income and capital, to cover the Society's expenditure in excess of the members' subscription income on an annual basis. A substantial level of unrestricted reserves of £1,916,729 is therefore necessary to ensure that the Society can run efficiently and meet the needs of current and future beneficiaries.

The Society's restricted funds consist of a number of different funds where the donor has imposed restrictions on the use of the funds which are legally binding. The purposes of these funds are set out in note 1.

STATEMENT OF TRUSTEES' RESPONSIBILITIES

Law applicable to charities in England and Wales requires the Council to prepare accounts for each financial year which give a true and fair view of the state of affairs of the Society and of its financial activities for that year. In preparing these accounts, the Trustees are required to:

- select suitable accounting policies and apply them consistently;
- make judgements and estimates that are reasonable and prudent;
- state whether applicable accounting standards have been followed, subject to any material departures disclosed and explained in the accounts;
- prepare the accounts on the going concern basis unless it is inappropriate to presume that the Society will continue in business.

The Council is responsible for ensuring proper accounting records are kept which disclose, with reasonable accuracy at any time, the financial position of the Society and enable them to ensure that the financial statements comply with applicable law. They are also responsible for safeguarding the assets of the Society and hence for taking reasonable steps for the prevention and detection of error, fraud and other irregularities.

MEMBERS OF THE COUNCIL

At the Anniversary Meeting on 23 November 2001, Professor J Hoppit succeeded Professor K Burk as Honorary Treasurer; the remaining Officers of the Society were re-elected.

The Vice-Presidents retiring under By-law XVII were Professor A J Fletcher and Professor C J Wrigley. Professor P J Corfield and Professor L J Jordanova were elected to replace them.

The Members of Council retiring under By-law XX were Dr I W Archer, Dr G W Bernard, Professor J C G Binfield and Professor R H Trainor. Dr S R Ditchfield, Dr M Finn and Professor F O'Gorman were elected in their place.

APPOINTMENT OF TRUSTEES

In accordance with By-law XVII, the Vice-Presidents shall hold office normally for a term of three years. Two of them shall retire by rotation, in order of seniority in office, at each Anniversary Meeting and shall not be eligible for re-election before the Anniversary Meeting of the next year. In accordance with By-law XIX, the Council of the Society shall consist of the President, the Vice-Presidents, the Treasurer, the Secretary, the Librarian, the Literary Directors and twelve Councillors. The President shall be *ex-officio* a member of all Committees appointed by the Council; and the Treasurer, the Secretary, the Librarian and the Literary Directors shall, unless the Council otherwise determine, also be *ex-officio* members of all such Committees. In accordance with By-law XX, the Councillors shall hold office normally for a term of four years. Three of them shall retire by rotation, in order of seniority in office, at each Anniversary Meeting and shall not be eligible for re-election before the Anniversary Meeting of the next year.

STANDING COMMITTEES 2002

The Society was operated through the following Committees during 2002:

Finance Committee	Dr S R Ditchfield	
	Mr P J C Firth	– non Council Member
	Professor P Mathias	– non Council Member
	Professor R J McKetterick	
	The six Officers * as above	
Membership Committee	Dr J E Burton	
	Professor H Meller	
	Professor J Miller	
	Professor P Stafford	Chair
	The six Officers * as above	
Publications Committee	Professor C M Andrew	
	Professor J A Green	
	Professor C D H Jones	Chair
	Professor F O'Gorman	
	Mrs S J Tyacke	
	The six Officers * as above	
Research Support Committee	Professor D N Cannadine	Chair
	Dr W Childs	
	Professor P J Corfield	
	Professor V I J Flint	
	Professor R J A R Rathbone	
	The six Officers * as above	
General Purposes Committee	Dr M Finn	
	Professor L J Jordanova	Chair
	Professor T A Reuter	
	Professor J A Tosh	
	The six Officers * as above	
Studies in History **Editorial Board**	Professor D S Eastwood	Convenor
	Professor M Braddick	– non Council Member
	Dr S J Gunn	– non Council Member
	Dr. J.E. Hunter	– non Council Member
	Professor C D H Jones	
	Professor M Mazower	– non Council Member
	Professor M. Taylor	–non Council Member
	Dr S Walker	– non Council Member
	A Literary Director	
	Honorary Treasurer	
Election of Officers Subcommittee: [Honorary Secretary]	The President – Chair	
	Professor C D H Jones	
	Professor T A Reuter	
	A Literary Director	
	Honorary Treasurer	

AUDITORS

A resolution proposing the appointment of auditors will be submitted at the Anniversary Meeting.

INDEPENDENT REPORT OF THE AUDITORS
FOR THE YEAR ENDED 30 JUNE 2002

We have audited the financial statements of The Royal Historical Society for the year ended 30 June 2002 which comprise the Statement of Financial Activities, the Balance Sheet, and the related notes. These financial statements have been prepared under the historical cost convention (as modified by the revaluation of certain fixed assets) and the accounting policies set out therein.

RESPECTIVE RESPONSIBILITIES OF TRUSTEES AND AUDITORS

As described in the Statement of Trustees' Responsibilities the charity's trustees are responsible for preparation of the financial statements in accordance with applicable law and United Kingdom Accounting Standards.

We have been as appointed auditors under section 43 of the Charities Act 1993 and report in accordance with regulations made under section 44 of that Act. Our responsibility is to audit the financial statements in accordance with relevant legal and regulatory requirements and United Kingdom Auditing Standards.

We report to you our opinion as to whether the financial statements give a true and fair view and are properly prepared in accordance with the Charities Act 1993. We also report to you if, in our opinion, the Trustees' Report is not consistent with the financial statements, if the charity has not kept proper accounting records or if we have not received all the information and explanations we require for our audit.

We are not required to consider whether the statement in the Trustees' Report concerning the major risks to which the charity is exposed covers all existing risks and controls, or to form an opinion on the effectiveness of the charity's risk management and control procedures.

We read the Trustees' Report and consider the implications for our report if we become aware of any apparent misstatements within it.

BASIS OF AUDIT OPINION

We conducted our audit in accordance with United Kingdom Auditing Standards issued by the Auditing Practices Board. An audit includes examination, on a test basis, of evidence relevant to the amounts and disclosures in the financial statements. It also includes an assessment of the significant estimates and judgements made by the Trustees in the preparation of the financial statements, and of whether the accounting policies are appropriate to the charity's circumstances, consistently applied and adequately disclosed.

We planned and performed our audit so as to obtain all the information and explanations which we considered necessary in order to provide us with sufficient evidence to give reasonable assurance that the financial statements are free from material misstatement, whether caused by fraud or other irregularity or error. In forming our opinion we also evaluated the overall adequacy of the presentation of information in the financial statements.

OPINION

In our opinion the financial statements give a true and fair view of the state of the charity's affairs as at 30 June 2002 and of its incoming resources and application of resources in the year then ended and have been properly prepared in accordance with the Charities Act 1993.

haysmacintyre
Chartered Accountants
Registered Auditors
20 September 2002

Southampton House
317 High Holborn
London
WC1V 7NL

THE ROYAL HISTORICAL SOCIETY

STATEMENT OF FINANCIAL ACTIVITIES
FOR THE YEAR ENDED 30 JUNE 2002

	Notes	Unrestricted Funds £	Restricted Funds £	Total Funds 2002 £	Total Funds 2001 £
INCOMING RESOURCES					
Donations, legacies and similar incoming Resources	7	5,277	–	5,277	6,333
Activities In Furtherance Of The Charity's Objects					
Grants for awards		–	6,500	6,490	3,393
Conferences		7,928	–	7,928	4,227
Subscriptions		56,101	–	56,101	53,543
Royalties		29,283	–	29,283	61,568
Activities To Generate Funds					
Investment income	3	107,345	4,886	112,231	102,489
Other		1,453	10,280	11,743	407
TOTAL INCOMING RESOURCES		207,387	21,666	229,053	231,960
RESOURCES EXPENDED					
Cost of Generating Funds					
Investment manager's fee		15,781	1,253	17,034	16,464
Charitable Expenditure					
Grants for awards	8	30,204	29,656	59,860	50,639
Conferences		22,742	–	22,742	14,769
Publications		63,243	–	63,243	110,775
Library		12,153	–	12,153	10,586
Support costs		53,792	6,445	60,237	47,368
Management and administration		13,824	–	13,824	13,904
TOTAL RESOURCES EXPENDED	9	211,739	37,354	249,093	264,505
NET OUTGOING RESOURCES		(4,352)	(15,688)	(20,040)	(32,545)
OTHER RECOGNISED GAINS AND LOSSES					
Unrealised (loss) on investments	3	(220,119)	(18,948)	(239,067)	(324,968)
NET MOVEMENT IN FUNDS		(224,471)	(34,636)	(259,107)	(357,513)
Balance at 1 July 2001		2,141,200	195,092	2,336,292	2,693,805
Balance at 30 June 2002		£1,916,729	£160,456	£2,077,185	£2,336,292

THE ROYAL HISTORICAL SOCIETY

BALANCE SHEET AS AT 30TH JUNE 2002

	Notes	2002 £	2002 £	2001 £	2001 £
FIXED ASSETS					
Tangible assets	2		390		1,600
Investments	3		2,011,500		2,250,106
			2,011,890		2,251,706
CURRENT ASSETS					
Stocks	4	30,471		42,136	
Debtors	5	29,405	13,212		
Cash at bank and in hand		30,492		75,018	
		90,368		130,366	
LESS: CREDITORS					
Amounts due within one year	6	(25,073)		(45,780)	
NET CURRENT ASSETS			65,295		84,586
NET ASSETS			£2,077,185		£2,336,292
REPRESENTED BY:	17				
Unrestricted – General Fund			1,916,729		2,141,200
Restricted – E M Robinson Bequest	16		98,321		114,330
Restricted – A S Whitfield Prize Fund	16		39,169		44,895
Restricted – BHB 2 (Andrew Mellon Fund)	16		12,511		35,867
Restricted – The David Berry Essay Trust	16		10,455		–
			£2,077,185		£2,336,292

Approved by the Council on 20 September 2002

President:

Honorary Treasurer:

The attached notes form an integral part of these financial statements.

THE ROYAL HISTORICAL SOCIETY

Notes to the Accounts for the Year Ended 30 June 2002

1. Accounting Policies

   (a) *Basis of Preparation*

   The financial statements have been prepared in accordance with the Statement of Recommended Practice 2000 "Accounting and Reporting by Charities" and with applicable accounting standards issued by UK accountancy bodies. They are prepared on the historical cost basis of accounting as modified to include the revaluation of fixed assets including investments which are carried at market value.

   (b) *Depreciation*

   Depreciation is calculated by reference to the cost of fixed assets using a straight line basis at rates considered appropriate having regard to the expected lives of the fixed assets. The annual rates of depreciation in use are:

   Furniture and equipment   10%
   Computer equipment   25%

   (c) *Stock*

   Stock is valued at the lower of cost and net realisable value.

   (d) *Library and archives*

   The cost of additions to the library and archives is written off in the year of purchase.

   (e) *Subscription income*

   Subscription income is recognised in the year it became receivable with a provision against any subscription not received.

   (f) *Investments*

   Investments are stated at market value. Any surplus/deficit arising on revaluation is   included in the Statement of Financial Activities. Dividend income is accounted for when the Society becomes entitled to such monies.

   (g) *Publication costs*

   Publication costs are transferred in stock and released to the Statement of Financial Activities as stocks are depleted.

   (h) *Donations and other voluntary income*

   Donations and other voluntary income is recognised when the Society becomes legally entitled to such monies.

   (i) *Grants payable*

   Grants payable are recognised in the year in which they are approved.

   (j) *Funds*

   Unrestricted: these are funds which can be used in accordance with the charitable objects at the discretion of the trustees.

   Restricted: these are funds that can only be used for particular restricted purposes defined by the benefactor and within the objects of the charity.

   (k) *Allocations*

   Wages and salary costs are allocated on the basis of the work done by the Executive Secretary and the Administrative Secretary.

   (l) *Pensions*

   Pension costs are charged to the SOFA when payments fall due. The Society contributes 10% of gross salaries to the personal pension plans of the two employees.

2. TANGIBLE FIXED ASSETS

	Computer Equipment £	Furniture and Equipment £	Total £
Cost			
At 1 July 2001	29,742	1,173	30,915
Additions	–	–	–
At 30 June 2002	29,742	1,173	30,915
Depreciation			
At 1 July 2002	28,142	1,173	29,315
Charge for the year	1,210	–	1,210
At 30 June 2002	29,352	1,173	30,525
Net book value			
At 30 June 2002	£390	£–	£390
At 30 June 2001	£1,600	£–	£1,600

All tangible fixed asset are used in the furtherance of the Society's objects.

3. INVESTMENTS

	General Fund £	Robinson Bequest £	Whitfield Prize Fund £	David Berry Essay Trust £	Total £
Market value at 1 July 2001	2,076,069	124,446	49,591	–	2,250,106
Additions	336,158	18,336	12,275	1,530	368,299
Disposals	(340,238)	(15,984)	(11,616)	–	(367,838)
Net realised/unrealised (loss)/ gain on investments	(220,119)	(13,611)	(5,337)	–	(239,067)
Market value at 30th June 2002	1,851,870	£113,187	£44,913	£1,530	£2,011,500
Cost at 30th June 2001	£1,781,248	£83,778	£30,603	£1,530	£1,897,159

	2001 £	2000 £
UK Equities	1,033,987	1,120,865
UK Government Stock and Bonds	823,429	879,337
Overseas equities	18,861	44,314
Uninvested Cash	135,223	205,590
	£2,011,500	£2,250,106
Dividends and interest on listed investments	111,725	101,874
Interest on cash deposits	506	615
	£112,231	£102,489

4. STOCK

	2002 £	2001 £
Transactions Sixth Series	2,076	3,994
Camden Fifth Series	9,636	17,234
Guides and Handbooks	7,214	4,047
Camden Classics Reprints	11,545	16,861
	£30,471	£42,136

5. DEBTORS

	2002 £	2001 £
Other debtors	19,358	7,079
Prepayments	10,007	6,133
	£29,405	£13,212

6. CREDITORS: Amounts due within one year

	2002 £	2001 £
Trade creditors	4,705	3,164
Sundry creditors	3,937	20,087
Subscriptions received in advance	9,557	16,301
Accruals and deferred income	6,874	6,228
	£25,073	£45,780

7. DONATIONS AND LEGACIES

	2002 £	2001 £
A Browning Bequest	96	81
G R Elton Bequest	4,176	3,243
Donations via membership	516	135
Sundry income	489	2,874
	£5,277	£6,333

8. GRANTS FOR AWARDS

	Unrestricted Funds £	Restricted Funds £	Total 2002 £	Total 2001 £
Alexander Prize	625	–	625	–
Sundry Grants	200	–	200	2,300
Research support grants (note 12) . .	20,404	–	20,404	20,830
Historical Association	2,500	–	2,500	–
Centenary fellowship	4,875	–	4,875	7,975
A-Level prizes	600	–	600	700
A S Whitfield prize	–	1,050	1,050	1,000
E M Robinson Bequest				
– Grant to Dulwich Picture Library . .	–	4,750	4,750	–
Gladstone history book prize . . .	1,000	–	1,000	400
P J Marshall Fellowship	–	6,500	6,500	–
BHB project grant	–	17,106	17,106	17,434
David Berry Prize	–	250	250	–
	£30,204	£29,656	£59,860	£50,639

GRANTS PAYABLE

	2001 £	2000 £
Commitments at 1 July 2001	20,087	5,829
Commitments made in the year	59,610	50,639
Grants paid during the year	(75,760)	(36,381)
Commitments at 30 June 2002 (Note 6)	£3,937	£20,087

9. DIRECT CHARITABLE EXPENDITURE

	Staff Costs £	Depreciation £	Other Costs £	Total £
Cost of Generating Funds				
Investment manager's fee . . .	–	–	17,034	17,034
Charitable Expenditure				
Grants for awards (Note 8) . . .	–	–	59,860	59,860
Conferences	5,094	–	17,648	22,742
Publications	13,923	–	49,320	63,243
Library	2,716	–	9,437	12,153
Support costs	26,778	1,210	32,249	60,237
Management and administration . .	–	–	13,824	13,824
TOTAL RESOURCES EXPENDED	£48,511	£1,210	£199,372	£249,093

STAFF COSTS

	2002 £	2001 £
Wages and salaries	40,938	38,025
Social Security costs	3,889	3,663
Other pension costs	3,684	3,294
	£48,511	£44,982

The average number of employees in the year was 2 (2001: 2)
There were no employees whose emoluments exceeded £50,000 in the year.

10. COUNCILLORS' EXPENSES
During the year travel expenses were reimbursed to 30 Councillors attending Council meetings at a cost of £6,012 (2001: £6,270).

11. AUDITOR'S REMUNERATION

	2002 £	2001 £
Audit fee	6,404	6,228
Other services	470	470

12. GRANTS PAID
During the year Society awarded grants to a value of £20,404 (2001: £20,830) to 83 (2001: 84) individuals (Note 8).

13. LEASE COMMITMENTS
The Society has the following annual commitments under non-cancellable operating leases which expire:

	2002 £	2001 £
Within 1–2 years	–	–
Within 2–5 years	7,281	2,326
	£7,281	£2,326

14. LIFE MEMBERS
The Society has ongoing commitments to provide membership services to 19 Life Members at a cost of approximately £42 each per year.

15. UNCAPITALISED ASSETS
The Society owns a library the cost of which is written off to the Statement of Financial Activities at the time of purchase.

This library is insured for £150,000 and is used for reference purposes by the membership of the Society.

16. RESTRICTED FUNDS

	Balance at 1 July 01 £	Incoming Resources £	Outgoing Resources £	Investment (Losses) £	Balance at 30 June 02 £
(i) E M Robinson Bequest	114,330	3,249	(5,647)	(13,611)	98,321
(ii) A S Whitfield Prize Fund	44,895	1,017	(1,406)	(5,337)	39,169
(iii) BHB/A.Mellon Fund	35,867	195	(23,551)	–	12,511
(iv) P J Marshall Fellowship	–	3,600	(3,600)	–	–
(v) David Berry Essay Trust*	–	10,705	(250)	–	10,455
	£195,092	£18,766	£(34,454)	£(18,948)	£160,456

* The assets of this Trust fund (£10,280) were transferred to the Society at the start of the year and are included in incoming resources.

(i) *E M Robinson Bequest*
Income from the E M Robinson bequest is used to provide grants to the Dulwich Picture Gallery.

(ii) *A S Whitfield Prize Fund*
The A S Whitfield Prize Fund is used to provide an annual prize for the best first monograph for British history published in the calendar year.

(iii) *BHB/A Mellon Fund*
The British History Bibliographies project funding is used to provide funding for the compilation of bibliographies in British and Irish History.

(iv) *P J Marshall Fellowship*
The P J Marshall Fellowship is used to provide a sum sufficient to cover the stipend for a one-year doctoral research fellowship alongside the existing Royal Historical Society Centenary Fellowship at the Institute of Historical Research in the academic year 2001–2002.

(v) *The David Berry Essay Trust*
The David Berry Essay Trust is to provide an annual prize for the best essay on a subject dealing with Scottish history.

17. ANALYSIS OF NET ASSETS BETWEEN FUNDS

	General Fund £	E M Robinso Bequest Fund £	A S Whitfield Prize Fund £	BHB/ Andrew Mellon Fund £	David Berry Essay Trust £	Total £
Fixed Assets	–	–	–	390	–	390
Investments	1,851,870	113,187	44,913	–	1,530	2,011,500
	1,851,870	113,187	44,913	390	1,530	2,011,890
Current Assets						
Stocks	30,471	–	–	–	–	30,471
Debtors	25,123	–	–	4,282	–	29,405
Cash at bank and in hand	13,478	–	–	7,839	9,175	30,492
	69,072	–	–	12,121	9,175	90,368
Less: Creditors	(4,213)	(14,866)	(5,744)	–	(250)	(25,073)
Net Current Assets	64,859	(14,866)	(5,744)	12,121	8,925	65,295
Net Assets	£1,916,729	£98,321	£39,169	£12,511	£10,455	£2,077,185